A Practical Approach to
Criminal Procedure

A Practical Approach to Criminal Procedure

Christopher J Emmins MA

of Middle Temple, Barrister
Senior Lecturer in Law at the Inns of Court School of Law

First published in Great Britain 1981 by Financial Training Publications Limited, Avenue House, 131 Holland Park Avenue, London W11 4UT

©Financial Training Publications Limited 1981

ISBN: 0 906322 08 1

Photoset by Top Type Phototypesetting Co. Ltd., London, W1
Printed in Great Britain by Livesey Limited, Shrewsbury

Contents

Table of Cases   ix

Table of Statutes   xix

Table of Statutory Rules and Orders and Statutory Instruments   xxvi

Preface   xxvii

PART 1   INTRODUCTION   1

1 Setting the Scene   3

1.1 Trial on indictment 1.2 Summary trial 1.3 Classes of offence
1.4 Indictable and summary offences

2 Commencing Prosecutions   6

2.1 Suspect charged by police officer 2.2 Application for summons by
police administrative officer 2.3 Private individuals 2.4 Considerations
relevant to commencing a prosecution 2.5 Roles of the law officers of the
Crown and the Director of Public Prosecutions

PART 2   TRIAL ON INDICTMENT   13

3 Committal Proceedings   15

3.1 Jurisdiction of the magistrates 3.2 Presence of the accused
3.3 Committals with and without consideration of the evidence 3.4 Procedure at committals with consideration of the evidence 3.5 Procedure at
committals without consideration of the evidence 3.6 Circumstances which
are appropriate for commital without evidence 3.7 Other orders and
applications made at committal proceedings 3.8 Evidence in writing other
than s.102 statements admissible at committals 3.9 Method of challenging
conduct of committal proceedings 3.10 Trial on indictment in the absence of
successful committal proceedings

4 The Crown Court   31

4.1 Crown Court judges 4.2 Organisation of the Crown Court 4.3
Magistrates as judges of the Crown Court 4.4 Rights of audience in the
Crown Court

5   *The Indictment*   37

5.1   Preferring the bill of indictment   5.2   Counts which may be included in
an indictment   5.3   Contents of the count   5.4   The rule against duplicity
5.5   Joinder of counts in an indictment   5.6   Joinder of defendants in an
indictment   5.7   Applications concerning the indictment

6   *Pleas*   53

6.1   The arraignment   6.2   Plea of 'not guilty'   6.3   Plea of 'guilty'   6.4
Plea of 'guilty' to a lesser offence   6.5   Change of plea   6.6   Plea bargaining
6.7   The accused who will not or cannot plead   6.8   Pleas of 'autrefois acquit'
and 'autrefois convict'   6.9   Judges' discretion to halt prosecution   6.10
Other possible pleas

7   *The Jury*   68

7.1   Eligibility for jury service   7.2   Summoning jurors   7.3   Empanelling a
jury   7.4   Challenges to jurors   7.5   Appeals based on errors in the
empanelling of the jury   7.6   Discharge of jurors or jury

8   *The Course of the Trial*   81

8.1 The role of counsel   8.2 The prosecution opening   8.3 The prosecution
case   8.4 Submission of no case to answer   8.5 The defence case   8.6
Counsel's closing speeches   8.7 The judge's summing up   8.8 Evidence given
out of the normal order   8.9 Power of judge to call witnesses

9   *The Verdict*   102

9.1 Retirement of the jury   9.2 Returning the verdict   9.3 Verdicts on counts
in the alternative   9.4 Verdicts of 'guilty' of an alternative offence   9.5
Majority verdicts   9.6 Discharging the jury from giving a verdict   9.7 Accepting the verdict

PART 3   SUMMARY TRIAL   113

10   *The Magistrates and their Courts*   115

10.1 Lay magistrates   10.2 Stipendiary magistrates   10.3 Organisation of the
courts   10.4 Magistrates' clerks

11   *Course of a Summary Trial*   121

11.1 Jurisdiction of a magistrates' court   11.2 The bench   11.3 The
information   11.4 Appearance of the accused   11.5 Legal representation
11.6 The course of the trial   11.7 Powers of sentencing after conviction for a
summary offence   11.8 The role of the clerk

12 Summary Trial of Offences Triable Either Way 139

12.1 Classification of offences   12.2 Determining the mode of trial   12.3 Commital to the Crown Court for sentence under section 38   12.4 Other circumstances in which magistrates may commit for sentence   12.5 The special procedure for criminal damage charges   12.6 Trial on indictment or summary trial

13 Trial of Juveniles 155

13.1 Trial of juveniles on indictment   13.2 Trial of juveniles in an adult magistrates' court   13.3 Trial of juveniles in a juvenile court   13.4 Sentencing juveniles

PART 4 SENTENCING 167

14 Procedure before Sentencing 169

14.1 The facts of the offence   14.2 The police officer's evidence   14.3 Reports on the offender   14.4 Mitigation   14.5 Taking other offences into consideration   14.6 Variation of sentence

15 Powers of Sentencing 181

15.1 Immediate imprisonment   15.2 Suspended sentences — Powers of Criminal Courts Act 1973, ss. 22-5   15.3 Fines   15.4 Probation: Powers of Criminal Courts Act 1973, ss 2-13   15.5 Absolute and conditional discharges   15.6 Community service orders — Powers of Criminal Courts Act 1973, ss. 14-17   15.7 Borstal training   15.8 Detention in a detention centre   15.9 Orders under the Mental Health Act 1959   15.10 Disqualification from driving and endorsement of driving licences   15.11 Recommendation for deportation   15.12 Deferring sentence — Powers of Criminal Courts Act 1973, s.1

16 Policy of Sentencing 214

16.1 The primary decision   16.2 Individualised sentences   16.3 Tariff sentences   16.4 Mitigating factors   16.5 Sentences above the tariff

PART 5 APPEALS 221

17 Appeals from the Crown Court 223

17.1 The Criminal Division of the Court of Appeal   17.2 The right of appeal against conviction   17.3 The right of appeal against sentence   17.4 Determination of appeals against conviction   17.5 Determination of appeals against sentence   17.6 Procedure for appealing   17.7 Other ways in which matters come before the Court of Appeal   17.8 Appeals to the House of Lords: Criminal Appeal Act 1968, s.33

18 Appeals from the Magistrates' Courts   250

18.1 Appeals to the Crown Court   18.2 Appeals to the Divisional Court by
case stated   18.3 Application for judicial review   18.4 Appeal from the
Divisional Court to the House of Lords

PART 6 MISCELLANEOUS   267

19 Preliminaries to Trial   269

19.1 Prosecuting authorities   19.2 Bringing the accused before the court
19.3 Police questioning of a suspect   19.4 Police powers of search   19.5
Obtaining evidence of identity   19.6 Special cases   19.7 Adjournments after
the first court appearance

20 Bail   303

20.1 Occasions on which a person may be granted bail   20.2 Principles on
which the decision to grant or refuse bail is taken   20.3 Requirements imposed
when granting bail   20.4 Procedure at an application for bail in a Magistrates'
Court   20.5 Applications to the Crown Court and High Court for
bail   20.6 Consequences of a defendant absconding   20.7 Detention of
defendant when bail is refused   20.8 Application for a writ of habeas corpus

21 Ancillary Financial and Property Orders   317

21.1 Legal aid   21.2 Orders to pay costs   21.3 Compensation orders   21.4
Restitution orders   21.5 Forfeiture orders   21.6 Criminal bankruptcy orders

Appendix 1   Schedule 1 to the Magistrates' Courts Act 1980   327

Appendix 2   The White Paper on Young Offenders (1980 Cmnd 8045)   329

Appendix 3   The Transport Act 1981   332

Appendix 4   The Report of the Royal Commission on Criminal
Procedure (the Philips Commission)   334

Appendix 5   Imaginary Brief   339

Subject Index   355

Table of Cases

Abbott [1955] 2 QB 497; [1955] 3 WLR 369; 119 JP 526; 99 SJ 544; [1955] 2 All ER
  899; 39 Cr App R 141   229
Abrahams (1895) 21 VLR 343   96
Aitken (Practice Note) [1966] 1 WLR 1076; 110 SJ 526; [1966] 2 All ER 453n; 50 Cr
  App R   227
Alderson v Booth [1969] 2 QB 216; [1969] 2 WLR 1252; 133 JP 346; 113 SJ 268; [1969] 2
  All ER 271; 53 Cr App R 301   275
Aldus v Watson [1973] QB 902; [1973] 2 All ER 1018; [1973] 2 WLR 1007; 137 JP 684; 117
  SJ 446   127
Alexander [1974] 1 WLR 422; 118 SJ 166; [1974] 1 All ER 539   103, 229
Allen and others [1977] Crim LR 163   293
Altrincham Justices ex p Pennington [1975] 1 QB 549; [1975] 2 All ER 78   123, 124
Amersham Justices ex p Wilson [1981] 2 All ER 315; [1981] 2WLR 887   159
Amos [1961] 1 WLR 308; 125 JP 167; 105 SJ 182; [1961] 1 All ER 191; 45 Cr App R
  42   203
Ashmore [1974] Crim LR 375   195
Assim [1966] 2 QB 249; [1966] 3 WLR 55; 130 JP 361; 110 SJ 404; [1966] 2 All ER 881;
  50 Cr App R 224   49, 50
Atkinson (1978) 67 Cr App R 200; [1978] 1 WLR 425; [1978] 2 All ER 460   57
Atkinson v USA Government [1971] AC 197; [1969] 3 WLR 1074; 113 SJ 901; [1969] 3
  All ER 1317   254
Attorney-General's Reference (No 1 of 1975) [1975] QB 733; [1975] 3 WLR 11; [1975] 2
  All ER 684   243
Attorney-General's References (Nos 1 and 2 of 1979) [1980] QB 180; [1979] 3 WLR 577;
  [1979] 3 All ER 143   243
Aughet (1919) 13 Cr App R 101   65
Baker 115 SJ 126; 55 Cr App R 182; [1971] Crim LR 300   193, 204
Ballysingh (1953) 37 Cr App R 28   44
Banks [1916] 2 KB 621; 85 LJKB 1657; 115 LT 457; 80 JP 432; 25 Cox CC 535; 12 Cr App
  R 74   81
Barker [1951] 1 All ER 479   149
Barker (1977) 65 Cr App R 287   52
Barnard [1980] Crim LR 235; (1980) 70 Cr App R 28   106
Barnes (1970) 114 SJ 952; 55 Cr App R 100   56, 59
Barrell and Wilson (1979) 69 Cr App R 250; [1979] Crim LR 663   46
Barry [1975] 1 WLR 1190; [1975] 2 All ER 760; 61 Cr App R 172   109
Barton [1977] Crim LR 435   205
Bathurst [1968] 2 QB 99; [1968] 2 WLR 1092; 112 SJ 272; [1968] 1 All ER 1175; 52 Cr
  App R   25   98, 292
Beresford (1971) 56 Cr App R 143   240
Berry (1977) 66 Cr App R 156   61
Best and others (1980) 70 Cr App R 21   44
Bibi [1980] 1 WLR 1193; (1980) 71 Cr App R 360   190
Bignell 111 SJ 773; 52 Cr App R 10; [1967] Crim LR 711   211
Blandford Justices ex p G (An Infant) [1967] 1 QB 82; [1966] 2 WLR 1232; 130 JP 260;
  110 SJ 465; [1966] 1 All ER 1021   251
Blick 110 SJ 545; 50 Cr App R 280; [1966] Crim LR 508   100

Box and Box [1964] 1 QB 430; [1963] 3 WLR 696; 127 JP 553; 107 SJ 633; [1963] 3 All
   ER 240; 47 Cr App R 284   78
Bracegirdle v Oxley [1947] KB 349   254
Brangwynne v Evans [1962] 1 WLR 267; [1962] 1 All ER 446; 126 JP 173; 106 SJ
   197   127
Brentford Justices ex p Catlin [1975] QB 455; [1975] 2 WLR 506; [1975] 2 All ER 201   280
Brentford Justices ex p Wong [1981] QB 445; [1981] 2 WLR 203; [1981] 1 All ER 884   128
Broad (1979) 68 Cr App R 281   60
Bros (1901) 66 JP 54; 85 LT 581; 18 TLR 39; 20 Cox CC 89   279
Brown (1857) E&B 757   262
Bryant and Dickson (1946) 110 JP 267; 31 Cr App R 146; 44 LGR 224   86
Bryant and Oxley [1979] QB 108; [1978] 2 WLR 589; (1977) 122 SJ 62; [1978] 2 All ER 689;
   1977) 67 Cr App R 157; [1978] Crim LR 307   97
Burles [1970] 2 QB 191; [1970] 2 WLR 597; 114 SJ 86; [1970] 1 All ER 642; 54 Cr App
   R 196   62
Burnham, Bucks Justices ex p Ansorge [1959] 1 WLR 1043; [1959] 3 All ER 505; 133 JP
   539   264
Burrows [1970] Crim LR 419   111
Cain [1976] QB 496; [1975] 3 WLR 131; 139 JP 598; 119 SJ 422; [1975] 2 All ER 900;
   61 Cr App R 186; [1976] Crim LR 464   57, 83, 218
Caird 114 SJ 652; 54 Cr App R 499; [1970] Crim LR 656   211, 299
Callaghan (1979) 69 Cr App R 88   88
Callis v Gunn [1964] 1 QB 495; [1963] 3 WLR 931; 128 JP 41; 107 SJ 831; [1963] 3 All
   ER 677; 48 Cr App R 36   299
Camberwell Green Justices ex p Christie [1978] QB 602; 67 Cr App R 39;
   [1978] 2 WLR 794; [1978] 2 All ER 377   16
Camberwell Green Justices ex p Sloper [1979] Crim LR 264   252
Camborne Justices ex p Pearce [1955] 1 QB 41; [1954] 2 All ER 850; [1954] 3 WLR 415;
   118 JP 488; 98 SJ 577   123, 124
Campbell (1911) 75 JP 216; 27 TLR 256; 55 SJ 273; 6 Cr App R 131   172
Canny (1945) 89 SJ 213; 30 Cr App R 143   99, 154
Cardiff Crown Court ex p Jones [1974] QB 113; [1973] 3 WLR 497; 117 SJ 634; [1973] 3
   All ER 1027; 58 Cr App R 85; [1975] Crim LR 626   227
Carter (1960) 44 Cr App R 225   96
Carter and Canavan [1964] 2 QB 1; [1964] 2 WLR 266; 128 JP 172; 108 SJ 57; [1964] 1
   All ER 187; 48 Cr App R 122   108
Cavanagh and Shaw [1972] 1 WLR 676; 116 SJ 372; [1972] 2 All ER 704; 56 Cr App R
   407; [1972] Crim LR 389   86, 87
Chandler [1964] 2 QB 322; [1964] 2 WLR 689; 128 JP 244; 108 SJ 139; [1964] 1 All ER
   761; 48 Cr App R 143   73
Chandler [1976] 1 WLR 585; [1976] 3 All ER 105; 140 JP 582; 120 SJ 96   291, 292, 293
Chan Wei Keung v R [1967] 2 AC 160; [1967] 2 WLR 552; 111 SJ 73; [1967] 1 All ER
   948; 51 Cr App R 257   89
Chapman and Lauday (1976) 63 Cr App R 75   77, 78
Charles (1979) 68 Cr App R 334   35, 99, 100
Chertsey Justices ex p Franks [1961] 2 QB 152; [1961] 1 All ER 825; [1961] 2 WLR 442;
   125 JP 305; 105 SJ 181; 59 LGR 260   262
Christie v Leachinsky [1947] AC 573; [1947] LJR 757; 176 LT 443; 63 TLR 231; 111 JP
   224; [1947] 1 All ER 567; 45 LGR 201   275
City of Oxford Tramway Co v Sankey (1890) 54 JP 564   129
Clarke (1931) 22 Cr App R 58   87
Clarke 136 JP 184; 116 SJ 56; [1972] 1 All ER 219; 56 Cr App R 255   226
Cleary (1963) 107 SJ 77; 48 Cr App R 116   288
Cocks (1976) 63 Cr App R 79   99, 100
Colchester Justices ex p North East Essex Building Co Ltd [1977] 1 WLR 1109   142
Cole [1965] 2 QB 388; [1965] 3 WLR 263; 129 JP 326; 109 SJ 269; [1965] 2 All ER 29;
   49 Cr App R 199   59
Collins [1938] WN 212; 159 LT 71; 54 TLR 842; 102 JP 328; 82 SJ 436; 31 Cox CC 83;
   [1938] 3 All ER 130; 26 Cr App R 177; 36 LGR 512   90

Collins [1947] KB 560; [1948] LJR 6; 203 LTJ 116; 111 JP 156; 63 TLR 90; 91 SJ 133;
    [1947] 1 All ER 147; 32 Cr App R 27; 145 LGR 104   179
Collison (1980) 71 Cr App R 249   51, 108
Commissioners of Customs and Excise v Harz and Power [1967] 1 AC 760; [1966] 3
    WLR 1241; 110 SJ 565; [1966] 3 All ER 433   287
Connelly v DPP [1964] AC 1254; [1964] 2 WLR 1145; 128 JP 418; 108 SJ 356; [1964] 2
    All ER 401; 48 Cr App R 183   63, 64, 65, 66,
Consett Justices ex p Postal Bingo [1967] 2 QB 9; [1967] 1 All ER 605; [1967] 2 WLR
    184; 131 JP 196; 110 SJ 850   137
Considine (1980) 70 Cr App R 239   153
Cooper [1969] 1 QB 267; [1968] 3 WLR 1225; 112 SJ 904; [1969] 1 All ER 32; 53 Cr
    App R 82   230
Cooper and McMahon (1975) 61 Cr App R 215   231, 242, 244
Coughlan and Young (1976) 63 Cr App R 33   63, 80
Coward (1980) 70 Cr App R 70   60, 83
Craske ex p Commissioner of Metropolitan Police [1957] 1 QB 591; [1957] 2 All ER
    772; [1957] 3 WLR 308; 121 JP 502; 101 SJ 592   145
Croydon Justices ex p Lefore Holdings [1980] 1 WLR 1465   258
Dallison v Caffery [1965] 1 QB 348; [1964] 3 WLR 385; 128 JP 379; 108 SJ 560; [1964] 2
    All ER 610   86, 275
Daly [1974] 1 WLR 133; (1973) 118 SJ 66; [1974] 1 All ER 290   324
Davis [1979] Crim LR 327   218
Dawson and Wenlock [1960] 1 WLR 163; 124 JP 237; 104 SJ 191; [1960] 1 All ER 558;
    44 Cr App R 87   40
Day (1940) 162 LT 407; 104 JP 181; [1940] 1 All ER 402; 27 Cr App R 168; 38 LGR
    155   100
Deputy Chairman of Inner London Sessions ex parte Metropolitan Police Commissioner
    [1970] 2 QB 80; [1970] 2 WLR 95   67
Dewing v Cummings [1972] Crim LR 38   254
Dillon v O'Brien and Davies (1887) 16 Cox CC 245   295
Dimes v Grand Junction Canal (1852) 3 HLC 759   123
DPP v Boardman [1975] AC 421; [1974] 3 WLR 673; 118 SJ 809; [1974]
    3 All ER 887; 60 Cr App R 165; [1975] Crim LR 36   47, 99
DPP v Doot [1973] AC 807; [1973] 2 WLR 532; 117 SJ 266; [1973] 1 All ER 940; 57 Cr
    App R 600; [1973] Crim LR 292   8
DPP v Humphrys [1977] AC 1; [1976] 2 WLR 857; 140 JP 386; [1976] 2 All ER 497; 63
    Cr App R 95   65, 66
DPP v Merriman [1973] AC 584; [1972] 3 WLR 545; 116 SJ 745; [1972] 3 All ER 42; 56
    Cr App R 766; [1972] Crim LR 784   48
DPP v Ottewell [1970] AC 642; [1968] 3 WLR 621; 112 SJ 687; [1968] 3 All ER 153; 52
    Cr App R 679   187, 220
DPP v Ping Lin [1976] AC 574; [1975] 3 WLR 419; 119 SJ 627; [1975] 3 All ER 175;
    [1976] Crim LR 53; 62 Cr App R 14   287
DPP v Stonehouse [1978] AC 55; [1977] 3 WLR 143; 121 SJ 491; [1977] 2 All ER 909; 65 Cr App R
    192; [1977] Crim LR 544   8
Doran 116 SJ 238; 56 Cr App R 429; [1972] Crim LR 392   100
Durham Quarter Sessions ex p Virgo [1952] 2 QB 1; [1952] 1 TLR 516; 116 JP 157;
    [1952] 1 All ER 466   251
Dyson (1943) 169 LT 237; 107 JP 178; 59 TLR 314; 41 LGR 230; (1943) 29 Cr App R
    104   309
Edmonds (1821) 4 B & Ald 471; 1 StTr (NS) 785   232
Ellis (James) 57 Cr App R 571; [1973] Crim LR 389   54
Elrington (1861) 1 B&S 688; 31 LJMC 14; 5 LT 284; 26 JP 117; 8 Jur (NS) 97; 10 WR 13; 9
    Cox CC 86   64
Epping and Harlow Justices ex p Massaro [1973] QB 433; [1973] 2 WLR 158; (1972) 117 SJ
    32; [1973] 1 All ER 1011; 57 Cr App R 499; [1973] Crim LR 109   89
Evans (1972) 56 Cr App R 854; [1972] Crim LR 574   205
Fennell (1881) 7 QBD 147; 50 LJMC 126; 44 LT 687; 45 JP 666; 29 WR 742; 14 Cox CC
    607   287

Ferguson v The Queen [1979] 1 All ER 877; [1979] 1 WLR 94   97
Flannagan v Shaw [1920] 3 KB 96   258
Fleming [1973] 2 All ER 401; 57 Cr App R 524; [1973] Crim LR 383   190
Flynn (1958) 42 Cr App R 15   101
Ford [1969] 1 WLR 1703   220
Ford and others (1976) 62 Cr App R 303; [1976] Crim LR 391   161, 165, 216
Forde [1923] 2 KB 400; 92 LJKB 501; 128 LT 798; 39 TLR 322; 87 JP 76; 67 SJ 539; 17
    Cr App R 99; 27 Cox CC 406   226
Foster (P) (Haulage) Ltd v Roberts [1978] RTR 302; 122 SJ 229; (1978) 67 Cr App R
    305; [1978] Crim LR 502; [1978] 2 All ER 751   251
Furlong [1950] WN 129; 66 TLR (Pt1) 558; 114 JP 201; 94 SJ 256; [1950] 1 All ER 636;
    34 Cr App R 79; 48 LGR 296   104
Galbraith [1981] 1 WLR 1039   92
Garfield v Maddocks [1974] QB 7; [1973] 2 WLR 888; 117 SJ 145; [1973] 2 All ER 303;
    57 Cr App R 372; [1973] Crim LR 231   252
Gateshead Justices ex p Tesco Stores Ltd [1981] QB 470; [1981] 2 WLR 419,
    [1981] 1 All ER 1027   260, 280, 282
Gelberg v Miller [1961] 1 WLR 459; 105 SJ 230; [1961] 1 All ER 618   244
Genese [1976] 1 WLR 958; 140 JP 460; 120 SJ 330; [1976] 2 All ER 600; 63 Cr App R
    152; [1976] Crim LR 459   193
Ghani v Jones [1970] 1 QB 693; [1969] 3 WLR 1158; 113 SJ 854; [1969] 3 All ER
    1700   296, 297, 335
Gilbert (1978) 66 Cr App R 237   109, 291, 292
Gilby [1975] 1 WLR 924; [1975] 2 All ER 743; 61 Cr App R 112   212
Goodson [1975] 1 WLR 549; [1975] 1 All ER 760; 60 Cr App R 266   103
Gortat and Pirog [1973] Crim LR 648   170, 171
Green [1950] 1 All ER 38; 34 Cr App R 33; 48 LGR 58   104
Gregory [1972] 1 WLR 991; 116 SJ 506; [1972] 2 All ER 861; 56 Cr App R 441; [1972]
    Crim LR 509   51
Grice (1978) 66 Cr App R 167   179
Griffiths [1969] 1 WLR 896; 133 JP 507; 113 SJ 364; [1969] 2 All ER 805; 53 Cr App R
    424   191, 192
Grondkowski and Malinowski [1946] KB 369; 31 Cr App R 116   49
Groom [1977] QB 6; [1976] 2 WLR 618; 140 JP 376; 120 SJ 198; [1976] 2 All ER 321; 62
    Cr App R 242   29
Guildford Justices ex p Harding (1981) *The Times,* 20 January   137
Gumbs (1926) 19 Cr App R 74   233
Gunnell 110 SJ 706; 50 Cr App R 242; [1966] Crim LR 515   207
Gurney [1974] Crim LR 472   212
Haddy [1944] KB 442; 113 LJKB 137; 170 LT 406; 60 TLR 253; 103 JP 151; [1944] 1
    All ER 319; 29 Cr App R 182   232
Hall v R [1971] 1 WLR 298   291
Hamberry [1977] QB 924; [1977] 2 WLR 999; 121 SJ 270; [1977] 3 All ER 561; 65 Cr App
    R 233   78
Hammond (1941) 166 LT 135; 106 JP 35; 86 SJ 78; [1941] 3 All ER 318; 28 Cr App R
    84; 40 LGR 1   89
Hanbury [1980] Crim LR 63   193, 195, 208, 209
Hannah (1968) 52 Cr App R 734   186
Harbax Singh [1979] QB 319; [1979] 2 WLR 100; [1979] 1 All ER 524; 68 Cr App R
    108   314, 315
Harden [1963] 1 QB 8; [1962] 2 WLR 553; 126 JP 130; 106 SJ 264; [1962] 1 All ER 286; 46
    Cr App R 90   8
Harnden 66 Cr App R 281; [1978] Crim LR 375   186, 215
Harrington 120 SJ 403; (1977) 64 Cr App R 1; [1976] Crim LR 702   72
Hassan [1970] 1 QB 423; [1970] 2 WLR 82; 113 SJ 997; [1970] 1 All ER 745; 54 Cr App
    R 56   26
Hatfield Justices ex p Castle [1981] 1 WLR 217; [1980] 3 All ER 509   152, 153, 263
Hawkes (1931) 75 SJ 247; 22 Cr App R 172   111
Hawkins v Bepey [1980] 1 WLR 419; [1980] 1 All ER 797   279

Hazeltine [1967] 2 QB 857; [1967] 3 WLR 209; 131 JP 401; 111 SJ 351; [1967] 2 All ER
671; 51 Cr App R 351   58
Heyes [1951] 1 KB 29; 114 JP 451; 94 SJ 582; [1950] 2 All ER 587; 34 Cr App R 161; 48
LGR 565   59
Hier 62 Cr App R 233; [1976] Crim LR 304   322
Highgate Justices ex p Lewis [1977] Crim LR 611   262, 319, 321
Hinds (1962) 46 Cr App R 327   225
Hogan [1974] QB 398; [1974] 2 WLR 357; 118 SJ 218; [1974] 2 All ER 142;
59 Cr App R 174; [1974] Crim LR 247   65
Hogan and Tompkins [1960] 2 QB 513; [1960] 3 WLR 426; 124 JP 457; 104 SJ 645; [1960] 3
All ER 149; 44 Cr App R 255   65
Hollyman [1980] Crim LR 60   219
Holmes (1843) 1 Car & Kir 248; 1 Cox CC 9   287
Hood [1968] 1 WLR 773; 132 JP 316; 112 SJ 292; [1968] 2 All ER 56; 52 Cr App R 265;
[1968] Crim LR 272   79
Horseferry Road Justices ex p Constable (1981) *The Times,* 27 January   144
Horseferry Road Magistrates' Court ex p Pearson [1976] 1 WLR 511; 140 JP 382; 120
SJ 352; [1976] 2 All ER 264   315
Howell (1981) *The Times,* 13 April   275
Hudson (1981) 72 Cr App R 163   276, 277, 288, 289
Hughes [1968] 1 WLR 560; 112 SJ 213; [1968] 2 All ER 53n; 52 Cr App R 214   186
Hunt [1978] Crim LR 697   325
Hussain [1962] Crim LR 712; 106 SJ 722   184
Hussien v Chong Fook Kam [1970] AC 492; [1970] 2 WLR 441; [1969] 3 All ER 1626   276
Hutchison [1972] 1 WLR 398; 116 SJ 77; [1972] 1 All ER 936; 56 Cr App R 307   171
Ibrahim v R [1914] AC 599; 83 LJPC 185; 111 LT 20; 30 TLR 383; 24 Cox CC 174   287
Ingle [1974] 3 All ER 811; 59 Cr App R 306; [1974] Crim LR 609   212
Inwood (1975) 60 Cr App R 70   324
Isequilla [1975] 1 WLR 716; 118 SJ 736; [1975] 1 All ER 77; 60 Cr App R 52;
[1974] Crim LR 599   110
Ithell [1969] 1 WLR 272; 133 JP 371; 113 SJ 104; [1969] 2 All ER 449; 53 Cr App R 210   191
Jackson [1973] Crim LR 356   26
Jackson and Hart [1970] 1 QB 647; [1969] 2 WLR 1339; 133 JP 358; 113 SJ 310; [1969] 2
All ER 453; 53 Cr App R 341   209
Jeffrey v Black [1978] 1 QB 490; [1977] 3 WLR 895; 121 SJ 662; [1978] 1 All ER 555;
[1977] Crim LR 555   295, 296, 335
Johal and Ram [1972] 3 WLR 210; 116 SJ 195; [1972] 2 All ER 449; 56 Cr App R 348   51
John [1973] Crim LR 113   299
Jones (No 2) [1972] 1 WLR 887; 116 SJ 483; 56 Cr App R 413; [1972] Crim LR 593   96, 236
Jones and others [1974] ICR 310; 118 SJ 277; 59 Cr App R 120; [1974] IRLR 117;
[1974] Crim LR 663   48, 52
Juett [1981] Crim LR 113   229
Kane (1977) 65 Cr App R 270   100
Kendrick and Smith (1931) 144 LT 748; 23 Cr App R 1; 29 Cox CC 285   64
Kent Justices ex p Machin [1952] 2 QB 355; [1952] 1 TLR 1197; 116 JP 242; 96 SJ 297;
[1952] 1 All ER 1123; 36 Cr App R 23   144, 154, 260
Ketteridge [1915] 1 KB 467; 84 LJKB 352; 112 LT 783; 31 TLR 115; 79 JP 216; 59 SJ
163; 11 Cr App R 54; 24 Cox CC 678   102
Kings Lynn Justices ex p Carter and others [1969] 1 QB 488; [1968] 3 WLR 1210; 113 JP 83;
[1968] 3 All ER 858; 53 Cr App R 42   143, 147, 148
Kray (1969) 53 Cr App R 412   74
Lake (1976) 64 Cr App R 172   49
Larkin [1943] KB 174; 112 LJKB 163; 168 LT 298; 59 TLR 105; 87 SJ 140; [1943] 1 All
ER 217; 29 Cr App R 18   110
Lattimore (1976) 119 SJ 863; 62 Cr App R 53   241
Launock v Brown (1819) 2 B & Ald 592   285
Lawrence v Same [1968] 2 QB 93; [1968] 1 All ER 1191; [1968] 2 WLR 1062; 132 JP
277; 112 SJ 212   135
Leeds Justices ex p Hanson [1981] 3 WLR 315   279

Lee Kun [1916] 1 KB 337; 85 LJKB 515; 114 LT 421; 32 TLR 225; 80 JP 166; 60 SJ
158; 11 Cr App R 293; 25 Cox CC 304   96
Leicester Justices ex p Lord [1980] Crim LR 581   153
Lemsatef [1977] 1 WLR 812; 121 SJ 353; [1977] 2 All ER 835; 64 Cr App R 242   289, 293
Lester (1940) 27 Cr App R 8   110
Lewis [1969] 2 QB 1; [1969] 2 WLR 55; 133 JP 111; 112 SJ 904; [1969] 1 All ER 79; 53
Cr App R 76   26, 232
Leyland Justices ex p Hawthorn [1979] QB 283; [1979] 2 WLR 28; [1979] 1 All ER 209;
68 Cr App R 269   134, 261
Lidster [1976] RTR 240; [1976] Crim LR 80   325
Lillis [1972] 2 QB 236; [1972] 2 WLR 1409; 116 SJ 432; [1972] 2 All ER 1209; 56 Cr App
R 573; [1972] Crim LR 458   106, 107
Lindley v Rutter [1981] QB 128; [1980] 3 WLR 660; 72 Cr App R 1   294
Linley [1959] Crim LR 123   90
Llandrindod Wells Justices ex p Gibson [1968] 1 WLR 598   261
Llewellyn (1977) 67 Cr App R 149; [1977] Crim LR 105   83
Lowe [1964] 1 WLR 609; 128 JP 336; 108 SJ 261; [1964] 2 All ER 116; 48 Cr App R 165   204
Lowe (1977) 66 Cr App R 122   219
Ludlow v Metropolitan Police Commissioner [1971] AC 29; [1970] 2 WLR 521; 114 SJ
148; 54 Cr App R 233   46, 47, 152
Lymm Justices ex p Brown [1973] 1 WLR 1039; [1973] 1 All ER 716; [1973] Crim LR 52   148
McCormack [1969] 2 QB 442; [1969] 3 WLR 175; 133 JP 630; 113 SJ 507; [1969] 3 All
ER 371; 53 Cr App R 514   106
McCready and Hurd [1978] 1 WLR 1376; 122 SJ 247; 67 Cr App R 345; [1978] 3
All ER 967   106, 107
McElligott ex p Gallagher [1972] Crim LR 332   124
McFadden and Cunningham 120 SJ 46; 62 Cr App R 187; [1976] Crim LR 193   82, 87
McKenna (1957) 40 Cr App R 65   101
McKenna [1960] 1 QB 411; [1960] 2 WLR 306; 124 JP 179; 104 SJ 109; [1960] 1 All ER
326; 44 Cr App R 63   110
McNally [1954] 1 WLR 933; 118 JP 399; 98 SJ 440; [1954] 2 All ER 372; 38 Cr App R 90   59
Majewski [1977] AC 443; [1975] 3 WLR 401; [1975] 3 All ER 296; 62 Cr App R 5; CA
[1977] AC 443; [1976] 2 WLR 623; [1976] 2 All ER 142; 62 Cr App R 262; HL   255
Mallinson [1977] Crim LR 161   230, 286
Manchester City Stipendiary Magistrate ex p Snelson [1977] 1 WLR 911; 121 SJ 442;
[1977] Crim LR 423   21, 64
Mansfield [1977] 1 WLR 1102; 121 S. 709; [1978] 1 All ER 134; 65 Cr App R
276   45, 109
Marquis [1974] 1 WLR 1087; [1974] 2 All ER 1216; [1974] Crim LR 556; 59 Cr App R
228   198, 227
Marwick (1953) 37 Cr App R 125   195
Marylebone Justices ex p Farrag [1981] Crim LR 182   261
Marylebone Justices ex p Westminster City Council [1971] 1 WLR 567; [1971] 1 All
ER 1025   251
Mason (1980) 71 Cr App R 617; [1980] 3 WLR 617   72, 73, 74, 75, 76
Maxwell (George) Developments Ltd [1980] 2 All ER 99   36
May (1952) 36 Cr App R 91   289
Mead (1916) 80 JP 382; 85 LJKB 1065; 114 LT 1172; 14 LGR 688   279
Melvin and Eden [1953] 1 QB 481; [1953] 2 WLR 274; 117 JP 95; 97 SJ 99; [1953] 1 All
ER 294; 37 Cr App R 1   105
Menocal [1980] AC 598; [1979] 2 WLR 876; [1979] 2 All ER 510   180
Ex p Meredith [1973] 1 WLR 435; 117 SJ 165; [1973] 2 All ER 234; [1973] RTR 228;
57 Cr App R 451; [1973] Crim LR 232   319
Metropolitan Police Commissioner ex p Blackburn (No 1) [1968] 2 QB 118; [1973] 1
All ER 763   271
Michaél v Gowland [1977] 1 WLR 296; [1977] 2 All ER 328   258
Middleton [1975] QB 191; [1974] 3 WLR 335; 118 SJ 680; [1974] 2 All ER 1190; 59 Cr
App R 18; [1974] Crim LR 667   287
Miller (1979) 68 Cr App R 56   324

Mitchell [1977] 1 WLR 753; 121 SJ 252; [1977] 2 All ER 168; 65 Cr App R 185   236
Moghal 65 Cr App R 56; [1977] Crim LR 373   49
Moylan [1970] 1 QB 143; [1969] 3 WLR 814; 133 JP 709; 113 SJ 624; [1969] 3 All ER
    783; 53 Cr App R 590   192
Mutch [1973] 1 All ER 178; (1972) 57 Cr App R 196; [1973] Crim LR 111   98
Neal [1949] 2 KB 590; 65 TLR 557; 113 JP 468; 93 SJ 589; [1949] 2 All ER 438; 33 Cr
    App R 189; 48 LGR 93   102, 103
Nelson (1977) 65 Cr App R 119   52, 82
Newcastle-upon-Tyne Justices ex p John Bryce (Contractors) Ltd [1976] 2 All ER
    611; [1976] 1 WLR 517; 140 JP 440; 120 SJ 64   128
Newsome and Browne [1970] 2 QB 711; [1970] 3 WLR 586; 114 SJ 665; 3 All ER 455;
    54 Cr App R 485   179
Nicholson [1947] WN 272; 63 TLR 560; 112 JP 1; [1947] 2 All ER 535; 32 Cr App R 98,
    127   65, 179
Norfolk Quarter Sessions ex p Brunson [1953] 1 QB 503; 117 JP 100; 97 SJ 98; [1953] 1
    All ER 346; 37 Cr App R 6   28
Northam 111 SJ 965; 52 Cr App R 97; [1968] Crim LR 104   287
Nottingham Justices ex p Davies [1981] QB 38; [1980] 3 WLR 15;
    [1980] 2 All ER 775   310
O'Brien v Brabner (1885) 49 JPN 227; 78 LTN 409   285
O'Coigley (1798) 26 St Tr 1191   74
O'Donnell (1917) 12 Cr App R 219   99
Oliphant [1905] 2 KB 67   8
Oliva [1965] 1 WLR 1028; 129 JP 500; 109 SJ 453; [1965] 3 All ER 116; 49 Cr App R
    298   85, 101
O'Neill (1950) 34 Cr App R 108; 48 LGR 305   88
Orpin [1975] QB 283; [1974] 3 WLR 252; 118 SJ 564; [1974] 2 All ER 1121; 59 Cr App
    R 231; [1974] Crim LR 598   36
Osbourne and Virtue [1973] QB 678; [1973] 2 WLR 209; [1973] 1 All ER 649; 57 Cr
    App R 297; [1973] Crim LR 178   290
Owen [1952] 2 QB 362; [1952] 1 TLR 1220; 116 JP 244; 96 SJ 281; [1952] 2 All ER
    1040; 36 Cr App R 16   103
Paling (1978) 67 Cr App R 299   29, 76
Palmer (1914) 10 Cr App R 77   299
Parks [1961] 1 WLR 1484; 105 SJ 868; [1961] 3 All ER 633; 46 Cr App R 29   240
Parsons v F. W. Woolworth and Co Ltd [1980] 1 WLR 1472   258
Pattinson (1974) 54 Cr App R 417   230
Payne v Lord Harris of Greenwich [1981] 1 WLR 754   189
Peace [1976] Crim LR 119   57
Peter [1975] Crim LR 593   185
Phillips and Quayle [1939] 1 KB 63; 26 Cr App R 200   17, 18
Podola [1960] 1 QB 325; [1959] 3 WLR 718; 103 SJ 856; [1959] 3 All ER 418; 43 Cr App
    R 220   61
Potter [1977] Crim LR 112   234
Potter, 15 September 1977 (unreported)   55
Power [1919] 1 KB 572; 88 LJKB 593; 120 LT 577; 35 TLR 283; 83 JP 124; 14 Cr App
    R 17; 26 Cox CC 399   229
Practice Direction [1966] 1 WLR 1184; 130 JP 387; 110 SJ 508; [1966] 2 All ER 929;
    50 Cr App R 271   172
Practice Direction [1967] 1 WLR 1198; 111 SJ 639; [1967] 3 All ER 137; 51 Cr App R
    454   108, 109
Practice Direction [1970] 1 WLR 916; 54 Cr App R 373   108
Practice Direction (1972) 56 Cr App R 52   33, 149, 252
Practice Direction [1973] 1 WLR 718; [1973] 2 All ER 592;
    57 Cr App R 798   322
Practice Direction (1973) 57 Cr App R 345   70
Practice Direction 30 June 1975   173
Practice Direction 120 SJ 541; [1976] Crim LR 561   57
Practice Direction [1977] 1 WLR 537; [1977] 1 All ER 540; 64 Cr App R 258   48, 322

Practice Direction [1977] 1 WLR 1435; [1978] 1 All ER 64   33
Practice Direction [1981] 1 WLR 1163   138
Practice Note [1962] 1 All ER 448   19, 134
Practice Note (1969) 50 Cr App R 290   236
Practice Note [1974] 1 WLR 770; 118 SJ 405; 59 Cr App R 159; [1974] 2 All ER 794   304
Practice Note [1980] 1 All ER 555   238
Prager [1972] 1 WLR 260; 116 SJ 158; [1972] 1 All ER 1114; 56 Cr App R 151   288, 289
Priestly (1966) 51 Cr App R 1   288
Prime (1973) 57 Cr App R 632   103
Quinn (1932) 23 Cr App R 196; 173 LTJ 474   218
R: For cases in which the Crown was prosecutor, see under the name of the defendant.
For applications for review of proceedings, see under the name of the court.
Ramsden [1972] Crim LR 547   236
Reading Crown Court ex p Malik 51 Gr App R 1 [1981] 2 WLR 473;
    [1981] QB 451; [1981] 1 All ER 249; 72 Cr App R 146   310, 313
Reeves (1972) 56 Cr App R 366   195
Rice v Connelly [1966] 2 QB 414; [1966] 3 WLR 17; 130 JP 322; 110 SJ 371; [1966] 2 All
    ER 649   289, 291
Richardson [1979] 3 All ER 247; [1979] 1 WLR 1316   78, 79
Roads [1967] 2 QB 108; [1967] 2 WLR 1014; 131 JP 324; 111 SJ 212; [1967] 2 All ER
    84; 51 Cr App R 297   104, 105
Robertson [1968] 1 WLR 1767; 133 JP 5; 112 SJ 799; [1968] 3 All ER 557; 52 Cr App R
    690   61
Robinson (Practice Note) [1953] 1 WLR 872; 97 SJ 474; [1953] 2 All ER 334; 37 Cr
    App R 95   225
Robinson (1969) 113 SJ 143; 53 Cr App R 314   173
Rose and Sapiano (1980) 71 Cr App R 296   220
Rouse [1904] 1 KB 184; 73 LJKB 60; 89 LT 677; 20 TLR 68; 68 JP 14; 52 WR 236; 20
    Cox CC 592; 48 SJ 85; [1900–03] All ER Rep Ext 1054   248
Ryan [1976] Crim LR 508   212
S (an infant) v Recorder of Manchester [1971] AC 481; [1970] 2 WLR 21; 113 SJ 872;
    [1969] 3 All ER 1230   59, 133, 252
Sahota [1980] Crim LR 678   104, 169
St Albans Crown Court ex p Cinnamond [1981] QB 480; [1981] 2 WLR 681;
    [1981] 1 All ER 802   254, 261, 265
St Albans Crown Court ex p Godman [1981] 2 WLR 882   159
Sanderson [1953] 1 WLR 392; 97 SJ 136; [1953] 1 All ER 485; 37 Cr App R 32   101
Sandwell Justices ex p West Midland Passenger Transport Board [1979] Crim LR 56   128
Sang [1980] AC 402; [1979] 3 WLR 263; [1979] 2 All ER 1222;
    69 Cr App R 282   296, 297, 299, 338
Sapiano (1968) 112 SJ 799; 52 Cr App R 674   193
Sartori [1961] Crim LR 397   287
Sawyer (1980) 72 Cr App R 283   79
Scarrott [1978] QB 1016; [1977] 3 WLR 629; 121 SJ 558; [1978] 1 All ER 672;
    65 Cr App R 125; [1977] Crim LR 745   47
Selvey v DPP [1970] AC 304; [1968] 2 WLR 1494; 132 JP 430; 112 SJ 461; [1968] 2 All
    ER 497; 52 Cr App R 443   248
Sheerin (1976) 64 Cr App R 68   39
Sheffield Crown Court ex p Brownlow [1980] QB 530; [1980] 2 WLR 892   75, 76
Sherman and Apps (1980) *The Times,* 9 December   277, 300
Shields and Patrick [1977] Crim LR 281   240
Skone 51 Cr App R 165; [1967] Crim LR 249   218, 234
Smith [1959] 2 QB 35; [1959] 2 WLR 623; 123 JP 295; 103 SJ 353; [1959] 2 All ER
    193; 43 Cr App R 121   287
Smith [1968] 1 WLR 636; 132 JP 312; 112 SJ 231; [1968] 2 All ER 115; 52 Cr App R
    224   93
Smith (David Raymond) [1974] QB 354; [1974] 2 WLR 20; (1973) 117 SJ 938; [1974]
    1 All ER 632; (1973) 58 Cr App R 320   225
Smith (M.S.) (1977) 64 Cr App R 116; [1977] Crim LR 234   212

Soanes 112 JP 193; 92 SJ 155; [1948] 1 All ER 289; 32 Cr App R 136; 46 LGR 218   58
Southampton Justices ex p Green [1976] QB 11; [1975] 3 WLR 277; [1975] 2 All ER
   1073   262, 265, 315
Southgate [1963] 1 WLR 809; 127 JP 538; 107 SJ 516; [1963] 2 All ER 833; 47 Cr App
   R 252   100
Springfield 113 SJ 670; 53 Cr App R 608; [1969] Crim LR 557   106
Stafford Justices ex p Ross [1962] 1 WLR 456   137
Stafford and Luvaglio v DPP [1974] AC 878; [1973] 3 WLR 719; 117 SJ 834; [1973] 3
   All ER 762; 58 Cr App R 256   231, 240, 241
Starie (1979) 69 Cr App R 239; [1979] Crim LR 731   202
Stone [1970] 1 WLR 1112; 114 SJ 513; [1970] 2 All ER 594; 54 Cr App R 364   55
Sullivan (1967) 51 Cr App R 102; 111 SJ 14; [1967] Crim LR 174   293
Sullivan [1971] 1 QB 253; 54 Cr App R 389   94, 95
Sullivan (1972) 56 Cr App R 541   238
Surrey Justices ex p Witherick [1932] 1 KB 450; [1931] All ER Rep 807; 95 JP 219; 101
   LJKB 203; 166 LT 164; 48 TLR 67; 75 SJ 853; 29 LGR 667; 29 Cox CC 414   126
Swales v Cox (1981) 72 Cr App R 171   275
Sykes (1913) 8 Cr App R 233   286
Taggart (1979) 1 Cr App R (S) 144   170
Tarry [1970] 2 QB 561; [1970] 2 WLR 1034; 114 SJ 283; [1970] 2 All ER 185; 54 Cr App
   R 322   193, 200
Taylor (1869) LR 1 CCR 194; 38 LJMC 106; 20 LT 402; 33 JP 358; 17 WR 623; 11
   Cox CC 261   106
Taylor [1979] Crim LR 649   225
Thames Magistrates' Court ex p Polemis [1974] 1 WLR 1371, [1974] 2 All ER 1219;
   [1974] 2 Lloyd's Rep 16   261
Thomas (1949) 33 Cr App R 200   64
Thompson v Knights [1947] KB 336; [1947] LJR 445; 176 LT 367; 63 TLR 38; 111 JP
   43; 91 SJ 68; [1947] 1 All ER 112   126
Thompson (1962) 126 JP 55; [1962] 1 All ER 65; 46 Cr App R 72   104
Thorne (1978) 66 Cr App R 6   50
Tonks [1980] Crim LR 59   219
Tower Bridge Magistrate ex p Osman [1971] 1 WLR 1109; 115 SJ 385; [1971] 2 All
   ER 1018; 55 Cr App R 434   148
Treacy v DPP [1971] AC 537; [1971] 2 WLR 112; (1970) 115 SJ 12; [1971] 1 All ER
   110; 55 Cr App R 113   8
Trigg [1963] 1 WLR 305; 127 JP 257; 107 SJ 136; [1963] 1 All ER 490; 47 Cr App R 94   232
Tucker [1974] 1 WLR 615; 118 SJ 330; [1974] 2 All ER 639; 59 Cr App R 71   200, 227
Turnbull [1977] QB 224; [1976] 3 WLR 445; 140 JP 648; 120 SJ 486; [1976] 3 All ER
   549; 63 Cr App R 132   92, 98, 248, 298
Turner [1944] KB 463; 114 LJKB 45; 171 LT 246; 60 TLR 332; [1944] 1 All ER 599;
   30 Cr App R 9   232
Turner [1970] 2 QB 321; [1970] 2 WLR 1093; 114 SJ 337; [1970] 2 All ER 281; 54 Cr
   App R 352   56, 57, 59, 82, 83, 219, 226, 232
Urbanowski [1976] 1 WLR 455, 140 JP 270; 120 SJ 148; [1976] 1 All ER 679; 62 Cr
   App R 229   53
Van Pelz [1943] KB 157; 112 LJKB 251; 168 LT 159; 59 TLR 115; 107 JP 24; [1943] 1
   All ER 36; 29 Cr App R 10; 41 LGR 93   172
Vivian [1979] 1 All ER 48; [1979] 1 WLR 291; 68 Cr App R 53   324
Walhein (1952) 36 Cr App R 167   110
Ware v Fox; Fox v Dingley [1967] 1 WLR 379; 131 JP 113; 111 SJ 111; [1967] 1 All
   ER 100   45
Watton (1979) 68 Cr App R 293   239
Weaver [1968] 1 QB 353; [1967] 1 All ER 277; [1967] 2 WLR 1244; 131 JP 173; 111
   SJ 174; 51 Cr App R 77   80
Wells Street Stipendiary Magistrate ex p Seillon [1978] 1 WLR 1002; 122 SJ 192;
   [1978] Crim LR 360; [1980] Crim LR 180   28, 262
West [1964] 1 QB 15; [1962] 3 WLR 218; 126 JP 352; 106 SJ 514; [1962] 2 All ER 624;
   46 Cr App R 296   44

West London Metropolitan Stipendiary Magistrate ex p Klahn [1979] 1 WLR 933;
   [1979] 2 All ER 221; 143 JP 390; 123 SJ 251   282
Whitehead v Haines [1965] 1 QB 200; [1964] 2 All ER 530; [1964] 3 WLR 197; 128 JP
   372; 108 SJ 336; 62 LGR 344   258
Whitehouse v Gay News Ltd and Lemon (1979) 68 Cr App R 381   269
Wilkins (1978) 66 Cr App R 49   172, 234
Williams (Roy) [1978] QB 373; [1977] 2 WLR 400; 121 SJ 135; [1977] 1 All ER 874; 64
   Cr App R 106; [1977] Crim LR 305   54
Wilson (R) (1979) 69 Cr App R 83   44
Wilson [1980] 1 WLR 376; [1980] 1 All ER 1093; 70 Cr App R 219   192
Wiltshire v Barrett [1966] 1 QB 312; [1965] 2 WLR 1195; 129 JP 348; 109 SJ 274;
   [1965] 2 All ER 271   278
Wong Kam-ming v The Queen [1979] 1 All ER 939; [1979] Crim LR 168   287
Woodage v Lambie [1971] 1 WLR 754; 115 SJ 588; [1971] 3 All ER 674; [1972]
   RTR 37   210
Woods, 25 October 1977 (unreported)   55
Wright v Nicholson [1970] 1 All ER 12; [1970] 1 WLR 142; 134 JP 85; 113 SJ 939   129
Zaveckas [1970] 1 WLR 516; 134 JP 247; 114 SJ 31; [1970] 1 All ER 43; 54 Cr App R
   202   287

Table of Statutes

Accessories and Abettors Act 1861 (24 & 25 Vict c 94)
s 8   48
Administration of Justice (Miscellaneous Provisions) Act 1933
s 2   28, 52
s 2(2)   40
Administration of Justice Act 1960 (8 & 9 Eliz 2, c 65)
s 1(1)(a)   265
s 15   316
s 16   261
Administration of Justice Act 1970 (c 31)
s 9   223
Bail Act 1976 (c 63)   303
s 3   308
s 3(2)   314
s 3(4)   278
s 3(5)   308
s 3(6)   278
s 3(8)   311
s 4   304, 305, 309, 311
s 5   311
s 6   133, 314
s 7   130, 306, 307, 313
s 7(1)   96, 313
s 7(3)   314
s 8(2)   310
sch 1   304, 305, 310
pt 1   305
  para 9   306
pt 2   307
Bankruptcy Act 1883 (46 & 47 Vict, c 52)
s 32   117
Bankruptcy Act 1914 (4 & 5 Geo 5, c 59)   325
Children and Young Persons Act 1933 (23 & 24 Geo 5, c 12)
s 34   157, 159, 300
s 34(1)   157
s 37   158
s 39   157
s 42   27, 28, 90
s 43   28, 90
s 46   157
s 47   158
s 49   159

Children and Young Persons Act 1933 – continued
s 53   160, 161, 164, 165, 174, 181, 216
s 53(1)   160, 161, 189
s 53(2)   156, 161, 189
s 55   160, 331
s 56   164
s 59   158
Children and Young Persons Act 1963 (c 37)
s 16(2)   171
s 18   157
s 28   158
s 29   159
Children and Young Persons Act 1969 (c 54)
s 1   31, 116, 161
s 2(12)   31
s 7(3)   330
s 7(7)(a)   161
s 7(7)(b)   162
s 7(7)(c)   163
s 7(8)   165
s 12   163
s 13   162
s 14   162
s 16(2)   171
s 17   162
s 18(2)   163
s 20   161
s 21(2)   161
s 23   315
s 24   161
s 29   303
s 29(1)   300
s 29(3)   300
s 29(5)   300
s 31   162
s 70   155
Coinage Offences Act 1936 (26 Geo 5 & 1 Edw 8, c 16)
s 4(1)   237
s 5(1)   238
Costs in Criminal Cases Act 1973 (c 14)
s 1   322
s 1(1)   323
s 1(2)   323
s 1(3)   321
s 1(4)   323

Costs in Criminal Cases Act 1973—*continued*
  s 2   322
  s 2(1)   323
  s 2(2)   160, 323
  s 2(3)   321
  s 3   322
  s 3(1)   323
  s 3(2)   253
  s 3(3)   321
  s 3(4)   323
  s 3(9)   323
  s 4(1)   323
  s 4(2)   322
  s 5   258, 264
  s 7(1)   242
  s 7(2)   242
  s 9   242
  s 16   322
Courts Act 1971 (c 23)
  s 1(1)   31
  s 4   31
  s 4(5)   33, 34
  s 5   35, 115, 252
  s 5(8)   35
  s 6   31
  s 7   34
  s 7(4)   53
  s 9   253
  s 9(4)   253
  s 10   259
  s 10(5)   260
  s 11   179, 180
  s 13(4)   252, 259, 304, 312
  s 13(6)   303
  s 16   32
  s 17   32
  s 18   32
  s 19   32
  s 20   32
  s 21   32
  s 24   32
  s 26   224
Criminal Appeal Act 1907 (7 Edw 7, c 8)   223
Criminal Appeal Act 1966 (c 31)
  s 1(1)   223
  s 1(3)   223
  s 2(1)   223
  s 2(3)   223
  s 2(4)   224
Criminal Appeal Act 1968 (c 19)
  s 1   226
  s 1(1)   224
  s 1(2)   224
  s 2   52, 229, 232
  s 2(1)   228
  s 2(2)   231
  s 3   105, 233
  s 3(2)   233
  s 4   233

Criminal Appeal Act 1968—*continued*
  s 6   244
  s 7   29, 232, 241
  s 9   227, 228
  s 10   227, 228
  s 11   233
  s 11(1)   228
  s 12   243
  s 13   243
  s 14   243
  s 15   244
  s 17   242
  s 18   235
  s 19   239, 304
  s 20   225, 235
  s 22   239
  s 23   232, 240
  s 23(1)   240, 241
  s 23(2)   240, 241
  s 29   225, 226, 233, 238, 242
  s 31   225, 237
  s 31(3)   238
  s 33   244
  s 35   244
  s 35(3)   244
  s 36   244, 304
  s 37   244
  s 45   223
  s 45(2)   224
  s 50   227
Criminal Damage Act 1971 (c 48)
  s 1   151
  s 1(1)   328
  s 1(2)   141
  s 1(3)   328
  s 2   328
  s 3   328
Criminal Evidence Act 1898 (61 & 62 Vict c 36)
  s 1   93
  s 1(b)   96
  s 1(e)   94
  s 1(f)   94, 248
  s 1(g)   94
  s 1(h)   94
  s 2   93
Criminal Justice Act 1925 (15 & 16 Geo 5, c 86)
  s 13   90
Criminal Justice Act 1948 (11 & 12 Geo 6, c 58)
  s 19   164
  s 19(1)   164
  s 20   149
  s 20(1)   203
  s 27   315
  s 37   259, 304, 312
  s 39   173
Criminal Justice Act 1961 (9 & 10 Eliz 2, c 39)
  s 1(2)   150, 203
  s 1(3)   150, 176, 204
  s 1(4)   150

Criminal Justice Act 1961—*continued*
  s 3   182, 185, 186, 187, 215, 329
  s 3(2)   182
  s 3(3)   182
  s 4(1)   205
  s 4(2)   205
  s 4(3)   205
  s 4(4)   205
  s 5   206
  s 7   206
  s 12   204
  s 37   176
  s 38(4)   186
Criminal Justice Act 1967 (c 80)   121
  s 1   16, 22
  s 2   18, 21, 22
  s 9   89, 90, 134
  s 10(4)   91
  s 11   26, 94, 95
  s 11(4)   100
  s 17   54
  s 22   304, 312
  s 56(5)   151
  s 56(6)   151
  s 60   182
  s 60(1)   189
  s 60(3)   190
  s 60(4)   188
  s 60(5A)   190
  s 61   189
  s 61(1)   161
  s 62(1)   188
  s 62(2)   188
  s 62(6)   150, 188
  s 62(7)   180
  s 67   188
Criminal Justice Act 1972 (c 71)
  s 35   189
  s 36   243
  s 36(7)   243
Criminal Justice Administration Act 1914
    (4 & 5 Geo 5, c 58)
  s 19   311
Criminal Law Act 1967 (c 58)   111
  s 2   273, 274, 275
  s 2(1)   273
  s 2(6)   295
  s 3   275, 285
  s 4   9
  s 4(1)   272, 328
  s 4(2)   105, 107, 108
  s 5   9
  s 5(1)   328
  s 5(2)   272
  s 6(1)   56
  s 6(1)(a)   63
  s 6(1)(b)   58
  s 6(1)(c)   60
  s 6(2)   58, 105, 107, 108, 135

Criminal Law Act 1967—*continued*
  s 6(3)   58, 105, 107, 108, 135
  s 6(4)   105, 107, 108, 135
  s 6(5)   58
Criminal Law Act 1977 (c 45)   121, 151
  s 20   144
  s 32(1)   194
  s 47   193
  s 48   134
  s 62   293, 294
Criminal Law Amendment Act 1867
    (30 & 31 Vict c 35)
  s 6   90
Criminal Procedure (Attendance of
    Witnesses) Act 1965 (c 69)
  s 1   25, 87
  s 1(2)   25, 87
  s 3   87
  s 4(2)   87
Criminal Procedure (Insanity) Act 1964
    (c 84)
  s 4   61
  s 4(2)   62
  s 5   61, 208
Diplomatic Privileges Act 1964 (c 81)   8
Factories Act 1961 (9 & 10 Eliz 2, c 34)   139
Firearms Act 1968 (c 27)
  s 47   296
Food and Drugs Act 1955 (4 & 5 Eliz 2,
    c 16)   139, 260
Forfeiture Act 1870 (33 & 34 Vict c 23)
  s 2   117
Forgery Act 1913 (3 & 4 Geo 5, c 27)   141
  s 2(2)(a)   327
  s 4   327
  s 7   327
Immigration Act 1971 (c 77)
  s 3(6)   211
Indecency with Children Act 1960 (8 & 9
    Eliz 2, c 33)   27
  s 2   129
Indictments Act 1915 (5 & 6 Geo 5, c 90)   37
  s 3   37, 40
  s 5(1)   51
  s 5(3)   47
  s 5(4)   51
Infanticide Act 1938 (1 & 2 Geo 6, c 36)
  s 1   107
Infant Life (Preservation) Act 1929
    (19 & 20 Geo 5, c 34)
  s 1   107
Interpretation Act 1978 (c 30)
  sch 1   4, 139
Juries Act 1974 (c 23)
  s 1   68, 77
  s 2   69
  s 5(1)   69
  s 5(2)   70
  s 5(3)   70

Juries Act 1974— *continued*
  s 6   70
  s 8   70
  s 9   70
  s 10   68
  s 11   70
  s 11(4)   76
  s 11(5)   76
  s 11(6)   76
  s 12   72
  s 12(3)   74
  s 12(4)   74
  s 12(6)   75
  s 13   103
  s 15   103
  s 16   78, 123
  s 16(2)   79
  s 17   108
  s 17(3)   108
  s 17(4)   108
  s 18   77, 78, 229
  s 20   70
  s 20(5)   69
  sch 1, pt 1   68
    pt 2   68
Justices of the Peace Act 1361 (34
  Edw 3, c 1)   115, 118, 202
Justices of the Peace Act 1968 (c 69)
  s 1(7)   202
Justices of the Peace Act 1979
  s 1   118
  s 2   118
  s 6   116, 118
  s 7   119
  s 8   118
  s 12   116
  s 13   118, 119
  s 16   123
  s 17   119
  s 19   119
  s 25   119
  s 26   119
  s 31   118, 119
  s 35   119
  s 64   124
Legal Aid Act 1974 (c 14)
  s 2   321
  s 28   317, 318
  s 28(8)   242
  s 29   318
  s 29(1)   318
  s 29(2)   318
  s 29(3)   320
  s 29(4)   318
  s 29(5)   320
  s 30(1)   321
  s 30(2)   320
  s 32   319
  s 32(1)   319

Legal Aid Act 1974—*continued*
  s 33   320
  s 37   317
  s 40(2)   320
  Pt. 1   318
  Pt. 11   317
Licensing Act 1964 (c 26)
  s 21   31
Magistrates' Courts Act 1952 (15 & 16
  Geo 6 & 1 Eliz 2, c 55)   121
Magistrates' Courts Act 1957
  (5 & 6 Eliz 2, c 29)   121
Magistrates' Courts Act 1980   121, 151
  s 1   125, 280, 282
  s 1(2)(b)   122
  s 1(3)   283, 285
  s 1(4)   285
  s 1(6)   283
  s 2(1)   121
  s 2(2)   122
  s 2(3)   116, 122
  s 2(4)   122
  s 2(6)   122
  s 3   122
  s 4   17, 144
  s 4(1)   16
  s 4(2)   16
  s 4(3)   16
  s 4(4)   16, 283
  s 5   302, 303
  s 6(1)   16, 25
  s 6(2)   16, 22, 23, 25
  s 6(3)   27, 303
  s 7   34
  s 8   24
  s 8(2)   24
  s 10   283, 302
  s 10(2)   130
  s 10(3)   137, 212, 302, 303, 304
  s 10(4)   302, 303
  s 11   129, 130, 283
  s 11(1)   129
  s 11(2)   129
  s 11(3)   132
  s 11(4)   132, 261
  s 12   129, 130, 131
  s 13   129, 130, 133, 283
  s 13(5)   132
  s 14   129
  s 15   132
  s 17   140, 327
  s 18   141, 142, 144
  s 18(2)   141
  s 18(3)   144
  s 18(4)   302, 303
  s 18(5)   141
  s 19   121, 141, 142, 144, 152
  s 19(2)(b)   141
  s 19(3)   142, 146, 147

Magistrates' Courts Act 1980— *continued*
s 19(4)   143
s 20   121, 141, 142, 144, 152
s 21   121, 141, 142, 144, 152
s 22   121, 151, 194
s 22(2)   153
s 22(7)   152
s 23   141, 283
s 23(1)   144
s 24   155
s 24(1)   157
s 24(3)   160
s 24(4)   160
s 25(2)   145
s 25(3)   145
s 28   145
s 29   156, 157, 159
s 30   137, 302, 303, 304, 308
s 31   146
s 31(1)   136
s 32(1)   146, 194
s 32(2)   146
s 33   152
s 33(1)   194
s 34(3)   194
s 36   160
s 37   149, 150, 151, 165, 166, 176, 192, 203
s 38   145, 146, 147, 148, 149, 150, 151, 152,
      179, 192, 194, 203, 210, 265, 303
s 42   124
s 43   277, 300, 303
s 43(1)   277
s 43(4)   277
s 49   299
s 75   194, 195
s 76   195
s 78   195
s 79   195
s 80   195
s 81   195
s 82   195
s 82(1)   194
s 83   195
s 84   195
s 85   195
s 86   195
s 87   195
s 88   195
s 89   195
s 97   134
s 102   18, 19, 21, 22, 23, 25, 27, 29, 39, 52,
      83, 84, 87, 90, 145, 169, 324
s 103   27, 28
s 105   27, 28, 90
s 106   18
s 108   250
s 108(1)   250
s 108(2)   250
s 108(3)   250

Magistrates' Courts Act 1980— *continued*
s 109   250, 253
s 110   250
s 111   253, 256
s 111(1)   253, 254
s 111(2)   255
s 111(3)   255
s 111(4)   259
s 111(5)   255
s 113   255, 303
s 113(1)   252
s 115   202
s 117   285, 303
s 120   315
s 121(1)   123
s 122   133
s 123   128
s 125(2)   285
s 125(3)   285
s 127   9, 127, 128, 260
s 128(4)   311
s 128(6)   302, 304
s 128(7)   315
s 129(1)   311
s 129(3)   311
s 131   311
s 133   136
s 133(1)   146
s 133(2)   146
s 142   135
s 142(1)   180
s 142(4)   180
sch I   146, 152, 327-8
sch IV   194, 195, 196
Mental Health Act 1959 (7 & 8 Eliz 2,
      c 72)   162, 181, 197
s 60   176, 206, 207, 215, 216, 227
s 60(1)   206
s 60(2)   133, 206
s 60(3)   207
s 62   206
s 62(3)   176
s 65   207
s 65(1)   207
s 67   207
s 72   208
s 75   208
Merchant Shipping Act 1894 (57 & 58
      Vic c 60)
s 686   8
Metropolitan Police Act 1839 (2 & 3
      Vict c 84)
s 66   296
Misuse of Drugs Act 1971 (c 38)   40, 45, 146
s 23   296
s 24   274
Murder (Abolition of Death Penalty)
      Act 1965 (c 71)
s 1(1)   182, 190

Oaths Act 1978 (c 19)
  s 1 17
  s 5 17
Offences Against the Persons Act 1861
  (24 & 25 Vict c 100)
  s 9 7
  s 16 327
  s 18 58, 106, 107, 108
  s 20 53, 58, 106, 135, 327
  s 38 327
  s 42 125
  s 47 327
  s 57 7, 327
Official Secrets Act 1911 (1 & 2
  Geo 5, c 28) 7, 9, 183, 272
  s 1 33
  s 10 7
Official Secrets Act 1920 (10 & 11
  Geo 5, c 75) 272
Official Secrets Act 1939 (2 & 3
  Geo 6, c 121) 272
Perjury Act 1911 (1 & 2 Geo 5 c 6) 271
  s 1 327
  s 3 327
  s 4 327
  s 8 7
  s 9 30, 52
Police Act 1964 (c 48) 271, 272
  s 49 271, 272
  s 51(1) 126, 136, 139
Powers of Criminal Courts Act 1973 (c 62)
  s 1 211
  s 1(1) 212, 213
  s 1(3) 212
  s 1(4) 213
  s 1(4A) 213
  s 1(5) 212, 213
  s 1(6A) 212
  s 1(7) 213
  s 1(8) 213
  s 2 197
  s 2(1) 197
  s 2(6) 198
  s 3 176, 197
  s 4 198
  s 5 198
  s 6 198
  s 6(6) 198
  s 7(1) 199
  s 8 198, 201
  s 8(1) 199
  s 8(6) 150, 199
  s 8(7) 198
  s 8(8) 198, 199
  s 8(9) 199
  s 13 200
  s 13(2) 200
  s 14 202
  s 14(1) 202

Powers of Criminal Courts Act
1973—*continued*
  s 14(2) 202
  s 14(2)(b) 175
  s 14(3) 202
  s 14(5) 202
  s 14(8) 202
  s 15 202
  s 16 202
  s 17 202
  s 17(2) 203
  s 17(3) 203
  s 18(1) 184
  s 18(2) 184
  s 19 216, 329
  s 19(1) 160, 182
  s 19(2) 176, 182, 185, 193
  s 19(3) 185
  s 20 185
  s 20(1) 176, 182, 185, 193
  s 20(2) 185
  s 20(3) 185
  s 21 177, 178, 182, 204, 206
  s 22 191
  s 22(1) 191
  s 22(2) 191, 193
  s 22(3) 193, 197, 199
  s 22(4) 191
  s 22(5) 194, 204
  s 23 191, 199, 200
  s 23(1) 191
  s 23(2) 191
  s 23(3) 206
  s 24 191
  s 24(2) 150, 192, 193
  s 25 191, 192
  s 26 199
  s 27 199
  s 28 182, 187, 188, 220
  s 28(2) 187
  s 29 182
  s 29(3) 188
  s 30 194
  s 31 195
  s 31(1) 194
  s 31(2) 194
  s 31(3) 194
  s 32 195
  s 35 323, 325
  s 35(1) 323, 324
  s 35(2) 323, 324
  s 35(3) 323
  s 35(5) 324
  s 38 324
  s 39 325
  s 42 146, 149
  s 43 325
  s 44 210
  s 46 176

Powers of Criminal Courts Act
1973—*continued*
  s 57(2) 193
Prevention of Corruption Act 1906
  (6 Edw 7, c 34) 9, 272
Prevention of Crime Act 1953
  (1 & 2 Eliz 2, c 14) 38, 274
Prevention of Crimes Act 1871
  (34 & 35 Vict c 112)
  s 18 173
Prevention of Offences Act 1851
  (14 & 15 Vict c 19)
  s 11 274
Prevention of Terrorism (Temporary
  Provisions) Act 1976 (c 8) 9
  s 12 300
Prison Act 1952 (15 & 16 Geo 6 & 1
  Eliz 2 c 52)
  s 45 204
  s 45(3) 204
  s 45(4) 204
Prosecution of Offences Act 1979
  (c 31) 10
  s 2(1) 271
  s 4 11
  s 6 10
Public Bodies Corrupt Practices Act 1889
  (52 & 53 Vict c 69) 9
Public Order Act 1936 (1 Edw 8 & 1
  Geo 6, c 6)
  s 1 9, 272
  s 2 9, 272
  s 5 139
  s 5A 9, 272
  s 7(3) 274
Rehabilitation of Offenders Act 1974
  (c 53) 173, 174
  s 4(1) 173
  s 7(2) 173
Representation of the Peoples Act 1949
  (12, 13 & 14 Geo 6, c 68)
  s 140 117
  s 141 117
  s 163 117
Road Traffic Act 1972 (c 20) 132
  s 3 126
  s 5 126, 139, 274
  s 6(1) 126, 139
  s 8 274
  s 9 139
  s 93(1) 209
  s 93(3) 209, 210, 331
  s 95 211
  s 100 274
  s 101 131, 208, 331
  s 101(4) 211
  s 102 197, 200, 211
  s 164(2) 274
  sch 4 107, 136, 208

Road Traffic Act 1972—
continued
  pt. IV 107
  para 3A 107
  para 4 135
Road Traffic Regulation Act 1967
  (c 76)
  s 78A 131
Sexual Offences Act 1956 (4 & 5 Eliz
  2, c 69) 27
  s 6 237
  s 10 272
  s 11 272
  s 13 237
  s 26 237
  s 37 9, 128, 272
Sexual Offences Act 1967 (c 60)
  s 4(1) 328
  s 8 272
State Immunity Act 1978 (c 33)
  s 20 8
Suicide Act 1961 (9 & 10 Eliz 2, c 60)
  s 2(1) 9
Summary Jurisdiction Act 1857
  (20 & 21 Vict, c 43)
  s 6 258
Supreme Court of Judicature (Consolidation)
  Act 1925 (15 & 16 Geo 5, c 49)
  s 31 312
Territorial Waters Jurisdiction Act 1878
  (41 & 42 Vict c 73)
  s 2 8
Theft Act 1968 (c 60) 139, 140, 323, 328
  s 1 71
  s 3 140
  s 7 140
  s 8 106
  s 8(2) 140
  s 9(1) 44
  s 9(1)(a) 45, 243
  s 9(1)(b) 45, 106
  s 12 58, 274
  s 22 45
  s 25(3) 274
  s 26 295, 335
  s 26(2) 296
  s 26(3) 295
  s 27(1) 49, 50
  s 28 324, 325
  s 30 273
  s 30(4) 9
Theft Act 1978 (c 31) 139, 140
  s 3 274
Tokyo Convention Act 1967
  (c 52)
  s 1 8
Trade Descriptions Act 1968
  (c 29) 9
Transport Act 1981 210, 332-3

Table of Statutory Rules and Orders and Statutory Instruments

Criminal Appeal Rules, SI 1968 No 1262
 r 2   235
 r 6   315
 r 12   238
 r 19   237
Crown Court Rules, SI 1971 No 1292
 (L 33)   35
 r 5   36
 r 6   250
 r 7   250, 252
 r 8   250
 r 9   250, 253
 r 10   253
 r 18   313
 r 18A   315
 r 19   53
 r 21   259
Indictments (Procedure) Rules, SI 1971
 2084   39
 r 5   39
Indictment Rules, SI 1971 No 1253   37
 r 6   37, 40, 52, 126
 r 7   44, 45
 r 9   45, 46, 47, 127, 152
Justices' Clerks (Qualification of Assistants)
 Rules, SI 1979 No 570   120, 137
Justices' Clerks Rules, SI 1970 No 231   282
Justices (Size and Chairmanship of Bench)
 Rules, SI 1964 No 1107   119
 r 2   123
Juvenile Courts (Constitution) Rules, 1954
 r 1   157
 r 5   158
 r 11   157
 r 12   158
Legal Aid in Criminal Proceedings
 (General) Regulations, SI 1968
 No 1231   320
Magistrates' Court Rules, 1968
 r 83   126

Magistrates' Courts (Forms) Rules, SI
 1981 No 553   124, 130, 282
Magistrates' Courts Rules, SI 1981
 No 552   125
 r 4   125
 r 6(4)   26
 r 7   17, 27, 28
 r 7(2)   17
 r 7(3)   17
 r 7(6)   20
 r 7(7)   20
 r 7(9)   20, 26
 r 13   135
 r 76   253, 255
 r 77   253, 258
 r 78   253, 255, 256, 258
 r 79   253
 r 80   253
 r 81   256
 r 98   280
 r 99   129
 r 100   276, 279
Prison (Amendment) Rules, SI 1968
 No 440   182
Prison Rules, SI 1964 No 388   182, 188
Prosecution of Offences Regulations, SI
 1978 No 1357   10
Rules of the Supreme Court (Revision)
 SI 1965 No 1776
 Ord 53   260, 263
 Ord 54   316
 Ord 54 r 4   316
 Ord 56   253
 Ord 56 r 1   259
 Ord 56 6   255
 Ord 79 r 9   312
 Ord 79 r 9(4)   312
 Ord 79 r 9(5)   312
 Ord 79 r 9(12)   312

Preface

In writing this book I have tried to avoid the two main pitfalls which are present in many of the more traditional books on procedure. On the one hand there are those so filled with detail that it is almost impossible for the reader to keep sight of the main outlines of the subject. On the other hand it is tempting, for the sake of clarity, to deal with the main elements of court procedure only, but in so doing, omit many points which are necessary detail for the serious student of the subject.

I believe that this book steers a middle course between these two extremes and I am grateful to my publishers who have presented the book in such a way as to highlight the more important parts of the text. Matters of detail or interest, not essential to a broad understanding of the subject, have been printed in small type, slightly indented from the remainder of the text. The reader may therefore make use of the book at either of two levels. He may gain an overall view of the subject just by reading those parts of the book which are in large type; or he may acquire more detailed knowledge through reading in addition the paragraphs in small type. I have also used examples of the documents most commonly used in connection with criminal procedure either at the appropriate point in the text or in an imaginary Brief to Counsel on the case of John Smith (see Appendix 5). This further ensures that the book fully justifies its title as *A Practical Approach* to Criminal Procedure.

The law is stated as at 6 July 1981, the day when the Magistrates' Courts Act 1980 came into force. This is a consolidating piece of legislation, replacing the Magistrates' Courts Act 1952 and 1957; the Criminal Justice Act 1967 ss.1-6, and the Criminal Law Act 1977 ss.18-29. The proposals for change made in the White Paper on Young Offenders (1980 Cmnd 8045) and by the Royal Commission on Criminal Procedure (the Philips Report — Cmnd 8092) are summarised in Appendices 2 and 4 respectively.

My thanks are due to my colleague at the Inns of Court School of Law, Miss Lynn Slater, BA, LLM, who has not only prepared the case and statute indexes, but also read the book as it was in the course of composition and made many invaluable suggestions for its improvement. My thanks also go to my publishers for their kindness and helpfulness, and, above all, to my parents for their unstinted support during the time the pages which follow were being written.

Walthamstow
17 September 1981

Part 1   Introduction

1 Setting the Scene

Criminal trials in England and Wales take one of two forms. They are either trials on indictment or summary trials. Trial in the juvenile court, which might at first sight appear to be a third distinct form of trial, is in fact a special form of summary trial. Part 2 of this book will deal in detail with the procedure for trial on indictment and Part 3 will deal similarly with summary trial. The following two paragraphs will give an indication of the salient characteristics of the two methods of trial.

1.1 TRIAL ON INDICTMENT

Trial on indictment is the method used for trying the more serious offences. The trial takes place before judge and jury in the Crown Court. The name 'trial on indictment' originates from the formal written statement of charges, and it is to the 'counts' contained in this indictment that the accused pleads 'Guilty' or 'Not guilty' at the beginning of his trial.

The trial is presided over by a paid professional judge, who is or was a practising barrister or, less frequently, solicitor. The judge controls the course of the trial, adjudicates on all matters of the admissibility of evidence, and is the sole arbiter of matters of law in the case.

Matters of fact are decided by the jury, which consists of lay men and women, drawn at random from a broad cross-section of the community, who are summoned for a period usually of two weeks. It is by no means unusual for this to be their only experience of the judicial system. They must accept the law as stated by the judge, but they alone decide matters of fact, to the extent that they need not give weight to, or even consider, the judge's view of the facts as expressed to them in his final summing up. Having heard the law and the evidence as to the facts, the duty of the jury is then to bring in the verdict.

Thus the general principle may be stated that at trial on indictment, 'the law is for the judge, and the facts are for the jury'.

1.2 SUMMARY TRIAL

Summary trial takes place in the magistrates' courts. It is also known as trial on information' because at the commencement of the trial the accused pleads guilty or not guilty to a charge contained in a document called an information. The case is heard and determined by magistrates (also known as Justices of the Peace) who are the judges of both law and fact. The great majority of magistrates are lay men and women, but since most magistrates serve as such for many years, and will normally sit in court at least twice a month, they become familiar with summary proceedings and are not 'complete amateurs' like the average juror. In practice, too, magistrates tend to be drawn from a narrower social and age range than jurors (for details on appointment of magistrates see Chapter 10). A minority of magistrates are stipendiaries, i.e. full-time, paid magistrates appointed from amongst barristers and solicitors of at least seven years' standing. One major difference between stipendiary magistrates and lay magistrates is that the former may, and normally do, sit alone to try cases, whereas at least two lay magistrates are required to try a case, and it is normal for them to sit in benches of three. Both lay and stipendiary magistrates are entitled to seek advice from their clerk on matters of law, admissibility of evidence and procedure, but the decision on these matters remains solely for the magistrates. Clerks are qualified lawyers (for details on appointment see Chapter 10), and, in addition to their duties in advising magistrates, they play an important role in the smooth functioning of the court, both in court (e.g. putting the information to the accused) and behind the scenes (e.g. working on the issue of summonses). The merits and demerits of trial on indictment as opposed to summary trial are much debated. Some of the arguments are mentioned in Chapter 12.

1.3 CLASSES OF OFFENCE

For purposes of the mode of trial there are three classes of offence, namely: those triable only on indictment, those triable only summarily, and those triable either way. Chapter 12 explains how to decide into which class a particular offence falls, but the broad principle is that the most serious offences (e.g. murder, manslaughter, rape, robbery and causing grievous bodily harm with intent to do so) are triable only on indictment. Offences of medium gravity, and especially offences which vary greatly in gravity depending upon the facts of the particular case, are triable either way. The least serious offences are triable only summarily. Theft, handling stolen goods, obtaining by deception, unlawful wounding, indecent assault and reckless driving are examples of offences triable either way. Perhaps the most serious offences triable only summarily are assaulting a police officer in the execution of his duty, and drinking and driving offences. It must be noted that where the accused is a juvenile (i.e. under 17) many offences, which in the case of an adult (i.e. 17 and over) would be triable only on indictment or triable either way, become triable only summarily, so that the juvenile must be tried either in the juvenile court or in an adult magistrates' court.

1.4 INDICTABLE AND SUMMARY OFFENCES

Many statutes refer to indictable offences and summary offences, not offences triable only on indictment, offences triable only summarily and offences triable either way. 'Indictable offence' means one which if committed by an adult is triable on indictment, whether it is triable only on indictment, or is triable either way. 'Summary offence' means one which if committed by an adult is triable *only* summarily. 'Offence triable either way' means one which if committed by an adult is triable either on indictment or summarily. The above definitions are contained in the Interpretation Act 1978, Schedule 1, and are all subject to a contrary intention appearing in the statute using the phrase. Confusion will arise unless it is carefully borne in mind that 'indictable offence', without further qualification, means not just offences triable only on indictment in the case of adults, but also offences which in the case of adults are triable either on indictment or summarily. A great many indictable offences are tried summarily; a summary offence can only be tried summarily.

2 Commencing Prosecutions

An unusual feature of the English system of criminal procedure is that the decision to begin a prosecution is normally taken by a non-lawyer. This is a consequence of another unusual aspect of the system, namely that there is no State prosecuting authority. The nearest approach to such an authority is in the work of the Law Officers of the Crown and the Director of Public Prosecutions (see Paragraph 2.5). The persons who are principally involved in the decision to prosecute are set out below.

2.1 SUSPECT CHARGED BY POLICE OFFICER

One way of commencing a prosecution is to charge the suspect at a police station. This is the appropriate method in the more serious type of case, especially in cases where the suspect has been arrested by a police officer acting without a warrant from a magistrate for that person's arrest. Charging is dealt with in Chapter 19, but briefly the procedure is that the charge is written down on a charge-sheet, signed by the arresting officer and read to the suspect. He is cautioned that he need not say anything. The decision to charge is taken by the arresting officer acting in conjunction with the station sergeant, and perhaps other officers investigating the offence.

Subsequently, if the case appears to warrant it, the papers may be referred to solicitors employed by the police authority for their view on the merits of the prosecution. If they consider the evidence too weak they may advise the discontinuance of the prosecution by offering no evidence. It should be noted, however, that many prosecutions in the magistrates' courts are handled entirely by police officers without the papers ever going to police solicitors. If the case is to be tried on indictment, the papers will be sent to police solicitors who can then instruct counsel for the trial.

2.2 APPLICATION FOR SUMMONS BY POLICE ADMINISTRATIVE OFFICER

The second method is for the prosecution to be commenced by 'laying an information' before a magistrate, or magistrates' clerk. This is particularly appropriate for minor offences, especially where the suspect has been warned of possible prosecution, but not arrested. Here, oral or written allegations are made to a magistrate or magistrates' clerk, who then issues a summons. This requires the accused to attend the magistrates' court at a specified time and date. Where the police are considering the use of this method, the decision to prosecute is taken by a senior police officer on the basis of the papers in the case, which are submitted to him. Chapter 19 deals with this matter in detail.

2.3 PRIVATE INDIVIDUALS

When a police officer lays an information, he merely does what any member of the public may do. Anyone may lay an information alleging any offence known to the criminal law, subject to obtaining the consent of the Attorney-General or the Director of Public Prosecutions in limited classes of cases. In practice, when the request for a summons comes from a private individual, the magistrate or clerk may consider the matter more carefully than when the request comes from a police officer.

Typical cases where a private individual might lay an information are allegations of minor assault arising out of a dispute between neighbours, and allegations of offences where, in the view of the informant, the police have failed in their duty by not initiating proceedings themselves. In the case of shoplifting, the usual procedure is for the store manager to call the police, who then arrest the suspect and charge him at the police station. Half-way between prosecutions by the police and prosecutions by private individuals are prosecutions commenced by officials of a government department or local authority laying an information. Examples of this are prosecutions on behalf of the Inland Revenue for tax offences, on behalf of the Department of Health and Social Security for social security frauds and on behalf of local authorities for contravention of food and health regulations.

2.4 CONSIDERATIONS RELEVANT TO COMMENCING A PROSECUTION

A police officer, considering whether to charge a suspect or considering whether to lay an information, is primarily concerned with the strength of the evidence available to him. The admissibility of evidence and its weight if admitted are, of course, matters beyond the scope of this book. Assuming that the officer considers that the evidence available to him affords a reasonable chance of securing a conviction he will normally commence a prosecution without further hesitation. In a minority of cases, he would not proceed because, for special reasons discussed below, any prosecution would be bound to fail.

2.4.1 Territorial jurisdiction of the English courts

English courts will try an accused for an offence allegedly committed in England or Wales irrespective of whether he is a British or foreign subject. They will not in general try even a British subject for offences committed outside England and Wales, and they will never try a foreign subject for offences allegedly committed on land outside England and Wales. Therefore, if the evidence available to the officer suggests the commission of an offence outside England and Wales the commencement of a prosecution would normally be pointless. However, by way of exception to the general rule, murder, manslaughter, perjury, bigamy and offences under the Official Secrets Act 1911 are all triable by the English courts wherever committed, provided the accused is a British subject (see Offences against the Person Act 1861 s. 9; Perjury Act 1911 s. 8; Offences against the Person Act 1861 s. 57, and Official Secrets Act 1911 s. 10 respectively).

Further examples of offences over which the English courts have jurisdiction even though committed outside England and Wales are:

(a) offences committed on board British ships on the high seas whether the accused is a British subject or a foreigner (Merchant Shipping Act 1894 s. 686);

(b) offences committed by British subjects on board any foreign ship to which they do not belong or in any foreign port or harbour (s. 686 supra);

(c) offences committed on board any ship, foreign or British, which is within territorial waters whether the accused is a British subject or a foreigner (Territorial Waters Jurisdiction Act 1878, s. 2), and

(d) offences committed on board British-controlled aircraft in flight outside United Kingdom air-space (Tokyo Convention Act 1967, s. 1).

Occasionally it is unclear whether an offence should be treated as having been committed in or outside England and Wales. The topic has produced a body of complex case law out of proportion to its practical importance, but it is worth noting that:

(a) If an offence is committed partly inside and partly outside England and Wales the English courts accept jurisdiction if the offence was *completed* within the jurisdiction. Thus, there is no jurisdiction to try an offence of obtaining property by deception where the deception is practised in England but the property is obtained outside the jurisdiction in Jersey (*R* v *Harden* [1963] 1QB 8) whereas there is jurisdiction to try an offence of false accounting committed by a person in Paris causing incorrect figures to be entered in an account in London (*R* v *Oliphant* [1905] 2KB 67). Lord Diplock has suggested obiter dicta in *Treacy* v *DPP* [1971] AC 537 that the courts should accept jurisdiction if any part of the offence took place in England or Wales.

(b) A conspiracy entered into abroad to commit an offence in England or Wales is triable by the English courts provided that the conspirators come within the jurisdiction at a time when the conspiracy is still in existance (*DPP* v *Doot* [1973] AC 807). Overt acts in England or Wales in furtherance of the conspiracy are probably necessary in order to show that it had not been abandoned before the conspirators reached England.

(c) An attempt to commit an offence which, if it had been completed, would have been triable in England is so triable even though none of the physical acts constituting the attempt took place in England or Wales (*DPP* v *Stonehouse* [1978] AC 55 – S was correctly tried in England for an offence of attempting to enable his wife to obtain a cheque from an insurance company by deception since, although the unsuccessful deception consisted in S faking his death by drowning off the coast of the United States, the cheque would have been given to his wife in England had the deception succeeded).

2.4.2 Claims to immunity

A second reason for not commencing a prosecution where the evidence available is ample is that the accused could and would claim immunity from prosecution. Details on this topic will be found in works on constitutional law, but, in brief, the Queen, foreign sovereigns or heads of state and members of their families are immune from prosecution: State Immunity Act 1978, s. 20. Diplomatic agents, administrative and technical staff of a diplomatic mission and members of the families of such agents and staff are also entitled to immunity, subject to waiver by the sending state. Members of the service staff of a diplomatic mission enjoy immunity in respect of acts performed in the course of their duties, again subject to waiver. The above-mentioned diplomatic immunities are subject to some modification where the person claiming immunity is a citizen of the United Kingdom or permanently resident in the United Kingdom (see, in general, the Diplomatic Privileges Act 1964).

2.4.3 Prosecutions out of time

A prosecution must be commenced within any time limit for so doing. By far the most important time limit on beginning prosecutions is contained in the Magistrates' Courts Act 1980, s. 127 which provides that an information alleging a summary offence must be laid within six months of the offence being committed (unless another statute expressly provides to the contrary). There is normally no time limit on commencing a prosecution for an indictable offence, but, amongst the exceptions to this rule, are prosecutions for unlawful sexual intercourse with girls aged 13 to 16 (which must be commenced within a year of the offence), prosecutions for certain homosexual offences (which again must be commenced within a year), and prosecutions under the Trade Descriptions Act 1968 (which must be commenced within 3 years of the offence or one year of its discovery whichever is the earlier). The statutes creating the above offences provide for the time limits mentioned.

2.4.4 Consent necessary for prosecution

The fourth and final special factor to consider before beginning a prosecution is whether any consent is required. The general rule is that a prosecutor can commence proceedings without asking anyone's permission, but in certain exceptional cases the consent of either the Attorney-General or the Director of Public Prosecutions is required. The Attorney-General's consent is required for prosecutions under:

(a) The Public Bodies Corrupt Practices Act 1889 (bribing members, officers or servants of public bodies such as county and borough councils),

(b) The Prevention of Corruption Act 1906 (bribing an agent or servant to show favour in connection with his principal's affairs),

(c) The Official Secrets Act 1911,

(d) Sections 1, 2 and 5A of the Public Order Act 1936 (wearing uniforms associated with a political organisation, organising a private army and stirring up racial hatred) and

(e) The Prevention of Terrorism (Temporary Provisions) Act 1976 (belonging to a proscribed organisation, failing to comply with an exclusion order etc).

The DPP's consent is required for:

(a) Prosecutions for theft or criminal damage where the property belongs to the spouse of the accused: Theft Act 1968 s. 30(4).

(b) Prosecutions brought under the Criminal Law Act 1967 ss. 4 and 5 for assisting offenders and for wasting police time,

(c) Prosecutions for homosexual offences where either or both the persons concerned are under 21: Sexual Offences Act 1967 s. 8,

(d) Prosecutions for incest: Sexual Offences Act 1956 s. 37 and

(e) Prosecutions for aiding and abetting suicide: Suicide Act 1961 s. 2(1).

The Attorney-General's consent tends to be required in cases where the decision to prosecute is likely to involve public policy considerations of a political or international nature. The requirement for the DPP's consent is a useful safeguard when enforcing the letter of the law could be oppressive to the individual or might bring the law into disrepute.

Even though consent is required for the bringing of a prosecution, a suspect may lawfully be arrested without consent having at that stage been obtained, and the validity of the arrest is unaffected by a subsequent refusal to permit prosecution (Prosecution of Offences Act 1979 s. 6).

2.5 ROLES OF THE LAW OFFICERS OF THE CROWN AND THE DIRECTOR OF PUBLIC PROSECUTIONS

It was stated at the beginning of this chapter that there is no state prosecuting authority in England. In so far as the system of prosecutions is nationally coordinated, this is done through the work of the law officers of the Crown, the Director of Public Prosecutions and the civil servants in their respective departments.

The law officers of the Crown (the Attorney-General and the Solicitor-General) are members of the government, although not normally in the Cabinet. The Attorney-General, in addition to his general duties of advising his colleagues in the government on difficult questions of law and appearing on behalf of government departments in important cases, plays an important part in the administration of the criminal law. He superintends the work of the Director of Public Prosecutions, he institutes proceedings in appropriate cases, he may take over a prosecution which has already begun or instruct the Director of Public Prosecutions so to do, and, as described in Paragraph 2.4.4 he may grant consent for certain prosecutions. Where a trial on indictment is pending or in progress he may, at any stage before judgment, enter a *nolle prosequi*, which puts an end to the prosecution. This power is not subject to control by the courts. It is used principally in cases where the accused is unfit to stand trial and is unlikely to be fit to do so in the future. Either prosecution or defence may apply to the Attorney-General to exercise his power to enter a *nolle prosequi*, or he may act on his own initiative. If the Attorney-General thinks it right to put an end to summary proceedings he could do so by taking over the prosecution and offering no evidence. In performing his non-political functions, the Attorney-General is obliged by convention to exercise independent discretion, not dictated by colleagues in the government, although he is at liberty to consult them. Where the Attorney-General is unable to act through illness or absence, or where he authorises the Solicitor-General to act in particular cases, the latter may discharge the former's functions.

The Director of Public Prosecutions is appointed by the Home Secretary. He must be a barrister or solicitor of at least ten years standing. His duties are set out in the Prosecution of Offences Act 1979, and the Prosecution of Offences Regulations 1978 (SI 1978 No 1357). He institutes or carries on criminal proceedings in cases which appear to him to be of major importance or difficulty, he can be directed to appear for the Crown in criminal appeals in the Court of Appeal or House of Lords, he may give advice to government departments, magistrates' clerks and chief officers of police in any criminal matter where he considers such advice to be called for, and, of course, his consent is required for certain prosecutions (see Paragraph 2.4.4). Chief officers of police must inform the DPP if there is a *prima facie* case for taking proceedings for various offences (e.g. murder, manslaughter, abortion, perjury, major robberies, some cases involving obscene publications and cases where the consent of the DPP or the Attorney-General is required for a prosecution). Having been informed, the DPP may advise as to the future conduct of the proceedings or intervene to take over the prosecution himself. By the Prosecution of Offences Act 1979, s. 4, the DPP has a general power, at any stage of criminal proceedings, to step in and carry on the case himself. If the DPP is conducting a prosecution he may employ a solicitor to act on his behalf in the matter.

Part 2   *Trial on Indictment*

3   Committal Proceedings

Trial on indictment always takes place in the Crown Court. However, nearly all trials on indictment are preceded by a preliminary hearing in a magistrates' court, called committal proceedings. These proceedings must not be confused with the trial itself. The accused is not asked during committal proceedings whether he pleads guilty or not guilty, nor are the magistrates concerned with whether, were they trying the case summarily, they would convict or acquit. The proceedings are designed merely to identify those cases where the prosecution would obviously fail to secure a conviction, so that in such cases the accused may be spared the strain and expense of a trial on indictment.

At committal proceedings, the question the magistrates have to answer is whether the evidence put before them raises a *prima facie* case that the accused has committed an indictable offence. If so, they commit (i.e. send) the accused to the Crown Court to be tried for that offence. If not, the accused is discharged. By a *prima facie* case is meant evidence on which a reasonable jury *could* convict the accused. This explains the statement made above that the magistrates are not, strictly speaking, concerned with whether they would want to convict on the evidence. In many cases, a magistrate might say to himself — 'I do not find the prosecution evidence convincing' — but, unless that evidence is so poor and unconvincing that no reasonable jury could convict on it, he is under a duty to commit the accused for trial. To put the same point yet another way, the standard of proof that the prosecution has to satisfy at committal proceedings is a very low one. For that reason most (though by no means all) committal proceedings end in the accused being sent for trial.

The procedures prior to committal proceedings are described in detail in Chapter 19, but it may be helpful to summarise what occurs in a typical case before the committal starts. The accused is arrested without warrant by a police officer and is taken to a police station. There, he is questioned under caution, and, when the investigating officers consider that they have sufficient evidence, he is charged with the offence. At that stage he is either released on bail under a duty to attend the magistrates' court at a stated time to answer the charge, or he is kept in custody at the police station and brought before the magistrates as soon as reasonably possible. On the occasion of the first court appearance neither prosecution nor defence is likely to have its case prepared, so the matter has to be adjourned. The magistrates either grant the accused bail or remand him in custody. The period of the adjournment is used by the accused to instruct his solicitors and possibly obtain legal aid, and by the prosecution to take all necessary statements and (if need be) arrange for their witnesses to be at court. The time between the first court appearance and the commencement of committal proceedings may be as short as a week or as long as two or three months depending on the complexity of the case, whether the police have further enquiries to make and the form the committal proceedings are to take.

3.1 JURISDICTION OF THE MAGISTRATES

A magistrates' court has jurisdiction to hold committal proceedings for an offence wherever the offence was allegedly committed, assuming, of course, that the offence is one over which English courts will accept jurisdiction (see Paragraph 2.4.1 on the territorial jurisdiction of the English courts). Thus, if the accused lives in Newcastle and is charged with an offence of theft committed in Newcastle he could nonetheless be brought before a magistrates' court in Plymouth for the purposes of committal proceedings. However, in practice, proceedings are usually brought in the magistrates' court for the area where the offence was allegedly committed irrespective of the address of the accused or the place where he was arrested. In contrast to the magistrates' geographically unlimited jurisdiction to hear committal proceedings, their jurisdiction to try summary offences is largely limited to offences occurring within the county where the court is situated. The Magistrates' Courts Act 1980, s. 2(3) deals with jurisdiction to hold committal proceedings. In the remainder of this chapter, references are to the Magistrates' Courts Act 1980 and the Magistrates' Courts Rules 1981 (SI 552) unless otherwise stated.

For the purposes of committal procedings, the court may consist of a single lay magistrate (s. 4(1), but two or more is usual. When magistrates conduct committal proceedings they are known as examining justices.

3.2 PRESENCE OF THE ACCUSED

Evidence given at committal proceedings must be given in the presence of the accused unless the examining justices consider that his disorderly conduct makes that impracticable, or he cannot be present for health reasons but is legally represented and has consented to evidence being given in his absence: s. 4(3) and (4). Committal proceedings are normally held in open court but the examining justices have a discretion to sit *in camera* if the ends of justice would not be served by an open-court hearing: s. 4(2).

> Committal proceedings may concern two or more accused persons. This is obviously appropriate where they are charged jointly with committing a single offence. It is also appropriate where the accused persons are charged with separate offences which are linked together in some way so that it is, in the interests of justice, to have a single set of proceedings: *R* v *Camberwell Green Magistrates* ex parte *Christie* [1978] 2WLR 794. Thus if two accused persons are charged with committing a robbery, a third is charged with taking without lawful authority the 'getaway car', and a fourth is charged with handling the proceeds of the robbery, the most convenient course of action is to deal with all four in one committal hearing.

3.3 COMMITTALS WITH AND WITHOUT CONSIDERATION OF THE EVIDENCE

Committal proceedings are either held with consideration of the evidence under s. 6(1), or without consideration of the evidence under s. 6(2). Prior to 1967 all committal proceedings were conducted with consideration of the evidence, and thus the Criminal Justice Act 1967, s. 1, was passed to introduce the alternative procedure in order to save the time of the court and unnecessary inconvenience for the witnesses. Most committals are now conducted without consideration of the evidence, and are known colloquially as 'Section 1' committals. Those conducted with the evidence are known as preliminary investigations, or 'old fashioned' committals.

3.4 PROCEDURE AT COMMITTALS WITH CONSIDERATION OF THE EVIDENCE

The stages of a committal with consideration of the evidence are detailed below.

3.4.1 Prosecution opening

The prosecution representative outlines his case to the examining justices, indicating the nature of the evidence he intends to call, and the charge or charges on which he will be suggesting that they should commit the accused for trial. The court will already know what the accused has been charged with at the police station, or the informations that have been laid against him. It may be that extra charges have been preferred or that the prosecution no longer seeks committal on some of the original charges. Such matters can be explained in the opening speech. If the committal is being contested the prosecution will probably choose to be legally represented by counsel or solicitor, both of whom have the right of audience in the magistrates' courts, but the case can be handled by the police officer principally involved. The accused is, of course, entitled to be legally represented, or he may choose to conduct his own defence.

3.4.2 The prosecution case

The prosecution presents its case by producing its evidence, which may be written or oral. Written evidence is read to the court. Oral evidence is given by calling witnesses in the same manner as in other criminal proceedings, namely by the witness going into the witness-box where he takes the oath, or if he objects to being sworn, affirms: Oaths Act 1978 ss. 1 and 5. The prosecution then conducts the examination-in-chief by asking questions which, while not suggesting any particular answer to the witness, are designed to elicit the relevant evidence. The witness is then cross-examined by the defence. The prosecution then re-examines the witness on matters which have arisen in cross-examination. The examining justices may put questions if they so wish. The clerk of the court writes down the evidence, and his note is then read to and signed by the witness at the earliest opportunity: Rule 7(2). This last procedure applies only in committal proceedings.

The note signed by the witness is termed the deposition. At the end of the proceedings one of the examining justices signs a certificate stating that all the depositions were taken in the presence of the accused (unless, of course, it was one of the exceptional cases where the court has dispensed with the presence of the accused — see Para. 3.2), and that the defence was given an opportunity to cross-examine the deponents: Rule 7(3).

The giving of oral evidence and the taking of depositions is a time-consuming process. It may also put the witnesses to some inconvenience. Moreover, it was held in *R v Phillips and Quayle* [1939] 1KB 63 that a committal based on depositions not taken in strict conformity with legislation then in force similar to s. 4 and r. 7 was a nullity, and accordingly any conviction on indictment following the invalid committal would have to be quashed. Judicial comment to the effect that the rules on taking depositions were unduly restrictive was followed eventually by legislation enabling written statements to be received in evidence at committal proceedings. The original provisions of the Criminal Justice Act 1967, s. 2, have been replaced by the Magistrates' Courts Act 1980, s. 102. A written statement is admissible if:

(a)   It is signed by the maker.

(b)   It contains a declaration by the maker that it is true to the best of his knowledge and belief, and that he made it knowing that if it were tendered in evidence he could be prosecuted for wilfully stating in it anything that he knew to be false or did not believe to be true.

(c)   The party proposing to put it in evidence gives a copy of it to each of the other parties to the committal proceedings before tendering it to the court.

(d)   None of the other parties objects to its being tendered in evidence.

A statement made under s. 102 is read out in full in court unless either the committal is without consideration of the evidence (see Para. 3.5) or the examining justices allow some or all of it to be summarised. Knowingly making a false statement which is tendered in evidence under s. 102 is an offence punishable on indictment with imprisonment for up to two years: s. 106.

> A statement under s. 102 should give the maker's age if under 21. If the maker cannot read, it should be read through to him before he signs it, and should contain a declaration that it was so read. (Note that it is not necessary for any witness to write his statement personally, provided that he reads it through before signing it.) Where the statement refers to another document as an exhibit (e.g. a police officer's statement might refer to a signed confession that he took from the accused in accordance with the Judges' Rules) a copy of the exhibit should be given to each of the other parties. The certificate signed by an examining justice after the proceedings to confirm that the depositions were properly taken should also list the statements tendered under s. 102. If a witness makes a statement to the police it is normally taken down on a standard form which incorporates the declaration that the statement is true etc. as required by s. 102. Examples of such statements will be found at pages 342 to 346.

3.4.3   Advantages and disadvantages of witnesses and depositions

Section 102 statements may only be tendered if all the parties wish that to be done. There is nothing to compel the party tendering the statement to present his evidence in that form rather than calling the maker of the statement as a witness. Each of the other parties, having read through his copy of the statement before the proceedings start, is fully entitled to object to the statement going into evidence. If there is an objection (albeit from only one of several parties involved in the committal proceedings) the statement cannot be received, although obviously the maker may be called as a witness. In what circumstances, then, would the prosecution and defence agree to a a s. 102 statement being read to the examining justices.

The obvious advantage of a written statement is that it saves the time, expense and possible inconvenience of calling its maker. For that reason the prosecution almost invariably serves on the defence copies of the s. 102 statements which they have taken from their potential witnesses in the hope that the defence will have no objection to the originals being tendered. The disadvantage to the defence of letting the statements go into evidence is that they have no opportunity to cross-examine the maker. Cross-examination is the means by which evidence is tested and challenged. Therefore, by forgoing the right to cross-examine, the defence in effect concedes, for purposes of the committal proceedings and for no other purposes, that the statement is correct. If the defence argues that the accused should not be committed for trial they will have to say to the examining justices — 'Assuming that the s. 102 statement read to you is correct, there is nonetheless not enough evidence for my client to be sent for trial.' Quite often the matters alleged in a s. 102 statement are uncontroversial (e.g. a statement by the victim of a burglary that his house was burgled between certain times and that certain items of property were stolen — the accused may well not dispute the fact of the burglary but will deny that he was responsible). In such cases it is clearly right for the defence to raise no objection to the statement being put in evidence. However, in many cases the defence may hotly dispute the accuracy of the contents of a statement but even so allow it to be tendered by the prosecution. The reason lies in the low standard of proof that the prosecution have to satisfy at committal proceedings (see beginning of this chapter and Para. 3.4.4). If the maker of the statement is called as a witness, skilled cross-examination may lead the examining justices to feel some doubt about his evidence, but only rarely will the cross-examination be so effective that they consider that no reasonable jury could believe him. Unless they do take this extreme view, they are obliged to take his evidence into consideration when deciding whether to commit. Moreover, if the defence does object to the s. 102 statements and cross-examines the witnesses vigorously, but nevertheless the examining justices commit the accused for trial, the nature of the defence case is to some extent revealed and the advantage of surprise is lost for the subsequent trial. It is therefore usually good tactics for the defence to allow the prosecution to tender statements under s. 102.

Without wishing to put forward hard and fast rules, one may summarise the position by saying that the defence will only want the prosecution to call a witness at committal if:
(a) they consider that by cross-examination his evidence will be so undermined that the examining justices will decide that no reasonable jury could believe it,
(b) they want to probe his evidence in the hope that lines of cross-examination may emerge which could be usefully pressed home at the trial on indictment, or.
(c) the case is one where identification of the accused is an issue, and the witness is to give evidence on that point (see Para. 3.5).

3.4.4 Submission of 'no case to answer'

After the prosecution have called their witnesses and read their written statements, the defence have the opportunity to submit that there is no case for the accused to answer — i.e. no *prima facie* case on which he should be sent for trial on indictment: r. 7 (6). Unless the submission is obviously ill-founded, the examining justices will invite the prosecution to reply. The test the justices should apply in deciding upon the submission has already been described in general terms. A more precise formulation may be derived from a Practice Note of the Divisional Court, Lord Parker CJ presiding (1962 1 All ER 448). Although dealing with submissions of no case to answer in summary trials, the Note seems equally relevant to such submissions in committal proceedings. Lord Parker said:

A submission that there is no case to answer may properly be made and upheld: (a) when there has been no evidence to prove an essential element in the alleged offence; (b) when the evidence adduced by the prosecution has been so discredited as a result of cross-examination or is so manifestly unreliable that no reasonable tribunal could safely convict on it.

It is important to remember that the examining justices must decide whether the prosecution evidence has disclosed a case to answer in respect of *any* indictable offence, not necessarily one of the offences with which the accused was charged at the police station. Thus, if the accused has been charged with murder, the examining justices may decide that, although there is no evidence on which a reasonable jury could find that the accused acted with malice aforethought, there is ample evidence of unlawful killing. They would then commit for trial on a charge of manslaughter but decline to commit on the charge of murder. Obviously, if the prosecution had expressly charged both murder and manslaughter the justices would again have had the option of committing on the latter but not the former charge. If the justices hold that there is no case to answer for any indictable offence the accused is discharged — i.e. he walks out of court a free man (unless he should happen to be in custody for any other matter). For the effect of a discharge at committal proceedings see Para. 3.4.7.

3.4.5 Charges to read to the accused, and the alibi warning

Those charges on which the court finds that there is a case to answer must then be read to the accused: r. 7(6). Where there is a charge which has not yet been written down, as where the examining justices find that there is no case to answer on a murder charge but that they wish to commit on manslaughter, the new charge must be put down in writing. The chairman of the examining justices must then ask the accused if he wishes to say anything in answer to the charge or charges: r. 7(7). If he is not legally represented the chairman warns him, in terms similar to the caution that a police officer gives to a suspect before questioning him, that he need not say anything unless he wishes to do so, that what he does say will be taken down and may be given in evidence, and that he should ignore any promise or threat that anybody may have made to persuade him to say something. It is rare for the accused to say anything as to do so might unnecessarily reveal the nature of his defence or give the prosecution material that they could use against him at the trial on indictment. If he does say something it is put into writing, read over to him and signed by an examining justice (and the accused himself if he so wishes). The chairman then warns the accused of the necessity to give notice to the prosecution should he wish to rely on an alibi, unless the chairman considers such a warning to be superfluous in the circumstances: r. 7(9) and see Para. 3.7.3.

3.4.6 The defence case

If the accused accepts the opportunity to say something in answer to the charge (see above) he makes his statement from the dock, which is the enclosed area where the accused sits during the course of the proceedings. Statements from the dock, whether in committal proceedings or in trials, are unsworn and are not subject to cross-examination, but, after the alibi warning, the accused is given the opportunity to testify like any other witness from the witness box on oath. If he does so he may, of course, be cross-examined by the prosecution. The accused may give evidence in the witness box whether or not he earlier made an unsworn statement from the dock. The defence may also call other witnesses and tender statements under s. 102.

The procedure for examining defence witnesses and taking depositions from them is exactly the same as for prosecution witnesses. Only rarely, however, does the defence choose to call evidence, whether from the accused or anyone else. The reasons are tactical, again springing from the low standard of proof placed upon the prosecution in committal proceedings. Given that a submission of 'no case to answer' has already failed, it is most unlikely that defence evidence would sway the examining justices sufficiently for them to hold that the case should not go for trial. Calling evidence would, however, reveal the nature of the defence case to the prosecution and expose the witnesses prematurely to cross-examination.

3.4.7 The decision to commit

If evidence has been called for the defence, the submission may again be made that the accused should not be sent for trial on indictment. The test to be applied by the examining justices is the same as that applied on a submission made at the close of the prosecution case (see Para. 3.4.4), but the decision is taken on all the evidence, prosecution and defence, not just on the prosecution evidence. However, as stated above, it is unusual for the defence to call evidence at committal proceedings, so, as contested hearings, many committals effectively end following the failure of a submission of 'no case to answer' after the prosecution evidence, although the formalities of asking the accused whether he wants to say anything and inviting the defence to call evidence must, of course, be complied with.

If the examining justices decide that there is not a case to answer, either at this stage or after the prosecution case, the accused is discharged, but discharge at committal proceedings is not equivalent to an acquittal. The prosecution can, therefore, prefer fresh charges for the same offence or offences and seek to persuade either the same examining justices or possibly a differently constituted bench of justices to commit for trial: *R v Manchester City Stipendiary Magistrate* ex parte *Snelson* [1977] 1WLR 911. If, on the other hand, the justices decide that there is a case to answer, they formally commit the accused to the Crown Court for trial on the charges for which there is sufficient evidence. A particular location of the Crown Court should be specified (see Para. 4.2).

The course adopted by the prosecution in ex parte *Snelson* of bringing fresh committal proceedings after an unsuccessful attempt to commit was appropriate for that case as there had not been a hearing on the merits. The prosecution had not been ready to proceed on the day fixed by the examining justices for the hearing, an adjournment was refused and, since the prosecution had literally no evidence available at court, the accused had to be discharged. If examining justices consider the prosecution evidence fully and decide that there is no case to answer, the better course of action is to apply to a judge in chambers for a voluntary bill of indictment (see Para. 3.10.1) rather than hoping that a re-run of the case before justices will produce a different result. Repeated unsuccessful attempts to commit for trial would amount to an abuse of the process of the court and could be restrained by the Divisional Court issuing an order of prohibition forbidding any further attempts.

3.5 PROCEDURE AT COMMITTALS WITHOUT CONSIDERATION OF THE EVIDENCE

The procedure introduced by the Criminal Justice Act 1967 s. 2 for reading statements at committal proceedings has undoubtedly saved much time. Even so, the procedure still takes up a certain amount of court time, and it was realised that in the majority of cases the defence could not seriously contest the prosecution's assertion that there was a case to answer. The only real advantage to the defence of committal proceedings in such cases was that they received forewarning of the prosecution case which would greatly assist them at the trial on indictment. Accordingly, the Criminal Justice Act 1967, s. 1 introduced a procedure by which the defence could agree to the examining justices committing the accused for trial without considering the evidence against him. The defence interest in knowing the prosecution case in advance was protected by the requirement that the prosecution evidence should be given to them in the form of copies of written statements admissible under s. 2 of the 1967 Act, now s. 102. Most committals now take place under the Magistrates' Courts Act 1980, s. 6(2) which has replaced s. 1 of the 1967 Act.

The accused may be committed for trial without the examining justices considering the evidence against him if:

(a)   all the evidence before the court consists of written statements tendered under s. 102,

(b)   each accused person is represented by counsel or solicitor, and

(c)   none of the counsel or solicitors representing the accused wishes to make a submission that there is no case to answer disclosed by the statements in respect of his client.

> Committals under s. 6(2) without consideration of the evidence are a pure formality, and take literally only two or three minutes to accomplish. The exact procedure may vary from court to court, but, in essence, the clerk reads the charge or charges to the accused. The police officer handling the case for the prosecution (they are unlikely to require the services of solicitor or counsel) hands the original witness statements admissible under s. 102 to the clerk. These are not read to the examining justices. The prosecuting officer and defence representative then tell the clerk what witness orders are required for the makers of the statements (see Para. 3.7.2). The defence representative is then asked whether there are any objections to the statements being put in evidence and whether a submission is to be made that they do not disclose a case, to both of which questions he answers 'no'. Sometimes the defence is asked even more simply — 'Do you agree to a committal without consideration of the evidence?' Next, if it is appropriate, the chairman of the examining justices gives the accused the alibi warning. The defence and, possibly, the prosecution are asked whether the warning is needed (see Para. 3.7.3). Finally, the justices formally commit the accused for trial at the Crown Court.

3.6   CIRCUMSTANCES WHICH ARE APPROPRIATE FOR COMMITTAL WITHOUT EVIDENCE

The procedure for committal without consideration of the evidence ought not to lead to the accused being unnecessarily committed for trial provided the defence representative reads carefully through the copies of the s. 102 statements which the prosecution have given to him, and only agrees to the committal if those statements clearly disclose a case to answer on all the charges preferred against the accused. For this reason committals without consideration of the evidence are only permitted where each of the accused is legally represented. If an unrepresented accused could forgo on his own behalf the right to have the evidence assessed by the examining justices, he might misguidedly, to save trouble, agree to a committal under s. 6(2) when in fact the evidence was inadequate. Counsel or solicitor representing the accused must be careful not to fall into a similar trap. Three main types of cases where a s. 6(2) committal would not be appropriate are as follows:

(a)   Where the statements of the prosecution witnesses, even if totally correct, do not reveal a case to answer. Here the defence may well be willing to have all the evidence tendered in written form under s. 102 and read to the examining justices. After that has been done, the defence submits that there is no *prima facie* case to answer.

(b)   Where the s. 102 statements, if correct, disclose a case to answer, but the defence considers that one or more of the statement makers could be so discredited in cross-examination that the examining justices would decide that no reasonable jury could believe them, and, taking away their evidence, there is no case to answer. Here, the defence would object to the disputed statements being tendered under s. 102, allow the remainder to be read, and submit that on the totality of the prosecution evidence (oral and written) there is no case to answer.

(c)   Where identification is in issue. In the mid-1970's a large measure of public concern arose about cases where an accused had been convicted largely on identification evidence — i.e. evidence from a witness who saw the offence being committed or the offender running away immediately after the offence, and picked out the accused at an identification parade. In a few much publicised cases it was subsequently established that the identification evidence had been mistaken and that the accused had been wrongly convicted. The fear was that in many other cases similar mistakes may have been made which had not come to light. To help prevent such miscarriage of justice the Attorney-General, in a written answer to the House of Commons (27 May 1976 Hansard Vol 912 No 115), laid down certain guidelines to cover cases where identification is likely to be an issue. One of the guidelines stated that where the DPP conducts a case, and it appears likely that identification is to be an issue, he will not seek a committal without consideration of the evidence and will call the witnesses as to identity to give oral evidence. The defence is thereby enabled to test and probe the evidence by cross-examination if desired. The hope is that by having the witnesses as to identity testify at a relatively early stage in the proceedings while the facts are fresher in their minds than would be the case at the trial on indictment, both sides will be able to form a better view as to the reliability of the evidence. Where it is clearly unreliable the examining justices can, of course, discharge the accused. Although the Attorney-General's guidelines were only directly relevant to the small minority of cases conducted by the DPP, both the Attorney-General and DPP expressed the wish that the guidelines be generally accepted by all prosecutors. However, the original guidelines have been modified by a written answer in the House of Commons by the Attorney-General (25 July 1979). The answer says that 'rigid adherence' to the requirements for calling witnesses as to identity at committal proceedings can 'itself lead to injustice' through unnecessary delay, or through emotionally distressed witnesses being twice put through the ordeal of giving evidence (i.e. once at committal proceedings and once at the trial on indictment) when neither side really desires it. Accordingly, where neither prosecution nor defence wish the witnesses as to identity to be called, and provided the court agrees, there may be a committal without consideration of the evidence, even though identification is likely to be an issue at the subsequent trial.

3.7   OTHER ORDERS AND APPLICATIONS MADE AT COMMITTAL PROCEEDINGS

The following additional matters may, and in some cases must, be considered at committal proceedings whether the latter be with or without consideration of the evidence.

3.7.1   Publicity

Proceedings in a magistrates' court prior to the commencement of committal proceedings and the committal proceedings themselves, can often give an impression of the case which is biased in favour of the prosecution. For example, where a bail application is made, the prosecution may resist that application on the grounds that on a previous occasion the accused was granted bail but failed to attend court when required. Reports in the media could lead members of the public to the conclusion that the accused had previously been in trouble. Thus a member of the public selected for jury duty in the case might be influenced by matters which are totally irrelevant to it.

Again, where the examining justices are asked to consider the evidence before committing for trial, the defence for purely tactical reasons often refrains both from challenging the prosecution evidence and calling its own evidence. If the prosecution evidence were to be reported in full and no balancing report given because the defence is being reserved for the trial on indictment, members of the public might form the view that the prosecution case is overwhelming and that there is simply no defence. The Magistrates' Court Act 1980 s. 8 therefore limits matters which may appear in reports of committal proceedings and any hearings, such as remand hearings, which may have preceded them. Section 8 permits the reporting of bare details of the case, and such reports may include the name of the court, the names of the justices, the names, addresses and occupations of the parties and witnesses, names of the legal representatives, the charges and whether the examining magistrates found that there was a case to answer on those charges, the court to which the accused was committed for trial, and whether bail and legal aid were granted. The court must, however, on the application of any accused person, lift the reporting restrictions, when the case may be reported in full as in any other hearing in open court: s. 8(2).

> This rule may have unfortunate effects where one of several accused persons requires the reporting restrictions to be lifted as is his right under s. 8(2), but the others do not. Equally unfortunate would be a 'majority vote' as this would prejudice the interests of a person wrongly accused who seeks publicity to find witnesses to clear his name. It will be vividly remembered that the publicity given to the committal proceedings in the Jeremy Thorpe trial came about solely on the application of one of four accused that reporting restrictions be lifted.
>
> Full reporting is permitted where all the accused persons are discharged by the examining justices. Similarly, where the committal proceedings are followed by trial on indictment, the committal proceedings may be reported in full after the subsequent trial on indictment or if two or more accused are committed for trial on one occasion but tried separately, after the last of their trials. Contravention of s. 8 is a summary offence punishable with a fine up to £500. The Attorney-General's consent is required for the bringing of a prosecution.

3.7.2   Witness orders

If the accused is committed for trial on indictment and pleads not guilty, it will almost certainly be necessary to call as witnesses at the Crown Court some or all of those who contributed evidence at the committal proceedings. To ensure that those who will be wanted at the Crown Court attend there at the appropriate time, the examining justices must make a witness order in respect of each person who testified at the committal or who made a written statement which was tendered under s. 102: Criminal Procedure (Attendance of Witnesses) Act 1965, s. 1. Witness orders may be full or conditional. A full order requires the subject to attend and give evidence before the Crown Court, a conditional one requires him to do so only if notice is subsequently given to him to that effect. Conditional witness orders are only appropriate where the evidence of the subject is unlikely to be required or unlikely to be disputed (s. 1(2) of the 1965 Act). If the accused is likely to plead guilty at the trial on indictment, conditional orders for all witnesses (except, perhaps, the police officer principally concerned in the case) will be made. The requirement to make witness orders does not extend to the accused himself should he testify at the committal proceedings, nor to witnesses that he may call solely as to his character.

> The choice between a full and a conditional witness order is nominally in the hands of the examining justices. In practice they make the orders requested by the prosecution and defence. If either the prosecution or the defence wish a witness to be fully bound to attend at the Crown Court, there is no point denying them their wish, as they can always cause an appropriate officer of the Crown Court to serve on the witness a notice converting a conditional order into a full one. At committals under s. 6(1), witness orders are most conveniently made after the taking of the subject's deposition or reading of his s. 102 statement; at committals under s. 6(2) the matter is dealt with when the s. 102 statements are handed to the clerk.
>
> Conditional witness orders should only be made where the evidence is not in dispute, or where it is not likely to be required. This is because a conditional witness order enables a deposition or s. 102 statement to be read out, and in these circumstances its veracity cannot be tested because of the absence of the witness. Thus, without the test of cross-examination, the jury may well assume it to be true. For the consequences of noncompliance with a witness order and the procedure in general for securing the attendance of witnesses at the Crown Court, see Para. 8.3.3.

3.7.3 Alibi warning

Committal proceedings ensure that the defence knows the nature of the prosecution case in advance of the trial on indictment. The prosecution has no similar advance warning of the defence case. At most trials on indictment this may not be a particularly grave handicap for the prosecution. Many defences are fairly predictable (e.g. mistaken identity on a robbery charge, no guilty knowledge on a charge of handling stolen goods or reasonable self-defence on an assualt charge), and anyway cross-examination of the prosecution witnesses alerts counsel to the likely defence. There is one situation, however, where lack of advance warning might unfairly hamper the prosecution in its attempts to test the strength of the defence. This is when the accused raises an alibi – i.e. says that he was somewhere other than the scene of the alleged offence at the relevant time and therefore could not possibly have committed it. Usually the defence call witnesses to confirm the accused's story. If the prosecution hear of the alibi defence only when the accused is in the witness box, it may be too late to check its truthfulness. Given time, they might obtain evidence from other witnesses who, if the accused's account is true, would have seen him at the place he puts himself, but who deny that he was there. Or, they might discover that the alibi witnesses the defence propose to call have previous convictions or some powerful reason to assist the accused. Lacking time, this cogent evidence might never come to light. Accordingly, the Criminal Justice Act 1967, s. 11 prevents the prosecution being taken by surprise by an alibi defence.

This section provides that, unless the accused gives notice of particulars of his alibi, he may not adduce evidence of the alibi at the trial on indictment as of right, but must rely on the judge giving him leave (for the circumstances in which a judge may properly refuse leave to adduce alibi evidence, see Para. 8.5.3). The notice must either be given in court during or at the end of the committal proceedings, or it must be given in writing to the prosecution not later than seven days from the end of the committal proceedings. Notice may be, and normally is, given by the defence solicitors on behalf of the accused. In addition to stating where the accused was at the relevant time, the notice should give the names and addresses of any witnesses to the alibi (other than the accused himself) who the defence are hoping to call. If those particulars are not given in respect of any witness he may only be called at the trial with leave, although, provided the notice is otherwise in order, the accused himself and the witnesses who were named etc. may be called as of right.

If the accused did not know of the onus resting on him to give notice of particulars of alibi it would clearly be unfair to refuse him leave to adduce the evidence even if notice should not be forthcoming. Rules 6(4) and 7(9) therefore require the court at committal proceedings to warn the accused of the effect of s. 11. This is done after the accused is given the opportunity of making an unsworn statement from the dock, or, if the committal is without consideration of the evidence, immediately before the formal committal for trial. The court may dispense with the alibi warning if, having regard to the nature of the offence charged, it appears unnecessary, but, if no warning was given at the magistrates' court, the Crown Court must give leave for the alibi evidence to be adduced, even if the accused has given no notice. The examining justices usually ask the defence and possibly the prosecution whether the alibi warning is appropriate.

For purposes of the Criminal Justice Act 1967, s. 11, 'alibi' is defined in a rather restrictive way. It means evidence 'tending to show that by reason of the presence of the (accused) at a particular place...at a particular time he was not...at the place where the offence is alleged to have been committed' at the relevant time. Thus, in *R v Lewis* [1969] 2QB 1, where the prosecution sought to support their allegation that L had dishonestly handled stolen postal orders on 14 February 1968 by evidence of L's cashing two of them on 16 February, L was under no duty to give notice of evidence he intended to call as to his whereabouts on the 16 February. The offence was allegedly committed on the 14th, so evidence about the 16th could not come within the s. 11 definition of alibi. Further, it was stated in *R v Hassan* [1970] 1QB 423 that the section appears 'to envisage an offence which necessarily involves the accused being at a particular place at a particular time'. Therefore, H, who was charged with living on the earnings of prostitution between 29 July and 21 August 1968 in Cardiff, did not have to give notice that on the morning of 20 August, he was at his brother's house, rather than being, as the prosecution alleged, at the prostitute's flat. The crime charged was 'anchored to no particular location', and so s. 11 did not apply. However, notice should be given under s. 11 even though the accused alone is to give evidence of the alibi: *R v Jackson* [1973] Crim LR 356.

3.7.4 Bail and legal aid

Having committed the accused for trial on indictment, the examining justices must then decide whether to grant bail and whether legal aid should be granted for the proceedings in the Crown Court.

Section 6(3) empowers the court to commit the accused for trial either in custody or on bail. Committal in custody means the accused is detained in prison, or, where the accused is under 21, a remand centre. Bail means that he is released under a duty to surrender to custody at the Crown Court on the day fixed for the trial. As months may elapse between committal and trial, the decision to grant or withhold bail at this stage is a most important decision. Bail is dealt with fully in Chapter 20.

It is usual for the examining justices to be asked to grant legal aid for the proceedings in Crown Court, and where it has already been granted for proceedings in the magistrates court, this follows almost automatically. Full discussion of legal aid may be found in Chapter 21.

3.8 EVIDENCE IN WRITING OTHER THAN s. 102 STATEMENTS ADMISSIBLE AT COMMITTALS

Although reliance on s. 102 is by far the most common way of securing the admission of written evidence at committal proceedings, there are three other statutory provisions which allow such evidence to be tendered.

(a) Depositions from persons dangerously ill. If a person is able and willing to give material information relating to an indictable offence, and he appears to a magistrate who has received medical advice on the matter to be dangerously ill and unlikely to recover, the magistrate may take in writing the deposition of the sick person on oath: s. 105. The deposition may be taken out of court (e.g. at the hospital where the sick person is being treated), and the procedure for taking the statement need not conform to Rule 7. It is admissible at committal proceedings for prosecution or defence, provided the party against whom it is tendered was given notice of the intention to take the deposition, and that party had the opportunity to cross-examine the deponent (either personally or through counsel or solicitor). This last requirement would appear to detract from the usefulness of s. 105, since it must be a rare disease which is so mortifying, yet which permits cross-examination.

(b) Written statements from children relating to sexual offences. Section 103 provides that a written statement made by or taken from a child (i.e. under 14) is admissible at committal proceedings for offences under the Sexual Offences Act 1956 or the Indecency with Children Act 1960. The statement need not be taken by a magistrate, and need not contain a s. 102 type declaration that it is true to the best of the maker's knowledge and belief etc. Other than this, s. 103 adds little to s. 102. Objection by the defence will prevent a statement from being admitted under s. 103, and, whilst the prosecution is in general obliged to use s. 103 statements rather than to call child witnesses, such a child witness must be called if he is required to establish the identity of any person.

(c) Depositions from juveniles. If a juvenile (i.e. under 17) is the victim of certain offences under the Sexual Offences Act 1956, or of any offence involving bodily injury to him, a magistrate may take a deposition from him out of court: Children and Young Persons Act 1933, s. 42. The magistrate must be satisfied, upon medical advice, that attendance at court would involve serious danger to the juvenile's life or health, which presumably includes mental health. The deposition is admissible at committal

proceedings for the prosecution or the defence, provided in the former case that notice
and opportunity to cross-examine were given to the accused: s. 43 of the 1933 Act.
Depositions out of court under s. 105 or s. 42 of the 1933 Act are also sometimes
admissible at the trial on indictment (see Para. 8.3.7). Section 103 statements are
admissible only at committal proceedings.

3.9   METHOD OF CHALLENGING CONDUCT OF
COMMITTAL PROCEEDINGS

There is no appeal as such against the examining justices' decision to commit or
not to commit for trial. However, if they refuse to commit, the prosecution may in
effect challenge the decision by applying to a judge in chambers for a voluntary bill
of indictment (see Para. 3.10.1). If they do commit, and the committal was a
complete nullity because (e.g.) the depositions were not taken in accordance with r.
7, the Court of Appeal will quash any conviction returned at the subsequent trial
on indictment: *R* v *Phillips and Quayle* [1939] 1KB 63. However, the hearing of
evidence from a witness who was in fact incompetent to testify or the reception of
inadmissible evidence will not nullify the proceedings or expose the committal for
trial to challenge: *R* v *Norfolk Quarter Sessions* ex parte *Brunson* [1953] 1QB 503.
The Divisional Court supervises the work of the magistrates' courts through the
prerogative orders of certiorari, mandamus and prohibition (see Chapter 18), and
these orders are theoretically available to control examining justices, but an order
would only be made in the most extreme case (e.g. where examining justices not
only refused to allow a relevant line of cross-examination but refused even to
consider argument that it should be allowed — see *R* v *Wells Street Stipendiary
Magistrate* ex parte *Seillon* [1978] 1WLR 1002 and [1980] Crim LR 180. The lack
of effective appeal from the decision of examining justices is not a source of
injustice as, if there was not truly a case to answer and the prosecution have not
supplemented their evidence by the time the case is tried on indictment, the judge
will direct the jury that they must acquit the accused.

3.10   TRIAL ON INDICTMENT IN THE ABSENCE OF
SUCCESSFUL COMMITTAL PROCEEDINGS

Trials on indictment are, in the great majority of cases preceded by committal
proceedings resulting in the committal of the accused to the Crown Court for trial. It
is possible, however, for the accused to be tried on indictment even though no
committal proceedings have been held in his case or where the proceedings ended in
his discharge. There are three ways in which this may occur: Administration of
Justice (Miscellaneous Provisions) Act 1933, s. 2.

3.10.1   Voluntary bills of indictment

A High Court judge may direct or consent to the preferment of a voluntary bill of
indictment. The terminology is explained in Chapter 4, but, in effect, the judge's
direction that a voluntary bill be preferred is equivalent to an order that an accused
be tried on indictment for those offences alleged in the bill. In theory the prosecution
could, in all cases, avoid the holding of committal proceedings by applying to a High

Court judge for the preferment of a voluntary bill. In practice, voluntary bills are only sought if either committal proceedings have been held and they resulted in the discharge of the accused, or committal proceedings, if held, would for some special reason be inconvenient or unsatisfactory. Thus, the voluntary bill procedure allows the prosecution to challenge the examining justices' refusal to commit for trial, although it is not in form an appeal against discharge. *R* v *Paling* [1978] 67 Cr App R 299 provides an example of the holding of committal proceedings being justifiably avoided. P was charged with assault. In the course of committal proceedings in relation to that charge he allegedly assaulted police officers involved in the case, and the examining justices adjourned. Rather than risk continuing the adjourned committal proceedings or commencing a committal for the assaults on the police officers, the prosecution sought a voluntary bill of indictment to cover all the assaults.

Committal proceedings may also be inconvenient where, after one accused has been committed for trial and an indictment signed against him, a second accused is arrested, the prosecution case against him being that he committed an offence jointly with the first accused. The prosecution will wish to have both accused tried together, but this can only be done if there is a single indictment against them both. Application may be made for a voluntary bill of indictment charging both accused. The indictment outstanding against the first accused will not be proceeded with. It seems that the same result could be achieved simply by holding committal proceedings for the second accused and then drafting an indictment against both accused (*R* v *Groom* [1977] QB 6) but the voluntary bill procedure may be swifter.

The procedure for obtaining a High Court judge's consent to the preferment of a voluntary bill of indictment is set out in the Indictments Procedure Rules 1971. The application must be in writing, signed by the applicant or his solicitor. It must be supported by an affidavit made by the applicant to the effect that any statements contained in the application are true to the best of his knowledge and belief. The bill of indictment it is proposed to prefer must also be sent with the application. If there have been no committal proceedings or if there have been successful committal proceedings, the application must state why it is being made (if there have been unsuccessful proceedings, the reason for the application is obvious). Where there have been committal proceedings, the applicant must provide copies of all depositions and s. 102 statements from those proceedings, together with proofs of evidence from any witnesses he intends to call at trial who did not give evidence or have their statements tendered at the committal. Where there have not been committal proceedings, proofs of evidence from the proposed prosecution witnesses are necessary. Normally, neither the applicant nor the witnesses attend before the judge — i.e. he makes his decision simply by reading the documents — and, even if they are ordered to attend, the proceedings are not in open court. The judge's decision is given in writing unless he otherwise directs.

3.10.2 Retrial by order of Court of Appeal

If an accused is convicted on indictment but, on appeal, the Court of Appeal quashes the conviction, he is in most cases treated as if he had been acquitted of the offence charged. Therefore, he cannot be retried for the offence. Where, however, an appeal to the Court of Appeal is successful because new evidence is adduced which was not available at the trial on indictment, then the Court of Appeal has power to order a retrial (Criminal Appeal Act 1968, s. 7, and see Para. 17.4.1). The Court of Appeal directs that a bill of indictment be preferred, and no further committal proceedings are required.

3.10.3   Direction to prosecute for perjury

If the judge of a court of record or the chairman of a bench of magistrates thinks that a witness in proceedings before him has committed perjury, he may order that witness to be prosecuted and commit him to the Crown Court to stand trial: Perjury Act 1911, s. 9. The section merely provides a quick way of bringing those suspected of perjury before a judge and jury. If no order is made, the prosecution are still entitled to prefer a charge of perjury, in which event committal proceedings will be held in the normal way.

4 The Crown Court

The Courts Act 1971 s. 1(1) provides that 'the Supreme Court shall consist of the Court of Appeal and the High Court, together with the Crown Court established by this Act'. The Crown Court thus replaces the many and ancient courts of assize and quarter sessions which formerly dealt with trials on indictment. It exercises the following jurisdiction:

(a)   All trials on indictment are heard before the Crown Court: Courts Act 1971, s. 6.

(b)   Magistrates courts may commit an offender to the Crown Court for sentence. This usually takes place where the accused, having been convicted summarily of an offence which may be tried either summarily or on indictment, is revealed to have such character and antecedents that the magistrates consider their powers of punishment to be insufficient (see Para. 12.3).

(c)   A person, summarily convicted by magistrates, may appeal either against conviction or sentence or both to the Crown Court (see Para. 18.1).

(d)   The Crown Court exercises limited jurisdiction in civil matters. For example, under the Children and Young Persons Act 1969, s. 2(12) it may hear appeals against care orders made by juvenile courts under s. 1 of that Act. It may also hear appeals against decisions of the licensing justices under the Licensing Act 1964, s. 21.

4.1 CROWN COURT JUDGES

High Court judges, circuit judges and recorders may sit in the Crown Court, and when they do so 'shall be deemed to be judges of the Crown Court': Courts Act 1971, s. 4.

4.1.1 High Court judges

The most serious cases are heard by a High Court judge sitting in the Crown Court. In practice, this judge will be drawn from the Queen's Bench Division as having experience in criminal matters, although in theory nothing prevents a judge of another division from sitting. In very exceptional circumstances, the Lord Chancellor, the head of the judiciary, may request a Lord Justice of Appeal to sit in the Crown Court. There are about twenty High Court judges sitting in the Crown Court at any one time.

4.1.2 Circuit judges

The office of circuit judge, like the Crown Court itself, was created by the Courts Act. There are around 340 circuit judges, most of whom spend the bulk of their time sitting in the Crown Court. Circuit judges and recorders (see Para. 4.1.3) handle most of the routine work of the Crown Court, and the circuit judge in particular may be regarded as the typical Crown Court judge. Circuit judges are appointed by the Queen on the recommendation of the Lord Chancellor. This is a full-time appointment which may not be combined with practice as a barrister or solicitor. Only barristers of at least ten years' standing and recorders who have held that office for at least three years are eligible for appointment. Retirement is normally at the age of 72 although the Lord Chancellor may authorise continuance in office until the age of 75. Conversely, the Lord Chancellor could remove a circuit judge from office before normal retiring age on grounds of incapacity or misbehaviour. For appointment, retirement etc. of circuit judges, see Courts Act 1971, s. 16-20.

Circuit judges may and, if possible, should sit in the county courts as well as the Crown Court. One of the suggestions made by Lord Beeching, on whose report the Courts Act was based, was that a reasonable 'mix' of civil work in the county courts and crime in the Crown Court would prevent circuit judges becoming jaded through lack of variety in their work. Accordingly, circuit judges are appointed to serve 'in the Crown Court and county courts': Courts Act 1971, s. 16. Obviously, some circuit judges will be predominantly Crown Court judges and other predominantly county court judges, but the intention was that they should not be exclusively one or the other. The increasing volume of criminal work may, however, force circuit judges to spend a larger proportion of their time in the Crown Court.

4.1.3 Recorders

Like circuit judges, recorders are appointed by the Queen on the recommendation of the Lord Chancellor. There are approximately 450 recorders. Unlike circuit judges, their appointment is a part-time one, and, when not sitting in the Crown Court, they may carry on in private practice. The appointment is for a fixed term, during which the recorder undertakes to make himself available to sit on an agreed number of occasions. Barristers or solicitors of at least ten years' standing are eligible for appointment. Provisions as to retirement and removal from office are similar to those which apply in the case of circuit judges, save that there is no discretion for the Lord Chancellor to allow a recorder to continue to act until he is 75. Appointment etc. of recorders is dealt with by the Courts Act, s. 21.

Perhaps the most interesting point to note about the appointment of recorders is that solicitors are eligible. Since a recorder who has held the office for at least three years may become a circuit judge, the Bar's monopoly of the higher judicial appointments is to some extent dented. In March 1981, however, only 19 of the 340 circuit judges were solicitors. Further, although circuit judges are occasionally raised to the High Court bench, that cannot happen in the case of a solicitor circuit judge as only barristers may be appointed High Court judges.

4.1.4 Deputy circuit judges

As a temporary measure, to assist the disposal of business in the Crown Court or county courts (e.g. when there is a substantial back-log of cases) the Lord Chancellor may appoint for a fixed period a deputy circuit judge under the Courts Act 1971, s. 24. For the period of his appointment a deputy circuit judge is in all ways equivalent to a circuit judge. Those eligible for appointment are barristers and solicitors of at least ten years' standing, together with retired Court of Appeal, High Court and circuit judges.

4.1.5 Mode of addressing Crown Court judges

High Court judges, all judges sitting at the Central Criminal Court and any circuit judge holding the office of honorary recorder of Liverpool or Manchester are addressed in court as 'My Lord' (or 'My Lady'). Except as stated above, circuit judges, recorders and deputy circuit judges are addressed as 'Your Honour'. The court list of cases for hearing in a particular court should refer to a circuit judge as 'His/Her Honour Judge...', and to a recorder as Mr/Mrs/Miss Recorder...' (see a practice direction given by the Lord Chief Justice: 1977 1WLR 1435).

4.1.6 Distribution of work between High Court judges and circuit judges etc.

Directions given by the Lord Chief Justice (1972, 56 Cr AppR 52), with the concurrence of the Lord Chancellor, under the Courts Act s. 4(5) establish a detailed system for distributing work between High Court judges and other Crown Court judges. The general principle is that the most serious offences must or normally will be tried by a High Court judge, the less serious ones, unless special circumstances apply, will be tried by a circuit judge or recorder.

The directions divide offences into four classes. Class 1 offences (e.g. murder and offences under s. 1 of the Official Secrets Act 1911) must be tried by a High Court judge. Class 2 offences (e.g. manslaughter, rape and sexual intercourse with a girl under 13) must be tried by a High Court judge unless the presiding judge of the circuit (see Para. 4.2) or someone acting with his authority allows an individual case to be tried by a circuit judge or recorder. Class 4 offences, comprising the great bulk of indictable offences, are normally listed for trial by a circuit judge or recorder. However, the Crown Court officer responsible for drawing up the lists of cases to be tried by the various judges sitting at a location of the Crown Court may decide that a particular case is especially serious, and list it for trial by a High Court judge. Class 4 offences include robbery, causing grievous bodily harm with intent to do so and all offences triable either way. Factors which should influence the listing officer in favour of having a Class 4 offence tried by a High Court judge include the offence involving serious violence or a large sum of money, the accused holding a prominent public position, and the case raising difficult questions of law. Class 3 offences are those not falling within any of the other classes. They are listed for trial by a High Court judge unless the listing officer decides that an individual case is more suitable for a circuit judge or recorder. A listing officer may only list a Class 4 offence for trial by a High Court judge or a Class 3 offence for trial by a circuit judge or recorder if he has first consulted the presiding judge (or judge acting for him) or is acting under general directions on the matter given by the presiding judge.

4.2 ORGANISATION OF THE CROWN COURT

The Crown Court is a single court but it sits in many different locations throughout the country. Strictly speaking, one should refer to the 'Crown Court sitting at Barchester' rather than the 'Barchester Crown Court'. One advantage of being a single court is that the Crown Court sitting anywhere in England or Wales may try any indictable offence over which the English courts have jurisdiction, irrespective of where it was allegedly committed (e.g. the Crown Court sitting at Plymouth can try an offence of theft allegedly committed in Newcastle and vice versa). The jurisdictional disputes which used to arise under the pre-Crown Court system, whereby a conviction might be quashed because the appellant had been tried at Loamshire Quarter Sessions when he should have been tried at Bricktown Assizes, are thus avoided. It is also easier to ensure an even distribution of work between the various locations of the

Crown Court. One of the few concessions to tradition made by the Courts Act is that when the Crown Court sits in the City of London (i.e. at the Old Bailey) it is still known as the Central Criminal Court, not the Crown Court sitting in London.

Locations of the Crown Court are classified as first, second and third tier locations. The first tier courts have facilities for handling High Court civil work and are attended by High Court judges. Those of the second tier have no facilities for civil work but do have the services of at least one High Court judge, and those of the third tier lack both facilities for civil work and High Court judges. The various locations of whatever tier are grouped together on a geographical basis into six circuits (Midland and Oxford, North-Eastern, Northern, South-Eastern, Wales and Chester, and Western). A High Court judge, known as the presiding judge, is assigned to have special responsibility for each circuit. Some of his functions have already been noted in Para. 4.1.6.

When a magistrates' court commits an accused for trial it must specify the location of the Crown Court at which the trial is to take place: Magistrates' Courts Act 1980, s. 7. In selecting the appropriate location the examining justices are to consider:

(a)   the convenience of the defence, prosecution and witnesses,

(b)   the expediting of the trial, and

(c)   any direction given by the Lord Chief Justice under the Courts Act, 1971 s. 4(5).

The Crown Court may on its own initiative vary the decision of the examining justices as to the place of trial. Further, either the prosecution or defence may apply to the Crown Court for a variation of the examining justices' original decision or for a further variation of any decision the Crown Court may have substituted for that original decision. Such applications must be heard by a High Court judge in open court: Courts Act 1971, s. 7. The defence might apply for a change in the venue of trial if the accused has been committed for trial at a location of the Crown Court near the scene of the crime and the offence has raised so much anger in the area that jurors from that area might not be able to consider the evidence in a dispassionate way. The prosecution might want a change of venue if they fear an escape from court by the accused, and the original location chosen would be difficult to guard.

The directions given by the Lord Chief Justice (see Para. 4.1.6) make the decision on the location of the trial a formality in the great majority of cases. If the offences for which the accused is committed (or one of them) fall within Classes 1-3 the committal must be to the most convenient location of the Crown Court where a High Court judge regularly sits, since it is at least probable that the case will have to be tried by a High Court judge. If the offences are in Class 4 the committal is to the most convenient location of the Crown Court, even if no High Court judge sits there. If the examining justices consider that a Class 4 offence should be tried by a High Court judge they may send a notice to that effect to the Crown Court, and commit to a location where a High Court judge sits. The factors which should influence the justices in favour of a trial by a High Court judge are the same as those which should influence a Crown Court listing officer to list a Class 4 offence for a High Court judge (see Para. 4.1.6). The examining justices do not normally need to pause to consider what may be the most convenient location of the Crown Court or the most convenient location where a High Court judge regularly sits, since each magistrates' court is notified of the location/s of the Crown Court to which it should usually commit (probably the locations nearest to the court in question). There are, however, instances where the location of the court assumes great importance.

The importance of having a case tried at a suitable location of the Crown Court is illustrated by *R v Charles* [1979] 68Cr App R 334. C and others were charged with several offences, including obtaining property by deception, arising out of complex business transactions. Although the offences alleged were Class 4 offences, the magistrates decided — rightly according to the Court of Appeal — that the accused should be committed to the Central Criminal Court rather than to a third tier Crown Court location. At the Central Criminal Court there are a number of judges who have had long experience of trying complicated commercial fraud cases. Unfortunately, the Central Criminal Court was, at the time, overloaded with work, and the appropriate officers of the court took the decision to transfer the case to the Crown Court sitting at Snaresbrook. The trial lasted some 35 days; C was convicted, but his conviction had to be quashed because of several shortcomings in the summing up (see Para. 8.7). The Court of Appeal implied that the difficulties had arisen through the case coming before a judge who had had no experience of cases of its type. That in turn was caused by its being heard at an inappropriatiate location of the Crown Court. Lawton LJ stated at p. 337:

> Now that court (the Crown Court sitting at Snaresbrook) plays an important part in the administration of justice in North East London. It has its own special problems arising out of delinquency in that area and the judges there are very experienced in dealing with cases reflecting the social needs of the people living locally. But commercial frauds of this kind and of this complexity are not the normal type of case dealt with at Snaresbrook Crown Court. It follows that there was a chance that the judge at that Court who was given the task of trying the case might not have had much experience in dealing with long, fairly complicated cases. Without making any criticism whatsoever of the judge who tried this case, the indications are that he had not had much experience.

4.3 MAGISTRATES AS JUDGES OF THE CROWN COURT

The primary role of magistrates in the judicial system is, of course, adjudicating in the magistrates' courts. They do, however, have a secondary role to play in the work of the Crown Court (see Courts Act 1971, s. 5; Crown Court Rules 1971 SI 1971 No 1292, and the Lord Chief Justice's directions). When the Crown Court is hearing an appeal from the decision of a magistrates' court or dealing with an offender upon committal for sentence, it must consist of a 'professional' judge, sitting with not less than two and not more than four magistrates. The professional judge may be a High Court judge, circuit judge or recorder, although the Lord Chief Justice's directions provide that these cases should normally be listed for hearing by a circuit judge or a recorder. If insisting upon the presence of two magistrates would cause unreasonable delay, the hearing may take place with only one assisting the professional judge, and, should any of the magistrates initially comprising the court have to withdraw, the hearing may be completed in his or their absence. Having regard to the availability of magistrates for work in the Crown Court, the Lord Chancellor may give directions that at certain locations of the Crown Court the above rules be relaxed.

Although appeals and committals for sentence are the only types of case where the presence of magistrates is essential, up to four of them may sit with a circuit judge or recorder in any Crown Court proceedings, including trials on indictment. It may be that by sitting with a professional judge a lay magistrate will gain experience which will help him in his work at the magistrates' court. However, even in cases where his presence is not essential, the magistrate is not there as a mere observer, and should play his full part in any decision the court takes. The Courts Act s. 5(8) provides that when magistrates sit in the Crown Court any decision of the court may be by a majority, although if the members of the court are equally divided the professional judge has a casting vote. The subsection applies not just to appeals and committals for sentence but to decisions which the court, as opposed to the jury, has to take during trial on indictment. In *R* v *Orpin* [1975] QB 283 the point arose as to the admissibility of a confession on the grounds of it having been gained voluntarily or otherwise. The Court of Appeal was asked to decide whether the magistrates and the judge were correct in having retired together to decide the point, and it was held that they were correct. In all cases, however, the magistrates must accept the professional judge's guidance on the law.

As has been seen, a magistrate, sitting in the Crown Court upon the hearing of an appeal or committal for sentence, plays a major role in the proceedings. If the appellant or offender were to find himself in the Crown Court before one of the magistrates who had previously decided against him, he might justifiably feel aggrieved. Rule 5 of the Crown Court Rules provides, therefore, that a magistrate who was involved in the proceedings in the magistrates' court may not be a member of the court for the appeal or committal for sentence.

4.4 RIGHTS OF AUDIENCE IN THE CROWN COURT

Barristers, of course, have the right of audience in the Crown Court. In addition, the Lord Chancellor has issued directions entitling solicitors to 'appear in, conduct, defend and address the court' in appeals and committals for sentence where they, or a member of their firm, represented the accused in the magistrates' court. At some of the remoter locations of the Crown Court (e.g. Caernarvon, Barnstaple and Bodmin) solicitors have a more general right of audience, being able to appear for the defence at trials on indictment for Class 4 offences. The prosecution at a trial on indictment must be legally represented but the accused has the right to defend himself if he so wishes (see *R* v *George Maxwell Developments Ltd* [1980] 2 All ER 99 in which Judge David QC at first instance restated and explained the rule that the prosecution must be legally represented).

This chapter has described the legal structure of the Crown Court. It may be useful to conclude with a brief description of the physical appearance of a location of the Crown Court. Externally, the court buildings vary enormously, from modern glass and concrete structures to ornate Victoriana. Internally, the court rooms themselves also vary, but one may detect a basic pattern. At the front of the court is the raised bench where the judge sits in a throne-like chair beneath the Royal coat-of-arms. Below the judge is the clerk at his desk. Facing the judge, either at the rear or in the middle of the court, is the accused in the partitioned off area known as the dock. In front of the dock are the seats for counsel. To one side of the court is the jury box — twelve seats, usually in two tiered rows of six — and, on the other side, is the witness box from where the witnesses give their evidence. At the back of court, or in a gallery looking down from above, are seats for the public. Special areas in court may also be set aside for probation officers or social workers. A room leading off the court is reserved for the use of the jury, and it is to that room, at the end of the trial, that they retire to consider their verdict.

5   The Indictment

The indictment is the formal document containing a list of the charges against the accused, to which he pleads either guilty or not guilty at the beginning of his trial on indictment. The law on drafting indictments is contained principally in the Indictments Act 1915 and the Indictment Rules 1971 (SI 1971 No 1253) made under the Act. References in this chapter are to the Indictments Act 1915 or the Indictment Rules unless otherwise stated.

On page 38 you will find the form of indictment which might be expected to follow from an imaginary incident involving three young men who, after a football match, attacked two supporters of the opposition team (Barry and Charles Johnson). The police arrived to find two of the young men (David Wilson and John Burton) kicking Barry Johnson as he lay on the ground. This caused sufficient severe bruising to require outpatient hospital treatment. The third young man (Paul Green) was threatening Charles Johnson with a broken milk bottle, with which he had already inflicted a facial wound requiring stitches but not sufficiently serious to leave a subsequent scar.

The indictment illustrates certain fundamental points about indictments which will be discussed in detail later in the chapter.

(a)   The heading or commencement to the indictment is always in a standard form. At the top is the word 'INDICTMENT', followed by the place of trial and the name of the case. The prosecution is always formally in the name of the Queen. After the name of the case comes the standard phrase 'AB, CD etc. are charged as follows', known as the presentment.

(b)   The offences alleged against the accused are set out in separate counts of the indictment. Each count must allege only one offence.

(c)   Each count is divided into a Statement of Offence and Particulars of Offence. The Statement of Offence gives the name of the offence, and, if it is a statutory offence, the relevant statute and section as required by Rule 6. The Statement of Offence for Count 1 in the illustration indictment does not mention a statute since assault occasioning actual bodily harm is a common law offence, although the punishment is prescribed by statute. The remaining two counts, being for statutory offences, mention the relevant legislation.

(d)   The Particulars of Offence give the names of the accused alleged to have committed the offence set out in the count, and the basic details of what they allegedly did (s. 3 and r. 6).

(e)   Although a count may allege only one offence, an indictment may contain two or more counts against an accused. Paul Green is charged with wounding Charles Johnson (the cut to the cheek) and with having an offensive weapon (the broken milk

No.

INDICTMENT

The Crown Court at BARCHESTER

THE QUEEN v DAVID WILSON, JOHN BURTON and PAUL GREEN

DAVID WILSON, JOHN BURTON and PAUL GREEN are CHARGED AS FOLLOWS:—

Count 1

Statement of Offence
Assault occasioning actual bodily harm.

Particulars of Offence
DAVID WILSON and JOHN BURTON, on the 28th day of March 1981, assaulted Barry Johnson thereby occasioning him actual bodily harm.

Count 2

Statement of Offence
Wounding contrary to s. 20 of the Offences against the Person Act 1861.

Particulars of Offence
PAUL GREEN, on the 28th day of March 1981, maliciously wounded Charles Johnson.

Count 3

Statement of Offence
Having an offensive weapon contrary to s. 1(1) of the Prevention of Crime Act 1953.

Particulars of Offence
PAUL GREEN, on the 28th day of March 1981, without lawful authority or reasonable excuse had with him in a public place, namely Cathedral Row, Barchester, an offensive weapon, namely a broken milk bottle.

Date

A. N. Other
Officer of the Crown Court

bottle). Had the injuries to Barry Johnson been more serious the prosecution might have included in the indictment a count for causing grevious bodily harm with intent against Wilson and Burton as well as the count for occasioning actual bodily harm. The jury could then convict on one count or the other depending on whether they thought the evidence established the more serious or the less serious offence. Green can, of course, be convicted on either or both of the counts against him.

(f) Two or more accused may be charged in a single count if the prosecution case is that they acted in concert to commit an offence. Wilson and Burton were both kicking Barry Johnson so it is proper to put them both in one count.

(g) Two or more accused may be charged in a single indictment even though they are not alleged to have committed any single offence together. Green was not involved in the attack on Barry Johnson, but since his attack on Charles Johnson and the attack by the other two on Barry Johnson were all part of one incident they may all be joined in one indictment.

(h) The indictment is signed by an officer of the Crown Court.

5.1 PREFERRING THE BILL OF INDICTMENT

Until an indictment is signed by an officer of the Crown Court it is, technically, a bill of indictment, not an indictment. If the bill of indictment has been drafted by counsel on behalf of the prosecution it has to be delivered to the Crown Court so that it can be signed, such delivery constituting preferment of the bill of indictment: Indictments (Procedure) Rules 1971 SI 1971, No 2084). Most bills of indictment are drafted by officers of the Crown Court, counsel's services only being thought necessary in important or complicated cases. A bill of indictment drafted by a Crown Court officer is deemed to have been preferred as soon as it is properly drafted. In an attempt to reduce the delay between committal for trial and the commencement of the trial on indictment, Rule 5 of the Indictment (Procedure) Rules provides that a bill of indictment must be preferred within 28 days of committal. However, the rule indicates what ought to occur rather than what must occur. A judge of the Crown Court may always allow a bill of indictment to be preferred out of time, and, even if no such application is made within the 28 day period, it has been held that the requirement in Rule 5 is merely directory so the late preferment of the bill will not lead to the indictment being quashed: *R* v *Sheerin* [1977] 64 Cr App R 68. The distinction between an indictment and a bill of indictment is only relevant in the context of preferment of a bill of indictment, so further references will be simply to drafting an indictment.

5.2 COUNTS WHICH MAY BE INCLUDED IN AN INDICTMENT

When the accused has been committed to the Crown Court for trial on indictment, the question arises as to what charge or charges are to be contained in that indictment. Whether he is an officer of the Crown Court or counsel instructed for the purpose, the person drafting the indictment will have at his disposal all depositions and s. 102 statements from the committal proceedings, and he will be informed of those charges upon which the examining justices committed the accused, and those upon which they refused to commit. The subsequent indictment may include counts for *any* indictable offence disclosed by the depositions and s. 102 statements whether or not the accused

was committed for trial in respect of that offence: Administration of Justice
(Miscellaneous Provisions) Act 1933 s. 2(2). Thus, where the prosecution evidence is
that the accused was found in possession of stolen goods an hour after they were
stolen and he has been committed on a charge of theft, the indictment may include
counts in the alternative for both theft and handling stolen goods to cover the
possibility or   , accused saying that he did not steal the goods but merely received
them. Again, where the committal is for manslaughter, the indictment could contain a
single count for murder and no count for manslaughter if counsel or the Crown Court
officer considers that there is sufficient evidence of malice aforethought. That would
be possible even if the examining justices had been specifically asked to commit on a
charge of murder, but had refused and merely committed for manslaughter. The
power to include a count for an offence for which the examining justices expressly
refused to commit should, however, be very carefully exercised: *R v Dawson* [1960]
1WLR 163.

5.3   CONTENTS OF THE COUNT

A count consists of a statement of offence, giving the short name of the offence and
the statute contravened if it is statutory, followed by particulars of the offence. Section
3 provides that the indictment shall contain 'such particulars as may be necessary for
giving reasonable information as to the nature of the charge'. Rule 6 is a little more
specific, saying that where the offence is a statutory one, the particulars must disclose
the 'essential elements of the offence', save that if the accused would not be 'prejudiced
or embarrassed in his defence' by failure to disclose an essential element that element
need not be mentioned. Where the accused is entitled to be acquitted if he can bring
himself within some exception or proviso, it is not necessary to state in the particulars
that he is outside the exception and the proviso. For example, a count alleging the
production or supplying or possession of a controlled drug need not state that the
accused falls outside those categories of persons who are entitled to produce, supply or
possess such drugs under the Misuse of Drugs Act 1971.

   The guidance on drafting particulars given by s. 3 and r. 6 is so vague that the
best advice to a person settling an indictment is to look up a precedent for any
count he wishes to include. 'Archbold Criminal Pleading Evidence and Practice'
contains specimen counts for all the common indictable offences, and the
practitioner can usually follow the form of wording in Archbold with safety.
Specimen counts for some offences are set out on pages 42-44, but the following
general comments may be helpful:

   (a)   The particulars start with the fore-name and surname of the accused charged in
the count. An error in giving the name will not be a good ground of appeal against
conviction provided the accused could reasonably be identified from the name stated.
Similarly, where any other person is referred to in the particulars, fore-name and
surname should be stated but errors will not defeat a conviction.

   (b)   The date of the alleged offence is then stated. Surprisingly, a conviction can be
upheld even where the prosecution evidence shows that the offence was committed on
a day other than that laid in the particulars, although if the change in date would
prejudice the accused in his defence (e.g. he has an alibi for the date in the particulars)
he should be granted an adjournment. If the exact date of the offence is unknown the

particulars may allege that it was on a day unknown between the day before the earliest day on which it could have been committed and the day after the latest day on which it could have been committed. Thus, if property was stolen on 1 January 1981 and found in possession of the accused on 31 January, the count would allege 'A.B., on a day unknown between the 31st day of December 1980 and the 1st day of February 1981 dishonestly received . . .'

(c)   The elements of the offence are alleged. It is not usually necessary to write out the elements in full. For example, in a count for theft, it is sufficient to allege that 'A.B. stole a wrist-watch belonging to C.D.' However, in counts for certain offences such as handling stolen goods a fuller form of particulars is recommended.

(d)   Where property is mentioned in the particulars, the owner should be named in order to identify the property, but the value need not be given. If the owner is unknown the property can be referred to as 'belonging to a person or persons unknown'. If the property relevant to a count is cash, it may be described simply as money without specifying the individual coins and bank-notes (e.g. 'A.B., on . . . . . . stole a purse and £5.50 in money').

(e)   The place where the offence occurred need not be alleged, unless the definition of the offence requires that it be committed in or with reference to a limited range of places. Thus, a count for reckless driving must specify the road where it occurred since the offence can only be committed on a road, and a count for burglary must specify the building burgled since the offence necessitates entering a building as a trespasser. Theft, on the other hand, can be committed anywhere so the count need not say where the property was stolen.

5.4   THE RULE AGAINST DUPLICITY

No one count may charge an accused with more than one offence although, as already stated, a single indictment may include several counts against one accused. Should a count allege more than one offence it is bad for duplicity, and the defence may move the judge to quash it (see Para. 5.7.3). If a motion to quash succeeds the accused is not asked to plead guilty or not guilty to the count concerned. Failure by the judge to quash a count which is bad for duplicity is a good ground of appeal. It should be noted that a motion to quash a count for duplicity is only appropriate where the wording of the count shows that it is alleging two or more offences. If the fact that the prosecution are alleging more than one offence only becomes apparent when they call their evidence in relation to the count, the correct remedy is to amend the indictment so as to have a separate count for each offence (see Para. 5.7.2 for applications to amend an indictment).

Usually it is obvious if a count is worded so as to allege more than one offence. Thus, if the particulars state that 'AB, on the 1st day of June 1981, stole a coat belonging to Harridges and on the 2nd day of June 1981 stole a dress belonging to Selfrods', the count is clearly bad as it mentions two different dates, two different victims and two different items of property. Were the count to name only one day but separate victims (e.g. 'AB, on the 1st day of June 1981, stole a coat belonging to Harridges and a dress belonging to Selfrods'), or one victim but separate days (e.g. 'AB, on the 1st day of June 1981, stole a dress and, on the 2nd day of June 1981, stole a coat both belonging to Harridges'), it would still be a duple count. However, a count which alleges that 'AB, on the 1st day of June 1981, stole a coat and a dress belonging

SPECIMEN FORMS OF COUNTS

Murder

STATEMENT OF OFFENCE

Murder

PARTICULARS OF OFFENCE

John SMITH, on the 1st day of January 1981, murdered Richard Brown.

Manslaughter

STATEMENT OF OFFENCE

Manslaughter

PARTICULARS OF OFFENCE

John SMITH, on the 1st day of January 1981, unlawfully killed Richard Brown.

Section 18
Offences against
the Person Act
1861

STATEMENT OF OFFENCE

Causing grievous bodily harm with intent contrary to s. 18 of the Offences against the Person Act 1861.

PARTICULARS OF OFFENCE

John SMITH, on the 1st day of January 1981, caused grievous bodily harm to Richard Brown with intent to do him grievous bodily harm.

Robbery

STATEMENT OF OFFENCE

Robbery, contrary to s. 8(1) of the Theft Act 1968.

PARTICULARS OF OFFENCE

John SMITH, on the 1st day of January 1981, robbed Richard Brown of a wallet and £10 in money.

Burglary

STATEMENT OF OFFENCE

Burglary, contrary to s. 9(1)(b) of the Theft Act 1968.

PARTICULARS OF OFFENCE

John SMITH, on the 1st day of January 1981, having entered as a trespasser a building known as 30, Acacia Avenue, London W30, stole therein a television set, a gramophone, two necklaces and £37 in money.

Theft

STATEMENT OF OFFENCE

Theft, contrary to s. 1(1) of the Theft Act 1968.

PARTICULARS OF OFFENCE

John SMITH, on the 1st day of January 1981, stole a watch belonging to Richard Brown.

Handling

STATEMENT OF OFFENCE

Handling stolen goods, contrary to s. 22(1) of the Theft Act 1968.

PARTICULARS OF OFFENCE

John SMITH, on a day unknown between the 31st day of December 1980 and the 1st day of February 1981 dishonestly received certain stolen goods, namely a camera belonging to Richard Brown, knowing or believing the same to be stolen goods.

Handling

STATEMENT OF OFFENCE

Handling stolen goods, contrary to s. 22(1) of the Theft Act 1968.

PARTICULARS OF OFFENCE

John SMITH, on the 1st day of January 1981, dishonestly undertook or assisted in the disposal of certain stolen goods, namely a watch belonging to Richard Brown, by or for the benefit of another, knowing or believing the same to be stolen goods.

Obtaining
by deception

STATEMENT OF OFFENCE

Obtaining property by deception, contrary to s. 15(1) of the Theft Act 1968.

PARTICULARS OF OFFENCE

John SMITH, on the 1st day of January 1981, dishonestly obtained from Richard Brown Televisions Limited a television set with the intention of permanently depriving Richard Brown Televisions Limited thereof by deception, namely, by falsely representing that he, the said John Smith, was one Paul Price and that a cheque which he, the said John Smith, tendered in payment for the said television set was a good and valid order for the payment of the price of the said television set.

Making off   **STATEMENT OF OFFENCE**
without payment Making off without payment contrary to s. 3 of the Theft Act 1978.

PARTICULARS OF OFFENCE

John SMITH, on the 1st day of January 1981, knowing that payment on the spot for a meal supplied to him by the Richard Brown Restaurant was expected of him and with intent to avoid payment of the amount due, dishonestly made off without having paid.

Reckless   **STATEMENT OF OFFENCE**
driving   Reckless driving, contrary to s. 2 of the Road Traffic Act 1972.

PARTICULARS OF OFFENCE

John SMITH, on the 1st day of January 1981, drove a motor vehicle on a road, namely Acacia Avenue, London W30, recklessly.

---

to Harridges' is not, on the face of its wording, bad for duplicity. This is because a count may allege more than one criminal act provided that those acts form part of one activity. A person who goes into a shop on one occasion and takes a number of items without paying performs several acts but, since those acts constitute a single activity, it is only necessary to have one count naming all the items taken. Even where the prosecution case is that the accused went into a department store and moved from department to department taking items from each department, one count is sufficient (*R* v *Wilson* (1979) 69Cr App R 83, distinguishing *R* v *Ballysingh* (1953) 37Cr App R 28). If the evidence were to show that the accused, having taken one item from a shop, left and returned later the same day to take another item, it is suggested that his leaving the shop breaks his conduct into two separate activities so that separate counts for theft would be required.

> Difficult problems of duplicity arise from statutes which do not make it clear whether they are creating one or several offences. Rule 7 provides that 'where an offence created...by an enactment...states any part of the offence in the alternative...the matters stated in the alternative in the enactment...may be stated in the alternative in an indictment charging the offence'. Thus, a count for criminal damage may allege that the accused damaged the property 'intending to damage it *or* being reckless as to whether such property would be damaged', because there is one offence of criminal damage which may be committed intentionally or recklessly. Similarly, it has been held that a count for being in possession of a controlled drug may allege that the drug was 'cannabis *or* cannabis resin' (*R* v *Best and others* (1980) 70Cr App R 21). If, however, a section of a statute, on its true interpretation, creates two or more separate offences, they must be alleged in separate counts. Section 9(1) of the Theft Act 1968, for example, provides that:

> A person is guilty of burglary if —
> (a) he enters any building...as a trespasser and with intent to (steal etc.); or
> (b) having entered any building...as a trespasser he steals...anything in the building...

The structure of the subsection shows that it is creating two separate offences, namely burglary contrary to s. 9(1)(a) and burglary contrary to s. 9(1)(b). A count which alleged that the accused 'entered as a trespasser with intent to steal or, having entered as a trespasser, stole...' would therefore be bad for duplicity, notwithstanding r. 7. Sometimes it is difficult to know whether a statute is creating one or several offences. Thus, in *Ware* v *Fox; Fox* v *Dingley* [1967] 1WLR 1209 it was held that a section in the predecessor to the Misuse of Drugs Act 1971 which made it criminal to 'permit premises to be used for the purpose of smoking cannabis...or of dealing in cannabis' created separate offences of permitting premises to be used for smoking cannabis and permitting premises to be used for dealing in cannabis. Prior to the court's decision, however, one could reasonably have thought that the section was creating one offence which could be committed in two different ways.

The difficulty discussed above also arises in relation to one of the commonest indictable offences. The Theft Act 1968, s. 22 provides that 'a person handles stolen goods if . . . knowing or believing them to be stolen goods he dishonestly receives the goods, or dishonestly undertakes or assists in their retention, removal, disposal or realisation by or for the benefit or another person, or if he arranges to do so.' The lack of any division of the subsection into paragraphs shows that only one offence of handling is created, so particulars which simply alleged dishonestly handling stolen goods would not be bad for duplicity. However, since the wording of s. 22 means that the handling could have been committed in any of eighteen different ways, it is generally fairer to the accused to specify the form of handling alleged. If the prosecution evidence shows that the accused did no more than assist in the retention of stolen goods for the benefit of another, the particulars should be to that effect; if the evidence shows receiving, the particulars should be correspondingly worded; if the prosecution are genuinely in doubt as to which form of handling can be proved, they should have two counts. In the particulars of the first count, they allege receiving the goods; in the particulars of the second count they allege in the alternative such of the other forms of handling as may be appropriate (e.g. 'dishonestly undertook or assisted in the disposal or realisation of certain stolen goods . . . by or for the benefit of another'). The advantage of this form of drafting is that, depending on the view they take of the evidence, the jury may convict either of receiving (which is generally considered the most serious form of handling) or one of the less serious forms.

5.5 JOINDER OF COUNTS IN AN INDICTMENT

The circumstances in which several counts against one accused may be put in one indictment are set out in r. 9, which says:

Charges for any offences may be joined in the same indictment if those charges are founded on the same facts, or form or are part of a series of offences of the same or a similar character.

The operation of the rule is illustrated by *R* v *Mansfield* [1977] 1WLR 1102, where M. was charged in an indictment containing ten counts. Three counts were for arson, alleging that on 12 December 1974 M. had started a fire in the Worsley Hotel, Bayswater, and that on 19 December and 28 December 1974 he had started fires in the Piccadilly Hotel in the West End of London. The three offences were a series of the same or a similar character, so counts for them were rightly put in one indictment. The remaining counts were for murder, based on the fact that seven people had died in the Worsley Hotel fire. Since these counts were founded on the same facts as the Worsley Hotel arson count, all ten counts could properly be joined in one indictment.

5.5.1 Requirement for counts to be 'founded on the same facts'

The simplest application of this part of r. 9 is in cases such as *R* v *Mansfield* where a single act by the accused (setting fire to an hotel) gives rise to several offences (arson and seven murders). The rule will also apply where, in a continuous course of conduct, the accused commits several offences. If the accused is stopped for driving a car at 60 mph in a 30mph area, and, upon the police making enquiries, they discover that the car has been reported as having been taken without the owner's permission, the accused could be charged in a single indictment with reckless driving and taking a motor vehicle without lawful authority. If it were further found that the accused was disqualified from driving, a count for that could be added, and, if the accused were searched and found to have in his pocket car keys but did not possess a car, there might be a count for going equipped for theft. Finally, r. 9 will also apply, even though the facts in relation to the counts are not substantially identical or virtually contemporaneous as in the examples given above, if the offence alleged in the second count would not have occurred without the occurrence of the facts mentioned in the first count. In *R v Barrell and Wilson* (1979) 69Cr App R 250, B. and W. were charged with offences of affray and assault arising out of an incident at a discotheque. W was further charged in a count in the same indictment with attempting to pervert the course of justice in that, after committal proceedings for the other charges, he had tried to bribe a prosecution witness. The Court of Appeal held that, despite the gap in time between the facts alleged in the assault counts and the facts alleged in the perverting the course of justice count, the latter was properly joined in one indictment with the former. Had it not been for the alleged assaults, there would have been no reason for W. to attempt to pervert the course of justice.

5.5.2 Requirement for the counts to be of 'the same or a similar character'

The meaning of this phrase was discussed by the House of Lords in *Ludlow* v *Metropolitan Police Commissioner* 1971 AC 29. Lord Pearson (their lordships all concurring) said that for two or more offences to form a series or part of a series of the same or a similar character there must be a nexus between them. The nexus must arise from a similarity both in law and in the facts constituting the offences. In *Ludlow*, L. was charged in the first count with attempted theft and in the second count with robbery. The element of attempted or actual theft in both counts provided a sufficient similarity in law. The facts of the first count were that L. was seen emerging from a window in the private part of a public house in Acton, the jury being asked to draw the inference that he had been disturbed when attempting theft. The facts of the second count were that 16 days later, at another public house in Acton, L. paid for a drink and then snatched the money back, punching the barman. The House of Lords held that there was a sufficient similarity between the facts of the two offences to justify the joinder of the counts in one indictment. This might seem a surprising decision, since the fact that both offences were committed in public houses appears purely coincidental, and otherwise the only similarity arises from the closeness in time and geographical location of the offences. The lesson to be drawn from *Ludlow* is that only a slight similarity on the facts is necessary to satisfy r. 9. Another point confirmed by *Ludlow* is that two offences are sufficient to constitute a series within r. 9.

5.5.3 Discretion to order separate trials

If the judge is of the opinion that the accused may be 'prejudiced or embarrassed in his defence' through a single trial of all the counts against him in an indictment, or if for any other reason separate trials of at least some of the counts is desirable, he may order a separate trial of any count or counts: s. 5(3). This sub-section is meant to deal with cases where technically the prosecution have been correct in putting more than one count in an indictment (r. 9 is satisfied), but if the accused were to be tried by a single jury on all counts there would be a risk of some matters not being fairly considered by the jurors. The application of s. 5(3) was explained by the House of Lords in *Ludlow*. The judge is under a duty to direct separate trials only if there is a special feature in the case which would make a joint trial of several counts prejudicial or embarrassing. Examples are cases where the evidence relevant to one count would be difficult to disentangle from the evidence relevant to the other counts, and cases where one of the counts is of a scandalous nature so that if the jury were satisfied that the accused had committed that offence they would be so prejudiced against him that they would convict on the other counts regardless of any lack of proof.

The argument for the appellant in *Ludlow* was that the offence of attempted theft was not sufficiently similar to the offence of robbery for the jury to be entitled to consider the evidence on one count when deciding whether the accused committed the offence alleged in the other count (see works on evidence and *DPP* v *Boardman* [1975] AC 421 on the need for a striking similarity between offences before evidence that the accused committed one offence can be admissible to prove that he committed the other). Therefore, it was argued, L. was inevitably prejudiced and embarrassed in his defence on the attempted theft charge through the jury hearing irrelevant accusations about the robbery. The same applied in reverse on the robbery charge. The House of Lords accepted the premise that *Ludlow* was not a 'similar fact evidence' case but rejected the argument founded on that premise. In a simple case, such as *Ludlow*, the jury were quite capable, given a suitable direction from the judge, of ignoring the evidence of the robbery when considering the attempted theft and vice versa. In more complicated cases, however, the difficulty of disentangling the evidence relevant on the various counts might necessitate an order for separate trials. In particular, where a single indictment contains more than one count alleging offences of a sexual nature against different victims (e.g. indecent assaults on different children) the counts should be tried separately, unless the similarity between the offences is sufficient to bring them within the similar fact evidence rule: see *DPP* v *Boardman* and *R* v *Scarrott* [1977] 3WLR 629.

5.5.4 Alternative counts

Sometimes the evidence available to the prosecution shows that the accused has committed an indictable offence but it is not obvious which offence. For example, if the evidence is that the accused was found in possession of stolen goods an hour after they had been stolen, and he says that he 'was only looking after them for a friend', the jury might believe (a) that the friend is a figment of the imagination and the accused stole the goods, or (b) that the accused had bought the goods from the thief knowing them to be stolen, or (c) that the accused knew they were stolen but really was just looking after them for a friend, or (d) that the accused was a gullible innocent who did not know them to be stolen. Here the indictment should contain a count for theft, a count for handling with particulars alleging receiving and a count for handling with particulars alleging assisting in the retention of stolen property. Although the indictment will not expressly say that the three counts are in the alternative, counsel and judge will explain to the jury that they may only convict on one count. If the jury are satisfied as in (a) above they will convict of theft; if satisfied as in (b) they will convict of receiving; if satisfied as in (c) they will convict of assisting in the retention of stolen property, and if they think there is a reasonable possibility that (d) may be true they will acquit.

> A topic linked with that of alternative counts is whether the prosecution are entitled to include in an indictment a count alleging conspiracy in that A. and B. conspired to commit certain offences, and a count for jointly committing one of the offences they allegedly conspired to commit. A Practice Direction issued by the Lord Chief Justice (1977 1WLR 537) states that the judge should require the prosecution to justify such a joinder of counts. If they cannot do so they must elect to proceed either on conspiracy or on the substantive count. Joinder can only be justified if either the evidence may turn out too weak to support convictions on the substantive charges but ample for the conspiracy charge, or a number of counts for relatively minor substantive offences would not truly reflect the gravity of the conduct of the accused: *R* v *Jones and others* (1974) 59Cr App R 120.

5.6 JOINDER OF DEFENDANTS IN AN INDICTMENT

A count in an indictment may charge two or more defendants with committing a single offence. Further, two or more counts in an indictment may charge different defendants with separate offences even though there is no one count against them all collectively. In order to distinguish conveniently between the singular and the plural, reference will be made in this section to the defendant or defendants, not to the accused.

5.6.1 Joint counts

All parties to a single offence may be joined together in a single count. This applies not only to principal offenders but also by the Accessories and Abettors Act 1861, s. 8, to aiders, abettors, counsellors and procurers. Thus, if A. provides information upon which B. and C. enter premises as trespassers and steal property, whilst D. keeps watch outside, then all four can be charged in a single count with burglary.

Even though the particulars in the count need not state the separate roles which were played by each defendant, there will be no injustice because the nature of the prosecution case against each of them will be apparent from the committal proceedings, and the severity of the sentence will depend upon the view the judge takes of the evidence presented at the trial on indictment.

Although it will be convenient to draft joint counts in most cases, there is nothing to prevent the prosecution from having separate counts where this is appropriate in the circumstances, for instance where, for the offence to be committed, the principal offender must be under a legal disability, such as being an undischarged bankrupt or under a driving disqualification, but where the aider and abettor need not share that disability. A separate count for aiding and abetting avoids giving the misleading impression that the aiders and abettors are under the disability.

The jury are entitled to convict one or more but acquit other defendants named in a joint count. Furthermore, although the prosecution will not include defendants in a joint count unless their evidence suggests that there was a joint enterprise or cooperation between them, it has been held by the House of Lords in *DPP* v *Merriman* [1973] AC 584 that any or all of them may be convicted on the basis that they committed the offence independently of the others charged in the count.

The judge always has a discretion to order separate trials of defendants who are accused of committing an offence jointly, but there are strong reasons for a single trial which usually outweigh any opposing arguments. In favour of a single trial are the saving of time and convenience to witnesses of only having the evidence given once; the desirability of the jury having a full picture of what occurred which is more likely to be given through a single trial, and the risk of differing verdicts being returned by different juries on virtually identical evidence should there be separate trials. These considerations led the Court of Appeal to state in *R* v *Moghal* (1977) 65Cr App R 56 that separate trials of those joined in a single count should only be ordered in very exceptional cases. However, the decision is essentially one for the judge. Although, in *R* v *Moghal*, the Court of Appeal disagreed with the judge's decision to order separate trials, they did not quash the conviction. The judge was exercising a discretion given to him, not to the Court of Appeal, and it could not be said that his decision had led to a miscarriage of justice. If a decision, whether for or against separate trials, is shown to have led to a miscarriage of justice an appeal would be upheld. However, the fact that a joint trial will lead to the jury hearing evidence against A., which is inadmissible against B. but highly prejudicial to him, does not oblige the judge to accede to an application by B. for separate trials (*R* v *Lake* (1977) 64Cr App R 172, the judge's refusal of a separate trial for L. was upheld even though L.'s co-defendants had made confessions in L.'s absence which implicated not only themselves but L. also). Similarly, the fact that A. and B. are going to put forward defences in which they put the entire blame for the offence on each other does not necessitate separate trials: *R* v *Grondkowski and Malinowski* [1946] KB 369. Of course, in cases resembling *R* v *Lake* and *R* v *Grondkowski and Malinowski*, a judge more sympathetic to the problems of the defence would be entitled to order separate trials, but, if no such order is made, an appeal on the basis that there was a single trial is unlikely to succeed. The principles concerning separate trials of counts or defendants outlined in this paragraph and in Para. 5.5.3 are subject to modification where a single trial would be very long or complicated (see Para. 5.6.3).

5.6.2 Separate counts

An indictment may include separate counts each naming a different defendant, no defendant being joined with any other defendant in a single count. The circumstances in which this may be done are not closely defined. It is a matter for the practice of the court, but there must be some linking factor between the offences to justify joining their alleged perpetrators in one indictment. The linking factor may be that the defendants were apparently acting in concert although committing separate offences, or that the offences all occurred in one incident (e.g. various assaults during a gang fight), or that they occurred successively (e.g. two witnesses at the same trial committing perjury one after the other). An example of correct joinder is *R* v *Assim* [1966] 2QB 249. Two defendants were charged in a single indictment, one with unlawfully wounding X. and the other with assaulting Y. occasioning him actual bodily harm. Since their respective acts of violence had separate victims they could not be charged in a single count. The joinder of the separate counts in one indictment·was, however, justified as they were the doorman and receptionist at the same night-club, and X. and Y. were customers who had failed to pay their bills. The offences were linked by proximity in time and place, and by their apparent motive of discouraging bad payers.

The Theft Act 1968, s. 27(1) provides for handlers of stolen property to be charged in one indictment. All persons who at any time handle any portion of the goods stolen in one theft may be jointly indicted and jointly tried. So, if A., in the course of a burglary, steals a watch and a necklace which he sells to B. and C. respectively, and C. sells on the necklace to D. — all four can be indicted and tried together. The separate counts of handling against B., C and D are properly put in one indictment because of s. 27(1), and the burglary count against A. is sufficiently linked with the handling counts to fall within the principle in *R* v *Assim*.

Where defendants are joined in one indictment but not charged in a joint count, the judge again has a discretion to order separate trials, even though the single indictment was justified. The arguments for and against splitting the indictment are similar to those rehearsed above in the context of defendants charged in a joint count, but the argument for a single trial is less strong where there is no joint count, as the evidence in the case of one defendant will not be so closely inter-twined with the evidence in the cases of the other defendants.

5.6.3 The undesirability of numerous defendants

The Court of Appeal does not, in general, encourage separate trials of counts or defendants where joinder in one indictment is *prima facie* justified either under r. 9 or the practice of the court (see above). A different attitude has, however, emerged recently in cases where failure to order separate trials will lead to an inordinately long single trial. In *R* v *Thorne* (1978) 66Cr App R 6, no fewer than fourteen defendants were tried together on a single indictment containing three counts for robbery, and numerous related offences such as conspiracy to rob, handling the proceeds of the robberies and attempting to pervert the course of justice in respect of the prosecution for the robberies. The trial, involving 27 counsel and ten firms of solicitors, lasted 111 working days and included a summing-up from the judge which went on for twelve days. The Court of Appeal was of the opinion that such a huge trial placed an unfair burden on judge and jury. Although they did not allow any of the appeals simply on the ground that there had been a long trial, they stated that two or three shorter trials would have been far preferable. They went on to say that 'overloading of indictments must stop', and that 'no more accused should be indicted together than is necessary for the proper presentation of the prosecution case against the principal accused. Necessity not convenience should be the guiding factor.' Whether the advice in *R* v *Thorne* will affect the practice of the courts only in cases where there is a risk of a very long trial, or will herald in all cases a greater willingness to order separate trials, remains to be seen.

5.7   APPLICATIONS CONCERNING THE INDICTMENT

The following applications may be necessary:

5.7.1   Application to sever the indictment

If the defence considers that two or more counts in the indictment against the accused should be tried separately, or that he should not be tried with the other defendants named in the indictment, application must be made to the judge to sever the indictment. The application is usually made immediately after the pleas to the indictment have been taken. At major locations of the Crown Court, such as the Central Criminal Court, such applications may be made to the trial judge in a pre-trial hearing.

5.7.2 Applications to amend the indictment

If the judge considers that the indictment is defective he must order it to be amended, unless such amendment would cause injustice: Indictments Act 1915, s. 5(1). The amendment may be ordered before or at any stage during the trial, the defence, if necessary, being given an adjournment to consider the way their position has been affected: s. 5(4). Subject always to not causing injustice, any defect in an indictment can be remedied by amendment, whether the defect be trivial (e.g. the mis-spelling of a name) or fundamental (e.g. omitting from the particulars an essential element of the offence charged in the count). Amendment is also appropriate where the evidence at the trial differs from the allegations in the particulars, although if such amendments are made at a late stage they may well cause injustice. For example, in *R* v *Gregory* [1972] 1WLR 991, the Court of Appeal quashed G.'s conviction on a count for handling a starter-motor because, after all the evidence had been given, the judge deleted from the particulars an allegation that the starter-motor belonged to 'W.A.W.' Much of the evidence had turned on whether a starter-motor, admittedly found in G.'s possession, was the one that had earlier been stolen from W.A.W. The defence contended that it was not, and that G. had legitimately bought the motor from a casual acquaintance whose name he did not know. By deleting the allegation as to ownership the judge altered the whole basis of the prosecution case, and, in effect, invited the jury to convict on the basis that even if G.'s story were correct, the circumstances of the purchase (at a quarter of the proper price) showed that the motor had been stolen from someone and that G. knew it to be stolen. Had the amendment been made before the indictment was put to the accused, with the defence being offered an adjournment, it is unlikely that any appeal could have succeeded.

Amendment may also take the form of inserting new counts in the indictment either in substitution for or in addition to those originally drafted. This may be done even after the accused has pleaded to the indictment: *R* v *Johal and Ram* [1972] 3WLR 210. Indeed, in *R* v *Collison* (1980) 72Cr App R 249, the Court of Appeal approved the addition of a count when, after the jury had retired to consider their verdict, they returned to court for further directions from the judge. In *R* v *Johal* and *R* v *Collison* the fresh counts were needed to solve purely technical problems that had arisen on the indictments as originally drafted but did not alter the nature of the prosecution case. If a count containing a genuinely fresh charge were to be added after the start of the evidence, it would almost certainly cause injustice.

Where an amendment appears necessary counsel for the prosecution should apply for it. If he fails to do so, the judge may raise the matter on his own initiative, asking for the views of prosecution and defence.

When a defect in a count goes unamended, a conviction on the count will not necessarily be quashed on appeal. Some allegations in a count are regarded as 'mere surplusage', so an error in what is alleged is only a ground of appeal if the accused was genuinely misled or otherwise prejudiced by the error. Even the alleged date of the offence falls into the category of 'mere surplusage'. An unamended defect which means that the count does not comply with the Indictment Rules is always a ground of appeal, but the

Court of Appeal can still apply the proviso contained in the Criminal Appeal Act 1968, s. 2 (i.e. dismiss the appeal if there has been no actual miscarriage of justice). In *R* v *Nelson* (1977) 65Cr App R 119, the count broke r. 6 by failing to give the statute and section creating a statutory offence, but the Court of Appeal did not allow the appeal on that ground.

5.7.3   Motion to quash the indictment

The defence may apply to the judge to quash the indictment. If the application (or motion) succeeds no further proceedings may take place on the indictment. It follows that the appropriate time for moving to quash is before the indictment is put, as success at that stage will mean that the accused does not even have to plead. The judge may, however, entertain an application at a later stage. A motion to quash may also be brought in respect of a single count in an indictment.

Motions to quash are not of great value to the defence for three reasons. First, even after a successful motion, the prosecution are entitled to commence fresh proceedings in respect of the same matters, hoping to avoid the mistake that led to the first indictment or count being quashed. Second, a suitable amendment to the indictment can often prevent the motion to quash from succeeding. Third, the grounds for a successful motion are very limited. Those grounds are that:

(a)   the bill of indictment was preferred without authority, or

(b)   the wording of the indictment or count reveals a fundamental defect, or

(c)   the count is for an offence in respect of which the examining justices did not commit for trial, and no case to answer for that offence is revealed by the depositions and s. 102 statements from the committal proceedings.

As to (a) above, there is authority to prefer a bill of indictment if either the accused has been committed for trial, or a High Court judge has directed the preferment of a voluntary bill, or the Court of Appeal has ordered a re-trial, or there has been an order under the Perjury Act 1911, s. 9 (see Administration of Justice (Miscellaneous Provisions) Act 1933, s. 2, and Para. 3.10 above). It is almost inconceivable that the prosecution would, in the absence of such authority, even try to prefer a bill. As to (b) it must be stressed that the judge is only entitled to look at the wording of the indictment to see if there is something fundamentally wrong (e.g. a count fails to allege an essential element of the offence charged or is bad for duplicity). Except as described in (c), he may not be asked to consider any inadequacies in the prosecution evidence foreshadowed in the committal documents. In other words, a motion to quash is not a way of challenging the examining justices' decision to commit for trial on a certain charge. If the indictment or count is defectively worded the prosecution may prevent a successful motion to quash simply by applying to amend.

Perhaps the most valuable use of motions to quash is that mentioned in (c) above. If the indictment contains a count alleging an offence for which the examining justices did not commit the accused for trial, the defence may invite the judge to read the committal documents, and, if they do not disclose a case to answer, to quash the count. It is the one situation where, on a motion to quash, the judge considers the evidence: *R* v *Jones and others* (1974) 59Cr App R 120. It is right that he should do so because either the examining justices held that there was not a case to answer for the offence charged in the count, or, at the very least, they were not invited to give a decision on the point.

6 Pleas

6.1 THE ARRAIGNMENT

A trial on indictment begins with the arraignment, which consists of putting the counts in the indictment to the accused so that he can plead guilty or not guilty. The clerk reads the indictment, pausing after each count to ask those charged in it whether they plead guilty or not guilty. A plea must be taken on each count, unless it is in the alternative to another count to which the accused has already pleaded guilty. The consequences of the accused giving an ambiguous answer when asked to plead, or saying absolutely nothing, or being incapable of pleading rationally are discussed in Paras. 6.3 and 6.7.

The trial should begin (i.e. the arraignment take place) not less than two and not more than eight weeks from the date of the committal for trial: Courts Act 1971, s. 7(4) and r. 19 of the Crown Court Rules 1971, SI 1971 No 1292. Like the parallel rule on preferring a bill of indictment within 28 days of committal (see Para. 5.1), the rule is an indication of what ought to happen rather than of what actually does happen. A judge of the Crown Court may, and normally would, give permission for a trial to start after the eight week period. Even if no permission is expressly given, a trial commencing outside that period would not be a nullity as s.7(4) is directory not mandatory: *R v Urbanowski* [1976] 1WLR 455. In fact, in the south-east of England, the average wait between committal and trial is around 15 weeks for those in custody, and 29 weeks for those on bail. Outside the south-east, the figures are 8 weeks and 12 weeks respectively.

The procedure on arraignment is that the accused is brought into the dock. If it is anticipated that he will plead not guilty to all counts in the indictment the men and women from whom the jury will be selected (the jury in waiting) may be permitted to sit at the back of court to hear him plead. If there is any chance of his pleading guilty to one count and not guilty to another, they should be kept out of court since, were they to know that he had admitted one charge, it might prejudice their trying him fairly on the others. They should also be kept out of court if some but not all the accused joined in the indictment are expected to plead guilty.

Although there is no rigid formula for what ought to be said, the clerk putting the indictment which appears on page 38 might say — 'David Wilson, John Burton and Paul Green, you are charged in an indictment containing three counts. The first count charges you David Wilson and you John Burton with assault occasioning actual bodily harm. The particulars of that offence are that, on the 28th day of March 1981 you assaulted Barry Johnson thereby occasioning him actual bodily harm. David Wilson, do you plead guilty or not guilty? . . . John Burton, do you plead guilty or not guilty? . . . The second count charges you, Paul Green, with wounding contrary to Section 20 of the Offences against the Person Act 1861. The particulars of the offence are that . . . ' and so on through the indictment.

Where an indictment contains counts which are in the alternative (e.g. theft and handling stolen goods, the prosecution case being such that the accused could not be found guilty on both counts), and he wishes to plead guilty to one of the counts, it is advisable to tell the court of his intentions. The count to which he is pleading guilty can then be put to him first (irrespective of whether it is first on the indictment), and the other count need not be put.

6.2 PLEA OF 'NOT GUILTY'

A plea of not guilty puts the whole of the prosecution case in issue. Thus, in order to secure a conviction, the prosecution must prove each element of the offence beyond reasonable doubt, unless in exceptional instances, statute or common law has transferred the onus of proof to the defence. Of course, in most trials only a few issues will effectively be in dispute, but should the prosecution fail to introduce sufficient evidence as to any element of the offence charged the accused is entitled to be acquitted, even if he does not in fact dispute the prosecution allegation on that particular point. For example, an accused pleading not guilty on a charge of assault may give instructions to his solicitors that he hit the victim but in reasonable self-defence. Should the victim fail to identify the accused as his assailant, and should the prosecution be unable to call any other evidence on the issue of identity, the judge would have to direct the jury to acquit the accused, even though he did not, in reality, dispute that he struck the victim. By pleading not guilty, the accused put in issue the entire prosecution case, and it was an essential element of their case to prove that the accused committed the *actus reus* of the offence.

The next step, following a plea of not guilty, is to empanel a jury to try the case (see Chapter 7). Occasionally, however, the services of a jury are not required as the prosecution offers no evidence. This might be the case if, for example, fresh evidence has been discovered between the committal and the arraignment indicating that the accused is not guilty. Where the prosecution propose to offer no evidence the judge may order that a verdict of not guilty be recorded, the verdict being equivalent to an acquittal by a jury: Criminal Justice Act 1967, s. 17.

The plea of not guilty should be made by the accused personally, not by counsel on his behalf. However, failure to take a plea of not guilty from the accused in the normal way will not necessarily lead to the conviction being quashed on appeal. In *R* v *Williams* [1977] 2WLR 400 it was thought, through an administrative muddle, that W. had pleaded not guilty. In fact, he had never been arraigned, although he undoubtedly intended to deny the charge. The trial proceeded exactly as if W. had been arraigned and pleaded not guilty. W., who was the only person in court who knew that he had not pleaded, failed to raise any objection. The jury convicted, and the Court of Appeal dismissed the appeal, holding that the irregularity in the proceedings had not been sufficiently material to justify quashing the conviction.

6.3 PLEA OF 'GUILTY'

Major points to notice are as follows:

(a) The plea must be entered by the accused personally. Counsel may not plead guilty on his behalf. If he purports to do so, the plea is a nullity, and will result in the Court of Appeal quashing the conviction entered upon the plea and ordering a re-trial: *R* v *Ellis* (1973) 57C App R 571. In *R* v *Williams* the Court of Appeal stated that 'no qualification of or deviation from the rule that a plea of guilty must come from him who acknowledges guilt is permissible. A departure from the rule in a criminal trial would necessarily render the whole procedure void and ineffectual.'

(b)   Following a plea of guilty there is no need to empanel a jury as the accused has convicted himself out of his own mouth. The court may proceed straight to sentencing. The procedure before sentence is passed is described in Chapter 14. In brief, prosecuting counsel summarises the circumstances of the offence. A police officer then gives evidence about the previous convictions, background, education, employment, financial circumstances etc. of the accused. Any reports on him are read. Counsel for the defence then presents his plea in mitigation, and the judge passes sentence. If the accused pleads guilty on one count and not guilty on other counts, the judge will postpone sentencing him for the offence to which he has pleaded guilty until after the trial of the pleas of 'not guilty'. Should the jury convict him, the judge can sentence him at one time for all the offences.

(c)   If two accused are charged in one indictment, and one pleads guilty and the other not guilty, the usual practice is for the judge to adjourn the case of the one who has pleaded guilty. He is remanded, either in custody or on bail, to come up for sentence at the conclusion of the trial of the accused pleading not guilty. The advantage of this course of action is that, during the trial before the jury, the judge learns from the evidence full details of the case against the accused who has denied the charge, and may also learn much that he would not otherwise have known about the case against the accused who has pleaded guilty. Should the former be convicted by the jury, the judge can sentence both accused at the same time, knowing from the evidence which, if either, of the two played the major role. Whether or not to adjourn is, however, a matter for the discretion of the judge. If he is satisfied that he has sufficient information about the accused who has pleaded guilty, he may sentence him forthwith without waiting for the other to be tried.

(d)   If the prosecution proposes to call the accused who has pleaded guilty to give evidence against his co-accused, there is a strong argument for sentencing the former before he gives his evidence. Not to do so leaves room for suspicion that, in testifying, he may have said what he thought the judge wanted him to say in order to receive a lighter sentence. Accordingly, it was until recently the invariable practice in this type of case to sentence the accused forthwith. Counsel, in mitigation, indicated the sort of evidence his client was going to give, and the judge would no doubt make an appropriate reduction in sentence. If the evidence subsequently given by the accused was not what had been anticipated the judge had no power to increase the sentence originally passed: *R* v *Stone* [1970] 1 WLR 1112. The former practice is still followed in many cases, and, where that is done, *R* v *Stone* remains good authority. However, in two unreported cases (*R* v *Woods* 25 October 1977 and *R* v *Potter* 15 September 1977) the Court of Appeal stated that, even where the accused is going to testify for the prosecution, the judge has a discretion either to sentence him forthwith or to postpone sentence until after the trial of the other accused.

(e)   Instead of merely saying 'Guilty', an accused sometimes responds to the indictment in an ambiguous way. For example, he may answer to a count for handling by saying — 'Guilty to receiving, but I wasn't sure if the goods were stolen'. The plea is ambiguous. He may mean — 'I believed them to be stolen, although nobody told me in so many words that such was the case', or he may mean — 'I was a bit suspicious about the goods, but didn't really think they were stolen'. In the former case, he should plead guilty, but not in the latter. The judge should try to elucidate the plea by explaining to the accused the elements of the offence charged. Then the indictment can be put to him again. If the plea remains ambiguous a not guilty plea must be entered on his behalf: Criminal Law Act 1967, s. 6(1). If the judge proceeds to sentence upon a plea which remains ambiguous, the Court of Appeal will set aside the conviction and sentence and order that the accused be sent back to the Crown Court to plead again to the indictment. Similar principles apply whenever the accused says something when the indictment is put but will not give a direct answer to it (e.g. in a case where the motive for the offence alleged appears to be political he might say — 'I do not recognise the authority of the court'). A plea of not guilty should be entered on his behalf, and the case proceeds as if he had actually pleaded not guilty.

(f) Not only must the plea of guilty come from the lips of the accused, but his mind must go with his plea. In other words, where a plea is extracted from the accused by pressure and the circumstances are such that he cannot genuinely choose between pleading guilty and pleading not guilty, then that plea is a nullity. If he appeals, the Court of Appeal will quash the conviction and order a re-trial. The pressure necessary for a plea of guilty to be rendered a nullity may come either from the judge or from counsel. An example of the former is provided by *R* v *Barnes* (1970) 55Cr App R 100. Half way through the prosecution case, in the absence of the jury but in the presence of B., the judge said in effect that B. was plainly guilty and was wasting the court's time. Even so, B. refused to change his plea to guilty, but, had he done so, the plea would have been a nullity. Allowing the appeal on other grounds, the Court of Appeal stated that the judge's conduct was 'wholly improper'.

A more subtle way in which the judge might pressurise the accused is illustrated by *R* v *Turner* [1970] 2QB 321. T. pleaded not guilty to a charge of theft. After some of the prosecution witnesses had given their evidence, there was a lengthy adjournment during which T. discussed the conduct of the case with his counsel and solicitor. At one stage counsel went to see the judge in his private room. On his return, counsel warned T. that if he persisted in a not guilty plea and was found guilty there was a 'very real possibility' that he would receive a sentence of imprisonment, but that if he pleaded guilty he would be dealt with by a fine or other non-custodial sentence. Counsel was, in fact, expressing his personal opinion of the case, but inevitably it appeared to T. that he was passing on what the judge had said. T. changed his plea to guilty. The Court of Appeal (Lord Parker CJ presiding) quashed his conviction and ordered a re-trial. Once T. felt that the advice his counsel gave him as to sentence was 'an intimation emanating from the judge, it is really idle in the opinion of this court to think that he really had a free choice in the matter' of his plea. Lord Parker went on to say that the judge should 'never indicate the sentence which he is minded to impose', unless he can say that 'whatever happens, whether the accused pleads guilty or not guilty, the sentence will or will not take a particular form, e.g. a probation order or a fine or a custodial sentence' (see *R* v *Turner* supra at p.327). The value of such an indication is that out of fear, let us say, of a custodial sentence, an accused may persist in a not guilty plea although he knows he is guilty and the evidence against him is overwhelming. If he can be told, on the judge's authority, that he will not go to prison, he may be willing to admit his guilt. No pressure is brought upon him to plead as the promise of a non-custodial sentence applies whether he pleads guilty or is found guilty by a jury. What the judge may not do, however, as a result of *R* v *Turner*, is to indicate expressly that a plea of guilty will be followed by a more lenient form of sentence than that which would follow a verdict of guilty by a jury. Nor may he impliedly give an indication to the same effect by saying what form the sentence will or will not take if there is a guilty plea, and leaving the accused to infer the consequences of a 'Not Guilty' plea.

The difficulties in *R* v *Turner* arose from counsel seeing the judge privately. The Court of Appeal did not criticise this practice, but gave some guidance on when this is appropriate (see Para. 8.1.3). In particular, if a discussion on sentence takes place between counsel and judge in private the accused should be informed of what took place. In *R* v *Cain* [1976] Crim LR 464, the Court of Appeal qualified this aspect of *R* v *Turner* by holding that a judge may, if he wishes, tell counsel privately and without knowledge of the accused the approximate level of sentence he has in mind. Counsel could then advise the accused without telling him that he had seen the judge. *R* v *Cain* is, however, doubtful authority. A Practice Direction (1976 Crim LR 561) has stated that where *R* v *Cain* and *R* v *Turner* are in conflict then the latter shall prevail. Recent cases have stressed that private discussions between counsel and judge should be kept to an absolute minimum (see Para. 8.1.3).

It should be noted that the principles in *R* v *Turner* apply equally to private discussions between counsel and judge, and to indications of sentence given in open court in the hearing of the accused: *R* v *Atkinson* [1978] 1WLR 425, where the offending indication was given at a pre-trial review of the case.

The second source of pressure capable of rendering a plea of guilty a nullity is that which may be exerted by the accused's own counsel. In the decided cases the Court of Appeal have held that the conduct complained of was not sufficient to deprive the accused of his free choice as to plea. However, advice by defence counsel along the lines that 'the prosecution case is so strong that your only possible course of action is to plead guilty whether you committed the offence charged or not' would cause any plea of guilty to be a nullity. The principles governing the advice that counsel should give the accused about his plea are discussed in *R* v *Turner* at p.326. It is counsel's duty to give the best advice he can, if need be in 'strong terms'. That advice may include his view on the strength of the prosecution case and the difficulties thrown up by the nature of the defence (e.g. he might warn the accused that a defence involving attacks on the characters of the prosecution witnesses would lead to his being cross-examined about his previous convictions if he chose to give evidence). The accused should also be told, if he does not know already, that a conviction upon a plea of guilty is likely to attract a more lenient sentence than a conviction following a not guilty plea. Counsel can also indicate his personal view of the sentence the judge is likely to pass. The mischief in *R* v *Turner* arose not from the nature of counsel's advice on sentence, but from the implication that the 'advice' was a repetition of what the judge had said. Finally, it must be emphasised to the accused that the choice of plea is one for him, not counsel, to make, and that he should only plead guilty if he is indeed guilty. The mere fact that the accused pleads guilty reluctantly after receiving strong advice from counsel does not make the plea a nullity. It is only a nullity if, when he makes it, the accused has lost the power to make a voluntary and deliberate choice: *R* v *Peace* [1976] Crim LR 119.

6.4 PLEA OF 'GUILTY' TO A LESSER OFFENCE

Half way between a plea of guilty and a plea of not guilty is a plea of guilty to a lesser offence. Where an accused pleads not guilty to a count the jury may sometimes return a verdict on that count of 'not guilty as charged but guilty of some other (lesser) offence': Criminal Law Act 1967, ss. 6(2) and 6(3) and see Chapter 9. Familiar examples are that on a count for murder the jury can convict of manslaughter, on counts for burglary contrary to the Theft Act 1968, s 9(1)(b) they can convict of theft, and on a count for wounding with intent contrary to the Offences Against the Person Act 1861, s. 18 they can convict of unlawful wounding contrary to s. 20. When a count is put to the accused on which the jury could find him guilty of a lesser offence, he may offer a plea of not guilty as charged but guilty of the lesser offence: Criminal Law Act 1967, s. 6(1)(b). If the plea is accepted he stands acquitted of the offence charged, and the court proceeds to sentence him for the lesser offence: Criminal Law Act 1967, s. 6(5).

The prosecution are not, of course, obliged to accept a proffered plea of guilty to a lesser offence. If they consider that their evidence will establish the full offence charged they are entitled to have the matter decided by a jury. Even if the prosecution are willing to accept the plea, the judge has a discretion to reject it: *R v Soanes* [1948] 1AER 289. A recent example of a judge's refusal to accept a plea of guilty to a lesser offence, manslaughter, in return for the withdrawal of the more serious charge of murder is the case of Peter Sutcliffe who was charged with the Yorkshire Ripper murders. The jury convicted on all the counts for murder, whereas had the judge accepted the plea, Sutcliffe would have stood acquitted of the murder charges. Strictly speaking, acceptance of the plea is only justified if there is something in the statements from the committal proceedings to suggest that the accused may not be guilty of the full offence, but, in view of the saving in time and money made by not having to hold a jury trial, it may be fairly easy to persuade the judge that the plea is a proper one. If either the prosecution or the judge refuse to accept the plea, a plea of not guilty to the count is entered on behalf of the accused, and his plea of guilty to the lesser offence is impliedly withdrawn. A jury is then empanelled in the normal way.

An odd consequence of rejecting a plea of guilty to a lesser offence is illustrated by *R v Hazeltine* [1967] 2QB 857. H. pleaded not guilty to wounding with intent to cause grievous bodily harm but guilty of unlawful wounding. The plea was not accepted. The trial proceeded, and the jury simply acquitted H. They did not, as they were entitled to, find him not guilty as charged but guilty of unlawful wounding. The judge nevertheless proceeded to sentence H. for that offence, relying on the fact that H. had originally pleaded guilty to it. The Court of Appeal quashed the sentence. When the court entered on H.'s behalf a plea of not guilty to wounding with intent, his plea to unlawful wounding was by implication withdrawn and could not subsequently be re-instated by the judge. Nor could the prosecution prefer a fresh charge for unlawful wounding as the jury's acquittal for wounding with intent amounted impliedly to an acquittal for unlawful wounding also, and any proceedings would have been countered by the plea of autrefois acquit (see Para. 6.8).

What may appear, from the prosecution viewpoint, to be the unfortunate consequence of *R v Hazeltine* can be avoided quite easily. If the accused tenders a plea of guilty to a lesser offence which is not acceptable to either the prosecution or the judge, the prosecution should apply to amend the indictment by adding a count specifically for the lesser offence. That count is put to the accused, who pleads guilty to it. The trial proceeds on the plea of not guilty to the original count entered on his behalf. If the jury convict, the accused is sentenced for that offence, and no separate sentence is passed for the lesser offence. Technically, his plea of guilty to the lesser offence does not rank as a second conviction as he has not been sentenced upon that plea. If the jury acquit, he can be sentenced upon his plea of guilty. That plea was upon a count quite separate from the count on which the jury have acquitted. Entering a plea of not guilty on the original count could not affect the validity of a plea which had been properly taken on the additional count. A similar procedure should be followed where there are two counts in the alternative, but one is more serious than the other (e.g. robbery and handling a small part of the proceeds of the robbery). If the accused is willing to plead guilty to the less serious count, a plea should be taken from him, and the trial may then proceed on the other count. Should the jury convict, the accused is sentenced only on the serious count; if they acquit, his plea of guilty to the less serious count stands and he can be sentenced accordingly: *R* v *Cole* [1965] 2QB 388.

6.5 CHANGE OF PLEA

Mention has already been made in the discussion of *R* v *Barnes* and *R* v *Turner* of the possibility of the accused changing his plea from not guilty to guilty. This may be done at any stage of the trial. Defence counsel asks for the indictment to be put again to his client, and, upon that being done, the accused pleads guilty. Like any other plea of guilty, it must come from the accused personally, not from counsel on his behalf. In addition, the jury, empanelled as a result of the original not guilty plea, must return a formal verdict of guilty. If they fail to do so, the change of plea is ineffective, and the trial rendered a nullity: *R* v *Heyes* [1951] 1KB 29. The judge in sentencing may give the accused some credit for having changed his plea, although not as much as if he had admitted his guilt from the outset.

A change of plea from guilty to not guilty is also possible, but is subject to the judge giving his consent. Applications to withdraw a guilty plea may be made at any stage before sentence is passed: *S (an infant)* v *Recorder of Manchester* [1971] AC 481. Such applications are often prompted by the accused using the period of an adjournment between his plea and the date fixed for him to be sentenced to obtain legal advice for the first time. In the light of that advice he may reconsider the wisdom of his plea. Whatever the reason for the application, acceding to or rejecting it is a matter entirely within the judge's discretion. In *R* v *McNally* [1954] 1 WLR 933 the Court of Criminal Appeal approved the judge's decision to reject M.'s application, M. having pleaded guilty to a straightforward charge of burglary in circumstances which were such that he could not have misunderstood the nature of the allegation.

6.6 PLEA BARGAINING

R v *Turner* was partly concerned with what Lord Parker described as the 'vexed question' of plea bargaining. The phrase is an imprecise one which may be used in at least four different senses. It can mean an agreement between the judge and the accused that if he pleads guilty to some or all of the offences charged against him the sentence will or will not take a certain form. As a consequence of *R* v *Turner* a guilty plea made in such circumstances is a nullity and the conviction liable to be quashed (see Para. 6.3). Second, plea bargaining can mean an undertaking by the prosecution that if the accused will admit to certain charges they will refrain from putting more serious charges into the indictment or will ask the judge to impose a relatively light sentence. This form of bargaining is not possible under the English system as the prosecution (or, more probably, a Crown Court officer) draw up the indictment quite independently of the defence, and, at the sentencing stage, the prosecution's function is merely to tell the judge the facts, not to suggest an appropriate sentence. Thirdly, plea bargaining may refer to the prosecution agreeing with the defence that if the accused pleads guilty to a lesser offence they will accept the plea (see Para. 6.4), and, lastly, it may refer to the prosecution offering no evidence on one or more counts in the indictment against the accused if he will plead guilty to the remainder.

Plea bargaining in the third and fourth senses described above is a frequent occurrence, approved by the courts. It is in the public interest that where the accused is prepared to admit to the more serious charges against him, court-time and money should not be wasted pursuing him to conviction on the less serious counts. Similarly, if there is something to indicate that the accused may not be guilty of the full offence charged in a count, it is convenient to accept a plea of guilty to a lesser offence. Such bargains are usually struck by prosecuting and defence counsel outside court before the commencement of the trial. The judge's agreement to a plea of guilty to a lesser offence is essential (see Para. 6.4). Where the prosecution propose to offer no evidence on one count in exchange for a plea on another count, they normally ask for the judge's consent to this being done. That consent is not automatically forthcoming (*R* v *Broad* (1979) 68Cr App R 28), and, in its absence, the prosecution would almost certainly feel obliged to call their evidence. Whether, technically, the judge could compel the calling of the evidence is open to doubt. Sometimes the judge is asked privately whether he would approve an arrangement agreed by the prosecution and defence, but it seems safer simply to ask for his consent in open court: *R* v *Coward* (1980) 70Cr App R 70.

When, following a 'bargain' with the defence, the prosecution offer no evidence on a count, it is usual for the count to be left on the court file, marked not to be proceeded with without leave of the court or leave of the Court of Appeal. Leave to proceed would only be given in the very unlikely event of the conviction on the count to which the accused pleaded guilty being quashed. Leaving the count on the file is more appropriate than the judge directing a verdict of acquittal to be entered, as the prosecution are not conceding that the accused is innocent of the offence alleged — they are merely choosing not to press that charge in view of the accused's pleas to other matters.

6.7 THE ACCUSED WHO WILL NOT OR CANNOT PLEAD

So far it has been assumed that when the accused is arraigned he says something rational in answer to the charges. What he says may fall short of a proper plea of guilty or not guilty, but, at least, his response shows that he has heard and understood the clerk's words to him. However, the accused may be unwilling to reply when the indictment is put, or he may be incapable of replying in a sensible way. The first possibility raises the question of 'mute of malice', the second the question of unfitness to plead.

6.7.1 'Mute of malice' and 'Mute by visitation of God'

The accused may remain silent by choice, or because he is incapable of speech.

In the former case he is deemed to be 'mute of malice'. A plea of 'Not guilty' is entered on his behalf, and he is then treated in all respects as though he had himself pleaded not guilty: Criminal Law Act 1967, s. 6(1)(c). The method of deciding whether he is or is not mute of malice is to empanel a jury to decide the issue of muteness, and the onus of proof is upon the prosecution to show beyond reasonable doubt that he is mute of malice. The prosecution may do this by medical evidence, or by a witness to the fact that he has recently heard the accused speak, or by whatever means are appropriate to the case.

Muteness by visitation of God most frequently arises where the accused is dumb, or deaf and thus cannot hear the arraignment, or some combination of these or similar afflictions. It may also occur where the accused suffers from defective intellect to the extent that he hears the indictment but has not enough intelligence to reply to it. Where the jury decide that the accused is mute by visitation of God, they are then asked further to specify the cause. If this is a communication problem, such as when the accused is deaf and dumb, then the court will be adjourned in order to obtain the services of an expert in sign language, or whatever assistance is required. If the problem is caused by the accused not speaking English, then the court will be adjourned for the procurement of a translator.

Defective intellect is dealt with in the next paragraph.

6.7.2 Unfitness to plead

An accused is unfit to plead or stand his trial if his intellect is defective, so that he cannot comprehend the course of the proceedings so as to make a proper defence to the indictment. Whether he can answer when arraigned is obviously one relevant factor. Other relevant factors are whether he is capable of challenging a juror to whom he might wish to object (see Chapter 7), whether he can instruct his legal representatives, and whether he would be able to follow the evidence. An accused is not unfit to plead merely because he is highly abnormal (*R* v *Berry* (1977) 66Cr App R 157), or because he is likely to act against his own best interests (*R* v *Robertson* [1968] 1WLR 1767), or even because he is suffering from amnesia so as not to be able to recall the alleged offence or the circumstances surrounding it: *R* v *Podola* [1960] 1QB 325. An accused who is unfit to plead is not acquitted. The court must order that he be admitted to a hospital specified by the Home Secretary, and, if his condition improves, he may be remitted to prison preparatory to his being tried: Criminal Procedure (Insanity) Act 1964, s. 5.

Where the accused may be unfit to plead, either the prosecution or the defence should, before the arraignment, bring the matter to the judge's attention. Although one would normally expect the defence to do this, the prosecution might feel it their duty to take the initiative if, for instance, the accused is unrepresented but is clearly in no fit state to understand the proceedings. A jury is empanelled to decide the issue, evidence is called, and the judge directs the jury about the meaning of 'unfitness to plead'. If the prosecution raises the issue they must prove beyond reasonable doubt that the accused is unfit: *R* v *Robertson*; if the defence raises it they must satisfy the jury as to the accused's unfitness on a balance of probabilities: *R* v *Podola*. On a finding of unfitness, a hospital order is made. On a finding that the accused is fit to plead, the indictment is put to him, and, if he pleads not guilty, another jury must be empanelled to decide the issue of guilt or innocence.

Deciding the issue of fitness to plead before the arraignment has one disadvantage in that if the accused is found unfit, he is compulsorily detained in hospital, even though, had the trial been held, he might have been acquitted and have walked out of court a free man. To lessen the risk of such an injustice occurring, the judge has a discretion to postpone consideration of fitness to plead until any time up to the opening of the defence case: Criminal Procedure (Insanity) Act 1964, s. 4. If he does so, a plea of not guilty is entered on behalf of the accused, a jury is empanelled, and the prosecution evidence is called in the normal way. At the end of the prosecution case, the defence may submit that there is no case to answer against the accused (see Chapter 8). If the submission succeeds, the jury acquits the accused on the judge's direction. If it fails, the issue of fitness has to be decided, either by the jury already trying the main case, or by a second jury sworn in for the purpose. The judge can postpone consideration of fitness to plead irrespective of whether the issue was raised by the prosecution or the defence, but he must be satisfied that postponement is 'expedient and in the interests of the accused': s. 4(2) of the 1964 Act. To determine that issue, the judge looks at the documents from the committal proceedings to assess the strength of the prosecution case, and at any medical reports on the accused. The weaker the prosecution case appears to be, and the less extreme the mental problems of the accused, the more likely it is that the judge will postpone the trial of fitness to plead until the latest possible time: *R* v *Burles* [1970] 2QB 191.

6.8   PLEAS OF 'AUTREFOIS ACQUIT' AND 'AUTREFOIS CONVICT'

The pleas of 'autrefois acquit' and 'autrefois convict' (i.e. the accused has, on a previous occasion, been acquitted or convicted of the offence alleged in a count of the indictment) give effect to the vital constitutional principle that no one shall be prosecuted twice to acquittal or conviction for the same offence. If one or other of the pleas is raised successfully it is a bar to all further proceedings on the count concerned. These pleas, together with the plea of pardon (see Paragraph 6.10), are known as special pleas in bar. Despite the importance of the pleas being available to prevent harassment of the individual by repeated prosecutions for one crime, it is rare in practice for the defence to be forced to have recourse to them. This is because court records are available to establish clearly whether a person has previously been prosecuted for an offence, and if so, the result of that prosecution. If it ended in his being acquitted or convicted the prosecution would not for a moment consider preferring fresh charges against him for the offence. Although infrequently pleaded, autrefois acquit and convict have led to a disproportionately large body of case law as the appellate courts have been called upon to define the precise limits of the pleas. The following paragraphs seek to describe the main applications of the pleas without delving over-deeply into the minutiae of the subject.

6.8.1   Procedure on a plea of 'autrefois acquit' or 'autrefois convict'

The plea is made in writing signed by defence counsel on behalf of the accused. The prosecution join issue with the defence through a written replication signed by an appropriate officer of the Crown Court. The common forms of words used are — 'John Smith says that the Queen ought not further to prosecute the indictment against him because he has been lawfully acquitted (or convicted) of the offence charged therein', and 'David Thomas joins issue on behalf of the Queen'. If the accused is unrepresented he may make the plea orally. The correct time to plead is before the arraignment but the court may entertain the plea at any stage of the trial. Once issue is joined, a jury must be empanelled to decide the matter, the burden of proof being on the defence to show on a balance of probabilities that the plea applies. Usually there is no dispute on the facts between the prosecution and defence, but complex questions of law are often raised. In such cases it is normal for the judge to give a strong direction to the jury, amounting almost to a ruling that the plea either does or does not apply (see *R* v *Coughlan and Young* (1976) 63Cr App R 33, where the Court of Appeal also approved the practice adopted by counsel of reading to the jury short statements of the material facts about the previous trial and the present case on which they would rely in making their respective submissions — the practice would obviously not be appropriate if the plea involved deciding contested questions of fact). If the plea fails, the indictment is put in the normal way. The accused's right to plead not guilty is not affected by his having raised autrefois unsuccessfully: Criminal Law Act 1967, s. 6(1)(a).

6.8.2 Applicability of the pleas

The following propositions are based upon the speech of Lord Morris of Borth-y-Gest in *Connelly* v *DPP* [1964] AC 1254 at pages 1305–6:

(a) A man cannot be tried for a crime in respect of which he has previously been acquitted or convicted. This is the straighforward application of autrefois acquit and convict. If the accused is charged with an offence, in law and on the facts identical to one of which he has already been acquitted or convicted, autrefois will bar any further proceedings on that charge.

(b) A man cannot be tried for a crime in respect of which he could on some previous indictment have been convicted. This extension of (a) is necessary because of the possibility of a jury bringing in a verdict of not guilty as charged but guilty of a lesser offence (see Para. 6.4 and Chapter 9). If the jurors are entitled to convict of a lesser offence but choose simply to acquit, they decide by implication that the accused was not guilty both of the offence charged and the lesser offence. Accordingly, autrefois acquit bars proceedings for both offences, for instance, an acquittal on a count for murdering X entitles the accused to raise autrefois if he is subsequently indicted for the manslaughter of X.

(c) A man cannot be tried for a crime which is in effect the same or is substantially the same as one of which he has previously been acquitted or convicted (or could have been convicted by way of a verdict of guilty of a lesser offence). This is the most difficult and least well-defined application of autrefois. Indeed, Lord Devlin in *Connelly* v *DPP* preferred not to extend the pleas beyond the situations mentioned in (a) and (b) above. However, there is at least one clear application of this head of autrefois, namely that where the prosecution indicts the accused for Offence A, but, in order to secure a conviction, it is necessary to prove Offence B of which the accused has already been acquitted, autrefois acquit applies. For example, if a count charges the accused with robbing X of £10, and the accused has already been acquitted, on the same facts, of stealing the money from X, autrefois acquit will bar proceedings on the count as any conviction for robbery would in effect reverse the acquittal for theft. Similarly, if the accused has been acquitted of the manslaughter of Y he cannot subsequently be indicted for Y's murder. So much is well settled, but it is difficult to know in what other situations it will be held that an offence is 'in effect the same' as one of which the accused was previously acquitted or convicted. The fact that the prosecution at the trial of a second indictment proposes to prove the same facts and call the same evidence as at an earlier trial ending in the acquittal or conviction of the accused, does not of itself entitle the accused to rely on the pleas (see (d) below). In *R* v *Kendrick and Smith* (1931) 23Cr App R 1 autrefois convict was unsuccessfully raised where K and S, who were indicted for uttering letters demanding money with menaces, had previously been convicted on the same facts of threatening to publish photographic negatives with intent to extort money. This case represents the most restrictive view that has been taken of the applicability of autrefois, and it is not easy to reconcile it with the principle that the prosecution should not prefer a series of charges, beginning with the least serious, for the same criminal act, as a device for having the accused put on trial on several occasions: *R v Elrington* (1861) B&S 688. For example, if the accused has been acquitted or convicted of unlawful wounding of X, the prosecution are barred from indicting him on the same facts for causing grievous bodily harm with intent. Lord Devlin, in *Connelly v DPP,* agreed with the principle, but ascribed it to a discretion which, he said, the judge has to prevent a prosecution continuing if it would be unfair or oppressive to the accused. If, following the accused's conviction for an assault on X, the latter dies, the accused may be indicted for murder or manslaughter as the death of the victim has introduced an entirely new element into the situation: *R v Thomas* (1949) 33Cr App R 200. Similarly, an acquittal for wounding with intent to murder does not bar proceedings for murder should the victim die, as proving murder does not necessarily involve proving that the accused had an intent to murder.

(d) It is immaterial that the facts under examination or evidence called at a later trial are identical to those in some earlier proceedings. This point is well illustrated by the facts of *Connelly v DPP.* C was charged with murder and robbery. The prosecution's case was that he and three other men had taken part in an office robbery, during the course of which a victim was killed. In accordance with the practice then prevailing the indictment was split, and the murder charge was tried first. C raised the defences of alibi and, if that should fail, no intent to murder. He was convicted. The Court of Criminal Appeal quashed the conviction, and he was therefore treated as if he had been acquitted of murder (see below). The prosecution sought to proceed on the second indictment for robbery, but were met with the plea of autrefois acquit. The judge, in effect, directed the jury that the plea did not apply. The House of Lords upheld his ruling. Even though the prosecution at the robbery trial alleged the same facts and called the same evidence as at the murder trial, the two offences were not in effect the same or substantially the same. Applying the tests mentioned in (b) and (c) above, the jury could not, on the indictment for murder, have convicted C of robbery, and, on the indictment for robbery, it was not necessary, in order to secure a conviction, to prove that C had murdered the victim. Hence, autrefois did not apply.

(e) The principles of autrefois acquit and convict apply equally in summary trials, although there is no special form of plea or procedure as there is at trials on indictment — the defence raise the issue on a simple not guilty plea.

Many of the cases on autrefois are about what amounts to an acquittal or conviction for purposes of the pleas. No distinction is drawn between acquittals or convictions on indictment and those following summary trial. However, for the pleas to apply, the court trying the case must have been acting within its jurisdiction (see *R v West* [1964] 1QB 15 where a purported acquittal by magistrates on a charge which they were not entitled to try did not prevent their subsequently committing W for trial or his being convicted at quarter sessions). Discharge of the accused by the examining justices after committal proceedings is not an acquittal (*R v Manchester City Stipendiary Magistrate* ex parte Snelson [1977] 1WLR

911), nor is the quashing of an indictment following a motion to quash. Where, however, the Court of Appeal quashes the accused's conviction he is generally treated as if he had been acquitted by the jury that tried him, and so can rely on autrefois acquit. The exception to this is that retrials can take place when either the Court of Appeal, having allowed the appeal because of evidence it has heard, orders a retrial, or the original trial that led to the quashed conviction was a complete mistrial at which the accused was never in danger of a valid conviction (see Chapter 17).

Turning to what amounts to a conviction, a finding of 'guilt' in disciplinary proceedings followed by the imposition of a penalty is not a conviction (*R v Hogan and Tompkins* [1960] 2QB 513, where prison escapees, who had been punished for the escape by the visiting committee of magistrates under the Prison Rules, could not rely on autrefois convict at a subsequent trial for the offence of escaping by force). Similarly, if a court takes another offence into consideration when sentencing an offender for an offence of which he has been convicted, there is no conviction in respect of the offence taken into consideration *R v Nicholson* [1947] 32Cr App R 98 and see Chapter 14. Acquittals or convictions before foreign courts or by courts martial are sufficient grounds for autrefois: *R v Aughet* (1919) 13 Cr App R 101.

6.8.3 Issue estoppel

When autrefois acquit or convict is raised the court is called upon to decide whether the accused has previously been acquitted or convicted, and, if so, of what. It is not concerned with ascertaining the facts that the jury (or magistrates) must have found proved or not proved. Occasionally, it was suggested on behalf of the accused that, in a case where autrefois was not applicable, the judge should look behind the verdict of acquittal at an earlier trial, and rule that the jury had found in favour of the accused upon an issue raised at that trial. The prosecution should then be estopped at the later trial from denying the correctness of the jury's finding at the first trial. In *Connelly* v *DPP* some of their Lordships were prepared to accept that this doctrine of issue estoppel had a place in criminal proceedings, but, on the facts of the case, C could not rely on it. Lord Devlin doubted whether issue estoppel would, in practice, be of much assitance to the defence, and his scepticism has proved justified, since there is no reported case of the defence successfully raising an issue estoppel. The difficulty is that most criminal trials involve more than one disputed issue. If the accused is simply acquitted, it is impossible to know on which of the disputed issues the jury found in his favour. However, *DPP* v *Humphrys* [1977] AC 1 gave the House of Lords the opportunity to rule on whether, in a suitable case, issue estoppel can be relied upon. H was acquitted of driving whilst disqualified on a certain date in 1972. He gave evidence that he had not driven at all during 1972, and was subsequently prosecuted for perjury in respect of that evidence. Among the witnesses called by the prosecution, to prove that H's evidence was false, was a police witness who had testified at the earlier trial, and who again gave evidence that, on the date named in the indictment for driving while disqualified, he had seen H driving. The only issue at the first trial had been whether H was driving on the date alleged — H admitted that, on that date, he was disqualified. The defence submitted unsuccessfully that the prosecution were estopped from alleging in the perjury trial that H had been driving on the day of the alleged driving while disqualified. The House of Lords held that the judge's rejection of the defence submission was correct, and that issue estoppel has no application to criminal proceedings, neither prosecution nor defence being able to rely upon it. The ruling of Lawson J at first instance in *R v Hogan* [1974] QB 398, that the prosecution could raise an issue estoppel was incorrect, and the suggestions in *Connelly* v *DPP* that the doctrine might be available to assist the defence should also not be followed.

6.9 JUDGE'S DISCRETION TO HALT PROSECUTION

Among the numerous questions explored by their Lordships' judgements in *Connelly* v *DPP* was that of whether a judge has a discretion to prevent the prosecution proceeding with its case. Their Lordships agreed that the courts have a discretion to prevent abuse of their own process, but Lord Morris of Borth-y-Gest and Lord Hodson took the view that, unless there is a reason in law why the prosecution should not proceed (i.e. the indictment would be quashed because it is defective etc., or the court has no jurisdiction to try the case, or autrefois applies, or the Attorney-General has entered a *nolle prosequi*), the judge has no power to stop the case, however much he may disapprove the prosecution's having brought it. Lord Morris stated that — 'it would be an unfortunate innovation if it were held that the power of a court to prevent any abuse of its process or to ensure compliance with correct procedure enabled a judge to suppress a prosecution merely because he regretted that it was taking place' (*Connelly* v *DPP* at p.1304) — and Lord Hodson's comment was that 'to exclude a litigant with a *prima facie* case, whether prosecutor or civil claimant, from the court seems to be...not justifiable unless an Act of Parliament so provides' (ibid at p. 1337). Lord Devlin, on the other hand, argues that where a prosecution is technically justified but its continuation would be unfair to the accused, the judge has a residual discretion to prevent it proceeding. Applying this to the issues raised by *Connelly* v *DPP*, if autrefois acquit and convict do not apply, the judge can nonetheless halt the trial where a previous conviction or acquittal on the same facts make it oppressive to have a second trial. On the facts of *Connelly* v *DPP*, the prosecution were not behaving oppressively. Lord Pearce and Lord Reid agreed with Lord Devlin. In the present state of the authorities it is difficult to say whether a judge does have the discretion argued for by Lord Devlin. The answer may be that the judge, although having the discretion, is only entitled to exercise it in the rarest of cases, which certainly would not include a case where he merely thinks that it was very unwise to bring the prosecution. Lord Edmund-Davies in *DPP* v *Humphrys* summarised the position as follows — 'a judge has not and should not appear to have any responsibility for the institution of prosecutions, nor has he any power to refuse to allow a prosecution to proceed merely because he considers that, as a matter of policy, it ought not to have been brought. It is only if the prosecution amounts to an abuse of the process of the court and is oppressive and vexatious that the judge has power to intervene. Fortunately such prosecutions are hardly ever brought...'

6.10 OTHER POSSIBLE PLEAS

For the sake of completeness, three other pleas should be mentioned, although they are hardly ever used in practice.

  (a) The plea of pardon (i.e. the Crown, on the recommendation of the Home Secretary, has pardoned the accused for the offence alleged) is the third special plea in bar, and, if successful, prevents further proceedings on the indictment. If the pardon was granted before trial, it should be pleaded before the indictment is put. If granted during the trial it should be pleaded at the first opportunity. In the ten years up until

August 1980 the Home Secretary is said to have recommended a pardon in about 2,000 cases. The usual reason for doing so is to avoid the necessity for an appeal against conviction in cases where it is established after the trial that the accused was innocent. Once a person has been pardoned, the sentence imposed on him is no longer effective, but it is not clear whether he remains a convicted person for purposes, for instance, of holding an office which is not open to those with certain convictions recorded against them.

(b) A plea to the jurisdiction,which must be in writing, is to the effect that the court has no jurisdiction to try the offence. It would be appropriate in the unlikely event of the indictment alleging a summary offence. It could also be relied upon where the defence argue that the offence was committed outside the territorial jurisdiction of the English courts (see Para. 2.4.1.), although the point could equally well be taken on an ordinary not guilty plea.

(c) A demurrer which, like a plea to the jurisdiction, must be in writing is an objection to the wording of an indictment. Any objection which could be taken on a demurrer can more conveniently be taken on a motion to quash. For that reason Lord Parker CJ expressed the wish that demurrer 'will be allowed to die naturally': *R v Deputy Chairman of Inner London Sessions* ex parte *Commissioner of Metropolitan Police* [1970] 2QB 80.

7 The Jury

If the accused pleads not guilty then, unless the prosecution chooses to offer no evidence, a jury must be empanelled (or, more colloquially, sworn in) to try the case.

7.1 ELIGIBILITY FOR JURY SERVICE

Jurors are drawn from a broad, though not complete, cross-section of the population. Subject to the exceptions mentioned below, everyone aged 18 to 65, who is registered as a parliamentary or local government elector is eligible for jury service, provided he has been ordinarily resident in the United Kingdom for any period of at least five years since attaining the age of 13: Juries Act 1974, s. 1. The residential qualification is a rough and ready way of ensuring that jurors have an adequate grasp of the English language and way of life. If it appears to a Crown Court officer that a person attending at the court for jury service may not have a sufficient understanding of English to be able to act effectively as a juror, he may bring that person before a judge of the court for a ruling that he be discharged from jury service: Juries Act 1974, s. 10. The present rules on eligibility for jury service may be contrasted with those before the Juries Act, under which only householders were eligible. This led to the criticism (or, depending on one's point of view, commendation) of juries, that they were 'middle-aged, middle-class and middle-income'. It would be difficult now to sustain such a charge.

By the Juries Act 1974, s. 1 and Schedule 1 Parts I and II, the following are precluded from sitting on juries:

(a)   The judiciary, which includes all holders of high judicial office, circuit judges, recorders, lay and stipendiary magistrates and all former holders of any such office.

(b)   Others concerned in the administration of justice. These include barristers and solicitors, whether practising or not, magistrates' courts clerks, articled clerks and barristers' clerks, members of the Parole Board, members of local review committees advising on the granting of parole and probation officers, police officers and some civilians employed by police authorities, and anybody who in the last ten years has fallen within any of the preceding categories.

(c)   The clergy, whether of the Church of England or any other religious denomination.

(d)   Persons who by reason of mental illness are resident in a hospital or regularly attend for treatment by a doctor.

(e)   Persons who have been sentenced in the United Kingdom to imprisonment for life or for a term of five years or more, or to be detained during Her Majesty's pleasure, and persons who, at any time during the last ten years, have served in the

United Kingdom any part of a sentence of imprisonment or detention for three months or more, or have been detained in borstal. Those in categories (a) to (d) are described as ineligible for jury service; those in category (e) are said to be disqualified from it.

The reasoning behind the exclusion of the above groups from jury service is fairly obvious. Judges, barristers, solicitors etc. might exert too great an influence over their lay colleagues on a jury, police officers could be suspected of bias towards the prosecution, and, conversely, probation officers could favour the defence. The exclusion of the clergy is a little surprising, and may spring from a feeling that a clergyman, by reason of his vocation, would not wish to sit in judgment on others. The only surprising point about the exclusion of certain convicted criminals is that the category is not larger than it is. For example, the passing of a suspended sentence of imprisonment (see Chapter 15) does not disqualify the offender from jury service since he does not serve any part of the sentence unless he commits a further offence, but quite serious offences of dishonesty or violence are commonly dealt with by means of a suspended sentence. In theory, anyway, an offender could be sentenced to a period of imprisonment suspended for two years on one day, and serve on a jury the next. The procedures for asking a juror to stand by and for challenging jurors (see Para. 7.3) are meant to prevent unsuitable, though eligible jurors, serving on the jury in a particular case.

A person who serves on a jury knowing that he is disqualified from or ineligible for jury service commits a summary offence punishable, in the former case, with a fine of up to £400, and in the latter case, a fine of up to £100: Juries Act, s. 20(5). In the period 1974-80 there were only two prosecutions for such offences, one resulting in acquittal and the other in a fine of £10.

7.2 SUMMONING JURORS

The Lord Chancellor is responsible for summoning jurors to attend for jury service in the Crown Court: Juries Act 1974, s. 2. He acts, of course, through officers of the Crown Court. The summons, which must be in writing, may be sent by post. It requires the juror to attend on certain days at a stated location of the Crown Court. The location should, if possible, be within reasonable daily travelling distance of the juror's home, and the average period for which a juror is asked to attend is two weeks. At some courts, such as the Central Criminal Court, which regularly deal with long cases, the period may be greater. If a lengthy case is anticipated it is normal to ask jurors whether they have any objection to being involved. Jurors are, of course, entitled to payment in respect of *inter alia* travelling and subsistence expenses and loss of earnings, but the rates of payment laid down by the Lord Chancellor may not provide full compensation for the losses incurred. The summons should be accompanied by a notice explaining the restrictions on eligibility for jury service, the penalties for non-attendance when summoned and the possibility of being excused from jury service.

The Lord Chancellor is also responsible, through the Crown Court officers, for drawing up lists (or panels) of the names, addresses and dates for attendance of those who have been summoned for jury service at the various locations of the Crown Court: Juries Act 1974, s. 5(1). The prosecution and defence are both entitled by s.

5(2) to inspect the panel from which the jurors to try their case will be, or have been, drawn. By s. 5(3), this may be done in advance of or during but not after the trial. The right to inspect the jury panel before trial enables the prosecution and defence, if they so wish, to make enquiries about the potential jurors with a view to objecting to one or more of them sitting on the jury.

The usual pattern is to summon many more jurors for service than are likely to be required. Should a miscalculation occur, however, so that a full jury cannot be made up from those on the jury panel, the court may summon, without written notice, any person in, or in the vicinity of, the court to complete the jury: Juries Act 1974, s. 6. The names of persons so summoned are added to the jury panel. There is only a very remote possibility of the court actually having to make use of s. 6.

A person who is eligible and summoned for jury service is under a duty to attend as required, and, unless excused from doing so, commits an offence by not attending without reasonable cause: Juries Act 1974, s. 20. The offence is punishable with a fine of up to £100. The matter may be tried summarily, or, more conveniently, it may be dealt with by a judge of the Crown Court as if a criminal contempt had been committed in the face of the court. This means that, if the juror does not admit the offence, the judge can hear evidence and decide if the case has been proved without the necessity of empanelling a jury. It must be shown that the summons was duly served on the juror at least 14 days before the date fixed in it for his first attendance at court. Sudden illness or bereavement would, no doubt, be a reasonable cause for not attending.

The following persons, although eligible for jury service, are entitled to be excused:

(a)   Those who have attended a court for jury service within the two years preceding the service of the summons on them.
(b)   Those whom a court has excused from jury service for a period which has not yet terminated (occasionally, after a very long case, the judge will express his thanks to the jurors by saying that they are excused any further jury service).
(c)   Members of Parliament.
(d)   Full-time serving members of the armed forces.
(e)   Doctors, nurses and other members of the medical professions.

With the exception of members of the armed forces, persons claiming to be in the above groups must satisfy an appropriate officer of the Crown Court that they are, indeed, entitled to be excused service. Appeal against his decision may be made to a judge of the Crown Court. In the case of members of the armed forces, the commanding officer of the person summoned certifies that the latter's absence from duty would be prejudicial to the efficiency of the service.

If the juror is not entitled to be excused but nevertheless has a good reason for not attending, the appropriate officer may grant him excusal. An obvious reason that might well be urged with success is that, the time he should attend court coincides with his annual holiday in Spain. He could also properly argue that he has a conscientious objection to jury service, although a Practice Direction (1973 57Cr App R 345) states that jurors should not be excused on more general grounds, such as race, religion, political beliefs or occupation. Again, there is a right of appeal to a Crown Court judge against the appropriate officer's refusal to excuse attendance.

Excusal from jury service is dealt with in the Juries Act 1974, ss. 8 and 9.

7.3   EMPANELLING A JURY

The next stage in the procedure is to select, from amongst the jury panel summoned to attend at a location of the Crown Court on a certain day, the twelve men and women who will form the jury to try a particular case. This is the empanelling or swearing-in of the jury.

Twenty or more members of the jury panel (known as the jury in waiting) are either in court when the accused pleads not guilty, or are brought into court by an usher immediately after the plea has been taken. The clerk of court calls the names of twelve of them, asking them to step into the jury box. He has the names of all the jurors in waiting, and must choose the ones he calls at random: Juries Act s. 11 — "the jury to try an issue before a court shall be selected by ballot in open court from the panel, or part of the panel, of jurors...". The ballot is normally carried out by giving to the clerk some cards, each card having on it the name and address of a juror in waiting. He shuffles the cards, and calls the names on the top twelve. Once twelve persons are in the jury box, the clerk says to the accused — 'John Smith, the names that you are about to hear called are the names of the jurors who are to try you. If therefore you wish to object to them or to any of them, you must do so as they come to the book to be sworn, and before they are sworn, and your objection shall be heard.' This is meant to inform the accused of his right to challenge jurors (see Para. 7.4.1). Whether an unrepresented accused, unfamiliar with court procedure, would understand exactly how he should object to a juror is open to some doubt. However, the obscurity, if there be any, in what is said matters little, since most accused are legally represented in the Crown Court, and the right to challenge a juror is always exercised by counsel on behalf of his client.

Next, the clerk calls individually on each juror in waiting in the jury box to take the juror's oath, which takes the form: 'I swear by Almighty God that I will faithfully try the several issues joined between our Sovereign Lady the Queen and the prisoner/s at the bar and give a true verdict according to the evidence'. The juror reads the words of the oath from a printed card while holding the appropriate book (New Testament for Christians, Old Testament for Jews) in his right hand. If he so wishes, he may affirm. Sometimes, in order to signify his objection, immediately before a juror would otherwise commence the oath, counsel for the prosecution says 'Stand by' or defence counsel says 'Challenge'. In either event, the juror is asked to leave the box, and is replaced by a juror in waiting. The replacement takes the oath (or is asked to stand by or is challenged). The number of times this may happen and the reasons for it are explained in Paras. 7.4.1 and 7.4.2. Once a full jury of twelve has been sworn, the clerk asks them if they are all sworn, and puts the accused in their charge. This is a traditional, although not strictly essential part of the procedure. The clerk says something to the effect that — 'John Smith stands indicted for the following matters. Theft contrary to Section 1 of the Theft Act 1968, the particulars being...(and so on through the indictment). To this indictment he has pleaded not guilty. It is your charge to say, having heard the evidence, whether he be guilty or not.' If the accused has pleaded guilty to some counts on the indictment and not guilty to others, the clerk must not give any indication that this has occurred. Once the accused is in the jury's charge prosecuting counsel begins his opening speech (see Chapter 8).

7.4 CHALLENGES TO JURORS

Two contrasting views may be held on the best way to select a jury. One is that the process should be left as much as possible to chance. Although certain groups may unavoidably have to be excluded from jury service (children, the mentally sick, professional lawyers, those guilty of serious crime etc.) these groups should be narrowly defined, and, provided a person is eligible for jury service, it should not be possible to object to his being on a jury for a particular case if, by whatever method of random selection is used, he has been picked for that jury. Lawton LJ in *R* v *Mason* [1980] 3WLR 617 suggested that this approach could lead to unfairness. For example, the jury to try an accused who, while out poaching, is alleged to have unlawfully wounded a gamekeeper might include a juror with several convictions for poaching, the convictions not having resulted in a sentence which would disqualify him from jury service. The counter argument is that the jury could just as well include a gamekeeper, and, anyway, the provisions for majority verdicts (see Chapter 9) prevent any one juror having a decisive influence on the case.

The second view on selecting a jury is that every effort should be made to choose jurors who have no discernible prejudices relevant to the case, whether it be a prejudice against the particular type of crime alleged, or for or against accused persons in general, or for or against the particular accused charged. This approach is adopted in some of the American states. It involves giving the parties the opportunity to examine a potential juror, call evidence about him and present argument about his suitability. The difficulty is that the process of selecting a jury can become almost as lengthy and expensive as the trial itself. It is probably no accident that the process has been developed in one of the wealthiest and most litigious societies in the world.

The approach of the English courts represents a compromise between the above views, although it leans in favour of random selection. The groups not entitled to serve on juries are fairly small (see Para. 7.1), the summoning of jurors from amongst those qualified is entirely at random (see Para. 7.2), and the selection from the jury panel of those who go into the jury box with a view to taking the oath and forming the jury is by ballot (see Para. 7.3). However, the random nature of the choice is qualified by the prosecution and defence both being able to prevent at least some of those originally picked sitting on the jury. Both prosecution and defence can challenge a juror for cause. The prosecution can ask a juror to stand by, and the defence can peremptorily challenge up to three jurors.

7.4.1 Peremptory challenges

The defence has three peremptory challenges (Juries Act 1974, s. 12) — that is, they can make a challenge without giving any reason for it, and, if it is made in the correct form, it must succeed. The correct form is for defence counsel to say 'Challenge' immediately before the juror he wishes to remove would otherwise commence taking the oath. The juror is then told to leave the box, and is replaced by a juror in waiting. If the challenge is not made until after the start of the oath, the judge has a discretion to allow it, but is not obliged to do so: *R* v *Harrington* (1977) 64Cr App R 1. Where two or more accused are joined in one indictment each has three challenges.

It is normal practice for counsel to exercise the right to peremptorily challenge on behalf of his client. He need not have specific instructions to challenge an individual juror, and, just as the accused would be entitled to challenge for any or no reasons, so counsel's motives for challenging cannot be questioned or made the subject of proceedings for professional misconduct (Annual Statement of the Bar Council 1973-4 at pages 52-3). If counsel were told that a member of the jury panel knew that the accused had previous convictions, he would almost certainly challenge him. In all probability a challenge for cause (see Para. 7.4.3) would succeed, but it is safer and simpler to make use of a peremptory challenge. It is, however, rare for the random summoning of jurors to throw up jurors who know or are known by the accused. Where the only information that counsel has about the jurors is what he can glean from seeing them walk into the jury box and hearing them answer to their names, his decision to challenge or not is inevitably based on intuition, guess work or prejudice. Sometimes middle-aged men conventionally dressed are challenged on the basis that they will favour the prosecution, or counsel for a white accused charged with an assault on a coloured victim will challenge coloured jurors, or in a case of rape the women on the jury may be kept to a minimum. In theory, by making use of their right to inspect the jury panel before trial, the defence could cause enquiries to be made into the character and background of everyone on the panel with a view to challenging those who might be pro-prosecution. In practice, this does not happen, because it would cost a great deal of money, and the legal aid fund would certainly not pay for it.

7.4.2 Jurors asked to stand by

The prosecution does not have the right to make a peremptory challenge, but can ask a juror to stand by. Prosecuting counsel says 'Stand by' before the juror would otherwise take the oath, and the juror is replaced by a juror in waiting. Prosecuting counsel is not asked his reason for requiring the juror to stand by, nor need he have a reason capable of founding a challenge for cause (see Para. 7.4.3). His position is therefore analogous to that of defence counsel making a peremptory challenge: *R* v *Mason* [1980] 3WLR 617 at p.625. If a full jury can be obtained from the jury panel without him, there is no possibility of the juror who was stood by being on the jury. If the panel is exhausted and the jury is still incomplete, the juror joins the jury unless the prosecution can show cause why he should not do so. The practice of summoning many more jurors for service than are likely to be needed means that the prosecution are able to ask several jurors to stand by without risk of the jury panel being exhausted. In this respect, the right to make peremptory challenges is less valuable than the right to have jurors stand by, for the former right can only be exercised in respect of three jurors but the latter is only limited by the size of the jury panel. The defence have no right to stand jurors by: *R* v *Chandler* [1964] 2QB 322.

Just as the defence could in theory conduct extensive enquiries into those on the jury panel, so the prosecution could try to discover whether any of them had ever expressed a sentiment hostile to the police. In practice the one investigation the prosecution are likely to make is into the criminal convictions, if any, of the jurors. In *R* v *Mason,* M was convicted before the Crown Court at Northampton of offences of burglary and handling stolen goods. Prior to the trial the police checked the hundred jurors on the relevant jury panel, and found that four definitely had convictions. Two of these were disqualified from jury service. Lawton LJ found these facts 'disturbing', commenting that 'if two disqualified jurors can turn up in Northamptonshire out of 100 summoned, the number is likely to be much greater when a panel is summoned from an urban area with a high level of crime' (*R* v *Mason* at p.620). At M's trial, prosecuting counsel asked four jurors to stand by. One of them was known to a police officer in the case, so it was obviously right to stand him by. As to the other three, counsel had been told that they had previous convictions, although in at least one case the convictions were not such as to disqualify from jury service. M appealed, arguing that counsel had misused the information given to him about the jurors' convictions so as to stand by a juror who was qualified to serve and could not have been challenged for cause. The Court of Appeal held, first, that the right to stand jurors by is not dependent upon counsel having a reason for doing so capable of founding a challenge for cause (see above). It followed that there was no irregularity in standing by the juror whose convictions did not disqualify him. Second, 'the practice of supplying prosecution counsel with information about potential jurors' convictions has been followed during the whole of our professional lives' and 'is not unlawful' (see p.625). Third, counsel should use the information responsibly, and not request a stand by unnecessarily. A conviction for reckless driving would not justify asking the juror to stand by if he was to try a case of burglary, but it might if the charge were causing death by reckless driving. Fourth, there is no obligation on the prosecution to inform the defence of their discoveries about the jurors' convictions. If, on the other hand, the prosecution knew that the jury panel included a relative of the principal prosecution witness, they should tell the defence.

> Some indication of when the police will check potential jurors for criminal convictions is afforded by recommendations from the Association of Chief Police Officers, issued in the light of the observations in *R* v *Mason*. Checks will be made if:
>
> (a) it appears that an attempt is being made to introduce disqualified persons onto a jury, or that a particular juror may be disqualified, or
> (b) it is believed that in a previous related abortive trial an attempt was made to interfere with jurors, or
> (c) it is thought particularly important to ensure that no disqualified person serves on the jury. The interpretation of (c) is likely to vary from police force to police force.
> The police will not check j .rors on behalf of the defence unless requested to do so by the Director of Public Prosecutions. Nor will they carry out checks in addition to the check on convictions unless authorised to do so under the Attorney-General's guidelines on jury-vetting (see Para. 7.4.4).

7.4.3 Challenges for cause

Both the prosecution and the defence are entitled to challenge as many individual jurors as they wish for cause. The challenge, which is normally entered orally, must be made before the juror is sworn: Juries Act 1974, s. 12(3). The burden of proof is on the challenging party to satisfy the judge that he has good cause for his challenge. The grounds are that the juror is not qualified to serve by reason of (s. 12(4)), or that he is biased, or that he may reasonably be suspected of bias. Numerous eighteenth and nineteenth century cases explore the meaning of bias. Jurors were successfully challenged when they were employed by or related to a party, or entertained at the house of a party, when they had expressed a wish or an opinion as to the outcome of the trial, and when they showed hostility to a party (*R* v *O'Coigley* (1798) 26St.Tr. 1191, in which case the juror, on looking at the accused, said 'Damned rascals'.) More recently, in *R* v *Kray and others* (1969) 53Cr App R 412, the judge accepted that jurors who had read certain lurid and probably inaccurate newspaper reports of the alleged activities of the accused might have been prejudiced against them by what they read. He therefore allowed defence counsel to examine the jurors on the matter before they were sworn. The facts of *R* v *Kray* were exceptional in that the newspapers concerned, following the accused's trial on one indictment and knowing that they were soon to be tried on a second indictment, not only reported at length the evidence in the first trial but dug up from the past many discreditable stories of doubtful veracity. The mere fact that a previous trial of the accused, ending in his conviction, received much publicity will not justify challenges to jurors at the later trial on grounds of bias.

The case of *R* v *Kray* was also exceptional in that counsel was permitted to question the jurors without first producing evidence to show that an individual juror had read the reports. The general rule is that a juror cannot be questioned with a view to showing that there is a ground for challenge unless *prima facie* evidence to that effect has first been adduced by the challenging party. Such evidence is rarely available, since neither the prosecution nor the defence normally make enquiries about the jury panel before trial (apart from the police possibly checking for previous convictions). It follows that challenges for cause are infrequent. Even where counsel does have evidence available which would lay a foundation for a challenge, he may well think it safer and simpler to ask the juror to stand by or peremptorily challenge him. In *R* v *Mason,* for example, prosecuting counsel did not challenge for cause the jurors who were disqualified by their previous convictions, but merely asked them to stand by.

Even if the prosecution and defence do not object to a juror, the judge, in order to see that there is a fair trial, may exclude him from the jury. This most commonly happens when the judge notices that the juror is infirm, or has difficulty in reading or hearing, and the case is going to involve the reading of documents or the understanding of complicated evidence.

A challenge to the whole jury panel may be made in addition to challenges to individual jurors. This is known as a challenge to the array, and is on the ground that the Crown Court officer appointed to summon the panel was biased or otherwise acted improperly. Although challenges to the array are preserved by the Juries Act 1974, s. 12(6), they are virtually unknown in modern times.

7.4.4   Jury vetting

The practice of 'jury vetting' (that is, making enquiries about the jury panel before trial so as to use the right to stand by and challenge jurors more effectively) has recently caused public controversy and, indeed, judicial disagreement. The extent to which vetting takes place in ordinary cases has been discussed in the preceding paragraphs. Essentially, the position is that it could happen in any case, but the only check actually likely to be carried out is by the police into the criminal convictions of the jurors. That form of vetting (although no other) has, of course, been sanctioned in *R* v *Mason*. However, in *R* v *Sheffield Crown Court* ex parte *Brownlow* [1980] 2WLR 892 a differently constituted Court of Appeal trenchantly expressed the opposite view. Lord Denning MR said (at p.900) — 'To my mind it is unconstitutional for the police authorities to engage in 'jury vetting'. So long as a person is eligible for jury service, and is not disqualified, I cannot think that it is right that, behind his back, the police should go through his record so as to enable him to be asked to 'stand by for the Crown', or to be challenged by the defence. If this sort of thing is to be allowed, what comes of a man's right of privacy? He is bound to serve on a jury when summoned. Is he thereby liable to have his past record raked up against him — and presented on a plate to prosecuting and defending lawyers — who may use it to keep him out of the jury — and, who knows, it may become known to his neighbours and those about him?' Another criticism of *R* v *Mason* which can be advanced is that Parliament, when it passed the Juries Act, could have disqualified from jury service all those with previous convictions, but it chose not to do so. If the prosecution habitually stand by jurors who are qualified but have convictions, they effectively alter Parliament's decision. However, whatever the merits of the competing arguments, the law is as stated in *R* v *Mason*. The comments in ex parte *Brownlow,* which was decided shortly before and mentioned in *R* v *Mason,* were *obiter dicta*.

In a small minority of cases, jury vetting by the prosecution may go beyond checking for convictions. This is dealt with in guidelines issued by the Attorney-General on 31 July 1980. In terrorist cases, and in cases involving national security where part of the evidence is likely to be heard in camera, the records of police special branches can be checked for information about members of the jury panel. Such checks are only allowed on the personal authority of the Attorney-General, and the results are given to the Director of Public Prosecutions, who decides how much of the information should be passed on to prosecuting counsel. The aim of the checks is to enable counsel to exclude from the jury those who (in national security cases) might be tempted to divulge evidence heard in camera, and those who (in either type of case) might not be able to try the case fairly because of their extreme political views. Under rather less stringent guidelines then in force, the Attorney-General, during the period 1974-9, sanctioned jury vetting in only 29 cases. In both *R* v *Mason* and ex parte *Brownlow* the Court of Appeal declined to express a view on the guidelines.

7.4.5 Issues triable by one jury

A jury empanelled to try a certain issue (e.g. whether the accused is guilty or not guilty on the indictment against him) cannot, after they have decided that issue, be kept together to try a further issue (e.g. whether the accused is guilty or not guilty on a second indictment outstanding against him). A fresh jury must be selected by ballot from the jury panel to try that issue. Of course, an individual juror, during the course of his jury service may sit on more than one jury, although in the example given above, any member of the jury which tried the first indictment against the accused would be kept off the jury for the second indictment against him. The exceptions to the rule that a jury shall only try one issue are that:

(a) A jury can try two or more issues if the trial of the second or last issue begins within 24 hours of its being constituted to try the first issue.

(b) Where the trial of the issue of fitness to plead is postponed until after arraignment the jury trying the accused on the indictment can, at the judge's discretion, decide fitness to plead as well (see Para. 6.7.2).

(c) A jury that has tried a special plea raised by the accused (autrefois acquit, autrefois convict or pardon) can, if the plea fails, try him on a not guilty plea.

In the cases where a jury is entitled to try a second issue, the parties are not deprived of any right they would otherwise have to challenge the jurors, because if the judge considers that a juror 'could be justly challenged or excused', or if the parties consent to it being done, the juror may be replaced by a member of the jury panel. This safeguard is particularly important in cases where the jury empanelled to decide the issue of muteness (an issue unlikely to take 24 hours to decide) is, after deciding that the accused was mute of malice, asked to try him on the not guilty plea entered on his behalf. When the jury was empanelled, the defence would not have been able to make any challenges, as the right to challenge only arises when the accused has answered to the indictment: *R* v *Paling* (1978) 67Cr App R 299. Challenges can, however, be made before the jury begin the trial of the general issue.

The rules set out above are contained in the Juries Act 1974, s. 11(4), (5) and (6).

7.5 APPEALS BASED ON ERRORS IN THE EMPANELLING OF THE JURY

It is in the public interest that the decisions of juries should be treated with respect, and should not be overturned unless there has been an error during the course of the trial (e.g. inadmissible evidence admitted or a misstatement of the law during the summing up) or the appellate court is left with a real feeling that a miscarriage of justice may have occurred. If an appellant seeking to have his conviction by a jury quashed were allowed to attack the characters of the jurors concerned, or suggest that they had decided the case from improper motives, or had refused to listen to the evidence, the respect accorded to a jury's verdict would be diminished. Furthermore, since an ingenious appellant could find in most cases a way of criticising at least one of the jurors (if only on the basis that he appeared uninterested in the proceedings), the work-load of the Court of Appeal would be greatly increased. To avoid this happening, Parliament and the Court of Appeal have made it very difficult for an appellant to challenge his conviction by criticising individual jurors or the way they came, as a group, to their decision. For example, the Court of Appeal will not enquire into the discussions that the jury had in their room when they were considering their verdict (see Chapter 9), and the Juries Act 1974, s. 18 imposes strict limitations on appeals based on the way the jury was empanelled or the qualifications of a member of it.

Section 18 provides that a judgement after verdict shall not be reversed (i.e. a conviction shall not be quashed) solely because:

(a)   the provisions of the Act about summoning or empanelling jurors or their selection by ballot have not been complied with, or
(b)   a juror was not qualified under s. 1 of the Act, or
(c)   a juror was misnamed or wrongly described, or
(d)   a juror was unfit to serve.

Section 18 does not apply to appeals arising out of a member of the jury panel having been impersonated so that someone who was not qualified for service sat on the jury. Nor does it apply to irregularities within (a) above if, at the time they occurred or as soon after as was practicable, objection was taken but the error was not corrected.

The effect of s. 18 is illustrated by *R* v *Chapman and Lauday* (1976) 63Cr App R 75. After the appellants had been convicted, it was discovered that one of the jurors was deaf. He had heard less than half the evidence and none of the summing up, but the Court of Appeal refused to quash the conviction. The appellants argued that the trial had been a nullity, but their only ground for so arguing was the presence of the deaf juror on the jury, and the effect of s. 18 is that the unfitness of a juror to serve is not in itself a sufficient reason to quash a conviction. The Court of Appeal acknowledged that the 'deficiency in a member of the jury', combined with other factors, might render a conviction unsafe or unsatisfactory and so justify quashing it despite s. 18 (see Chapter 17 on the grounds for allowing an appeal). On the facts of *R* v *Chapman and Lauday,* however, the conviction appeared perfectly safe because the same verdict would have been returned even without the assistance of the deaf juror. The jury convicted unanimously. Had the juror's unfitness been discovered before he was sworn, and had he been replaced by a juror who was in favour of an acquittal, the jury could still have convicted by a majority of 11 to 1 (see Chapter 9). Had the unfitness been discovered during the trial, the judge would have discharged him from the jury, and the remaining eleven would again have been entitled to convict. The case would have been different if the conviction had not been unanimous, but by the smallest permissible majority, namely 10-2. On the assumption that the deaf juror was in the majority, his vote was crucial to the conviction — without his assistance the jury could not have reached a verdict.

> Sometimes, after conviction, the defence discover that a juror was biased, or may reasonably be suspected of bias. The reasoning in *R v Chapman and Lauday* enables them to appeal, notwithstanding s. 18, if they can show that the bias renders the conviction unsafe or unsatisfactory. However, the Court of Appeal is very reluctant to allow such appeals. For example, a conviction will not be quashed beause a juror knew the accused had previous convictions: see *R v Box and Box* [1964] 1QB 430, where the juror knew that the appellants were ex-burglars, villains and associates of prostitutes, and that one of them had recently been released from prison. Even so, their Lordships did not approve of the juror's behaviour. A juror who knows the accused or has heard that he has a criminal record should ask to be excused from being on the jury. But, unless from the outset of a trial a juror was determined to convict whatever the evidence might be, an appeal based on his bias will not succeed. In *R v Box and Box*, the juror who knew of B's convictions also stated to an acquaintance that 'he did not need to hear the evidence' and 'he would get B ten years'. However, he made this comment after hearing all the evidence, and the Court was not satisfied that he had decided at the outset of the case to convict irrespective of the evidence. Since the evidence of bias in *R v Box and Box* seems very cogent, one is left wondering just what evidence is required to induce the Court of Appeal to allow an appeal on this basis.

7.6 DISCHARGE OF JURORS OR JURY

Once a jury has been empanelled, the normal course of events is that those twelve men and women hear the entire case and return a verdict at the end of it. The judge may, however, discharge up to three members of the jury and allow the case to continue with the remainder. He may also discharge the entire jury from giving a verdict.

7.6.1 Discharge of individual jurors

This is a matter for the discretion of the judge, although the Court of Appeal will review the way he exercises it if either he has made an error of law (e.g. he discharges a juror for a reason which could not, in law, be adequate) or he behaves capriciously or unreasonably.

Section 16 of the Juries Act 1974 provides that if, during the course of the trial, a juror dies or is discharged by the judge 'whether as being through illness incapable of continuing to act or for any other reason' the remainder of the jury may complete the hearing of the case and return a verdict provided that their number is not reduced below nine. Discharge of a juror is justified only if there is an 'evident necessity' for it (see *R v Hamberry* [1977] QB 924), but it is not difficult to show such a necessity. The following would all justify the judge, in his discretion, discharging a juror:

(a) travelling difficulties so that the juror is unlikely to arrive at court within a reasonable time of the scheduled restart of the case following an overnight adjournment;

(b) the death of the juror's husband during an overnight adjournment (*R v Richardson* [1979] 3AER 247);

(c) the fact tnat the trial will not finish until two or three days after the juror had planned to go away on holiday (*R v Hamberry* supra, in which case the juror who had

only been summoned for service until 30 July and had been assured that H's case, commencing on 16 July, would only last three or four days, was discharged on the afternoon of the 30th so as to allow her to travel on the 31st as she had arranged), and
(d)   misconduct by the juror.

The most familiar example of misconduct by a juror is his talking to a prosecution witness. This does not in itself necessitate his discharge, but the judge should ascertain what was said, and, if there is any danger of prejudice to the accused, discharge either the individual juror or the whole jury: *R* v *Sawyer* [1980] 72 Cr App R 283. Similarly, if the judge discovers during the trial that a juror knows of the accused's bad character, he should at least discharge him if not the entire jury (*R* v *Hood* [1968] 1 WLR 773 — contrast the position where this is discovered after conviction and an appeal brought: see Para. 7.5). Chapter 9 deals with another possible form of misconduct by a juror, namely separating himself from the rest of the jury after they have retired to consider their verdict.

Trials for murder may only continue with less than twelve jurors if both prosecution and defence give their written consent: Juries Act 1974, s. 16(2). In other cases, the consent of the parties is not required, and, indeed, the judge can exercise his power to discharge otherwise than in open court and without even announcing in open court what he has done (*R* v *Richardson* supra, where the juror whose husband had died telephoned the court on the morning the trial was to resume, the judge ordered that she be told not to come to court, but failed to mention in court what he had done, so that counsel at the time did not even realise that a juror was missing — the conviction was upheld).

7.6.2   Discharge of the whole jury

The judge has a discretion to discharge the whole jury from giving a verdict. If he does so, the accused does not stand acquitted of the offence charged and can be retried by a different jury on the same indictment. The main situations where a judge is likely to discharge the jury are as follows:

(a)   where a juror has died, or could be discharged from the jury, but the judge considers it better to have a fresh jury empanelled rather than continue with less than twelve jurors;
(b)   where inadmissible evidence, prejudicial to the accused, has accidentally been given before the jury, and
(c)   where the jury cannot agree upon their verdict.

As to (a) above, if a juror has misconducted himself by talking to a prosecution witness, and has found out matters prejudicial to the accused which he ought not to know about, it is safer to discharge the whole jury, unless he has clearly had no opportunity to pass on the information to his colleagues. If the jury has already been reduced to nine, and a juror dies or circumstances arise in which he ought to be discharged, then clearly the judge has no option but to discharge the whole jury.

The jury is not, as a general rule, entitled to know that the accused has criminal convictions. Where none of the exceptional circumstances allowing evidence of previous convictions to be introduced have arisen, but a witness nevertheless mentions that the accused is of bad character, there is a good chance that the judge will accede to an application to discharge the jury. It is, however, a matter for his discretion. Relevant factors include the explicitness of the reference to previous convictions, and the degree, if any, to which the defence were to blame, through ill-advised cross-examination, for the evidence coming out: *R v Weaver* [1968] 1QB 353. The likely impact on the jury of what was said is also important. In *R v Coughlan and Young* (1976) 63Cr App R 33, the Court of Appeal refused to interfere with the judge's decision not to discharge the jury in a case where a co-accused, giving evidence on his own behalf, said that C had a previous conviction of some gravity. Prosecuting counsel continued with his cross-examination as if nothing untoward had happened, and counsel for C forebore from taking any action until the co-accused had completed his evidence — then he asked, in the jury's absence, for them to be discharged. The Court of Appeal held that the sensible way in which counsel had dealt with the co-accused's outburst had minimised its likely effect on the jury, and, in all the circumstances, there was no prejudice to C sufficient to necessitate discharging them.

Discharging the jury where they cannot agree upon their verdict is discussed in Chapter 9.

8 The Course of the Trial

8.1 THE ROLE OF COUNSEL

Both prosecuting and defence counsel will wish, naturally, to present their respective cases as skilfully as possible. Even so, there is (or ought to be) a difference in the manner in which they each approach their duties.

8.1.1 Prosecuting counsel

Counsel for the prosecution is not in court to win the case at all costs. Of course, he should present the prosecution case as persuasively as he can by cross-examining the defence witnesses with all proper vigour and guile, and, in his closing address to the jury, by emphasising the strong points of the prosecution case. Nevertheless, as Avory J. put it in *R* v *Banks* [1916] 2KB 621, prosecuting counsel 'ought not to struggle for the verdict against the prisoner, but they ought to bear themselves rather in the character of ministers of justice assisting in the administration of justice'. One aspect of this role is that, should the defence suggest a plea of guilty to a lesser offence or guilty on some but not all the counts in the indictment (see Chapter 6), prosecuting counsel does not consider only whether the evidence he has available might secure a conviction on all counts as charged, but whether the proposed pleas represent a fair way of dealing with the case. If they do, and subject to any comments by the judge, he should accept the pleas, even though that means giving up the chance of 'extra' convictions. Again, if the prosecution knows that one of its witnesses has previous convictions, there is a duty to reveal to the defence the nature and occasion of those convictions, although by doing so the defence is presented with a useful line of cross-examination. The duty of the prosecution does not, however, extend to informing the jury of the convictions if the defence choose not to cross-examine on the matter (e.g. because it might lead to the accused being questioned about his own convictions). The principle is that the prosecution should be scrupulously fair to the accused, but need not be quixotically generous. In the situation mentioned above, some prosecuting counsels would elect to introduce evidence of their witness' previous convictions, even though not obliged to do so.

8.1.2 Defence counsel

Counsel for the defence is not placed under the same constraints as prosecuting counsel. He is under no duty to be fair to the prosecution or to regard himself as a minister of justice. Subject to what is said below, he may use all means at his disposal to secure an acquittal. For example, if he notices a purely technical flaw in the prosecution case, which could be easily corrected if dealt with at an early stage of the trial, he need not draw his opponent's or the court's attention to the matter before the last possible moment (see *R* v *Nelson* (1977) 65Cr App R 119 where the Court of Appeal did not criticise N.'s counsel for waiting until after N. had been convicted to mention that there was a defect in the indictment — his only motive for not mentioning it sooner was to make it harder to remedy the defect by amendment). Again, if defence counsel knows that his client or one of his witnesses has previous convictions he is under no obligation to tell the prosecution. Further examples of this difference between the prosecution and defence approach to the case will become apparent in the remainder of this chapter.

The greater latitude afforded to defence counsel should not be exaggerated. Like all counsel, he owes a duty not just to his client but to the court. It follows that he must not deliberately mislead the court, or behave unethically in any other way. Although he need not reveal that the accused or his witness has convictions, he must not positively assert that they are of good character if he knows that to be false. He should also avoid wasting the court's time through prolixity or repetition. Perhaps the clearest statement of defence counsel's role is to be found in some principles outlined by the Chairman of the Bar (see 62Cr App R 193). The statement followed criticism by the judge Melford Stevenson J. in the case of *R* v *McFadden and Cunningham* (1976) 62 Cr App R 187 of the way in which defence counsel had presented their case and cross-examined police witnesses. The Chairman of the Bar said that defence counsel's duty is to present to the court, 'fearlessly and without regard to his personal interests', the defence of the accused. His personal opinion of the truth or falsity of the defence, or of the character of the accused, or of the nature of the charge should all be left out of account — 'that is a cardinal rule of the Bar, and it would be a grave matter in any free society were it not'. Of course, if the accused tells counsel that he is guilty, it would not be right for counsel to call evidence suggesting the opposite, as he would be acting contrary to his instructions and deliberately misleading the court. If the accused insists on pleading not guilty notwithstanding what he said to counsel, it is probably safest for counsel to withdraw from the case, although he could continue to represent the accused, but confine himself to cross-examining the prosecution witnesses with a view to showing that their evidence does not establish guilt beyond reasonable doubt. Provided, however, that the accused has not admitted to him that he is guilty, counsel may, and indeed is under a duty to, present the defence put forward as persuasively as possible, even though his personal opinion is that the defence is a tissue of lies. The proper limits of defence cross-examination of prosecution witnesses are discussed in para. 8.3.4.

8.1.3 Counsel seeing the judge in private

Lord Parker CJ in *R* v *Turner* [1970] 2QB 325 (see also Para 6.3) stated that there 'must be freedom of access between counsel and judge' (at p.326). He qualified this by saying:

> It is of course imperative that, as far as possible, justice must be administered in open court. Counsel should, therefore, only ask to see the judge when it is felt to be really necessary, and the judge must be careful only to treat such communications as private where, in fairness to the accused person, this is necessary.

Since *R* v *Turner* the Court of Appeal has emphasised in several cases that private access to the judge should be restricted to the 'very limited circumstances' mentioned by Lord Parker: see *R* v *Llewellyn* (1977) 67Cr App R 149. In *R* v *Turner* Lord Parker gave two examples of where it is proper for counsel to see the judge privately. One is where defence counsel, who is to present mitigation following the conviction of his client, knows that the latter is suffering from an incurable disease but is unaware of his condition. Clearly the judge should be told of the accused's ill-health, so as to avoid, if at all possible, passing a sentence which would result in his dying in prison. Equally clearly, to mention the fact in open court with the accused listening could have disastrous consequences. The second example given was that of prosecuting counsel who might wish to ask the judge about the advisability of accepting a plea of guilty to a lesser offence.

Lord Parker's first example is as useful today as when it was given, but *R* v *Coward* (1980) 70Cr App R 70 suggests that in the second situation mentioned prosecuting counsel should make up his own mind whether to accept the plea, and then ask the judge's view in open court. Similarly, if defence counsel is in doubt about how to advise the accused on the likely sentence, he must simply make the best estimate he can without seeking a private indication from the judge (*R* v *Coward* supra — defence counsel 'could not and should not expect a judge, save in wholly exceptional circumstances, to give any guidance whatsoever about the kind of sentence to be passed'). In the light of *R* v *Coward,* the more permissive approach to counsel asking the judge about sentence, approved in *R* v *Cain* [1976] Crim LR 464 (see Para. 6.3) is of doubtful validity. The principle emerging from recent cases (e.g. *R* v *Coward* and *R* v *Llewellyn*) is that private conversations between counsel and judge should be kept to the absolute minimum, and matters such as the way the indictment should be split, the appropriateness of suggested pleas and the likely sentence should be discussed in open court unless there is a very good reason to the contrary.

When the judge is seen privately, both prosecuting and defence counsel should be present, together with the defence solicitor if he so wishes. The accused should be told of what took place, unless there is a good reason why he should be kept in ignorance.

8.2 THE PROSECUTION OPENING

After the accused has been put in the charge of the jury, prosecuting counsel opens his case to them. The prosecution opening gives the members of the jury an overall view of the case. Counsel will remind them of the charges against the accused, which the clerk has just read out to them, explaining any relevant points of law which may not be familiar to lay persons. Probably he will tell them that the prosecution has to prove its case so that they are sure of the accused's guilt, and, if they are not so convinced, they must acquit. Whenever counsel refer to the law it is usual to warn the jury that what they (counsel) say about the law is merely intended as a guide, and is subject to whatever the judge may rule — the jury take the law from the judge not from counsel.

After his explanation of the charges, counsel summarises the evidence he intends to call. In his brief, he has copies of the depositions and statements under the Magistrates' Courts Act 1980 s. 102 tendered at the committal proceedings. Basing himself on these he tells the jury the main facts which (he hopes) his various witnesses will prove, and shows how the pieces of testimony fit together so as to show, beyond reasonable doubt, that the accused committed the offence charged. Having had a general picture of the case, the jury will be able to appreciate the significance of each witness' evidence as it is given. Three detailed points relevant to the opening are that:

(a)   If counsel is told by the defence that they intend to object to certain pieces of prosecution evidence, that evidence should not be included in the prosecution's opening to the jury.

(b)   It is sometimes advisable to 'open the case low' — i.e. slightly to underplay what a witness is expected to say. If counsel puts great weight on what a witness is going to prove, and then, in the event, the evidence is not quite as strong as the jury were led to expect, they may think that the whole prosecution case has been undermined. Had less been made of the evidence in the opening, there would be no risk of their so reacting.

(c)   As part of his duty not to 'struggle after the verdict' counsel should avoid unnecessarily emotive language. Indeed, in cases where the facts alleged are likely to cause especial sympathy for the victim or repugnance towards the criminal, it is desirable for the opening to warn the jury against such natural feelings. They should return a verdict upon the evidence, not upon feelings of sympathy or horror.

8.3   THE PROSECUTION CASE

Next, the prosecution call witnesses to give oral evidence and tender in evidence written statements which are read to the jury. At this point the subjects of evidence and procedure become intertwined. This book does not attempt to deal with evidence per se. Reference should be made to books on evidence for information on topics such as the swearing of witnesses and their competence and compellability; the questions which may be asked in examination in chief, cross-examination and re-examination, the cross-examination of the accused about his previous convictions or bad character, and the matters about which a witness may not give evidence. However, some matters which are, in a sense, part of the law of evidence, also have important procedural aspects, and these will be considered in the succeeding paragraphs.

8.3.1   The witnesses the prosecution should call

The defence naturally expects that a witness who was called by the prosecution at committal proceedings or whose statement was tendered by the prosecution under s. 102 of the Magistrates' Courts Act 1980 will also be called by the prosecution to give evidence at the trial on indictment. Accordingly, no steps are taken to secure the attendance at the Crown Court of such persons, nor do they take statements from them for fear of allegations that they are seeking to tamper with potential prosecution witnesses. If, in the event, the prosecution do not call one of their witnesses at the trial, the defence are usually pleased — it means that there is one less person supporting the case against the accused. However, there are occasions when the lack of a prosecution witness could prejudice the defence. Examples are provided by a witness who, although expected to give evidence generally confirming the accused's guilt, differs in his recollection of events from other prosecution witnesses, and by a witness who in cross-examination will probably testify to matters helpful to the defence which are not contained in his deposition or s. 102 statement from committal proceedings. In either case it would be unfair to deprive the defence of the benefit of the witness' evidence. Therefore, the general rule is that the prosecution must call as witnesses all persons who gave evidence oral or written for the prosecution at committal proceedings. These persons are referred to as 'witnesses whose names appear on the back of the indictment', the term deriving from the old practice of literally writing the names on the reverse of the indictment.

The prosecution must call the witnesses on the back of the indictment so that they may be cross-examined, vigorously if necessary, by the defence. As each side is limited as to the extent of questioning allowed of witnesses called on its own behalf, it follows that for the prosecution merely to ensure the presence of the witnesses on the back of the indictment would deny to the defence the opportunity of such vigorous cross-examination, unless the judge were persuaded to declare such witness hostile. The lines of questioning thus denied to the side calling its own witness would include:

(a)   Leading questions designed to invite the witness to change his evidence.

(b)   Questions concerning previous statements which are not consistent with the evidence which the witness is now giving.

(c)   Questions attacking the witness character by referring to, for example, previous convictions.

Had the witness been called by the opposite party, all the above questions and more could have been asked in the course of cross-examination. Thus, if the prosecution call a witness who gives evidence which is, in part at least, favourable to the defence, it is often impossible to challenge that evidence except by calling other witnesses to contradict what the first prosecution witness has said.

The general rule about calling the witnesses on the back of the indictment is subject to the following exceptions:

(a)   The prosecution do not need to call or even have present at court those persons whose statements they intend to tender in evidence (see Para. 8.3.7 for when the prosecution may tender written statements). The usual reason for the prosecution being able to put a statement in evidence is that, at committal proceedings, the defence agreed to the maker of the statement being made the subject of a conditional witness order. In effect, the witness is not called because the defence did not want him called.

(b)   If the evidence of a witness whose name is on the back of the indictment does not appear to be capable of belief, the prosecution need not call him, but should have him present at court so that the defence may call him if they wish: *R* v *Oliva* [1965] 1 WLR 1028. Normally, if a person does not appear to be capable of belief the prosecution would not call him at committal proceedings or make use of any statement he may have made, so his name would not be on the back of the indictment anyway. Occasionally, they are taken by surprise, as they were in *R* v *Oliva*. The victim of an offence of causing grievous bodily harm with intent, who had made a statement to the police identifying O. as the culprit, gave evidence to that effect on the first day of committal proceedings, but, following an overnight adjournment, he reversed his evidence. It was suspected that he had been threatened with further violence should he continue to implicate the accused. O. was nevertheless committed for trial, and, at his trial, the prosecution rightly did not call the victim as a witness. His change of story at the committal procedings showed that he was not capable of belief. If the judge considers that the prosecution ought to call a certain witness, he may indicate that opinion, and if the prosecution refuses, he can call the witness himself. It is not certain whether he can order prosecuting counsel to call the witness.

(c)   Where the prosecution wishes to call a witness, but is prevented from doing so by circumstances beyond its control (e.g. the witness has disappeared or has gone to live abroad) the judge may either adjourn the case in the hope that the witness may eventually be brought to court, or proceed in his absence even though his name is on the back of the indictment. In a case where the prosecution are willing to proceed without the witness but the defence wish him to attend, the judge, in deciding whether to adjourn, will consider especially the extent to which the absent witness' evidence would be likely to assist the accused and the prospects of securing his attendance within a reasonable time: see *R* v *Cavanagh* [1972] 1WLR 676.

8.3.2   Further duties of the prosecution in relation to witnesses

In the course of their investigations into an offence, the police may take a statement from a person who, if called as a witness, is likely to assist the defence rather than the prosecution case. He may have given a description of the criminal which does not fit the accused, or his version of what occurred may lay the foundation for some defence such as acting in reasonable self-defence on an assualt charge, or he may confirm an alibi which the accused has put forward. Obviously, the prosecution will not want to undermine its own case by making use of that person's statement or calling him as a witness, whether at committal proceedings or at the trial on indictment. The prosecution must not, however, keep the existence of the potential witness secret, but must make him available to the defence by giving them his name and address: *R* v *Bryant and Dickson* (1946) 31Cr App R 146. Whether they should also give the defence a copy of his statement to the police is not clear. According to the Court of Criminal Appeal in *R* v *Bryant and Dickson* there is no duty to do so, and Diplock LJ in *Dallison* v *Caffery* [1965] 1QB 348 at p.376, while approving the prosecution's decision in the circumstances of that case to provide a statement, thought they had done more than was required of them. Lord Denning MR., on the other hand, observed in that case at p.369:

> The duty of prosecuting counsel or solicitor, as I have always understood it, is this: if he knows of a credible witness who can speak of material facts which tend to show the prisoner to be innocent, he must either call that witness himself or make his statement available to the defence.

Failure to supply a statement could cause injustice where, for example, the witness' memory of the relevant events has faded in the period between his making the statement to the police and his being interviewed by the defence.

In cases where identification will be in issue, the Attorney-General's guidelines (27 May 1976, Hansard Vol 912 No 115) state that the Director of Public Prosecutions will make available any material likely to assist the defence. In particular, he will on request supply to defence solicitors the name and address of any person who claims to have seen 'the criminal in the circumstances of the crime', together with that person's description of the criminal. Although they only apply directly to cases conducted by the Director of Public Prosecutions, the guidelines should be followed by all prosecutors.

A problem similar to that described in the preceding paragraph arises when, unbeknown to the defence, the prosecution have in their possession a statement by one of their witnesses which is materially inconsistent with the evidence he gives. Cross-examination about previous inconsistent statements is one of the most effective ways of discrediting a witness, but, obviously, it is dependent upon the cross-examining party knowing about the previous statement. The rule, therefore, is that if the prosecution has an inconsistent statement by its own witness of which the defence are unaware, the defence should be informed of that fact, and the better view is that they should provide a copy of the statement: see *R* v *Clarke* (1931) 22Cr App R 58. Since the defence, as a result of committal proceedings, always have copies of the depositions or statements under s. 102 of the Magistrates' Courts Act 1980 that the prosecution witnesses have made, the need for the prosecution to inform them of an inconsistent statement is only likely to arise where the witness has made statements to the police in addition to his s. 102 statement.

8.3.3 Securing the attendance of witnesses

In *R* v *Cavanagh* (see Para. 8.3.1) the prosecution were willing but not able to call a witness. It is a problem which may beset both the prosecution and defence, but the court does assist the parties in securing the attendance of the witnesses they need. The examining justices must make either full or conditional witness orders in respect of all persons who gave evidence or whose statements were tendered at committal proceedings, apart from the accused himself and persons whose evidence or statements related only to the accused's character: Criminal Procedure (Attendance of Witnesses) Act 1965 s. 1, and see Para 3.7.2. Further, either the High Court or the Crown Court may issue a witness summons requiring a person to attend to testify for the purposes of any criminal proceeding in the Crown Court: s. 2 of the 1965 Act. A witness summons is useful where the prosecution or defence wish to call a witness who was not involved at the committal proceedings, and who therefore is not subject to a witness order. If a witness who is subject to a witness order or summons fails to attend before the Crown Court when required, the judge can order that a notice be served on him telling him to attend at a time specified in the notice. Alternatively, if a notice has already been served or if there are reasonable grounds for believing that the witness has failed to attend without just excuse, the judge can issue a warrant to arrest him and bring him before the court: s. 4 (2). He can then be remanded in custody or on bail until he gives his evidence. Failure to obey, without just excuse, a witness order or summons is a contempt of court punishable with up to 3 months imprisonment: s. 3.

While the the 1965 Act is a useful aid in securing the attendance of reluctant witnesses, it is worth bearing in mind that no legislation can force a witness to give the evidence desired by the party calling him. A reluctant witness may be a difficult witness, who does more harm than good to the case of the party calling him.

8.3.4 Limits set on defence cross-examination

Broadly speaking, defence counsel may, in the cross-examination of prosecution witnesses, ask any question provided it is relevant to an issue in the case or to the credibility of the witness. Such questions may not, of course, concern inadmissible evidence such as hearsay, and there is some limitation put upon the freedom of defence counsel to cast unfair aspersions upon prosecution witnesses see the Bar Council's Rules contained in the Annual Statement for 1965 at p.27. Although the Rules may be quoted in court, and are of persuasive value, they have no legal force. A barrister who conforms to them cannot be committing an offence against professional discipline, but if a judge orders him to desist from a line of questioning apparently sanctioned by the Rules he must obey the judge: *R* v *McFadden and Cunningham* (1976) 62Cr App R 187.

The Rules provide:

(a) That defence counsel should not 'wantonly or recklessly' attribute the crime with which the accused is charged to another person. Before making such a suggestion, counsel should be satisfied that there are 'facts or circumstances or rational inferences to be drawn from them' so as to raise a 'not unreasonable suspicion' that the crime may have been committed by the person to whom guilt is imputed.

(b)   That when counsel is cross-examining a prosecution witness as to his credit (i.e. suggesting that he is not the kind of person to be believed because of discreditable incidents in his past having no direct relevance to the case) he should only ask a question if he has reasonable grounds for thinking that the imputation conveyed by the question is true. The defence solicitor saying that in his opinion the imputation is true is sufficient grounds for counsel to ask the question. Even if counsel is absolutely confident that the imputation is true, he still should not ask the question if, in his opinion the matter would not affect the witness' credibility (e.g. because it happened a long time ago).

(c)   That when counsel is cross-examining a prosecution witness as to the issues in the case (i.e. matters directly relevant to the guilt or innocence of the accused) he may, and indeed should, put allegations to him that he has been guilty of grave misconduct, provided those allegations are genuinely part of the accused's case. For example, the allegation might be that the witness has totally and deliberately fabricated his evidence, or beat the accused in order to obtain a confession. There is no need for counsel to think that the allegation is, or even might be, true — it is sufficient that the defence put forward by the accused involves the making of the allegation. This is another aspect of the principle that defence counsel's participation in and conduct of the case is divorced from his personal view of its merits. One qualification to the principle has, however, been suggested, namely that counsel should not allege that a prosecution witness obtained a confession from the accused by improper means or was otherwise guilty of grave misconduct towards him unless he intends to call him as a witness. That was the view of Lord Goddard CJ in *R* v *O'Neill* (1950) 34Cr App R 108 and of the Court of Appeal in *R* v *Callaghan* (1979) 69Cr App R 88. However, the Court of Appeal's comments in *R* v *Callaghan* have since been modified extra-judicially. Waller LJ, who gave the judgment of the court in *R* v *Callaghan,* has stated that defence counsel may put the allegations, but he should warn the accused that the judge, in his summing up, will probably comment unfavourably on his failure to testify.

8.3.5   Defence objections to proposed prosecution evidence

The defence may wish to object to part of the prosecution evidence on the grounds that it is inadmissible. If this defence submission is upheld by the judge, it would clearly be prejudicial to the defence case if the jury were to hear reference to such evidence. Thus a procedure is necessary to prevent such an occurrence.

The procedure is that defence counsel, before the start of the trial, warns the prosecuting counsel that he intends to object to certain evidence. No reference is then made to that evidence in the prosecution opening speech. The prosecution evidence is then called in the normal order but, immediately before the disputed evidence would otherwise be introduced, the prosecution will tell the judge that a point of law has arisen and that is is desirable for the jury to retire. If the prosecution fail to do so, the defence may intervene by raising the same point.

In the absence of the jury defence counsel then outlines the nature of his objection. Prosecuting counsel is given an opportunity to reply, and the judge rules on the success or otherwise of the objection. The jury return to court. Whether they hear the disputed evidence or not depends, of course, on the judge's ruling but, in either event, they are told nothing of what occurred in their absence.

Sometimes the judge can only rule on the admissibility of the evidence if he first makes findings of fact about how the evidence was obtained. This most frequently happens when the defence argue that a confession made by the accused is inadmissible because it was involuntary or obtained through a breach of the Judge's Rules. In such a case the prosecution and defence may both call evidence before the judge about how the disputed evidence was obtained. The witnesses, who are liable to cross-examination, give their testimony on a special form of oath, known as the 'voire dire'.

The wording of the oath is — 'I swear by Almighty God that I will true answer make to all such questions as the court shall demand of me.' The hearing before the judge is known as a hearing 'on the voire dire' or, more colloquially, a 'trial within a trial'. Once the judge has heard the evidence and argument from counsel, he rules on whether the disputed evidence is admissible. If it is, the defence may again call, this time before the jury, their evidence on how it was obtained, but only for the purpose of persuading the jury to attach less weight than they would otherwise do to the disputed evidence: *Chan Wei Keung* v *R* [1967] 2AC 160.

The practice of delaying an objection to evidence until the witness is about to give it need not be followed in all cases. If the evidence is crucial to the prosecution case so that without it counsel would find it difficult to make his opening speech, the admissibility of the evidence can be decided as a preliminary issue immediately after the jury have been empanelled (*R* v *Hammond* [1941] 3AER 318). If the evidence is ruled inadmissible, the prosecution might choose to offer no evidence; if it is admitted counsel's problem with his opening speech is overcome.

8.3.6 Additional evidence

A witness may be called for the prosecution at a trial on indictment even though they did not call him at or tender his statement at committal proceedings. The obvious reason for not making use of a witness' evidence at committal proceedings but calling him at the trial is that the prosecution only became aware that the witness could give relevant evidence during the period between committal and the trial's commencement. However, even where the prosecution, at the time of the committal proceedings, know of the evidence the witness is able to give and intend to call him at the Crown Court, they are under no duty to call him or tender his statement before the examining justices: *R* v *Epping and Harlow Justices* ex parte *Massaro* [1973] QB 433. In fact, there is little or nothing to be gained by not revealing the evidence at committal proceedings, since the prosecution at the trial on indictment are not allowed to take the defence by surprise with evidence of which they have given no prior warning. The rule is that a notice of intention to call an additional witness, together with a written account of the evidence it is proposed he should give, should be served by the prosecution on both the defence and the court. Usually they serve a copy of a statement signed by the witness and complying with the requirements of the Criminal Justice Act 1967, s. 9 (see Para. 8.3.7). The advantage of so doing is that, if the defence do not object, the original statement can be tendered in evidence, thus avoiding the need to call the witness.

Where no notice is served, the defence should be granted an adjournment so that they can deal properly with the additional evidence.

8.3.7 Depositions and written statements as evidence

The general rule is that a person who can give evidence about an offence charged in the indictment must be called as a witness at the trial, so that he can be examined by the party calling him and also cross-examined by the other parties. However, some statutes permit depositions and written statements to be tendered in evidence, so that their makers do not have to be called as witnesses. The statutory provisions are available to assist both the prosecution and the defence, but it is usually the prosecution who take advantage of them. The underlying principle which seems to run through the various provisions is that statements are only allowed in evidence where e 'her the matters dealt with in the statement are not disputed, or it is impossible or highly undesirable to call the maker of the statement as a witness. Depositions and written statements are admissible at the trial on indictment in the following circumstances:

(a)   Section 13 of the Criminal Justice Act 1925 (as amended) provides that depositions and statements under s. 102 of the Magistrates' Courts Act 1980 which were made or tendered at the committal proceedings resulting in the accused's committal for trial, may be read as evidence at the trial on indictment if — either the maker of the deposition or statement was made the subject of a conditional witness order by the examining justices and has not subsequently been given notice that he must attend as a witness (see Para. 3.7.2); or he is proved to be dead, insane or too ill to be able to travel; or it is proved that he is being kept out of the way by the accused or his agents. It must also be proved that the deposition or s. 102 statement was correctly made/tendered at the committal proceedings. This may be done by means of a certificate signed by one of the examining justices. Note that where s. 13 applies, the judge is not obliged to allow the deposition or statement to be read but merely has a discretion to permit it. Thus, if all the prosecution witnesses have been conditionally bound to attend at the Crown Court on the assumption that the accused was going to plead guilty, but he in fact pleads not guilty, the judge should adjourn the case so that the witnesses can be called rather than let all the prosecution evidence be read out: *R* v *Collins* [1938] 3AER 130. Similarly, in *R* v *Linley* (1959) Crim LR 123 Ashworth J refused to allow the reading of a deposition taken from a witness who would never be fit enough to attend court, since his evidence was substantially the case for the prosecution and to deprive the defence of the opportunity of challenging that evidence by cross-examination would have been unfair.

(b)   A deposition taken out of court under the Magistrates' Courts Act 1980, s. 105 from a witness who is dangerously ill and unlikely to recover (see Para. 3.8.1) may be read as evidence at the trial of indictment if it is proved that the witness is dead or so ill that there is no reasonable probability of his ever being able to travel to court to give evidence (Criminal Law Amendment Act 1867 s. 6 as amended). The party against whom the deposition is to be read must have been given notice of the intention to take the deposition and an opportunity to cross-examine the witness.

(c)   A deposition taken out of court under the Children and Young Persons Act 1933, s. 42 from a child or young person who was the victim of an assault etc. (see Para. 3.8.3) is admissible in evidence at the trial on indictment if the court is satisfied, upon medical evidence, that the attendance of the child or young person before the court would involve serious danger to his life or health (s. 43 of the 1933 Act). The deposition is only admissible against the accused if he was given notice of the intention to take it and an opportunity to cross-examine the child or young person.

(d)   The Criminal Justice Act 1967, s. 9 which complements s. 102 of the Magistrates' Courts Act 1980, provides for the admissibility of written statements in criminal proceedings other than committal proceedings. To be admissible under s. 9 the statement must be in the same form as a s. 102 statement. In particular, it must be signed and contain a declaration that it is true to the best of the maker's knowledge and belief etc. The party proposing to tender the statement in evidence must serve a copy of it on each of the other parties. If one of those parties, during the period of seven days from the date of the service of the copy on him, serves notice on the party wishing to use the statement that he objects to it going into evidence, the statement cannot be tendered. Thus, s. 9 statements, like s. 102 statements at committal proceedings, are only admissible if all the parties agree, but whereas an objection to a s. 102 statement can be made orally at court, an objection to a s. 9 statement should be made in writing within seven days of a copy being served on the objecting party. Even where a statement is admissible under s. 9 the court may require that the maker attend to give oral evidence. This would be appropriate where the defence dispute the the contents of a s. 9 statement but, through inadvertence, failed to serve notice objecting to it being tendered. Section 9 applies both to summary trials and to trials on indictment. At the latter, it is chiefly used where the prosecution wish to adduce evidence additional to that which they used at committal proceedings (see Para. 8.3.6).

8.3.8 Formal admissions

Reading a witness' deposition or written statement (see preceding paragraph) is a convenient method of proving facts which are not in dispute. Another way of proving an undisputed fact is for the party against whom evidence of the fact would otherwise be led to admit formally that the fact is true. The formal admission is conclusive evidence of the fact admitted, so no evidence on the matter need be adduced. The Criminal Justice Act 1967, s. 10 which applies both to summary trials and to trials on indictment, governs the making of formal admissions.

Section 10 provides that any fact of which oral evidence may be given in criminal proceedings may be formally admitted, for purposes of those proceedings, by either the prosecution or defence. The admission may be made at or before trial, but if made outside court it must be in writing and signed. An admission by the defence must be made by the accused personally or by counsel or solicitor on his behalf. If the admission is made by the accused personally before trial, it must be approved by counsel or solicitor on his behalf either at the time it is made or subsequently. The admission only binds the party making it in the criminal proceedings for purposes of which it was made and in any subsequent criminal proceedings, such as a retrial or appeal, arising out of the original proceedings. Thus, if the defence at a trial on indictment for reckless driving formally admit that on January 1 1981 the accused was driving car number ABC 123 in Acacia Avenue, they cannot deny that fact either at the trial or on an appeal to the Court of Appeal against conviction, but if the accused is subsequently prosecuted for driving while disqualified on the same occasion or is sued in civil proceedings based on the alleged reckless driving, he is free to deny that he was driving the car. The formal admission in the reckless driving proceedings might be used as evidence against him in the other proceedings, but it would not be conclusive evidence. Even in the proceedings for purposes of which it was made a formal admission can be withdrawn with leave of the court: s. 10(4).

A formal admission by the defence under s. 10 must not be confused with a confession by the accused in which he informally admits to facts and matters which are against his interest. A confession, provided it is voluntary and not excluded on account of a breach of the Judges' Rules etc., is admissible evidence to prove the facts stated in it. Often it is very powerful evidence, but it is not conclusive evidence of the facts admitted as a formal admission is. The defence may, and often do, agree that the accused made a confession, but deny the truth of the facts confessed; if they have made a formal admission they cannot deny the fact admitted, unless the court gives leave for the admission to be withdrawn. Unlike an out of court formal admission, a confession need not be in writing and need not be approved by the accused's counsel or solicitor — if it did have to be so approved it is hard to imagine the approval ever being given.

8.4 SUBMISSION OF NO CASE TO ANSWER

After the prosecution evidence, oral and written, has been adduced, prosecuting counsel closes his case by saying 'that is the case for the prosecution', or words to that effect. Defence counsel may then, if he so wishes, submit that there is no case to answer, a submission similar to that which may be made at committal proceedings. If the accused is unrepresented, or even if he is but counsel apparently is not going to make a submission when one is called for, the judge can raise the matter on his own initiative. The submission may be made on all or any of the counts, or on behalf of all or any of the accused joined in the indictment. If a submission on a count succeeds the judge directs the jury to acquit on that count the accused on whose behalf the submission was made.

The procedure is that the jury are asked to leave court. This is so that counsel and the judge can comment freely upon the quality and significance of the evidence without the risk of the jury being influenced by what is said. Once the jury have gone, defence consel makes his submission. The test applied is whether the prosecution have adduced evidence upon which a jury properly directed could properly convict: *R* v *Galbraith* [1981] 1WLR 1039. The judge should not uphold a submission merely because he thinks the prosecution witnesses are not telling the truth — it is for the jury to decide who is a reliable witness and who is not: *R* v *Barker* 65Cr App R 287. The question for the judge is whether the minimum evidence necessary to establish that the accused committed the crime alleged has been called. If it has, the case should be left to the jury, but if it has not they should be told to acquit. Where there is no evidence to link the accused with the offence (e.g. because the main prosecution witness has failed to give the evidence that he was expected to give) the prosecution have obviously failed to adduce the minimum evidence required. Even where there is some evidence against the accused, the judge should uphold the submission if the evidence is tenuous or vague or inherently weak so that, if the jury were to give it all the weight it might reasonably be given, they still could not properly convict. Where, however, the prosecution witnesses have given evidence which, if accepted as truthful, clearly establishes that the accused committed the offence, the jury should determine where the truth lies, even if the judge happens to think that each of the witnesses is lying.

After defence counsel has made his submission, the prosecution are given an opportunity to reply. The judge then announces his decision, and the jury are brought back into court. If the judge has decided that there is no case to answer on all counts, he explains briefly to the jury the decision he has reached. He then asks them to appoint a foreman to speak for them, and the clerk of court takes from the foreman on each count a verdict of not guilty upon the judge's direction. If the decision was that there is no case to answer on one or more counts, but there is a case to answer on other counts, the judge tells the jury that at the end of the trial he will be directing them to return a verdict of not guilty on the counts in respect of which there is no case, and so, for the remainder of the trial, they should ignore those counts. However, on the remaining counts, the case will proceed as normal. If the submission failed on all counts, the jury are told nothing of what went on in their absence.

In one important type of case the correct approach to submissions of no case has been explained by the Court of Appeal with some precision. Where the main issue in the case is one of mistaken identity (i.e. the case against the accused depends substantially on the correctness of one or more identifications of him which the defence allege to be mistaken), the judge should assess the quality of the identifying evidence. If it is poor, and if there is no other evidence to support the correctness of the identification, the judge should withdraw the case from the jury: *R* v *Turnbull and others* [1977] QB 224. Identification evidence is poor if the witnesses only saw whoever committed the offence for a short space of time, or saw him in circumstances of fear or confusion, or if the lighting conditions were bad, or if a long time elapsed between seeing the culprit and picking out the accused at an identification parade. The detailed guidance given to judges on how they should decide submissions of no case in identification cases is necessary because judicial experience has shown mistaken identifications by honest witnesses to be a prime factor in wrongful convictions.

8.5 THE DEFENCE CASE

After the prosecution case has been closed or, if a submission of no case to answer is made, after that, the defence presents its case. Since it is for the prosecution to prove each element of the offence charged beyond reasonable doubt, the defence is under no obligation to adduce any evidence whatsoever. Defence counsel can, without calling evidence of his own, submit to the jury in a closing speech that the accused should be acquitted as the prosecution evidence fails to establish their case to the requisite standard of proof. Such a strategy may be right when the prosecution's case is weak, but in general there are obvious dangers in the jury only hearing evidence favouring the prosecution. It is therefore unusual for the defence not to call evidence, although sometimes they adopt a tactic which is, in effect, half way between doing and not doing so. This tactic is to have the accused make an unsworn statement from the dock (see Para. 8.5.2).

8.5.1 Defence opening speech

If defence counsel is calling evidence as to the facts of the case other than or in addition to the evidence of the accused, he has the right to make an opening speech to the jury. In that speech he may both outline his own case and criticise the evidence which has been called by the prosecution. Where the only defence evidence is from the accused, or from the accused and witnesses who speak only as to his good character, defence counsel does not have an opening speech: Criminal Evidence Act 1898, s. 2.

8.5.2 Defence evidence

The accused is a competent but not compellable witness for the defence (Criminal Evidence Act 1898, s. 1) — i.e. he is entitled, but cannot be forced, to give evidence. If he does testify he is nearly always the first defence witness. The precise position is that if the accused is the only defence witness as to the facts he must be called immediately after the prosecution case or submission of no case, and before any character witnesses (Criminal Evidence Act 1898, s. 2). If others also testify to the facts for the defence, the accused's evidence should still be given first, unless one of the other witnesses gives evidence which is not in dispute and it is convenient to hear him before the accused (e.g. because he has an urgent appointment): see *R v Smith* [1968] 1 WLR 636. This is partly because he is the person best able to tell the jury what the defence case is, and partly because he is in court throughout the trial, unlike the other witnesses (both for the prosecution and defence) who are kept out of court until they come to give their evidence. Should the accused testify after his other witnesses, there would be room for suspicion that he had adjusted his evidence to fit in with the evidence he had heard from them. Whether or not the accused is called, the defence may call other witnesses to testify as to the facts in dispute at the trial and perhaps the character of the accused. In addition, the defence may take advantage of the various statutory provisions permitting the reading of depositions and written statements (see Para. 8.3.7).

Details about the accused as a witness must be sought in the books on evidence. Very briefly, the position is that he is treated like any other witness expect that:

(a)   He can be asked questions which tend to incriminate him as to the offence charged, and to that extent cannot, as witnesses normally can, claim a privilege against self-incrimination: Criminal Evidence Act 1898, s. 1(e). It would obviously be absurd if the accused could give evidence exonerating himself and then avoid any questions in cross-examination which might tend to show that he had committed the offence for which he is being tried.

(b)   Again unlike other witnesses, he is protected from questions in cross-examination designed to discredit him by showing that he has previous convictions or is of bad character. He loses this protection if his defence has cast imputations on the character of a prosecution witness, or if he has given evidence of his own good character, or if his evidence has made it less likely that another accused joined in the same indictment will be acquitted: Criminal Evidence Act 1898, s. 1(f).

Nothing should be said or done to suggest to the jury that the accused, as a witness, is inferior to the other witnesses in the case. This is illustrated in a symbolic way by the fact that in the absence of compelling reasons to the contrary (e.g. the risk of violence or attempted escape), the accused should testify from the witness box not the dock: Criminal Evidence Act 1898, s. 1(g). However, being treated essentially like the other witnesses is often a dubious advantage for the accused, as he is exposed to cross-examination by prosecuting counsel. This is particularly damaging where he has previous convictions, but has lost the protection against questions about previous convictions mentioned above. Sometimes, rather than run the risks inherent in cross-examination, the accused does not give evidence, but makes an unsworn statement about the case while standing in the dock. He is not then subject to questioning, either by his own counsel or prosecuting counsel or anybody else. The advantage of an unsworn statement is that it avoids cross-examination; the disadvantage is that, for that very reason, the jury are unlikely to attach much weight to it. The right to make a statement is preserved by the Criminal Evidence Act 1898, s. 1(h). The proper time for it is at the end of the defence case, immediately before the prosecution closing speech.

8.5.3 Alibi evidence

The Criminal Justice Act 1967, s. 11 (see Para. 3.7.3) provides that, unless notice of particulars of alibi is given to the prosecution at or within seven days of the close of committal proceedings, the defence may only adduce evidence in support of the alibi with leave of the judge. Similarly, if the notice does not give sufficient particulars in respect of one of the proposed alibi witnesses, that witness can only be called with leave. In *R* v *Sullivan* [1971] 1QB 253 the Court of Appeal held that the judge's discretion to allow alibi evidence notwithstanding failure to comply with s. 11 of the 1967 Act must be exercised judicially. The aim of the legislation was not to limit the time the defence had to 'exercise their ingenuity for the purpose of inventing an alibi' (per Salmon LJ at p.258), but to ensure that the prosecution have enough warning of an alibi to check on its genuineness and secure the attendance at court of any witnesses who might be able to disprove it. Accordingly, the fact that notice is given outside the statutory seven day period does not by itself justify a judge in excluding alibi evidence. The question is whether the prosecution have had, or could by means of an adjournment be given, sufficient opportunity to investigate the defence allegations. If so, leave to call the evidence should be granted. An example of a case where leave could properly be refused is one where the prosecution can prove to the judge's satisfaction that the information in the notice is spurious or useless (e.g. old or false addresses are given for proposed alibi witnesses).

> The facts of *R* v *Sullivan* (supra) were that S., having been committed for trial on 10 April 1969, did not obtain legal representation until 9 June, two days before the scheduled start of his trial. Realising that no notice of particulars of alibi had been served, his solicitors immediately wrote to the prosecution with some of the necessary information. The particulars were completed by further details given on what should have been the first day of the trial. The prosecution were given a three week adjournment to investigate the alibi. Nevertheless, at the resumed hearing the judge did not allow the defence to call alibi evidence, holding that the purpose of s. 11 was to limit the time for fabricating alibis. The Court of Appeal's decision was that the adjournment had given the prosecution sufficient time to check the alibi. Therefore — 'on the basis of the only evidence before the [judge], the court has no hesitation in concluding that the [judge] wrongly exercised his discretion in excluding the alibi evidence on the ground which he gave, namely, that it had been supplied too late' (per Salmon LJ at p.259). At the appeal allegations were made that the defence had been deliberately unhelpful about supplying particulars, and had, in particular, given inaccurate addresses for two of the three witnesses they proposed to call. Had those allegations been made and properly proved at the trial, the judge might have had grounds for excluding the evidence of alibi.

8.5.4 More than one accused in the indictment

If two or more accused are charged in one indictment and are separately represented their cases are presented in the order in which their names appear on the indictment. Thus, if Robert Smith precedes John Brown on the indictment, counsel for Smith makes his opening speech (if he has the right to one), calls Smith and calls his other witnesses; counsel for Brown then opens his case and so forth. There is little authority on who should be named first on an indictment, although the accused who is regarded as the principal offender is normally put first. It may seem strange, however, that the order of the defence cases depends on how prosecuting counsel or an officer of the Crown Court chooses to draft the indictment.

Where two of more accused are jointly represented they are treated as, in effect, presenting a joint defence. Counsel has one opening speech on behalf of both accused, and may then call them in turn to give evidence.

8.5.5 The unrepresented accused

Although an accused at the Crown Court is encouraged to obtain legal representation, he is entitled to conduct his own defence throughout, or, indeed, to start with the benefit of legal representation and dismiss his counsel at any stage of the trial. The judge should assist an unrepresented accused in matters such as the cross-examination of the prosecution witnesses, the giving of his own evidence, and the examination in chief of any witnesses he may choose to call. Often a judge has to explain to the accused that when he cross-examines a witness he must ask questions rather than make a speech of his own disagreeing with what the witness has said. It is particularly important that at the close of the prosecution case the accused should be told that he may give evidence himself or make a statement from the dock, and that he may also call witnesses. The judge's failure to ask the accused if he wishes to call evidence in his defence may lead to any conviction being quashed: *R* v *Carter* (1960) 44Cr App R 225.

8.5.6   Presence of the accused

The accused must be present at the commencement of a trial on indictment in order to plead. After he has pleaded the trial may proceed in his absence only in 'very exceptional circumstances': *R* v *Lee Kun* [1916] 1KB 337, per Lord Reading CJ at p. 341. It is a matter of elementary fairness that the accused should hear what is said for and against him, and be in a position to answer the prosecution case. His presence may, however, be dispensed with if he makes it impossible for the trial to continue with him there, either by behaving in an unruly fashion or by deliberately absenting himself. In the latter case the judge has a choice between proceeding with the trial without the accused, and discharging the jury from giving a verdict so that, on his eventually being brought before the court, the accused can be tried by a fresh jury. Where, as is usually the case, the accused's absence, either at the start of the trial or at some later stage, is due to his failure to attend court to answer to his bail, the judge may issue a warrant for his arrest: Bail Act 1976, s. 7(1).

> An example of a judge correctly continuing a trial in the accused's absence is provided by *R* v *Jones* (No 2) [1972] 1WLR 887. Jones, who was one of several accused charged with conspiracy to defraud and other offences, was granted bail for the period of the trial. After a prosecution case lasting four weeks, counsel submitted unsuccessfully that there was no case to answer. On the next day, it was discovered that J had 'deliberately, to use a colloquialism, jumped his bail' (per Roskill LJ at p.888). The judge rejected a defence application to discharge the jury. J was convicted and sentenced to 5 years imprisonment in his absence. In giving their judgment on the propriety of the judge's decision, the Court of Appeal adopted the language of Hood J in *R* v *Abrahams* (1895) 21 Vict LR 343 — 'the judge may proceed without the presence of the prisoner, where the absence is voluntary. He has in law a discretion, but that discretion should be exercised with great reluctance and with a view rather to the due administration of justice than to the convenience or comfort of anyone'. On the facts of *R* v *Jones* the judge plainly exercised his discretion properly.
>
> If the absence of the accused is not genuinely voluntary (e.g. he has been threatened with violence should he attend court and give evidence in his own defence which implicates a co-accused), or if he absconds at a very early stage of the trial (e.g. just after the prosecution opening) the judge should discharge the jury rather than proceed in his absence.

8.6   COUNSEL'S CLOSING SPEECHES

After the close of the defence case (or the last of the defence cases where there are more than one accused separately represented) prosecuting counsel may sum up his case to the jury. In doing so he should continue to regard himself as a 'minister of justice' (see Para. 8.1.1), not an advocate striving at all costs for a conviction. In his speech he can for example remind the jury of the most cogent parts of the prosecution evidence, and comment upon any implausibilities in the defence case. He may not comment upon the failure of the accused to give evidence: Criminal Evidence Act 1898, s. 1(b). The only situation where the prosecution does not have the right to a closing speech is where an unrepresented accused did not have the right to an opening speech (i.e. did not call evidence as to the facts other than his own). It does not follow, however, that whenever counsel has the right to a speech he should necessarily make one. If no evidence is called in the defence of a represented accused there will rarely be any need for a prosecution speech, although they are entitled to one: *R* v *Bryant and Oxley* [1978] 2WLR 589. In *R* v *Bryant and Oxley,* Watkin J stated *obiter dicta* that 'the majority of speeches by prosecuting and defence counsel should bear the becoming hallmark of brevity' — advice which, perhaps, is not followed on all occasions.

The last word, in a criminal trial, leaving aside the judge's summing up, belongs to the defence. After the prosecution closing speech, defence counsel sums up his case to the jury. He has a broad discretion to say anything he considers desirable on the whole case, but he should not allege as fact matters of which no evidence has been given. The latter rule applies equally to prosecuting counsel, but defence counsel may be more tempted to transgress it. If there are two or more accused separately represented the speeches on their behalves are given in the order in which their names appear on the indictment. An unrepresented accused can, of course, make both a closing and, if he is entitled to one, an opening speech on his own behalf.

8.7 THE JUDGE'S SUMMING UP

The final and very significant stage of a trial on indictment is the judge's summing up. In it he directs the jury on the law and assists them in their task of deciding the facts. While it is impossible to know the reasons for a jury returning a certain verdict, a reasonable assumption is that the judge's apparent view of the case sways them considerably. Having heard persuasive and eloquent speeches from the various counsel in the case which usually arrive at directly opposite conclusions, the jurors turn with relief to the impartial judge who can put the arguments in perspective, identify the 'red herrings' and clarify the issues. Counsel, of course, are not always as convinced of the impartiality and wisdom of the judge as the jurors may be.

The following matters are nearly always dealt with in a summing up:

(a) The judge explains to the jury his and their respective roles — i.e. the judge decides on the law, and they must accept whatever he says about the law; the jury decide what facts have been proved, in which task they may be helped but are in no way bound by what he says.

(b) The jury are told that it is for the prosecution to prove the guilt of the accused, that the accused does not have to prove anything, and that, unless they are satisfied beyond reasonable doubt on all the evidence that the accused committed the offence charged, they must acquit him. The Court of Appeal's guidance on how best to explain to a jury the standard of proof has not been consistent. Sometimes they have urged the abandonment of the classic formula — 'You must be satisfied beyond reasonable doubt' — in favour of 'You must be satisfied so that you are sure'. The most recent case on the subject (*Ferguson* v *The Queen* [1979] 1AER 877) suggested an amalgam of the two phrases — 'You must be satisfied beyond reasonable doubt so that you feel sure of the defendant's guilt'.

(c) The judge defines the offence charged, explaining the matters which the prosecution have to prove in order to establish guilt. If possible he keeps his statement of the law simple and basic. For example, if Smith is charged with stealing Jones' umbrella and the defence is mistaken identity, the judge might say something like — 'Members of the jury, you all know what is meant by stealing — it is taking somebody else's property dishonestly, knowing it does not belong to you, and intending that they shall not get it back again. Now, Mr Jones has told you that at 1pm he left his umbrella in the cloakroom, and that at 2pm when he returned to collect it it had gone, and he did not see it again until he was shown it at the police station. That evidence was not disputed by the defence, so you may not have much difficulty in deciding — it's a matter entirely for you, ladies and gentlemen — that somebody stole the umbrella. The question is, was it this defendant?...' If the defence raised by Smith was mistake (he took the umbrella thinking it was his own) or an unauthorised loan (he took the umbrella for use in a heavy shower intending to return it), the judge would have to emphasise, in the one case, that the appropriation must be dishonest and, in the other, that there must be an intention permanently to deprive.

(d)   Depending on the evidence called in the particular case, it may be necessary to explain some evidential points to the jury. For example, the basic direction on the burden and standard of proof is inadequate where, on an assault charge, the accused raises the defence of acting in reasonable self defence, for the jury might be left with the impression that the accused has to show that he was so acting. The judge should therefore tell the jury expressly that it is for the prosecution to prove beyond reasonable doubt that the accused was not acting in reasonable self defence. Similar principles apply where the defence raised is one of alibi. Conversely, if the burden of establishing a defence is, by way of exception to the general rule, upon the accused (e.g. where a defence of diminished responsibility is raised upon a charge of murder) the judge explains both that and the standard of proof required of the defence (i.e. upon a balance of probabilities). Questions of corroboration often call for a careful direction in the summing up. If for example an accomplice testifies for the prosecution, the judge must warn the jury of the danger of convicting on his uncorroborated evidence, define for them what is meant by corroboration, and indicate the evidence in the case which is and which is not capable of being corroboration. Similarly, where the defence is mistaken identity the judge should mention the special need for caution before convicting on the basis of the evidence from the identifying witnesses (see *R* v *Turnbull and others* [1977] QB 224 for full details of what the judge should say in mistaken identity cases). If the accused's character, good or bad, has been put into evidence, the judge should explain the bearing it has upon the case — usually the direction will be that it may help the jury in deciding what weight to attach to the accused's evidence but it does not directly go to prove that he did or did not commit the offence charged. Lastly, the judge may have to deal with the fact that the accused stayed silent when questioned by the police about the offence and that he may have chosen not to give evidence at the trial. He should emphasise that, at least after caution, it is the right of the accused to say nothing, and it is also his right not to testify. Although the Court of Appeal's decisions are not entirely consistent, criticisms by the judge of the accused's failure to disclose his defence to the police have usually led to any conviction being quashed. In commenting on failure to testify the judge may say that the jury have been deprived of the opportunity of hearing the accused's story tested in cross-examination, but he must also say that they must not assume that the accused is guilty because he has not gone into the witness box (see *R* v *Bathurst* [1968] 2QB 99 and *R* v *Mutch* [1973] 1AER 178 for the stronger comment permissible in exceptional cases). The above is merely a list of evidential points which commonly arise — depending on the evidence in the particular case many other points may have to be considered in the summing up.

(e) If two or more accused are joined in one indictment, the judge must direct the jury to consider the case of each accused separately. In particular, if evidence has been given against A which, although inadmissible against B, is prejudicial to his defence (e.g. A has made a confession in B's absence which implicates both himself and B), the jury must be told to ignore that evidence when reaching their verdict on B. Similarly, if an accused is charged in one indictment with two or more offences, the jury are warned to give separate consideration to each count. The fact that they have decide to convict or acquit the accused on count one is irrelevant to their decision on count two, and vice versa. Where there is a striking similarity between the offence charged in one count and that charged in a second count (see *DPP* v *Boardman* [1975] AC 421) the judge has the difficult task of explaining that, while the evidence in respect of each count is admissible to support the prosecution case on the other count, the jury must nonetheless reach independent verdicts on each count.

(f) The last part of the summing up deals with the evidence in the case. Using the note of evidence which he takes during the trial, the judge reminds the jury of the evidence they have heard and comments upon it. Judges vary in the way they discharge this part of their duty. Some merely read out the significant parts of each witness' evidence, concentrating upon the evidence in chief, others seek to define the issues in the case, and relate the evidence to those issues. Some keep their own view of the case discreetly hidden, others, whether directly or indirectly, let the jury know their opinion of the facts. In *R* v *Charles* (1979) 68Cr App R 334, Lawton LJ commented upon the desirable method of summing up in a long case. In a trial which lasted for a total of 35 days and involved complex allegations of fraudulent business dealings, the summing up took three days. After an introductory survey of the law and issues relevant to the case, the judge adopted the technique of reading out from his notes what each witness had said. The Court of Appeal criticised his approach because, in long fraud cases especially, it is important for the judge to 'analyse the issues and relate the evidence to the issues' (p.341). Merely reading a note of the evidence is unsatisfactory, not least because 'it must bore the jury to sleep' (p.339). In general, judges 'should not indulge in long-winded summings up which are more likely to confuse than help the jury' (p.341). Whatever method of summing up the judge uses, it is essential that he put the defence before the jury in a form which they can appreciate. He is entitled to express his opinion on that defence (or, indeed, on any of the facts of the case), provided that he leaves the issues of fact to the jury to determine. Thus, in *R* v *O'Donnell* (1917) 12Cr App R 219, a conviction was upheld where the judge said that the prisoner's story was a 'remarkable' one and contrary to previous statements he had made, but in *R* v *Canny* (1945) 30Cr App R 143 repeatedly telling the jury that the defence was 'absurd' and that there was no foundation for defence allegations amounts to a direction to find the case against the accused proved. The conviction was therefore quashed.

(g) At the very end of the summing up, the judge advises the jury to appoint one of themselves to be their foreman. The foreman will act as their spokesman and, in due course, announce their verdict. Finally, the judge tells them to retire, consider their verdict and seek to reach a unanimous decision.

Before he starts summing up, the judge may ask counsel to assist him on the law and facts with which he is to deal, but he should never seek counsel's help after the jury have retired, and only in exceptional circumstances should he discuss the law with counsel after finishing his summing up but before the jury's retirement: *R* v *Cocks* (1976) 63Cr App R 79. Asking counsel to interrupt the summing up in order to correct any errors as they are made is also unwise as it may disrupt the jury's train of thought and appear to undermine the judge's authority (*R* v *Charles* supra, where counsel intervened 33 times in the course of a three day summing up). If, having listened to the summing up, prosecuting counsel appreciates that there has been some misdirection of law or fact, he may raise the matter with the judge before the jury retire so that the error can be corrected. It is not clear if there is an obligation upon defence counsel to mention any error that he may notice. James LJ in *R* v *Cocks* (supra at p.82) thought there was not, but dicta in *R* v *Southgate* (1963) 47Cr App R 252 and *R* v *Charles* (supra) are to the contrary. The difficulty is that defence counsel owes a duty to both the court and his client, and it may be in the latter's interest for an error to go uncorrected so that, should there be a conviction, it will be quashed on appeal.

Counsel should take a note of the summing up. This will assist him when advising on the merits of an appeal and drafting the initial Grounds of Appeal, at which stage a transcript of the shorthand writer's note of the summing up is unlikely to be available.

8.8   EVIDENCE GIVEN OUT OF THE NORMAL ORDER

The prosecution may not in general call evidence after they have closed their case, or even cross-examine the accused about matters which they could have proved as part of their case had they so chosen.

The rule is illustrated by *R* v *Day* [1940] 1AER 402 and *R* v *Kane* (1977) 65Cr App R 270. In the former case, D's conviction for forging a cheque was quashed because, after the defence had closed their case, the judge allowed the prosecution to call a handwriting expert to compare the writing on the cheque with a sample of D's writing. In *R* v *Kane,* also, the conviction was quashed, prosecuting counsel having cross-examined K about admissions he allegedly made in the course of an 'off the record' conversation with a police officer — no evidence of the conversation had been produced by the prosecution in their case.

The exceptions to the general rule are as follows:

(a)   Evidence to disprove an alibi may, subject to the court's directions, be given before or after the evidence in support of it: Criminal Justice Act 1967, s. 11(4).

(b)   If, in the course of the defence case, a matter arises *ex improviso*, which no human ingenuity can foresee, the prosecution may adduce evidence to rebut the defence evidence on the matter. In *R* v *Blick* (1966) 50Cr App R 280, for example, B who, according to the police, was arrested following a chase and charged with robbery, testified that at the time of the chase he was in a public lavatory. The prosecution were correctly allowed to reopen their case and call evidence that at the relevant time the lavatory was closed for repairs. No human ingenuity could have foreseen that access to a public lavatory would be relevant to the case against B. (The difficulty which arose in *R* v *Blick* would today be avoided by the defence having to give notice of particulars of alibi, and the court being able, in all cases where alibi is in issue, to direct that the evidence to disprove it be given after the evidence in support — see (a) above). *R* v *Blick* may be compared with *R* v *Day* (supra) where the prosecution should have anticipated that a handwriting expert would be needed to help establish that the writing on the cheque was D's.

(c)   The judge has a discretion to allow the prosecution to call a witness who was not available to them before they closed their case, even though his evidence does not go to rebut a matter raised *ex improviso* by the defence. Cases where it is proper to exercise the discretion are rare. Leave to call the witness should be refused if the only reason for the prosecution not calling him before they closed their case was that they wished to 'keep him up their sleeve' or had not been sufficiently diligent in preparing the case. In *R* v *Doran* (1972) 56Cr App R 429 prosecuting counsel was informed, after he had closed his case, that two members of the public sitting in the gallery, had realised that they could give relevant evidence. He was allowed to call them, and the Court of Appeal confirmed the conviction because, although the case did not fall within the principle of (b) above, the prosecution could not have found out about the witnesses before closing their case.

(d)   Where the prosecution inadvertently omit to lead evidence of a purely formal nature the judge may allow them to reopen their case and repair the omission. Evidence that a steamroller is made mainly of iron or steel comes within the category of evidence of a purely formal nature (*R* v *McKenna* (1957) 40Cr App R 65, where M was charged with exporting manufactured goods 'wholly or mainly of iron or steel'). The principle has been extended somewhat to cover cases where the prosecution by mistake fail to call evidence identifying the accused as the person who committed the *actus reus* of the offence. Even in a case where identity is not in dispute, this could hardly be said to be evidence of a purely formal nature, but it seems that the court has a discretion to let prosecuting counsel reopen his case.

(e)   The rule of evidence that a party cross-examining the other side's witness about matters going only to the witness' credibility, not the issues in the case, cannot adduce his own evidence to rebut the answer he receives in cross-examination does not apply if the witness is asked about his previous convictions, previous inconsistent statement or bias. Therefore, if prosecuting counsel asks a defence witness about, for example, his previous convictions and the witness denies having any, the prosecution can adduce evidence to prove the convictions even though their case will obviously have been closed before the defence witness was called to testify.

Where there are proper grounds for allowing the prosecution to reopen their case, their evidence may be called during or at the close of the defence case, or even after counsel's closing speeches: *R* v *Flynn* (1958) 42Cr App R 15. The judge also has a broad discretion to allow the defence to reopen their case. In *R* v *Sanderson* [1953] 1WLR 392, where a defence witness did not arrive until the summing up was virtually completed, the judge rightly allowed the witness to testify at the end of the summing up, and then delivered a supplementary summing up dealing with his evidence.

8.9   POWER OF JUDGE TO CALL WITNESSES

The judge has a right to call a witness if, in his opinion, it is necessary for him to do so in the interests of justice.

The judge asks the witness questions, and then allows either or both counsel to cross-examine. However, the judge's power to call a witness should be exercised sparingly. If the witness is likely to favour the prosecution and they have already closed their case, the judge should only call him if the circumstances are such that he could accede to a prosecution application to reopen their case were one to be made. One situation where a judge might call a witness is where the witness is named on the back of the indictment but the prosecution decline to call him (see *R* v *Oliva* [1965] 1WLR 1028 and Para. 8.3.1).

The judge has a discretion to recall for further questioning witnesses who have been called by the prosecution or defence, provided this does not allow the prosecution improperly to reopen their case. The power to recall witnesses includes power to recall the accused himself if he has testified. Where assertions are made by counsel or witnesses in the course of the defence case which should have been put to a prosecution witness in the course of cross-examination, the witness can be recalled to deal with the assertions. It is wrong, however, to recall a witness merely so that his evidence can be heard twice over.

9   The Verdict

9.1   RETIREMENT OF THE JURY.

When the judge has finished his summing up, a court usher takes an oath to keep the jury in some 'private and convenient place', to prevent anybody speaking to them without leave of the court, and not to speak to them himself 'except it be to ask them if they are agreed upon their verdict'. Having so sworn, the usher, who is referred to as the jury bailiff, leads the jury to their room and stations himself outside. During the period of their retirement the jury are kept together so that through discussion and argument they can arrive at a unanimous verdict (or, at least, at a verdict upon which ten of them are agreed). As far as possible, they are kept apart from everybody else, because no outside influences should affect a jury's verdict. They and they alone must reach a decision on the guilt or innocence of the accused, and they should reach that decision solely on the basis of the evidence and speeches they have heard in court combined with their own experience of life and good sense. Three interconnected rules are designed to ensure that nothing untoward occurs while the jury are considering their verdict.

First, the jury must stay in the custody of the jury bailiff. This means that the jury bailiff must be in a position to prevent anybody speaking to the jury or any individual member of it. He should not himself go into the jury room or speak to the jurors unless the judge orders him to do so (e.g. to pass on a message from the judge or ask a question). Convictions have been quashed where either the whole jury or a juror left the jury bailiff's custody. In *R* v *Neal* [1949] 2KB 590, the jury, with the judge's permission but after having retired to consider their verdict, left the court building to go to a restaurant for lunch. The jury bailiff did not go with them. Having lunched, they returned to court and convicted N. The conviction was quashed because they had been out of the bailiff's custody for a substantial period, during which time numerous persons could have spoken to them about the case. Similarly, in *R* v *Ketteridge* [1915] 1KB 467, Ketteridge's conviction was quashed because a member of the jury, instead of retiring with his colleagues to the jury room, by mistake left the court building and was absent for fifteen minutes before rejoining the other jurors. Just as in *R* v *Neal* there was ample opportunity for non-jury members to speak to the juror.

Second, the jury should not leave the jury room except to return to court to ask questions or receive further directions from the judge. Permission to leave their room can, however, be given by the judge in cases of 'evident necessity': *R* v *Neal* supra. Although the Court of Criminal Appeal in *R* v *Neal* did not find it necessary to decide whether the judge could properly have allowed the jury to go to a restaurant in the custody of the jury bailiff, the obtaining of refreshments away from the court building could hardly now amount to an 'evident necessity' as the jury may have sandwiches brought into them (they may be allowed reasonable refreshment at their own expense — Juries Act, 1974 s. 15). Where the jury are far from agreement and it is getting late, the judge may decide that there is an evident necessity for them to be taken to a hotel for the night, so that they can return to their room the next morning refreshed by a good sleep. This is only appropriate in very long or complex cases where it is reasonable for the jury to take a day or more to consider their verdict. Normally, if a jury have been given several hours to deliberate and are still nowhere near a verdict, the judge discharges them from giving a verdict (see Para 9.6). If the jury are kept at an hotel for the night or allowed to leave their room for any reason, they must still remain in the custody of the jury bailiff.

The third rule, which is really a corollary of the second, is that the jury must not separate, except, again, in cases of evident necessity with the permission of the judge: Lord Goddard CJ in *R* v *Neal* (supra) summed up the position — 'No doubt if a juror is taken ill or wishes to relieve himself the court can permit the bailiff to take him from the jury room for the purpose of medical attention or of going to the water closet but he must remain in the charge of the bailiff' — otherwise the jurors must stay together in their room. Prior to their retiring to consider their verdict, however, the judge has an unfettered discretion to allow the jury to separate (Juries Act 1974, s. 13) which he will automatically exercise so as to allow them to leave the court building at midday adjournments and return home for overnight adjournments. On the first occasion when the jury separate the judge should warn them not to talk about the case to anybody not on the jury: *R* v *Prime* (1973) 57Cr App R 632.

An infringement of the rules described above, however trivial, is an irregularity in the course of the trial. but it will not lead to a conviction being quashed by the Court of Appeal unless it 'goes to the root of the case'. Thus, in *R* v *Alexander* [1974] 1WLR 422 a conviction was upheld where, after the jury had left court in the charge of the jury bailiff, one of them returned to collect an exhibit (the judge had told them that they might see any exhibit they wanted). Technically the juror had both separated himself from his colleagues and left the custody of the jury bailiff, but since the separation was for a matter of seconds only and since he had been observed by defence counsel throughout those few seconds, the irregularity did not go to the root of the case. In *R* v *Goodson* [1975] 1WLR 549, on the other hand, the jury bailiff allowed a juror to leave the jury room to use a telephone. By chance, prosecuting counsel discovered what was happening, and took steps to prevent the juror rejoining his colleagues. The judge discharged him from the jury, and the remaining eleven convicted. The Court of Appeal held that the irregularity was such that the conviction had to be quashed. The bailiff's error, for which the court had to take ultimate responsibility, had deprived G 'of the voice of one juror in the jury room' (per James LJ at p.552).

9.1.1 Questions from the jury

Even though they have retired to consider their verdict, the jury may ask the judge for further explanation of matters of law arising in the case. They may also ask him to remind them of any part of the evidence. If they ask for information about a point on which no evidence has, in fact, been given the judge must tell them there is no evidence on the matter and that they must decide the case on the evidence they have heard. It is an absolute rule that no evidence shall be adduced before the jury after they have begun to consider their verdict: *R* v *Owen* [1952] 2QB 362.

Where the jury have a question or communication for the judge, they should write it down and give it to the jury bailiff, who passes it on to the judge. The note should also be shown to counsel. If the matter can be very simply dealt with, such as by a 'yes' or 'no' answer, the reply may be delivered through the jury bailiff without the jury leaving their room. Otherwise the jury are brought into court, the judge confirms with them the question they wish to raise and gives his reply to it. When the jury do not return to court the communication from them and the judge's reply must be read in open court before the bailiff delivers the reply. This is to avoid any suggestion that a secret message has been passed to the jury, inducing them to convict.

> A deviation from the procedure described above amounts to an irregularity in the conduct of the trial, but it will not lead to a conviction being quashed unless it goes to the root of the case (*R* v *Furlong* [1950] 1AER 636 — the principle is the same as that governing appeals on the basis that the jury left the bailiff's custody or wrongly separated). *R* v *Sahota* (1980) Crim LR 678 and *R* v *Green* [1950] 1AER 38 provide examples of deviations sufficiently serious to result in successful appeals, but in *R* v *Furlong* (supra), where the jury's question and the judge's reply were read in open court after the reply was delivered to the jury, the irregularity did not go to the root of the case.

9.1.2   The privacy of the jury room

The extreme reluctance of the Court of Appeal to quash a conviction because of any inadequacy, or apparent bias, or misconduct by a juror has already been noted (see Para. 7.5). This reluctance is complemented by a total refusal to enquire, for purposes of an appeal, into what took place in the jury room. The general public interest requires that jurors should feel free, in the privacy of their room, to express whatever view they wish about the case, without the fear that a wrong word could be seized upon by the defence, following a conviction, and made the subject of an appeal. While the broad principle is understandable it may sometimes work apparent injustice in the case of an individual appellant. In *R* v *Thompson* [1962] 1AER 65 the Court of Criminal Appeal refused to hear evidence that the jury, in a case where T's character had not been revealed in evidence, were going to acquit until the foreman read to them a list of T's previous convictions which, in some unexplained way, had come into his possession. Similarly, in *R* v *Roads* [1967] 2QB 108 evidence that one of the jurors had not agreed with the verdict of guilty was not received by the court.

9.2   RETURNING THE VERDICT

At the end of his summing up the judge directs the jury to try to reach a unanimous verdict. For when the jury can return a verdict by a majority, see Para 9.5. If they succeed in reaching a unanimous verdict, they come into court, and the clerk of the court asks the foreman if they have reached a verdict on which they are all agreed. He answers 'yes', after which their verdict on each count is announced. The jury must return a verdict on each count, and in respect of each accused joined in a count, unless they are discharged from giving a verdict on a certain count (see Para. 9.3). They can, of course, find an accused guilty on some counts and not guilty on others, or they can find one accused guilty and his co-accused not guilty. They can also find the accused guilty of, for example, stealing a part but not all of the goods named in a count for theft: *R* v *Furlong* [1950] 1AER 636. In asking for the verdicts, the clerk says something like — 'On count one, which charges the defendant with theft, do you find the defendant guilty or not guilty?... On count two, which charges the defendant with going equipped to steal, do you find him guilty or not guilty?'... and so on, through the indictment. If there are more than one accused joined in the indictment the clerk obviously has to name the accused in respect of whom he requests a verdict, rather than just referring to the defendant. Where, after a submission of no case to answer, the judge ruled that there was no case on count one, but that the trial should proceed on count two, the clerk says — 'On count one, charging the defendant with...do you, upon His Honour's direction, find the defendant not guilty?' The foreman obediently replies 'Not guilty', and the verdict on count two is taken in the normal way. Unless one of them protests at the time, it is conclusively presumed that the jurors are in agreement with the verdicts returned on their behalves: *R* v *Roads* [1967] 2QB 108.

9.3 VERDICTS ON COUNTS IN THE ALTERNATIVE

The prosecution case on two counts is sometimes such that the accused may be found guilty on one count or the other but not on both (e.g. if the prosecution evidence shows that the accused, who was found in possession of stolen goods shortly after they were stolen, failed to give an explanation of how he came by the goods, the jury could convict him of either theft or handling — see Para. 5.5.4 on alternative counts). If, on an indictment containing alternative counts, the jury convict on, say, count one and are discharged from giving a verdict on count two, the Court of Appeal have power to quash the conviction on count one and substitute a conviction on count two provided it appears to them that the jury must have been satisfied of facts which proved the accused guilty on that count: Criminal Appeal Act 1968, s. 3. If, on the other hand, the jury convict on count one and actually acquit on count two, the Court of Appeal cannot overturn the latter verdict: *R* v *Melvin and Eden* [1953] 1QB 481. Therefore, if the count one conviction has to be quashed, the accused will stand acquitted on both counts, even though the Court of Appeal consider that he richly deserved to be convicted on the second count. To avoid such a miscarriage of justice, the foreman of the jury should be asked, in a case where there are counts in the alternative, whether the jury find the accused guilty on either count. If the answer is 'yes', he is further asked to name the count on which they wish to convict, and the verdict is taken on that count. The judge then discharges them from giving a verdict on the other count. If the answer is 'no', the clerk confirms that the jury acquit the accused on both counts.

9.4 VERDICTS OF 'GUILTY' OF AN ALTERNATIVE OFFENCE

Normally, when the jury are considering their verdict on a count, they have a simple choice between acquitting and convicting the accused. Sometimes, however, a third option is open to them. They can find the accused not guilty as charged in the count, but guilty of some other (lesser) indictable offence. The circumstances in which they may do this are set out in the Criminal Law Act 1967, ss. 6(2)-6(4) and s. 4(2).

9.4.1 The general provision

If the allegations in a count for an offence other than treason or murder 'amount to or include (expressly or by implication) an allegation of another (indictable) offence', the jury may find the accused not guilty of the offence charged but guilty of the other offence: Criminal Law Act 1967, s. 6(3).

A count by implication includes an allegation of another offence if, by reference to the indictment alone and ignoring the prosecution evidence as foreshadowed in the committal statements, it can be shown that proof of the offence charged would necessarily involve proof of the other offence: *R* v *Springfield* (1969) 53Cr App R 608. Thus, if a count alleges that 'AB on the 1st day of January 1981 robbed CD of a handbag', AB could be convicted of theft of the handbag because, having regard to the definition of robbery ('a person is guilty of robbery if he *steals,* and in order to do so, he uses force...' — Theft Act 1968 s. 8) the prosecution could not prove the robbery without incidentally proving the theft (*R* v *Barnard* (1980) 70Cr App R 28 where the point is made *obiter dicta*). Similarly, a count for unlawful sexual intercourse with a girl under 16 necessarily involves an allegation of indecent assault on her (*R* v *McCormack* [1969] 2QB 442), and a count for unlawful wounding contains an allegation of common assualt: *R* v *Taylor* (1869) LR 1CCR 194. The fine distinctions to which s. 6(3) gives rise are illustrated by comparing *R* v *Taylor* with *R* v *McReady and Hurd* [1978] 1WLR 1376 where counts against M and H alleged causing grievous bodily harm with intent to do grievous bodily harm contrary to the Offences against the Person Act 1861, s. 18, and convictions for common assault and unlawful wounding were quashed. The reasoning was that a s. 18 offence can be committed for example by poisoning the victim. Since that would not amount to either an assault or a wounding, it was possible for the prosecution to prove the offences charged without proving the offences of which M and H were convicted.

A count expressly includes an allegation of another offence if, having struck out the allegations in the count which the prosecution may be unable to prove, there is still a valid count for the other offence. In *R* v *Lillis* [1972] 2QB 236, L was charged with burglary contrary to the Theft Act 1968, s. 9(1)(b) in that he had entered a building on a certain date as a trespasser and had stolen therein a lawnmower. The prosecution evidence in fact showed that he had had permission both to enter the building and to take the lawnmower, but that he had failed to return it. The judge ruled that there was no case to answer in respect of burglary, but that the jury could convict L of theft in that he had appropriated the mower by keeping it when it should have been returned. The jury did so convict, and L argued on appeal that a count which essentially alleged that he had stolen property inside a building on a certain day should not expose him to the risk of conviction on the basis that he had subsequently stolen the property outside the building. The argument was rejected. The Court of Appeal held that, having struck out everything in the count the prosecution could not prove (namely the entry as a trespasser and the place where the offence occurred), there was still a valid count for theft — i.e. 'L on...stole a lawnmower'. Admittedly, the date alleged for the theft was incorrect, but a variation between the date laid in the indictment and the evidence as to when the offence was committed has never been regarded as material (see Para. 5.7.2).

The difficulty arising from the decision in *R* v *McReady and Hurd* (supra) that a count for causing grievous bodily harm with intent contrary to s. 18 of the Offences against the Person Act 1861 does not impliedly include an allegation of unlawful wounding or assault can be overcome by wording a s. 18 count so that it expressly includes an allegation of the lesser offence. Thus, if the count is for wounding (not causing grievous bodily harm) with intent to do grievous bodily harm contrary to s. 18 the jury can convict of unlawful wounding contrary to s. 20 of the 1861 Act, and if the count is for causing grievous bodily harm by assaulting the victim with intent etc. contrary to s. 18 there can be a conviction for common assault or assault occasioning actual bodily harm. The inclusion of the words 'by assaulting' in a s. 18 count is unnecessary in the sense that a count without those words is perfectly valid, but the Court of Appeal in *R* v *McReady and Hurd* suggested that putting the words in would avoid the problem encountered in that case.

9.4.2 Specific provisions

The Criminal Law Act 1967, s. 6(3), which makes general provision for verdicts of guilty of a lesser offence, is supplemented by three further subsections of the 1967 Act and a Paragraph in the Road Traffic Act 1972, Schedule 4, which all deal with the verdicts which may be returned in particular types of case. If the jury find the accused not guilty of the offence charged in the count then:

(a) On a count for murder they may convict of any one of the following — manslaughter; causing grievous bodily harm with intent to do so contrary to the Offences against the Person Act 1861, s. 18; infanticide contrary to the Infanticide Act 1938, s. 1; child destruction contrary to the Infant Life (Preservation) Act 1929 s. 1; attempt to commit any of the aforesaid offences, or attempted murder: Criminal Law Act 1967, s. 6(2).

(b) On a count for a completed offence the jury may convict of an attempt to commit that offence or of an attempt to commit another offence of which the accused could be convicted on the count: Criminal Law Act 1967, s. 6(4). Thus, if the accused is charged with robbery, the jury could convict him of attempted robbery or attempted theft. In the converse case of the accused merely being charged with the attempt but the evidence showing that the completed offence was committed, the jury may convict of the attempt or the judge may, in his discretion, discharge the jury from giving a verdict so that a fresh indictment may be preferred alleging the completed offence.

(c) On a count for an arrestable offence (one punishable with five years imprisonment or more) the jury, if satisfied that the offence charged (or another offence of which they could convict the accused on the count) was committed by someone, may convict the accused of assisting the offender by impeding his apprehension or prosecution: Criminal Law Act 1967, s. 4(2). Thus, combining s. 4(2) and s. 6(2) of the 1967 Act, the accused on a murder count may be convicted of assisting an offender who has committed murder, manslaughter or any of the offences listed in (a) above.

(d) On a count for reckless driving or causing death by reckless driving the jury may convict the accused of driving without due care and attention or driving without reasonable consideration (Road Traffic Act 1972, Schedule 4 Part IV Para. 3A). This is an unusual provision in that it allows a jury to convict of a summary offence.

9.4.3 Judge's discretion

Where the prosecution introduce the possibility of a verdict of guilty of a lesser offence and, by doing so, significantly alter the basis of the prosecution, the judge should consider granting the defence an adjournment to review the changed position. He might even discharge the jury. The accused should not be taken by surprise by a charge markedly different from that he had been expecting to meet (see *obiter dicta* comments in *R* v *Lillis* supra). The judge also has a discretion as to whether, in his summing up, he tells the jury about the possibility of convicting of a lesser offence. If both prosecution and defence have ignored the possibility, so that the accused has not had the opportunity to deal with the matter in evidence, it may be fairer for the judge to ignore the matter also. In *R* v *Carter and Canavan* [1964] 2QB 1, however, a conviction for a lesser offence was upheld where prosecuting counsel had, but the judge had not, mentioned the possibility.

The wording of s. 6(2)-(4) and s. 4(2) of the Criminal Law Act 1967 requires that, before the jury can convict the accused of an alternative offence, they must find him not guilty of the offence charged. In *R* v *Collison* (1980) 71Cr App R 249 a strange situation arose in that the jury trying a single count for wounding with intent contrary to the Offences against the Person Act 1861, s. 18 were agreed that C should be convicted of unlawful wounding but could not agree that he was not guilty of the s. 18 offence. The ironic possibility arose that the jury would have to be discharged from giving a verdict since they could not convict of unlawful wounding, on which they were agreed, until they were prepared to acquit of wounding with intent, about which they found it impossible to agree. The judge rescued the situation by amending the indictment to add a separate count for unlawful wounding (see Para. 5.7.2).

9.5 MAJORITY VERDICTS

Until 1967 the verdict of a jury had to be unanimous. This may have helped prevent mistaken convictions, but it had the disadvantage that one obstinate or unreasonable juror could prevent the jury reaching a verdict when, in truth, the evidence one way or the other was absolutely clear. Also the sinister possibility arose that a juror could be threatened or bribed into refusing to agree to a conviction. The Criminal Justice Act 1967, therefore, departed from centuries of tradition by introducing majority verdicts. The present legislation is contained in the Juries Act 1974, s. 17.

Section 17 provides for verdicts by a majority of 11 to 1 or 10 to 2, or, if the jury is reduced below twelve, by a majority of 10 to 1 or 9 to 1. If the jury is reduced to nine they must be unanimous. A jury can both acquit and convict by a majority, although if they convict the foreman must state in open court what the majority was: s. 17(3). Juries empanelled to try preliminary issues such as unfitness to plead may also decide the issue by a majority. The chief restriction upon majority verdicts is that before one may be accepted by the court the jury must have had two hours, or such longer period as the judge 'thinks reasonable having regard to the nature and complexity of the case', in which to try to reach a unanimous verdict: s. 17(4). It is for this reason that the judge, at the end of his summing up, directs the jury that they must seek a verdict on which they are all agreed — the time when the judge can accept a verdict which is not the verdict of them all has not yet arrived. The two hour minimum period laid down in s. 17 has, in effect, been extended slightly by a Practice Direction (1970 1WLR 916), which states that at least two hours and ten minutes must elapse between the jury leaving their box and their returning with a majority verdict. The extra ten minutes is meant to allow them time for going to their room, settling down in their room, returning to court with any questions and any other trivia which reduce the period they actually spend deliberating their verdict.

The procedure for the taking of majority verdicts is set out in a Practice Direction of 1967 (1 WLR 1198). Should the jury come into court, apparently with a verdict, before the two hours and ten minutes or such longer period as the judge considers reasonable has elapsed, the clerk asks the foreman if they have reached a verdict on which they are all agreed (see Para. 9.2). If they have, the verdict is taken in the usual way; if not, the judge sends them out again with a further direction to arrive if possible at a unanimous verdict. If the jury return to court or are sent for by the judge after the two hour ten minutes or longer period, they are again asked if they have agreed unanimously. At this stage, however, should the foreman answer 'no', the judge gives them the majority verdict direction — i.e. he tells them they should retire once more and endeavour to reach a unanimous verdict, but if they cannot he will accept a majority verdict. He then informs them what the permissible majorities are. When the jury finally return to court after the majority verdict direction, the clerk asks — 'Have at least ten (or, in the case of a ten man jury, nine) of you agreed upon your verdict?' If they have, the verdict is taken, the clerk stressing that the foreman should only answer 'Guilty' or 'Not Guilty'. This is to avoid the foreman saying 'Not Guilty by a majority', as the whole aim of the rather elaborate procedure prescribed by the Practice Direction is to prevent the public knowing, if it be the case, that the accused, although acquitted, was only acquitted by a majority. Accordingly, if the verdict is not guilty, nothing further is said. If, however, the jury convict they are asked if their decision was by a majority, and, if so, the foreman states the majority. On an appeal against conviction the Court of Appeal may, in a border line case, be swayed in their decision by the fact that the verdict was only by a 10 to 2 majority. Although the Court of Appeal have stressed the importance of the procedure in the 1967 Practice Direction being followed, the direction does not have the force of law and failure to comply with it will not in itself lead to a conviction being quashed: *R* v *Gilbert* (1978) 66Cr App R 237. The position is different where s. 17 itself is contravened through a majority verdict being returned within the two hour period or the foreman failing to say by what majority the jury decided to convict. The verdict then is not 'a proper or lawful one', so an appeal must succeed: *R* v *Barry* [1975] 1WLR 1190.

> The readiness of the judge to accept a majority verdict varies depending upon the gravity and complexity of the case and the views of the individual judge on the desirability of unanimity. In *R* v *Mansfield* [1977] 1WLR 1102, for example, Cobb J twice had the jury back into court to stress the 'utter desirability' of a unanimous verdict, and delayed for over six hours before giving a majority verdict direction. Melford Stevenson J, on the other hand, in *R* v *Gilbert* (supra) told the jury that he would accept a majority verdict after only the bare statutory minimum period had elapsed. In both *R* v *Mansfield* and *R* v *Gilbert* the accused was charged with murder, although the former was admittedly the more serious case in that there were seven counts of murder and three of arson. The evidence in *R* v *Mansfield* was also more complicated than that in *R* v *Gilbert*. Even so, the reluctance in the one case and the readiness in the other to accept a majority verdict seemed to spring essentially from the attitude of the judges concerned to such verdicts.
>
> In a case which is not especially serious or complicated one would normally expect the judge to give the majority verdict direction after the jury have been out for about two and a half hours.

9.6 DISCHARGING THE JURY FROM GIVING A VERDICT

Where a jury cannot agree upon their verdict, the judge discharges them from giving one. The procedure is that, after giving them the majority verdict direction, the judge allows them whatever time he thinks reasonable for further deliberations. If they still do not return with a verdict, he has them brought back into court and finds out from the foreman whether there is any real possibility of their arriving at a decision. Should the answer be that they are so badly split that, even given more time, they would not reach a verdict, the judge discharges them. Discharge of the jury from giving a verdict is not equivalent to an acquittal. Therefore, the accused may be tried again by a fresh jury on the same indictment, and a plea of autrefois acquit will fail. In theory, there could be an infinite number of trials for the same offence, with the jury failing to agree and being discharged on each occasion. In practice, if two juries have disagreed, the prosecution offer no evidence at the start of what would otherwise be the third trial, and the judge enters a verdict of not guilty. Occasionally, the prosecution do not even insist upon a second trial. When the jury trying the accused for offences arising out of the rioting in the St Paul's area of Bristol in April 1980 failed to agree upon their verdicts in respect of some of the accused, the Director of Public Prosecutions decided to offer no evidence at the second trial. He feared that a second contested trial would have exacerbated racial tensions.

Failure by the jury to agree is regrettable because a second trial involves extra public expense and inconvenience for the witnesses. In *R* v *Walhein* (1952) 36Cr App R 167, the Court of Criminal Appeal approved a form of direction which may encourage the jury to agree. The direction was chiefly aimed at the mischief of the one obstinate juror who, in the days of unanimous verdicts, could prevent the jury returning a verdict. Suitably modified to take account of the possibility of majority verdicts, the direction may still be used today, but judges should bear in mind that the chief problem the direction was meant to solve is now overcome by majority verdicts: see *R* v *Isequilla* [1975] 1WLR 716. The direction essentially is that, while he must always be loyal to his oath to give a true verdict according to the evidence, each juror should listen to the arguments of his colleagues and modify his own views accordingly if he thinks it right to do so having regard to his oath. The judge may also mention the expense and inconvenience occasioned by a split jury. Whether or not the judge gives a '*Walhein*' direction' is entirely within his discretion.

However anxious the judge is for the jury to agree he must not pressurise them into doing so. Subject to being discharged from giving a verdict, the jury must be allowed as much time as they need to deliberate freely and reach a proper verdict. If the judge does exert undue pressure, any conviction will be quashed. An example is provided by *R* v *McKenna* [1960] 1QB 411. At 2.40pm, after the jury had been considering their verdict for two and a quarter hours, the judge told them that he was leaving court within ten minutes, and if they had not by then agreed they would have to be 'kept all night'. The reason for this ultimatum was that the judge was anxious to catch a train. After six minutes the jury returned with a verdict of guilty. Describing the judge's words as a threat, and pointing out that the jury might have thought that they would be locked in their room until the next morning, the Court of Criminal Appeal quashed the conviction. Cassels J stated at p.422 — 'It is a cardinal principle of our criminal law that in considering their verdict...a jury shall deliberate in complete freedom, uninfluenced by any promise, unintimidated by any threat'.

9.7 ACCEPTING THE VERDICT

In general, the judge has no power to reject the jury's verdict however much he may disagree with it: *R* v *Lester* (1940) 27Cr App R 8 — for exceptions, see below. Nor should he ask the jury any questions about the verdict (e.g. the reason why they convicted of manslaughter and not murder — *R* v *Larkin* [1943] KB 174). Once the jury have completed giving their verdict they are discharged. If the accused has been acquitted on all counts, he is discharged as well. If he has been convicted on any count, the judge either proceeds to sentence him forthwith, or adjourns so that reports on him can be prepared. The accused may be released on bail or kept in custody for the period of the adjournment. The procedure before sentence is passed is dealt with in Chapter 14.

In the following cases the judge is not obliged to accept the first verdict returned by the jury:

(a)   If their verdict is one which, on the indictment, they have no power to return the judge can ask them to reconsider it. An example is if the jury purport to convict of an offence not charged in the indictment which does not fall within the provisions of the Criminal Law Act 1967 on alternative verdicts.

(b) If a verdict on a count is ambiguous the judge should not accept it in the form it is given, but should ask questions to resolve the ambiguity and, if need be, further direct the jury on the law. Usually the verdict is an unambiguous guilty, not guilty or guilty of another offence, but occasionally something more is said which raises a doubt as to what the jury's decision really is. In *R* v *Hawkes* (1931) 22Cr App R 172 the foreman said 'Guilty' when asked the jury's verdict on a count for driving while unfit through drink, but a moment later he added 'We find the defendant guilty of being under the influence of drink'. This remark introduced an element of ambiguity into the original verdict, since it might have meant that the jury, although satisfied that H had consumed alcohol, were not satisfied that it had impaired his ability to drive. The judge failed to take steps to clear up the ambiguity, so the conviction had to be quashed.

(c) If a verdict appears, having regard to the evidence adduced at the trial, to be inconsistent with another verdict returned by the jury in the same case the judge may ask them to reconsider the verdicts. He should only do this if the verdicts genuinely cannot be reconciled. If there is a possible, though unlikely, view of the evidence on which they can be supported, the judge should accept them. In *R* v *Burrows* (1970) Crim LR 419, where the jury were trying three accused on a joint count for theft of a purse and one of the three on a second count, in the alternative, for handling the purse, the judge thought that acquittals of all three on the theft count were inconsistent with a conviction on the handling count. He asked the jury how they could convict the handler when they had found that the purse was not stolen by acquitting all the alleged thieves. The Court of Appeal held that the verdicts were not inconsistent. The jury might have been satisfied that one of the three accused had stolen the purse, but unable to say which it was.

If the judge, in a proper case, declines to accept the jury's first verdict, and, as a result of his further directions, they alter their verdict, the second verdict is the operative one. If, despite the judge's efforts, the jury insist upon their first verdict it seems that it would have to be accepted.

Part 3   Summary Trial

10   The Magistrates and their Courts

The office of justice of the peace, or magistrate, is an ancient one first mentioned in 1264. As early as 1361 the Justices of the Peace Act provided for the appointment in each county of 'one lord and three or four of the most worthy in the county with some learned in the law' whose duty it would be to 'pursue, arrest...and chastise' offenders and rioters, and take surety of good behaviour 'towards the King and his people' from those who were not 'of good fame'. The magistrates retain their original function of assisting in the keeping of the peace, and, to further that end, can still bind a person over to keep the peace or be of good behaviour even though no offence has been proved against him.

Over the centuries the work of the magistrates widened in scope. By the eighteenth century they had extensive judicial and administrative powers. Administratively, they were responsible for, *inter alia,* the licensing of ale houses, the appointment of overseers of the poor and surveyors of highways, the levying of rates in their counties, and the transaction of important county business. Judicially, they not only tried minor cases summarily but, at quarter sessions, benches of two to nine magistrates presided over trials by jury. Only the most serious of indictable offences were excluded from the jurisdiction of quarter sessions and reserved for the assize courts. However, in the late nineteenth and early twentieth centuries the magistrates' powers were reduced. Their administrative functions were transferred to elected local authorities, although traces of the old system can still be seen in, for example, the work of the licensing justices who control the granting of licences to sell alcohol. Their judicial functions were not expressly reduced, but the introduction of a rule that at quarter sessions the bench must always have a legally qualified chairman (usually the sort of person who today would be appointed a circuit judge or recorder) meant that lay magistrates had much less influence than formerly. The role of the magistrates at quarter sessions is reflected today in their being allowed to sit with a professional judge at trials on indictment in the Crown Court, and in the requirement that two of them be present at appeals and committals for sentence: Courts Act 1971, s. 5 and see Para. 4.3.

Although the powers of magistrates are not as great as they were, they still play a very important part in the administration of the criminal law. In summary, their work is as follows:

(a)   They can issue either a warrant for the arrest of a person against whom an offence is alleged or a summons requiring him to attend at a magistrates' court to answer the allegation (see Chapter 19). In practice, this does not form a major part of their work as proceedings against a person for a serious offence normally begin with an arrest without warrant by a police officer, while the issuing of a summons, which is the appropriate way to commence proceedings in less serious cases, can be and usually is done by a magistrates' clerk rather than the magistrate himself.

(b) They sit as examining justices for the hearing of committal proceedings (see Chapter 3).

(c) They try cases summarily in the adult magistrates' courts (see Chapter 11).

(d) They try in the juvenile courts cases brought against juveniles (i.e. those under 17). Only magistrates who have been appointed by their colleagues to the juvenile court panel are eligible to sit in the juvenile court (see Chapter 13).

(e) They have a minor role to play in the work of the Crown Court (see Para. 4.3).

The magistrates' jurisdiction is by no means limited to criminal proceedings. Details are outside the scope of this book, but it may be noted that magistrates have power, for example, to make maintenance orders as between the parties to a marriage and to deal with the custody of children of the family. Frequently, a wife will choose to apply to the magistrates for a maintenance order rather than commence divorce proceedings in the county court. Affiliation proceedings are also a matter for the magistrates, while the juvenile court deals with care proceedings brought in respect of juveniles under the Children and Young Persons Act 1969, s. 1. Mention has already been made of the work of the licensing justices in granting licences to sell alcohol. Magistrates appointed to Betting Licensing Committees perform a similar function in granting permits to bookmakers and in licensing premises for gaming. In short, the administration of justice in England and Wales depends to a greater extent than, perhaps, most people realise on the work of magistrates.

10.1 LAY MAGISTRATES

In January 1981 there were over 25,000 active lay magistrates in England and Wales. Lay magistrates are so called because their work is unpaid, although they can claim allowances for travelling, subsistence and loss of earnings: Justices of the Peace Act 1979 s. 12. Most lay magistrates are also 'lay' in the sense that they have no legal qualifications, but there is no bar to lawyers or, indeed, holders of high judicial office becoming magistrates. Academic lawyers may find work as lay magistrates a suitable way in which to serve the community.

10.1.1 Appointment of lay magistrates

Lay magistrates are appointed by the Lord Chancellor 'on behalf and in the name of Her Majesty': Justices of the Peace Act 1979, s. 6. About 1,800 appointments are made each year to replace magistrates who die or whose names are placed on the supplemental list (see Para. 10.1.3), or to cope with an increase in the amount of work to be done. It is said that the number of suitable candidates for appointment considerably exceeds the vacancies to be filled. In deciding whom to appoint, the Lord Chancellor is principally concerned that the appointee will, by character and ability, be suited for the work of a magistrate, and that he will be recognised by his fellows as being so suited. The major statutory limitation on eligiblity for appointment is a residential one (see Para. 10.3) but certain categories of persons will not, in practice, be considered (e.g. those aged 60 or over, members of the armed forces or the police and those with convictions for serious crime). Those convicted of treason or corrupt practices at elections are statutorily disqualified from being appointed or, if already appointed, holding office as magistrates (Forfeiture Act 1870, s. 2 and Representation of the People Act 1949 ss. 140, 141 and 163). Undischarged bankrupts are also disqualified (Bankruptcy Act 1883, s. 32). Why Parliament should have picked on these groups as the only groups to be barred by law from the magistrates' bench is a matter for conjecture. Political affiliations are ignored when making appointments except that the magistrates in a particular area should not be heavily weighted in favour of one party or the other. As well as trying to maintain a political balance, the Lord Chancellor tries to maintain a balance between the sexes (in fact, there are roughly three male to every two female magistrates), and to introduce younger people in their thirties or early forties to the magistracy. Criticism of the approach to appointing magistrates is usually based on an assertion that magistrates do not represent a sufficiently broad cross-section of the local community. Too often, it is said, they are drawn from what, for want of a better term, may be described as the upper social classes. If this is so, the reason probably is that wealthier people have more time available to do what is essentially voluntary work.

The preceding paragraph referred to the Lord Chancellor being concerned about the character and ability of appointees as if he personally assessed the suitability of each candidate. It would, of course, be impossible for the Lord Chancellor to carry out such a task, so in making appointments he acts on the advice of local advisory committes. There are over a hundred such committees and many of them are assisted by area subcommittees. To avoid unseemly lobbying, the names of members of the committees are kept secret, save that the name and address of the secretary are published. Any individual or organisation can give to the secretary particulars of a person they consider should be made a magistrate. The committee then decides whom to recommend to the Lord Chancellor for appointment.

10.1.2 Training and court attendance of lay magistrates

Before appointment magistrates undertake to complete, within one year of appointment, a course of basic instruction in the duties which they will be carrying out. It is the responsibility of Magistrates' Courts Committees (see Para. 10.3) to administer training schemes for the areas for which they are responsible. The aim of the training is to impress upon the new magistrate the necessity of acting judicially, to give him a grounding in law and evidence which will enable him to follow intelligently the types of case he will normally encounter, to inform him of the nature of the sentences he will be able to pass, and to help him understand the role of others who work in the courts (e.g. the clerk, court staff and legal representatives). The training should include, in addition to formal lecturing, visits to courts and penal institutions, and group discussions of the problems magistrates frequently face.

Magistrates are expected to sit in court at least 26 times during a year. No doubt, the frequency with which they actually do sit varies greatly, but the average attendance (outside London) is around 35 times a year. The significance of this is that through their initial training and through their regular attendance at court, often over many years, magistrates become knowledgeable about the work of their courts. Although the adjective 'lay' is used to describe them, they are far from being almost ignorant of the ways of the court as is the average juror.

10.1.3   Removal and 'retirement' of magistrates

Lay magistrates can be removed from office by the Lord Chancellor: Justices of the Peace Act 1979, s. 6. This is only appropriate in extreme cases where for instance the magistrate has been convicted of serious crime. If a magistrate is infirm or it is expedient for any other reason that he should cease to exercise judicial functions, or if he fails to attend court as often as he ought, the Lord Chancellor can order that his name be placed on the supplemental list: Justices of the Peace Act 1979, s. 8. A magistrate on the supplemental list retains the status of justice of the peace but the only powers he can exercise are trivial ones in connection with the witnessing of documents — he cannot sit in court or even issue a summons or warrant. At the age of 70 (75 in the case of one who holds or has held high judicial office) a magistrate is automatically placed on the supplemental list. In effect, therefore, lay magistrates retire at the age of 70.

10.2   STIPENDIARY MAGISTRATES

Stipendiary magistrates, as the name implies, are paid a salary. They are appointed by the Queen on the Lord Chancellor's recommendation from amongst barristers and solicitors of at least seven years standing: Justices of the Peace Act 1979, ss. 13 and 31. Up to 60 metropolitan stipendiary magistrates may be appointed for work in the courts of inner London, and up to 40 non-metropolitan stipendiaries may be appointed for work outside London. Various statutory provisions give to metropolitan stipendiaries slightly wider jurisdiction than that possessed by non-metropolitans, but the differences are not significant. A stipendiary may be removed from office by the Lord Chancellor for inability or misbehaviour. Otherwise he retires from office at the end of the completed year of service during which he attains the age of 70, unless the Lord Chancellor gives special authority for him to continue up to the age of 72.

Except when he is sitting in the juvenile court, a stipendiary magistrate can try a case by himself whereas at least two lay magistrates must be present for the purposes of a summary trial. This fact, together with his legal qualifications and experience, normally enables a stipendiary to dispose of cases more expeditiously than his lay colleagues. Nevertheless, it is only in inner London that stipendiaries play a significant part in the work of the magistrates' courts. Outside London there were, in January 1981, only eleven stipendiaries, whereas the number of metropolitan stipendiaries was 43, and some of the busiest and best known London courts (e.g. Bow Street and Marlborough Street) depend heavily on their stipendiaries.

10.3   ORGANISATION OF THE COURTS

The appointment of justices of the peace under the Justices of the Peace Act 1361 (see beginning of the chapter) was on the basis of one lord and three or four worthy men being appointed for each county. Today a magistrate is appointed to act for a commission area not a county, but the change is one of nomenclature as, outside London, there is a commission area for each county whether metropolitan or non-metropolitan. In London there are six commission areas, namely the City of London, the inner London area, the north-east, south-east and south-west London areas, and the Middlesex area: Justices of the Peace Act 1979, ss. 1-2. Henceforward, the commission areas will be referred to as counties. Unless the Lord Chancellor otherwise directs, a magistrate must live in or within 15 miles of the county for which he acts: Justices of the Peace Act 1979, s. 7. Generally speaking, magistrates only have jurisdiction to try summary offences allegedly committed within the county for which they act (see Chapter 11).

The counties are subdivided into petty sessional divisions, with a magistrates' court in each division. Although a magistrate can sit in any of the courts for his county, he is assigned to the bench for the division in which he lives or works, and normally would only sit in the court for that division. Where proceedings are begun against a magistrate in his own petty sessional division it is convenient to have magistrates from another division of the county deal with the case, so as to avoid the embarrassment of the accused magistrate being tried by his colleagues on the bench.

The Lord Chancellor decides in which courts stipendiary magistrates shall sit. A non-metropolitan stipendiary is, by virtue of his office, a justice of the peace for the county in which he is appointed to work, and metropolitan stipendiaries are, by virtue of their office, justices for each of the London commission areas, and for Essex, Hertfordshire, Kent and Surrey: Justices of the Peace Act 1979, ss. 13 and 31.

Each year the magistrates for a petty sessional division must elect by secret ballot a chairman and one or more deputy chairmen: Justices of the Peace Act 1979, s. 17. If a chairman or deputy chairman so elected is present at a sitting of the magistrates' court he is entitled to preside over the proceedings. His powers are no greater than those of his colleagues with him in court (see Chapter 11) but he speaks for the bench — e.g. giving the accused the alibi warning in committal proceedings and announcing the court's decisions. If none of the elected chairmen are present, the longest serving magistrate acts as chairman. An elected chairman does not have the right to preside when sitting with a stipendiary magistrate, or when sitting in the juvenile court. The procedure for electing chairmen is set out in the Justices (Size and Chairmanship of the Bench) Rules 1964 (SI 1964 No 1107).

Section 19 of the 1979 Act provides that a magistrates' courts committee shall be set up in each non-metropolitan county, in each district of the metropolitan counties, and in each London commission area, other than inner London. The committee is made up of magistrates chosen from the benches for the various petty sessional divisions which make up the area for which the committee is responsible. The committee deals, amongst other things, with administrative matters such as the running of training schemes for magistrates, the review of the boundaries between petty sessional divisions, and the appointment of magistrates' clerks. A High Court judge, circuit judge or recorder may, with his consent be co-opted onto the committee. Section 35 provides for a committee of magistrates in inner London, similar to the magistrates' court committees elsewhere, but the importance of stipendiaries in inner London is reflected in the fact that the committee always has on it more stipendiary than lay magistrates.

10.4 MAGISTRATES' CLERKS

One or more magistrates' clerks may be appointed for each petty sessional division: Justices of the Peace Act 1979, s. 25. The appointments are made by the relevant magistrates' courts committee from amongst barristers and solictors who are either of at least five years' standing or have worked for at least five years as assistant to a magistrates' clerk (s. 26). The duties of the magistrates' clerk are such that he could not, in a busy court, carry them out unaided. The magistrates' courts committee may, therefore, after consultation with the clerk, employ staff to assist him. The assistants to the magistrates' clerk need not be, but often are, legally qualified.

The nature of the work done by the magistrates' clerk and his assistants is described in later chapters. Briefly, they play a major part in the behind the scenes administration of the court (e.g. issuing summonses and processing legal aid applications), and, in court, they advise the magistrates on the law. The Justices' Clerk (Qualifications of Assistants) Rules 1979 (SI 1979 No 570) provide that an assistant shall not act as a clerk in court unless he has, at the very least, attended a course leading up to the Common Professional Examination or Part I of the Law Society examinations. Many assistant clerks in fact choose to qualify as barristers or solicitors rather than being content with satisfying the minimal requirements mentioned above.

11   Course of a Summary Trial

All summary offences are tried in a magistrates' court. Offences triable either way (see Para. 1.3) are tried in a magistrates' court if, essentially, both the magistrates and the accused agree. Because the most commonly committed offences (e.g. all but the most serious road traffic offences) are summary, and because many accused charged with an offence triable either way elect, if given the option, to have the matter dealt with summarily no less than 98% of criminal cases are disposed of by magistrates. The procedure at a summary trial is the same whether the offence charged is summary or triable either way. In the latter case, however, the procedure set out in the Magistrates' Courts Act 1980, ss. 19-22 for determining the more suitable mode of trial must be complied with before the start of the summary trial (see Chapter 12).

The conduct of a summary trial is governed principally by the Magistrates' Courts Act 1980, which repeals and reenacts without amendment several earlier statutes, including the Magistrates' Courts Acts 1952 and 1957 and parts of the Criminal Justice Act 1967 and the Criminal Law Act 1977. Where, in this chapter, there is a reference to a section of a statute but the name of the statute is not given it is a reference to a section of the Magistrates' Courts Act 1980. Where a case is quoted as being relevant to the interpretation or application of a section of the Magistrates' Court Act 1980 it is a case on the equivalent pre-1980 legislation. Notice also that the terms 'summary trial', 'trial on information' and 'trial by the magistrates' may be used interchangeably.

11.1 JURISDICTION OF A MAGISTRATES' COURT

A magistrates' court has jurisdiction to try any summary offence committed within the county, but, subject to the exceptions mentioned below, cannot try a summary offence committed outside the county: s. 2(1). In fact, summary offences are normally tried by the court for the petty sessional division in which the offence occurred. The advantage of restricting the magistrates' jurisdiction over summary offences to those committed in the locality for which they act is that local knowledge may assist in the determination of cases (e.g. knowledge of the road where a traffic offence allegedly occurred). The disadvantage from the accused's viewpoint is that contesting a charge against him may involve a long journey to court. For example, if the accused lives in Newcastle and, while on his annual holiday in Devon, he allegedly commits an offence of driving without due care and attention, the case would have to be heard in a Devon magistrates' court. Assuming that the accused has returned home before the hearing date, he has the unattractive options of pleading guilty by post, being found guilty in his absence or making a long journey to contest the charge. If he were charged with reckless driving, a magistrates' court in Newcastle would have jurisdiction to hold committal proceedings or, if the accused consented, try the case summarily. That is because reckless driving is an offence triable either way, and a magistrates' court's jurisdicition in respect of such offences is not limited to those occurring within the county. It does not follow, however, that proceedings would, in fact, be taken in a Newcastle court. Where any of several magistrates' courts could exercise jurisdiction, the prosecution in effect decide where the case should proceed by (if the accused is in custody at a police station) bringing him before Court A rather than Court B, or, if he is at liberty, applying to a magistrate on the bench for Court A for a summons requiring the accused to attend at Court A to answer the charge. In the example given above, the Devon police would probably find it more convenient to have a charge of· reckless driving dealt with in a Devon magistrates' court. They would therefore apply to a Devon magistrate for the issue of a summons, and ignore the possibility of proceedings in Newcastle.

In the following two situations a magistrates' court has jurisdiction to try a summary offence even though the offence was committed outside the county:

(a) A magistrates' court which tries a person for an offence (which may be triable either way or summary) has jurisdiction to try him in addition for any other summary offence wherever committed: s. 2(6). The purpose of s. 2(6) is to enable charges outstanding against an accused in different counties to be dealt with by a court for one of the counties concerned. The additional jurisdiction to try given by the subsection is limited to summary offences because, if an accused is being tried for an offence by a magistrates' court in Loamshire and he is further charged with an indictable offence committed in Clayshire, the Loamshire court can deal with the indictable matter on the basis that a magistrates' court's jurisdiction in respect of indictable offences is never limited to those committed within the county: s. 2(3) and (4).

(b) If one accused is being proceeded against for an offence in a magistrates' court for Loamshire, and it is 'necessary or expedient, with a view to the better administration of justice' that he be tried 'jointly with or in the same place as' another person, a Loamshire magistrate can issue a summons or warrant for arrest to bring that other person before the Loamshire court. Once he appears before the Loamshire court, the court has jurisdiction to try him for any summary offence with which he is charged, even if it was committed in Clayshire: s. 2(2).

The rather complicated provisions described above may be made clearer by an example. John Smith is driving his car in Loamshire, and Paul Brown is his passenger. Smith goes through a red traffic light. He is seen by a police officer who follows him in his police car, waiting for an opportunity to stop him. Smith's journey takes him across the county boundary into Clayshire, at which stage he realises he is being followed and accelerates rapidly, breaking the speed limit. He then decides that running away will only make matters worse, and pulls in to the side of the road. While the police officer is speaking to Smith, Brown becomes agitated and, despite the officer's request that he be silent, repeatedly interrupts the conversation and jogs the officer's arm as he tries to write in his notebook. All three possible offences (failure to comply with traffic directions and speeding against Smith, and obstructing a police constable in the execution of his duty against Brown) are summary. Even though only one of them took place in Loamshire, the Loamshire magistrates have jurisdiction to try all three. The offence of going through a red light occurred in Loamshire, so s. 2(1) applies. Since they are trying Smith for that offence, the Loamshire magistrates also have jurisdiction to try him for speeding in Clayshire: s. 2(6). As Brown's offence of obstructing the police officer is linked with Smith's offences, a magistrate for Loamshire can issue a summons requiring Brown to appear before the Loamshire court, s. 1(2)(b), and, upon his appearing, that court can try the case: s. 2(2).

To avoid meritless disputes on whether an offence was committed in one county or another s. 3 provides that offences committed within 500 yards of a county border and offences begun in one county and completed in another may be treated as having been committed in either of the counties concerned. Similarly, an offence committed against a person who or property which, at the time of the offence, was in a vehicle engaged on a journey through two or more counties can be dealt with in a court for any of the counties.

11.2   THE BENCH

'A magistrates' court shall not try an information summarily...except when composed of at least 2 justices...' s. 121(1). The maximum number who may sit is seven (r. 2 of the Justices of the Peace (Size and Chairmanship of Bench) Rules 1964 — SI 1964 No 1107). Usually three sit in order to avoid the risk of being equally divided as to the verdict. Except in the juvenile court, a stipendiary magistrate may and normally does sit alone: Justices of the Peace Act 1979, s. 16. Where, exceptionally, a stipendiary magistrate sits with lay justices, he acts as their chairman. The chairman of a bench of lay justices is either one of the chairmen chosen at the annual elections held by the bench (see Para. 10.3) or, if none is present, the most senior magistrate present.

Where a magistrate has any direct pecuniary interest, however small, in the outcome of a case he is disqualified from hearing the matter and should withdraw. The same applies if he has a non-pecuniary interest which is such as to create a real likelihood of bias. If he fails to withdraw, an application may be made to a Divisional Court of the Queen's Bench Division for an order of *certiorari* to quash the court's decision. The principle stated above is merely an aspect of the rule of natural justice that no man may be a judge in his own cause, and applies equally to judges in the High Court, Crown Court etc. It is of special significance in relation to magistrates because the local nature of their jurisdiction makes it more likely that somebody known to them will appear as a prosecutor, defendant or witness in a case which they would otherwise be entitled to try.

An applicant for *certiorari* to quash a magistrates' court's decision, on the basis that a magistrate had an interest in the case, need not show that the magistrate actually was biased. If a pecuniary interest can be established, *certiorari* will be granted even if nobody could really suppose that the magistrate's view of the case was affected by his interest. The principle is illustrated by *Dimes* v *Grand Junction Canal* (1852) 3HLC 759 where decrees granted by the then Lord Chancellor in favour of the canal company were set aside by the House of Lords because the Lord Chancellor owned shares in the company. It was not suggested that the Lord Chancellor would be swayed by the thought that his shares might rise a little in value if he held in favour of the company, but nonetheless his ruling could not stand. What is true for Lord Chancellors is also, of course, true for magistrates — 'for a justice to adjudicate on a matter in which he has a pecuniary or proprietary interest is often a very serious dereliction of duty' (per Lord Widgery CJ in *R* v *Altrincham Justices* ex parte *Pennington* [1975] 1QB 549 at p.552), and, in all cases, it will render the court's decision liable to be quashed.

If an interest of a non-pecuniary nature is alleged it will not necessarily lead to the Divisional Court granting *certiorari*. The applicant must show that by reason of the interest there is 'a real likelihood of bias, or at all events that a reasonable person advised of the circumstances might reasonably suspect that the judicial officer was incapable of producing the impartiality and detachment' which the judicial function requires (see Lord Widgery CJ in ex parte *Pennington* supra at p.552). In ex parte *Pennington* a county council successfully prosecuted P for underweight deliveries of carrots to two of its schools. The chairman of the magistrates who convicted P was a co-opted member of the council's education committee, which had negotiated the contract with P for supply of vegetables to the schools. She was also a governor of two other schools, not those named in the informations against P, which received their vegetables from P. Her interest in the good running of the local schools was sufficient to disqualify her from hearing P's case, and the convictions were accordingly quashed. *R* v *Camborne Justices* ex parte *Pearce* [1955] 1QB 41 provides an interesting comparison with ex parte *Pennington*. There, a magistrates' clerk, to whom the rule against bias equally applied, was under no duty to withdraw from a case in which a county council of which he was a member was prosecuting a trader for offences under food and drugs legislation. The clerk was not a member of the council's health committee which had advised the prosecution, whereas in ex parte *Pennington,* of course, the magistrate was a member of the education committee which, even if it had not advised the prosecution, certainly had an interest in its outcome. Section 64 of the Justices of the Peace Act 1979 deals specifically with a problem similar to those raised in ex parte *Pennington* and ex parte *Pearce.* It provides that magistrates who are members of local authorities shall not adjudicate in proceedings brought by or against their authority. The section does not apply to magistrates' clerks or to co-opted members of committees who are not actually members of the local authority.

If, in deciding an application by the accused to be released on bail for the period prior to his trial, a magistrate learns that he has previous convictions the magistrate may not take part in the trial of the accused: s. 42. If a magistrate knows by some other means that the accused has previous convictions (e.g. he has tried and convicted him on a previous occasion) there is no rule of law that he should withdraw from the case, but it is desirable that other magistrates should deal with the matter: *R* v *McElligott* ex parte *Gallagher* (1972) Crim LR 332.

11.3 THE INFORMATION

The information is the charge to which the accused pleads guilty or not guilty at the beginning of a summary trial. In addition, the laying of an information is the pre-condition for the issue of a summons requiring the accused to attend at the magistrates' court to answer the allegation made against him in the information. This Paragraph is concerned principally with the first mentioned function of an information, but, in order to understand what an information is and the form it takes, it is necessary to know something of its other function.

The first appearance of the accused in a magistrates' court is usually secured in one of three ways. He may be arrested without warrant and detained at the police station in custody until he can be brought before the court; or, having been arrested without warrant, he may be bailed from the police station on terms that he appear at court on a certain date; or a summons may be served on him. The summons states the time and place where he is to appear and the charge which he is to answer. In general, a summons is appropriate where the prosecution is to be for a summary or one of the less serious indictable offences — the graver the crime of which the accused is suspected the more likely it is that he will be arrested without warrant. Where a summons is considered the proper way to bring the accused before the court, application for one must be made to a magistrate or a magistrates' clerk, who may only issue such summons upon information being laid before him. Laying an information simply means alleging that a certain person has committed an offence, and giving reasonable particulars of that offence. Although the information need not be in writing, prosecuting authorities (e.g. the police, local authorities, Department of Health and Social Security) have arrangements with their local magistrates' courts by which, if one of their officers believes that AB has committed an offence, a written information signed by the officer is posted or otherwise delivered to the court, and the magistrate or clerk can then issue a summons to AB without any oral allegation being made before him. A private individual who wishes to commence a prosecution would be more likely to lay his information orally, probably upon oath. He may also be asked to sign a deposition repeating the contents of his information.

The Magistrates' Courts (Forms) Rules 1981 (SI 1981 No 553) set out a standard form for an information. The information on the page opposite follows that form. The

INFORMATION (M.C. Act 1980, s. 1; M.C. Rules 1981, r. 4)
CASTERBRIDGE Magistrates' Court (Court Code 1234)

Date: 13th July 1981

Accused: John David DOE

Address: 1, Port Bredy Road,
CASTERBRIDGE,
Hardyshire

Alleged offence: On the 12th day of July 1981 John David DOE did assault and beat Richard Roe contrary to s. 42 of the Offences against the Person Act 1861

The information
of: Richard Roger ROE

Address: 3, Port Bredy Road,   Telephone No.
CASTERBRIDGE,
Hardyshire

who upon oath states that the accused committed the offence of which particulars are given above.

Taken and sworn before me

John Justice
Justice of the Peace

Note: The above information is based upon the form for an information given in the Magistrates' Courts (Forms) Rules 1981 (SI 1981 No 553). It is a form which a magistrate (or magistrates' clerk) can use in order to take down in writing an information laid orally before him. Private prosecutors, such as Richard Roe, often commence their prosecutions by laying an oral information, but the police and other prosecuting agencies prefer to deliver their information to the court in writing without anybody going before a magistrate or clerk. In such a case, the information is signed by the informant (police officer, official of the Department of Health and Social Security, local government officer etc.), not by the magistrate or clerk. It will give, like the information above, particulars of the offence alleged; the name and address of the accused, and the name of the informant together with an appropriate address (e.g. the address of the police station in the case of a police information). For further details — see Para. 19.2.4.

person who lays the information is, formally, the prosecutor in the case, even if he is not the chief witness or victim of the offence. For most purposes, laying the information is regarded as the commencement of the prosecution. In cases which commence with the accused being arrested without warrant and brought before or bailed to appear before the court, there is no need to lay an information. The charge against him, however, is written down on the charge sheet at the police station prior to his being charged under Rule III of the Judges' Rules. By convention, the charge-sheet serves as the information against the accused, and the clerk's reading out of the charge at the first court appearance can be treated as the laying of the information, since the charge is read in the presence of the magistrates.

A full account of the laying of informations to obtain the issue of a summons is contained in Chapter 19. The following points are especially relevant to the information in its role as the charge which is put to the accused at the beginning of a summary trial:

(a)   An information may be likened to a count in an indictment. Like a count it must not charge more than one offence, but it may allege in the alternative different ways of committing a single offence. Thus, an information for being in charge of a motor vehicle 'while under the influence of drink *or* drugs' is valid because the Road Traffic Act 1972, s. 5 creates one offence which can be committed under the influence of either drink or drugs, but an information for driving 'without due care and attention *or* without reasonable consideration' is bad for duplicity since s. 3 of the Act creates one offence of driving without due care, and a second of driving without reasonable consideration (see *Thompson* v *Knights* [1947] KB 336 and *R* v *Surrey Justices* ex parte *Witherick* [1932] 1KB 450 — see also Para. 5.4 for the parallel problem in relation to counts in an indictment).

(b)   The contents of an information are similar to the contents of a count. Using, as far as possible, non-technical language, it must give reasonable particulars of the nature of the charge, but it need not state every element of the offence alleged. Where the offence is statutory it must refer to the statute and section contravened. It is not necessary, however, to allege specifically that the accused falls outside the ambit of any defence provided by the statute creating the offence (see r. 6 of the Indictment Rules 1971 for a similar rule in relation to counts in an indictment). The main difference between an information and a count is that the former, unlike the latter, is not split into a Statement of Offence and Particulars of Offence. Below are two examples of informations:

John Smith on the 1st day of January 1981 did assault Richard Brown, a constable of the county of Barsetshire, in the execution of his duty contrary to s. 51(1) of the Police Act 1964.

John Smith on the 1st day of January 1981 did drive a certain motor vehicle, namely a Ford Cortina number ABC 123W, on a certain road called High Street, Barchester, he having consumed alcohol in such a quantity that the proportion thereof in his blood, as ascertained from a laboratory test for which he subsequently provided a specimen under s. 9 of the Road Traffic Act 1972, exceeded the prescribed limit at the time he provided the specimen contrary to s. 6(1) of the said Act.

Rule 100 of the Magistrates' Courts Rules 1981 governs the drafting of informations.

Precedents are to be found in 'Okes — Magisterial Formulist' and 'Stone's Justices Manual'.

(c) Two or more informations against one accused may only be tried together if he expressly or impliedly consents to that being done: *Brangwynne* v *Evans* [1962] 1 WLR 267. There is here a significant difference between trial on information and trial on indictment, which may be illustrated by the facts of *Brangwynne* v *Evans*. B was charged in three informations with having, on February 3, 1961 gone into three different shops in Neath and stolen articles from each shop. After he had agreed to be tried summarily and had pleaded not guilty to the first information, his solicitor objected to the three charges being heard together. The magistrates over-ruled the objection. B pleaded not guilty to the other two informations also, but was convicted of all three offences. The Divisional Court quashed the convictions because, far from consenting to the single trial, the defence had expressly objected to it. However, had B been tried on indictment there is no doubt that counts for the three thefts could have been included in one indictment and tried by a single jury. The offences formed a series of the same or a similar character, being offences of shoplifting committed on the same day in the same town (see r. 9 of the Indictment Rules and Para. 5.5). Lord Parker CJ in *Brangwynne* v *Evans* went as far as to state that before hearing two or more informations at the same time the magistrates should expressly ask the accused whether he consents to that course. It seems, however, that where the accused is legally represented and, although not asked if he consents to the single trial, neither he nor his counsel or solicitor objects to a single trial taking place, the silence of the defence on the matter amounts to an implied consent.

(d) Two or more accused may be charged in one information with having committed an offence jointly. If so charged, they may be tried together whether or not they consent. If two or more accused are charged in separate informations, they can only be tried together if each expressly or impliedly consents — i.e. the rule in *Brangwynne* v *Evans* (supra) applies both to several informations against one accused and to several informations each charging a different accused. The strictness of the rule is shown by *Aldus* v *Watson* [1973] QB 902, where four motor cyclists were convicted after a joint trial on separate informations alleging that each of them had driven without reasonable consideration. The prosecution case was that they had ridden as a group in the centre of the road, preventing other road-users overtaking them. Although the case against each accused was inextricably linked with the cases against his three co-accused, and although the defence on appeal conceded that there could have been a single information against all four, the Divisional Court quashed the convictions. The fact of the matter was that there had been separate informations, and the accused had been tried jointly on those informations without expressly or impliedly consenting to the joint trial.

(e) The court may not try an information for a summary offence unless the information was laid within six months of the offence being committed: s. 127. Where the offence is indictable but triable either way, a summary trial for it may take place even though the information was laid outside the six month period, unless the statute creating the offence lays down a time limit for commencing prosecutions for the offence and the information was laid outside that period. Thus, an accused may be tried summarily on a charge of theft however long after the alleged offence the information was laid, but he may not be tried (either summarily or on indictment) for an offence of unlawful sexual intercourse with a girl aged 13 to 16 if the information was laid more than a year after the incident, since the Sexual Offences Act 1956 s. 37 provides that prosecutions for unlawful sexual intercourse must be commenced within a year. It is, of course, unusual for there to be any time limit on prosecutions for indictable offences (see Para. 2.4.3). The purpose of s. 127 was succinctly expressed by May J in *R* v *Newcastle-upon-Tyne Justices* ex parte *John Bryce (Contractors) Ltd* [1976] 1WLR 517 where he said that the section existed:

> To ensure that summary offences are charged and tried as soon as reasonably possible after their alleged commission, so that the recollection of witnesses may still be reasonably clear, and so that there shall be no unnecessary delay in the disposal by magistrates' courts... of the summary offences brought before them to be tried.

Where the aims of the section are indirectly thwarted by a prosecutor laying an information and obtaining a summons just within the six month period, and then failing to serve the summons for another four months, the magistrates have a discretion to refuse to try the case on the ground that there has been an abuse of the process of the court: *R* v *Brentford Justices* ex parte *Wong* [1981] 2WLR 203. In ex parte *Wong* the only reason for the police prosecutor's delay in serving the summons was that, presumably through pressure of work, he had not decided whether or not to prosecute W. Had he, at the time he laid the information, definitely intended to proceed against W, and had he thereafter taken reasonably prompt steps to serve the summons, a delay in service (e.g. through W having changed his address) would not have been fatal to the proceedings.

(f)   The magistrates have a discretion to allow, at any stage of the hearing, an amendment to the information. In addition, s. 123 provides that defects in the form or substance of an information and variations between the allegations in it and the evidence adduced by the prosecution at the trial are not grounds for objecting to the information. Where, however, the accused has been misled by a variance between the information and the prosecution evidence he must, on application, be granted an adjournment.

> Section 123 is so widely worded that, if read literally, it would enable the prosecution to support a conviction however grossly inadequate or misleading the information was. In fact, numerous cases have given a restricted meaning to the section. The cases establish that where the defect in the information, or variation between it and the evidence, is trivial, so that the accused is not prejudiced or misled by it, any conviction upon the information will stand even though the information is not amended. Mis-spellings of the accused's name or of place names provide examples of such trivial errors. In *R* v *Sandwell Justices* ex parte *West Midland Passenger Transport Board* (1979) Crim LR 56 a variation between the evidence (that the Board had put on the road a bus with a defective rear off-side tyre) and the information (which alleged that the defective tyre was the rear near-side one) was stated by the Divisional Court to be so slight that, even in the absence of the amendment which was in fact made, the conviction would have stood. The Board had always been aware of which tyre was the subject of complaint, and, indeed, brought it to court for examination. The position of the tyre on the bus was a matter of no conseqence.
>
> Where the variation between the information and the evidence is substantial, the prosecution should apply for an amendment. If they allow the amendment, the magistrates should consider whether the accused has been misled by the original information, and, if he has, they must grant him an adjournment. Failure to obtain an amendment, or failure by the magistrates to allow the accused an adjournment when he is entitled to one, will lead to any

conviction being quashed. In *Wright* v *Nicholson* [1970] 1WLR 142, for example, the Divisional Court quashed W's conviction for inciting a child to commit an act of gross indecency contrary to the Indecency with Children Act 1960, s. 2. The information, which was not amended, alleged that the offence occurred on 17 August 1967. The evidence of the child was vague as to when the incident happened — it could have been any time in August. W, who had called alibi evidence in respect of August 17, was convicted on the basis that he committed the offence some time in August. The information misled W, it was not amended, and it may have caused him grave injustice because, in the absence of an adjournment, he was unable to call alibi evidence for other days in August.

Amendment of the information and, if appropriate, the granting of an adjournment can remedy almost any defect in it. Where, however, the information is laid against the wrong person (e.g. a company secretary and not the company itself) the defect is so fundamental that even an amendment will not assist the prosecution: *City of Oxford Tramway Co* v *Sankey* (1890) 54JP 564.

11.4 APPEARANCE OF THE ACCUSED

A major difference between summary trial and trial on indictment is that in the latter case the accused must be present to plead to the indictment, and should normally be in court throughout his trial (see Para. 8.5.6). Summary trials, on the other hand, may and often do take place in the accused's absence. Section 12 permits the accused to plead guilty by post, sections 11 and 13 set out the options open to the magistrates when an accused, who has not intimated under s. 12 that he wishes to plead guilty, fails to appear at the time appointed for trial.

11.4.1 Proceeding in the accused's absence under section 11

If the accused does not appear at the time and place fixed for summary trial, the magistrates have a discretion to proceed in the absence of the accused: s. 11(1). If they do so, a plea of not guilty to the information is entered on behalf of the accused, and the prosecution proceed to call their evidence. In the circumstances, they are unlikely to have much difficulty in proving their case, but should the evidence for any reason prove insufficient (e.g. an essential witness fails to give the evidence which was expected of him) the magistrates would be obliged to find the accused not guilty. The position is different where the accused pleads guilty by post under s. 12 (see Para. 11.4.2).

It would obviously be unfair to proceed without the accused if he did not know of the proceedings against him. Accordingly, if the proceedings began with the laying of an information and the issue of a summons requiring the accused to appear at court, the magistrates may not begin to try the case without him unless it is proved that the summons was served on him a reasonable time before the hearing date, or he appeared on a previous occasion in answer to the summons when the case was adjourned: s. 11(2). A summons can be served by sending it through the post to the accused's last known address. Where that method of service is adopted, and the offence charged is indictable, the prosecution in order to prove service must prove that the summons actually came to the knowledge of the accused. If the offence charged is summary, proof that the summons was sent by registered letter or recorded delivery to the last known address is sufficient proof of service: Magistrates' Courts Rules 1981 r. 99. That gives rise to the possibility that the prosecution may be able to prove service when the accused is, in fact, totally unaware of the summons (e.g. because he has moved from the address to which the summons was sent). Section 14 accordingly provides that where proceedings commence with the issue of a summons, and the accused is tried in his absence, he may deliver to the magistrates' clerk a statutory declaration to the effect that he did not know of the summons or the proceedings until a date after the trial's commencement. The declaration should normally be delivered within 21 days of the date on which the declarant found out about the proceedings.

Where proceedings begin, not with the issue of a summons, but with the accused being arrested, either with or without warrant, the fact of the arrest alerts him to the charge against him. Accordingly, if he is bailed from the police station to appear at the magistrates' court but fails to do so, the magistrates can try him in his absence without any formal proof that he knows of the hearing. In fact, if the offence charged is serious enough to justify an arrest, the magistrates would be unlikely to deal with it without the accused.

Two final points should be noticed about proceeding in the absence of the accused. First, although he can be tried summarily in his absence for an offence triable either way, he must normally be present for the hearing at which it is decided to deal with the case summarily (see Chapter 12). Second, if the magistrates, as often happens, do not try the case on the first occasion it comes into their list but adjourn it to another day, the adjourned hearing cannot proceed unless all parties have had adequate notice of the date to which the case was adjourned: s. 10(2).

> Even if the magistrates have power to try the information without the accused they may choose not to do so if for example the offence alleged seems fairly serious. If there is apparently a good reason for the accused's non-appearance (e.g. the police officer in the case says that he is in hospital) the magistrates may simply adjourn, and trust that on the date the hearing is to resume the accused will be present. Should there be no satisfactory explanation for his absence, the magistrates will want to issue a warrant for his arrest. Where the accused was on bail and has failed to surrender to custody in answer to his bail, the court can issue a bench warrant: Bail Act 1976, s. 7. If he is not on bail but has merely failed to appear in answer to a summons, s. 13 provides that a warrant for arrest can only be issued if:
> (a)   the information is substantiated on oath;
> (b)   there is proof of service of the summons, and
> (c)   the offence charged is punishable with imprisonment.
> If the information was not originally laid on oath, the condition in (a) can be satisfied by the prosecutor swearing before the magistrates that the information's contents are correct. The condition in (c) does not apply to juveniles.

11.4.2   Pleas of guilty by post

Proceeding in the absence of the accused under s. 11 has at least three disadvantages. The court's time is wasted hearing evidence which nobody is present to challenge, the prosecution witnesses are inconvenienced, and the accused has no opportunity to tell the magistrates about any mitigating circumstances which ought to reduce the penalty imposed upon him. These disadvantages are overcome by the s. 12 procedure for pleading guilty by post. The procedure can only be used where the accused is summoned to appear before a magistrates' court other than a juvenile court to answer an information alleging a summary offence for which the maximum penalty does not exceed three months imprisonment. The procedure is as follows:

(a)   The prosecutor serves on the accused, together with the summons, a notice explaining how he can plead guilty by post and what will happen if he does so. A form for the notice is given in the Magistrates' Courts (Forms) Rules 1981 (SI No 553). In addition, the prosecutor serves a brief statement of the facts of the alleged offence, which may either be on a separate form or printed at the bottom of the summons. The statement of facts is necessary because the accused may admit that he committed the offence described in the summons but be unwilling to forgo attending court unless he knows what the prosecution will say about the manner in which he committed the offence.

(b) The prosecutor notifies the magistrates' clerk that the documents referred to in (a) have been served.

(c) The accused, if he so wishes, notifies the clerk in writing that he wants to plead guilty without appearing before the court. With the notification, he can send a statement of any mitigating facts which he would like to be brought to the court's attention.

(d) The clerk informs the prosecutor of the accused's intentions, so, on the day of the hearing, neither prosecution nor defence appear at court. Formal proof is given of the service of the summons and other documents on the accused; the clerk reads out the prosecution's brief statement of facts, together with the accused's guilty plea and statement of mitigating circumstances, and the magistrates may proceed to sentence. It is a strict rule that the only statement which may be put before the court on behalf of the prosecution is the brief statement of facts served on the accused. Therefore, when the accused pleads guilty by post he knows exactly what the prosecution case against him will be.

(e) If, having given notice that he wished to plead guilty, the accused changes his mind, he may notify the clerk in writing that he wants his original notification to be withdrawn. The case is not dealt with under s. 12, and the accused is entitled to attend court and plead not guilty in the usual way.

(f) The magistrates always have a discretion not to accept a plea of guilty by post. If the accused's statement of mitigating circumstances should allege facts which, if accepted, would amount to a defence to the charge it would clearly be wrong to proceed on the guilty plea. Instead, the court should adjourn the case. Notice is then given to the accused of the adjournment and the reason for it, and the case proceeds as if no notification of a guilty plea had ever been given.

A great many minor summary offences are disposed of through pleas of guilty by post. The procedure is especially well-suited to road traffic offences, as may be seen in the following example. The information laid against John Smith in that 'on the 1st day of January 1981 he drove a motor vehicle on a restricted road called The High Street, Barchester, at a speed exceeding 30 miles per hour contrary to s. 78A of the Road Traffic Regulations Act 1967'. The information is set out in the summons served on Smith, but if that was all he was told about the offence he would be ill-advised to plead guilty by post as the speed at which he was driving is highly relevant to the sentence which will be imposed. The brief statement of facts served with the summons solves the problem. The statement may say that Smith drove for half a mile along the High Street at a speed which varied between 38 and 40 mph; that there was no danger to pedestrians or other road-users, and that, when stopped, he said 'Why don't you go and catch some burglars?' Smith may feel that, although not absolutely accurate, the statement of facts is substantially correct. He therefore posts to the magistrates' court a letter containing his guilty plea and a description of any mitigating circumstances (e.g. his speed was not as stated by the prosecution, but only around 33 mph, and he was anxious to get home to his wife as he had received a message that she was unwell). He must also send to the court his driving licence because speeding is an endorsable offence (i.e. particulars of the conviction will be endorsed on the licence — Road Traffic Act 1972 s. 101). When the case is heard, and Smith's letter is read to the magistrates, they will take into account the mitigation he has put forward when fixing the amount of the fine he should pay.

11.4.3   Sentencing an accused in his absence

The magistrates may not, for obvious reasons, sentence an offender to imprisonment
in his absence: s. 11(3). If, having convicted an absent accused, they consider that a
sentence of imprisonment may be appropriate, they should adjourn and issue a
warrant for his arrest: s. 13(5). Indeed, the magistrates should adopt this course of
action whenever, after embarking on a case without the accused, they find that the
offence alleged is graver than they had anticipated so that to continue without him is
undesirable. If the magistrates convict the accused in his absence following a plea of
guilty by post, but do not proceed to sentence him because they are considering
imprisonment or the matter otherwise appears too grave to deal with in his absence,
they may not on that occasion issue a warrant for his arrest. Instead the matter is
adjourned. The accused is then given notice of the reasons for the adjournment, and, if
he fails to appear at the adjourned hearing, a warrant may be issued under s. 13(5).
The magistrates may disqualify from driving an offender who is not present, but only
if his case has first been adjourned and a notice served on him stating that the reason
for the adjournment is that the magistrates are considering disqualification: s. 11(4).
This frequently happens when the accused pleads guilty by post to an endorsable
offence, and the magistrates discover, on looking at his licence, that he is liable to a
six month disqualification under the 'totting-up' provisions of the Road Traffic Act
1972 (see Chapter 15). The magistrates automatically adjourn the case. If the accused
fails to appear at the adjourned hearing, he can be disqualified in his absence, or, if
the magistrates consider that it is a particularly bad case, they can adjourn again and
issue a warrant for his arrest.

11.4.4   Non-appearance of the prosecution

If the prosecution fail to appear at time and place fixed for summary trial, the
magistrates have a discretion either to dismiss the information or adjourn the case: s.
15. If the case has been adjourned part-heard from a previous occasion, and the
prosecution do not appear for the adjourned hearing, the magistrates have the
additional option of proceeding in the absence of the prosecution. The evidence given
for the prosecution on the previous occasion will then be the case against the accused,
and in meeting that case he has the obvious advantage of not facing any prosecution
challenge to his evidence or arguments.

11.5   LEGAL REPRESENTATION

Both barristers and solicitors have the right of audience in the magistrates' courts. In
contrast to the position in the Crown Court, the prosecution do not have to be legally
represented in magistrates' courts. It is common where a prosecution is initiated by the
police for a police officer to conduct the case. Similarly, a private individual who has,
for instance, laid an information alleging that his neighbour assaulted him may
himself prosecute the neighbour. Whether it is desirable for persons as closely involved
in the case as police officers or private prosecutors to act, in effect, as prosecuting
counsel is open to question. Prosecuting counsel at a trial on indictment should regard
himself as a minister of justice, acting fairly towards the accused (see Para. 8.1.1) but
one wonders whether a police officer who may have originally been responsible for the

arrest of the accused, or a person who considers himself to have been the victim of an offence can adopt the same attitude when presenting the case against the accused in a magistrates' court.

The accused may, of course, defend himself if he so wishes. Where he is not legally aided and the consequences of a conviction are unlikely to be serious, he would be well advised to save money by doing so. Although the clerk should not 'step into the arena' and conduct a party's case for him, the court may allow him to assist an unrepresented accused (e.g. by telling him the sort of questions which sould be asked in cross-examination of the prosecution witnesses, and by reminding him of any items of prosecution evidence with which he ought to deal). An accused (or, indeed, any party) who is represented by counsel or solicitor is deemed not to be absent even though he is not physically present in court: s. 122. Thus, counsel or solicitor for an absent accused can nonetheless cross-examine prosecution witnesses, call witnesses for the defence other than the accused, and, if his client is convicted, present mitigation on his behalf. However, if the accused has been bailed to appear at court he must attend personally. Should he fail to do so, the presence of counsel or solicitor on his behalf will not be a defence to a charge of absconding under s. 6 of the Bail Act 1976 (see Chapter 20). Similarly, the accused must, generally speaking, be personally present at committal proceedings (see Para. 3.2) and at proceedings for determining the mode of trial of an offence triable either way (see Para 12.2). However, a warrant for the arrest of an absent accused may not be issued under s. 13 (see Paras. 11.4.1 and 11.4.3) if he is deemed to be present through the attendance of counsel or solicitor.

11.6 THE COURSE OF THE TRIAL

The course of a summary trial is, to a large degree, identical to the course of a trial on indictment. Proceedings begin with the clerk putting the information to the accused, and asking him if he pleads guilty or not guilty. If he pleads guilty, the magistrates may proceed immediately to sentence him, or they may adjourn the case to obtain reports on him. If the plea is ambiguous and questions from the bench cannot resolve the ambiguity, a plea of not guilty is entered. Similarly, if the accused stays silent, the case proceeds as on a not guilty plea. There is no special procedure for determining questions of autrefois acquit and convict, but the issues can be raised on an ordinary not guilty plea., The issue of unfitness to plead cannot, however, be raised at a magistrates' court. If the accused appears to have mental problems and the offence charged is triable either way, it is probably safer to have the matter committed for trial. If the offence is summary, a not guilty plea may be entered on behalf of the accused, and if the magistrates are satisfied that he committed the *actus reus* of the offence, and that he is suffering from mental illness or severe abnormality, they may, without convicting him, make an order that he be admitted to a mental hospital: Mental Health Act 1959, s. 60(2). An order under s. 60(2) can only be made if the offence charged is punishable with imprisonment. Like a judge at the Crown Court, the magistrates have a discretion to allow a change of plea. In particular, they may allow the accused to withdraw a plea of guilty at any stage of the trial before sentence is passed: *S. (An Infant)* v *Manchester City Recorder* [1971] AC 481.

Following a not guilty plea, the prosecution have the right to an opening speech. Unless the case is particularly complicated, counsel or solicitor keeps the speech short, or even forgoes completely his right to address the magistrates — being more experienced in trying cases than are jurors, magistrates do not need the preliminary explanations which assist jurors. The prosecution witnesses are then called. If either the prosecution or defence wish to call a witness, but have reason to think that he will not attend court voluntarily, they should apply before trial to a magistrate or a magistrates' clerk for a summons requiring the witness to attend: s. 97. If the summons is not obeyed and there appears to be no just excuse for the disobedience, the magistrates may issue a warrant for the witness' arrest provided that they are satisfied by evidence on oath that the witness is likely to be able to give material evidence, that he has been served with the summons, and has been paid a reasonable sum to cover the costs of his court attendance. The magistrates may also adjourn the case until the witness is brought to court. In extreme cases, where a magistrate is satisfied by evidence on oath that a summons issued under s. 97 is unlikely to be obeyed, he may before trial issue a warrant to arrest the witness, a procedure which also applies to committal proceedings. At summary trials as at trials on indictment, the prosecution are under a duty to make available to the defence a witness who can give material evidence but whom they do not intend to call (see Para. 8.3.2 and *R* v *Leyland Justices* ex parte *Hawthorn* [1979] QB 283 for a case where failure by the police to tell the defence of a witness who could have given evidence helpful to H led to his conviction being quashed on the ground that the hearing by the magistrates had been in breach of the rules of natural justice). If a prosecution witness gives evidence which is materially different from a statement which he has previously made and which is in the prosecution's possession, the defence should be told of that fact, and preferably be given a copy of the statement. Sections 9 and 10 of the Criminal Justice Act 1967 (admissibility of written statements and formal admissions by the parties respectively — see Paras. 8.3.7 and 8.3.8) apply to summary trials as they do to trials on indictment.

After the prosecution case has been closed, the defence may submit that there is no case to answer. The submission should be upheld if either there is no evidence to prove an essential element of the offence alleged in the information, or the prosecution evidence has been so discredited as a result of cross-examination or is so manifestly unreliable that no reasonable tribunal could safely convict on it (see Practice Note 1962 1AER 448 issued by the Divisional Court, Lord Parker CJ presiding). If the submission is upheld, the accused is found not guilty and discharged.

If no submission is made, or a submission is made unsuccessfully, the defence may call evidence. Just as at trial on indictment, there is no obligation upon the defence to adduce any evidence. The accused is a competent but not a compellable witness, and he may make a statement from the dock instead of giving sworn evidence. A point of contrast with trial on indictment is that the defence do not have to disclose particulars of any alibi evidence which they intend to adduce, but that advantage is more than outweighed by the fact they are not entitled to any advance notice of the prosecution evidence. Usually the prosecution will give to defence counsel or solicitor before the hearing a general indication of the nature of their case. Before a trial on indictment, on the other hand, the defence, as a result of committal proceedings and notice of any additional evidence, know precisely what evidence the prosecution witnesses are expected to give. The Criminal Law Act 1977, s. 48, allows rules to be made requiring the prosecution to disclose to the defence facts and matters of which they intend to adduce evidence in proceedings before magistrates, but no rules have as yet been made under the section. Further discussion of the advantages and disadvantages of summary trial as compared with trial on indictment will be found in Para. 12.6.

The prosecution have no right to a closing speech. The defence have either an opening or a closing speech, and nearly always choose to make a closing speech so as to have the advantage of the last word (Magistrates' Courts Rules 1981, r. 13). Either party may, at the court's discretion, be allowed to make a second speech. If that discretion is exercised, the other party must be given a second speech also. Any second speech by the prosecution must be made before the defence second speech, so as not to deprive the defence of the last word.

A stipendiary magistrate sitting alone normally announces his decision immediately after the defence closing speech. Lay magistrates nearly always retire to consider their verdict. They need not be unanimous. In the event of an even numbered court being equally divided, the chairman has no casting vote. The magistrates can either adjourn the case for rehearing by a differently constituted bench, or acquit the accused. If, after convicting an accused, the magistrates have second thoughts about the correctness of their decision, they may direct that the case be reheard by different justices: s. 142. Such a direction must be given within 28 days of the conviction. The court giving the direction must consist of either the same magistrates who constituted the 'convicting court' or, if that court consisted of three or more magistrates, a majority of them. A direction may be given in cases where the accused appeared and pleaded not guilty, and in cases where the magistrates proceeded in his absence with a plea of not guilty being entered on his behalf. The effect of a direction is that the conviction and any sentence subsequently imposed are nullified. The magistrates who rehear the case may, of course, convict the accused and pass whatever sentence they consider fit.

The Criminal Law Act 1967, s. 6(2)-(4), which permits juries to return verdicts of not guilty as charged but guilty of some other offence, does not apply to magistrates. Accordingly, a magistrates' court has no power to find the accused guilty of a lesser offence (*Lawrence* v *Same* [1968] 2QB 93, where a conviction for common assault upon an information alleging unlawful wounding contrary to the Offences against the Person Act 1861, s. 20 was quashed by the Divisional Court). A quasi-exception to this rule is found in the Road Traffic Act 1972, Schedule 4 Part IV para. 4, which provides that magistrates who are of the opinion that an information alleging reckless driving is not proved may permit or direct the preferring of a charge for careless driving or driving without reasonable consideration. They may do this during or immediately after the hearing of the reckless driving charge, and may then proceed immediately to hear the new charge unless an adjournment is necessary to avoid prejudice to the accused. The evidence which has already been given for purposes of the reckless driving charge is admissible on the new charge, but the defence must be given an opportunity to recall any prosecution witness for further cross-examination. The defence should also be given the opportunity to answer the new charge in any other proper way (e.g. by calling further evidence or by making a closing speech relevant to the new charge rather than the reckless driving charge). The magistrates may then dismiss the information for reckless driving but find the careless driving or driving without reasonable consideration proved.

11.7 POWERS OF SENTENCING AFTER CONVICTION FOR A SUMMARY OFFENCE

The powers of the courts when sentencing offenders and the restrictions placed on the imposition of each form of sentence are dealt with in Chapter 15. This Paragraph concerns certain additional restrictions placed on the magistrates' powers to sentence an offender who has been convicted of one or more summary offences. The restrictions on the magistrates' powers to sentence an offender who has been summarily convicted of an offence triable either way are set out in Para. 12.3.1.

The maximum penalties which may be imposed upon conviction for a summary offence are set out in the statute creating the offence. To take two random examples, the Police Act 1964, s. 51 provides that a person who assaults a police constable in the execution of his duty 'shall be... liable on summary conviction to imprisonment for a term not exceeding six months or to a fine not exceeding £1,000 or to both', while Schedule 4 to the Road Traffic Act 1972 prescribes a fine of up to £500 plus obligatory endorsement of the licence and discretionary disqualification as the penalty for careless driving. The magistrates' powers to imprison are thus regulated by the statute creating the offence. Where, however, the statute provides for imprisonment in excess of six months upon summary conviction, the Magistrates' Courts Act 1980, s. 31(1) reduces the maximum term the magistrates can impose to six months. The only situation where s. 31(1) does not operate to limit the maximum term is where the statute allowing more than six months imprisonment expressly states that the sub-section is not to apply.

When a court, be it the Crown Court or a magistrates' court, passes a sentence of imprisonment it may make the sentence take effect either after or at the same time as any other sentence of imprisonment which the offender may be serving. In the former case, the sentence is consecutive to the sentence already being served; in the latter case, it is concurrent with it. Similarly, where a court on one occasion sentences an offender to separate terms of imprisonment for two or more offences, the court can order that the terms run consecutively to or concurrently with each other. The magistrates' powers to order consecutive sentences are, however, limited in that if they sentence an offender for two or more summary offences, the aggregate sentence imposed must not exceed six months: s. 133. If, therefore, the magistrates convict an offender of two offences of assaulting a police officer in the execution of his duty, they could sentence him to two terms of six months imprisonment to run concurrently, or to two terms of three months to run consecutively, but they could not sentence him to four months and three months to run consecutively.

There are, of course, many other methods of dealing with offenders in addition to imprisoning them or fining them (see Chapter 15). These other forms of sentence are, in general, available for the magistrates to use. For example, they can conditionally or absolutely discharge an offender; they can put him on probation; they can order that he perform community service, and, in the case of a young offender, they can order that he go to a detention centre or attend at an attendance centre. There are, however, important restrictions on the magistrates' powers of sentencing a juvenile (one under the age of 17) who has been convicted in the adult magistrates' court (see Chapter 13). Another major restriction on their powers is that they cannot pass a sentence of Borstal training either upon a juvenile or upon an offender who has attained the age of 17. Chapter 12 describes the course of action which is open to them when they consider that an offender should be sent to Borstal. Suspended sentences of imprisonment may be passed by the magistrates, but the term which they suspend must not exceed the maximum term which they could impose as an immediate sentence of imprisonment.

Upon the accused pleading guilty or being found guilty by them, the magistrates may proceed immediately to sentence him, but often they feel that to sentence him properly they must learn more about him. If so, they may adjourn so that inquiries can be made (for instance through the preparation by a probation officer of a social enquiry report), but the adjournment must not be for more than four weeks: s. 10(3). If the offender is remanded in custody for the period of the adjournment, it must not exceed three weeks. Section 10(3) is supplemented by s. 30, which provides that if the magistrates are satisfied that the accused committed the *actus reus* of the offence, and if they are also of the opinion that an inquiry should be made into his physical or mental condition to enable them to decide how to deal with him, they must adjourn for medical reports to be prepared. The maximum period of the adjournment is again either three or four weeks depending on whether the accused is remanded in custody, and if he is granted bail, it must be on condition that he attend at a hospital etc. for the preparation of the reports. The magistrates may adjourn under s. 30 for medical reports even though they have not convicted the accused, provided that they are satisfied he committed the *actus reus* of the offence. If the medical reports show that he is suffering from mental illness or severe abnormality they may order that he be detained in a mental hospital without the necessity of recording a conviction against him (see also Para. 11.6).

11.8 THE ROLE OF THE CLERK

The court clerk plays a major role in the conduct of summary proceedings. He is not necessarily the magistrates' clerk himself, but may be an assistant clerk qualified to act as a clerk in court under the Justices' Clerks (Qualification of Assistants) Rules 1979 (SI 1979 No 570 — see Para. 10.4). During the course of a hearing, the clerk's tasks include putting the information to the accused; taking a note of the evidence; helping an unrepresented accused in the presentation of his case, and advising the magistrates upon points of law or procedure as they arise. This last is probably his most important function, for, although the magistrates are the judges of both law and fact, lay magistrates do, as a matter of practice, accept their clerk's advice on matters of law. Because of the importance of his advice, it is desirable that when a point of law has to be decided during a hearing (e.g. as to the admissibility of evidence) the clerk should give his advice publicly so that the parties know what he has said. Similarly, if there is a point of law which has not been argued by the parties but which the clerk feels should be brought to the magistrates' attention, he should refer to the point in open court so that the parties have an opportunity of commenting upon the matter.

When the magistrates retire to consider their verdict, the clerk may retire with them, but only to advise them on the law and, if they are minded to convict, on their powers of sentencing. He should not join the magistrates in their retirement unless asked to do so, and, as soon as he has advised on the point of law, he should return into open court. However, in a complicated case where issues of fact and law are closely intertwined, the clerk may stay with the magistrates during virtually the whole period for which they are retired: *R* v *Consett Justices* ex parte *Postal Bingo* [1967] 2QB 9. The essential point is that the clerk should neither interfere with the magistrates' decision on the facts, nor, through retiring with them when there is no good reason for doing so, put himself in a position where he might appear to be interfering with their decision. Thus, in *R* v *Stafford Justices* ex parte *Ross* [1962] 1WLR 456 the Divisional Court quashed R's conviction because, during the trial, the clerk had passed a note to the magistrates in which he suggested that R's defence was implausible. Similarly, in *R* v *Guildford Justices* ex parte *Harding* ('The Times' 20 January 1981) the conviction could not stand because, in a case where the law was absolutely straightforward, the clerk had retired with the magistrates to advise them on the standard of proof. The Divisional Court appeared to regard this reason for wanting the clerk's advice as little better than a pretence.

A Practice Direction from Lord Lane CJ ([1981] 1WLR 1163) summarises the functions of the clerk.

12   Summary Trial of Offences Triable Either Way

12.1 CLASSIFICATION OF OFFENCES

An offence is either summary or indictable (see Para. 1.4). An indictable offence is one for which an adult (i.e. a person who has attained the age of 17) either must or may be tried on indictment; a summary offence is one which must be tried summarily: Interpretation Act 1978, Schedule 1. As the definition of indictable offence implies, some are only triable on indictment and some may be tried either on indictment or summarily. The latter are known as offences triable either way.

12.1.1 Summary offences

Summary offences are all statutory. The statute creating a summary offence shows that it is summary by specifying a maximum penalty which may be imposed on summary conviction without specifying a second greater penalty for offenders convicted on indictment. For example, s. 51 of the Police Act 1964 provides that:

> any person who assaults a constable in the execution of his duty...shall be guilty of an offence and liable on *summary* conviction to imprisonment for a term not exceeding six months or to a fine not exceeding £1,000 or to both.

Since s. 51 does not mention a penalty imposable following conviction on indictment, the offence of assaulting a constable in the execution of his duty is summary.

A large variety of minor and occasionally not so minor offences are summary. They include keeping a dog without a licence, dropping litter, taking a pedal cycle without lawful authority (the only summary offence under the Theft Acts 1968 and 1978), offences under the Food and Drugs Act 1955 (e.g. selling food which is unfit for human consumption), offences under the Factories Act 1961 (e.g. not maintaining machinery in a safe condition) and most road traffic offences (e.g. careless driving, speeding, failing to comply with traffic directions, failing to stop after an accident and many more). Among the most serious summary offences are using threatening words or behaviour likely to cause a breach of the peace contrary to s. 5 of the Public Order Act 1936, drink/driving offences contrary to ss. 5, 6 and 9 of the Road Traffic Act 1972 and assaulting a constable.

12.1.2 Indictable offences

All common law offences (e.g. murder, manslaughter and attempts) are indictable. Statutory offences are indictable if the statute creating the offence specifies a penalty to be imposed following conviction on indictment. For example, the Theft Act 1968 shows that theft and robbery are indictable offences by providing in s. 7 that — 'a person guilty of theft shall on *conviction on indictment* be liable to imprisonment for a term not exceeding ten years' — and in s. 8(2) that 'a person guilty of robbery... shall on *conviction on indictment* be liable to imprisonment for life'. Where a statute creating an offence provides for two separate penalties, one to be imposed on summary conviction and the other on conviction on indictment, the offence created is indictable but triable either way. An example is reckless driving which is punishable on summary conviction with six months imprisonment and a £1,000 fine and punishable on conviction on indictment with two years imprisonment and an unlimited fine. It should be noted, however, that many offences are triable either way even though the statute creating them does not provide for a penalty on summary conviction (see below).

12.1.3   Offences triable either way

Offences triable either way fall into two groups. They are either, like reckless driving, made triable either way by the statute creating them, or they are included in Schedule 1 to the Magistrates' Courts Act 1980. Section 17 of the Act provides that 'the offences listed in Schedule 1... shall be triable either way'. Extracts from the Schedule will be found at page 327 in Appendix One.

As one would expect, the most serious offences are triable only on indictment. Offences triable either way tend to be those which, although serious enough to be indictable, are never, even at worst, very grave (e.g. reckless driving or making off without payment contrary to s. 3 of the Theft Act 1978), and those which vary greatly in gravity depending upon the facts of the particular case (e.g. criminal damage or theft). The table below lists some of the most common indictable offences according to whether they are triable only on indictment or triable either way.

NATURE OF OFFENCE	TRIABLE ONLY ON INDICTMENT	TRIABLE EITHER WAY
Offences against the person	Murder, manslaughter, child destruction, attempt to procure abortion, causing grievous bodily harm with intent to do so.	Unlawful wounding, assault occasioning actual bodily harm.
Sexual offences	Rape, intercourse with girl under 13, buggery, incest.	Unlawful sexual intercourse with girl under 16, indecency between men, indecent assault, living on the earnings of prostitution.
Offences under the Theft Acts 1968 and 1978	Robbery, aggravated burglary, blackmail, assault with intent to rob, burglary comprising the commission of or intention to commit an offence triable only on indictment (e.g. entry as a trespasser with intent to rape), burglary in a dwelling if any person	All offences under the Acts apart from those which are triable only on indictment and taking a pedal cycle, which is summary. They include theft, handling stolen goods, obtaining property by deception, most forms of burglary, going equipped, obtaining

	therein was subjected to violence or the threat of it.	services by deception, evading liability by deception, making off without payment.
Offences under the Forgery Act 1913	Forgery of wills, deeds, bonds or bank notes.	Forgery of documents evidencing the payment of money, or authorising the payment of money or transfer of goods where the value involved is £1,000 or less.
Criminal damage	Damage or arson charged under s. 1(2) of the Criminal Damage Act 1971 (offence committed with intent to endanger life or being reckless as to the endangering of life).	Criminal damage offences where no intent etc. to endanger life is alleged.
Road traffic offences	Causing death by reckless driving.	Reckless driving, driving while disqualified, taking a motor vehicle without lawful authority.

Attempts and incitement to commit offences triable either way are themselves triable either way, but conspiracy is only triable on indictment.

Leaving aside road traffic offences and other minor summary offences carrying no real social stigma, the offences which occur most frequently are triable either way. Therefore, the procedure for determining the mode of trial for these offences is of major importance.

12.2 DETERMINING THE MODE OF TRIAL

The procedure for deciding whether an offence triable either way shall be tried on indictment or summarily, where the accused is 17 or over, is laid down in the Magistrates' Courts Act 1980, ss. 18-21 and 23. The procedure must be carried out before any evidence is called for the purpose of committal proceedings or summary trial: s. 18(2). The committal or summary trial will probably take place immediately after the mode of trial has been determined, but an adjournment may be necessary for example because the parties are not ready to proceed or there is not enough time for the hearing. Like committal proceedings, the procedure for determining the mode of trial can take place before a single lay justice, but it is more usual for the court to consist of at least two lay justices: s. 18(5). The following are the steps in the procedure:

(a) The clerk reads the charge to the accused.

(b) First the prosecution and then the defence are given the opportunity to make representations as to whether trial on indictment or summary trial would be the more suitable method of trial: s. 19(2)(b). The factors relevant to that question, to which the prosecution or defence might refer in their representations, are indicated in (c) below.

(c) The magistrates consider which of the two methods of trial is the more suitable. They must bear in mind the representations, if any, made by the prosecution and defence, and they must have regard to the nature of the case, whether the circumstances make the offence one of serious character, whether the punishment which a magistrates' court would have power to inflict for it would be adequate, and any other circumstances which make the case more suitable for one method of trial rather than the other: s. 19(3).

(d)   If the magistrates consider that the offence is more suitable for summary trial, the court clerk tells the accused that the magistrates have taken that view. He then informs him that he may, if he consents, be tried by the magistrates, but that if he wishes he can choose to be tried by a jury instead. However, if he is tried by the magistrates and found guilty information will be obtained about his character and antecedents, and if, because of these, the magistrates consider that greater punishment should be imposed than they have power to inflict, they may send him to the Crown Court to be sentenced. The clerk then puts the accused to his election — he asks 'Do you wish to be tried by this court or do you wish to be tried by a jury?' If, and only if, the accused consents, the magistrates proceed to summary trial with the accused pleading guilty or not guilty to the charge against him. If the accused does not consent to summary trial, committal proceedings must be held: s. 20.

(e)   If the magistrates consider that trial on indictment is more appropriate, the accused is told of their decision, and committal proceedings take place: s. 21.

The essence of the procedure laid down by ss. 18-21 is that there can be a summary trial for an offence triable either way only if both the magistrates and the accused agree to it. Of the matters mentioned in s. 19(3) to which the magistrates must pay regard in considering the more suitable method of trial (see (c) above) by far the most important is whether, in the event of a conviction, they would have power to inflict adequate punishment. Their powers of sentencing upon convicting an offender of an offence triable either way are described in Para. 12.3. In essence, they can pass a sentence of six months imprisonment and a £1,000 fine in respect of any one offence triable either way. If they deal with an offender for two or more offences triable either way they can fine him up to £1,000 for each offence, but, although they can pass prison sentences for each offence to run consecutively, the aggregate sentence must not exceed 12 months. So, having listened to any representations from the prosecution or defence, the magistrates look at the nature of the case (is the accused charged with theft of £10 or theft of £10,000? — did the unlawful wounding alleged against him result in the victim suffering a slight graze or a deep cut requiring several stitches?), they bear in mind any circumstances which make the offence one of serious character (e.g. the accused, occupying a position of trust, abused that trust in order to commit the offence), and then they ask themselves — 'is six months imprisonment and a £1,000 fine a sufficient penalty for this offence?' If the answer is no, they should not agree to try the case. If the answer is yes, then summary trial would appear the more suitable method of trial, but there might still be other factors which make trial on indictment more appropriate (e.g. although the offence charged is trivial in itself, the accused is a prominent public figure, whose career would be ruined by a conviction).

In considering whether their sentencing powers are adequate, the magistrates assume that the accused is a man of entirely good character. If he has previous convictions, they must not be told about them: *R v Colchester Justices* ex parte *North East Essex Building Co. Ltd.* [1977] 1WLR 1109. However, some offences triable either way are so serious that, even when committed by a man of otherwise exemplary character, six months imprisonment and a £1,000 would be a much too lenient punishment. Lord Parker CJ made the point forcefully in *R* v *Kings Lynn Justices* ex parte *Carter and others* [1969] 1QB 488 where the magistrates agreed to deal summarily with a charge of stealing almost £3,500 worth of ladies garments. He said:

> This is a very serious charge, and it is very difficult to think how the magistrates could have felt that they had power to inflict punishments appropriate to the offence...I would like to repeat what Lord Goddard CJ said in a number of cases in the past, that magistrates must not deal summarily with serious cases of this nature, which can only properly be tried on indictment...In the present case if the justices had applied their minds to the charge, they could not properly have agreed to try it summarily.

The ravages of inflation make it difficult to say precisely how valuable the goods stolen must be before magistrates today should decline to try the case. Possibly, theft of garments valued at £3,500 might today just be within the magistrates' proper jurisdiction. Nonetheless, the principle of ex parte *Carter* is as important now as it was in 1969 — the magistrates should not try serious cases.

Except as mentioned below, the prosecution cannot insist upon trial on indictment. Their views on the appropriate method of trial are, however, given great weight by the magistrates, who may feel that the police are the people in the best position to know how serious the alleged offence is. Therefore, if the prosecution are content with summary trial, and the defence indicate that the accused wishes to opt for summary trial, the magistrates may, in practice, agree without enquiring minutely into whether their sentencing powers will be adequate. Conversely, if the prosecution wish to go for trial on indictment, the defence may have a difficult task in persuading the magistrates that the matter is suitable for them to deal with. If the prosecution is being carried on by the Attorney-General, Solicitor-General or Director of Public Prosecutions, and he applies for trial on indictment, the magistrates must comply with his wishes and hold committal proceedings: s. 19(4).

In the majority of cases the procedure for determining the mode of trial will not take nearly as long to carry out as it has taken to describe. The prosecution representative — who may, of course, be a barrister or solicitor but very often is the police officer in the case — is asked whether the prosecution are asking for summary trial. If he says that they are, defence counsel or solicitor is asked for his comments. He may indicate that the accused also wants the case dealt with summarily. If so, the magistrates will probably agree to summary trial without more ado. Should the charge seem more serious than is normally tried summarily, they may enquire further into how grave the case really is before accepting jurisdiction (e.g. they may ask whether all the property allegedly stolen has been recovered, or whether the victim of an assault has suffered any permanent injury, or whether the accused abused a position of trust in order to commit the offence). Immediately the magistrates have said that they consider summary trial appropriate, the clerk informs the accused of his right to be tried by a jury etc. (see stage (d) of the procedure), and the accused elects summary trial.

Where the prosecution ask for summary trial, but the defence wish the case to go for trial on indictment, there is little point in counsel or solicitor making lengthy representations to show that the case is one fit for the Crown Court, as it cannot in any event be tried by the magistrates unless the accused consents. Accordingly, counsel or solicitor may simply say that his client is electing trial by judge and jury, the magistrates say that they consider summary trial appropriate, and the clerk proceeds to put the accused to his election. Having asked for summary trial, the prosecution cannot be criticised for having inflicted on the public the extra expense of a judge and jury trial. The only situations in which determining the mode of trial is likely to lead to any real argument are where the prosecution say that trial on indictment is appropriate but the defence are anxious that the case stay in the magistrates' court, and where both prosecution and defence are content with summary trial but the magistrates have doubts about the adequacy of their sentencing powers.

12.2.1   Failure to comply with the procedure

The magistrates' jurisdiction to try offences triable either way derives solely from the Magistrates' Courts Act 1980, ss. 18-20. Therefore, if the procedure laid down in those sections is not strictly complied with but the court nevertheless proceeds to try an accused for an offence triable either way, the magistrates act in excess of their jurisdiction and any conviction is liable to be quashed. In *R v Kent Justices* ex parte *Machin* [1952] 2QB 355 magistrates, purporting to act under jurisdiction given to them by legislation then in force similar in effect to ss. 18 to 20, convicted M of larceny and obtaining credit by fraud. Although M had, through his solicitor, consented to summary trial, the conviction and subsequent committal to Quarter Sessions for sentence were quashed because the clerk had failed to explain to M the possibility of his being sentenced at Quarter Sessions. Presumably, M's solicitor had explained to him that he might be committed for sentence, but failure to follow the statutory procedure was fatal to the conviction. In *R v Horseferry Road Justices* ex parte *Constable* ('The Times' 27 January 1981) the Divisional Court (Donaldson LJ) was equally insistent that the procedure set out in sections of the Criminal Law Act 1977 identical to ss. 18 to 20 of the Magistrates' Courts Act 1980 should be followed to the letter. C had consented to summary trial of an offence triable either way, but the Divisional Court could not be certain that he had first been asked whether he had any representations to make as to the more suitable method of trial. Since he apparently wanted summary trial, and since the magistrates had agreed that summary trial was more suitable, any representations from C on the subject might seem superfluous. Even so, the Divisional Court held that C could withdraw his consent to summary trial. It was of 'fundamental importance' that the procedures laid down in the Criminal Law Act 1977, s. 20 (now Magistrates' Courts Act 1980, s. 19) should be complied with, and failing to ask C for his view on the more suitable method of trial was a departure from those procedures.

12.2.2   Presence of the accused

The accused should normally be present for proceedings under ss. 18-21 to determine the mode of trial. His presence can be dispensed with, however, in circumstances similar to but a little wider than those in which an accused need not be present for committal proceedings (see Para. 3.2). The court can proceed in his absence if his disorderly conduct makes it impracticable to continue the proceedings in his presence: s. 18(3). It can also proceed in his absence if there is a good reason for so doing, and he is represented by counsel or solicitor who states that he (the accused) consents to the proceedings being conducted without him: s. 23(1). The 'good reasons' for proceeding without the accused are not limited to reasons of health, but might include the accused having an important prior engagement for the day in question (compare s. 4 which permits committal proceedings to be held in the accused's absence only if he is disorderly or too ill to attend). If the magistrates consider that summary trial is more appropriate, the accused's consent to the magistrates dealing with the case can be signified by counsel or solicitor on his behalf. The magistrates could then proceed immediately to try the case or adjourn to give the accused an opportunity to attend. If the case is more suitable for trial on indictment or the accused's consent to summary trial is not signified, committal proceedings must be held, and the magistrates adjourn unless the circumstances are such that they can hold committal proceedings without the accused being there.

12.2.3   Changing the original decision

The decision in favour of summary trial or trial on indictment as the case may be is not irreversible. If the decision is for summary trial and the accused pleads not guilty to the information, the magistrates may, at any stage before the close of the prosecution case, discontinue the summary trial and hold committal proceedings instead: s. 25(2). This is appropriate where the prosecution evidence shows the offence to be more serious than the magistrates had at first realised, so that their powers of punishment would not after all be adequate in the event of their convicting. Conversely, the magistrates may, at any stage of committal proceedings, decide that the case is less serious than they originally thought, and give the accused the opportunity of having it tried summarily: s. 25(3). They must first ask for representations from prosecution and defence about the proposed change of method of trial, and the clerk should explain to the accused the possibility of his being committed for sentence if that has not already been done. Any switch to summary trial is, of course, dependent upon the accused's consent. If the prosecution is being conducted by the Attorney-General, Solicitor-General or Director of Public Prosecutions, it is also dependent upon his consent. Where the magistrates do switch to summary trial, oral evidence given already for purposes of the committal proceedings is deemed to have been given for purposes of the summary trial, so that evidence does not need to be repeated (s. 28), but the section does not apply to written statements tendered in the committal proceedings under s. 102 (see Para. 3.4.2). Consequently, if the party who tendered the statement wishes to use the evidence in it for the summary trial, he must call the maker of the statement as a witness.

Where the accused has consented to summary trial, the magistrates have a discretion to allow him to withdraw his consent at any stage before evidence is heard. Thus, if the accused agrees to summary trial and, after a plea of guilty, the magistrates adjourn the case for reports, they have a discretion at the resumed hearing (a) to let the accused change his plea to not guilty (see Para. 11.6), and (b), if they do permit a change of plea, to let him withdraw his consent to summary trial: *R v Craske* ex parte *Commissioner of Metropolitan Police* [1957] 1QB 591. Permitting a withdrawal of consent to summary trial is, however, always a matter for the magistrates' discretion. Unless they have refused even to consider exercising their discretion or have approached the question upon a completely wrong basis, the Divisional Court will not interfere with their insisting that the case be tried summarily. The fact that the accused gave his consent to summary trial when he was not legally represented does not entitle him to withdraw consent after obtaining representation, but it would be an argument for the magistrates exercising their discretion in his favour.

12.3   COMMITTAL TO THE CROWN COURT FOR SENTENCE UNDER SECTION 38

Where an accused who has attained the age of 17 is summarily convicted of an offence triable either way the magistrates may commit him to the Crown Court to be sentenced if, on obtaining information about his character and antecedents, they are of the opinion that they are such that greater punishment should be inflicted for the offence than they have power to inflict: Magistrates' Courts Act 1980, s. 38. The committal for sentence may be in custody, or the offender may be bailed to appear at the Crown Court, but committals for sentence on bail are rare because by committing for sentence the magistrates generally imply that they consider a sentence of imprisonment to be the appropriate punishment, and they would not want to release on bail an offender whom they believe should be sent to prison. When the offender comes before the Crown Court to be sentenced, he may be dealt with for the offence as if he had just been convicted of it on indictment: Powers of Criminal Courts Act, 1973, s. 42.

12.3.1 Powers of sentencing after summary conviction of an offence triable either way

Upon convicting an offender of an offence triable either way, the magistrates may:

(a)   If the offence is one of those listed in Schedule 1 to the Magistates' Courts Act 1980, sentence the offender to up to six months imprisonment and fine him £1,000: s. 32(1).

(b)   If the offence is made triable either way by the statute creating it, the maximum sentence of imprisonment the magistrates can impose is six months or the maximum laid down in the statute creating the offence, whichever is the *less* (s. 31 — see also Para. 11.7). Thus, although the Misuse of Drugs Act 1971 provides that several offences involving drugs can be punished with up to a year's imprisonment upon summary conviction, the operation of s. 31 means that in fact the maximum prison sentence the magistrates can pass is six months. If the statute creating the offence provides for, say, three months imprisonment upon summary conviction, that is the maximum the magistrates can impose, not six months.

(c)   The maximum fine the magistrates may order to be paid for an offence made triable either way by the statute creating it is £1,000 or the amount mentioned in the relevant statute whichever is the *greater:* save that if the relevant statute was passed after 1977, the maximum fine is the figure mentioned in the statute, whether more or less than £1,000: s. 32(2).

(d)   Where the magistrates sentence an offender for two or more offences triable either way, they may pass sentences of imprisonment for each offence and make the sentences run consecutively to each other (and consecutively to sentences of imprisonment passed in respect of any summary offences of which they have also convicted the offender). The aggregate term of the sentence must not, however, exceed twelve months: s. 133(2). Thus, if magistrates convict an offender of two offences of theft and one of assaulting a police constable in the execution of his duty (i.e. of two offences triable either way and one summary offence), they may sentence him to six months imprisonment for each offence to run concurrently; or they may sentence him to four months for each offence to run consecutively, but they may not sentence him to six months for each offence to run consecutively. If the offender was convicted of only one offence of theft and one of assaulting a police constable, the aggregate term would be restricted to six months (s. 133(1) and see Para. 11.7).

12.3.2 Circumstances in which magistrates may commit for sentence under s. 38

The magistrates should only agree to try an offence triable either way if they consider that, in the event of a conviction, they could inflict adequate punishment for it: s. 19(3) and see Para. 12.2. However, when they agree to summary trial, they are ignorant of matters which have a major bearing upon the sentence which it is proper to impose. They know nothing about the character or background of the accused. In particular, they do not know whether he has any previous convictions. An offence of, for example, 'shoplifting' involving theft of £100 worth of clothes could, in the case of a first offender, be dealt with by means of a fine or probation or even a conditional discharge. In the case of an offender with several previous similar convictions who is in breach of a suspended sentence passed for 'shoplifting', six months and £1,000 fine might well be inadequate. For that reason s. 38 enables the magistrates to commit the offender to the Crown Court to be sentenced, and the Crown Court will have ample sentencing powers.

The magistrates' power to commit for sentence under s. 38 only arises if the offender's 'character and antecedents' make their powers of punishment inadequate. If, setting aside the offence of which he has just been convicted, the offender is of good character and antecedents, a s. 38 committal for sentence will be in excess of jurisdiction, and is liable to be quashed by an order of *certiorari* issued by the Divisional Court. Undoubtedly, the most important element in an offender's character is the number of previous convictions, if any, which he has. As a rule of thumb, one can say that an offender with no previous convictions who is summarily convicted of an offence triable either way is not at risk of being committed to the Crown Court for sentence. However, the phrase 'character and antecedents' does not refer merely to previous convictions or the lack of them. On the contrary, Lord Parker CJ in *R* v *Kings Lynn Justices* ex parte *Carter and others* [1969] 1QB 488 stated that the expression is 'as wide as it possibly can be' (p. 497). 'Antecedents' merely means background information about the age, education, family situation, income and past and present employment of the offender. That information is given to the magistrates by a police officer before they sentence the offender (see Chapter 14). The officer also tells them about the offender's previous convictions. If he has convictions, other than for minor matters carrying no real social stigma, he is clearly not of good character for the purposes of s. 38, and the magistrates can commit for sentence. If he has no convictions he is not necessarily of good character. For example, he may plead guilty to one offence triable either way and ask for another offence to be taken into consideration (see Chapter 14). When an offence is taken into consideration, the offender admits he committed the offence but he is not actually convicted of it. At the time the magistrates agree to summary trial they do not know that the offender is going to ask for another offence to be considered. Obviously, that offence reflects as badly on the offender's character as would a previous conviction, so the magistrates are entitled to commit him to the Crown Court to be sentenced for the offence to which he pleaded guilty — despite his lack of previous convictions, his character, as revealed by the other offence which he wanted taken into consideration, makes the magistrates' sentencing powers inadequate.

A more difficult question is whether the magistrates can commit for sentence under s. 38 when the offender has no previous convictions and does not ask for any other offences to be taken into consideration. The answer is that they can if facts about the offence of which they have convicted the offender, which were not known to them when they agreed to summary trial, cast an unexpectedly bad light on his character. The point is illustrated by ex parte *Carter* (supra). C, S and W were jointly charged with theft of about £3,500 worth of ladies garments. The charge merely alleged that they had stolen the goods between 1 October 1967 and 10 January 1968. They pleaded guilty, and the prosecution, outlining the facts of what had occurred to the magistrates, explained that during the period mentioned in the charge the accused had on numerous occasions appropriated bags of clothing belonging to their employers, who were the owners of a chain of clothing shops. C was the deputy supervisor at his employers' warehouse. He persuaded S and W, who were cleaners at the warehouse, to conceal bags of clothing amongst the rubbish which, as part of their duties, they took out to a rubbish bay. S and W then transferred the bags to the boot of C's car. C, S and W had no previous convictions and did not ask for any other offences to be taken into consideration. Even so, the Divisional Court (Lord Parker CJ presiding) held that their committals for sentence were valid. C was in a position of trust as deputy supervisor, he abused that trust in order to commit the offence and he also corrupted two junior employees. Those facts were not known to the magistrates when they agreed to summary trial. The justification for committing S and W for sentence seems less clear cut, but their committals were upheld because the method of committing the offence showed calculated dishonesty over a period of months — it was not a case of yielding on one occasion to the temptation of the moment. Had these aggravating factors in the circumstances of the offence not been present, C, S and W could not have been committed for sentence. The magistrates were undoubtedly wrong in agreeing to summary trial in the first place as the value of the property stolen made the case unfit for summary trial (see Para. 12.2), but if the case had been no more serious than it appeared from the charge sheet they could not have remedied their original mistake by committing for sentence. Similarly, if the aggravating factors had been made known to the magistrates before they agreed to summary trial, any committal would have been invalid.

The principle in ex parte *Carter* is further illustrated by a comparison of *R* v *Lymm Justices* ex parte *Brown* [1973] 1WLR 1039 and *R* v *Tower Bridge Magistrate* ex parte *Osman* [1971] 1WLR 1109. In the former case, the magistrates agreed to deal with B summarily for what, on the face of the informations against B, appeared to be minor offences of theft. B pleaded guilty, and when the prosecution outlined the facts the magistrates discovered that, while on duty as an airport policeman, B had stolen clothing on display in showcases belonging to the airport authority. This breach of trust by B made the offences far more serious than the magistrates had realised them to be when they accepted jurisdiction, casting an unexpectedly bad light on B's character, and therefore justifying his committal to the Crown Court for sentence. In ex parte *Osman*, on the other hand, nothing in the facts of the three offences of theft to which O pleaded guilty rendered them more serious than a magistrate reading the informations would expect them to be. Admittedly, O had stolen from his employer, but the nature of the informations, alleging minor thefts widely separated by time, must have alerted the stipendiary magistrate to the fact that the case was one of petty pilfering by an employee even before he agreed to summary trial. Accordingly, the Divisional Court quashed O's committal for sentence.

12.3.3 Powers of the Crown Court

When magistrates commit an offender for sentence under s. 38 of the Magistrates' Courts Act 1980 they should commit him to the most convenient location of the Crown Court, where the case is normally listed for hearing by a circuit judge or recorder (see the Lord Chief Justice's Practice Directions 1972 56Cr App R 52). The professional judge should sit with two magistrates (see Para. 4.3). The offender is asked whether he admits that he was convicted by the magistrates and committed by them to the Crown Court for sentence. In the absence of an admission, the prosecution must call evidence to prove those facts (*R* v *Barker* [1951] 1AER 479), probably the evidence of a police officer who was present at the magistrates' court when the committal for sentence was made. Once the convictions and committal have been admitted or proved, the proceedings before sentence is passed are the same as those which follow a guilty plea on indictment (see Chapter 14).

When dealing with an offender who has been committed to it for sentence under s. 38, the Crown Court can pass any sentence which it could have passed on him as though he had just been convicted on indictment: Powers of Criminal Courts Act 1973, s. 42. The maximum sentence upon a committal for sentence is consequently greater, and often much greater, than that which the magistrates have power to impose. For example, an offender convicted on indictment of theft may be sentenced to ten years imprisonment and an unlimited fine. If he is convicted of two or more thefts, prison sentences for those offences may be made to run consecutively even if the aggregate term exceeds ten years. An offender who has been committed for sentence under s. 38 in respect of offences of theft may be similarly sentenced. On the other hand, had he been sentenced by the magistrates, the maximum for one offence of theft would have been six months imprisonment and a £1,000 fine, and the maximum prison term for several offences of theft would have been one year. Of course, the Crown Court would not in practice consider passing a sentence anywhere near the maximum it could pass for offences of theft which the magistrates considered suitable for summary trial. However, it is common for the Crown Court upon a committal for sentence to inflict punishment considerably more severe than that which the magistrates could have inflicted.

12.4 OTHER CIRCUMSTANCES IN WHICH MAGISTRATES MAY COMMIT FOR SENTENCE

Section 38 of the Magistrates' Courts Act 1980 is by no means the only provision enabling magistrates to commit for sentence. It is desirable, at this stage, to describe these other powers to commit although, since they may be exercised without there having been a summary conviction for an offence triable either way, they are not strictly speaking part of the primary topic of this Chapter.

12.4.1 Committal with a Borstal recommendation

Neither an adult magistrates' court nor a juvenile court has power to pass a sentence of Borstal training (see Chapter 15). However, where a juvenile court (in the case of a person aged 15 or 16) or the adult magistrates' court (in the case of a person aged 17 to 20 inclusive) considers that Borstal is appropriate for an offender, s. 37 of the Magistrates' Courts Act 1980 empowers it to commit him to the Crown Court in custody or on bail to be sentenced by the Crown Court in accordance with the provisions of s. 20 of the Criminal Justice Act 1948. This is known as a committal with a Borstal recommendation, because s. 20 of the 1948 Act allows the Crown Court either to follow the magistrates' suggestion and send the offender to Borstal, or to deal with him in any way the magistrates could have dealt with him. The Crown Court does not have power, as it does when the offender has been committed under s. 38 of the 1980 Act, to sentence him as if he had just been convicted on indictment.

The power to commit under s. 37 is available in respect of offenders who:

(a)   are aged 15 to 20 inclusive on the date of conviction by the magistrates;

(b)   have been convicted of an offence punishable with imprisonment, and

(c)   should, in the view of the magistrates, be detained for training for not less than six months.

Before deciding that the offender should be detained as in (c) above, the magistrates should have regard to the circumstances of the offence, the offender's character and previous conduct, and any report on him made by or on behalf of the Home Secretary: see Criminal Justice Act 1961, s. 1(2)-(4). If the offender was under 17 on the day of his conviction the magistrates should also, before committing with a Borstal recommendation, be satisfied that no other method of dealing with him is appropriate.

It will be realised that in many cases where the magistrates can commit under s. 37 they can also commit for sentence under s. 38. It is then preferable to make use of s. 38 since the powers of the Crown Court, when it deals with the offender, will be wider (see above). In particular, on a s. 38 committal the Crown Court may sentence the offender to more than six months imprisonment. In fact, any sentence of imprisonment exceeding six months would have to be for three years or more or, in certain circumstances, for 18 months or more (see Chapter 15). The cases in which magistrates may be able to commit under s. 37 but will not be able to commit under s. 38 are where:

(a)   The offender is aged 15 or 16, or

(b)   He is of previous good character so his character and antecedents do not make the magistrates' powers of punishment inadequate (see Para. 12.3.2), or

(c)   He is convicted of a summary offence punishable with imprisonment.

12.4.2   Miscellaneous powers to commit for sentence

Sections 37 and 38 of the Magistrates' Courts Act 1980 are those which the magistrates most frequently use when committing for sentence. However, they can also commit for sentence if:

(a)   They have convicted an offender of an offence committed during the currency of a probation order or conditional discharge made by the Crown Court: Powers of Criminal Courts Act 1973, s. 8(6); or

(b)   They have convicted an offender of an offence punishable with imprisonment committed during the operational period of a suspended sentence passed by the Crown Court: Powers of Criminal Courts Act 1973, s. 24(2), or

(c)   They have convicted of an indictable offence an offender who, having been released from prison on parole, is still under licence: Criminal Justice Act 1967, s. 62(6).

The magistrates need to be able to commit for sentence in these circumstances because they could not themselves deal with the offender for the breach of probation etc.

Probation, conditional discharge, suspended sentences and release from prison on parole are described in Chapter 15.

12.4.3 Committal for sentence under s. 56 of the Criminal Justice Act 1967

Where magistrates convict an offender of two or more offences they may decide that for one of those offences he should be committed to the Crown Court for sentence under, for example, s. 38 of the Magistrates' Courts Act 1980, but that in respect of the other offences neither that section nor any of the others so far discussed gives them power to commit. If an offender is to be dealt with for several matters, it is desirable that one court should deal with them all on one occasion, otherwise the cumulative effect of the sentences passed on different occasions may be unduly harsh. Accordingly, s. 56 of the Criminal Justice Act 1967 provides that where magistrates commit an offender to the Crown Court under s. 37 or s. 38 of the 1980 Act or under one of the sections mentioned in Para. 12.4.2 above to be dealt with for an offence (the 'relevant offence'), they may also, if the relevant offence is indictable, commit him to be dealt with for:

(a) Any other offence of which they have convicted him.

(b) Breach of a probation order or conditional discharge made on a previous occasion by their court.

(c) Breach of a suspended sentence passed by any magistrates' court.

If the relevant offence is summary, they have no power to commit for breach of probation or conditional discharge as in (b) above, and they only have power to commit the offender for another offence of which they have convicted him if that offence is punishable with imprisonment or disqualification from driving. Should the magistrates commit an offender for sentence in respect of one matter but be unable to commit him for something else, they would probably adjourn the latter matter until the former had been dealt with by the Crown Court.

In dealing with an offender for a matter in respect of which he was committed to it under s. 56, the Crown Court may pass any sentence or make any order which the magistrates could have made had they not committed for sentence: s. 56(5) and (6).

12.5 THE SPECIAL PROCEDURE FOR CRIMINAL DAMAGE CHARGES

The Criminal Law Act 1977 contained many provisions, now repealed and re-enacted in the Magistates' Courts Act 1980, for simplifying the law on the mode of trial of offences, and also for redistributing the work of the criminal courts so that a greater proportion of cases would be heard in the magistrates' courts than had been so previously. Offences such as driving with excess alcohol in the blood-stream and assaulting a police constable in the execution of his duty, which had formerly been triable either way, became summary, and offences ranging from bigamy to failing to provide one's apprentice with sufficient food, which had before been triable only on indictment, became triable either way. However, the most controversial proposal for shifting work to the magistrates only reached the statute book in an attenuated form. The Criminal Law Bill contained provisions which would have made minor offences of theft, obtaining property by deception and criminal damage triable only summarily, but the outcry at this restriction on the right to jury trial was such that only the provisions in respect of criminal damage offences became law. The present legislation is contained in the Magistrates' Courts Act 1980, s. 22.

If the accused is charged with criminal damage contrary to the Criminal Damage Act 1971, s. 1, or an attempt to commit such an offence, then, unless the offence involved damage or attempted damage by fire, the magistrates must proceed as follows:

(a)   They consider, having regard to any representations made by the prosecution or defence, the value involved in the offence — i.e. the cost, in a case where property was allegedly destroyed or damaged beyond repair, of replacing the property, or, in other cases, the cost of repair.

(b)   If the value involved is clearly under £200, the magistrates proceed as if the offence were triable only summarily. They do not follow the procedure in s. 19 to 21 of the Act (see Para. 12.2), and the accused has no right to a trial on indictment.

(c)   If the value involved is clearly over £200, the charge is dealt with like any other offence triable either way. The magistrates hear any representations as to the more suitable mode of trial, and, if they consider that summary trial is appropriate, the clerk asks the accused if he consents to the magistrates dealing with the case.

(d)   Where the case is tried summarily under (b) above, the maximum sentence the magistrates can impose is three months imprisonment or a £500 fine: Magistrates' Courts Act 1980, ss. 33. They cannot commit for sentence to the Crown Court under s. 38 of the 1980 Act, but they could commit with a Borstal recommendation under s. 37.

(e)   Where the case is tried summarily under (c) above, the maximum sentence is that which can be imposed for any other of the offences triable either way listed in Schedule 1 to the 1980 Act — i.e. six months imprisonment and a £1,000 fine. In addition, the magistrates may commit for sentence under s. 38.

(f)   If the magistrates are not sure whether the value involved is more or less than £200, the clerk asks the accused if he consents to summary trial. If he does so and is convicted, the maximum penalty is as in (d) above and, again, he cannot be committed for sentence under s. 38. The clerk explains the maximum penalty to the accused before asking for his consent to summary trial. If he does not want to be tried summarily, the normal ss. 19—21 procedure for determining the mode of trial comes into operation.

The special procedure does not apply when a criminal damage charge is one of two or more offences with which the accused is charged, and those offences constitute or form part of a series of offences of the same or a similar character: s. 22(7). Thus, if the accused is charged with three offences of throwing a brick through the window of a house, the apparent motive being that in each window was displayed a poster urging the public to vote for the candidate of a political party of which the accused disapproved, the special procedure will not apply to any of the charges. They are identical in law (each is for criminal damage), and they are similar on the facts. Even if the total value of the damage is less than £200, the magistrates proceed immediately under ss. 19—21 of the 1980 Act, and do not consider how much damage was done save in so far as that is relevant to the adequacy of their powers of punishment in the event of summary conviction. In other words, the accused has a right to trial on indictment on each charge.

In cases less clear cut than the example given above, the courts have had difficulty in deciding whether or not offences form a series of a similar character within the meaning of s. 22(7). According to *R v Hatfield Justices ex parte Castle* [1981] 1 WLR 217 the test is whether there is a similarity in law and on the facts between the offences. This is the same test as is applied in determining whether counts can be joined in one indictment under r.9 of the Indictment Rules (see *Ludlow v Metropolitan Police Commissioner* [1971] AC 29 and Para. 5.5.2). Thus, in *ex parte Castle* the Divisional Court granted an order of prohibition to prevent magistrates holding committal proceedings in respect of a charge of criminal damage to a police officer's tunic, value £23, even though the accused was also charged with three other offences arising out of the same incident, namely assaulting the officer in the execution of his duty, obstructing him in the execution of his duty and using threatening words or behaviour likely to cause a breach of the peace. Since there was no similarity in law between the criminal damage charges, they did not form a series of a similar character, and the special procedure therefore applied. The magistrates had to proceed as if the offence were triable only summarily. The Divisional Court also held that for the special procedure not to apply the other offences said to form a series with the criminal damage offence must themselves be indictable, not summary as was the case in *ex parte Castle*. The decision in *ex parte Castle* is difficult to reconcile with that in *R v Leicester Justices ex parte Lord* [1980] Crim LR 581, where the facts were analagous to those in *ex parte Castle*. It is submitted, however, that the decision in the latter case is to preferred.

It should be noted that even where the special procedure applies and the value involved in the offence is less than £200, s. 22(2) merely requires the *magistrates* to proceed as if the offence charged were triable only summarily — it does not provide that the offence shall be deemed to be summary for all purposes. Accordingly, if an accused has been committed for trial on a charge of, for instance, burglary, and the committal statements disclose a case to answer for criminal damage to a value of less than £200, the officer of the Crown Court drafting the indictment can include counts for both burglary and criminal damage (*R v Considine* (1980) 70 Cr App R 239, where the value involved in the criminal damage count was only £34).

12.6 TRIAL ON INDICTMENT OR SUMMARY TRIAL

Where the accused has a choice of trial on indictment by judge and jury, or summary trial by magistrates, the following points should be borne in mind as to the advantages and disadvantages of each method.

Summary trial is less expensive and less time-consuming than trial on indictment. If the accused elects to be tried by the magistrates and is found guilty, any order to pay some of the prosecution's costs or contribute towards his own legal aid costs will almost certainly reflect the fact that he has chosen the less costly form of trial. In addition, the sentence itself may well be less severe than if he had been tried at the Crown Court. If his character and antecedents are such that he cannot be committed for sentence, the punishment will not of course, exceed six months imprisonment and a £1,000 fine (twelve months if convicted of two or more offences triable either way). Even if the magistrates have power to commit for sentence, they may well deal with the offender themselves in cases where, had he been convicted on indictment, the Crown Court judge would have passed a sentence in excess of that which the magistrates may pass. For these reasons, accused persons charged with offences triable either way, who intend to plead guilty, usually want their case to be heard by the magistrates. Amongst those intending to plead not guilty, the general view is that trial by a jury offers a better prospect of an acquittal.

Three reasons may be advanced in support of the above view. First, at a trial on indictment the defence, as a result of committal proceedings and any notice of additional evidence, have the advantage of knowing the prosecution's case in advance. At a summary trial, the only knowledge defence counsel or solicitor has of the prosecution case is what the prosecution may choose to tell him (see Para. 11.6). Second, it is difficult at a summary trial to object effectively to evidence which may be inadmissible, since the magistrates, as judges of both law and fact, must decide themselves on its admissibility, even if they act on the advice of their clerk. Having heard the evidence so as to rule on its admissibility, the magistrates will find it difficult to put that evidence out of their minds should they hold it inadmissible. At trial on indictment, the judge decides on the admissibility of evidence in the jury's absence (see Para. 8.3.5). Finally, it is suggested that jurors are more likely to believe the accused than are magistrates, especially in cases where there is a conflict between police evidence and defence evidence. Some would say that this is because magistrates are less gullible than juries, others that through often sitting in court magistrates become 'prosecution-minded'. Whatever the reason, there are even judicial comments suggesting that the accused's chances may be better before a jury. In *R* v *Kent Justices* ex parte *Machin* [1952] 2QB 355, Lord Goddard CJ commented on the fact that defendants with several previous convictions sometimes did not agree to summary trial because they knew of the 'curious verdicts' (i.e. unjustified acquittals) which juries occasionally returned. Similarly, in *R* v *Canny* (1945) 30Cr App R 143, the Court of Criminal Appeal, holding that a judge should not tell the jury in his summing up that the accused's defence is absurd, stated that — 'a prisoner is entitled to take his chance of finding a stupid jury and is entitled to put his defence before the jury with a view to persuading them to acquit him' (Humphreys J at p. 146). No doubt, there are defendants today who, to paraphrase Humphreys J, elect trial on indictment simply because they hope to find a jury stupid enough to believe them.

13   Trial of Juveniles

A juvenile is normally tried in a juvenile court. In the circumstances described in Para. 13.1 he may or must be tried on indictment; in the circumstances described in Para. 13.2 he may or must be tried in an adult magistrates' court. In all other cases he is tried in a juvenile court, even if the offence charged is one which, if he were an adult, either could or would have to be tried on indictment.

By a juvenile is meant a person who has not attained the age of 17. Juveniles are either children, who have not attained the age of 14, or young persons, who have attained the age of 14 but are not yet 17: Children and Young Persons Act 1969, s. 70. For purposes of criminal procedure, children under the age of ten may be ignored as they have not yet reached the age of criminal responsibility. As far as method of trial is concerned, all persons aged 17 and over are treated in exactly the same way, and are referred to in this chapter simply as adults. However, if a person aged 17 to 20 inclusive is convicted of an offence, several methods of dealing with him are open to the courts which are not available in respect of offenders who have attained the age of 21.

13.1   TRIAL OF JUVENILES ON INDICTMENT

Section 24 of the Magistrates' Courts Act 1980 provides that a juvenile must be tried summarily (i.e. in an adult magistrates' court or a juvenile court) unless any of the following apply.

(a)   The juvenile is charged with an offence of homicide. 'Homicide' includes murder and manslaughter, and probably also includes causing death by reckless driving. Since all three offences are triable only on indictment, the magistrates before whom the juvenile appears have no discretion as to the method of trial, but must hold committal proceedings and, if the prosecution can show a case to answer, commit the juvenile to the Crown Court for trial.

(b)   The juvenile and an adult are jointly charged with an indictable offence, and the magistrates before whom they appear consider it necessary in the interests of justice to commit them both for trial. The reason for this provision is that it is, generally speaking, desirable to have two or more accused, who are jointly charged with having together committed an offence, tried together (see Para. 5.6.1). If the offence charged is triable only on indictment in the case of an adult, or if it is triable either way but the adult does not consent to summary trial, it is impossible for the adult to be tried summarily. Accordingly, the only way to bring about a joint trial is to commit the juvenile for trial with the adult. The magistrates must, however, balance the desirability of a joint trial against the undesirability of having youngsters put through the possibly traumatic experience of a trial in the Crown Court. The younger the juvenile and the less serious the offence charged, the more likely it is that the magistrates will decide that the interests of justice do not require that the juvenile be committed for trial. If they do so decide, the juvenile should be asked if he pleads guilty or not guilty to the charge. Where he pleads not guilty, he may and normally would be remitted to a juvenile court for trial: s. 29 of the 1980 Act.

(c)   The juvenile has attained the age of 14 and the magistrates consider that, if he is convicted on indictment of the offence charged, he could properly be sentenced under the Children and Young Persons Act 1933 s. 53(2). This section enables the Crown Court, in a case where a juvenile has been convicted on indictment of an offence which if he were an adult would be punishable with 14 years imprisonment or more, to order that the juvenile be detained in accordance with the Home Secretary's directions for any period not exceeding the period of the maximum prison sentence which could be imposed (see Para. 13.4.2). An order for detention under s. 53(2) is only appropriate in really serious cases. Therefore, magistrates should only commit a young person for trial on the basis that such an order might be made if the charge against the young person is grave. If a young person is charged with handling a small quantity of stolen goods, or breaking into a house, or snatching a lady's handbag in the street, he should not be committed for trial. Although handling stolen goods, burglary and robbery each carry 14 years imprisonment or more, the particular offences alleged are not serious enought to warrant an order under s. 53(2). If the allegation were that the young person had snatched a bag and, in the course of so doing, caused serious and permanent injury to the victim of the offence, then the magistrates might commit for trial.

The magistrates also have a supplementary power to commit for trial which arises when they commit a juvenile charged jointly with an adult (see (b) above). If the juvenile is charged individually with another indictable offence, which arose out of circumstances the same as or connected with the circumstances of the joint charge, he may be committed for trial on that charge as well as on the joint charge. For example, if Smith, aged 17, and Brown aged 16 are jointly charged with taking a car without the owner's consent, and Brown is charged with driving the car recklessly, the magistrates would probably offer to Smith the option of summary trial. If Smith elects for trial on indictment and the magistrates consider it in the interests of justice for Smith and Brown to be tried together, they will commit them both on the charge of taking the car. They may also commit Brown on the reckless driving charge, since the circumstances of that offence are linked to those of the joint offence.

A general point to note about the way in which juveniles are tried is that they do not have a choice in the matter. If the charge against the juvenile falls within (a) above, he must be tried on indictment. If the charge could come within (b) or (c), the magistrates decide whether the juvenile shall be tried on indictment or summarily. Even in a case where an adult charged jointly with a juvenile is given the option of summary trial, the magistrates do not ask the juvenile if he consents to be tried by them. If the adult elects for summary trial, the juvenile is, in effect, bound by his decision; if the adult goes for trial at the Crown Court, the juvenile goes with him, whatever his views on the matter, if the magistrates consider that to be in the interests of justice.

Once the decision that a juvenile should be tried on indictment has been taken, the procedure is not significantly different from the procedure in respect of adults. If he is jointly charged with an adult, committal proceedings take place in the adult magistrates' court, or if he is charged alone, they are held in a juvenile court. Just as in the case of an adult, the committal may be with or without consideration of the evidence (s. 24(1) of the 1980 Act). At the trial on indictment, the juvenile has the same rights as an adult accused (e.g. to challenge jurors), and his defence is conducted in the same way as that of an adult. The court may require the attendance of the juvenile's parents or guardians at all or part of the proceedings, unless satisfied that it would be unreasonable to make them attend (Children and Young Persons Act 1933, s. 34(1), which applies also to proceedings against a juvenile in the adult magistrates or juvenile court). The court may also order that the media shall not reveal the name, address, school or any other identifying details of the juvenile charged or any juvenile who is a witness in the case: Children and Young Persons Act 1933, s. 39. Sentencing of juveniles by the Crown Court is considered in Para. 13.4.

13.2 TRIAL OF JUVENILES IN AN ADULT MAGISTRATES' COURT

By a combination of s. 46 of the Children and Young Persons Act 1933 and s. 18 of the Children and Young Persons Act 1963, it is provided that a juvenile who is to be tried summarily shall be tried in a juvenile court unless:

(a)   He is charged jointly with an adult; or

(b)   He appears before the magistrates together with an adult, they are charged in separate informations, and the information against the adult is that he aided and abetted the offence alleged against the juvenile or vice versa; or

(c)   He appears before the magistrates together with an adult, and the charge against him arises out of circumstances the same as or connected with the circumstances giving rise to the charge against the adult; or

(d)   The adult magistrates' court began to hear the proceedings against him in the erroneous belief that he was an adult.

Where (a) above applies, the adult magistrates' court *must* try the juvenile unless the adult with whom he is jointly charged pleads guilty and he pleads not guilty, in which case the court may, and probably would, remit him to a juvenile court to be tried: Magistrates' Courts Act 1980, s. 29. Where (b) to (d) above apply the adult court merely has a discretion to hear the case if it so wishes.

Sections 34 and 39 of the Children and Young Persons Act 1933 (requiring the attendance of the juvenile's parents or guardians and orders restricting the reporting of the juvenile's name etc. — see Para. 13.1) apply to trials of juveniles in an adult magistrates' court.

13.3 TRIAL OF JUVENILES IN A JUVENILE COURT

The great majority of charges against juveniles are tried in the juvenile courts. The magistrates for each petty sessional division must meet together every third year to appoint from amongst their number a panel of magistrates who are specially qualified for dealing with juvenile cases. This is known as the juvenile court panel, and the magistrates who sit in the juvenile court for that division must be drawn from the panel: Juvenile Courts (Constitution) Rules 1954 r. 1 and r. 11. Where convenient, two or more petty sessional divisions may combine to have a single juvenile court panel. Also, special rules apply to the composition of juvenile courts in the Inner London area. A lay magistrate who has attained the age of 65 may not be a member of the panel: r. 5. Vacancies occurring in the membership (e.g. through a magistrate dying or attaining the age of 65) may be filled as they arise. A stipendiary magistrate is a member of the juvenile court panel for his area by virtue of his office, even if he is over 65. Thus a juvenile court is made up of magistrates who are suited to handle juvenile work. It is a special form of magistrates' court, differentiated from the ordinary adult courts in the ways described below.

The following are some of the special rules applying to juvenile courts:

(a)   A juvenile court must not sit in a room which is also used for the sittings of a court other than a juvenile court unless at least an hour elapses both between the conclusion of that other court's sitting and the commencement of the juvenile court sitting, and between the conclusion of the juvenile court sitting and another sitting of the other court: Children and Young Persons Act 1933, s. 47. The purpose of s. 47 is to prevent juveniles mingling with adult offenders, which might easily occur if, immediately after the adult magistrates' court has finished its sitting, the room it was using could be immediately taken over by the juvenile court. Ideally, a juvenile court should sit in a room, or even a building, which is only used for that purpose.

(b)   The general public are excluded from juvenile courts. Only the parties and their legal representatives, officers of the court (e.g. court ushers), witnesses after they have given their evidence and others directly concerned in the case, probation officers and social workers, and members of the press are allowed in: Children and Young Persons Act 1933, s. 47. In addition, the court may especially authorise other persons to be present (e.g. law students). Proceedings against juveniles in the adult magistrates' courts or Crown Court are normally in open court, but there is power to clear the court whenever a juvenile is called as a witness in those courts in relation to an offence against decency or morality: Children and Young Persons Act 1933, s. 37.

(c)   The bench of magistrates hearing the case must consist of no more than three magistrates, and must include a man and a woman: Juvenile Courts (Constitution) Rules 1954, r. 12. If, through unforeseen circumstances, the members of the juvenile court panel available for a sitting of a juvenile court are all male or all female, they can waive the above rule and form a single-sex court should they not consider it expedient to adjourn. A stipendiary magistrate should not normally sit alone in the juvenile court, but may do so if he is the only member of the panel present and does not think it expedient to adjourn.

(d)   When the charge is put to the juvenile he is usually asked whether he admits or denies the offence, rather than being asked if he pleads guilty or not guilty. All witnesses in the case, whether juvenile or adults, 'promise before Almighty God to tell the truth, the whole truth' etc. instead of swearing by Almighty God that they will do so. The different form of oath for juvenile courts was introduced by the Children and Young Persons Act 1963, s. 28. It is also used by juveniles giving evidence in other courts. If the magistrates decide that the juvenile committed the offence charged, they do not convict him, but record a finding of guilt. When they deal with him for the offence, they do not sentence him but make an order upon a finding of guilt: Children and Young Persons Act 1933, s. 59. The same terminology should be employed when a juvenile is 'convicted' or 'sentenced' in the adult magistrates' court.

(e)   Where the juvenile is not legally represented the court may permit his parent or guardian to assist him in conducting his defence (e.g. by cross-examining prosecution witnesses on his behalf). If the parents or guardians are not present the court may require their attendance: Children and Young Persons Act 1933, s. 34 and see Para. 13.1.

(f) The media may not report the name or any other identifying details of the juvenile charged or any other juvenile involved in the proceedings: Children and Young Persons Act 1933, s. 49. The prohibition may be lifted if the court thinks that to be necessary in order to avoid injustice to the juvenile. Thus, in the adult magistrates' courts and in the Crown Court, the juvenile's name etc. may be published unless the court makes an order to the contrary; in the juvenile court, the position is the opposite.

(g) In general, the atmosphere in a juvenile court is more relaxed and less formal than in an adult court. The juvenile charged does not go into a dock, but sits on a chair facing the magistrates, with his parents alongside or behind him. The magistrates are usually seated behind a slightly raised table. They address the juvenile by his Christian name, and, when making an order upon a finding of guilt, may talk to him in a semi-informal fashion. Some have argued that the proceedings are, in fact, too informal, because a greater display of the majesty of the law might impress a juvenile delinquent with the gravity of his conduct.

> A juvenile becomes an adult on his 17th birthday. Where the dividing line is likely to cause problems, as where proceedings are commenced before the accused's 17th birthday but not fully disposed of until after that date, then the Children and Young Persons Act 1963, s. 29 applies to enable the juvenile court to deal with the matter as though the accused had not attained that age. Proceedings are begun for purposes of s. 29 when the accused makes his first appearance in court: *R* v *Amersham Justices* ex parte *Wilson* [1981] 2WLR 887. If he is under 17 at that date the juvenile court can deal with him, whatever his age at the conclusion of the proceedings. If on the other hand, he was under 17 when charged at the police station but reaches 17 before his first court appearance the juvenile court does not have juristriction.
>
> It is suggested that *ex parte Wilson* (supra) is good authority even though a differently constituted Divisional Court in *R* v *St. Albans Crown Court ex parte Godman* [1981] 2WLR 882 held that G., who was under 17 when he pleaded not guilty to a charge of theft in the juvenile court but attained 17 before his case could be heard, had the right to elect trial on indictment. As explained in *ex parte Wilson,* the court in *ex parte Godman* reached their decision without reference to s. 29, both counsel apparently thinking that the section had no bearing upon the case.

13.4 SENTENCING JUVENILES

This Paragraph must be understood in conjunction with Chapter 15 which deals with the sentencing powers of the courts in relation to adults, since some forms of sentence are available for both juveniles and some or all adults. The Paragraph concentrates upon those sentences which are available only in the case of juveniles, and any special rules governing the application to juveniles of sentences which may also be passed in respect of adults. It also describes attendance centre orders since these are mainly used in the cases of juveniles although also available for adults who have not attained the age of 21.

13.4.1 Sentences available for juveniles and adults

A juvenile who has been found guilty of an offence may, like an adult, be fined for it or given an absolute or conditional discharge (see Paras. 15.3 and 15.5 respectively). If he is aged 15 or 16 at the date of conviction he may be sentenced to Borstal training; if he is a young person he may be sentenced to detention in a detention centre (see Paras. 15.7 and 15.8 respectively).

Some special rules apply to the fining of juveniles. The maximum fine which may be imposed on a juvenile found guilty by a magistrates' court (juvenile or adult) is £200 in the case of young person and £50 in the case of a child: Magistrates' Courts Act 1980, s. 24(3) and (4), and s. 36. There is no limit on the fine which may be imposed on a juvenile following his conviction on indictment, but if the court intends the juvenile, rather than his parents, to pay the money it must obviously keep the amount to be paid low, probably well under the above figures. The court may, however, order that the parent or guardian of the juvenile pay the fine: Children and Young Persons Act 1933, s. 55. Such orders can be made by a juvenile court, adult magistrates' court or Crown Court, unless the court is satisfied that the parent or guardian did not help to bring about the offence by failing to 'exercise due care or control' of the juvenile. If the court is not so satisfied it must, in a case where the juvenile is a child, and may in a case where he is a young person order the parent or guardian to pay the fine. A juvenile may also be ordered to pay some or all of the prosecution's costs, and pay compensation to the victim of the offence (see Chapter 21 for costs and compensation orders). The Children and Young Persons Act 1933, s. 55 applies to such orders as it does to fines. There is no special limitation on the amount of compensation payable by a juvenile but the amount of costs which a juvenile or adult magistrates' court orders him to pay personally must not exceed the amount of any fine they impose: Costs in Criminal Cases Act 1973, s. 2(2). If the parent or guardian is ordered to pay the costs the above limitation does not apply.

The following sentences are available in the cases of adults but not in the cases of juveniles:

(a)   Imprisonment (see Para. 15.1). Section 19(1) of the Powers of Criminal Courts Act 1973 provides that no court may impose imprisonment on a juvenile. 'Imposing imprisonment' includes passing a sentence of immediate imprisonment, passing a suspended sentence and committing a person to prison for non-payment of a fine.

(b)   Probation (see Para. 15.4). Probation is not available for juveniles because they can be made the subject of a supervision order, the effect of which is similar to probation   (see Para. 13.4.4).

(c)   Community service order (see Para. 15.6). The White Paper on the treatment of young offenders (1980 Cmnd 8045—see Appendix 2) recommends that community service should be made available as a method of sentencing juveniles who have attained the age of 16.

13.4.2   Detention under the Children and Young Persons Act 1933, s. 53

A person convicted of murder, who was under 18 at the time he committed the offence, is not sentenced to imprisonment for life (the mandatory sentence in all other cases of murder) but the Crown Court must order him to be detained during Her Majesty's pleasure: Children and Young Persons Act 1933, s. 53(1). His release from detention is at the Home Secretary's discretion, but he may only exercise that discretion and release the offender if (a) he has been recommended to do so by the

Parole Board (see Para. 15.1.5) and (b) he has consulted with the Lord Chief Justice and, if available, the trial judge: Criminal Justice Act 1967, s. 61(1).

A juvenile convicted on indictment of an offence, other than murder, which is punishable in the case of an adult with 14 years or more imprisonment may be sentenced by the Crown Court to be detained in accordance with the Home Secretary's directions for a period not exceeding the maximum prison term (s. 53(2) of the 1933 Act). As explained in Para. 13.1, such sentences are only appropriate in the most serious cases, although the Crown Court can make an order under s. 53(2) which is designed to deter others rather than to rehabilitate the juvenile (e.g. *R* v *Ford and others* (1976) 62Cr App R 303, see Para. 16.1). The offender must not be detained for longer than the period ordered by the court, but the Home Secretary, if so recommended by the Parole Board, may order his release at any time during that period.

Sentences under s. 53(1) and (2) must not be confused with detention centre orders. The latter are for short periods (three to six months), and involve the offender being sent to a custodial institution (the detention centre) where the regime is such as to give him a short, sharp shock. An offender detained under s. 53 is kept at such place and under such conditions as the Home Secretary thinks fit — e.g. he might be sent to a mental hospital, or to a community home where juveniles subject to care orders are living, or to a hostel, or even to prison. As explained above, his release is essentially within the discretion of the Parole Board and the Home Secretary.

13.4.3 Care orders

A juvenile found guilty of any imprisonable offence other than murder may be made the subject of a care order: Children and Young Persons Act 1969, s. 7(7)(a). By a care order, the subject is committed to the care of the local authority in whose area he resides, and, subject to the earlier discharge of the order, he remains in their care until he attains the age of 18, or, 19 if when the order was made he had already attained the age of 16: see s. 20 of the 1969 Act. On the application of the subject or the local authority, a juvenile court may discharge the care order: s. 21(2). Unless the subject has attained the age of 18, it may replace the care order with a supervision order. During the currency of the care order, the local authority has the same powers and duties with respect to the subject as his parents would have had if the order had not been made. In particular, the authority may restrict the subject's liberty: s. 24. However, care orders are not intended as punishment for the juvenile concerned, and, indeed, an order can be made in respect of a juvenile who has not even committed an offence, for instance on the basis that he is being neglected and is in need of care or control: s. 1. Whether the subject of the order is a juvenile offender or is in care through no fault of his own, the aim of the order is to provide him with an environment in which he can develop into a responsible, law-abiding citizen.

Local authority social workers decide where the subject of a care order is to live. If the home background is reasonable, and his offences have not been such that society needs to be protected from him, they may allow him to continue living at home. If not, they can send him to a local authority-run community home, or possibly to a home run by a voluntary organisation. One of the complaints which magistrates have made about the working of the Children and Young Persons Act 1969 is that, once they have made a care order, they have no control over what happens to the subject. The local authority may allow him to return home, and he may promptly reoffend. Even if he is sent to a community home, there is a problem in that, by and large, community homes are not, and should not, be made secure like prisons. The lack of security, however, can make it relatively easy for the youngsters to abscond, and commit offences while on the run. The White Paper on the treatment of young offenders (1980 Cmnd 8045—see Appendix 2) recommends that in certain circumstances the juvenile court should be empowered to make a residential care order under which the subject would not be allowed to remain at home for a period of up to six months.

Where the subject of a care order has attained the age of 15 and is being kept at a community home, the local authority, with the Home Secretary's consent, may bring him before a juvenile court with a view to the court ordering that he be removed to a Borstal institution: s. 31. The court may only so order if satisfied that his behavour in the community home is so bad as to be detrimental to the others living there.

13.4.4   Supervision orders

A juvenile found guilty of any offence other than murder may be made the subject of a supervision order: Children and Young Persons Act 1969, s. 7(7)(b). The supervisor may be the local authority for the area where the subject of the order resides, or a probation officer (s. 13), but it is unusual for the latter to be the supervisor where the subject has not attained the age of 13. The local authority, of course, acts through social workers. The order lasts for three years or such shorter period as the court specifies (s. 17), unless it was made upon the discharge of a care order, in which case, it cannot continue beyond the subject's eighteenth birthday.

While the order is in force, it is the duty of the supervisor to 'advise, assist and befriend' the subject: s. 14. In addition, the court may include any or all of the following requirements in the order:

(a)   A requirement that the subject be of good behaviour.

(b)   A requirement that the subject reside with a person who is named in the order, and who agrees to the requirement being made.

(c)   If the subject is of school age, a requirement that he comply with the arrangements made for his education (i.e. does not play truant from school).

(d)   A requirement that he submit to treatment for a mental condition which, although it needs to be treated, is not such as to warrant his compulsory detention in hospital under the Mental Health Act 1959. Evidence must be obtained from an approved medical practitioner that the subject is suffering from such a condition. The treatment ordered may be treatment by or under the direction of a doctor, or treatment as an out-patient at a place specified in the order, or treatment as a resident in a hospital or mental nursing home. If the subject has attained the age of 14 he must consent to the requirement being included.

(e)   Any requirement (other than a residential requirement or requirement as in (d) above) which the court considers appropriate to prevent the subject committing further offences. The consent of the subject or, if he is a child, the consent of his parent is necessary for the inclusion of such a requirement.

(f)   A requirement that for or on a certain number of days, which must not in aggregate exceed 90, the subject shall live at a place and/or report to a person and/or take part in activities specified in directions given by his supervisor. This requirement enables the supervisor, by giving appropriate directions, to ensure that the subject attend at a course of instruction or other activity designed to be beneficial to him, even if that means him living away from home for a time. Thus, the subject receives treatment which is intermediate between the treatment he would receive under a care order and that he would receive under an ordinary supervision order. The court may fix the period for which the subject is to comply with the supervisor's directions at less than the full ninety days, and the supervisor need not, in any event, give directions for all the days on which the order entitles him to give them.

The supervision order may also contain any provisions the court considers appropriate to assist the supervisor in carrying out his duties under the order (e.g. a provision that the subject visit the supervisor at stated intervals). The requirements and provisions described above are set out in s. 12 and s. 18(2) of the 1969 Act. It should be noted that, except as mentioned in (d) and (e) above, neither the making of an order, nor the inclusion in it of conditions is dependent upon the subject's consent (contrast the making of probation orders in the cases of adults).

There is a system for discharging or varying supervision orders which makes the operation of the orders very flexible. On the application of the supervisor or subject, the court may do any or all of the following:

(a) Discharge the order;

(b) Discharge the order and, if the subject is under 18, replace it with a care order;

(c) Insert new requirements or provisions in the order in addition to or in substitution for those originally in it;

(d) If the subject is proved to have failed to comply with any requirement of the order, fine him up to £50 or make an attendance centre order in respect of him (see Para. 13.4.6);

(e) If the subject has attained the age of 17, and the order is being discharged, sentence him for the offence for which he was placed under supervision. If the offence is indictable, the penalty must not exceed six months imprisonment and a £1,000 fine.

Where the subject is under 18, application is made to a juvenile court, where 18 or over, it is made to an adult magistrates's court. If the application is made by the supervisor a magistrate can issue a summons or warrant to secure the subject's attendance before the court. Applications to vary or discharge an order are appropriate if for instance the supervision has been a success, and the supervisor considers that the order need not run its full course. Conversely, if the subject has been uncooperative, the supervisor may want the order strengthened by the insertion of a requirement as in (f) above, or he may even feel that a supervision order is inadequate for the subject's needs and a care order is required. The commission by the subject of an offence during the currency of an order does not entitle the court finding him guilty of that offence to make orders in respect of the supervision order, but the order the court makes in dealing with the later offence may reflect the fact that it was committed while under supervision.

13.4.5 Recognisance by parent

Where a juvenile is found guilty of any offence other than murder, the court may order that his parent of guardian enter into a recognisance to take proper care of him and exercise proper control over him: Children and Young Persons Act 1969, s. 7(7)(c). The order may only be made if the parent or guardian consents. The effect of the parent or guardian entering into a recognisance is that if he fails to take the required care of the juvenile, a magistrates' court may declare the recognisance to be forfeited. He (the parent or guardian) then has to pay the court the sum of money mentioned in the recognisance. The recognisance must not be for a sum exceeding £200 or for a period exceeding three years. When he enters into the recognisance, the parent or guardian does not pay any money to the court, the liability only arising if he is subsequently in breach of his undertaking to exercise due care and control in respect of the juvenile.

13.4.6   Attendance centre orders

Attendance centre orders may be made by a magistrates' court (juvenile or adult) when dealing with a person under 21 in respect of whom they have power, or would have had power if it were not for his age, to impose imprisonment: Criminal Justice Act 1948, s. 19. Attendance centre orders are available, therefore, when a person under 21 is summarily convicted of an imprisonable offence, or when he is being dealt with for non-payment of a fine. They can also be made for non-compliance with the requirements of a probation or supervision order (see Chapter 15 and Para. 13.4.4 above). The order specifies a number of hours (not less than 12 except in the case of a child for whom 12 hours would be excessive, and not more than 24) during which the subject of the order must attend at a centre. Usually, the centres are opened on Saturday afternoons, and one of the aims of an order is to punish the offender by depriving him of his leisure. Another aim is to teach him, through the activities provided at the centre, something about the constructive use of leisure. Physical training is considered to be an important part of the regime at the centres. If the subject of the order fails to attend or is in serious breach of the centre's rules, he may be brought before a magistrates' court, which can revoke the order and deal with him in any other lawful way for the matter which led to the order being made.

An attendance centre order may only be made if a centre for persons of the offender's age and sex is available within reasonable travelling distance of his home. In fact, there are few centres where the regime is suitable for persons aged 17 and over, so attendance centre orders, although not restricted to juveniles, are much more likely to be made in their cases than in the cases of adults. An order may be an appropriate way of dealing with a child's first or second offence, but it is unlikely to be of much value in dealing with a more hardened delinquent. It is specifically provided that a person who has been sentenced to imprisonment, Borstal training or detention in a detention centre shall not be made the subject of an attendance centre order (proviso to s. 19(1) of the 1948 Act). Despite regular suggestions that attendance centres are the way to deal with football hooligans, the government seems unwilling to make provision for more senior centres.

13.4.7   Sentencing powers of the juvenile, adult magistrates', and Crown Court

Following conviction of a juvenile on indictment, the Crown Court may deal with him in any of the ways described above, save that it may not make an attendance centre order. In cases other than homicide, however, it should remit the offender to a juvenile court to be sentenced, unless satisfied that it would be undesirable to do so: Children and Young Persons Act 1933, s. 56. Where the Crown Court judge considers that the proper sentence is one which the juvenile court does not have power to pass (e.g. Borstal training), or where he is quite sure what the sentence ought to be so that any remittal would be a waste of time, he will pass sentence himself and not remit to the juvenile court.

A juvenile court cannot sentence an offender to detention under s. 53 of the Children and Young Persons Act 1933 (see Para. 13.4.2) or to Borstal training. The maximum fine it can impose is restricted (see Para. 13.4.1), and its power to make detention centre orders is also more restricted than the Crown Court's power (see Para. 15.8). Otherwise a juvenile court possesses the same sentencing powers as does the Crown Court, with the additional option of an attendance centre order. If the court considers that the juvenile should be sent to Borstal, it may commit him to the Crown Court with a Borstal recommendation under the Magistates' Courts Act 1980, s. 37 (see Para. 12.4.1).

Where a juvenile is found guilty before an adult magistrates' court, that court's powers of dealing with him are limited. It can fine him, or absolutely or conditionally discharge him, or make an order that his parent or guardian enter into a recognisance. It can also make any order which may be combined with a conditional discharge (e.g. endorsement of any driving licence the juvenile has or may obtain; disqualification from driving, and orders ancillary to a sentence, such as an order to pay costs to the prosecution, or compensation to the victim of the offence). If, in the court's opinion, the case cannot properly be dealt with by any of these methods, it must remit the juvenile to the juvenile court to be sentenced: Children and Young Persons Act 1969, s. 7(8). It follows that, if the adult court considers that Borstal is appropriate for the juvenile, it cannot commit him direct to the Crown Court under s. 37 of the Magistrates' Courts Act 1980, but must remit him to a juvenile court, which may then, if it thinks fit, commit him to the Crown Court.

13.4.8 General approach to sentencing juveniles

In deciding how to sentence an offender, a court takes a primary decision between passing either an individualised or a tariff sentence (see Chapter 16). An individualised sentence is the one which the court considers best suited to the needs and eventual rehabilitation of the individual offender. A tariff sentence is one primarily related to the gravity of the offence, and the need to punish and deter offenders. The great majority of sentences passed on juveniles come into the category of individualised sentences. For example, supervision orders and care orders are designed purely to help the subject, and the court's choice between them will depend more on what it perceives to be the juvenile's needs than on the gravity of the offences he has committed. Even a detention centre order, although intended as a punishment, is meant to shock a young person out of his criminal ways. The period of the order (three to six months — see Para. 15.8) is so short that it does not really fit into the category of a tariff sentence. The one form of sentence for juveniles where the needs of society clearly take precedence over the needs of the juvenile, is a sentence of detention under the Children and Young Persons Act 1933, s. 53. The judge may order the juvenile to be detained for the period during which, in the judge's view, he would otherwise be a danger to the public. He may even make an order designed to deter other potential offenders (see *R* v *Ford and others* supra Para. 13.4.2). Even so, the Home Secretary's discretion to release the offender means that he need not be detained for anything approaching the full period to which he was sentenced. Borstal training may be thought of as a tariff sentence, but it is, as its name implies, meant to give training in useful skills as well as to punish. In any event, only a small minority of juveniles are sent to Borstal — it is primarily a sentence for the 17-20 age range.

The circumstances in which the various types of sentence available for use in the juvenile courts are likely to be imposed may be illustrated by an imaginary case. Johnny Smith appears twice before the juvenile court when aged 11. On the first occasion he is found guilty of stealing a record from one shop and chocolates from another shop, and on the second occasion he admits taking another boy's pedal cycle. Reports before the court indicate that his home background is good, and Johnny seems duly repentant. The magistrates therefore deal with the cases by a combination of conditional discharge, attendance centre order and small fine (which, it is stressed, Johnny and not his parents should pay — it is not a case where the parents have failed to exercise due care and control). For two years, Johnny stays out of trouble. When he is nearly 14, he and older friends break into a school, steal expensive electrical equipment, and do £1,000 worth of damage. Johnny is still under 14 when the court deals with him. He is too young to be sent to a detention centre, so, despite the gravity of the offences, the magistrates make a supervision order. They consider carefully the possibility of a care order, but decide that in view of his good home a supervision order is sufficient. At the age of 15, Johnny acquires a liking for cars, and admits to taking three cars without the owner's consent and driving while under age. He is still under supervision, and a report from his social worker indicates that he is not cooperating with her efforts to befriend him. A report from his school shows him to be playing truant. The court considers that the time has come for a 'short, sharp shock', and they send Johnny to a detention centre for three months. Almost immediately after his release from detention centre, he is back before the court, again for taking a car. The offence, however, was committed before he went to detention centre, so, bearing that in mind, the court deals with it by way of a conditional discharge. Another year or so passes. Johnny leaves school, finds a job but is dismissed for insolence and bad time-keeping. Shortly before his seventeenth birthday, he is found guilty of two offences of 'mugging'. One of the victims required hospital treatment. The magistrates look back over his record. He has been, in effect, 'let off' with conditional discharges; he has been dealt with leniently through an attendance centre order; he has been given the advantage of supervision, and he has been taught a lesson at detention centre. Now, through his own fault, he is out of work. Reluctantly, they decide that Borstal training is the only appropriate sentence, and commit him for sentence under the Magistrates' Courts Act 1980, s. 37.

Part 4   Sentencing

14 Procedure before Sentencing

If the accused pleads guilty, or is found guilty by a jury or magistrates, the court proceeds to sentence him. It may do so immediately upon his being convicted. Alternatively, it may adjourn so that reports on him can be obtained, or so that the trial of a co-accused can take place and they both be sentenced together if the co-accused is convicted (see Paras. 6.3, 9.7 and 11.7). Where the court adjourns before sentencing, the offender is either kept in custody or granted bail. This Chapter describes the procedure in the Crown Court after conviction and before sentence is pronounced. The procedure is essentially the same in the magistrates' courts, although the information about the offender given to the magistrates may be less full than the information given to the judge in the Crown Court. For example, if the offender has committed a road traffic offence, the only evidence of previous convictions likely to be before the court is that provided by the endorsements, if any, on his licence.

In the magistates' courts the decision on what sentence to impose, like the decision as to verdict, may be taken by a majority of the magistrates. In the Crown Court, the responsibility for sentencing rests solely upon the judge and any magistrates with whom he may be sitting. The only way a jury may try to influence sentence is by adding a rider to their verdict recommending leniency. They very rarely do so. Since counsel in their speeches and the judge in his summing up do not refer to the possibility of recommending leniency, the jurors probably do not even know that they could make such a recommendation. Moreover, in *R* v *Sahota* (1980) Crim LR 678, where the jury asked if they could recommend leniency and the judge answered 'yes', the Court of Appeal stated that he should have told them that matters of sentencing were not for their consideration.

The procedure before sentencing is divided into the presentation of the facts of the offence by the prosecution; the giving of evidence about the offender by a police officer; the reading of any reports on the offender, and mitigation by the defence.

14.1 THE FACTS OF THE OFFENCE

Where the offender has pleaded not guilty and has been convicted by the jury, the Crown Court judge, having heard the evidence, knows full well the facts of the offence, and does not need to be reminded of them. If the offender pleads guilty, on the other hand, it is prosecuting counsel's duty to summarise the facts of the offence. He does this partly to assist the judge, partly to establish the prosecution version of how the offence was committed, and partly so that the public may know what occurred and form their own views on the justice of the sentence passed.

In summarising the facts, counsel makes use of copies, given to him in his brief, of the statements under s. 102 of the Magistrates' Courts Act 1980 made by the prosecution witnesses for purposes of the committal proceedings. He explains how the offence was committed, mentioning facts especially relevant to its gravity — e.g. if it was an offence of theft, he tells the judge the value of the property stolen and the amount which has been recovered; if it was an offence of violence, he recites the injuries suffered by the victim; if it was an offence committed when in a position of trust, he describes the position held by the offender. He goes on to describe the arrest of the offender, and his reaction when asked about the offence. If the offender was immediately cooperative, admitting his guilt to the police, it is a point in his favour which may result in the sentence being lighter than it would otherwise have been. Therefore, prosecuting counsel should acknowledge, if it be the case, that the offender did frankly confess to the crime. If the offender has made a written statement, counsel could either read it in full, or, more probably, summarise its contents and leave the defence to refer to it in more detail if they so wish.

At the sentencing stage the prosecution take a neutral attitude towards the case, neither under-estimating the seriousness of the offence, nor necessarily agreeing with the defence version of how it was committed. On the other hand, they do not ask for any particular sentence to be passed, or even urge the judge to pass a severe sentence. Prosecuting counsel is still to regard himself as a minister of justice (see Para. 8.1.1), conceding to the defence those points which, in the prosecution's view, can fairly be made on behalf of the offender.

> One problem which frequently arises, and to which there is no completely satisfactory solution, is the problem of the prosecution and defence differing about the facts of the offence. Prosecuting counsel puts forward one version of what occurred, but defence counsel in mitigation, while conceding that his client committed the offence, asserts that it was not committed in the manner or circumstances postulated by the prosecution. For example, in *R v Taggart* (1979) 1Cr App R (S.)144, T pleaded guilty to unlawful wounding, but denied the prosecution allegation that he had used a knife. Use of a knife or of any weapon is not a necessary element of an offence of unlawful wounding. Therefore, T's plea was the correct one. On the other hand, if he did use a knife, the judge would be entitled to pass a significantly more severe sentence than if the injuries had been inflicted during the course of a fist fight. Having heard the evidence given in the trial of T's co-accused, the judge decided that T had used a knife, and sentenced him accordingly. The sentence was confirmed, and it was held that the judge is not bound to accept the version of events put forward in mitigation, but can decide what occured on the basis of the information put before him. If he is left in doubt, however, that doubt must be resolved in favour of the offender.
>
> Where the differences between the prosecution and defence are such as to have a significant bearing upon the proper sentence it may be better, notwithstanding the decision in *R v Taggart*, for the judge to hear evidence from the prosecution and defence of what occurred (in *R v Taggart* the only evidence before the judge was that given in the co-accused's trial). In *R v Gortat and Pirog* (1973) Crim LR 648, Cusack J, before sentencing G and P on their pleas of guilty to conspiracy to rob, heard evidence about when the offenders had abandoned their enterprise. Mitigation for the offenders had suggested that they gave up the plan to commit a robbery even before they were arrested. The prosecution did not accept this, but asserted that, had the offenders not been arrested, they would have carried out the crime. The judge decided that they had not abandoned the enterprise before arrest but they had had misgivings about it. Another way to deal with the situation would have been for G and P to plead not guilty. The defence could than have cross-examined the prosecution witnesses and called G and P, while making it clear that their object was not to secure G and P's acquittal but to show the circumstances of the offence.
>
> Sometimes the prosecution suggest in their summary of the facts that the offence charged in the indictment is a sample offence. In other words, the offender committed numerous similar offences over a period of time. If the defence accept the prosecution suggestion, the judge proceeds to sentence on that basis. If not, the sentence should be on the basis that the offence

charged was not accompanied by others. The prosecution can, of course, charge the offender with the other offences. If they are proved, the offender will be separately sentenced for them. In *R* v *Hutchison* [1972] 1AER 936, H, who pleaded guilty to one count of incest with his daughter, denied the suggestion in her statement to the police that there had been regular intercourse over a long period, and said that it had only happened once. The judge, before sentencing, heard evidence from H and the daughter. He believed the daughter, and sentenced H to four years imprisonment. The Court of Appeal halved the sentence. By adopting the course he did, the judge in effect deprived H of his right to trial by jury in respect of the other alleged acts of incest. The situation was different from that in *R* v *Gortat and Pirog,* because in that case, on any view of the matter, there had only been one conspiracy to rob. In *R* v *Hutchison* the question was whether there had been one offence of incest or several.

14.2   THE POLICE OFFICER'S EVIDENCE

After prosecuting counsel has summarised the facts, he calls one of the police officers dealing with the case to tell the judge what is known about the offender. The officer gives his evidence on the special form of oath known as the 'voire dire' — 'I swear by Almighty God that I will true answer make to all such questions as the court shall demand of me'. The normal rules of evidence are relaxed at this stage. Counsel can ask leading questions and the officer's testimony consists of his reading out a type-written document containing what are known as the offender's antecedents. A copy of the antecedents is given to the defence not later than the jury's retiring to consider their verdict, or, in the case of a guilty plea, the entry of the plea. A copy is also given to each member of the court and to the shorthand writer, and to prosecuting counsel in his brief.

The antecedents should contain details of the offender's age, education, past and present employment, his domestic circumstances and income, the date of his arrest, whether he has been remanded in custody or on bail, and the date of his last release from prison or other custodial institution. There should also be a summary of his previous convictions and findings of guilt. This may include findings of guilt made when the offender was under 14, despite the Children and Young Persons Act 1963, s. 16(2) which provides that in proceedings against a person who has attained the age of 21 findings of guilt when under 14 shall be disregarded for the purposes of evidence relating to previous convictions. Attached to the antecedents is a form giving full details of the offender's criminal record, save that, unlike the summary, it omits mention of s. 16(2) findings of guilt. As regards each conviction or finding of guilt on it, the form states the name of the convicting court, the offence dealt with, the sentence passed, and the date of release if the sentence was a custodial one. Convictions which are spent (see Para. 14.2.2) are included in both the summary of convictions and the previous convictions form, but they should be marked as such on the latter. The defence are entitled before or at any stage during the trial to be supplied with details of the accused's previous convictions. The judge also knows about them, in contrast to magistrates trying a case summarily who, if possible, are kept in ignorance of the accused's criminal record until after conviction.

A convenient way to give the antecedents evidence is for prosecuting counsel to ask the officer for the age and date of birth of the offender. The officer replies by reading the details from his copy of the antecedents form. Then he is asked to summarise the previous convictions and findings of guilt, or counsel may deal with them in the form of a leading question (e.g. 'Is it right that this defendant has three previous convictions for burglary, one for causing grievous bodily harm with intent and two findings of guilt as a juvenile?' — the officer answers 'yes'). Next counsel and the officer turn to the full details of convictions given in the previous convictions form. If the convictions are numerous the judge will not want to hear about them all, but may say 'last three only' or 'last four only'. Counsel then asks the officer about the three or four most recent court appearances. Then the officer returns to the antecedents proper, and, suitably prompted by questions from counsel, tells the court about the offender's education, employment etc.

When prosecuting counsel has finished his examination, counsel for the defence may question the officer. One favourite question is — 'Is it right, officer, that my client cooperated with the police, and immediately admitted his guilt?' It is only advisable to ask the question if one knows in advance that the answer will be in the affirmative. Where the offender's circumstances have changed since the antecedents were prepared (e.g. he has found a job, or has become engaged to marry) the officer may be asked to confirm what has happened. Usually, he will not be in a position to confirm or deny the suggestion put to him.

A Practice Direction issued by Lord Parker CJ (1966 1WLR 1184) deals with the contents of the antecedents and the way in which the evidence should be given. Examples of antecedents and previous convictions forms will be found at pages 00.

After the police officer has testified the prosecution case is closed.

14.2.1 Challenges to the antecedents

Although the rules of evidence do not apply in their normal strictness to the giving of antecedents, the defence may challenge any of the assertions made by the police officer. Should they do so, the prosecution may put forward proper proof of the assertion — i.e. evidence of a type which would be admissible during the trial of a not guilty plea, and not, for example, inadmissible hearsay. If the prosecution fail to satisfy the judge of the truth of the assertion, he should ignore it in passing sentence and state that he is ignoring it: *R* v *Campbell* (1911) 6Cr App R 131.

The police officer should, in any event, be restrained from making generalised allegations, prejudicial to the offender, which are incapable of strict proof or disproof. In *R* v *Van Pelz* (1942) 29Cr App R 10, where VP had been convicted of an offence of larceny, the Court of Criminal Appeal criticised the prosecution for allowing the officer giving the antecedents to say that VP had led a loose and immoral life, was very well known as a prostitute, had associated constantly with thieves, and was regarded as a very dangerous woman indeed. Even where an allegation is specific enough for the defence, assuming it to be untrue, to challenge it effectively, the allegation should be made by an officer with first-hand knowledge of the matter, not by an officer relying upon what others have told him. In *R* v *Wilkins* (1978) 66Cr App R 49, the Court of Appeal reduced W's sentence for living on the earnings of prostitution from three years to two years because the officer giving the antecedents evidence testified that some 82 women, who had worked for an escort agency run by W, had stated that they used the agency as a medium for prostitution. The evidence at W's trial, while satisfying the jury that he had lived on the earnings of prostitution, had not suggested that he was involved in the organisation of prostitution on such a substantial scale. Clearly, the officer in making his allegations was not speaking of matters within his first-hand knowledge — he was repeating what the prostitutes had said. In all probability he had not even interviewed the prostitutes personally, but was telling the judge what other officers had told him of the prostitutes' allegations. The Court of Appeal emphasised the irregularity in the giving of the antecedents by reducing W's sentence even though, by the time the appeal was heard, he had been released from prison — a point of principle was involved. If allegations in the antecedents are likely to be disputed it may be advisable for the prosecution to give the defence advance notice of them, and of the evidence they intend to adduce in support of them: see *R v Robinson* (1969) 53Cr App R 314.

If the defence challenge the correctness of the prosecution evidence about the offender's previous convictions, the principles described above apply, and the prosecution must provide strict proof of the conviction. They can do this by producing, if the conviction was on indictment, a certificate, signed by the court clerk or other appropriate officer of the Crown Court, which sets out the substance of the indictment and conviction. If the conviction was summary, a copy of the record of the conviction signed by a magistrate or court clerk is produced. There must also be evidence of identity to show that the person named in the certificate or record of summary conviction is the offender before the court: Prevention of Crimes Act 1871, s. 18. Where (a) the police criminal records contain the finger-prints of whoever was convicted of the offence of which the offender allegedly stands convicted, and (b) the offender has been remanded in custody and had his finger-prints taken, the prosecution may prove that the offender is the person who was convicted of the offence by tendering certificates which establish that the two sets of finger-prints are identical: Criminal Justice Act 1948, s. 39.

14.2.2 Spent convictions

The Rehabilitation of Offenders Act 1974 is meant to enable offenders to 'live down' their past. Broadly speaking, the scheme of the Act is that after the elapsing from the date of conviction of a certain period of time (known as the 'rehabilitation period'), the offender becomes a rehabilitated person and his conviction is spent. A rehabilitated person is treated 'for all purposes in law as a person who has not committed... or been convicted of or sentenced for the offence or offences' of which he was convicted (s. 4(1) of the Act). This means, for example, that when a rehabilitated person applies for a job he does not, generally speaking, have to disclose his spent convictions, and any questions on the job application form about the applicant's criminal record are deemed not to relate to such convictions. Similarly, in most civil proceedings questions about spent convictions and evidence of the offences to which they related are inadmissible.

Section 4(1) is subject to the remainder of the Act, which contains provisions restricting the circumstances in which the subsection is to apply. Thus, a person wishing to follow certain professions or occupations designated by the Home Secretary may be asked about spent convictions by a person assessing his suitability for the profession or occupation. Not surprisingly, any would be barristers, solicitors of judges must declare their spent convictions. More to the point as far as criminal procedure is concerned, s. 7(2) provides that s. 4(1) is not to apply at all to criminal proceedings — i.e. there is no statutory restriction on the evidence which may be given of, and questions which may be asked about spent convictions that does not apply equally to convictions which are not spent. However, in a Practice Direction of 30 June 1975, Lord Widgery CJ recommended that both courts and counsel should give effect to the general intention of Parliament expressed in the debates leading up to the passing of the Act, and should not refer to a spent conviction when that can reasonably be avoided. At the sentencing stage of proceedings, the record supplied to the court of the offender's convictions should mark those which are spent. No reference should be made in open court to a spent conviction without the judge's authority, and that authority should only be given if the interests of justice so require. The judge himself, when passing sentence, should not mention a spent conviction unless he has to do so to explain the sentence he is passing (e.g. in a case where the sentence would seem unreasonably severe unless the public were made aware that, in the relatively recent past, the offender had committed an offence similar to that for which he is now being sentenced).

The period after which a conviction becomes spent (the rehabilitation period) depends upon the sentence passed for the offence. The periods are as follows:

(a) If the offender was sentenced to imprisonment for life or for a term exceeding 30 months, the conviction is never spent.

(b) If the sentence was for more than six months, but not more than 30 months imprisonment, the rehabilitation period is ten years.

(c) If the sentence was one of imprisonment for six months or less, or Borstal training, the period is seven years.

(d) If the sentence was a fine or detention under the Children and Young Persons Act 1933, s. 53 for a term exceeding six months but not exceeding thirty months, the period is five years.

(e) If the sentence was detention under s. 53 for six months or less or detention in a detention centre, the period is three years.

(f) If the offender was conditionally discharged, placed on probation, or made the subject of a care order or a supervision order, the period is one year or that for which the order remains in force, whichever is the longer.

(g) If the offender was disqualified from driving, the period is that for which he remains disqualified.

Where more than one sentence is imposed for a conviction (e.g. for a drink/driving offence the offender is sentenced to six months imprisonment suspended for two years; is fined £100, and disqualified from driving for three years), the rehabilitation period is the longest of the relevant periods (i.e. in the example given above, seven years for the suspended prison sentence, not five years for the fine or three years for the disqualification).

If, during the rehabilitation period for one offence, the offender is convicted of an indictable offence, and the sentence for the latter offence is such that rehabilitation is possible, both convictions become spent on the later of the two relevant rehabilitation dates. Using again the example given in the preceding paragraph, if the offender, three years after his conviction for drink/driving, were convicted of theft and conditionally discharged for two years, his conviction for theft would become spent after four, not two years (i.e. on the date when the drink/driving conviction becomes spent). If, on the other hand, he were sentenced to two years imprisonment for the theft, both that conviction and the drink/driving conviction would become spent ten years from the date of the former; if he were sentenced to three years for theft, that conviction would never become spent, but the rehabilitation date for the drink/driving offence would be unaffected. Finally, if he were convicted not of theft but of careless driving (a summary offence) the rehabilitation date for each conviction would be unaffected by the existence of the other conviction.

14.2.3 Suspended sentence etc.

If the offence of which the offender has been convicted was committed during the operational period of a suspended sentence, the Crown Court or, in certain circumstances, a magistrates' court can bring the suspended sentence into effect (see Para. 15.2). Also, if the offence was committed during the currency of a conditional discharge or probation order, the court may sentence the offender for the offence in respect of which the order was made (see Paras. 15.5 and 15.4). When it becomes apparent during the evidence of previous convictions that the offender is in breach of a suspended sentence, conditional discharge or probation, he should be asked whether he admits the breach. If he does, the court may deal with him for that matter when it sentences him for the present offence. If he does not, strict proof must be provided of the previous conviction and sentence (see Para. 14.2.1). Upon such proof, the court may deal with the breach.

14.3   REPORTS ON THE OFFENDER

After the antecedents evidence, the judge reads any reports which have been prepared on the offender. The defence are given copies of the reports. Counsel may refer to their contents in mitigation, but it is not normal practice to read them out in full. Where medical or psychiatric reports are concerned, it is obviously necessary to use them with discretion for fear that the offender should learn something about his physical or mental condition which it would be better for him not to know.

The main types of reports are as follows:

(a)   Social Enquiry reports — These are prepared by probation officers. Probation officers are appointed by committees of magistrates known as 'probation and after-care committees'. A limited number of non-magistrates may also be co-opted onto the committees. There is a committee either for a single petty sessional division or for a combined group of petty sessional divisions, and it is the committee's duty to appoint, for the area for which it has responsibility, sufficient probation officers to carry out the work of the probation service in that area. The work of the probation service includes supervising offenders who are placed on probation or who have been released from prison on licence (see Chapter 15). It also includes preparing social enquiry reports when requested to do so by the court. Since at least two probation officers must be appointed for each petty sessional division and at least one officer assigned to each location of the Crown Court, there should always be an officer available to receive the court's request for a report.

Before writing his report, the probation officer interviews the offender unless the offender refuses to see him. The report will usually contain an expanded version of the antecedents, describing the offender's background, circumstances, income and any particular social problems that he has. If the offender is pleading guilty, and was prepared to talk about his reasons for committing the offence, the report may set out those reasons. At the end of the report, the probation officer usually makes a recommendation as to how the offender could be dealt with. He will assess, in particular, the offender's likely response to probation, and he may go on to assess the likely response to other forms of punishment or treatment. If the report makes no recommendation, it is probably because the probation officer sees no real alternative to a custodial sentence. Home Office Circulars No 59/1971 and No 118/1977 give guidance on the preparation of social enquiry reports.

Before making a community service order (see Para. 15.6) the court must consider a report by a probation officer: Powers of Criminal Courts Act 1973, s. 14(2)(b). Before passing a sentence of imprisonment on an offender who is under 21 or who has not previously been sentenced to imprisonment the court will in most cases have to obtain a social enquiry report (Powers of Criminal Courts Act 1973 ss. 19(2) and 20(1), and see Para. 15.1.3). Although there is no absolute requirement to do so, one would expect the court to consider a report before sentencing an offender to Borstal or detention centre, and before sentencing a woman to immediate imprisonment. In general, reports are appropriate in the cases of young offenders and offenders whose wrong-doing seems to spring from inadequacy or personality disorders rather than calculated wickedness. Strangely, there is no rule that the court must have a report before putting an offender on probation, but clearly a judge or magistrate would be reluctant to make an order without a favourable report from a probation officer.

A copy of the social enquiry report must be given to counsel or solicitor for the offender, or, if he is unrepresented, to the offender himself. If the offender is a juvenile and unrepresented, the report may be given to his parent or guardian: Powers of Criminal Courts Act 1973, s. 46. The defence can require the probation officer who prepared the report to give evidence, so that for instance they can challenge unfavourable comment about the offender contained in the report.

(b)   Reports made on behalf of the Home Secretary. Before passing a sentence of Borstal training the Crown Court must consider any report on the offender made on behalf of the Home Secretary: Criminal Justice Act 1961, s. 1(3). The defence are entitled to a copy of the report: s. 37. Usually the report is drawn up during the period of a remand in custody before the offender is sentenced, and it gauges his likely reaction to a custodial sentence.

(c)   Medical and Psychiatric Reports — The court may request that a duly qualified medical practitioner make a report on the physical and mental condition of the offender. Such reports are desirable whenever the health of the offender apparently had something to do with his committing the offence. They are essential if the court is to make orders under the Mental Health Act 1959, s. 60 or the Powers of Criminal Courts Act 1973, s. 3 (orders for compulsory detention in a mental health hospital and probation orders with a condition attached that the probationer receive treatment for a mental condition — see Paras. 15.9 and 15.4). Where the offender is legally represented, a copy of the report must be given to counsel or solicitor, but if he is unrepresented the substance of the report only is to be disclosed to him: Mental Health Act 1959, s. 62(3). The practitioner who prepared the report may be required to attend to give oral evidence, and evidence may be called on behalf of the offender to rebut that contained in the report.

(d)   In the cases of juveniles, there may be reports from social workers involved with the juvenile and his family. Where the juvenile, prior to being dealt with for the offence, is remanded in the care of a local authority, detailed reports may be prepared on him covering matters such as his intelligence, behaviour in care, reaction to persons in authority and relationships with his peers. There may also be a report from his school.

14.4   MITIGATION

Once the reports have been read and, if necessary, the makers of the reports called to give evidence, defence counsel presents the mitigation on behalf of the offender. Much of it may be foreshadowed in the reports, and counsel can refer the judge to passages in them which are of especial assistance to his argument. Usually, counsel deals with the immediate circumstances of the offence, stressing any factor which may lessen its gravity. If it is an offence of dishonesty, he may be able to say that it was committed on the impulse of the moment, when temptation was suddenly and unexpectedly placed in the offender's way, or, if it is an offence of violence, he could point to extreme provocation which led the offender to lose his temper. Counsel must be careful, however, not to put forward in mitigation anything which in fact amounts to a defence to the charge — e.g. he should not assert that an assault was committed in self-defence. Where there is nothing that can sensibly be said with a view to making the offence appear less serious, it is best to turn rapidly to the circumstances of the offender. If the offence was committed when the offender was going through a period of difficulty, financial or otherwise, that may provide some explanation for what occurred. Looking to the future, there may have been a change in the offender's circumstances which offers hope for him staying out of trouble — he may have found a good job, or been reconciled with his wife, or accepted treatment for a drink problem which contributed to his offending. Finally, a cooperative attitude with the police when arrested, and a plea of guilty in court are both good points in mitigation.

In addition to his speech in mitigation counsel may call character witnesses on behalf of the offender to say (e.g.) that the offence was completely out of character and that they are convinced nothing like it will ever happen again. If the offender has no previous convictions it is, of course, a very strong argument in mitigation whether or not any character witnesses are called.

The offender may decline legal representation and put forward his mitigation in person if he so wishes. Generally speaking, however, it is of assistance to the court to have counsel or solicitor emphasise those matters which genuinely argue for a light sentence — an offender in person, through ignorance, may concentrate upon points which if anything exacerbate the offence and ignore some which are good mitigation. Legal representation for the offender is especially important where he is in danger of receiving a certain form of custodial sentence for the first time. Except as a last resort when it is really unavoidable, the courts do not want for instance to send to prison an offender who has not previously been there, because having experienced prison he may become hardened to it, and not deterred by the risk of it as he was before serving his sentence. So that all possible alternatives to imprisonment can be explored, it is desirable to have a lawyer mitigate for the offender. Therefore, the Powers of Criminal Courts Act 1973, s. 21 provides that a court shall not pass a sentence of imprisonment, Borstal training or detention in a detention centre on an offender who is not legally represented, and who has not previously been sentenced to that punishment unless either (a) he has applied for legal aid but his means made him ineligible for it or (b) he has been informed of his right to apply for legal aid, has had the opportunity to do so but has failed to make any application. Broadly speaking, the effect of s. 21 is that if a court is considering a custodial sentence for an offender who has not previously been so sentenced it must tell him that he can apply for legal aid, and grant, say, a week's adjournment to allow him to make the application. If he makes the application and is represented at the resumed hearing, the object of the section has been achieved. If he fails to make any application and is still unrepresented, the court has done all it reasonably could to persuade him to be represented, and is at liberty to pass any custodial sentence which it thinks fit. The means test applied to applications for legal aid in criminal matters is anything but a strict one, so it is unlikely that an offender who makes an application will be turned down on the grounds that his means make him ineligible. For purposes of s. 21, a suspended sentence of imprisonment which has not been brought into effect (see Para. 15.2) is disregarded — i.e. an offender who has never been sentenced to immediate imprisonment but has been given a suspended sentence which has remained suspended is within the ambit of s. 21.

14.5   TAKING OTHER OFFENCES INTO CONSIDERATION

A suspect who is questioned by the police about an offence and admits that he committed it may be further questioned about other crimes, as yet unsolved, which bear some similarity to the crime to which he has confessed. If the suspect is responsible for some or all of these other crimes, he might nevertheless be unwilling to acknowledge responsibility should each crime appear as a separate count on an indictment against him. A system has therefore developed which allows an offender to admit to other offences without actually being convicted of them. It is known as taking other offences into consideration when passing sentence. The procedure can be used in both the magistrates' courts and Crown Court.

The police prepare a list of the other offences which they believe or suspect the offender has also committed. The offender studies the list, and, if he so wishes, indicates that he did commit at least some of the offences. He then signs the list, those offences which he denies having beer deleted. Committal proceedings will then take place in respect, probably, of the offence for which the offender was arrested and one or two of the most serious of the other offences. The indictment is drafted accordingly. At the trial, the offender pleads guilty to the counts in the indictment. During his summary of the facts, prosecuting counsel tells the judge that he understands that the offender wishes to have other offences taken into consideration. The judge, who is given the list of offences which the offender has signed, asks him whether he admits committing each of the offences and whether he wants them taken into consideration when sentence is passed. Upon the offender answering 'yes' the judge will nearly always comply with his request. Prosecuting counsel will not give full details of the way the other offences were committed, but he may tell the judge for instance the total value of the property stolen in the other offences and the amount recovered.

In passing sentence, the maximum sentence the court may impose is the maximum for the offences of which the offender has been convicted. This, in practice, is not a significant limitation on the court's powers. Typically, offences are taken into consideration where an offender has committed several offences of dishonesty, none of which are, for offences of that type, exceptionally serious. He may, for example, plead guilty to an indictment containing two counts for burglary from dwelling houses and one for taking a motor vehicle without the owner's consent. He then asks for two other offences of burglary and three of taking motor vehicles to be taken into consideration. Burglary is punishable with imprisonment for up to 14 years, taking motor vehicles with imprisonment for up to three years, and any prison sentences can be made to run consecutively to each other. For the three counts in the indictment the offender could, in theory, be sentenced to 31 years imprisonment. In fact, for both the offences on the indictment and those taken into consideration the judge is most unlikely to impose more than, say, a sixth of the theoretical maximum. The magistrates' powers of sentencing are, of course, much more restricted than the Crown Court's, but, assuming the offender is aged 17 or over and has been convicted of an offence triable either way, they can commit him to the Crown Court for sentence under the Magistrates' Courts Act 1980, s. 38 if the offences he wants taken into consideration make the punishment they can inflict inadequate.

The judge should not automatically take other offences into consideration merely because the prosecution and defence wish him to do so. Where the other offences are of a different type from those charged in the indictment, it may not be right to agree to the request to take them into consideration. Certainly, an offence which is punishable with endorsement of the driving licence and discretionary or obligatory disqualification from driving should not be taken into consideration when none of the offences on the indictment are so punishable: *R v Collins* [1947] KB 560. The reason is that, since the court's powers of sentencing are limited to those it possesses in respect of the counts in the indictment, an offender who was allowed to 't.i.c.' an endorsable offence when none of the offences on the indictment carried endorsement, would unfairly escape endorsement of his licence and possible disqualification. It is also wrong for magistrates to take into consideration offences which they have no jurisdiction to try — i.e. they should not 't.i.c.' offences triable only on indictment.

Where an offence is taken into consideration, the offender is not convicted of it and accordingly could not successfully raise the plea of autrefois convict if subsequently prosecuted for the offence: *R v Nicholson* [1947] 2ALL ER 535. In practice, the police would never consider instituting proceedings for an offence which was taken into consideration. The 't.i.c.' system helps them to reduce the list of unsolved crimes by encouraging offenders who have little option but to admit to one offence to admit, at the same time, to other offences which, in the absence of such admission, it would be difficult or impossible to prove against them. The obvious question is — why should an offender admit to and ask to have taken into consideration other offences when, if the police had had sufficient evidence against him, they would have arrested him for those other offences? The answer is that, although the judge may increase his sentence somewhat because of the 't.i.c.' offences, the increase is unlikely to be significant, and the offender has the advantage of having his 'slate wiped clean'. When he has served his sentence, he can lead an honest life without worrying about the police uncovering evidence which would enable them to prosecute him for one of his past crimes.

The above discussion of taking offences into consideration has proceeded on the assumption that the offender is pleading guilty to the counts in the indictment or the informations preferred against him. However, there is nothing to stop the police asking an accused who is pleading not guilty whether, in the event of a conviction, he would like to have other offences considered, or there may be an opportunity between conviction and sentence to raise the matter with him. In general, though, the 't.i.c.' system is geared to the offender who is pleading guilty.

14.6 VARIATION OF SENTENCE

The sentence imposed or other order made by the Crown Court when dealing with an offender may be varied or rescinded within a period of 28 days beginning with the date of sentence: Courts Act 1971, s. 11. If two or more persons are jointly tried on an indictment, the period is 28 days from the conclusion of the joint trial or 56 days from the imposition of the sentence which is to be varied or rescinded, whichever is the shorter. Section 11 can be used to increase a sentence, but that should only be done in the most exceptional circumstances. A comparison of *R v Grice* (1978) 66Cr App R 167 and *R v Newsome and Browne* [1970] 2QB 711 illustrates the point. In *R v Grice* the judge, upon G undertaking that he would not in future see certain people including the victim of the offence, passed a suspended sentence of imprisonment. Within the 28 day period, G broke the undertaking. He was brought before the judge who altered the suspended sentence to one of immediate imprisonment. The Court of Appeal held that it was quite wrong to use s. 11 to effect a fundamental change in the sentence which was to the detriment of the offender. In *R v Newsome and Browne,* on the other hand, the Court of Appeal upheld an increase of one month in a prison sentence which had originally been for six months. The judge increased the sentence because, under legislation then in force, a six month sentence would have had to have been suspended.

Once the period specified in s. 11 has elasped the Crown Court has no power to vary or rescind its sentence. Thus, an order made outside the relevant period that the offender should forfeit money which he had been carrying in order to facilitate the commission of drugs offences, was quashed by the House of Lords because the addition of a forfeiture order amounted to a variation of sentence, and so had to be made within the s. 11 time limits (*R* v *Menocal* [1979] 2WLR 876).

A magistates' court can also within 28 days vary or rescind a sentence or other order made when dealing with an offender: Magistrates' Courts Act 1980, s. 142(1). The court which makes the change in the sentence must consist either of all the magistrates who made up the original court, or, if that original court comprised three or more magistrates, a majority of them: s. 142(4). Similar provisions apply when a magistrates' court has convicted an accused, and the magistrates who made up the court have doubts about the correctness of their decision (see Para. 11.6).

15   *Powers of Sentencing*

An account of the procedure before sentencing would be incomplete without a description of the various types of sentence the courts may pass and the circumstances in which they may pass them. This chapter will concentrate upon the points of principal importance. Reference should also be made to Para. 11.7 and 12.3.1. for restrictions upon the sentencing powers of the magistrates' courts, and to Para. 13.4 for sentencing of juveniles. The latter Paragraph deals with four forms of sentence which are largely or totally confined to juveniles, namely orders for detention under the Children and Young Persons Act 1933, s. 53, care orders, supervision orders and attendance centre orders. Of the sentences and other orders mentioned in this chapter, fines, conditional and absolute discharges and orders under the Mental Health Act 1959 are available for offenders of all ages. Imprisonment, suspended sentences, community service orders and probation are available in the cases of all adults, and Borstal training and detention centre orders are available in the cases of offenders aged under 21 but over 15 and 14 respectively. Some of these methods of dealing with an offender are intended principally to punish and deter (e.g. imprisonment, both immediate and suspended, and fines). Others are used as an alternative to punishment (e.g. probation and conditional and absolute discharges). Yet others contain elements of both punishment and training for the offender (e.g. Borstal and community service orders).

At the same time as they pass sentence, judges or magistrates may make ancillary orders connected with the case (e.g. orders that the offender pay costs to the prosecution, or contribute to his own legal aid costs, or pay compensation to the victim of the offence). Such orders are not, strictly speaking, part of the sentence. A compensation order, for example, merely gives to the victim a convenient means of recovering from the offender at least some of the damages which he could claim in a civil action. Since these orders are merely ancillary to the sentence, they are dealt with in a later chapter (see Chapter 21). However, the possible effect of ancillary orders should be borne in mind when considering the court's powers of sentencing. An offender who is fined £100 might think that he has been dealt with leniently. If he then learns that he is to pay £100 costs to the prosecution, £100 contribution to his own legal aid costs, £100 compensation to the victim of the offence, and to forfeit £100 which, at the time of his arrest, he had in his possession in order to facilitate the commission of an offence, he may feel that the judge has not been so lenient after all.

The method adopted for describing the sentences and orders dealt with in this chapter is to list the main points about each of them in summary form, and then give further explanation beneath as required.

15.1 IMMEDIATE IMPRISONMENT

(a)   Subject to the special restrictions on the powers of magistrates' courts to imprison, the maximum term which may be imposed for one offence is, in the case of a common law offence, imprisonment for life and, in the case of a statutory offence, the maximum prescribed by the statute creating the offence.

(b)   A court imposing a sentence of imprisonment may make it run concurrently with or consecutively to any sentence of imprisonment which the offender is currently serving for some other matter. A court passing sentences of imprisonment for two or more offences may order that the terms run concurrently with or consecutively to each other, even if, in the latter case, the aggregate term which the offender is to serve is greater than the term which could have been imposed for any one offence. This is again subject to the condition mentioned in (a) above.

(c)   No court may impose imprisonment on an offender who is under 17 (Powers of Criminal Courts Act 1973, s. 19(1) and see Para. 13.4.1).

(d)   No court may impose imprisonment on an offender who is under 21, or pass a sentence of imprisonment on an offender who has attained the age of 21 but has not previously been sentenced to imprisonment, unless no other method of dealing with him is appropriate: Powers of Criminal Courts Act 1973, ss. 19(2) and 20(1). Unlike the phrase 'pass a sentence of imprisonment', the words 'impose imprisonment' include committing an offender to prison for non-payment of a fine. See also Para. 14.4 for s. 21 of the 1973 Act and the need to adjourn so that an offender who has not previously been sentenced to imprisonment may apply for legal aid.

(e)   No court may pass a sentence of imprisonment on an offender who is within the age limits which qualify for Borstal training (i.e. under 21 at the date of conviction) unless that sentence is for a term of three years or more, or six months or less: Criminal Justice Act 1961, s. 3. This does not apply if the offender is currently serving a prison sentence: s. 3(2). If he has already served a sentence of Borstal training or a sentence of at least six months imprisonment, a sentence of 18 months imprisonment or more may be passed: s. 3(3).

(f)   The Prison Rules 1964 (SI 1964 No 388 as amended by Prison (Amendment) Rules SI 1968 No 440) provide for remission of one third of a sentence for good behaviour. Any time the offender spends in custody before sentence, whether before or after conviction, counts towards the serving of his sentence.

(g)   After the offender has served twelve months or one third of his sentence, whichever is the greater, he may be released on licence by the Home Secretary: Criminal Justice Act 1967, s. 60. The Home Secretary may only thus release him if recommended to do so by the Parole Board.

(h)   Recidivist offenders (i.e. those who repeatedly commit offences) may have extended terms of imprisonment imposed upon them. The term may be longer than that which would normally be imposed for the offence of which the offender has been convicted, and special provisions apply as to his release: Powers of Criminal Courts Act 1973, ss. 28 and 29.

(j)   An offender convicted of murder who, at the time of the offence, was aged 18 or over, must be sentenced to imprisonment for life: Murder (Abolition of Death Penalty) Act 1965, s. 1(1). An offender who was under 18 at the relevant time must be sentenced to be detained during Her Majesty's pleasure (see Para. 13.4.2).

15.1.1 Maximum terms of imprisonment

The maximum terms of imprisonment which may be imposed for the most important or common offences are as follows:

(a) For manslaughter, causing grievous bodily harm with intent, rape, forgery of certain documents (e.g. banknotes, wills and deeds), criminal damage committed by use of fire or with an intent etc. to endanger life, aggravated burglary and robbery — imprisonment for life.

(b) For burglary, handling stolen goods, blackmail, offences under the Official Secrets Act 1911 and supplying controlled drugs in Classes A and B — 14 years.

(c) For theft, obtaining property by deception and non-aggravated criminal damage — 10 years.

(d) For perjury, bigamy, living on the earnings of prostitution, making or accepting corrupt payments in relation to public contracts and having possession of a Class A controlled drug — 7 years.

(e) For unlawful wounding, assault occasioning actual bodily harm, causing death by reckless driving, obtaining services by deception, evasion of liability by deception and having possession of a Class B controlled drug — 5 years.

(f) For taking a motor vehicle without the owner's consent and going equipped — 3 years.

(g) For reckless driving, forgery of any document for which a higher maximum is not fixed, making or accepting corrupt payments otherwise than in relation to public contracts, making off without payment, having an offensive weapon, unlawful sexual intercourse, indecent assault and having possession of a Class C controlled drug — 2 years.

(h) For driving while disqualified, and common assault tried on indictment — 1 year.

(i) For assaulting a police constable in the execution of his duty, drink/driving offences and conduct conducive to a breach of the peace — 6 months.

(j) For being in charge of a motor vehicle when under the influence of drink or drugs, or with excess alcohol in the blood — 3 months.

(j) For obstructing a police constable in the execution of his duty — 1 month.

As will be seen from the above, the maximum terms roughly, but only roughly, reflect the relative gravity of the various offences. There are apparent anomalies, such as burglary being punishable with a sentence twice as long as perjury. For many indictable offences, including burglary, handling, theft and criminal damage, the maxima are much higher than the terms which would be imposed in all but the gravest cases, but fixing the maximum term high allows for suitable punishment for the man who steals the Crown jewels or damages the National Gallery's most valuable painting. It should not be thought that the penalty which could theoretically be imposed plays a major part in determining the penalty which is actually imposed on a particular offender for a particular crime — i.e. a judge does not pass a sentence of five years imprisonment for an offence of theft which he regards as being of average gravity on the basis that the maximum for theft is ten years. Subject, of course, to not exceeding the lawful maximum, the sentence will reflect the character of the offender and the gravity of his conduct, not the label (robbery, burglary, theft, handling or whatever) which is attached to that conduct. For example, a person who enters a restaurant with no money, orders and consumes an expensive meal for which he never had any intention of paying, and leaves without paying when the waiter is not looking, could be convicted of obtaining property by deception (the food he has eaten) or obtaining services by deception (the services of the waiter and kitchen staff). Notwithstanding that the former offence is punishable with up to ten years and the latter with up to five years imprisonment, the sentence he will receive will be exactly the same whether he is convicted of either, or for that matter both, offences.

Although an offender convicted on indictment of a common law offence may on the face of it be sentenced to imprisonment for life, statute sometimes limits the Crown Court's sentencing powers. Thus, an attempt to commit an offence is a common law offence, but the maximum term imposed for an attempt must not exceed the maximum which could be imposed for the completed offence even if that is substantially less than life imprisonment: Powers of Criminal Courts Act 1973, s. 18(2). Where the Crown Court has power, at common law or by statute, to pass a sentence of life imprisonment it may, except in cases of murder, pass a sentence of imprisonment for a determinate period, or even refrain from passing a prison sentence at all. Ironically, a sentence of life imprisonment may sometimes be more favourable to the offender than a lengthy sentence for a fixed term of years, because under the former he may possibly be released on licence at an earlier stage than he could be under the latter. The mandatory sentence of life imprisonment for murder is dealt with in Para. 15.1.6.

Where a statute creates an indictable offence and provides that it shall be punishable with imprisonment, but fails to state the maximum term of imprisonment which is permissible, it is punishable with up to two years imprisonment upon conviction on indictment: Powers of Criminal Courts Act 1973 s. 18(1).

15.1.2   Concurrent and consecutive sentences

Where a single act by an offender gives rise to two or more offences of which he is convicted the court dealing with him should not pass consecutive sentences of imprisonment. Returning to the example given in Para. 15.1.1 of a man who orders a meal at a restaurant and leaves without paying, if he is convicted of obtaining property by deception, obtaining services by deception and making off without payment and the court decides to pass a prison sentence, the sentences for the three offences should be made to run concurrently. He has, effectively, committed only one criminal act. If he is spotted leaving by a waiter and assaults the waiter in an attempt to avoid apprehension, that constitutes a second distinct criminal act, and he could properly be sentenced for it to a consecutive term of imprisonment. *R v Hussain* [1962] Crim LR 712 illustrates the appellate court's attitude to consecutive and concurrent sentences. H, who tried unsuccessfully to smuggle Indian hemp through customs at Heathrow airport, was given three years for possessing a dangerous drug and two years to run consecutively for unloading prohibited goods from an aircraft. The Court of Criminal Appeal held that since both offences arose out of a single act it was wrong to impose consecutive sentences. H's pleasure at a successful appeal was short-lived, because the sentence was varied to one of five years imprisonment for each offence to run concurrently.

Where an offender is convicted of several similar offences committed at different times, he could be sentenced to consecutive terms of imprisonment. The danger with such an approach is that the individual sentences may, in themselves, be short and well justified by the criminal conduct in respect of which they are passed, but taken in the aggregate they can amount to an unreasonably severe punishment. To avoid this danger, a judge sentencing an offender for, say, five offences of burglary from dwelling houses committed over a six month period, will probably decide on the penalty appropriate for the offender's over-all criminal conduct during that period (it might be three years imprisonment). He will then pass a sentence of three years imprisonment for the most serious of the burglaries and make the sentences for the other burglaries run concurrently with each other and with the three year sentence.

The judge or presiding magistrate should expressly state whether the prison sentences imposed are to run concurrently or consecutively. If nothing is said, the sentences are presumed to be concurrent.

15.1.3 Restrictions on imprisonment

Of the five restrictions on the courts' powers to pass sentences of imprisonment which have been mentioned (limitations on the powers of magistrates' courts; no imprisonment to be imposed on juveniles; adjournment for legal aid application where an unrepresented offender is to be sentenced to imprisonment for the first time, and the restrictions mentioned in propositions (d) and (e) of the summary of powers of imprisonment) only the latter two call for further consideration here.

Sections 19(2) and 20(1) of the Powers of Criminal Courts Act 1973 provide that the court, in order to decide whether a prison sentence is the only appropriate method of dealing with an offender under 21 or one who has attained that age but has not previously been sentenced to imprisonment, 'shall obtain and consider information about the circumstances, and shall take into account any information before the court which is relevant to the offender's character and physical and mental condition'. Probably a social enquiry report and, in the case of an offender under 21, a report prepared on behalf of the Home Secretary dealing with his suitability for Borstal training, will be before the court. If they are, the court must take them into consideration, together with any other reports on the offender, such as medical or psychiatric reports. If no reports have been prepared, the court is not obliged to adjourn so as to obtain them (*R* v *Peter* [1975] Crim LR 593), but will nearly always do so, at least if it is considering immediate imprisonment. In *R* v *Peter*, however, the Court of Appeal upheld a sentence of imprisonment on an offender who had not previously been so sentenced because, although the judge had no reports before him when he sentenced, his observation of P during a long trial in which P had given evidence and put his character in issue, gave him sufficient information about P to conclude that no method of dealing with him, other than prison, was appropriate.

An offender who has not previously been sentenced to immediate imprisonment, but has had a suspended sentence passed on him which has not been brought into effect is within the ambit of s. 20: s. 20(3). If a magistrates' court imposes imprisonment on an offender under 21 or passes a sentence of imprisonment in respect of a 's. 20 offender' it must state its reasons for concluding that no other method of dealing with him is appropriate: ss. 19(3) and 20(2) respectively.

The purpose of s. 3 of the Criminal Justice Act 1961 (for its terms, see proposition (e) of the summary of powers of imprisonment) is to encourage a judge who could sentence an offender to either Borstal training or prison to employ the former rather than the latter sentence. If sent to Borstal, the offender should receive instruction in crafts and skills which would not be available in the young prisoners' wing of a prison.

However, Borstal training, which usually results in the offender's release after about nine months, would not provide sufficient protection for the public where the offender has been convicted of a really serious crime. Conversely, if the offender has been convicted of a relatively minor offence which nonetheless calls for a custodial sentence, and is nearly 21, a short sentence of imprisonment is called for rather than Borstal. Accordingly, s. 3 permits the court to impose on an offender aged under 21 at the date of conviction either a prison sentence of such length that, given the youth of. the offender, it can only be justified if the offence is grave, or a prison sentence of such brevity that the court would consider it, in most cases, too lenient. In the majority of cases, having decided that either prison or Borstal is called for, the judge is effectively forced to pass a sentence of Borstal training.

The approach to sentencing the judge should adopt when s. 3 applies, and the problems raised by the section, are illustrated by *R* v *Harnden* (1978) 66 Cr App R 281. H, a student aged 20, was convicted of supplying a controlled drug. The judge decided that Borstal was inappropriate because the training and instruction given there would not be suited to the needs of an academically gifted young man. Nevertheless, a custodial sentence of more than six months was called for to mark the gravity of the offence. He therefore passed the minimum prison sentence in excess of six months that he could lawfully pass, namely three years. The Court of Appeal replaced that sentence with one of Borstal training. They stated that, when s. 3 applies and the judge's provisional view is that a prison sentence should be passed, he should calculate the proper length of the sentence, and, if a sentence of that length is. prohibited by s. 3, he should pass a sentence of Borstal training instead. In H's case, the offence was not sufficiently grave to warrant three years imprisonment, bearing in mind that H was only 20. Therefore, he had to be sent to Borstal, even though the Court of Appeal readily understood the judge's reasons for thinking Borstal inappropriate.

Where an offender has served a sentence of Borstal training but, after his release, reoffends, the arguments for sending him to Borstal again rather than to prison are much less strong than they are in the case of an offender who has never experienced Borstal. Section 3(3) therefore permits offenders who have served a sentence of Borstal training (and those who have served a prison sentence of at least six months) to be sentenced to imprisonment for six months or less, or 18 months or more (not three years or more). An offender who absconds from Borstal and commits offences 'on the run' has not served a sentence of Borstal training within the meaning of s. 3(3), and so for him a sentence of 18 months imprisonment would be unlawful: *R* v *Hughes* [1968] 1WLR 560.

Although an offender who is serving a prison sentence can be sentenced to Borstal training, it is generally undesirable so to do — Borstal should precede rather than follow an experience of prison: *R* v *Hannah* (1968) 52Cr App R 734. For this reason, s. 3 does not apply to offenders who are serving a sentence of imprisonment. The court has a complete discretion in such cases to pass a sentence of imprisonment of any length, or, if Borstal would be of value despite the offender's experience of prison, to send him to Borstal. If a sentence of Borstal training is passed, that takes effect immediately and the prison sentence merges into it. An offender who has been released from prison on licence (see Para. 15.1.5) is still deemed to be serving a sentence of imprisonment, and so is outside the provisions of s. 3.

Where an offender is sentenced to imprisonment for two or more offences, the terms of imprisonment passed are treated as a single term whether they are made to run concurrently with or consecutively to each other: Criminal Justice Act 1961, s. 38(4). Therefore, an offender to whom s. 3 applies who is convicted on indictment of three offences of theft may be sentenced to 12 months imprisonment on each count to run consecutively, but may not be sentenced to 12 months on each to run concurrently. In the former case, the sentence is treated as a single sentence of three years imprisonment; in the latter case, as a single sentence of one year's imprisonment. However, where the offender is in breach of a suspended sentence (see Para. 15.2) the court may pass for the present offence a sentence complying with s. 3, and bring into effect the suspended sentence to run consecutively to the sentence for the present offence, even though the total sentence is for a period prohibited by s. 3. For example, an offender to whom s. 3 applies who is in breach of a suspended sentence of six months imprisonment, may be sentenced to, say, three months imprisonment for his present offence, and, in addition, the suspended sentence may be brought into effect to run consecutively to the three month sentence. Although the total term of the present sentence and the suspended sentence is nine months, s. 3 is not contravened.

Note that the White Paper on the treatment of young offenders (1980 Cmnd 8045 — see Appendix 2) recommends the repeal of s. 3 of the Criminal Justice Act 1961 and the introduction of a sentence of 'youth custody' to replace imprisonment for offenders under 21.

15.1.4   Extended sentences

Extended sentences are designed to meet the problem of the persistent offender who never commits an offence which, in itself, is serious enough to warrant a long term of imprisonment. An extended term differs from an ordinary term of imprisonment in that:

(a)   If the maximum term of ordinary term imprisonment that may be imposed is less than 5 years, an extended term of up to 5 years may be imposed; if the ordinary maximum is 5 years or more but less than 10 years, an extended term of up to 10 years is permissible: Powers of Criminal Courts Act 1973, s. 28(2). However, a term of imprisonment may be ordered by the court to be an extended term even though it is for a period within the maximum period of ordinary imprisonment which could be imposed *DPP* v *Ottewell* [1970] AC 642. In *DPP* v *Ottewell*, O pleaded guilty to two offences of assault occasioning actual bodily harm, an offence which is punishable with up to five years imprisonment. The House of Lords upheld the imposition of extended terms on both counts made to run consecutively, each term being for a period of only two years.

(b)   The provisions governing remission and release on licence for a prisoner serving an extended term differ from those which apply to a prisoner serving an ordinary term of imprisonment (see Para. 15.1.5). In particular, if the former is released before his sentence has run its full course, he is always subject to supervision and the possibility of being recalled to prison if he misbehaves, whereas the latter is only subject to such conditions if he is released on parole rather than being granted remission under the Prison Rules (see proposition (f) of the summary of powers of imprisonment).

(c)   When the court imposes an extended term it may be for a period sufficient to protect the public from the offender, even if that period is longer than that justified by the gravity of the offence committed were one to apply normal 'tariff' principles of sentencing (see Chapter 16 for tariff sentences). Thus, four years imprisonment for two offences of assault occasioning actual bodily harm would normally be too severe a sentence even though it is well within the statutory maximum, but because the judge passed extended terms he was entitled to make the sentence long enough to protect the public, and a total sentence of four years was upheld — see *DPP* v *Ottewell* (supra).

Relatively few extended sentences are passed because the conditions which must be satisfied before an offender is liable to be so sentenced are numerous and strict. To over simplify somewhat a very detailed piece of legislation, s. 28 provides that an offender is at risk of an extended sentence if:

(a)   He is over 21; and
(b)   He is convicted on indictment of an offence punishable with at least two years imprisonment; and
(c)   The offence mentioned in (b) was committed within three years of his being convicted

of or released from prison after serving a sentence for such an offence (i.e. an offence punishable with at least two years imprisonment); and

(d)   On at least three separate prior occasions since attaining the age of 21 he has been convicted on indictment of (or committed to the Crown Court for sentence for) such offences; and

(e)   Those convictions were dealt with by sentences of imprisonment totalling 5 years or more in length, and including at least two sentences which resulted in his serving time in prison (either because the sentence was one of immediate imprisonment or because it was a suspended sentence subsequently brought into effect); and

(f)   The court is satisfied that, by reason of his previous conduct, it is expedient to protect the public from him for a substantial time.

Notice must be given to the offender at least three clear days before the extended sentence is passed of the prosecution's intention to prove the convictions and sentences which make him liable to such a sentence: s. 29(3). This enables the defence to check that the offender is indeed within the ambit of s. 28, and to challenge any inaccuracies in the prosecution's account of the previous convictions.

15.1.5   Remission and release on licence

Except as mentioned below, a prisoner is automatically granted remission of up to one third of his sentence for good behaviour (the Prison Rules SI 1964 No 388 as amended). In addition, the time he spends in custody prior to sentence being passed counts towards the serving of his sentence: Criminal Justice Act 1967, s. 67. A prisoner who is released with remission under the Prison Rules is released unconditionally. Although he may be offered help from probation officers or other suitable persons, he is not obliged to accept that help. Nor is he liable to be recalled to prison.

A prisoner who is released on licence after serving twelve months or one third of his sentence, whichever is the greater, is still, in a sense, serving his sentence. He must comply with any conditions specified in the licence, for example a condition that he be under the supervision of a probation officer or other suitable person: Criminal Justice Act 1967, s. 60(4). At any time the Parole Board (see below) may recommend to the Home Secretary that he revoke the licence and recall the licencee to prison, or, in cases of urgency, the Home Secretary may revoke the licence on his own initiative without consultation with the Parole Board (s. 62(1) and (2) of the 1967 Act). Of even more significance is the fact that if a licencee is convicted on indictment of an imprisonable offence the Crown Court may, in addition to punishing him for the offence, revoke the licence. If he is convicted summarily of an offence punishable on indictment with imprisonment, the magistrates may commit him to the Crown Court to be dealt with for the breach of licence, and again the Crown Court may revoke the licence: s. 62(6) and (7). Where a licence is revoked the prisoner normally serves whatever is left of his sentence less any remission that he is entitled to under the Prison Rules. If the Crown Court has revoked the licence because of the commission of a further offence, it may order that any prison sentence it passes for that offence shall take effect either concurrently with or consecutively to the remainder of the sentence in respect of which the offender was released on licence. Subject to prior revocation, and subject to the exceptions mentioned below, a licence expires on the 'remission date' — i.e. the date when, had he not been released on licence, the licencee would with remission have been released under the Prison Rules.

The Home Secretary may only release a prisoner on licence (i.e. grant him parole) if recommended to do so by the Parole Board or, in some cases, a local review committee: s. 60(1). The Parole Board, consisting of at least five members appointed by the Home Secretary, must include a person who holds or has held judicial office, a qualified psychiatrist, a person experienced in the supervision of discharged prisoners and an expert in criminology. In addition, there exists for each prison a local review committee established in accordance with rules laid down by the Home Secretary, and including a probation officer and a member of the prison board of visitors but no prison officer other than the governor. The system for granting parole is helpfully summarised in the judgments of their Lordships in *Payne* v *Lord Harris of Greenwich* [1981] 1WLR 754.

First, the prisoner is interviewed by a member of the local review committee. He must be given an opportunity to make any representations which he wishes to be considered by the committee. The member of the committee makes a writen report of the interview which incorporates any representations from the prisoner. Second, the local review committee considers the prisoner's case. It has before it the report of the interview with the prisoner. In addition, the prisoner has the right to submit his own written representations. The committee draws up a report for the Home Secretary on the prisoner's suitability for parole. Third, the Home Secretary refers the case, together with the local review committee's report, to the Parole Board. If necessary, a member of the Board can interview the prisoner, or the Board can rely upon the report of the interview which the prisoner had with the member of the local review committee. If the Board recommends parole the Home Secretary may, but need not, release the prisoner. In certain classes of cases, determined by the Home Secretary after consultation with the Parole Board, he may release the prisoner upon being recommended to do so by the local review committee without referring the case to the Board: Criminal Justice Act 1972 s 35.

The system described above is criticised for being secretive and over-dependent upon administrative discretion. An unsuccessful applicant does not even have the right to know why parole was refused: *Payne* v *Lord Harris of Greenwich* (supra). In addition, the tension an applicant must feel during the period his application is being considered may easily be imagined. On the other hand, parole enables many prisoners to spend significantly less time in prison than they would otherwise have to do, with about 60% of all eligible prisoners being granted parole for an average period of nearly nine months.

For three groups of prisoners the rules about remission and release on licence are different from those described above.

(a) Offenders sentenced to imprisonment for life cannot earn remission of sentence, but they can be released on licence at any stage. For this reason, an offender convicted of (e.g.) manslaughter on the grounds of diminished responsibility may be given a life sentence in preference to a fixed term of imprisonment, because under the former he may be considered for parole as soon as his mental problems have been overcome, whereas under the latter he would inevitably have to serve twelve months or one third of the sentence whichever was the longer. However, a life sentence means what it says in the sense that, if released, the offender is on licence for the rest of his life. Before releasing a 'lifer' on licence the Home Secretary must consult with the Lord Chief Justice and the judge who passed the sentence, if he is available: s. 61. Similar provisions apply to young offenders sentenced to be detained during Her Majesty's pleasure or for life in accordance with the Home Secretary's directions under s. 53(1) and (2) of the Children and Young Persons Act 1933 (see Para. 13.4.2).

(b)   In the cases of prisoners serving extended terms of imprisonment, the Home Secretary may direct that, instead of being granted remission of sentence, they shall be released on licence: s. 60(3). This is without prejudice to his power to release them on licence, in the normal way, before they have served two thirds of their sentence. In either case, the licencee remains on licence until the expiration of his sentence, not merely until the remission date.

(c)   In the cases of prisoners under the age of 22 serving sentences of 18 months or more imposed on them when under 21, the Home Secretary may direct that they be released on licence instead of receiving remission of sentence. The licence expires when the sentence expires or when the licencee attains the age of 22, whichever is the earlier. When a person under the age of 22 is released on licence in the normal way (i.e. before the date on which, if he were over 22, he would be entitled to release with remission under the Prison Rules) he remains on licence, generally speaking, until he attains the age of 22 or until the remission date, whichever is the later: s. 60(5A).

15.1.6   The sentence for murder

Except when the offender was under 18 at the time the offence was committed, the sentence for murder must be one of life imprisonment: Murder (Abolition of Death Penalty) Act 1965, s. 1(1). The judge may recommend to the Home Secretary a minimum period of time which should elapse before the offender is released on licence. There is no appeal against the sentence itself, since it is fixed by law, nor against the recommended minimum term since it is merely a recommendation, not a sentence. The power to recommend a minimum term only arises where a judge is passing sentence for murder — it does not arise where he passes a sentence of life imprisonment for (e.g.) manslaughter: *R* v *Fleming* [1973] 2ALL ER 401. In the remainder of this Chapter, where a sentence is stated to be available whenever an offender of a certain description is 'convicted of an offence' or of an 'offence punishable with imprisonment', the statement should be understood as referring to convictions for offences other than murder, because for murder the sentence is fixed by law.

15.1.7   General approach of the courts to imprisonment

The restrictions on passing sentences of imprisonment described in Para. 15.1.3, which were all statutory, indicate Parliament's attitude to imprisonment — it should be employed as a last resort when the gravity of the offence, or the need to protect the public, or the offender's history of offending and failure to respond to other methods of dealing with him, make it a sad necessity. In *R* v *Bibi* (1980) 71Cr App R 360, Lord Lane CJ urged the courts to adopt a similar attitude. He referred to the dangerous overcrowding in prisons, and stated that the courts should be particularly careful to examine each case to ensure that, if an immediate custodial sentence is necessary, it is kept as short as possible. Of course, the courts have to protect the public and punish and deter the criminal, but for many offenders six or nine months imprisonment would be as effective as 18 months or three years. The Lord Chief Justice mentioned, in particular, the offender who is guilty of the less serious types of factory or shop breaking, of minor sexual indecency, of petty fraud, or of fringe participation in a more serious crime — such offenders could properly be dealt with by shorter sentences. Longer sentences were still necessary in most cases of robbery, in cases involving serious violence, in cases of burglary from private dwelling houses, and in cases where there was planned crime for wholesale profit. Of course, the Lord Chief Justice was merely giving illustrations of the types of cases where short sentences would or would not be appropriate. In general, he urged judges and magistrates to ask themselves whether there was any compelling reason why a short sentence should not be passed. If there was not, they should keep the sentence short.

15.2 SUSPENDED SENTENCES — POWERS OF CRIMINAL COURTS ACT 1973, ss. 22–5

(a)   A court passing a sentence of imprisonment for not more than two years may order that the sentence shall be suspended (s. 22(1)), provided the case is such that, in the absence of a power to suspend, a sentence of immediate imprisonment would have been appropriate: s. 22(2).

(b)   When it passes a suspended sentence, the court specifies the operational period of the sentence. That period, which runs from the date of sentence, must be not less than one and not more than two years: s. 22(1). If, during the operational period, the offender commits no offence punishable with imprisonment, the suspended sentence is never brought into effect.

(c)   If the offender is convicted of an offence punishable with imprisonment committed during the operational period, he is in breach of his suspended sentence. A court having power to deal with him for that breach may either:

(i)   Bring the suspended sentence into effect with its term unaltered; or

(ii)   Bring the suspended sentence into effect with a shorter term substituted for the original term; or

(iii)   Vary the length of the operational period so that it lasts until a date not more than two years after the date of variation; or

(iv)   Make no order with respect to the suspended sentence: s. 23(1).

However, the court must make an order as in (i) above unless it would be unjust to do so having regard to all the circumstances, including the facts of the subsequent offence, which have arisen since the suspended sentence was passed.

(d)   The court must state its reasons for not making an order as in (i) above: s. 23(1).

(e)   If brought into effect, the suspended sentence may be ordered to run consecutively to or concurrently with any sentence of imprisonment which the court passes for the subsequent offence: s. 23(2). Normally the two terms of imprisonment are made to run consecutively: *R* v *Ithell* [1969] 1WLR 272.

(f)   When passing a suspended sentence the court must explain to the offender the consequences of being in breach of it: s. 22(4).

(g)   A magistrates' court may deal with a breach of a suspended sentence passed by that or any other magistrates' court, but it may not deal with breach of a suspended sentence passed by the Crown Court. The Crown Court may deal with breach of any suspended sentence: s. 24.

15.2.1   Consequences of breach of a suspended sentence

The normal consequence of being convicted of an offence punishable with imprisonment committed during the operational period of a suspended sentence is that the sentence is brought into effect, with its term unaltered, and made to run consecutively to any sentence of imprisonment passed for the subsequent offence. The Court of Appeal will not interfere with the Crown Court's decision to activate the suspended sentence with its term unaltered merely because the offence for which it was passed was different in type from the subsequent offence (*R* v *Griffiths* [1969] 1WLR 896 where G's suspended sentence of 12 months for burglary was brought into effect and made to run consecutively to a sentence of nine months imprisonment for reckless driving and assaulting a police constable in the execution of his duty — the Court of Appeal confirmed the sentence). Where, however, the subsequent offence is both trivial and different in type from the suspended sentence offence it may be necessary to, at least, reduce the term of the suspended sentence, or even not to activate it at all (*R* v *Moylan* [1970] 1QB 143 — M was convicted of criminal damage to a window and being drunk and disorderly, the offences being committed during the operational period of an 18 month suspended sentence for theft of a television set. He was given three months for the subsequent offences with the suspended sentence brought into effect and made to run consecutively, but the Court of Appeal reduced the term of the suspended sentence to six months). Another strong argument for not fully activating a suspended sentence is that the subsequent offence was committed at the very end of the operational period (*R* v *Wilson* [1980] 1WLR 376 where 22 months of the two year operational period had elapsed before W committed the subsequent offence).

It should not be thought that judges and magistrates will inevitably bring suspended sentences into effect whenever, according to a strict interpretation of s. 23(1) and cases such as *R* v *Griffiths,* they really ought to do so. A lenient judge, faced with facts similar to those in *R* v *Griffiths,* might find in the difference between burglary and reckless driving a sufficient reason for non-activation of the suspended sentence. If he took that view, the prosecution would have no means of challenging his decision, since they cannot appeal against a sentence they consider too light. The significance of the decision in *R* v *Griffiths* is that if, in such circumstances, the suspended sentence is activated an appeal against sentence by the defence has little chance of succeeding.

15.2.2   Magistrates' powers upon breach of a Crown Court suspended sentence

When a summary conviction for an imprisonable offence puts the offender in breach of a suspended sentence passed by the Crown Court, the magistrates have no power to deal with the offender for the breach (see proposition (g) of the summary of suspended sentences). Two options are open to them in respect of the breach. They can commit the offender to the Crown Court to be dealt with for it, or they can decline to commit but give notice of the conviction to the Crown Court under s. 24(2). In the latter event, a judge of the Crown Court may issue a summons or warrant for arrest to secure the attendance of the offender before the Crown Court so that he can be dealt with for his breach: s. 25.

A committal to the Crown Court to be dealt with for breach of a suspended sentence may be in custody or on bail. At the same time as they commit for the breach, the magistrates commit the offender to be sentenced for the offence of which they have just convicted him, so that one court can deal with both matters. The latter committal may, if the offender has been convicted of an offence triable either way, be under s. 38 of the Magistrates' Courts Act 1980 (see Para. 12.3), or, if he has been convicted of a summary offence, under s. 56 of the Criminal Justice Act 1967 (see Para. 12.4.3) or s. 37 of the 1980 Act (see Para. 12.4.1).

If the magistrates choose merely to notify the Crown Court of the breach, they sentence the offender for the subsequent offence. By not committing him, they obviously indicate their view that the subsequent offence does not require activation of the suspended sentence, but the decision is one for the Crown Court not them. Therefore, they should not deal with the subsequent offence in a way which would make it impossible for the Crown Court to bring the suspended sentence into effect.

Since a conviction which results in the offender being placed on probation, or discharged conditionally or absolutely is deemed not to be a conviction, magistrates should not use any of those methods when sentencing an offender in breach of a Crown Court suspended sentence: *R* v *Tarry* [1970] 2QB 561. If they think that probation etc. is appropriate they should commit the offender to the Crown Court under s. 24(2), (for breach of the suspended sentence) and under the Criminal Justice Act 1967, s. 56 for the subsequent offence, and hope that the Crown Court judge will share their view of the case.

15.2.3 Circumstances in which a suspended sentence may be passed

Section 22(2) provides that suspended sentences may only be passed where immediate imprisonment would otherwise be appropriate. This is to prevent the use of suspended sentences as an easy option in circumstances where the court is not sure what sentence is appropriate. The effect of the subsection is illustrated by *R* v *Hanbury* [1980] Crim LR 63 where a sentence of six months imprisonment suspended for two years for dangerous driving was quashed by the Court of Appeal because H was a man of previous good character and, even in a bad case of dangerous driving such as this was, a sentence of immediate imprisonment upon a man of good character would not have been appropriate. The term of imprisonment which is suspended must not, of course, exceed two years. Where an offender is sentenced on one occasion for several offences and two or more prison sentences are passed, the terms are treated as a single term irrespective of whether they are made to run concurrently with or consecutively to each other (s. 57(2) of the 1973 Act). Consequently, an offender convicted on indictment of three offences of theft may be given suspended sentences of two years imprisonment on each count, provided the terms are made to run concurrently with and not consecutively to each other.

An offender may, for one offence be both fined and given a suspended sentence. This applies even if the offender falls within the ambit of s. 19(2) or 20(1) of the 1973 Act (i.e. is an offender who may not be sentenced to imprisonment unless no other method of dealing with him is appropriate — see *R* v *Genese* [1976] 1WLR 958). A suspended sentence may not, however, be combined with probation, even if the offender is being dealt with for two or more offences on one occasion s. 22(3). The Crown Court can, however, achieve the effect of having the offender on probation and subject to a suspended sentence by making a suspended sentence supervision order (see Para. 15.4.2).

If an offender is currently serving a sentence of imprisonment or Borstal training, it is wrong in principle to pass a suspended sentence: *R* v *Baker* (1971) 55Cr App R 182. Similarly an offender should not be sentenced on one occasion to immediate imprisonment (say six months) for one offence and a suspended sentence (say two years suspended for two years) for a second offence. Suspended sentences and sentences of immediate imprisonment fall into different categories and should not be combined: *R* v *Sapiano* (1968) 52Cr App R 674. An interesting provision in s. 47 of the Criminal Law Act 1977, which would allow a court passing a sentence of six months to two years imprisonment to order that a quarter to three quarters of the total term be served immediately and the remainder be held in suspense, has not yet been brought into force. Given the time that has elapsed since the passing of the Criminal Law Act 1977, there can be no guarantee that the section will ever be made effective.

A suspended sentence may be passed in respect of an offender aged 17 to 20 provided the length of the term suspended is such that it could have been imposed as a sentence of immediate imprisonment (i.e. it must be for six months or less or for 18 months to two years — see Para. 15.1.3). If such a sentence is subsequently brought into effect for a term of three to six months at a time when the offender is still under 21, the court may order that he serve the sentence in a detention centre, not in prison. If an offender subject to a suspended sentence is subsequently sentenced to Borstal training he ceases to be liable to be dealt with for any breach of the suspended sentence: s. 22(5).

15.3 FINES

(a)   All offences other than murder (and high treason) are punishable by means of a fine.

(b)   There is no statutory limit on the size of the fine which the Crown Court, following conviction on indictment or a committal for sentence under s.38 of the Magistrates' Courts Act 1980, may order the offender to pay: Criminal Law Act 1977, s.32(1). The fine may be imposed in addition to any sentence of imprisonment, immediate or suspended, which the Crown Court passes for the offence: Powers of Criminal Courts Act 1973, s.30.

(c)   Following conviction for a summary offence, a magistrates' court may fine the offender an amount not exceeding the maximum prescribed by the statute creating the offence. If that statute provides for punishment by means of imprisonment but does not make provision for fining the offender, the court may, instead of sentencing him to imprisonment or other custodial penalty, impose a fine not exceeding £200: Magistrates' Courts Act 1980, s.34(3). The powers of a magistrates' court to fine an offender who has been summarily convicted of an offence triable either way are set out in Para. 12.3.1. Whether magistrates may fine an offender in addition to or only as an alternative to passing a sentence of imprisonment on him for the offence depends on the wording of the relevant statute (e.g. if the offender is summarily convicted for an offence of criminal damage where the value involved exceeds £200, the magistrates may imprison him for up to six months or fine him up to £1,000 or do both, but if the value involved was less than £200 and the magistrates proceeded under the special procedure in the Magistrates' Courts Act 1980, s.22, they may imprison him for up to three months or fine him up to £500 but may not do both — see ss.32(1) and 33(1) of the 1980 Act respectively).

(d)   For the power of the Crown Court, adult magistrates' court or juvenile court to order that a juvenile's parent pay a fine instead of the juvenile, and for the limitations on the fines which an adult magistrates' court or juvenile court may order a juvenile to pay — see Para. 13.4.1.

(e)   When either the Crown Court or a magistrates' court fines an offender the court may, and normally should, give the offender time to pay or order payment by instalments instead of requiring immediate payment: Powers of Criminal Courts Act 1973, s.31(1) and (3) in respect of the Crown Court, and Magistrates' Courts Act 1980, ss.75 and 82(1) in respect of the magistrates' courts. At the time the Crown Court fines an offender it must fix a term of imprisonment to be served in default of payment of the fine (s.31(2) of the 1973 Act), but that term must not exceed twelve months in respect of a fine for any one offence (s.31(3) of the 1973 Act). When a magistrates' court imposes a fine it does not usually fix a term in default, but non-payment may result in the offender being brought before the court and, either on that occasion or subsequently, being committed to prison for the failure to pay. The maximum periods for which an offender may be committed to prison for non-payment of a magistrates' court fine are set out in Schedule 4 to the 1980 Act.

15.3.1 When a fine is appropriate

Where the offence is sufficiently grave to warrant immediate imprisonment the court should not refrain from imposing that penalty merely because the offender has the means to pay a substantial fine (*R* v *Markwick* (1953) 37Cr App R 125 where M., who was convicted of stealing some small change from trousers hanging in the changing room of his golf club despite trying to put the blame on club servants, unwisely appealed to the Court of Criminal Appeal and had his sentence varied from a £500 fine to two months imprisonment — Lord Goddard CJ stated that 'persons of means should not be given an opportunity of buying themselves out of being sent to prison'. Note that unlike the Court of Appeal today, the Court of Criminal Appeal when *R* v *Markwick* was decided had power to increase an appellant's sentence). Conversely, if the offence is not of a gravity to justify imprisonment, the offender should not be sentenced to imprisonment merely because he is too poor to pay a substantial fine (*R* v *Reeves* (1972) 56Cr App R 366) or so rich that even a substantial fine would be as nothing to him: *R* v *Hanbury* [1980] Crim L R 63. In many cases the gravity of the offence and the character of the offender are such that either imprisonment or a fine could be justified. Despite cases such as *R* v *Markwick* and *R* v *Reeves*, the choice between the two forms of punishment may then turn on whether the offender is capable of meeting a substantial fine.

Having decided to punish the offender by means of a fine, the judge or magistrates should consider what amount the offender ought to pay having regard to the gravity of the offence and any mitigating factors in the case. If that amount would be beyond his means, he should be ordered to pay a sum which, given time to pay, he can reasonably afford: *R* v *Ashmore* (1974) Crim L R 375. Care must be taken not to impose too great a financial burden on the offender for fear that he might commit further offences to pay his fine.

15.3.2 Combining a fine with other sentences or orders

For one offence the Crown Court can always and a magistrates' court can sometimes both pass a sentence of imprisonment and impose a fine (see propositions (a) and (b) of the summary of fines). In addition, a fine and an order that the offender be detained in a detention centre can be imposed for one offence, although that is in practice an unlikely combination of penalties. However, a fine can be, and very often is, combined with an order for endorsement of the offender's driving licence or his disqualification from driving. It can also be combined with any of the ancillary orders the court may make when it passes sentence (e.g. compensation orders, restitution orders or orders to pay costs to the prosecution — see Chapter 21). Such ancillary orders can sometimes be as onerous as the fine itself, although it is wrong in principle to impose a very small fine and a very heavy order for costs — those two orders should be kept in step with each other. Because probation, absolute and conditional discharges, community service and Borstal are all alternatives to sentencing an offender in another way for an offence, he cannot for one offence be both fined and dealt with by one of those methods. If, however, he is dealt with on one occasion for two or more matters, he could be fined for one matter and put on probation etc. for another.

15.3.3 Enforcement of fines

The ways in which a reluctant offender may be compelled to pay a fine are set out in the Powers of Criminal Courts Act 1973, ss.31 and 32, and in the Magistrates' Courts Act 1980, ss.75 to 89 and Schedule 4. The subject is complex, and not of great interest to practising lawyers since an offender is very rarely legally represented when he appears before magistrates for non-payment of a fine. Below is a summary of the procedure.

When it imposes a fine, the court, be it Crown Court or magistrates', always may, and usually must, give the offender time to pay or order that he pay in stated instalments. The exceptional cases in which the court need not allow time to pay are:

(a) the offence is punishable with imprisonment and he appears to have sufficient means to pay the fine forthwith; or

(b) he is of no fixed abode, or is unlikely to remain in the United Kingdom long enough for the fine to be enforced if he is given time to pay; or

(c) he is already serving a term of imprisonment or detention in a detention centre; or

(d) on the occasion that it fines him, the court also sentences him to immediate imprisonment or detention in a detention centre.

The Crown Court always fixes a term of imprisonment, not exceeding 12 months, which the offender must serve in default of payment of the fine. If no time to pay is allowed, and the offender does not have sufficient money with him to meet the fine, he is committed to prison and kept there until either he has arranged for payment or he has served the term ordered in default. Except in cases where it need not grant time to pay, a magistrates' court does not, on the occasion it imposes a fine, fix a term of imprisonment in default of payment. In the exceptional cases (i.e. when it can refuse time to pay) the court may issue a warrant committing the offender to prison in default of payment. The maximum period for which the court may order the offender to be detained under the warrant is determined by Schedule 4 to the 1980 Act, and increases in proportion to the size of the fine (e.g. for a fine not exceeding £25 the maximum period is 7 days; for a fine exceeding £50 but not exceeding £200 it is 30 days; for a fine exceeding £500 but not exceeding £1,000 it is 90 days). Of course, if the offender pays the fine he is released from prison forthwith, unless liable to be detained there for some other reason. As an alternative, in the exceptional cases, to issuing a warrant immediately, the court can postpone its issue upon such conditions as to payment of the fine as it thinks fit, and at the same time fix the term of imprisonment to be served if subsequently the warrant has to be issued. One power which both the Crown Court and the magistrates have whenever they impose a fine, but which is especially useful should they be considering refusing time to pay, is the power to order the offender to be searched so that any money found on him can be used in satisfaction of the fine, unless the money does not belong to him or the loss of it would be more injurious to his family than his detention in prison for non-payment.

If the offender is given time to pay, enforcement of the fine is through a magistrates' court. In the case of a Crown Court fine, the fine-order names the court which is to enforce it or, if none is named, it is enforced by the court which committed the offender to the Crown Court for trial or sentence. In the case of a magistrates' court fine, the court which imposed the fine enforces it. In either case, the court initially having responsibility for enforcement can transfer its functions to the court for the petty sessional division in which the offender is residing.

The offender can always apply to the court for more time to pay. If he fails to pay within the time originally specified by the court imposing the fine or, where he has been granted more time to pay, within the time so extended, the court enforcing the fine holds a means inquiry. The offender's presence at the inquiry can be secured, if necessary, by the issue of a summons or warrant for his arrest. He can also be ordered to supply the court with a statement as to his means. If, as a result of the means inquiry, the court is satisfied that the default in payment is due to his 'wilful refusal or culpable neglect' and other methods of enforcing payment appear unlikely to succeed, the court can issue a warrant committing the offender to prison. The maximum period he can be detained under the warrant is, if the fine was imposed by a magistrates' court, the period mentioned in Schedule 4 to the 1980 Act. If it was a Crown Court fine, he is ordered to be detained for the period the Crown Court fixed in default of payment. In both cases, the periods are reduced in proportion to any part-payment of the fine which has been made. Similarly if, having been committed to prison under the warrant, the offender makes part-payment of the amount outstanding the term he has to serve is reduced proportionately. If he makes full payment he is, of course, released immediately.

Where the court has power to issue a warrant committing the offender to prison, it may choose to give him one last chance of paying the fine without going to prison by postponing the issue of the warrant upon such conditions as it considers just — e.g. payment of the amount outstanding at so much per week. At the time it postpones issuing the warrant, the court fixes the term of imprisonment which will be served if it is issued. If the offender fails to comply with the court's conditions, the warrant can be issued even in his absence, and, upon his arrest, he is committed to prison.

If the court cannot issue a warrant (because the offender's default in payment was not due to wilful refusal etc.) or if it chooses not to issue a warrant, there are still various ways of obtaining payment. The simplest is to make an attachment of earnings order (i.e. an order directed to the offender's employer that he deduct a certain amount from the offender's wages and pay it to the court until the fine has been satisfied). Unfortunately, persons who default in paying fines are often the very people who are not in regular employment. Another method is to issue a warrant of distress under which goods belonging to the offender may be seized and sold in satisfaction of the fine. Yet another method is to appoint for instance a probation officer to supervise payment. The court may also remit the whole or part of the fine, but, if it was imposed by the Crown Court, may only do so with that court's consent.

Offenders aged 17 to 20 may be sent to a detention centre for non-payment of a fine, instead of being committed to prison, but the period they are ordered to spend in detention centre must not exceed six months. A juvenile who is in default may be ordered to attend at an attendance centre.

Where an offender is both sentenced to imprisonment and fined for an offence, the term the court fixes in default of payment may be made to run consecutively to the prison sentence, even if the combined length of the terms is greater than the maximum prison sentence the court could lawfully impose.

15.4 PROBATION: POWERS OF CRIMINAL COURTS ACT 1973, ss.2—13

(a) The Crown Court or a magistrates' court may place on probation any offender who, at the date of conviction, had attained the age of 17: s.2(1).

(b) The effect of a probation order is that for a period specified in it, which must be not less than six months and not more than three years, the probationer must remain under the supervision of a probation officer (see Para. 14.3 for a brief description of the appointment and work of probation officers).

(c) Since a probation order under s.2(1) is made instead of sentencing the offender, he cannot for one offence be both put on probation and punished by, for example, a fine. However, the making of a probation order does not prevent the court disqualifying the offender from driving (Road Traffic Act 1972, s.102), nor does it prevent it making any of the ancillary orders which a court is empowered to make when passing sentence (e.g. order to pay compensation or prosecution costs). Where an offender is dealt with for two or more offences on one occasion he can be given probation for one offence and fined, for example, for another, but he may not on one occasion be both placed on probation and have a suspended sentence passed on him (s.22(3) of the 1973 Act).

(d) The court may attach such requirements to the probation order as it considers necessary to ensure the good conduct of the probationer and to avoid his re-offending. Typically, a probationer may be required to 'be of good behaviour and keep the peace'. An order may also contain a requirement as to where the probationer should reside (e.g. an order that for a specified period he should live in an approved probation hostel or other institution). Whether or not any requirements are expressly attached to the order, the probationer is still subject to the fundamental duty of remaining under the supervision of his probation officer.

(e) Where the court is satisfied by evidence from a duly qualified medical practitioner that the offender's mental condition is such as to need treatment but is not such as to warrant the making of an order under the Mental Health Act 1959 for his compulsory detention in hospital, the order may include a requirement that for part or the whole of the period for which he is on probation he submit to treatment by or under the direction of a doctor named in the order: s.3. The order may leave the form of treatment at the discretion of the doctor, or it may specifically require the probationer to go into a hospital or nursing home, or attend at a hospital or other institution as an out-patient. Before including such requirements in an order, the court must be satisfied that arrangements have been made for the probationer to receive the treatment specified. Similar requirements may be included in supervision orders (see Para. 13.4.4).

(f)   If, in the petty sessional division in which the probationer resides, there is a day training centre which he can attend, the probation order may include a requirement that for a certain number of days, not exceeding 60, he attend at the centre in accordance with his probation officer's instructions: s.4. The activities and training provided at the centres are geared principally to help the socially inadequate. Therefore, an order should only require attendance at a centre if the probationer appears to be the sort of person who would be helped by such activities.

(g)   Before an offender is placed on probation the court must explain to him the effect of the order, and of any additional requirements included in it. The order can only be made if the offender consents: s.2(6). That consent may not be obtained by, in effect, threatening him with a custodial sentence if he does not consent: *R* v *Marquis* [1974] 1WLR 1087.

(h)   The consequences of failure to comply with a requirement of a probation order or committing a further offence while on probation are explained fully below (see Para. 15.4.1). Essentially, a probationer who is found to be in breach of a requirement (e.g. failing to keep in touch with his probation officer) may be fined up to £50 or dealt with for the offence for which he was put on probation (the original offence) as if he had just been convicted of it: s.6. If the probationer is fined for non-compliance with the requirement, the probation order continues to run; if he is sentenced for the original offence, it ceases to be effective: s.5. Where an offender is convicted of an offence committed during the currency of a probation order, he may be dealt with both for the subsequent offence and the original offence: s.8. The court may always choose not to deal with him for the original offence, in which case the probation order continues in force. If, however, the offender is sentenced for the original offence the consequence again is that the probation order is nullified: s.5.

(j)   For the status of a conviction which results in the offender being put on probation — see Para. 15.5.

15.4.1   Consequences of a breach of probation order

The court with the primary responsibility for ensuring that a probation order is properly enforced is the magistrates' court for the petty sessional division in which the probationer resides (known as the 'supervising court'). If an information, alleging that the probationer is in breach of a requirement of his order, is laid before a magistrate for the supervising court (or, if the order was made by a magistrates' court other than the supervising court, a magistrate for that court) he may issue a summons or warrant to secure the probationer's attendance before the court. If the court is satisfied that the probationer has failed to comply with a requirement, it may deal with him as described in proposition (h) above, save that if the order was made by the Crown Court it cannot sentence him for the original offence. Should the magistrates feel that a fine is not an adequate way of dealing with breach of a requirement in a Crown Court order, they may commit the probationer in custody or on bail to the Crown Court which may then, if satisfied that a breach has occurred, either fine him up to £50 or deal with him for the original offence: s.6(6). When an offender has been convicted on indictment of an offence committed while he was on probation, or when he has been committed to the Crown Court to be sentenced for such an offence, the Crown Court may deal with him for both the subsequent offence and the original offence: s.8(7) and (8). If, however, the probation order was made by a magistrates' court the Crown Court's powers of sentencing for the original offence are limited to those that a magistrates' court would possess: s.8(8). A magistrates' court which convicts an offender of an offence committed during the currency of a Crown Court probation order may not deal with him for the original offence, but may commit him to the Crown Court so that the Crown Court can sentence him: s.8(6). Probably, the magistrates will also commit him to be sentenced for the offence of which they have convicted him, for instance under s.56 of the Criminal Justice Act 1967.

If an offender is summarily convicted of an offence committed during the currency of a magistrates' court probation order, the convicting court may deal with him for the original offence if either it is also the court which ordered probation, or it is the supervising court, or one of those two courts has given it permission to deal with the matter: s.8(9).

Where an offender has been convicted of an offence committed while on probation, but no court with power to sentence him for the original offence has considered whether or not to exercise that power, a summons or warrant for arrest may be issued to bring him before the appropriate court: s.8(1). Thus, if a magistrates' court convicts an offender of an offence committed while subject to a Crown Court probation order, but does not commit him to the Crown Court under s.8(6) to be dealt with for the original offence, a judge of the Crown Court may issue a summons or warrant to secure the offender's appearance before the Crown Court. He may then be sentenced for the original offence.

15.4.2 Suspended sentence supervision orders

As the name implies, suspended sentence supervision orders are a form of suspended sentence rather than a form of probation, but as they have much in common with probation it may be easier to appreciate the way they operate now that both suspended sentences and probation have been described. Section 26 of the Powers of Criminal Courts Act 1973 provides that where a court passes a suspended sentence for a term of more than six months for a single offence it may add to the suspended sentence a supervision order. Since a magistrates' court cannot for a single offence pass a sentence of imprisonment, suspended or otherwise, for more than six months, suspended sentence supervision orders can only be made by the Crown Court.

The effect of the order is that for a period specified in it, which must not exceed the operational period of the suspended sentence, the offender must remain under the supervision of a probation officer. If he fails to keep in touch with the probation officer, the supervising court (the magistrates' court for the area in which he lives) may fine him up to £50, but the supervision order continues to run (s.27 of the 1973 Act). Should he commit an imprisonable offence during the operational period of the suspended sentence then s.23 of the 1973 Act applies in the normal way (i.e. the suspended sentence will in all probability be brought into effect — see Para. 15.2.1). If the suspended sentence is brought into effect the supervision order is discharged.

The advantage of a suspended sentence supervision order is that the offender is both deterred from wrong-doing by the threat of the suspended sentence being activated, and encouraged in well-doing by the support of his probation officer. If it were not for s.26 the court could not achieve this effect because even where an offender is sentenced for two or more offences he cannot on one occasion be given a suspended sentence and be put on probation: s.22(3).

15.5 ABSOLUTE AND CONDITIONAL DISCHARGES

(a) Where an offender of any age is to be dealt with for an offence, the court (Crown Court or magistrates' court) may, if it is of the opinion that to punish the offender would be inexpedient and that probation would be inappropriate, make an order absolutely or conditionally discharging him: Powers of Criminal Courts Act 1973, s.7(1).

(b) An absolute discharge is equivalent to doing nothing about the offence. It is only appropriate where the offender technically has committed an offence but no blame whatsoever attaches to him. Absolute discharges are rare.

(c)   The period of a conditional discharge, which is specified by the court when it makes the order, must not exceed three years. If the offender is convicted of an offence committed during that period he may be sentenced for the offence in respect of which he was conditionally discharged (the original offence).

(d)   Since both absolute and conditional discharges are ordered where punishment is not expedient, an offender cannot, for one offence, be both discharged and subjected to some penalty (e.g. a fine), although he may be disqualified from driving (Road Traffic Act 1972, s.102) or ordered to pay compensation, prosecution costs etc. If an offender is dealt with for two or more offences on one occasion, it is common for him to be subjected to a substantial penalty for the most serious offence or offences and conditionally discharged for the less serious ones.

(e)   Where a conviction for an offence is dealt with by means of a probation order or conditional or absolute discharge, it is deemed not to be a conviction save for purposes of an appeal against conviction or for purposes of proceedings against the offender in respect of a breach of the order: Powers of Criminal Courts Act 1973, s.13. Thus, s.13 does not prevent for instance an offender who commits an offence during the period of probation or conditional discharge being sentenced for the original offence, but it does prevent the Crown Court activating a suspended sentence when the offender, having been summarily convicted of an offence committed during the operational period, is placed on probation for the offence (*R* v *Tarry* [1970] 2QB 561 — see Para. 15.2.2). The reason is that s.23 of the 1973 Act allows a suspended sentence to be brought into effect when an offender 'is convicted' of an imprisonable offence committed during the operational period, and in *R* v *Tarry*, having been given probation, T. was deemed not to have been convicted. For similar reasons an offender who is discharged or put on probation by the Crown Court cannot appeal to the Court of Appeal against the order (*R* v *Tucker* [1974] 1WLR 615 — see Chapter 17), although he can appeal against the conviction which led to its being made. Notwithstanding s.13, however, convictions dealt with by probation or discharge do appear on the antecedents given to the court before it sentences an offender.

(f)   If, having been placed on probation or conditionally discharged, the offender is subsequently dealt with for the original offence, s.13 no longer applies, and the conviction for the offence is, for all purposes, treated like any other conviction: s.13(2). The only exception is where the offender was under 17 when convicted of the original offence — in that case, the conviction continues to be deemed not to be a conviction.

15.5.1   Offences committed during the period of a conditional discharge

Where an offender is convicted of an offence committed during the operational period of a conditional discharge the consequences are the same as when an offender commits an offence while on probation, but there is not the complicating factor of responsibility for dealing with the matter being shared by a supervising magistrates' court. Thus, when the Crown Court deals with the offender for the subsequent offence following a conviction on indictment or committal for sentence, it may also deal with him for the original offence, whether or not the conditional discharge was ordered by a magistrates' court, but subject, in the case of a magistrates' court order, to not exceeding the powers of sentencing that a magistrates' court would have if dealing with the original offence. If a magistrates' court convicts an offender and discovers that he is in breach of a Crown Court discharge, it may commit him to the Crown Court; if it discovers that he is in breach of a discharge ordered by itself on a previous occasion, it may deal with him for the original offence; if it discovers that he is in breach of a discharge ordered by another magistrates' court, it may, with that court's permission, deal with him for the original offence: Powers of Criminal Courts Act 1973, s.8.

Superficially, conditional discharges and suspended sentences may seem to have much in common. In both cases, the offender is not immediately punished for his offence. Indeed, in both cases, provided he does not commit an offence during the specified period (the period of the conditional discharge or the operational period of the suspended sentence as the case may be), he is never punished for the offence. One difference between the two orders is that in the case of a suspended sentence the penalty for the offence (i.e. so many months imprisonment) is fixed at the time sentence is passed but not then brought into effect, whereas if a conditional discharge is breached the sentence for the original offence is entirely in the hands of the court dealing with the breach — the court ordering discharge has no influence over what will happen if it is breached. Perhaps a more significant difference from the viewpoint of an offender is that the commission of an imprisonable offence during the operational period of a suspended sentence usually leads to a sentence of imprisonment for the subsequent offence and the suspended sentence being activated. On the other hand, if an offence is committed during the period of a conditional discharge, both the subsequent offence and the original offence can often be dealt with leniently. Obviously, the breach of conditional discharge is an aggravating factor, but the court's decision as to sentence will be influenced chiefly by the gravity of the subsequent offence and the offender's general character rather than his committing the offence during the period of a discharge.

15.5.2 Binding over to be of good behaviour

The power of a court to bind a person over to keep the peace or be of good behaviour is distinct from its power to order a conditional discharge, but since a binding over has some similarities with a conditional discharge, and since it might be ordered in some types of case where the court would otherwise order a conditional discharge, it is convenient to describe the power at this stage.

A person bound over to keep the peace or to be of good behaviour enters into an undertaking (a recognisance) that for a specified period he will keep the peace and be of good behaviour, upon pain of forfeiting a certain sum of money, if he does not abide by the undertaking. Essentially, a binding over is a measure of preventive justice designed to avoid potential assaults or breaches of the peace. Although the court can order an offender to be bound over in addition to or in lieu of any other sentence it may impose for an offence, a person who has not been convicted (e.g. an acquitted accused, or a witness or even the victim of an alleged offence) may be ordered to be bound over. However, a pre-condition of a binding-over is that there must be material before the court leading it to fear that, unless steps are taken to prevent it, there might be a breach of the peace (e.g. a further assault by an offender who has just been convicted of an assault). An offender convicted of an offence of theft could not be bound over to be of good behaviour because the court would not have any reason to suppose that a further offence of theft would lead to a breach of the peace.

One type of case often dealt with by means of binding over is where A. and B., who are neighbours, have a heated argument. A. takes out a summons against B. alleging that B. assaulted A., and B. takes out a summons alleging that A. assaulted B. Sometimes A. and B. can be persuaded to abandon their respective prosecutions upon each entering into a recognisance to keep the peace, sometimes the magistrates convict one or both and then order them to be bound over, sometimes they acquit them both but still order a binding over.

If an offender is convicted of an offence which constitutes a breach of a bind-over, the court which bound him over may order that he forfeit all or part of the sum in which he was bound over. Thus, if A. is convicted by Barchester Magistrates' Court of assaulting B. and is bound over for six months in the sum of £25 to keep the peace, he may, on being convicted by the same court three months later of an assault on C., be sentenced for the assault on C. and ordered to pay the £25 in which he was bound over. If the conviction for the assault on C. was by Fulchester Magistrates' Court, that court cannot deal with the breach of the binding-over but a complaint alleging the breach could be made by B. to the Barchester court, which could then order forfeiture.

Where the person who is ordered to be bound over refuses to comply with the order and will not enter into the necessary undertaking, he may be committed to prison. If the binding-over is ordered by a magistrates' court the maximum period for which he can be so committed is six months. The power of the magistrates to bind a person over is contained in the Magistrates' Courts Act 1980, s.115, and in the Justices of the Peace Act 1361. The power of the Crown Court to do so is confirmed by the Justices of the Peace Act 1968, s.1(7).

15.6   COMMUNITY SERVICE ORDERS: POWERS OF CRIMINAL COURTS ACT 1973, ss.14-17

(a)   An offender who at the date of conviction for an offence punishable with imprisonment has attained the age of 17 may be made the subject of a community service order — i.e. an order requiring him to perform unpaid work: s.14(1).

(b)   A community service order may be made by either the Crown Court or a magistrates' court. The number of hours work to be performed is fixed by the court within limits of a minimum of 40 and a maximum of 240 hours. An offender who is dealt with for two or more offences on one occasion may be ordered to perform community service for each offence, but if the hours of service are made to run consecutively the aggregate must still not exceed 240 hours: s.14(3).

(c)   The work is performed under the direction of a probation officer (or other suitable person appointed for the purpose), and should normally be completed within a period of 12 months beginning with the date of the orders: s.15. The work he is required to do should not interfere with the offender's attendance at school, other educational establishment or place of paid employment. Nor should it conflict with his religious beliefs.

(d)   Before making an order the court must be satisfied, having considered a report by a probation officer, that the offender is a suitable person to perform community service and that work can be provided for him to do: s.14(2). The offender himself must consent to the making of the order after its effect and the consequences of non-compliance with it have been explained to him: s.14(2) and (5).

(e)   A community service order is an alternative to dealing with the offender in any other way for an offence, and so cannot, for one offence, be combined for example with a fine. However, s.14(8) specifically provides that when a court orders an offender to perform community service it may also disqualify him from driving or make any of the ancillary orders a court may make when passing sentence (e.g. an order to pay compensation or prosecution costs). An offender who is dealt with on one occasion for two or more offences may be given community service for one offence and for instance fined for another offence, but it would be bad sentencing practice to combine community service for one offence with a suspended sentence for another: *R* v *Starie* (1979) 69 Cr App R 239.

(f)   The consequences of not complying with a community service order are broadly similar to the consequences of not complying with a requirement in a probation order. If the magistrates' court for the area where the offender resides is satisfied that he has, without reasonable excuse, not complied with the instructions given by the probation officer supervising his work, it can fine him up to £50, in which case the order continues in force. Alternatively, if the order was made by a magistrates' court, it can revoke the order and deal with the offender for the offence in respect of which the order was made (the original offence). If the order was made by the Crown Court, it can commit him to the Crown Court which can fine him up to £50 or sentence him for the original offence: s.16.

(g)   Where a community service order is in force in respect of an offender who is sentenced by the Crown Court following his conviction on indictment or committal for sentence, the Crown Court may revoke the order, or revoke it and deal with the offender for the original offence: s.17(3). A magistrates' court which sentences an offender subject to a community service order has no power to revoke etc. the order. However, if the probation officer directing the offender's work considers that in view of the later conviction and sentence the order should be revoked (e.g. because the offender is serving a prison sentence) he may apply to the magistrates' court for the area where the offender lives (or did live before he was sent to prison) for revocation of the order. The court may, if the order was made by a magistrates' court, revoke the order, or it may revoke it and sentence the offender for the original offence: s.17(2). If the order was made by the Crown Court it may commit the offender to the Crown Court, which may then revoke the order etc. The offender or the probation officer can always apply for the order to be revoked — e.g. on the grounds that most of the work has been completed and, because the offender is studying for examinations, it would be particularly difficult for him to complete the remaining hours.

> Community service is often advocated as a method of dealing with offenders because it combines punishment (deprivation of leisure time) with recompense to society for the wrong done in the form of useful, unpaid work. It also, of course, avoids sending the offender to prison or other custodial institution. It seems that community service orders are successful in the sense that offenders usually perform the work they are ordered to do. Whether they are more successful than other punishments or methods of treatment in preventing offenders from re-offending is open to question.

15.7 BORSTAL TRAINING

(a) An offender who, on the date of his conviction for an offence punishable with imprisonment, has attained the age of 15 but is not yet 21 may, in lieu of any other sentence, be sentenced by the Crown Court to Borstal training: Criminal Justice Act 1948, s.20(1).

(b) A sentence of Borstal training may follow the offender's conviction on indictment or his summary conviction and committal for sentence under s.37 or s.38 of the Magistrates' Courts Act 1980 (see Paras. 12.4.1 and 12.3 respectively). It is not necessary that the offence of which he stands convicted should be indictable — it merely has to be punishable with imprisonment.

(c) Borstal training may only be ordered if, having regard to the circumstances of the offence and the offender's character and previous conduct, the court is of the opinion that he should be detained for training for not less than six months: Criminal Justice Act 1961 s.1(2). If Borstal is the appropriate punishment it may be ordered even though the maximum prison sentence which could be imposed for the offence of which the offender has been convicted is less than six months, although the shortness of the maximum prison sentence in relation to the time the offender is likely to spend in detention if sent to Borstal is a relevant factor in deciding whether or not to make an order: *R v Amos* [1961] 1WLR 308.

(d) An offender under 17 on the date of his conviction may only be sent to Borstal if no other method of dealing with him is appropriate (proviso to s.1(2) of the Criminal Justice Act 1961).

(e) Before passing a sentence of Borstal training the court must consider any report made on the offender by or on behalf of the Home Secretary: Criminal Justice

Act 1961, s.1(3). Usually such a report will be available. If not, there is no absolute obligation on the court to adjourn for reports (*R* v *Lowe* [1964] 1WLR 609), but since it is considering a custodial sentence for a young offender the court will probably think it right to obtain reports before so sentencing him.

(f) A sentence of Borstal training is unusual in that the court does not specify the period which the offender is to spend in custody. The maximum period the offender may be kept in Borstal is two years running from the date of sentence, the normal minimum is six months, although the Home Secretary can direct his release before six months have elapsed if he thinks fit: Prisons Act 1952, s.45. Within those limits his release is at the discretion of the Home Secretary — i.e. of the Borstal authorities — and will depend upon his response to the regime and training provided by Borstal. The normal time spent in Borstal is around nine months.

(g) Since Borstal training is in lieu of any other sentence, an offender cannot for one offence be sent to Borstal and have an additional penalty (e.g. a fine) imposed upon him. If he is dealt with on one occasion for two or more offences, it is generally bad sentencing practice to pass a sentence of Borstal training for one offence and impose a fine for another offence. Nor should Borstal be combined with a suspended sentence: *R* v *Baker* (1971) 55Cr App R 182. Where an offender who is already subject to a suspended sentence is sentenced to Borstal training, he ceases to be liable to be dealt with in respect of the suspended sentence: Powers of Criminal Courts Act 1973, s.22(5). An order for Borstal training can, however, be combined with the offender's disqualification from driving for the offence for which he is sent to Borstal or his being ordered to pay costs, compensation etc. for that offence.

(h) Section 21 of the Powers of Criminal Courts Act 1973 (adjournment so that an unrepresented offender can apply for legal aid) applies where the court is considering a sentence of Borstal training in the case of an offender who has not previously been so sentenced — see Para. 14.4.

Note that the White Paper on the treatment of young offenders (1980 Cmnd 8045 — see Appendix 2) recommends that sentences of Borstal training be replaced by sentences of 'youth custody'.

The regime in a Borstal institution varies depending upon whether it is an 'open' or 'closed' Borstal. The latter, as the name implies, provide a higher degree of security for those who have committed serious offences or have absconded from open Borstals. In both open and closed Borstals the aim is not only to punish the offender by deprivation of liberty but to train him in useful skills (e.g. through work in a craft work-shop or on the farm attached to the institution). There are also periods for physical training, and for educational and leisure pursuits.

Upon release from Borstal, the offender is placed under the supervision of a probation officer or other suitable person or society specified by the Home Secretary: Prisons Act 1952, s.45(3). The Home Secretary may further specify requirements (e.g. as to keeping in touch with the supervisor) with which the offender must comply during the period of supervision. Unless earlier terminated by the Home Secretary, the supervision lasts for one year from the date of release. If the Home Secretary is satisfied that an offender under supervision has failed to comply with any of the requirements specified, he may order his recall to a Borstal institution. He may then be detained in Borstal until two years have elapsed from the date of his sentence or six months have elapsed from his recall, whichever is the later, but the Home Secretary may order his release at any time: s.45(4) of the 1952 Act.

If an offender under supervision is convicted of an imprisonable offence the court may order that he be returned to Borstal: Criminal Justice Act 1961, s.12. This is instead of dealing with him in any other manner for the offence. An offender returned to Borstal by the court is treated as if he had been recalled there by the Home Secretary. Either the Crown Court or a magistrates' court may order return to Borstal. The Crown Court could, alternatively, pass a fresh sentence of Borstal training, which it has power to do not only when dealing with offenders under supervision after release from Borstal, but also when dealing with those detained in Borstal. In the latter case, the fresh sentence and the original sentence run concurrently, but the imposition of the fresh sentence might lead the Borstal authorities to delay the offender's release unless, when it passes the fresh sentence, the Crown Court makes it clear that he is to be freed at what the authorities consider to be the optimum time: see *R* v *Evans* (1972) 56Cr App R 854.

15.8   DETENTION IN A DETENTION CENTRE

(a)   An offender who has attained the age of 14 but is not yet 21, and who has been convicted of an imprisonable offence, may be ordered to be detained in a detention centre: Criminal Justice Act 1961, s.4(1).

(b)   The Crown Court, an adult magistrates' court and the juvenile court may make detention centre orders. In the case of a juvenile, the sentence *must* be one of detention for a period of three months unless the juvenile is convicted on indictment of an offence carrying more than three months imprisonment, in which case the sentence may be for not less than three and not more than six months detention. Again subject to the offence carrying more than three months imprisonment, an offender aged 17 to 20 inclusive can be sentenced to three to six months detention irrespective of whether he is convicted on indictment or summarily: s.4(2) of the 1961 Act.

(c)   A court may not make a detention centre order in respect of an offender unless it has been notified by the Home Secretary that a centre is available to receive from that court persons of the offender's class or description: s. 4(3). Since no girls' detention centres have been established, this effectively means that detention centre sentences are limited to boys and young men.

(d)   An offender who has served a sentence of Borstal training or imprisonment for a term of at least 'six months should not, in the absence of special circumstances, be sent to a detention centre: s.4(4). Before ordering detention in the case of such an offender, the court must consider any report made on him by or on behalf of the Home Secretary. If no report is available, a magistrates' court (but not the Crown Court) must adjourn to obtain one. In fact, a court which is considering a detention centre sentence is likely to adjourn for reports whether or not there is any statutory requirement on it to do so (*R* v *Barton* [1977] Crim L R 435 where the Court of Appeal stated that it is, in general, wise to have a social inquiry report before passing custodial sentences on young persons).

(e)   Where an offender who has attained the age of 17 is sentenced on one occasion to two or more terms of detention, the terms may be made to run consecutively, but not so that the aggregate term exceeds six months. Similarly, an offender who has attained the age of 17 and is already serving a term in a detention centre may be sentenced to a further term to commence on the expiration of the term he is serving. In such a case the aggregate of the two terms may exceed six months but should not exceed nine months. If a term of detention is made to run consecutively to another term, it may be for a period of less than three months (e.g. an offender serving a term of six months detention who appears to be sentenced for a further offence could be given one month's detention to commence on the expiration of the term he is serving). Terms of detention imposed on juveniles cannot be made to run consecutively (s.7 of the 1961 Act).

(f)   Section 21 of the Powers of Criminal Courts Act 1973 (adjournment so that an unrepresented offender can apply for legal aid) applies where the court is considering a detention centre order in the case of an offender who has not previously been so sentenced — see Para. 14.4.

Note that the White Paper on the treatment of young offenders (1980 Cmnd 8045 — see Appendix 2) recommends that the permissible periods for detention centre sentences be changed to a minimum of three weeks and a maximum of four months.

> While in a detention centre, the detainee is subject to intensive discipline and training, often with an emphasis on physical exercise. If he is of school age he receives full-time education as well as other training. However, the term of detention, as explained above, is never long, and, through good behaviour, the detainee can earn remission of sentence. Therefore, detention centre is referred to, as a 'short, sharp shock', designed to demonstrate to a youngster who has committed three or four offences which may not, in themselves, be all that serious, that if he continues to offend the consequences will be serious. In 1979 the Home Secretary introduced at two detention centres a regime which was designed to provide an even sharper shock than that provided at other detention centres. This did not amount to a new form of sentence — it merely meant that if an offender sentenced to detention had the misfortune to live in the 'catchment area' for one of the new strict centres, he could as a matter of administrative decision be sent there rather than to an ordinary detention centre.
>
> Upon release from detention centre the ex-detainee is placed under supervision for a year. If he fails to comply with any of the requirements of the supervision he can be returned to detention centre for 14 days or, if he was released with remission, for the number of days of his sentence which had not expired when he was released, whichever is the greater.
>
> An offender aged 17 to 20 inclusive who is liable to be committed to prison for non-payment of a fine, may instead be committed to a detention centre for a period not exceeding six months (s.5 of the 1961 Act). Similarly, a court which brings into effect a suspended sentence for a term of not less than three and not more than six months may, if the offender is aged 17 to 20, order that he shall serve the sentence in a detention centre: Powers of Criminal Courts Act 1973, s.23(3).

15.9   ORDERS UNDER THE MENTAL HEALTH ACT 1959

Both the Crown Court and magistrates' court may make hospital orders under s.60 of the Mental Health Act, 1959 if:

(a)   An offender has been convicted of an offence punishable with imprisonment. In certain circumstances, magistrates may make an order without even convicting the person concerned: s.60(2) — see Para. 11.6. Note that a person of any age can be made the subject of a s.60 order.

(b)   The court is satisfied, on the written or oral evidence of two qualified medical practitioners (at least one of whom must have special experience in the diagnosis or treatment of mental disorders), that the offender is suffering from mental illness, psychopathic disorder, subnormality or severe subnormality which warrants his detention in hospital for medical treatment. The medical evidence may take the form of written reports, but copies must be given to counsel or solicitor for the offender, who may require the practitioner who signed the report to attend for oral examination: s.60(1) and s.62.

(c) The court is of the opinion that a s.60 order is the most suitable method of dealing with the case. The court should have regard to the circumstances of the offence, the character and antecedents of the offender and the other ways in which he could be sentenced. A s.60 order need not be made merely because the offender's mental condition would warrant it. The court may feel that, despite that condition, he deserves to be punished, and so sentence him to imprisonment: *R* v *Gunnell* (1966) 50Cr App R 242.

(d) Arrangements have been made for the offender's admission to a mental hospital: s.60(3).

The effect of a s.60 order is that the offender is admitted to the hospital named in the order. Once there he is treated like any non-offender patient who is compulsorily detained, and will be discharged when the doctors consider on medical grounds that he ought to be. He has, essentially, the same rights as other patients, including being able to apply to a Mental Health Review Tribunal for his release. Although the s.60 order lapses after a year, it can be renewed by the hospital managers if they consider that necessary. Section 60 also allows the court, as an alternative to ordering admission to a hospital, to place the offender under the guardianship of a local social services authority.

A hospital order under s.60 might, by itself, provide insufficient protection for the public in a case where a mentally ill offender has committed or is liable to commit grave offences (e.g. of violence). For example, an offender who absconds from hospital and stays at large for 28 days or six months (depending on the type of mental disorder he is suffering from), cannot be taken back into custody under the s.60 order. Furthermore, the hospital authorities, in their natural anxiety to do what is best for their patient, might when considering the discharge of an offender (patient) give less weight than they should to the possibility of his illness recurring with disastrous results. Therefore, s.65 of the 1959 Act provides that when the Crown Court makes an order under s.60 it can add to it a restriction order which imposes special restrictions on the offender's discharge from hospital. The restriction order may be ordered to apply for a period stated in it or for an unlimited period. While it is in force the offender can only be discharged with the Home Secretary's consent, and, if he absconds from hospital, he may be returned there irrespective of the length of time for which he has been at large. Often the hospital to which the offender is sent when a restriction order is made is one of the special high security hospitals (Broadmoor, Rampton or Moss Side).

Before making a restriction order the Crown Court must be satisfied, having regard to the nature of the offence, the antecedents of the offender and the risk of his committing further offences if set at large, that the order is necessary for the protection of the public: s.65(1). The court must also hear oral evidence from at least one of the medical practitioners whose evidence about the mental condition of the offender is relied upon to justify the making of a hospital order (see above). Magistrates have no power to make a restriction order. If, in the case of an offender who has attained the age of 14, they consider that one is necessary, they may commit him in custody to the Crown Court which may then make a hospital order (with or without a restriction order), or deal with the offender in any way the magistrates could have dealt with him: s.67.

Where an accused is found not guilty by reason of insantiy or unfit to plead the Crown

Court must make an order that he be admitted to a hospital specified by the Home Secretary: Criminal Procedure (Insanity) Act 1964, s.5 and see Para. 6.7.2. The Home Secretary can also direct that an offender serving a sentence of imprisonment be transferred from prison to a mental hospital (s.72 of the 1959 Act). He must first have reports from two medical practitioners indicating that the prisoner is suffering from mental illness etc. such as to warrant his detention in hospital. The power to order a transfer to mental hospital is particularly useful in the case of an offender convicted of murder because in such a case the mandatory sentence of life imprisonment prevents the court making a hospital order, even if the judge thinks that one would be desirable. When he makes a transfer to mental hospital, the Home Secretary can give a direction restricting discharge: s.75. The direction ceases to have effect when the offender's sentence expires.

15.10   DISQUALIFICATION FROM DRIVING AND ENDORSEMENT OF DRIVING LICENSES

Most offenders convicted of road traffic offences are dealt with by means of a fine. Many road traffic offences are not punishable with imprisonment, and even those which are (e.g. reckless driving, driving with excess alcohol in the blood and driving while disqualified) rarely result in a sentence of imprisonment unless the offence is a bad one of its type and the offender has previous convictions of a similar nature. In *R v Hanbury* [1980] Crim LR 63 (see Para. 15.2.3), for example, H.'s offence of dangerous driving was a grave one of its type in that he not only drove his car up onto the pavement but in the process drove it over a policeman's toe, and, furthermore, was suspected (though not proved) to have been drinking. The Court of Appeal nevertheless set aside the suspended sentence passed on him because, given that H. was of previous good character, the offence was not serious enough to warrant imprisonment. Therefore, most motorists who are caught speeding, or driving without due care and attention, or even driving recklessly are not so much worried about the penalty for the offence, in the sense of being imprisoned or fined a large sum, but about having their driving licence endorsed or even being disqualified from driving.

Many of the offences connected with the driving and keeping of motor vehicles carry obligatory endorsement of the licence — i.e. an offender convicted of the offence is not only fined etc. for the offence but particulars of the conviction are entered on his licence and remain there for four years: Road Traffic Act 1972, s.101. Virtually all offences which relate to the manner of driving (e.g. reckless and careless driving, driving while unfit and driving with excess alcohol in the blood, speeding and failing to comply with traffic directions) are endorsable. Some offences relating to the condition of the vehicle used (e.g. using a vehicle with defective tyres) are also endorsable, as are some which relate to the driving licence itself (e.g. driving without a licence and driving while disqualified). Stealing or attempting to steal a motor vehicle, taking or attempting to take a motor vehicle without the owner's consent and going equipped for theft when committed with reference to the theft or taking of motor vehicles also carry endorsement. Schedule 4 to the Road Traffic Act 1972 gives a full list of offences in respect of which the offender's licence must be endorsed. If at the time he is convicted of an endorsable offence the offender is not the holder of a licence, but he subsequently obtains one, particulars of the conviction are endorsed on the licence which he obtains. ·

A full description of the subject of disqualification from driving is beyond the scope of this book, but, to summarise, disqualification may be ordered when:

(a) *An offender is convicted of an offence carrying discretionary disqualification.* All endorsable offences involve at least discretionary disqualification, but, if disqualification is discretionary, the court is unlikely to order it unless the offence is a particularly serious one of its type. Thus, in *R v Hanbury* (supra) the Court of Appeal did not interfere with H.'s disqualification for one year, but in a less gross case of reckless driving the offender might retain his licence, and certainly an offender convicted merely of careless driving would not expect to be disqualified.

(b) *An offender is convicted of an offence carrying obligatory disqualification.* Where there is a conviction for causing death by reckless driving, driving or attempting to drive when unfit through drink or drugs, driving or attempting to drive with excess alcohol in the blood, or failing to provide a specimen of blood or urine for a laboratory test the court must disqualify the offender for at least twelve months unless, for special reasons, it thinks fit to order him to be disqualified for a shorter period or not to order him to be disqualified at all: Road Traffic Act 1972, s.93(1). If within the ten years preceding his committing a drink/driving offence carrying obligatory disqualification, the offender has been convicted of another such offence, the minimum period of disqualification, in the absence of special reasons, is three years. The special reasons put forward for not disqualifying when the offender is convicted of an offence carrying obligatory disqualification must be directly connected with the circumstances of the offence. Thus, if the offender's drink was 'laced' without his knowledge, or if he drove in an unexpected emergency which could only be met by his driving and not by use of public transport, the court is no longer obliged to disqualify him, although it could still choose in its discretion to do so. The courts are usually reluctant to find that special reasons have been established. Thus, in *R v Jackson and Hart* [1970] 1QB 647, the Court of Appeal held that a medical condition, of which the offender was unaware and which caused him to retain alcohol in his blood for an unusually long time, did not amount to a special reason.

(c) *An offender is convicted of an offence involving obligatory or discretionary disqualification; he has, within the three years preceding the commission of the offence, been convicted on at least two occasions of such offences, and particulars of those convictions have been endorsed on the licence.* Such an offender must be disqualified for at least six months unless the court is satisfied that, having regard to all the circumstances, there are grounds for not disqualifying or for disqualifying for less than six months: Road Traffic Act 1972, s.93(3). Disqualifications under s.93(3) are known as 'totting-up' disqualifications. Any such disqualification should normally run consecutively to any other period of disqualification imposed on the same or a previous occasion. Thus, where a conviction for driving with excess alcohol in the blood renders the offender liable to a totting-up disqualification, he is normally disqualified for a year for the offence itself and, in addition, he is disqualified for six months under s.93(3). If he were also convicted on the same occasion of speeding he could receive a second six month 'totting-up' disqualification, making a total of two years disqualification, but if the court felt that to be an unduly long period it could hold that the need to keep the total disqualification in proportion to the gravity of the offender's conduct was a sufficient ground for not imposing further disqualification in respect of the speeding. It should be noted that liability to a 'totting-up' disqualification depends upon the offender's licence having been endorsed on at least two separate occasions during the three years before the *commission* of the offence for which he is before the court. Offenders often think that because, at the date of conviction, they have two endorsements on the licence, both within the preceding three years, they are necessarily within the 'totting-up' provisions, but that will not be so if one of the endorsements was recorded after the date when the offence of which they have just been convicted was committed. Conversely, an offender may be within the ambit of s.93(3) even though the two endorsements on his licence were recorded more than three years before the date of his present conviction if, at the date of the offence, less than three years had elapsed since the earlier endorsement. If, however, there is only one endorsement on the licence, the offender cannot be liable to a 'totting-up' disqualification, even if the endorsement records that on one occasion he was convicted of several offences. The circumstances which justify not disqualifying when s.93(3) *prima facie* applies are much wider than the special reasons which justify not disqualifying for an offence involving obligatory disqualification. The circumstances of the present and the earlier offences are relevant, although it should be remembered that s.93(3) is designed for the motorist who repeatedly commits minor offences, so the mere fact that his offending has not been serious is unlikely to enable the offender to keep his licence: see *Woodage* v *Lambie* [1971] 1WLR 754. However, the personal hardship which would be caused to an offender through disqualification (e.g. losing his job if that involves driving or extreme difficulty in getting to work by public transport) is a good ground for not disqualifying, often relied upon with success. If, on the other hand, an offence carries obligatory disqualification, personal hardship, even if extreme, is not a special reason for non-disqualification.

(d) *An offender is convicted on indictment of, or committed to the Crown Court under s.38 of the Magistrates' Courts Act 1980 to be sentenced for, an offence punishable with at least two years imprisonment, and a motor vehicle was used to commit, or to facilitate the commission of, the offence.* In such a case the Crown Court may order the offender to be disqualified for such period as it thinks fit: Powers of Criminal Courts Act 1973, s.44. Note that the offender disqualified need not have used the vehicle himself in committing the offence, nor need he have any connections with the vehicle apart from being a party to the crime for purposes of which it was used. The magistrates have no power to disqualify under s.44.

Note that the Transport Act 1981 contains provisions which, when in force, will alter the law on 'totting-up' disqualifications (see (c) above). The relevant sections, which are described in Appendix 3 are not expected to be brought into effect until the Autumn of 1982.

An offender who wishes to establish special reasons for not being disqualified in a case which would otherwise attract obligatory disqualification must adduce evidence to prove on a balance of probabilities the truth of the facts said to constitute such a reason. This will usually involve the offender himself giving evidence. Similarly, an offender facing a 'totting-up' disqualification should give evidence of the grounds justifying the court in not disqualifying: *Woodage* v *Lambie* [1971] 1WLR 754. Outside of special reasons and 'totting-up' cases it is, of course, very unusual for the offender to give evidence at the sentencing stage, since mitigation is best presented through counsel making a speech not through the offender testifying about what occurred.

The period of disqualification is entirely at the discretion of the court, although the trend is against overlong disqualifications because they merely invite further offending in the form of driving while disqualified. Except when a period of disqualification is imposed under the 'totting-up' provisions, a disqualification must run from the date of sentence, and must run concurrently with any other disqualifications imposed at the same time or already in force as a result of previous convictions. Application for removal of a disqualification may be made to the court which ordered it. Such an application may only be made after two years if the disqualification was for less than four years; after half the period of the disqualification if it was for four to nine years inclusive, and after five years in all other cases: Road Traffic Act 1972, s.95.

A person charged with an endorsable offence must deliver or post his licence to the court or have it with him at the hearing: s.101(4). If he is convicted, the licence is produced to the court which, in passing sentence, takes into account any convictions endorsed on it. An offender who has not delivered his licence to the court etc. thereby commits a further offence, unless he satisfies the court that he has applied for a new licence and not received it. In addition, his licence is suspended until such time as it is produced to the court.

Although an order for disqualification is valid where no other penalty is imposed for the offence (*R* v *Bignell* (1968) 52Cr App R 10), endorsement and disqualification are almost invariably ordered in conjunction with imprisonment, or a fine, or some other order in respect of the offence. An offender may be disqualified or have his licence endorsed even though he is put on probation or absolutely or conditionally discharged for the offence: Road Traffic Act 1972, s.102.

15.11 RECOMMENDATION FOR DEPORTATION

Where a non-patrial (i.e. someone without the right of abode in the United Kingdom) who has attained the age of 17 is convicted of an imprisonable offence , the court may recommend that he be deported: Immigration Act 1971, s.3(6). Both the Crown Court and a magistrates' court may make such recommendations. The recommendation is made to the Home Secretary, who, in deciding whether to act upon it, may take into account matters which could not properly be considered by the court (e.g. the possibility of the offender being persecuted if returned to his own country). A recommendation for deportation may be made in addition to any other penalty (custodial or otherwise) imposed for the offence. Even if no custodial sentence is passed the offender may be detained pending the Home Secretary's decision. The court may not recommend deportation unless the offender has been given notice in writing explaining that patrials are not liable to deportation, and describing the persons who fall within that category. The notice must be given at least seven days before the recommendation is made.

A full enquiry into the circumstances of the case should be made before deportation is recommended, and reasons for a recommendation should be given. If considering making a recommendation, it is advisable for a judge to ask counsel for the offender to address him 'on the matter. The court must consider whether the offender's continued presence in the United Kingdom would be to the country's detriment (*R* v *Caird* (1970) 34Cr App R 499), but the fact that he has a criminal record is not in itself a sufficient reason for deporting him. The question is whether, in the light of the present offence and his previous record, he is likely to re-offend. If he is, that would be a good ground for recommending his deportation.

15.12 DEFERRING SENTENCE — POWERS OF CRIMINAL COURTS ACT 1973, s. 1

Counsel mitigating for an offender often makes optimistic or even extravagant claims on his behalf. If given a chance by the court (i.e. not sent to prison) his client will cease to commit crime; settle down in society; hold a steady job; marry his girl-friend, and make full reparation to the victims of his past offences. The court, having perhaps heard such claims on many previous occasions and not always found them borne out by subsequent events, may not be convinced by counsel's argument, but nevertheless may feel that the offender deserves a chance to prove himself. Time will show whether he can live up to the promises made on his behalf. To give him that time, the court may defer sentencing him.

The Powers of Criminal Courts Act 1973, s. 1(1) provides that the Crown Court or a magistrates' court may defer passing sentence on an offender for a period of not more than six months. The date on which sentence is to be passed should be specified when deferment is made, but the court does not lose its jurisdiction to sentence merely because the offender does not come before it on the day fixed: *R v Ingle* [1974] 3All ER 811. The reasons for deferring sentence are set out in s. 1(1). They are to enable the court to take into account, when it does pass sentence, the offender's conduct after conviction and any change in his circumstances. 'Conduct after conviction' may include his making reparation for his offence, and 'change in circumstances' would cover, *inter alia*, his marrying or finding employment. Of course, staying out of further trouble is of prime importance. The offender must consent to sentence being deferred: s. 1(3).

When the court defers sentence it does not bail the offender to appear on the date fixed for sentencing, but simply released him (s.1 (6A)). If he fails to attend to be sentenced a summons or warrant for his arrest may be issued: s. 1(5). Having deferred sentence once under s. 1(1), the court cannot defer again under the subsection, but a magistrates' court could adjourn for three or for four weeks for reports under s. 10(3) of the Magistrates' Courts Act 1980, and the Crown Court always has inherent jurisdiction to postpone sentencing. However, unless there are very strong reasons to the contrary (e.g. the offender is soon to be tried on other outstanding charges) the court should sentence on the date fixed when sentence was deferred, doing the best it can with the information available. As to the sentence it should pass, it is wrong in principle to pass a substantial custodial sentence after deferment of sentence if any report on the offender's conduct and any change in his circumstances are not unfavourable to him: *R v Gilby* [1975] 1WLR 924. However, merely avoiding further convictions may not be enough to save the offender from a substantial penalty. In *R v Smith* (1977) 64Cr App R 116, S, who had four previous convictions for offences of dishonesty, pleaded guilty to three burglaries, one attempted burglary and had five other offences taken into consideration. As a result of his previous offending he had already been sentenced to both suspended and immediate terms of imprisonment. The Crown Court deferred sentence to see whether he would (a) reduce his drinking and (b) work regularly. Although S did not commit any offences during the period of deferment, he failed to cut down his drinking and refused offers of work. The Court of Appeal upheld the sentence of 18 months imprisonment passed on him. Had he kept the promises made on his behalf when sentence was deferred it would have been quite wrong to send him to prison, but the most that could be said for S was that he had not reoffended. In the circumstances, that was not a sufficient reason for passing a non-custodial sentence.

The offender should if possible be sentenced by the same judge or same magistrates as deferred sentence. Where that is not possible the sentencing court should be told why the original court deferred sentence: *R v Gurney* [1974] Crim L R 472. Counsel who represented the offender when sentence was deferred should also do his utmost to appear for the sentencing: *R v Ryan* [1976] Crim L R 508. A magistrates' court which has deferred sentence cannot commit the offender to the Crown Court to be sentenced for the offence: s. 1(8).

If, before the period of deferment expires, the offender is convicted of a further offence, the court which deferred sentence may sentence him forthwith for the offence in respect of which sentence was deferred: s. 1(4). It may issue a summons or warrant to bring him to court: s. 1(5). Alternatively, the court convicting of the subsequent offence may sentence the offender both for that offence and the deferred sentence offence, save that a magistrates' court may not sentence an offender for an offence in respect of which the Crown Court deferred sentence, and the Crown Court, when dealing with an offence in respect of which a magistrates' court deferred sentence, is limited to the powers that the magistrates would have in dealing with the case: s. 1(4A).

Section 1(7) of the 1973 Act preserves the Crown Court's common law power to bind an offender over to come up for judgement either on a day fixed when he is bound over, or on a day subsequently notified to him. This power is similar to the power the court has to bind a person over to keep the peace or be of good behaviour (see Para. 15.5.2). The offender enters into a recognisance under which, if he fails to attend for judgement when required, he may be ordered to forfeit the sum of money specified in the recognisance. In that sentence is postponed, a bind-over to come up for judgement is similar to deferring sentence. It differs from deferring sentence in that more than six months may elapse between the date of the bind-over and the date when the offender is to appear, and there is a sanction for non-appearance through the possibility of the recognisance being forfeited. Also, the court may defer sentence only for the reasons set out in s. 1(1), but the power to bind-over to come up for judgement may be exercised whenever the judge considers that there is good reason for doing so. One appropriate situation for a bind-over is where the offender is appealing against his conviction, and the judge does not wish to sentence him when there is a possibility that the conviction will be quashed.

16   Policy of Sentencing

The two preceding Chapters have described respectively the information given to a judge before he passes sentence, and the sentencing options available to him. The topic dealt with in this Chapter is the process by which he decides upon the correct sentence for the particular offender before him. On passing sentence, judges do not always give reasons, and even if they do they need to keep the reasons short and simple so that the offender can readily understand what is being said to him. Therefore, it is from judgments of the Court of Appeal when disposing of appeals against sentence, not from the words of the sentencing judges themselves, that the principles governing the sentencing process are to be deduced.

It should, however, be emphasised that precedent plays a relatively small part in sentencing. This is for three reasons. First, the truism that every case turns upon its own facts is never truer than in the context of sentencing. No two offenders and no two offences are ever precisely the same, whatever the similarities between them. Therefore, if told about a Court of Appeal decision in a comparable case, a judge can always find a reason for distinguishing it if he so chooses. In fact, it is very rare for counsel to quote any cases when mitigating. He does not even suggest a precise sentence, but merely argues for a certain form of sentence. For example, he might say — 'if this offence is so serious that a prison sentence is required, then it should be suspended and not immediate', or 'in the light of my client's previous good character and regular income, the case can suitably be dealt with by means of a fine', but he would not say that in the case of X the Court of Appeal reduced a five year prison sentence to three years and therefore, since the present case is a little less serious than X's, the proper sentence is two years. Such an argument might be used before the Court of Appeal, but not in mitigation before the sentencing judge. Second, the Court of Appeal does not attempt to prescribe the one right sentence for a particular case. Instead, their Lordships allow Crown Court judges a broad discretion, and, in general, only interfere to reduce a sentence if it is outside the range of sentences appropriate to the gravity of the offence when taken in conjunction with any mitigating factors. Third, there is no procedure which enables the Court of Appeal to pronounce a sentence too light. The prosecution cannot appeal against a sentence they consider over-lenient, while if the defence appeal (against conviction or sentence) the Court of Appeal has no power to increase sentence. The most their Lordships can do is state that, far from the sentence being too severe, they would, if they had been sitting in the Crown Court, have imposed a harsher penalty.

Despite these limitations, the Court of Appeal's decisions in the numerous appeals against sentence which come before it provide a useful guide on the way judges arrive, or should arrive, at their sentencing decisions. See also 'The Principles of Sentencing' by David Thomas.

16.1 THE PRIMARY DECISION

The first stage in the sentencing process is for the judge to take a primary decision between an individualised sentence and a tariff sentence. The former is a sentence primarily related to the needs of the individual offender. It is meant to reform and rehabilitate him by providing support and treatment. It is not intended to be a punishment, although there may well be elements in it which the offender will perceive to be unpleasant or inconvenient and therefore regard as a punishment. A tariff sentence, on the other hand, is primarily related to the offender's culpability. Its main object is to mark society's abhorrence of the crime by a suitable penalty, and to deter others from committing similar crimes. It may incidentally reform the offender, if only by making him so afraid of the consequences of crime that he does not reoffend, but that is not its primary purpose. Sometimes deterrence and reform can both be furthered by a single sentence. For example, a recidivist offender whose offences are apparently caused by a drinking problem might best be reformed through a prison sentence of medium length, because that would enable him to be treated in a special prison alcoholic unit. The passing of a prison sentence would also have the advantage of deterring others. Often, however, the sentence appropriate to the crime will do nothing to reform, or might even hinder the reformation, of the offender. In *R v Harnden* (1978) 66 Cr App R 281 (see Para. 15.1.3), for example, a tariff sentence required that H be sent to Borstal since the prison sentence that would otherwise have been appropriate was prohibited by the Criminal Justice Act 1961, s. 3. The Court of Appeal conceded that the training provided in Borstal was not appropriate for H, who was a student aged 20. Possibly, although the Court of Appeal did not say this, the likelihood of H reoffending might even have been increased through his keeping bad company in Borstal. Even so, H was sent to Borstal because the broader interests of society required that others should be deterred from committing offences of the kind H had committed (supplying a controlled drug). Had the trial judge taken a primary decision in favour of an individualised sentence, H might have been put on probation or even conditionally discharged.

Imprisonment, both immediate and suspended, and fines are the clearest examples of tariff sentences. Probation, which is ordered instead of sentencing an offender, conditional and absolute discharges, which are ordered when punishment would be inexpedient, and, in the cases of juveniles, supervision and care orders, are all individualised forms of sentence. Orders under s. 60 of the Mental Health Act 1959, even with a restriction order included, are also individualised sentences, because the purpose of such orders is that the offender should be discharged from hospital as soon as that can safely be done, not that he should be punished. Borstal can be categorised as either a tariff or an individualised sentence depending on whether the judge's purpose in ordering it is genuinely to remove the offender from a bad environment and provide him with training which will be beneficial for him, or, as in *R v Harnden* (supra) simply to punish him and deter others. Detention centre is also difficult to categorise because it has in it elements of a tariff sentence (it is meant to punish), but at the same time the shock given to the offender is meant to reform him. In addition, the sentence is so short (three to six months) that the courts cannot adequately distinguish between serious and less serious offences — if a juvenile court finds a young person guilty of theft and decides to send him to a detention centre, it must send him there for three months whether he stole a sheep or a lamb. Detention during

Her Majesty's pleasure or in accordance with the Home Secretary's directions under s. 53 of the Children and Young Persons Act 1933 is intended principally to protect the public from juveniles who commit serious crimes. It can, however, be used as a deterrent sentence: *R* v *Ford and others* (1976) 62Cr App R 303 — see Para. 13.4.2.

The strongest argument in favour of an individualised sentence is the youth of the offender. Only in the most serious cases could a deterrent, tariff sentence be justified for a juvenile. Where the offender has attained the age of 17 but is not yet 21, there are still powerful reasons for individualising the sentence. This has been impliedly recognised by Parliament through its passing the Powers of Criminal Courts Act 1973, s. 19 (no imprisonment to be imposed on offenders aged under 21 unless no other method of dealing with the case is appropriate) and the Criminal Justice Act 1961, s. 3, (sentences of imprisonment passed on those of Borstal age to be for six months or less or three years/18 months or more). The case of *R* v *Ford* (supra) is, however, an example of the argument for individualisation giving way to an overwhelming need for deterrence. F and three other appellants were jointly tried and convicted on an indictment containing ten counts, each count alleging an offence of robbery or theft committed by snatching a bag from a woman in the street. On some occasions, violence was used, and on all occasions, the offences were committed by a group of young men operating as a gang. The appellants were not convicted of all the offences alleged in the indictment, but F, for example, was found guilty on two counts of robbery and two of theft, and, on at least one occasion, the evidence was that he played the leading role in the offence. F, who was aged 16, was sentenced to five years detention under s. 53. His co-appellants, who had attained the age of 17 but were of an age for Borstal, were sentenced to five years imprisonment. The gravity of the offences, involving as they did gang activity and violence, and the prevalence of such offences in the Brixton and Clapham areas of London where they were committed, meant that deterrent sentences were justified despite the youth of the offenders. Accordingly, the appeals were dismissed.

A second good ground for an individualised sentence is that the offender is of previous good character, but, if the offence is sufficiently serious, that will not be enough to save him from a prison sentence. Somebody over the age of 21 who takes part in an armed robbery can expect to go to prison for it for a long time, however excellent his antecedents. Offenders in need of psychiatric treatment may also hope to receive an individualised sentence — e.g. a hospital order under s. 60 of the Mental Health Act 1959 or a probation order with a requirement for treatment in a mental hospital. Frequently, too, adult recidivist offenders who have already served two or three terms in prison, are given one last chance to reform in the shape of, for instance, probation. If they reoffend after that last chance, they may well receive a long extended term sentence.

16.2 INDIVIDUALISED SENTENCES

Once the judge has decided upon an individualised sentence the only task that remains is to identify the form of sentence which will best assist the offender's reformation and rehabilitation. Usually the sentence will be much preferable, from the offender's viewpoint, to any tariff sentence which could have been passed. Occasionally, in their desire to help the offender, judges or magistrates may make an order which to him seems unduly onerous. For example, a juvenile who is made the subject of a care order may feel that he has been treated unfairly by way of comparison with his co-defendant who is conditionally discharged or put under supervision, but the only reason for the court's decision is that the magistrates, perhaps having regard to the juvenile's home background, feel that it is in his interests to be looked after by the local authority. Similarly, an offender in respect of whom a hospital order is made may well be deprived of his liberty for a longer time than he would have been had a prison sentence been passed. Nevertheless, it is, in general, in the offender's interests for an individualised sentence to be passed.

16.3 TARIFF SENTENCES

Although human ingenuity is such that the definition of any particular offence will be wide enough to allow it to be committed in a vast number of different ways, experience shows that within the scope of any legal definition a variety of typical factual situations will recur. It is this which makes tariff sentencing possible. The idea is that by studying the decisions of the Court of Appeal one can identify, for each typical factual situation, an upper and a lower sentencing limit within which, leaving aside any mitigating features peculiar to the offender himself, the sentence should normally fall. This is the tariff for the offence, or the 'range' or 'bracket' of sentence appropriate to the offence. If the judge or magistrates exceed the tariff, or if, having regard to the tariff, they appear to have ignored mitigating factors which should have been taken into account, the Court of Appeal will reduce the sentence.

The working of the tariff may be illustrated by the offence of rape. The statutory penalty is imprisonment for life which, on the face of it, leaves the sentence entirely at the discretion of the Crown Court judge. Court of Appeal decisions have, however, established the following tariffs which control the judges in the exercise of their sentencing discretion without putting close limits on what they should and should not do. In the overwhelming majority of cases the Court of Appeal has upheld the imposition of tariff sentences. The least serious of the commonly recurring factual situations is that of the young man who rapes a young woman, using minimal force after the victim has consented to some degree of familiarity. The tariff for such an offence is said to be about two to three years. At the other end of the scale are rapes accompanied by aggravating factors, such as the use of a high degree of violence in addition to the violence required to perpetrate rape, or the rape of a girl by a group of men. Here the tariff is put at five to eight years. In between come the 'average' rapes where the man has intercourse with a woman previously unknown to him who does not consent to any initial acts of familiarity, but little or no actual force is used. The tariff is three to five years. Off the normal scale, as it were, are offences by a young man of previous good character who 'goes too far' with his girl friend. He might escape with a suspended sentence. At the other extreme, the man who has committed a series of rapes and deliberately terrorised his victims in the process might be given a life sentence.

Having decided into which broad category the offence falls, and being aware of the tariff for that category, the judge next fixes the precise position of the offence on the relevant scale. If the rape involved a high degree of violence, just how much was used and has the victim suffered permanent injury? If it was an 'average' rape was any force at all used or was it a rape by threat? Did the offender carry a weapon? Having answered such questions, the judge arrives at the tariff for the offence, but one very important adjustment still has to be made. The judge may and nearly always will reduce the sentence to take account of any mitigating factors peculiar to the offender. He might, in a case where it was particularly important to deter others from committing similar offences, ignore the mitigation and pass an unadjusted tariff sentence, but in general the offender is entitled to credit for the matters mentioned below.

16.4 MITIGATING FACTORS

A great variety of mitigating factors may be pleaded on behalf of an offender. Two of the most cogent are his youth and previous good conduct. Even if they do not sway the judge to pass an individualised sentence, they should at least result in a much reduced tariff sentence. The offender's circumstances at the time he committed the offence may also provide mitigation — e.g. emotional difficulties or, if it was an offence of dishonesty, financial pressures. An offence committed on the spur of the moment when temptation suddenly presented itself is also likely to attract a lighter sentence than a carefully planned offence. Further mitigating factors are dealt with in the next two Paragraphs.

16.4.1 Plea of guilty

A judge must not increase the sentence he passes because the accused pleaded not guilty, even if he considers that the accused, in giving evidence in his own defence, committed perjury: *R* v *Quinn* (1932) 23Cr App R 196. Nor must he increase sentence because the nature of the defence involved grave allegations against the police officers in the case (*R* v *Skone* (1967) 51Cr App R 165), or because, by pleading not guilty, the accused forced the prosecution to call witnesses who might well have found giving evidence particularly distressing or even harmful (e.g. child witnesses to a sexual offence). The principle is, however, slightly unreal because, provided the sentence does not exceed the tariff maximum and provided the judge does not actually say that he has added to the sentence because of the not guilty plea, he can in fact pass a severer sentence than he would otherwise have done. Furthermore, it is well established that a guilty plea attracts a somewhat lighter sentence than a conviction following a not guilty plea (*R* v *Cain* [1976] Crim L R 464), and, if the accused does not know this before he decides on his plea, he should be told it by counsel. In other words, a guilty plea is an excellent reason for reducing sentence, but a not guilty plea is no justification for increasing sentence beyond the tariff maximum. Pragmatism is probably the major reason for treating a guilty plea as mitigation. If every defendant pleaded not guilty, the legal system could not cope with the extra work involved. If there is nothing to be gained by pleading guilty, why should any defendant give up the chance, however slight, of an acquittal? Therefore, the guilty are encouraged to plead guilty by giving them a discount in their sentence. In mitigation, counsel may say that by pleading guilty the offender has shown his contrition for his past, and his determination to reform.

One interesting question is the extent to which an offender may hope to have his sentence reduced because of a guilty plea. In *R* v *Davis* [1979] Crim L R 327, the judge indicated to counsel for D that if D changed his plea to guilty he could expect a discount of 20% to 30% in his sentence. The Court of Appeal criticised the judge for giving such a precise indication as he came very close to breaking the rule in *R* v *Turner* (see Para. 6.3), but no criticism was made of the percentages mentioned. A more difficult point is whether a judge can properly make the type of sentence he passes turn upon the plea. In *R* v *Hollyman* [1980] Crim L R 60, H and another were jointly charged with theft of miniature bottles of gin to a value of £5. H, who pleaded not guilty but was convicted, was sentenced to three months imprisonment; his co-accused, who pleaded guilty but who had taken the leading role in the offence, received a suspended sentence of two months. Both men were of previous good character. The Court of Appeal held that the different treatment meted out to the two offenders was wholly justified by their different attitudes to the offence when it was discovered. By refusing to acknowledge his guilt H had shown that, unless punished, he could not be trusted not to reoffend. In *R* v *Tonks* [1980] Crim L R 59, on the other hand, a differently constituted Court of Appeal reduced T's sentence of six months immediate imprisonment for drugs offences to three months because his co-accused had been given suspended sentences, and the only significant difference between him and them was that they had pleaded guilty. Although their Lordships agreed that a plea of guilty was a powerful mitigating factor, T would have been left with a sense of legitimate grievance had it been allowed to make all the difference between immediate and suspended imprisonment. The logic of their Lordships' view seems to demand the complete quashing of the sentence of imprisonment or its replacement with a suspended sentence, but it may be, although this is not clear from the report, that at the time the appeal was heard T had already served two months or more in prison and so, on his sentence being reduced, he was entitled to immediate release.

16.4.2 Cooperation with the police

Cooperation with the police, in the sense of not resisting arrest and confessing frankly to the offence at the police station, is good mitigation, although it may not add much to the effect of a guilty plea. Cooperation in the sense of giving evidence for the prosecution against one's accomplices should lead to a substantial reduction in sentence (see Para. 6.3 for a discussion of whether the offender should be sentenced before or after he testifies for the Crown). Even greater reductions are available for the handful of offenders who give information and/or evidence which leads to the conviction of large numbers of their criminal associates. The case of *R* v *Lowe* (1977) 66Cr App R 122 illustrates the point. L was arrested on charges of robbing a garage and having a sawn-off shot gun. He offered 'to tell the police everything', and was as good as his word. He made statements in which he admitted to 91 offences including 15 robberies (some armed), 11 conspiracies to rob and 31 burglaries. More importantly, he implicated 45 other people, many of whom were arrested and charged. The police officer in charge of the investigation told the Court of Appeal that as a result of L's information the police were in the process of clearing up most of the serious gangs of criminals throughout the East End of London. L's information also enabled the police to recover no less than £400,000 worth of stolen property. L was only indicted for a total of 12 offences, but those included the most serious of the offences in which he was concerned (robbery of over a thousand cases of whisy). The Crown Court judge sentenced him to ten years imprisonment for that; concurrent sentences on the other counts, and activated a suspended sentence of 18 months to run consecutively to the ten years, making a total of $11^1/_2$ years. The Court of Appeal reduced the total sentence to five years. Only by information such as L gave could criminal gangs be broken up. It was in the public interest that criminals who have become involved in gang activities should be encouraged to assist the police. Unless credit was given to people like L when they were sentenced, others would not come forward. Accordingly, L received a sentence which was far below the tariff for the offences he had committed. The amount by which the sentence of a 'supergrass' is reduced will depend on the criminality of the admitted offences, weighed against the assistance which he has given to the police: *R* v *Rose and Sapiano* (1980) 71Cr App R 296.

16.5   SENTENCES ABOVE THE TARIFF

Where the judge passes an extended sentence of imprisonment under s. 28 of the Powers of Criminal Courts Act 1973 (see Para. 15.1.4), the term may exceed the tariff for the offence of which the offender has been convicted: *DPP* v *Ottewell* [1970] AC 642. In other cases, a judge passing a tariff sentence must not exceed the maximum allowed by the tariff, even if his motive is benevolent. In *R* v *Ford* [1969] 1WLR 1703 F was sentenced to 27 months imprisonment for burglary. His co-accused, who had a far worse record for dishonesty than did F and was also sentenced for other offences at the same time, received a shorter sentence. F was sentenced so severely because he had a drinking problem and the judge hoped that he would be sent to a prison alcoholic unit for treatment. If given a shorter sentence, the prison administrators would not send him to the unit. Although the relatively long sentence was intended for F's good, the Court of Appeal reduced the sentence to normal tariff levels.

Part 5   Appeals

17   Appeals from the Crown Court

Appeals against conviction on indictment, against sentence following conviction on indictment, and against sentence passed following committal to the Crown Court for sentence, are all heard in the Criminal Division of the Court of Appeal. Decisions of the Crown Court in matters not relating to trial on indictment (e.g. in disposing of appeals from magistrates' courts) may be challenged by appealing by way of case stated to a Divisional Court of the Queen's Bench Division, or by applying for judicial review and one of the prerogative orders (certiorari, mandamus or prohibition). Since appeals by case stated and applications for judicial review are chiefly used to correct errors made by magistrates, they are described in Chapter 18. The subject of this Chapter is appeals to the Criminal Division.

17.1   THE CRIMINAL DIVISION OF THE COURT OF APPEAL

The Criminal Appeal Act 1966, s. 1(1), now repealed and re-enacted as s. 45 of the Criminal Appeal Act 1968, abolished the old Court of Criminal Appeal and transferred its jurisdiction to the Court of Appeal (Criminal Division). The Court of Criminal Appeal, established by the Criminal Appeal Act 1907, had for the first time provided a person convicted on indictment with a general right of appeal. Prior to 1907 an appeal was only possible if the trial judge, in his discretion, reserved a point of law for the consideration of the Court for Crown Cases Reserved. The Court of Criminal Appeal consisted of the Lord Chief Justice and the judges of the Queen's Bench Division. The Criminal Division of the Court of Appeal, on the other hand, comprises all the Lords Justices of Appeal, and Queen's Bench Division judges are not members of the Criminal Division as such. However, they continue to play an important role in disposing of the business of the Division, because the Lord Chief Justice, after consultation with the Master of the Rolls, may at any time request any High Court judge to sit as a member of a court of the Criminal Division: Criminal Appeal Act 1966, s. 1(3). So as to comply with the rule of natural justice that no man shall be a judge in his own cause, s. 2(3) of the 1966 Act provides that the judge before whom an appellant was convicted or by whom an appellant was sentenced may not take or share in any of the decisions connected with the appeal. Although it is possible for any Lord Justice of Appeal and any High Court judge to sit in the Criminal Division, one would normally expect the work of the Division to be carried on by those who, as puisne judges, have had experience in criminal matters.

Any number of courts of the Criminal Division may sit at the same time: s. 2(1) of the 1966 Act. The Administration of Justice Act 1970, s. 9, provides that a court must consist of at least three judges when determining: (a)   Appeals against conviction and sentence.   (b)   Applications for leave to appeal from the Criminal Division to the House of Lords.   (c)   Applications for leave to appeal to the Criminal Division where the application has not already been refused by a single judge.

Parliament is, however, considering the proposal that a court consisting of two judges should be enabled to hear appeals against sentence. For all other purposes (e.g. refusing an application for leave to appeal already refused by a single judge) the court may consist of two judges. Except when a two judge court is permissible, there must be an uneven number of judges so as to avoid the embarrassment of their being equally divided as to their decision. Only in cases of exceptional importance or difficulty, perhaps when the court is considering departing from the decision of an earlier court, will there be five or more judges. Whatever the number of judges, only one judgement is given, unless the judge presiding over the court states that the question raised by the appeal is, in his opinion, one of law on which it is convenient that separate judgements should be pronounced by the members of the court: Criminal Appeal Act 1966, s. 2(4).

In addition to determining appeals, the Criminal Division must make many decisions preliminary to and incidental to the hearing (e.g. decisions to grant leave to appeal, or to release an appellant on bail, or to order a witness to attend at court for examination). Such decisions may be and, in practice, normally are taken not by a court of the Division but by a single judge (see Para. 17.6.4 for the procedure). If the decision goes against the appellant, he may renew his application to the court which may consist of two or three judges. By 'a single judge' is meant 'any judge of the Court of Appeal or of the High Court': Criminal Appeal Act 1968, s. 45(2).

The administration of the work of the Criminal Division is carried out by the Registrar of Criminal Appeals, together with the assistant and deputy assistant registrars and their staff. The Registrar, who must be a barrister or solicitor of at least ten years standing, is appointed by the Lord Chancellor (Courts Act 1971, s. 26), as are his assistants and deputy assistants. Notices of appeal and notices of application for leave to appeal (see Para. 17.6.1) are served on the Registrar, whose responsibilities then include obtaining any necessary transcript of the note taken by the shorthand writer of the proceedings at the Crown Court, obtaining from the Crown Court exhibits and information it may have relevant to the appeal, instructing counsel to represent an appellant who does not have a solicitor, and giving notice of the time fixed for the hearing of the appeal.

17.2   THE RIGHT OF APPEAL AGAINST CONVICTION

A person convicted on indictment may appeal to the Court of Appeal against his conviction: Criminal Appeal Act 1968, s. 1(1). However, leave to appeal must be given by the Court of Appeal unless either the appeal is on grounds of pure law, or the trial judge at the Crown Court has granted a certificate that the case is fit for appeal on a ground involving a question of fact or mixed law and fact: s. 1(2) of the 1968 Act. Certificates from the trial judge that a case is fit for appeal are rare. In 1979, the last year for which statistics are available, out of 1,418 appeals against conviction only three followed the granting of a certificate. Perhaps trial judges are reluctant to acknowledge that a trial for which they had ultimate responsibility may have had a wrong result or perhaps it simply does not occur to defence counsel to ask for a certificate. Whatever the reason, the overwhelming majority of appeals based on fact or mixed law and fact involve an application to the Court of Appeal for leave to appeal, not a certificate that the case is fit for appeal.

17.2.1   Appeal on grounds of pure law

No leave to appeal is necessary when the ground of appeal involves a question of law alone. Differentiating between a question of law and a question of mixed law and fact is notoriously difficult, because any question of law arises in a factual context and, in that sense, involves both law and fact. If the trial judge misdirected the jury as to the elements of the offence charged (e.g. if he said that the offence could be committed by a person who was reckless as to the consequences of his actions when intent to bring about a certain consequence is required) the appeal would be on law. So would an appeal based on a misdirection as to the burden of proof (e.g. telling the jury that, where the accused is charged with an offence of assault, it is for him to prove that he was acting in reasonable self-defence). On the other hand, an appeal arising out of the judge's admitting into evidence an allegedly involuntary confession after a 'trial within a trial' would involve mixed law and fact.

The Court of Appeal itself decides whether a point raised by an appellant in his Grounds of Appeal is one of pure law or not (*R* v *Hinds* (1962) 46Cr App R 327 — the fact that counsel in drafting the grounds has 'labelled' one or more of the grounds 'law only' or words to that effect is irrelevant). In fact, the Court appears to find in most grounds at least an element of fact. Out of the 1,418 appeals against conviction in 1979 only 28 were on a point of pure law. Where an appeal is on two or more grounds, one of which involves a question of law alone, the appellant will still need leave to appeal on the remaining grounds, even though his appeal on the ground of law is of right (*R* v *Robinson* (Practice Note) 1953 1WLR 872).

The unfettered right to appeal on a point of pure law could, in theory, lead to the Court of Appeal's time being wasted by clearly unmeritorious appeals. The scarcity of appeals on law suggests that this is not, in practice, a problem, but unmeritorious appeals are discouraged in two ways. First, if the Registrar considers that an appeal purporting to be on law alone has no substantial basis, he may refer it to the Court for summary determination. If the Court is of the opinion that the appeal is 'frivolous or vexatious' they may dismiss it summarily, without a full hearing and without hearing argument (s. 20 of the 1968 Act). A point of law may be substantial enough to demand a full hearing even though it is unlikely to succeed (*R* v *Majewski* [1975] 3 All ER 296), but if, upon argument, it could not possibly succeed it comes within the heading of frivolous or vexatious: *R* v *Taylor* (1979) Crim L R 649. The second way in which unmeritorious appeals are discouraged is through s. 29 of the 1968 Act (see Para. 17.6.5) which provides that the Court of Appeal may direct that any time the appellant has spent in custody between commencing his appeal and having it dismissed shall not, as it normally would, be reckoned as part of the term of any custodial sentence passed on him by the Crown Court. If the court's time has been wasted through an appeal on a point of law which had no chance of succeeding, it might seriously consider a direction under s. 29.

A certificate by the trial judge that a case is fit for appeal on a ground of law is a nullity: *R* v *Smith* (David Raymond) 1974 QB 354. It would, in any event, serve no useful purpose since no leave is required for the appeal. The advantage of having a trial judge's certificate when the appeal is on fact or mixed law and fact is that the appellant does not have to surmount the initial hurdle of obtaining leave to appeal.

17.2.2   Leave to appeal

Most appellants against conviction do not have an automatic right to bring their case before the Court of Appeal, but must first obtain leave to appeal. The power to grant leave to appeal is one of the powers of the Court of Appeal which may be, and most frequently is, exercised not by a court but by a single judge (see s. 31 of the 1968 Act). The procedure for applying to a single judge for leave to appeal is described in more detail in Para. 17.6.4, but, in essence, it involves the papers in the case being handed to him for his consideration. The papers will include the appellant's 'Notice of Application for Leave to Appeal' and 'Grounds of Appeal'. They may also include a transcript of the trial judge's summing up and possibly, depending on the nature of the points raised in the Grounds of Appeal, a transcript of part of the evidence. The judge reads through the papers privately. He could, but hardly ever does, call on counsel for the appellant to present argument. Having read the papers, he decides whether to grant leave or not. If leave is refused, the appellant has the right to have the application decided by a court of the Criminal Division. The risk, from his point of view, in exercising that right is that if the court, like the single judge, refuses leave, it may well order that time he has spent in custody since the commencement of the appeal shall not count as part of any custodial sentence imposed upon him (see s. 29 and Para 17.6.5 on directions for loss of time). Most appellants who are refused leave to appeal by a single judge do not renew the application before the court. Where an application is renewed, it is decided in open court with reasons for the decision being given, but argument on behalf of the appellant is not usually heard.

In granting or refusing leave to appeal the single judge acts as a kind of filter, ensuring that cases do not go before a court for a full hearing unless there is an arguable point. In 1979, out of 1,418 appellants against conviction all but 39 required leave to appeal. Of those requiring leave, 202 abandoned their appeal before the papers went before the single judge, 835 were refused leave, and 345 obtained leave. The vital role of the single judge in keeping the work load of the Criminal Division down to manageable proportions is revealed in those figures.

17.2.3 Appeal against conviction following guilty plea

In entitling persons convicted on indictment to appeal against conviction, s. 1 of the 1968 Act does not differentiate between those who pleaded guilty at the Crown Court and those who pleaded not guilty. On the face of it, the former have as much right to appeal as the latter. However, an appeal against conviction on a guilty plea will succeed only when:

(a) The plea of guilty was in error because the facts alleged by the prosecution did not, in law, amount to the offence admitted by the appellant: *R v Forde* [1923] 2KB 400, per Avory J at p. 403; or

(b) The appellant did not appreciate the nature of the charge, or did not intend to admit that he was guilty of it; or

(c) The plea was induced by a wrong ruling in law by the trial judge.

The proposition in (b) above permits an appeal where the guilty plea was ambiguous or a nullity because the appellant did not make it of his own free will: *R v Turner* [1970] 2QB 321 — see Para. 6.3. The proposition in (c) is illustrated by *R v Clarke* (1972) 1All ER 219. C originally pleaded not guilty to a count alleging shoplifting, but changed her plea after the judge ruled that her defence of putting the goods into her bag in a moment of absent mindedness amounted to a plea of not guilty by reason of insanity — C obviously preferred being convicted and fined to being found insane and made the subject of a Mental Health Act 'order. The judge's ruling was wrong; the ruling induced the guilty plea, and therefore the appeal against conviction succeeded.

17.3 THE RIGHT OF APPEAL AGAINST SENTENCE

Appellants to the Court of Appeal against sentence fall into two categories — those who were sentenced for an offence following conviction on indictment, and those who were sentenced for an offence following summary conviction and committal to the Crown Court for sentence.

17.3.1 Sentence following conviction on indictment

Section 9 of the Criminal Appeal Act 1968 provides that a person who has been convicted of an offence on indictment may appeal to the Court of Appeal against sentence. The right of appeal does not apply when the offender has been convicted of murder, because then the sentence is fixed by law. Nor may the offender appeal against a recommendation to the Home Secretary as to the minimum period of his life sentence that he should serve in prison. Such a recommendation is neither binding on the Home Secretary nor an order of the court, and is not therefore part of the sentence passed: *R v Aitken* [1966] 1WLR 1076.

Section 50 of the 1968 Act provides that in the Act 'sentence' includes 'any order made by a court when dealing with an offender'. This wide definition means that offenders may appeal not only against orders which are obviously part of a sentence (e.g. imprisonment, fine, Borstal training) but also against hospital orders under s. 60 of the Mental Health Act 1959, recommendations for deportation, disqualification from driving, orders to pay costs to the prosecution, and orders to pay compensation to the victim of the offence. An order that the offender should contribute to his own legal aid costs is not, however, part of the sentence because such an order may be made even when a legally aided person is acquitted: *R v Cardiff Crown Court* ex parte *Jones* [1973] 3 All ER 1027. There is thus no appeal against such an order. Nor is there, generally speaking, any appeal against a probation order or conditional or absolute discharge: *R v Tucker* [1974] 1WLR 615. This is because a conviction resulting in probation or discharge is deemed not to be a conviction (Powers of Criminal Courts Act 1973, s. 13), and the right of appeal under s. 9 only extends to those who have been convicted on indictment. Where the probation order is made unlawfully, however, the order may be appealed against (*R v Marquis* [1974] 1WLR 1087 — M's consent to probation was obtained through threatening him with a custodial sentence). Appeal also lies in respect of a sentence subsequently passed on an offender for an offence that was orginally dealt with by probation or conditional discharge.

17.3.2 Sentence following summary conviction

An offender sentenced by the Crown Court for an offence following a summary conviction and committal for sentence by the magistrates may appeal to the Court of Appeal under s. 10 of the 1968 Act against his sentence if:

(a) For the offence (or for that offence and others for which sentence was passed on the same occasion) he was sentenced to imprisonment for a term of six months or more; or

(b) The sentence for the offence was one which the magistrates could not have passed (e.g. Borstal training); or

(c)   The sentence included a recommendation for deportation or disqualification from driving.

The general effect of the section is that if the Crown Court passed a sentence as severe or more severe than the greatest sentence the magistrates could have imposed, appeal lies to the Court of Appeal. If the Crown Court sentence is within the magistrates' powers of sentencing, appeal to the Court of Appeal is unnecessary because the Crown Court obviously took a less serious view of the offence than did the magistrates when they decided to commit for sentence.

Section 10 also gives a right of appeal to an offender who is dealt with by the Crown Court for an offence in respect of which he was originally put on probation or conditionally discharged by magistrates. The appeal lies in the same circumstances as does an appeal against sentence following committal for sentence. In addition, there may be an appeal against a Crown Court order bringing into effect or varying the operational period of a suspended sentence passed by magistrates. Thus, if O is convicted on indictment of an offence of theft committed while subject to a probation order made following his summary conviction for assault, and the Crown Court sentences him to three months imprisonment for theft and three months for assault to run consecutively, he may appeal to the Court of Appeal against both sentences. Since he was convicted on indictment of theft, appeal against that sentence lies under s. 9. Appeal against the three months for assault lies because the Crown Court has dealt with him for an offence in respect of which magistrates originally put him on probation, and the total sentence for that offence and another offence (i.e. the theft) passed on the same occasion was six months. Had O been in breach not of probation but of a suspended sentence passed by the magistrates, he could similarly have appealed against any Crown Court decision to bring it into effect.

17.3.3   Leave to appeal

An appeal against sentence, whether under s. 9 or s. 10 of the 1968 Act, lies only with leave of the Court of Appeal: s. 11(1). Leave is necessary even when the appellant claims that the sentence passed on him was wrong in law. As with applications for leave to appeal against conviction, the procedure is that the papers go before a single judge with the option, if he refuses leave, of renewing the application before a court. In 1979, out of 4,048 applications for leave to appeal against sentence only, 628 were abandoned before the papers were put before the single judge; 2,350 were refused, and 1,070 were granted.

17.4   DETERMINATION OF APPEALS AGAINST CONVICTION

The Court of Appeal shall allow an appeal against conviction if they think that:

(a)   The conviction should be set aside because, in all the circumstances of the case, it is unsafe or unsatisfactory; or

(b)   The trial judge made a wrong decision on any question of law; or

(c)   There was a material irregularity in the course of the trial: Criminal Appeal Act 1968, s. 2(1).

This is subject to the proviso that, even where the point raised in the appeal might be decided in favour of the appellant, the Court may dismiss the appeal if they consider that no miscarriage of justice has actually occurred.

The phrases 'wrong decision on any question of law' and 'material irregularity in the course of the trial' are largely self-explanatory, and cover a wide variety of mistakes by the judge and departures from correct procedure. Many errors could be classified as either a wrong decision on law or a material irregularity but nothing turns upon the nomenclature that ought to be applied. All that matters is that the error mentioned in a ground of appeal can be brought under one or other or both headings. Examples of wrong decisions on law are: allowing a case to continue on an indictment which is bad for duplicity or otherwise defective, wrongly admitting or excluding evidence, wrongly allowing the accused to be cross examined about his previous convictions, misdirecting the jury in the summing up about the law applicable to the offence charged, misdirecting them about the burden or standard of proof, failing to warn them about the danger of convicting on uncorroborated evidence where the warning is required as a matter of practice, and implying that the accused's silence when questioned after caution could be evidence of guilt. Note that, although the appellant complains of an error of law, most of the examples given above raise questions of mixed law and fact so leave to appeal is needed.

Material irregularities in the course of a trial include: failing to sever an indictment, errors in empanelling the jury (although see Juries Act 1974, s. 18 and Para. 7.5 for the restrictions on such appeals), misconduct of a juror, inadvertently informing the jury of the accused's previous convictions, constant interruptions by the judge prejudicial to the defence, misdirecting the jury in the summing up about the evidence given in the trial, failing to explain the defence adequately, and wrongful separation of the jury after they have retired to consider their verdict. Sometimes the court holds that an irregularity has occurred but it is too trivial to be classified as a 'material irregularity'. A minor misdirection as to the testimony of a witness which could not, in the circumstances of the case, have affected the verdict, would be an irregularity, but not a material one. Similarly, in *R* v *Alexander* [1974] 1WLR 422 (see Para. 9.1) the irregularity, consisting in a juror momentarily separating himself from his colleagues, was so minor that it did not 'go to the root of the case', and so was not a good ground of appeal.

Where, after the prosecution case, the judge wrongly rejects a defence submission of no case to answer, he makes an error of law which leads to a material irregularity in the trial because the accused remains at risk of a conviction when he should have been acquitted on the judge's direction. If no evidence is given during the remainder of the trial on which a reasonable jury could convict the accused, then clearly an appeal against conviction must succeed. If, on the other hand, evidence emerges (e.g. in cross examination of the accused should he testify, or as part of a co-accused's case) entitling the jury to convict, the Court of Appeal will be presented, should the accused appeal, with a difficult problem. They may either look at all the evidence which was before the jury, and hold that the appellant's conviction was justified, or they may hold that the appellant ought to have been acquitted even before the damaging evidence against him was given, and should not be prejudiced through the judge trying his case making a mistake. The first approach was adopted in *R* v *Power* [1919] 1KB 572, and the appeal was dismissed. The second approach was favoured in *R* v *Abbott* [1955] 2QB 497 and *R* v *Juett* [1981] Crim L R 113, where the appeals succeeded. Which of the two approaches is correct is still an open question.

The first ground for allowing an appeal mentioned in s. 2 — namely, that the conviction is unsafe or unsatisfactory — is less precise than the other two. Although often put forward merely to supplement a suggestion that there has been an error of law or a material irregularity, it is, like them, an independent ground of appeal, which may be advanced even if there has not been any specific error or irregularity. The test applied when an appellant claims his conviction to be unsafe is a subjctive one. Each member of the court asks himself — 'Do the circumstances of the case leave me with lurking doubts, causing me to wonder whether injustice has been done?' If the answer is in the affirmative, the conviction is unsafe, and must be quashed. The 'lurking doubt' test was put forward in *R v Cooper* [1969] 1QB 267, where C had been convicted of assault on the basis of evidence from the victim who had picked him out on an identification parade. C denied the offence, but admitted being on the scene shortly after it occurred, which could have explained why he was picked out on the identification parade. At the trial, C called evidence from a man of good character that another person, bearing a close resemblance to C and with a record for violence, had admitted to him (the witness) that he committed the offence. For obvious reasons this other person was not called to testify. The weakness of the prosecution evidence, and the plausible suggestion that somebody else had committed the offence, left the Court of Appeal with lurking doubts about the correctness of the conviction. Accordingly, the appeal succeeded.

Most appeals are decided after their Lordships have heard argument from counsel for the appellant and counsel for the Crown, and have read the papers in the case, which will include a transcript of the judge's summing up and, sometimes, a transcript of some or all of the evidence. Although they have the power to hear evidence, they do not usually do so. It is very rare for a witness who gave evidence at the trial on indictment to repeat his testimony in the Court of Appeal. Therefore, when asked to allow an appeal because the conviction is unsafe or unsatisfactory, the Court is conscious that the jury heard the evidence whereas it merely has the written record of what the witnesses said. Even though a case looks weak on paper, the jury, able to assess the demeanour and attitude of the witnesses, may have been absolutely right to convict. As Lord Widgery CJ expressed it in *R v Cooper* (supra):

> The court must recognise the advantage which a jury has in seeing and hearing the witnesses, and if all the material was before the jury and the summing up was impeccable...the court shall not lightly interfere.

'Not lightly interfering' means that an appellant must do more than show that the case against him was a weak one — he must point to some special factor which will leave the court with a lurking doubt. Such a factor was present in *R v Pattinson* (1974) 58Cr App R 417. The incriminating evidence against P came entirely from police officers who testified that P had made oral admissions to committing a serious offence of robbery. An argument that the conviction was unsafe because there was no written confession and no independent evidence linking P with the offence would probably have failed: see *R v Mallinson* [1977] Crim L R 161. P's appeal succeeded, however, because of the bizarre circumstances in which he allegedly made his admissions. According to the police officers, P, while in custody at the police station, asked to shave, and, in the course of shaving, began to talk to himself. Unaware that the officers could hear what he was saying, he made disjointed remarks from which it could be inferred that he had committed the offence charged. This continued for about twenty minutes. The officers made no contemporaneous notes, but an hour and a half later were able to record in their notebooks exactly what P had said. This the Court of Appeal described as 'a remarkable feat of memory'. Suspicions were also raised because the admissions were made after P had been charged — i.e. at a stage when he could not have been questioned about the offence. Bearing in mind all the circumstances, the Court of Appeal was left with a lurking doubt, and accordingly allowed the appeal.

In cases where the Court of Appeal itself receives evidence (see Para. 17.6.8), the question for the court is whether, in the light of that evidence and all the circumstances of the case the conviction is unsafe or unsatisfactory: *Stafford and Luvaglio* v *DDP* [1974] AC 878. The court is not obliged to uphold the appeal merely because the jury, had they heard additional evidence heard by the Court of Appeal, might have acquitted — the decisive factor is what their Lordships think about the conviction not what the jury might have done.

The case of *R* v *Cooper and McMahon* is a vivid illustration of the difficulty sometimes encountered in putting lurking doubts into the minds of the judges in the Court of Appeal. C, McM and a co-accused, Murphy, were convicted of the murder of a Luton subpostmaster in the course of an unsuccessful robbery. At their trial in 1970, Matthews, who was not prosecuted, gave evidence for the Crown that he had been peripherally involved in the attempted robbery, if not in the murder. He named C, McM and Murphy as the principal offenders. His testimony was almost the only evidence against the three men. Their applications for leave to appeal failed because, although the prosecution case was weak in that it rested on the largely uncorroborated evidence of an accomplice, the jury were entitled to convict on that evidence, and they had had the advantage of seeing and hearing the witnesses. In 1973, however, Murphy succeeded in having his conviction quashed on the basis of fresh alibi evidence which had not been available at the trial, but was called before the Court of Appeal. In 1975, C and McM's cases were referred to the Court by the Home Secretary (see Para 17.7.1 for Home Secretary's references). They argued that, since Matthews' evidence about Murphy had been wrong, their convictions, also based on his evidence, were unsafe. The Court of Appeal did not hear evidence from Matthews but held that in implicating Murphy he could have made a genuine mistake; that in C and McM's cases there was less room for mistake, and that their convictions were therefore safe. In 1976 the Home Secretary again referred the matter to their Lordships. This time Matthews testified before them, and they concluded that his evidence was unconvincing and, in parts, a 'cock and bull story'. Nevertheless, they held that in the crucial part of his evidence, where he named C and McM as having been involved in the murder, he was telling the truth. Accordingly, the convictions stood. There was yet another unsuccessful reference to the Court in 1978, this time on the basis of fresh alibi evidence, and eventually, in July 1980, the Home Secretary ended the saga by remitting the remainder of C and McM's life sentences.

The case is reported in (1975) 61Cr App R 215, but only on the question of whether, in refusing to certify that a case involves a point of law of general public importance, the Court of Appeal should give reasons. The case was before the Court on five occasions. They were — 26 February 1971 (applications for leave to appeal refused); 13 November 1973 (Murphy's conviction squashed), and 22 February 1975, 22 July 1976 and 11 April 1978 (successive Home Secretary's references in the cases of Cooper and McMahon). For details of the case, the reader is referred to the book 'Wicked beyond Belief' by Ludovic Kennedy, which includes a contribution by Lord Devlin.

17.4.1 The effect of a successful appeal

If the Court of Appeal allows an appeal, it must quash the appellant's conviction: Criminal Appeal Act 1968, s. 2(2). The effect of quashing a conviction is to put the appellant into precisely the position he would have been in had he been acquitted by the jury who tried him. This means that if he is again prosecuted for the offence which resulted in his quashed conviction he may rely upon the plea of autrefois acquit — in other words, a successful appellant does not face the possibility of a retrial. The rule is subject to two exceptions.

First, if the Court of Appeal allows an appeal solely because of evidence it has received, or had the opportunity of receiving, under s. 23 of the 1968 Act (see Para. 17.6.8) it may quash the conviction but order the appellant to be retried: s. 7. Second, the Court of Appeal still has power to grant the old writ of venire de novo, the effect of which is to set aside the conviction and order the Crown Court to empanel a fresh jury to try the case. However, the writ may only be issued in very limited circumstances, where the original proceedings in the Crown Court were so fundamentally flawed that they amounted to a complete mistrial, so that the appellant was never in danger of a valid conviction. Denying an accused the right to challenge jurors is one example of an irregularity which turns a trial into a mistrial, and so gives rise to the possibility of a venire de novo (*R* v *Edmonds* (1821) 4B&Ald 471), but today the writ is only likely to be needed when an appellant's conviction on a guilty plea is quashed because pressure put on him made the plea involuntary and a nullity (see *R* v *Turner* [1970] 2QB 321 and Para. 6.3). In 1979, the Court of Appeal ordered a retrial in only one of the 109 cases in which there was a successful appeal against conviction.

17.4.2   Application of the proviso

Since a successful appellant is normally not retried, criminals might unjustly avoid the consequences of their crimes if every wrong decision on law or material irregularity led to their convictions being quashed. It often happens that a judge makes a minor error in directing the jury on the law, or allows evidence to be given which is inadmissible, but the prosecution case is so strong that, even had no mistake been made, the accused would inevitably have been convicted. If, in such a case, the accused appeals against his conviction, the Court of Appeal may apply the proviso.

The proviso to s. 2 of the 1968 Act states that where a point raised in an appeal might be decided in favour of the appellant the Court may nevertheless dismiss the appeal if their Lordships consider that 'no miscarriage of justice has actually occurred'. Where an error in a Crown Court trial deprives the appellant of a chance of an acquittal which was fairly open to him, a miscarriage of justice occurs, and the proviso cannot be applied, even if the members of the Court of Appeal subjectively think that the appellant is guilty. The proviso is only applicable if their Lordships are satisfied that on the whole of the facts, and with no error of law or material irregularity, the only proper verdict would have been one of guilty: *R* v *Haddy* [1944] KB 442. Whether or not the proviso may be applied will obviously turn upon the facts of the individual case before the Court of Appeal, but it has been stated that, in a case where a judge wrongly fails to warn the jury about the dangers of convicting on uncorroborated evidence, it is most unlikely that the conviction could be upheld: *R* v *Trigg* [1963] 1WLR 305. Similarly, the proviso will probably not be applicable if the trial judge wrongly allowed the accused to be cross examined about his previous convictions, or wrongly refused him leave to call alibi evidence: see *R* v *Turner* [1944] KB 463 and *R* v *Lewis* [1969] 2QB 1.

17.4.3 Partially successful appeals

If an appellant was convicted at the Crown Court on two or more counts, and appeals against all those convictions, the Court of Appeal may, of course, allow the appeal on some but not all the counts. Further, where the indictment against the appellant was such that the jury could have convicted him on it of an offence other than the one of which they did convict him, the Court may substitute for the jury's verdict a verdict guilty of that other offence: s. 3. The Court of Appeal must take the view that the jury must have been satisfied of the facts proving the appellant guilty of the other offence. Section 3 may apply in two situations. First, if the jury, on a count in the indictment, convicted the appellant as charged, but could have returned a verdict of not guilty as charged but guilty of a lesser offence, the Court of Appeal can substitute for their verdict a conviction for the lesser offence. Second, if the jury convicted of one of two counts on the indictment in the alternative, and were discharged from giving a verdict on the other count, the Court of Appeal can reverse the verdicts (i.e. quash the conviction and enter a verdict of guilty of the offence in respect of which the jury were discharged from giving a verdict) (see Para. 9.3).

In 1979, the Court of Appeal heard 372 appeals against conviction. Of those, 109 resulted in the appellant's convictions being completely quashed, 16 were successful on some counts but not on others, 5 were dealt with by quashing the conviction and substituting a verdict of guilty of a lesser offence, and the remainder were completely unsuccessful.

17.5 DETERMINATION OF APPEALS AGAINST SENTENCE

On an appeal against sentence, the Court of Appeal may quash any sentence or order which is the subject of the appeal, and replace it with the sentence or order it considers appropriate provided:

(a)   The sentence it passes or order it makes is one which the Crown Court could have passed or made, and

(b)   Taking the case as a whole, the appellant is not more severely dealt with on appeal than he was by the Crown Court: s. 11 of the 1968 Act.

Unlike the old Court of Criminal Appeal, the Court of Appeal does not have the power to increase sentence. Where, however, the Court allows an appeal in respect of one count but confirms the conviction in respect of another count, it may increase the sentence for the count on which the appellant still stands convicted, provided it does not make the sentence more severe than the total sentence passed by the Crown Court on both counts: s. 4. If the Court of Appeal substitutes for the jury's verdict a verdict of guilty of a lesser offence (see Para. 17.4.3) it may pass a sentence for the lesser offence which again must not be more severe than the Crown Court sentence: s. 3(2). Despite the prohibition on increasing sentence, an appellant serving a custodial sentence may find that his sentence has in effect been increased through the court directing that the time he has spent in custody pending determination of his appeal shall not count as part of his sentence. Section 11 (no increase in sentence) should therefore be considered in conjunction with s. 29 (directions for loss of time).

The Court of Appeal does not reduce a sentence merely because the members of the court would, if they had been dealing with the appellant in the Crown Court, have passed on him a somewhat different sentence. Crown Court judges are given a broad discretion in sentencing matters, and the Court of Appeal only interferes if the sentence passed was manifestly excessive in view of the circumstances of the case or wrong in principle: *R* v *Gumbs* (1926) 19Cr App R 74. A sentence which is above the tariff for the offence, or which apparently takes no account of cogent mitigating factors, is manifestly excessive. A tariff sentence passed in a case which clearly called for an individualised sentence would be wrong in principle. A sentence may also be reduced because the judge, in passing it, apparently allowed himself to be influenced by irrelevant factors (e.g. *R* v *Skone* (1967) 51Cr App R 165 — trial judge increasing his sentence because S's defence had involved allegations against the police), or because inadmissible and prejudicial comments were made by the police officer when giving antecedents evidence (e.g. *R* v *Wilkins* (1978) 66Cr App R 49 — see Para. 14.2.1). If two offenders with roughly similar antecedents are convicted of the same or related offences, and one receives a markedly more severe sentence than the other, the disparity between the two sentences is a ground for reducing the more severe sentence, even if it is not, taken by itself, manifestly excessive: *R* v *Potter* [1977] Crim L R 112. The question is whether the difference between the two sentences is so great that the offender more harshly dealt with might have a justifiable sense of grievance. If the difference is slight, the Court of Appeal will not interfere with a merited sentence merely because a co-offender was fortunate in being sentenced a little more leniently than he deserved.

In 1979, out of 1,060 appeals against sentence only heard by the Court of Appeal, 729 were successful.

17.6 PROCEDURE FOR APPEALING

The main stages in making an appeal are as follows:

(a)   Within 28 days of conviction or sentence, depending on which the appeal is against, the appellant must serve on the Registrar a Notice of Application for Leave to Appeal (or, if he does not require leave, a Notice of Appeal). The Notice must be accompanied by Grounds of Appeal, either drafted by the appellant himself, or settled and signed by counsel on his behalf.

(b)   At least where the appeal is against conviction, the initial Grounds of Appeal accompanying the Notice of Application for Leave to Appeal are unlikely to be sufficiently detailed or precise to be put before a single judge with a view to his granting leave to appeal. This is because counsel, in drafting them, will have had to rely upon his memory of what occurred at the trial, together with his long-hand note of the proceedings. The final, or perfected, Grounds of Appeal should specify exactly the inadmissible evidence, or error in the summing up, or other matter of which the appellant complains. To do this, it is usually necessary to have a transcript of the summing up. Sometimes a transcript of at least part of the evidence is also necessary. Therefore, in his initial Grounds of Appeal, counsel asks for a transcript, and the Registrar, if he considers the request reasonable, obtains a copy of it for him. Having read the transcript, counsel may amend and perfect his initial Grounds of Appeal.

(c)   The papers in the case are put before the single judge. In the light of the Grounds of Appeal, transcript and any other relevant documents (e.g. documentary exhibits from the Crown Court trial), he decides whether to grant leave to appeal. If he does grant leave, he may at the same time consider for instance releasing the appellant on bail pending determination of the appeal, ordering a witness to attend court for the hearing of the appeal so that the Court may receive testimony from him if it so wishes, and granting the appellant legal aid so that he may be represented on the appeal.

(d) The appellant is notified of the single judge's decision. If leave to appeal is refused, the appellant has 14 days in which to serve notice on the Registrar that he wishes to renew the application before a court of the Criminal Division. Sometimes the court hearing the application for leave to appeal treats the application as a hearing of the appeal, and determines it forthwith. Otherwise, once leave to appeal has been given, whether by the single judge or the court, the Registrar ensures that the papers are in order (e.g. obtains any extra transcript which the single judge has indicated is necessary), and fixes the hearing date.

(e) At the hearing, counsel for the appellant presents argument. If the appeal is against conviction, the Crown will almost certainly be represented, and may be called upon to oppose the appellant's case. Sometimes witnesses are called by the appellant (e.g. alibi witnesses, whose identity could not reasonably have been known at the time of the trial on indictment), but usually the appeal is based on the transcript and counsel's argument. At an appeal against sentence only the Crown is not usually represented as it is not the prosecution's task, either at trial or on appeal, to argue for a high sentence.

The above sequence of events may be varied by the Registrar not referring an application for leave to appeal to the single judge, but listing it straightaway for hearing before the Court. Alternatively, the single judge on reading the papers may feel that the Court ought to decide the application, and will accordingly refer it to them. Another possibility is that the single judge will consider the Grounds of Appeal to be inadequately drafted, and will have them sent back to counsel to be properly perfected. Where the appeal lies without leave, it is listed for a full hearing by the Court, subject only to the possibility of the Registrar referring it for summary determination under s. 20 of the 1968 Act (see Para. 17.2.1).

17.6.1 Notice of application for leave to appeal

The appellant's Notice of Application for Leave to Appeal must be given on a standard form provided by the Criminal Appeal Office: Criminal Appeal Rules 1968, r. 2. An example of a Notice is printed at page 246. As will be seen, it contains the essential details about the appeal, including the name of the appellant, his address or, if he is in custody, the address of the prison etc. where he is detained, the name of the court at which and the judge before whom he was tried, the offences of which he was convicted and the sentences for those offences, and whether he is appealing against conviction or sentence or both. The form may also be used to inform the Court that the appellant is applying for legal aid, or for bail pending the hearing of the appeal, or for leave to be present at or call witnesses at the hearing. The form must be signed by the appellant or by solicitors on his behalf. If the appellant does not need leave to appeal, he simply gives Notice of Appeal. Where an appellant who does not need leave gives notice of application for leave, it is treated as a notice of appeal, and vice versa.

The Notice should be served on the Registrar within 28 days of conviction or sentence: s. 18 of the 1968 Act. The court has a discretion to give the appellant leave to apply for leave to appeal out of time, but there must be good reasons for the Notice not having been served within the statutory period. The fact that the appellant absconded before the conclusion of his trial on indictment and was not recaptured until more than 28 days had elapsed from the date the jury convicted him in his absence, is not a sufficient reason for extending time for appealing, even though the appellant had indicated before his disappearance that if convicted he wanted to appeal: *R* v *Jones* (No. 2) [1972] 1WLR 887. Even if a decision of the Court of Appeal made in another case soon after the appellant's time for giving notice expired indicates that there was an error of law in the conduct of the appellant's trial, the court need not necessarily grant him leave to appeal against conviction out of time: *R* v *Ramsden* [1972] Crim LR 547. However, in *R* v *Mitchell* [1977] 1WLR 753 the Court's discretion was exercised in M's favour because he had, within time, appealed against sentence, and not to have granted him leave to appeal against conviction would have placed their Lordships in the position of determining an appeal against sentence, knowing that, in the light of their decision in a case subsequent to his trial, M's conviction ought to be quashed.

The fairly strict enforcement of the 28 day limit for giving Notice ought not to lead to injustice. If the appellant was legally represented at the Crown Court, counsel or a representative of the solicitors will normally see him after the verdict and sentence, and advise informally on whether there are grounds for appeal. Most defendants at the Crown Court are legally aided, and that legal aid covers a written advice from counsel on the merits of an appeal and, if so advised, the drafting of Grounds of Appeal. Having received the Grounds from counsel the solicitors obtain a Notice form from the Criminal Appeal Office or the Crown Court, complete it on behalf of the appellant, and serve it, together with the Grounds, on the Registrar. If the appellant is unrepresented, or his representatives advise against an appeal, he may complete the forms himself. If he is in custody, the forms are available at the prison etc. where he is detained.

17.6.2 Grounds of appeal

In preparing his Grounds of Appeal, which should accompany the Notice, the appellant must again make use of a standard form from the Criminal Appeal Office. The Grounds form asks for many of the details already included in the Notice form. In addition, at the bottom of the form, is a space in which the appellant may write out his Grounds. However, if counsel settles and signs the Grounds they are typed on a separate sheet, which is served on the Registrar together with the Notice and Grounds' forms. As already explained, the Grounds as initially settled may not be fit to go before the single judge. Once perfected, they should enable the single judge or Court to identify the particular matters put forward by the appellant for their consideration. It is not enough to state in general terms that 'the conviction is unsafe or unsatisfactory' or 'the sentence was too severe in all the circumstances of the case without giving reasons for those assertions. No particular formality is required in the phrasing of the Grounds, provided the point or points the appellant wishes to raise are made clear. A convenient method of drafting is to deal with the errors of which complaint is made in chronological order — e.g. ground one might deal with the trial judge failing to sever the indictment, ground two with his failing to uphold a submission of no case to answer, ground three with his wrongly allowing the appellant to be cross examined about his previous convictions, and ground four with various misdirections in the summing up. The Grounds should refer by page number and letter to relevant passages in the transcript, and should cite authorities on which counsel intends to rely. Where the appellant wishes to call a witness at the hearing of the appeal, the reasons for doing so should be fully developed. If counsel settles grounds. he should only include those which are reasonable, and which, in his opinion, afford some real chance of success (Practice Note 1969 50Cr App R 290). If no such grounds exist, the appellant must be left to pursue his appeal in person if he so wishes. An example of Grounds of Appeal appears on pages 248-9.

Sometimes counsel cannot be sure, at the stage when he is asked to draft the initial

Grounds of Appeal, whether there are any reasonable grounds or not. For example, he may think that the judge made a mistake in the summing up, but needs to read the transcript to make certain, or the viability of the appeal may depend on the evidence which fresh witnesses, who have not yet been interviewed by solicitors, may be able to give. In such difficult cases, Notice of Application for Leave to Appeal should be served within the 28 days as normal, but it should be accompanied not by Grounds of Appeal but by a Note to the Registrar of Provisional Grounds of Appeal. The Note explains what the provisional grounds are, and asks the Registrar for any assistance he can give (e.g. a transcript of the summing up, or legal aid so that solicitors can interview potential fresh witnesses). Once counsel has the information he needs he either advises that the appeal should be discontinued or drafts Grounds of Appeal.

17.6.3 Transcripts

A shorthand writer takes a note of any proceedings in the Crown Court upon which an appeal may lie to the Court of Appeal. The Registrar and any 'interested party' has a right to be supplied with a transcript of the note, but only upon payment of a fixed charge: Criminal Appeal Rules 1968, r. 19. The cost of a transcript would inhibit most appellants from obtaining one, but the Registrar has a discretion to order a transcript and supply a copy free of charge to any legally aided appellant. Most appellants are legally aided, so, essentially, the supplying of transcripts depends on the Registrar's discretion. In his initial Grounds of Appeal, counsel specifies those parts of the transcript which he needs (e.g. the whole of the summing up and the evidence of John Smith who was called on the second day of the trial). Counsel should not ask for a transcript of the whole of the evidence unless that really is essential to the appeal, as asking for unnecessary transcript wastes both time and money. The Registrar may decline to order some or all of the transcript which counsel requests. If dissatisfied with the Registrar's decision, counsel may have the question referred to a single judge.

For an appeal against conviction, a transcript of the summing up and of any evidence said to be inadmissible will probably be required. For an appeal against sentence, a transcript of counsel's mitigation and any remarks the judge made when passing sentence is usually needed. A transcript of the prosecution's summary of the facts, where there was a guilty plea, and of the antecedents evidence may also be obtained.

17.6.4 Applications to a single judge: Criminal Appeal Act 1968, s. 31

Applications for leave to appeal are most frequently decided by a single judge. The single judge may also exercise, whether at the time he decides an application for leave or otherwise, certain other of the Court of Appeal's powers. He may give leave to appeal out of time, allow an appellant to attend at proceedings connected with his appeal even though he has no right to be present, order a witness to attend court on the day fixed for hearing of the appeal so that the Court may receive evidence from him if it so wishes, grant bail to the appellant pending determination of the appeal, and give directions concerning loss of time. Although any of these powers could be exercised by the single judge in open court following argument from counsel, the usual procedure, as already explained, is for him to read through the papers in the case privately, and reach a decision simply on the basis of the papers. That is one reason why the Grounds of Appeal should be as clear as possible.

If the single judge grants leave to appeal he will almost certainly grant legal aid for the hearing, although if counsel will apparently need no instructions beyond those contained in the papers already prepared the legal aid will cover representation by counsel only, not by counsel and solicitor. He might also make observations to be brought to counsel's attention (e.g. as to an extra ground of appeal which counsel appears to have overlooked), or he might direct that some additional transcript be obtained. A direction to expedite the hearing would be appropriate in a case where there seem to be strong grounds of appeal and the appellant is serving a short custodial sentence (i.e. there is a risk of his serving his full sentence and then having his conviction quashed). Where there is an appeal against sentence, the single judge might order up to date reports on the appellant, including reports on his progress at prison, Borstal etc.

The appellant is notified of the single judge's decision. If he is refused leave to appeal, he has the right to have the application determined by the court (s. 31(3)), provided he serves on the Registrar a notice in the prescribed form. The notice must be served within 14 days of his being notified of the judge's decision: Criminal Appeal Rules 1968, r. 12. Although the Court of Appeal has power to extend the period of giving notice, it only does so if the appellant can show a good reason for not having acted within the proper time — merely having a change of mind after the 14 days is not a good enough reason: *R* v *Sullivan* (1972) 56Cr App R 541. To assist the appellant in deciding whether to renew his application before a court, the notification of the judge's decision includes some observations by him as to why he refused leave. If the application is renewed, it may be determined by a two judge or three judge court. The decision is reached in open court, but an appellant in custody has no right to be present, and counsel do not usually attend. The procedure described above applies not only when the single judge refuses leave to appeal but whenever he declines to exercise one of his powers in favour of an appellant.

17.6.5   Directions concerning loss of time: Criminal Appeal Act 1968, s. 29

Unless a direction to the contrary is given, the time that the appellant spends in custody between commencing his appeal and its being determined counts as part of any custodial sentence which he is serving, whether the sentence was imposed in the Crown Court proceedings which are the subject of the appeal or on some previous occasion. A direction to the contrary (i.e. a direction for loss of time) may be given by the single judge on refusing an application for leave to appeal, or by the court on an unsuccessful renewal of an application for leave to appeal, or by the court when dismissing an appeal on a ground of pure law. Directions for loss of time are a means of penalising an appellant for commencing a meritless appeal which wastes the time of the court.

In a Practice Note (1980 1AER 555) the Lord Chief Justice indicated when directions are likely to be made. Where counsel has settled and signed the Grounds of Appeal and supported them with a written opinion, the single judge will not order loss of time because it would be unfair to blame an appellant for pursuing an appeal advised by his legal representatives. If, however, counsel has not advised an appeal, and the single judge refuses the application for leave to appeal, he will give 'especial consideration' to making a direction, and 'it may be expected that such a direction will normally be made'. Similarly, when an application for leave is unsuccessfully renewed before the court, a direction will probably be made. At that stage, the appellant is not even protected by counsel having settled the Grounds of Appeal and advised the further application to the court.

A direction for loss of time may relate to part only of the time the appellant has been in custody since commencing his appeal. Thus, in a case where grounds have not been settled by counsel, the single judge could order that the appellant lose, say, a month's time, and, if he were unwise enough to renew the application, the court could order that he lose a further two months.

> Whether the Court of Appeal should have power to make directions for loss of time is an arguable point. Certainly, the knowledge that his custodial sentence might, in effect, be increased if he is thought to be wasting the court's time, will discourage a frivolous appeal. Time-wasting applications for leave to appeal need to be discouraged because they delay the consideration of applications which have merit. The counter argument is that fear of a direction for loss of time might discourage not only the worthless but some worthwhile appeals. It may also seem unfair that those who have not received custodial sentences may appeal with impunity, whereas those who are serving custodial sentences and, *prima facie,* have more urgent reasons for appealing, are liable to possible sanctions if they do so.

17.6.6 Bail pending hearing of the appeal: Criminal Appeal Act 1968, s. 19

The Court of Appeal's power to grant bail to an appellant, pending determination of his appeal, is exercisable by a single judge. The procedure is to indicate on the Notice of Application for Leave to Appeal form that the appellant is also applying for bail. In addition, a form giving details of the application must be served on the Registrar. Bail is rarely granted as, in the event of the appeal failing, the appellant will suffer the trauma of being returned to prison. The question is — 'Are there exceptional circumstances which would drive the court to the conclusion that justice can only be done by the granting of bail?': *R* v *Watton* (1979) 68Cr App R 293. The fact that the single judge has granted leave to appeal against conviction does not in itself justify bail, but the appellant might be bailed where either the appeal seems likely to succeed, or he is serving a short custodial sentence which, in the absence of bail, is likely to be completed before the appeal is heard.

> A relevant factor in connection with both directions for loss of time and bail pending determination of the appeal is the period which may be expected to elapse between giving notice of application for leave to appeal and the appeal being determined. Unfortunately, the length of that period varies so much depending on the nature and complexity of the case that it is difficult to indicate how long it is likely to be. The time between giving notice and the single judge granting leave to appeal is measured in months rather than weeks, but will turn upon (e.g.) how much transcript is required and whether the Grounds of Appeal have to be returned to counsel to be perfected. From obtaining leave to having the appeal heard might average around three months, but in difficult cases, requiring extra preparation, the delay will be longer. In the cases of young appellants and those serving short custodial sentences every effort is made to expedite the appeal.

17.6.7 Presence at the appeal: Criminal Appeal Act 1968, s. 22

An appellant need not be present for his appeal. An appellant who is not in custody has, like any other member of the public, a right to be present when his appeal is heard, or when applications ancillary to the appeal are decided in open court as opposed to being decided privately by a single judge. An appellant in custody has no right to be present at his application for leave to appeal or other ancillary applications. He is entitled to attend the actual hearing of the appeal, unless it is on a ground of law alone. Where an appellant in custody does not have the right to be present, a single judge or the court may give him leave to be present.

17.6.8 Evidence called before the Court of Appeal: Criminal Appeal Act 1968, s. 23

The Court of Appeal must receive evidence if:

(a) It appears to them likely to be credible; and
(b) It would have been admissible at the trial on indictment; and
(c) It was not adduced at the trial on indictment, but there is a reasonable explanation for failure to adduce it: s. 23(2).

Even if the above conditions are satisfied the Court of Appeal need not hear the evidence if it is apparently of such marginal significance that it would afford no ground for allowing the appeal.

The question of whether the evidence is 'likely to be credible' is decided by considering the testimony which, it is anticipated, the witness will give in the context of the case as a whole: *R* v *Parks* [1961] 1WLR 1484. Relevant factors are whether the witness' proof of evidence is intrinsically credible, and whether it fits in with at least some of the other evidence in the case. The explanation for not adducing the evidence at the Crown Court is closely examined by the court. The general principle is that all the relevant evidence should be put before the jury so that they can make a once and for all decision on the issues of fact. As Edmund Davies LJ expressed it in *R* v *Stafford and Luvaglio* (1969) 53Cr App R 1 at p. 3.

> public mischief would ensue and legal process could become indefinitely prolonged were it the case that evidence produced at any time will generally be admitted when verdicts are being reviewed.

Thus, counsel's considering at the time of the trial that the risk of calling a witness was too great in view of the cross examination to which he might be subjected is not an explanation for failing to call him which will oblige the Court of Appeal to hear his evidence — the defence stand or fall by the tactical decision they make at trial about the evidence: *R* v *Shields and Patrick* [1977] Crim L R 281. If the evidence the appellant wishes to call before the Court has only just become available, the Court must be satisfied that it could not with reasonable diligence have been obtained for use at the trial. 'Reasonable diligence' involves an accused cooperating with his solicitors for instance by giving them the names and addresses of alibi witnesses: *R* v *Beresford* (1971) 56Cr App R 143. If, however, the defence could not trace a witness before trial because for example his address was not known to the accused, but he comes forward after the trial as a result of reading newspaper reports about the accused's conviction, the accused, on appeal, would *prima facie* have a reasonable explanation for not having adduced the evidence before the jury.

Even where the Court of Appeal are under no duty to receive evidence, they may 'if they think it necessary or expedient in the interests of justice' receive the evidence of any competent witness: s. 23(1). In theory, the subsection is wide enough to allow the court to re-try a case, hearing all the witnesses who testified at the trial on indictment and any additional witnesses the parties might wish to put forward. In fact, their Lordships are reluctant to receive evidence except in those cases where s. 23(2) obliges them to do so. The reason is that explained above — the jury, not the Court of Appeal, are the tribunal of fact, and all the relevant evidence should be put before them. Where, however, the evidence the appellant wishes to adduce appears exceptionally cogent the court will, in the interests of justice to the individual, hear it. Such a case was *R* v *Lattimore* (1976) 62Cr App R 53. L and his two co-accused were convicted of the murder of C. The prosecution case rested largely upon confessions to the police in which the defendants admitted strangling C, leaving his body in his house, and setting fire to the house so as to destroy the evidence of the murder. According to the confession, the arson of the house took place immediately after the murder. The Court of Appeal received medical and scientific evidence which showed that at least three hours had elapsed between the two crimes. That in turn showed that the confessions were unreliable since the true murderer must have known that the arson did not follow straight after the murder, and, having decided to confess, he would have had no reason to tell lies on the point. The doubt cast upon the confessions rendered the convictions unsafe, and they were accordingly quashed. All the evidence heard by the Court of Appeal could have been adduced by the defence at the trial on indictment. Indeed, some of the witnesses before the Court of Appeal also testified at the trial, but the significance of the evidence they could give was not at that time appreciated. Clearly, the court was not obliged under s. 23(2) to allow the witnesses to testify, but, because their evidence was so vital to the appellants' case, it was received by their Lordships under s. 23(1).

Having heard evidence, the members of the court ask themselves whether in the light of that evidence and all the circumstances of the case the conviction is unsafe or unsatisfactory. They do not have to allow the appeal merely because the evidence appeared capable of belief, or even because the jury, had they heard the evidence, might have reached a different verdict, although gauging the likely effect of the evidence on the jury would, in many cases, provide the best means of determining whether the conviction is safe: *Stafford and Luvaglio* v *DPP* [1974] AC 878. If the appeal is allowed solely on the basis of evidence received under s. 23, the Court of Appeal has a discretion to order a retrial (s. 7 of the 1968 Act).

An appellant who wishes to adduce evidence before the court should indicate on his Notice of Application for Leave to Appeal form that he is also asking for leave to call a witness. A form should be served on the Registrar giving details of the application. If the appellant fears that the witness will not attend voluntarily to testify, and he would have been a compellable (not merely a competent) witness at the trial on indictment, the single judge may order him to attend for the hearing of the appeal. Although the single judge can order a witness to attend, only the court itself can give the appellant leave to call him. The next stage, therefore, is for counsel for the appellant, at the hearing of the appeal, to preview the evidence which the witness can give, and seek to persuade the court either that they are under a duty to receive his evidence or that they should, in the exercise of their discretion, receive it. If the witness is compellable, he may be called by the court, rather than by one of the parties, examined in chief by a member of the court, and then tendered to both parties for cross examination. If the court does not call the witness but gives leave for one of the parties to call him, the normal procedure for examining witnesses applies — the party calling him examines him in chief, the other party cross examines and the court may ask any questions it thinks fit. Normally it will be the appellant who wishes the court to receive evidence, but the prosecution may seek to call a witness to rebut the evidence the court has heard on behalf of the appellant.

When determining appeals against sentence, the Court of Appeal often has the benefit of social, medical, psychiatric and other reports. Up to date reports of the progress the appellant is making in the prison, Borstal or other custodial institution in which he is detained are also of value. When an appeal against conviction involves an allegation of a material irregularity in the course of the trial, such as the judge constantly interrupting the defence or bringing improper pressure to bear on the accused to persuade him to plead guilty, the court may accept informal 'evidence' of what occurred in the shape of statements by counsel or a note from the judge.

17.6.9   Legal aid and costs

A person wishing to appeal to the Court of Appeal may be granted legal aid for that purpose. The order for legal aid can be made only by the Criminal Division, not by the Crown Court: Legal Aid Act 1974, s. 28(8). The Criminal Division may exercise its powers through the Registrar or a single judge and may initially limit a grant of legal aid to that necessary for obtaining advice on the merits of an appeal and the drafting of Grounds of Appeal. Most appellants will have had the benefit of legal aid for the proceedings against them in the Crown Court. In such cases, the Crown Court legal aid covers also advice on appeal and the preparatory work in connection with making an appeal (serving the Notice of Application for Leave to Appeal, drafting the grounds, applying for bail etc.). It does not cover oral argument before the court. Therefore, the single judge, on granting leave to appeal, usually grants legal aid for representation at the hearing. Depending on how much paper work needs to be done in preparation for the hearing, the legal aid may be for counsel only or for counsel and solicitor.

A successful appellant against conviction may be awarded his costs out of central (i.e. government) funds: Costs in Criminal Cases Act 1973, s. 7(1). The prosecution costs may always be paid out of central funds: s. 7(2). Costs awarded under s. 7 may include costs incurred in the Crown Court proceedings. When an appeal or application for leave to appeal is dismissed the appellant may be ordered to pay costs to 'such person as may be named in the order': s. 9 of the 1973 act. The costs may include the expense of obtaining a transcript.

Much useful information about the procedure for appealing will be found in a booklet, obtainable from the Criminal Appeals Office, entitled — 'Preparation for Proceedings in the Court of Appeal Criminal Division'.

17.7   OTHER WAYS IN WHICH MATTERS COME BEFORE THE COURT OF APPEAL

The great majority of cases heard in the Criminal Division of the Court of Appeal are appeals against conviction and/or sentence, but a minority come before the court in other ways.

17.7.1   Reference by the Home Secretary: Criminal Appeal Act 1968, s. 17

The Home Secretary may at any time refer to the Court of Appeal the case of a person who has been convicted on indictment. The Court then treats the case as if it were an appeal by the person convicted. Alternatively, the Home Secretary may, without referring the whole case to it, ask for the Court's opinion on a particular point arising in the case. The Home Secretary may refer a case whether or not the person convicted has asked for that to be done. The latter cannot possibly be prejudiced by having his case referred since, where the Home Secretary makes a reference, the Court of Appeal has no power to give a direction under s. 29 for loss of time. Home Secretary's references are especially valuable when, long after the time for appealing against conviction has past or after an unsuccessful appeal has been made, fresh evidence is discovered or other circumstances arise which cast doubt upon the correctness of the conviction. The case of *R* v *Cooper and McMahon* (see Para. 17.4) was extraordinary in that, as additional evidence kept coming to light, the matter was referred to the

Court of Appeal no less than four times, but in general, Home Secretary's references are infrequent. In 1979, 5,461 appeals against conviction and/or sentence were commenced; only 8 references by the Home Secretary were made.

17.7.2 Reference by the Attorney-General: Criminal Justice Act 1972, s. 36

Until 1972, no procedure existed for testing the correctness of a decision or statement of law made by a judge during the course of a trial on indictment which ended in the acquittal of the accused. This was because the prosecution could not, and still cannot, appeal against an acquittal on indictment, and Home Secretary's references depend upon there having been a conviction. The absence of any method of appeal left open the possibility that a ruling by a Crown Court judge which was unduly favourable to the accused might be reported, and become accepted as representing the law, when it was, in fact, mistaken. To avoid this happening, s. 36 of the Criminal Justice Act 1972 provides that where a person has been tried on indictment and acquitted (whether on the whole indictment or some counts only), the Attorney-General may refer to the Court of Appeal for their opinion any point of law which arose in the case. Before giving their opinion on the point referred, the Court must hear argument by or on behalf of the Attorney-General. The person acquitted also has the right to have counsel present argument on his behalf. However, despite his right to be represented at the hearing, the person acquitted is not put in peril by the proceedings. Whatever the opinion expressed by the Court of Appeal — even if they decide that the trial judge was wrong and the facts of the case were such that the accused clearly ought to have been convicted — the acquittal is unaffected: s. 36(7). By making a reference, the Attorney-General may obtain a ruling which will assist the prosecution in future cases against other defendants, but he cannot set aside the acquittal of the particular defendant whose case gave rise to the reference.

In *Attorney-General's Reference (No. 1 of 1975 — 1975 QB 733)* Lord Widgery CJ stated that references by the Attorney-General should not be confined to cases where 'very heavy questions of law arise', but should also be made when 'short but important points require a quick ruling ·of (the Court of Appeal) before a potentially false decision of law has too wide a circulation in the courts.' The usefulness of Attorney-General's references is illustrated by References Nos. 1 and 2 of 1979 (1979 3AER ·143) where 'burglars' surprised when committing the offence, had been acquitted following rulings that, although there was evidence of entering a building with intent to steal anything of value which might be found therein, s. 9(1)(a) of the Theft Act 1968 required an intent to steal a specific item within the building entered, and the prosecution were unable to prove such an intent. The rulings could be interpreted as a 'burglar's charter', but the Attorney-General was able to refer the point of law to the Court of Appeal which quickly clarified the position — on a charge of burglary with intent to steal, the accused is guilty even if he intended to steal only if he found something in the building worth stealing. Had the Attorney-General not made the reference, the mistaken view of the law expressed by the Crown Court judges might have taken hold, with amending legislation the only way of remedying the situation.

17.7.3 Appeal against verdicts of 'Not guilty by reason of insanity': Criminal Appeal Act 1968, ss. 12 to 14

A person who is found not guilty by reason of insanity may appeal to the Court of Appeal against the verdict. The provisions as to leave to appeal and determination of the appeal parallel those which apply to appeals against conviction. If the appeal is allowed on a ground relating to the finding that the appellant was insane, the Court of Appeal may substitute a verdict of guilty of the offence charged (or guilty of a lesser offence) for the verdict of the jury. The appellant may then be sentenced for the offence. If the appeal is allowed on other grounds (i.e. even in the absence of a finding of insanity, a conviction could not have been sustained), the Court of Appeal replaces the jury's verdict with a straightforward acquittal. It may, however, order that the appellant be admitted to a mental hospital specified by the Home Secretary.

A person who has been found unfit to plead may appeal against the finding: s. 15. If the issue of fitness to plead was determined after arraignment, and the Court of Appeal thinks that before it was determined the appellant should have been acquitted, the court may quash the finding of unfitness and substitute a verdict of acquittal. In other cases where the appeal is allowed, the court makes such orders as are necessary to secure the appellant's attendance at the Crown Court to be tried.

An appellant against conviction may argue that he should have been found unfit to plead or not guilty by reason of insanity instead of being convicted. If the Court of Appeal agrees with him, it quashes the conviction without making a finding of unfitness or insanity, but must nonetheless make an order that the appellant be admitted to a mental hospitl: s. 6.

17.8   APPEALS TO THE HOUSE OF LORDS: CRIMINAL APPEAL ACT 1968, s. 33

Either the prosecution or defence may appeal to the House of Lords from a decision of the Criminal Division of the Court of Appeal, but the appeal is subject to:

(a)   The Court of Appeal certifying that the decision which it is sought to appeal involves a point of law of general public importance, and

(b)   Either the Court of Appeal or the House of Lords giving leave to appeal because it appears to them that the point of law is one which ought to be considered by the House.

An application to the Court of Appeal for leave to appeal to the House of Lords should either be made orally immediately after the court's decision, or it should be made within 14 days of the decision, notice of the application being served on the Registrar in the prescribed form. There is no appeal against a refusal by the Court of Appeal to certify that a point of law of general public importance is involved (*Gelberg v Miller* [1961] 1WLR 459); nor is it the practice of the court to give reasons for such a refusal: *R v Cooper and McMahon* (1975) 61Cr App R 215. If the Court of Appeal is willing to certify that a point of law of general public importance is involved, but nevertheless refuses leave to appeal, an application may be made to the House of Lords within 14 days of the Court of Appeal's refusal. Such applications are referred to an appeal committee consisting of three Lords of Appeal. If leave to appeal is granted, at least three Law Lords must be present for the hearing (s. 35) but it is usual to have five deciding the case. In disposing of the appeal, the House of Lords may exercise any powers of the Court of Appeal or remit the case to it: s. 35(3).

The Court of Appeal may grant an appellant bail pending determination of his appeal to the House of Lords: s. 36. If the prosecution are appealing to the House of Lords against the Court of Appeal's decision to allow an appeal and, but for his successful appeal, the appellant in the Court of Appeal would be liable to be detained in pursuance of a custodial sentence, the Court of Appeal may order that he be detained until the appeal is decided: s. 37. Should the prosecution's appeal succeed and the conviction be reinstated, no problems arise about returning him to prison. Alternatively, the Court of Appeal may order that he be released on bail instead of being released unconditionally, which would, of course, be the normal consequence of his having his conviction quashed.

SEE NOTES ON BACK	**CRIMINAL APPEAL ACT, 1968**	(See R2 Form 2)

COURT OF APPEAL CRIMINAL DIVISION **N**	NOTICE OF APPLICATION FOR LEAVE TO APPEAL AND OF OTHER APPLICATIONS (See Note 7)	To the Registrar, Criminal Appeal Office REF. No. Royal Courts of Justice, Strand, LONDON, W.C.2A 2LL

Write legibly in black   PART 1

Particulars of APPELLANT	FULL NAMES Block letters	FORENAMES THOMAS	SURNAME JONES	Age on Conviction 18
	ADDRESS If detained give address where detained	H.M. BORSTAL at BOXALL HILL	Index number if detained 36415	

COURT where tried and/or Sentenced. (see note 3)	DATES of appearances at the Court including dates of conviction (if convicted at the Court) and sentence. JULY 27th & 28th 1981.	Name of Court GRESHAMSBURY CROWN COURT
		Name of Judge HIS HONOUR JUDGE ALLWORTHY

Particulars of OFFENCES of which convicted. (State whether convicted on indictment or by a magistrates Court) and particulars of SENTENCES and ORDERS.	OFFENCES	Convicted on INDICTMENT or by MAGISTRATES COURT	SENTENCES AND ORDERS
	ROBBERY	1	BORSTAL TRAINING

Offences TAKEN INTO CONSIDERATION when sentenced. NONE	TOTAL SENTENCE BORSTAL TRAINING

PART 2

The appellant is applying for:— (*Delete if inapplicable)

*EXTENSION of time in which to give notice of application for leave to appeal.

*LEAVE to appeal against CONVICTION.   *BAIL.

*LEAVE to appeal against SENTENCE.   see note 8   *LEAVE to be present at hearing.

*LEGAL AID.   *LEAVE to call WITNESSES.

SLOW and BIDEAWHILE Solicitors (Signed) (Appellant)	Date 11.8.1981	Address of person signing on behalf of Appellant. (See Note 6) 10, COURT STREET, GRESHAMSBURY

This notice was handed in by the appellant today. (Signed) (Officer)	Date	**N**	Received in the Criminal Appeal Office. FORMS N.G. Date

E.D.R.

Form 1458 31431—5-5-70 XBD

The contents of a Notice of Application for Leave to Appeal and the drafting of Grounds of Appeal may be illustrated by the case of *R* v *Thomas Jones*. Jones, aged 18, was convicted by a jury following his plea of not guilty to a charge of robbing Deborah Wilkins. The case against him rested upon the evidence of Mrs Wilkins and P.C. Blifil. The former stated in evidence that as she was walking home at around 10.30pm on the night of January 30th 1981 she heard footsteps rapidly approaching her from behind. Then she felt her bag, which she was carrying in her hand, being pulled. She resisted, but was pulled to the ground, and in the process suffered bruising and abrasions but no serious injury. The bag was eventually torn from her grasp. It contained £25 which she had won playing Bingo. Her assailant made off. Although the road she was walking along was dimly lit, the incident happened near to a street lamp, and, during the struggle she obtained a good look at her attacker. She recognised him as a young man who until recently, had worked in the large department store where she was employed. She did not know his name, but when the police checked with the store they discovered that only one person answering to the general description Mrs Wilkins had given of the offender had left their employment in the past six months. That person was Tom Jones. He was arrested, put on an identification parade, and picked out by Mrs Wilkins. He was then interviewed under caution by P.C. Blifil and another officer. According to the police officers, he said — 'I suppose I might as well tell you what happened. I was hard up because I was out of work, and I saw this woman walking all by herself with a bag, just ahead of me. I suppose the temptation was just too much for me. I just grabbed the bag. I didn't mean to hurt her, and I'm sorry now for what I did — just my bad luck to pick on somebody who knew me.'

At the trial, Jones gave evidence in his own defence, and stated that at the time of the offence he was at a bus-stop, about half a mile from the scene of the crime, waiting for a bus to take him home. He had got into conversation with a girl called Sophia, who was also waiting for a bus, but, although he had taken her telephone number at the time with a view to meeting again, he had lost it, and had also forgotten her surname. Therefore, Jones had no witness who could support his alibi. He denied making any admissions to P.C. Blifil. He had said to him that he was hard up, and that he thought he knew the lady who had picked him out on the parade, but he had not said anything about grabbing the bag. He might have said that he was sorry the lady had been hurt. Prosecuting counsel, in cross-examination, asked him whether he was suggesting that P.C. Blifil was deliberately lying. Jones said — 'I don't know, but he's certainly got it all completely wrong.' His Honour Judge Allworthy, trying the case, held that Jones' evidence amounted to an assertion that Blifil was deliberately fabricating his evidence. He therefore allowed Jones to be cross-examined about a previous conviction for assault occasioning actual bodily harm. In his summing up, Judge Allworthy said:

> Members of the jury, you must approach the evidence of Mrs Wilkins with especial care. She picked out this defendant on an identification parade as the person who snatched her bag, but you must bear in mind that mistakes can be made when this type of evidence is given. It is easy for a witness to over-estimate the accuracy of his or her memory and powers of observation. So you must ask youselves — could Mrs Wilkins be making a mistake? Well, it's a matter for you, ladies and gentlemen, but remember that she told you that she had a good look at her attacker, and she recognised him as somebody she happened to know well from her

place of work. Does that help you to decide where the truth lies in this case.?

After the jury convicted, the judge was handed a social enquiry report which recommended that Jones be put on probation, and a report prepared on behalf of the Home Secretary which stated that detention for training would be of no particular value in Jones' case. Jones was sentenced to Borstal training. In passing sentence the judge said:

> You are a young man who already has one conviction for violence. You have attacked and injured a defenceless woman, and stolen her bag. Such offences have been occurring much to frequently of late. Young men like you must learn that it has got to stop. The sentence is one of Borstal training.

A week after Jones' conviction, a Miss Sophia Western contacted his solicitors, stating that she had read a report of the case in the local newspaper, and had realised that she was the girl Jones had been talking to at the bus-stop. She could confirm everything he had said, and remembered that date because it was the day before her birthday. She had been disappointed that Jones had not telephoned her, as he had promised, but now everything was explained.

The perfected Grounds of Appeal in Jones' case might read as follows:

GROUNDS OF APPEAL

The grounds of appeal against conviction are:

1. The learned judge wrongly allowed the appellant to be asked about his conviction for assault occasioning actual bodily harm. The appellant in his evidence did not make any imputations against the character of P.C. Blifil or any other prosecution witnesses. In denying the truth of parts of P.C. Blifil's evidence the appellant did no more than assert his own innocence of the charge, and so was protected by s. 1(f) of the Criminal Evidence Act 1898 against questions tending to show that he had a previous conviction. The appellant will rely upon *R* v *Rouse* [1904] 1KB 184 and *Selvey* v *DPP* [1970] AC 304. The appellant also relies upon the submissions made by defence counsel at the trial (p. 25B-27D).
2. The learned judge erred in failing to prevent cross-examination of the appellant about his said previous conviction on the grounds that its prejudicial effect exceeded its probative value.
3. The learned judge in his summing up misdirected the jury in that:
    (i) He reminded them of certain matters which tended to confirm the correctness of Deborah Wilkins' identification of the appellant as the person who had robbed her, but failed to remind them of other matters which cast doubt upon the identification. In particular, he failed to remind them that the witness saw the person who robbed her at night, in a dimly-lit road, for only a few seconds, at a time when she was frightened and confused (p. 40A-C).
    (ii) He told them that Deborah Wilkins recognised the person who robbed her as 'somebody she happened to know well from her place of work' whereas her evidence was that she did not know the appellant's name, and only knew him by sight (p. 10D and p. 40C).

The appellant will rely upon *R* v *Turnbull* [1977] QB 224.

4. The appellant wishes to call one Sophia Western to give evidence before this Honourable Court that at the time of the offence occurred she was with the appellant at a distance of approximately half a mile from the scene of the offence. The witness did not come forward until after the appellant's conviction. Her name and address could not with reasonable diligence have been discovered by the defence in time for her to be called at the trial.

5. In all the circumstances of the case the appellant's conviction is unsafe and unsatisfactory.

The grounds of appeal against sentence are:

1. The sentence was too severe in all the circumstances of the case.

2. The learned judge failed to give any or any sufficient weight to the recommendation in the social enquiry report on the appellant that he be placed on probation.

3. The learned judge failed to give any or any sufficient weight to the statement in the report on the appellant prepared on behalf of the Home Secretary that detention for training would be of no particular value.

4. In view of the fact that the appellant had only one previous conviction and no convictions for offences of dishonesty, the sentence was too severe.

5. In passing sentence, the learned judge was apparently influenced by the prevalence of offences similar to that of which the appellant had been convicted, rather than by the facts of the appellant's case.

> W. Partridge
> Counsel for the Appellant

18 Appeals from the Magistrates' Courts

A decision by a magistrates' court can be challenged by:

(a) Appeal to the Crown Court, or

(b) Application to the magistrates to state a case for the opinion of the High Court, or

(c) Application to the High Court for judicial review of the magistrates' decision and the issue, as appropriate, of the orders of *certiorari,* mandamus or prohibition.

Appeal to the Crown Court is only by a person convicted. The other two procedures are available to any person aggrieved by a magistrates' court decision, which includes both a convicted accused and an unsuccessful prosecutor. Decisions of the Crown Court, not made in connection with its jurisdiction over trials on indictment, may also be challenged through a case stated for the opinion of the High Court or an application for review. The jurisdiction of the High Court in these matters is exercised by a Divisional Court of the Queen's Bench Division.

18.1 APPEALS TO THE CROWN COURT

Appeals to the Crown Court from a magistrates' court are governed by the Magistrates' Courts Act 1980, ss. 108 to 110, and Rules 6 to 9 of the Crown Court Rules 1971 (SI 1971 No 1292).

18.1.1 The right of appeal

A person convicted by a magistrates' court following a plea of not guilty may appeal to the Crown Court against his conviction and/or his sentence. A person sentenced by the magistrates following a guilty plea may only appeal against his sentence: s. 108(1) of the 1980 Act.

An appeal to the Crown Court against sentence may be brought in respect of any 'order made on conviction by a magistrates' court' other than a probation order, conditional or absolute discharge or order to pay prosecution costs: s. 108(3). Although the making of a probation order or conditional discharge cannot be appealed, a person subsequently sentenced for an offence originally dealt with by probation or discharge may appeal against that subsequent sentence: s. 108(2). An 'order made on conviction' includes a disqualification from driving, an order to pay compensation or a recommendation for deportation. It would probably not include an order to contribute towards the legal aid costs of conducting the defence since such an order can be made even where the legally aided person has been acquitted, and so is not an order made on conviction.

Although a person who genuinely pleaded guilty before the magistrates cannot appeal to the Crown Court against conviction, an appellant may argue that his apparent plea of guilty was not genuine but an equivocal plea. If the argument succeeds, the Crown Court remits the case to the magistrates with a direction that a not guilty plea be entered. A plea is equivocal if something in the proceedings before the magistrates indicates that it should not be accepted at its face value. The clearest example of such a plea arises when, at the time the information is put to him, the accused says 'guilty' but adds words which indicate that he really believes himself not guilty (e.g. charged with assault, he answers 'guilty but I hit him in self-defence'). The magistrates must not proceed to sentence upon such a plea, but must explain to the accused that if he acted in reasonable self-defence he is not guilty of the charge. If he then unequivocally admits his guilt the magistrates may sentence him. Otherwise, the case should proceed as if he had denied the charge, and, if it does not, the Crown Court on appeal will remit the matter to the magistrates with a direction to try it on a not guilty plea.

The Crown Court will also remit a case to the magistrates if, although nothing was said to cast doubt on the correctness of the plea at the moment it was entered, something emerged in the hearing of the case, prior to sentence being passed, which should have alerted them to the fact that the accused did not genuinely admit his guilt. In *R* v *Durham Quarter Sessions* ex parte *Virgo* [1952] 2QB 1, the Divisional Court held that a plea of guilty to theft of a motorcycle was equivocal because when, after the presentation of the facts by the prosecution, the accused was asked if he had anything to say in mitigation (he was not legally represented) he replied that he had taken the cycle by mistake, thinking that it belonged to a friend who had given him permission to use it. Similarly, in *R* v *Blandford Justices* ex parte *G* [1967] 1QB 82, G's admission of guilt when charged in the juvenile court with theft of jewellery from her employer was rendered equivocal by her claiming, in a statement to the police which was read to the magistrates, that she had merely borrowed the jewellery intending to return it. On the other hand, if nothing known to the magistrates when they passed sentence could reasonably have alerted them to the fact that the accused might have a defence to the charge, the Crown Court cannot entertain an appeal against conviction or remit the case to the magistrates, even if the would be appellant now suggests that his guilty plea was entered in error: *R* v *Marylebone Justices* ex parte *Westminster City Council* [1971] 1WLR 567.

The Divisional Court, in *P Foster (Haulage) Ltd* v *Roberts* [1978] 2All ER 751, adopted a slightly different approach to the question of equivocal pleas from that adopted in the cases discussed above. They drew a distinction between a plea which was equivocal at the time it was made, and one which was only put in doubt at a later state of the proceedings (e.g. the pleas in ex parte *Virgo* and ex parte *G*). In the former case, the magistrates were simply not entitled to accept the plea as it stood. In the latter case, they had a discretion to allow the accused to withdraw his plea of guilty, but were not obliged to exercise that discretion in his favour. Unless they failed to consider exercising their discretion, or had exercised it wrongly, the Crown Court would have no power to remit the case to them for reconsideration. In *Foster (Haulage) Ltd* v *Roberts* the magistrates did in effect consider allowing a change of plea, and reasonably decided not to do so. Therefore, the Crown Court had been right in not remitting the case. Applying the reasoning in *Foster Haulage Ltd* v *Roberts* to ex parte *Virgo,* the magistrates in that case erred through failing even to consider proposing to the accused a change of plea.

If the Crown Court does remit to the magistrates with a direction to try on a not guilty plea the case of an appellant whose plea it considers was equivocal, the magistrates are not obliged to comply with the direction. They can hold that, notwithstanding the Crown Court's view, the original plea was a valid one so their jurisdiction in the matter is at an end: *R* v *Camberwell Green Justices* ex parte *Sloper* [1979] Crim LR 264. The unseemly conflict between the two courts can then only be resolved by an application to the Divisional Court for an order of mandamus to compel the magistrates to hear the case (see 18.3.1).

The Crown Court's limited power to remit cases in which an appellant pleaded guilty before and was sentenced by magistrates should be contrasted with its powers in relation to an offender who appears before it on a committal for sentence after a guilty plea in the lower court. In the latter type of case, the Crown Court can remit to the magistrates whether or not the plea was equivocal if it considers that the offender really should have pleaded not guilty: *S (an infant)* v *Manchester City Recorder* [1971] AC 481. When the case again comes before the magistrates, they must allow the change of plea and try the case; ex parte *Sloper* supra.

18.1.2 Procedure on appeal

Notice of appeal must be given in writing to the clerk of the relevant magistrates' court and to the prosecutor within 21 days of sentence being passed: Crown Court Rules 1971, r. 7. The appellant has 21 days from the date of sentence even if that is after the date of conviction and he is only appealing against conviction. No particular form is prescribed for the notice but it must state whether the appeal is against conviction or sentence or both. The grounds of appeal need not be given, although the appellant may choose to state in very general terms why he considers the magistrates' decision was wrong. The Crown Court may give leave to appeal out of time. If notice of appeal is given by an appellant upon whom the magistrates have passed an immediate custodial sentence, they may bail him to appear at the Crown Court at the time fixed for the hearing of the appeal: Magistrates' Courts Act 1980, s. 113(1). If the magistrates refuse to grant bail, application may be made to the Crown Court under the Courts Act 1971, s. 13(4), or to a High Court judge in chambers. Bail pending the appeal is particularly important because any custodial sentence imposed by a magistrates' court is necessarily short, so if not granted bail the appellant may have served much of his sentence by the time the appeal is heard.

An appeal is normally listed for hearing by a court presided over by a circuit judge or recorder (Lord Chief Justice's Practice Directions 1972 56Cr App R 52), who should sit with two magistrates: Courts Act 1971 s. 5. It takes the form of a rehearing of the case. If the appeal is against conviction, counsel for the Crown makes an opening speech and calls his evidence, the appellant may submit that there is no case to answer, and, if that submission is rejected, may give evidence himself and/or call other witnesses. The parties are not limited to the evidence which they called at the magistrates' court, but, if evidence has become available to them since the earlier hearing, they may call it before the Crown Court. However, the Crown Court on appeal has no power to amend the information on which the appellant was convicted by the magistrates: *Garfield* v *Maddocks* [1974] QB 7. After a closing speech on behalf of the appellant the court announces it decision. Where the appeal is against sentence, the procedure is again just as it was in the magistrates' court with the facts of the offence being summarised, the antecedents given, and mitigation presented.

18.1.3 Powers of the Crown Court

The powers of the Crown Court in disposing of an appeal are extensive. It may confirm, reverse or vary the decision appealed against, it may remit the matter to the magistrates with its opinion thereon (e.g. where it considers the plea to be equivocal), or it may make such other order in the matter as it thinks just (e.g. in the case of a successful appeal, an order that the costs of the defence in the magistrates' court be paid by the prosecution or out of central funds: Courts Act 1971, s. 9). Varying the decision appealed against includes increasing the sentence imposed by the magistrates, even in a case where the appeal is only against conviction, but the Crown Court sentence must not exceed that which the magistrates could have passed: s. 9(4). In fact, it is unusual for the Crown Court to increase sentence, but the reason it, unlike the Court of Appeal on appeals from the Crown Court, has retained the power to do so may be that leave is never required for appeals to the Crown Court unless they are out of time. The possibility of an increase in sentence may therefore inhibit unmeritorious appeals. Another way of dealing with time wasting appeals is to order the appellant, upon dismissal of the appeal, to pay costs to the Crown. As between the parties to an appeal, the Crown Court may 'make such order for costs as it thinks just': Crown Court Rules 1971, r. 10. It may also, if the appeal arose out of a conviction or sentence for an indictable offence, order that the prosecution costs be paid out of central funds. If an appeal against conviction for an indictable offence succeeds, the defence may be awarded costs out of central funds: Costs in Criminal Cases Act 1973, s. 3(2).

> The appellant may abandon his appeal by giving notice in writing to that effect to the clerk of the magistrates' court and to the prosecution: Crown Court Rules 1971, r. 9. A copy of the notice should also be sent to the appropriate officer of the Crown Court. The notice should be given at least three days before the hearing of the appeal. If notice to abandon an appeal is duly given, the magistrates may order the appellant to pay costs in respect of expenses properly incurred by the prosecutor before he received the notice: Magistrates' Courts Act 1980, s. 109.

18.2 APPEALS TO THE DIVISIONAL COURT BY CASE STATED

An appeal by way of case stated is an appeal on a point or points of law, which are identified in a document (the case) drawn up by the clerk of the magistrates' court in conjunction with the magistrates whose decision is being questioned. The appeal is to the High Court which exercises its jurisdiction through a Divisional Court of the Queen's Bench Division. One can refer, therefore, either to an appeal to the High Court or to an appeal to the Divisional Court.

Appeals by case stated are governed by the Magistrates' Courts Act 1980, s. 111, Rules 76 to 81 of the Magistrates' Courts Rules 1981 (SI 1981 No 552), and Order 56 of the Rules of the Supreme Court 1965.

18.2.1 The right of appeal

Any party to proceedings before a magistrates' court, or any person aggrieved by a 'conviction, order, determination or other proceeding of the court', may challenge the court's decision on the grounds that it is wrong in law or in excess of jurisdiction: s. 111(1) of the 1980 Act. He does so by applying to the magistrates who formed the court to state a case for the opinion of the High Court on the question of law or jurisdiction said to be wrongly decided. Magistrates' decisions in both civil and criminal cases may be appealed by case stated. The main points to note about the availability of the procedure in criminal matters are:

(a)   Both the prosecution and defence can appeal. This means that an acquittal by a magistrates' court, unlike an acquittal on indictment, is not necessarily final. The prosecution can appeal under s. 111, and, if they are successful, the Divisional Court remits the case to the magistrates with a direction to convict and proceed to sentence.

(b)   The appeal may only be on one or other or both of the two grounds mentioned in s. 111. In other words, the appellant must contend either that the magistrates acted in excess of jurisdiction (e.g. purported to try a case which was only triable on indictment) or made an error of law (e.g. received inadmissible evidence or misunderstood the elements of the offence charged). Generally speaking, the magistrates' decision as to where the truth lies on a disputed issue of fact cannot be appealed by case stated, although the defence may, of course, appeal to the Crown Court. The exception to the above rule is that where magistrates make a finding of fact which is unsupported by any evidence or which could not, on the evidence, have been made by any reasonable bench of magistrates, they err in law, and so an appeal to the High Court lies: *Bracegirdle* v *Oxley* [1947] KB 349.

(c)   Since there is greater scope for errors of law when trying a case following a not guilty plea than when sentencing an offender, appeals by case stated are likely to aim at setting aside a summary acquittal or conviction. However, a sentence which is in excess of jurisdiction (e.g. seven months imprisonment for one offence) or wrong in law (e.g. an 18 year old given a total of 12 months imprisonment for two indictable offences) could be appealed under s. 111. Further, a sentence which is so harsh and oppressive that no reasonable court could have passed it without misdirecting itself is also wrong in law or in excess of jurisdiction, and can therefore be appealed by case stated, even though it is within the statutory maximum for the relevant offence; *R* v *St. Albans Crown Court* ex parte *Cinnamond* [1981] 2WLR 681. In ex parte Cinnamond the remedy sought by and granted to C was *certiorari* (see Para. 18.3.1). However, Donaldson LJ at p. 684 stated — 'I treat this application as if it could equally well have come before the court· by case stated'. Therefore, the case, apparently the first of its kind, is authority for holding that in the circumstances described an offender may challenge his sentence either through an appeal by case stated or by an application for *certiorari*. If the sentence is merely severe or even surprisingly severe, but not harsh and oppressive, case stated is not appropriate, although the offender may, of course, appeal to the Crown Court.

(d)   Section 111 presupposes that the proceedings before the magistrates which are the subject of appeal have resulted in a final determination of the case by the court — i.e. an acquittal, conviction or sentence: see *Atkinson* v *U.S.A. Government* [1971] AC 197. Since committal for trial is only a preliminary step in the proceedings against an accused, a decision to commit cannot be challenged by case stated: *Dewing* v *Cummings* [1972] Crim LR 38. Similarly, if magistrates in the course of a trial admit evidence which one of the parties considers to be inadmissible he cannot at that stage apply to them to state a case, although if the final decision goes against him he could appeal then on the basis that the court had erred in law by admitting inadmissible evidence. By parity of reasoning with *Dewing* v *Cummings* (supra), a decision to commit for sentence may not be appealed by way of case stated. However, the conviction which preceded the committal may, of course, be the subject of appeal, and, if that appeal succeeds, the committal is nullified.

18.2.2 Procedure on appeal

An application for the magistrates to state a case must be made within 21 days of acquittal or conviction, or, if the magistrates convicted an accused and ajourned before sentencing him, within 21 days of sentence: s. 111 (2) and (3) of the 1980 Act. The application, which must be in writing, should identify the question of law or jurisdiction on which the High Court's opinion is sought: Magistrates' Courts Rules 1981, r. 76. If it is suggested that there was no evidence on which the magistrates could reasonably have come to a particular finding of fact, the fact in question should be specified. The application is sent to the clerk of the relevant magistrates' court. Where the magistrates consider that an application to state a case is frivolous they may refuse to comply with the application, but must give the applicant a certificate stating that his application has been refused: s. 111(5). The applicant may then apply to the Divisional Court for an order of mandamus compelling the magistrates to state a case.

A statement of case should set out the facts as found by the magistrates, but not the evidence which led them to those findings of fact. The only exception to the rule arises when the appellant contends that there was no evidence on which the magistrates could reasonably have reached a finding of fact, in which case a short statement of the relevant evidence must be included. The case also sets out the charge or charges heard by the magistrates, the contentions of the parties on the questions of law or jurisdiction raised, any authorities cited, the magistrates' decision, and the question for the High Court. The clerk to the magistrates is principally responsible for drafting the case. He consults with the magistrates, and takes into account any representations by the parties. After any necessary alterations have been made to the case as initially drafted by the clerk, it is signed by at least two of the magistrates whose decision is being appealed, or by the clerk on their behalf. It is then sent to the appellant or his solicitor (Magistrates' Courts Rules 1981, r. 78), who, within ten days of receiving it, must lodge it in (i.e. deliver it to) the Crown Office at the Royal Courts of Justice: Rules of the Supreme Court 1965, Ord. 56 r. 6. Unless time for lodging the case is extended by the Divisional Court, failure to lodge it within the ten days will lead to the appeal being struck out. The appellant must also serve on the respondent to the appeal a notice of entry of the appeal and a copy of the case. This is done within four days of the case being lodged. The appeal is not normally heard until at least eight clear days after the service of the notice.

Where magistrates have passed on an appellant an immediate custodial sentence, they may grant him bail pending the hearing of his appeal: Magistrates' Courts Act 1980, s. 113. The terms of bail are that, unless the appeal succeeds, he must appear at the magistrates' court within ten days of the Divisional Court's judgement being given, the precise date being fixed by the magistrates after the appeal. If the magistrates refuse bail, an application for bail may be made to a High Court judge in chambers.

An example of a case stated is shown overleaf. Below are more details of the rather elaborate procedure for drawing up a case.

> After an application for the magistrates to state a case has been received, the clerk immediately prepares a draft case. If necessary he consults with the magistrates and he can also discuss the application informally with either or both the parties so as to elucidate the

Case stated (M.C. Act 1980, s. 111; M.C. Rules 1981, rr. 78, 81)

In the High Court of Justice
Queen's Bench Division

Between   Mohammed KHAN   Appellant
                 and
                 Peter CONSTABLE   Respondent

Case stated by the justices for the county of Loamshire, acting in and for the
Petty Sessional Division of Loamtown in respect of their adjudication as a
Magistrates' Court sitting at 1, High Street, Loamtown.

CASE

1. On the 27th day of July 1981 an information was preferred by the
Respondent against the Appellant that he on the 13th day of July 1981 had with
him in a public place namely Clay Road, Loamtown, an offensive weapon,
namely a knuckleduster, without lawful authority or reasonable excuse, contrary
to s. 1(1) of the Prevention of Crime Act 1953.

2. We heard the information on the 10th day of September 1981. The
appellant elected summary trial, and we found the following facts proved:

(a) On the 13th day of of July 1981 the Respondent, who is a police officer,
observed the Appellant and a white youth fighting in Clay Road, Loamtown. The
appellant is a Pakistani aged 19. The white youth ran away, but the Respondent
was able to arrest the Appellant for conduct likely to occasion a breach of the
peace. The Respondent searched the Appellant, and found in his trouser pocket a
knuckleduster. The knuckleduster was made for use for causing injury to the
person.

(b) Clay Road, Loamtown is a public highway to which the public have
access at all times.

(c) During a period of roughly a month before the 13th day of July 1981 three
Pakistani youths walking at night in the Clay Road area of Loamtown had, in
separate incidents, been assaulted by white youths referred to as 'skinheads'. The
last attack occurred on the 3rd day of July 1981. The Appellant had never himself
been assaulted prior to July 13th. He claimed that the white youth he was fighting
when seen by the Respondent attacked him without cause. We made no finding
on the point as the information we were trying did not directly concern the said
fight.

(d) On Mondays and Wednesdays the Appellant attended evening classes
which finished at approximately 10.00pm. His journey home necessitated his
walking through the Clay Road area. After the first attack on a Pakistani youth
he began to carry on the evenings when he attended evening classes the

knuckleduster which the Respondent found in his possession. His reason for doing so was to protect himself should be be attacked, but he did not in fact use it during the fight on July 13th.

3. It was contended by the Appellant that he had a reasonable excuse for having the knuckleduster with him because, as a result of the attacks on Pakistani youths which had taken place, he was in immediate fear of attack on the occasions when he walked through the Clay Road area.

4. It was contended by the Respondent that the permanent carrying of weapons is prohibited by the Prevention of Crime Act 1953, and that, in the absence of any very recent attack upon the Appellant personally, he had no reasonable excuse for having a knuckleduster. Recent attacks upon persons belonging to the ethnic group to which the Appellant belongs could not be a reasonable excuse for the Appellant carrying an offensive weapon.

5. We were referred to the following cases —

Evan v *Hughes* [1972] 3 All ER 412

R v *Peacock* [1973] Crim. LR 639

Bradley v *Moss* [1974] Crim LR 430

Pittard v *Mahoney* [1977] Crim LR 169

6. We were of the opinion that the Appellant had the burden of proving that he had a reasonable excuse for having the knuckleduster with him in a public place. This he failed to do because he had never himself been attacked or put in fear of attack, and furthermore ten days had elapsed since the last attack on a Pakistani youth in the Clay Road area. Accordingly we convicted the appellant and conditionally discharged him for 12 months.

QUESTION

7. The question for the opinion of the High Court is whether we were right in holding, as a point of law, that the Appellant's explanation for carrying the knuckleduster could not be a reasonable excuse within the meaning of s. 1(1) of the Prevention of Crime Act 1953. If we were incorrect in so holding the Court is respectfully requested to reverse or amend our decision or remit the matter to us with the opinion of the Court thereon.

Dated the 1st day of December 1981

J. Smith

R. Brown

Justices of the Peace for Loamshire on behalf of all the Justices adjudicating.

issues. Occasionally, the appellant himself might be allowed to prepare the draft, or, if the hearing was before a stipendiary magistrate, he might wish to undertake the task. Within 21 days of receiving the application, the clerk sends the draft case to the appellant and respondent or their respective solicitors. They then have 21 days from when they receive the draft case to make representations about it, pointing out any apparent inaccuracies or suggesting improvements. In the light of any representations received the magistrates and clerk agree upon the final form of the case, which is then signed. This must be done within 21 days of the last day on which representations about the draft case could have been made. The signed case is sent forthwith to the appellant or his solicitor. The above procedure is set out in Rules 77 and 78 of the Magistrates' Courts Rules 1981.

The time limits mentioned in Rules 77 and 78 can all be extended where necessary, but the 21 day period within which the initial application to the magistrates to state a case must be made is prescribed by statute, and cannot be varied even by the High Court: *Michael* v *Gowland* [1977] 1WLR 296. Where an application is made within time but it does not comply with r. 76 in that it fails to identify the question of law or jurisdiction on which the High Court's opinion is sought, the Divisional Court will still accept jurisdiction if the defect is subsequently remedied, even if that is done out of time (see *Parsons* v *F W Woolworth and Co Ltd* [1980] 1WLR 1472 and *R* v *Croydon Justices* ex parte *Lefore Holdings* [1980] 1WLR 1465 where, by slightly different reasoning, differently constituted Divisional Courts arrived at substantially the same conclusions).

18.2.3   Hearing of the appeal

The appeal is heard by a Divisional Court of the Queen's Bench Division. The court consists of at least two judges of the Division, but often three judges sit, including the Lord Chief Justice. If a two judge court is equally divided, the opinion of the judge agreeing with the court below prevails and the appeal therefore fails: per Scrutton LJ at p. 107 in *Flannagan* v *Shaw* [1920] 3KB 96. No evidence is called before the court. The appeal takes the form of legal argument for the appellant and respondent, based solely upon the facts stated in the case. If those facts give rise to a point of law not taken before the magistrates which might, if it had been taken, have provided the appellant with a good defence to the charge against him, the Divisional Court will consider the point, so long as it does not depend upon any further findings of fact: *Whitehead* v *Haines* [1965] 1QB 200. In disposing of the appeal, the Divisional Court can 'reverse, affirm or amend' the magistrates' decision, or remit the matter to the magistrates with its opinion thereon, or make any other order it thinks fit in respect of the matter, including an order as to costs: Summary Jurisdiction Act 1857, s. 6. The powers of the Divisional Court thus include both substituting for an appellant's conviction an acquittal, and, where the prosecution appeal following an acquittal, remitting the case to the magistrates with a direction that they convict and proceed to sentence. Alternatively, if the magistrates have acquitted on a ground that is wrong in law but the respondent might have a defence on some other groud, the case could be remitted with a direction for a rehearing (or, if a submission of no case to answer was upheld, a direction that the magistrates continue the original hearing). Costs may be awarded to either party out of central funds: Costs in Criminal Cases Act 1973, s. 5. There is also power to order the unsuccessful party to pay his opponent's costs. The costs awarded may cover both the costs of the appeal and the costs incurred in the proceedings before the magistrates.

18.2.4   Appeal by case stated from the Crown Court

Appeal by way of case stated may be used not only to question the decisions of magistrates, but also to question the Crown Court's decisions in matters not relating to trial on indictment: Courts Act 1971, s. 10. When disposing of an appeal, the Crown Court is exercising a jurisdiction which is in no way connected with trial on indictment. It follows, therefore, that after an appeal to the Crown Court against conviction or sentence by the magistrates, either party to the appeal may apply to the Crown Court to state a case for the opinion of the High Court. If the appeal to the Crown Court succeeds the prosecution (i.e. the respondents to the Crown Court appeal) can seek to have the conviction reinstated; if it fails, the appellant may hope for better fortune in the Divisional Court. As with appeals by case stated direct from a magistrates' court, the Crown Court's decision may only by challenged on the grounds that it was wrong in law or in excess of jurisdiction.

An application to the Crown Court to state a case should be made to the appropriate officer of the court within 14 days of the decision challenged being made: Crown Court Rules 1971, r. 21. Like the magistrates, the Crown Court may refuse to state a case if the application is considered frivolous. Unlike the magistrates, it may extend the time for making the application. It can also require an appellant to enter into a recognisance to prosecute the appeal without delay. The form in which the case should be drafted is not prescribed by the Crown Court Rules, but normally it will correspond in contents and lay out to a magistrates' court case. On receiving the case, the appellant should lodge it in the Crown Office, together with copies of the judgements or orders made in both the Crown Court and the magistrates' court: Rules of the Supreme Court Ord. 56 r. 1. The appeal should normally be entered for hearing within six months of the Crown Court decision. Pending hearing of the appeal, the appellant may be granted bail by either the Crown Court or a High Court judge in chambers: Courts Act 1971, s. 13(4), and Criminal Justice Act 1948, s. 37. On disposing of the appeal, the Divisional Court's powers are identical to those it possesses in disposing of an appeal from the magistrates.

Upon an application being made to magistrates to state a case for the opinion of the High Court, the applicant loses any right he had to appeal to the Crown Court: Magistrates' Courts Act 1980, s. 111(4). Therefore, if a person convicted by magistrates is dissatisfied both with the view of the facts they apparently took, and with their ruling on any question of law which arose, he is well advised to appeal to the Crown Court against conviction and refrain from asking the magistrates to state a case. At the rehearing in the Crown Court, the evidence is again called, and all questions of both fact and law may be fully ventilated. If the appeal fails, the appellant still has the right to ask the Crown Court to state a case for the High Court's opinion on the question of law. Had he appealed on the law direct from the magistrates' court to the Divisional Court, he would have lost the chance of having the evidence reheard in the Crown Court.

18.3 APPLICATION FOR JUDICIAL REVIEW

One of the High Court's tasks is to supervise the work of inferior tribunals. The principal way in which it does this is through issuing one or more of the three prerogative orders — namely, *certiorari,* mandamus and prohibition. An order of *certiorari* quashes a decision of an inferior tribunal, mandamus compels an inferior tribunal to carry out its duties, and prohibition prevents an inferior tribunal acting unlawfully or in excess of jurisdiction.

The prerogative orders are only issued upon an application being made to the High Court for judicial review of the inferior tribunal's decision. In the field of administrative law, judicial review is of great importance, being used to control the way in which a wide variety of tribunals and other persons under a duty to act judicially exercise their powers. It is also available in respect of decisions by magistrates (whether those decisions were made in the exercise of their civil or criminal jurisdiction), and in respect of decisions by the Crown Court when it is not exercising its jurisdiction in matters relating to trial on indictment: Courts Act 1971, s. 10(5). It is a useful supplement to appeal by case stated in that a person aggrieved by a decision of a magistrates' court or by a decision of the Crown Court on an appeal from the magistrates may sometimes be able to obtain judicial review when he could not have asked the magistrates or the Crown Court to state a case.

An applicant for judicial review must have a sufficient interest in questioning the decision which it is sought to review. Whatever may be the precise meaning of 'sufficient interest' — and the concept has caused considerable difficulty in cases where the High Court has been asked to review the decision of an inferior tribunal in a civil matter — it is clear that the prosecution and defence each have a sufficient interest to apply for judicial review both of a magistrates' court's decision in a criminal case and of a Crown Court decision upon appeal from the magistrates. The application is made to a Divisional Court of the Queen's Bench Division. The procedure is governed by Order 53 of the Rules of the Supreme Court 1965 (as amended).

18.3.1 Scope of the orders

The effect of *certiorari* is to quash the inferior tribunal's decision, leaving the parties free to take fresh proceedings in the inferior tribunal in respect of the same matter. Thus, in *R v Kent Justices* ex parte *Machin* [1952] 2QB 355 (see Para. 12.2.1), where M successfully applied for *certiorari* to quash his convictions by the magistrates, the Divisional Court acknowledged that the order could not prevent his being tried again on the same charges. Lord Goddard CJ hoped that that would not happen, as M had already spent a considerable time in custody awaiting the outcome of the application, but the decision was in the hands of the prosecution, not of the court. The powers of the Divisional Court upon an appeal by way of case stated are wider in that the court may not only set aside a conviction by the magistrates but substitute for it an acquittal.

An order of *certiorari* is issued (or '*certiorari* will go' as it is often expressed in the judgements) in three main situations.

First, the order is made when the inferior tribunal acts in excess of jurisdiction. Ex parte *Machin* (supra) provides an example. The magistrates tried M for offences triable either way without first explaining to him the possibility of being committed to Quarter Sessions for sentence. Since the procedure set out in the relevant statute, which alone could give them jurisdiction to try an indictable offence, had not been followed, the magistrates acted in excess of their powers in trying M, and accordingly *certiorari* issued to quash his convictions. Similarly, in *R v Gateshead Justices* ex parte *Tesco Stores Ltd* [1981] 2WLR 419, Tesco's conviction for an offence under the Food and Drugs Act 1955 was quashed because no information alleging the offence had been validly laid within six months of its commission. The magistrates therefore had no jurisdiction to try the offence (see Magistrates' Courts Act 1980, s. 127 and Para. 11.3). A sentence passed by magistrates may also be in excess of jurisdiction. In *R v Llandrindod Wells Justices* ex parte *Gibson* [1968] 1 WLR 598 for example, G's disqualification from driving was quashed because, having pleaded guilty by post, he was disqualified in his absence without the magistrates first adjourning and notifying him of the reason for the adjournment. In those circumstances, the court had no power to disqualify him (see s. 11(4) of the 1980 Act and Para. 11.4.3). In *R v St. Albans Crown Court* ex parte *Cinnamond* [1981] 2 WLR 681 the concept of a sentence in excess of jurisdiction was extended to cover a sentence which was harsh and oppressive (see Para. 18.2.1). In cases such as ex parte *Cinnamond* where the Divisional Court does not quash an applicant's conviction, it may reduce without completely quashing the sentence imposed by the court below: Administration of Justice Act 1960, s. 16. Thus, in ex parte *Cinnamond* the court halved the sentence of 18 months disqualification from driving which the Crown Court, on an appeal from the magistrates, had passed for an offence of careless driving.

Secondly, *certiorari* will go where the inferior tribunal acted in breach of the rules of natural justice. The modern approach to alleged breaches of the rules of natural justice is to state, simply but vaguely, that a tribunal must act fairly having regard to the nature of the inquiry on which it is engaged. Traditionally, the rules of natural justice have been defined with a little more precision, and are said to involve two main principles — no man may be a judge in his own cause, and the tribunal must hear both sides of the case. Breaches of both so called rules have led to convictions by magistrates being quashed through the issue of *certiorari*. Numerous cases have concerned alleged breaches of the first rule through a magistrate or a clerk taking part in a case when he has a pecuniary interest in its outcome, or a non-pecuniary interest which is such as to give rise to a real likelihood of bias (see Para. 11.2). The second rule may be invoked where procedural irregularities have occurred which possibly prejudiced the applicant. Failure to give the accused reasonable time to prepare his defence (*R v Thames Magistrates' Court* ex parte *Polemis* [1974] 1 WLR 1371), announcing a verdict of guilty before hearing a closing speech by counsel on behalf of the accused (*R v Marylebone Justices* ex parte *Farrag* [1981] Crim LR 182), and not notifying the defence of witnesses who could support their case (*R v Leyland Justices* ex parte *Hawthorn* [1979] QB 283) have all been held to be breaches of the rules of natural justice. The last case is particularly interesting because *certiorari* issued even though the responsibility for not giving the defence the necessary information lay with the police not the court.

The third situation in which *certiorari* will be granted is where there is an error of law apparent on the face of the record of the inferior tribunal's proceedings — i.e. just by reading the record, and without receiving evidence on affidavit or otherwise as to what occurred in the court below, the Divisional Court can tell that a mistake has been made. Historically, *certiorari* was developed to correct such patent errors, the effect of the order (or writ as it then was) being to remove the record into the King's Bench where it would be rectified. Today, appeal by way of case stated provides a remedy for errors of law much broader in scope than the remedy provided by *certiorari*. The problem in relying on *certiorari* when one wishes to have a magistrates' court decision quashed is that magistrates never give written reasons for their decisions, and such oral reasons as they may choose to give are usually of the briefest.

If the magistrates do give oral reasons, it has been held that they may be incorporated into the record of the court's proceedings (*R* v *Chertsey Justices* ex parte *Franks* [1961] 2QB 152), but in the absence of such reasons the record will consist only of the charges against the accused, his pleas, the verdict and the sentence passed. The only errors likely to be revealed by such basic information are jurisdictional errors such as those already discussed (e.g. passing a sentence in excess of the statutory maximum for the offence of which, according to the record, the accused was convicted). One device by which the record can be augmented is illustrated by the case of *R* v *Southampton Justices* ex parte *Green* [1976] QB 11. G applied to the Divisional Court to quash a decision by magistrates that she should forfeit the sum of £3,000, that being the amount in which she had stood surety for her husband who had 'jumped bail'. The record of the magistrates' court proceedings simply showed that they had made the order complained of. Since that order was undoubtedly within their powers, no error appeared, and the application for *certiorari* failed. G appealed to the Court of Appeal against the Divisional Court's decision. The Court of Appeal had before it affidavits sworn by the chairman of the magistrates and the clerk. They showed that the bench had approached its decision on whether to estreat the recognizance on a basis which was wrong in law. The affidavits were treated as part of the record (see Browne LJ's judgement at p. 22), and therefore an error appeared on the face of the record, which enabled the Court of Appeal to issue *certiorari*. However, there is no obligation on magistrates to make affidavits explaining the reasoning behind their decisions, and, if they do not, the problem remains that any errors of law they may have made are unlikely to be patent on the face of the record.

The function of the orders of mandamus and prohibition is implicit in their names. Mandamus may be used to compel an inferior tribunal to adjudicate upon a case which is within its jurisdiction (e.g. *R* v *Brown* (1857) E& B 757 where the order was issued against magistrates who had refused to hear an information on the clearly inadequate ground that in their view other persons, in addition to the accused, should have been charged with the offence). Mandamus is also appropriate where magistrates fail to consider properly whether to exercise a power which they possess. Thus, in *R* v *Highgate Justices* ex parte *Lewis* [1977] Crim LR 611, L applied for an order to require the magistrates to grant him legal aid. On the facts, the application failed, but had L been able to show that, in turning down his legal aid application, the magistrates had approached the matter improperly or erred in principle, mandamus could have been granted. The order would not have forced the magistrates to grant legal aid, but it would have forced them to reconsider L's application, this time applying the correct principles. The actual decision in ex parte *Lewis,* refusing to issue mandamus, shows the limited value of the order. Where an inferior tribunal fails to exercise a discretionary power, the person aggrieved by that failure can only obtain mandamus if either the inferior tribunal did not even consider exercising the power or it considered the question on wrong principles. Similarly, although mandamus may compel an inferior tribunal to hear a case, it is not a means of controlling the way the case is conducted. In *R* v *Wells Street Stipendiary Magistrate* ex parte *Seillon* [1978] Crim LR 360, for example, the Divisional Court refused to grant an order which would have forced the magistrate, who was conducting committal proceedings, to allow a line of cross examination which she considered to be inadmissible. Essentially, mandamus is a remedy appropriate where the inferior tribunal fails to exercise its jurisdiction, but not where it exercises that jurisdiction wrongly.

The order of prohibition is the reverse of mandamus. It prevents an inferior tribunal acting or continuing to act in excess of its jurisdiction. One recent example of the issue of the order is provided by *R* v *Hatfield Justices* ex parte *Castle* [1981] 1 WLR 217 (see Para. 12.5). In that case, magistrates decided to hold committal proceedings in respect of a charge of criminal damage, even though the value involved was only £23. They adjourned before commencing the committal, and during the adjournment the prosecution applied for prohibition. The application was successful. The value of the damage was well under £200, the charge was not, on a true construction of the phrase, one of a series of the same or a similar character, and therefore the magistrates did not have jurisdiction to hold committal proceedings. Prohibition was therefore appropriate.

18.3.2 Procedure for an application

The procedure for applying for judicial review is contained in Order 53 of the Rules of the Supreme Court 1965. The procedure falls into two main stages — namely, an application for leave to apply for review and, if leave is granted, the application itself. The steps to be taken are as follows:

(a) Notice of application is given by filing in the Crown Office a statement setting out the applicant's name and description, the relief sought and the grounds upon which it is sought, the name and address of the applicant's solicitors, and his address for service. An affidavit verifying the facts contained in the statement must also be filed. The applicant is not limited to asking for just one of the prerogative orders, but can ask for two or more of them cumulatively or in the alternative (e.g. he might seek *certiorari* to quash proceedings in excess of jurisdiction which have already taken place and prohibition to prevent any resumption of them, or he might seek *certiorari* to quash a refusal to make an order in his favour and mandamus to compel reconsideration of the matter applying the correct principles). Notice of application should normally be given within three months of the grounds for the application arising.

(b) The application for leave to apply is made ex parte (i.e. without notice being given to the other interested parties who therefore do not attend court). It is made to a High Court judge who may determine it without a hearing unless a request for one is made by the applicant. If a hearing is requested, it need not take place in open court. If there is no hearing the judge considers the applicant's statement and supporting affidavit privately, and decides whether they establish a *prima facie* case for judicial review which should go before the Divisional Court. This system for determining applications for leave to apply for review only came into operation in January 1981, so it is too early to say what proportion of applicants insist upon a hearing.

(c) A copy of the judge's order is sent from the Crown Office to the applicant. If leave to apply is refused, the applicant may renew his application before a Divisional Court of the Queen's Bench Division. In order to do so he must, within ten days of being served with notice of the judge's refusal, lodge in the Crown Office a notice of intention to renew the application. The application may be renewed whether or not the judge's refusal followed a hearing.

(d) If leave to apply is granted, the application itself is made by originating motion to a Divisional Court of the Queen's Bench Division. Notice of motion, together with a copy of the statement the applicant filed in the Crown Office, must be served on all persons who will be directly affected by the court's decision. In the context of applications arising out of criminal matters, this simply means that where the prosecution are applying for review they must serve notice on the defence and vice versa. Notice must also be served on the clerk of the court below.

(e) Evidence at the hearing before the Divisional Court, whether it be for the applicant or the respondent, is normally in the form of affidavits. Evidence might be required to show for example that a member of the court below was biased or that, through not complying with the proper procedure, the court below was acting in excess of jurisdiction. A party proposing to use an affidavit must, on demand, supply a copy to any other party. Any party may apply by summons to a master for an order that the maker of an affidavit attend at the hearing for cross examination, or for orders for discovery or interrogatories. Such orders are more likely to be of value where the application for review arises out of civil proceedings than when it arises from a criminal matter.

(f) The Divisional Court hears argument for the applicant. Unless given leave to amend, he is limited to seeking the relief mentioned in his statement. The grounds he relies upon should also be those foreshadowed in the statement. In opposition to the application, the court hears any person who appears to it to be a proper person to be heard. At an application relating to a criminal matter, the only persons likely to wish to be heard are the prosecutor and the accused and, perhaps, the magistrates or judge in the court below.

(g) The court reaches its decision. If *certiorari* is granted, it may also order that the case be retried, applying the law as it has stated it to be. The issue of any of the prerogative orders is a discretionary matter, so that an order which is *prima facie* justified may be refused if for example the applicant has more convenient remedies at his disposal. Furthermore, the court, in the exercise of its discretion, is unlikely to grant *certiorari* to quash a conviction if the applicant pleaded guilty in the magistrates' court: (*R v Burnham Bucks Justices* ex parte *Ansorge* [1959] 1WLR 1043, but compare ex parte *Machin* — see Para. 18.3.1 — where *certiorari* issued despite M's guilty plea because the magistrates had acted in excess of jurisdiction). Costs may be awarded either against the unsuccessful party or out of central funds: Costs in Criminal Cases Act 1973, s. 5.

Bail pending the hearing of an application for judicial review may be granted by a judge in chambers or, if the application is in respect of one of its decisions, by the Crown Court. Magistrates do not have power to grant bail to a person who is challenging their decision by judicial review, although they do have power to bail somebody who is appealing against their decision by way of case stated (see Para. 18.2.2).

18.3.3   A comparison of judicial review and appeal by case stated

The functions of mandamus and prohibition on the one hand, and appeal by case stated on the other are quite distinct. The appellant by case stated argues that the magistrates have made a mistake in exercising jurisdiction. The applicant for mandamus or prohibition argues either that the magistrates have failed to exercise their jurisdiction or that they should be prevented from exercising a jurisdiction which they do not lawfully have. *Certiorari* and appeal by case stated, on the other hand, serve similar purposes. The effect of both remedies is to set aside the decision of the court below, and counsel advising a person aggrieved by a decision of a magistrates' court or of the Crown Court on appeal from the magistrates may find the choice between the remedies difficult. Most of the points relevant to that choice have already been touched upon, but, in summary, the position is that:

(a)   Where the magistrates or Crown Court have acted in excess of jurisdiction both *certiorari* and appeal by case stated are available.

(b)   Where an error of law has been made, but the inferior tribunal was acting within its jurisdiction, appeal by case stated is the obvious remedy. If the error of law is patent on the face of the record of the inferior tribunal's proceedings, *certiorari* could also be used, but, as explained in Para. 18.3.1, most errors of law are latent rather than patent. Only through the statement of case will the latent error be revealed.

(c)   If the rules of natural justice have been broken, the appropriate remedy is *certiorari*. When a magistrate tries a case in which he has a pecuniary interest, or the prosecution fail to notify the defence of potential witnesses who might corroborate the accused's story, no error of law is made which could found a successful appeal, but an application for *certiorari* will succeed.

(d)   *Certiorari* is again the only remedy where the defence wish to quash a committal for trial or sentence. Appeal by case stated will not lie because there has not been a final determination in the case (see Para. 18.2.1). In fact, an application for *certiorari* to quash a committal for trial is most unlikely to succeed (see Para. 3.9), but it is at least theoretically available. Applications to quash a committal for sentence under s. 38 of the Magistrates' Courts Act 1980 will succeed where the committal was in excess of jurisdiction because the character and antecedents of the offender did not make the magistrates' powers of punishment inadequate (see Para. 12.3.2).

(e)   Where both *certiorari* and appeal by case stated are available, the advantage may lie with the former in that it is likely to provide the speedier remedy — the elaborate procedure for drafting a case with its 21 day periods and opportunity for making representations, is a time consuming affair. Certainly, in *R* v *St Albans Crown Court* ex parte *Cinnamond* [1981] 2WLR 681 where C could have proceeded either by case stated or *certiorari*, the Divisional Court on the application for leave to apply for judicial review advised *certiorari* in preference to case stated 'in order to minimise the delay' (per Donaldson LJ at p. 684).

18.4   APPEAL FROM THE DIVISIONAL COURT TO THE HOUSE OF LORDS

The decision of a Divisional Court of the Queen's Bench Division in a criminal cause or matter may be appealed to the House of Lords: Administration of Justice Act 1960, s. 1(1)(a). The circumstances in which the appeal will lie are analagous to those in which an appeal lies from the Criminal Division of the Court of Appeal to the House of Lords — i.e. the Divisional Court must certify that there is a point of law of general public importance involved, and either the Divisional Court or the House of Lords must grant leave to appeal.

Where the Divisional Court's decision was not in a criminal cause or matter, appeal lies first to the Court of Appeal and thence to the House of Lords. For details on leave to appeal and the possibility of a 'leap-frogging' appeal, readers are referred to text books on civil procedure. Occasionally magistrates or the Crown Court make a decision which is linked with criminal proceedings although it is not a decision in a criminal matter. Should such a decision be taken to the Divisional Court on an appeal by case stated or application for judicial review, any appeal from the Divisional Court is first to the Court of Appeal. An example is provided by *R* v *Southampton Justices* ex parte *Green* [1976] QB 11 where the Divisional Court's refusal to issue *certiorari* to quash the magistrates' decision to estreat G's recognizance was appealed to the Court of Appeal not the House of Lords. Proceedings in respect of a surety's recognizance are not criminal proceedings because the surety is not charged with an offence — the surety is, in effect, being forced to pay a civil debt.

Part 6   Miscellaneous

19 Preliminaries to Trial

The preceding Chapters have described the sequence of events from the moment committal proceedings or summary trial commence to the conclusion of an appeal. It is now necessary to return to the beginning of the criminal process for a summary of what occurs before the accused makes his first appearance in court. The topic will involve discussion not only of procedure but also of evidence, constitutional law and police organisation and practice. It will only be possible to give a broad outline of what happens in typical cases — for further details readers are referred to books on evidence and constitutional law. The Report of the Royal Commission on Criminal Procedure (Chairman Sir Cyril Philips — Command 8092), as well as being of interest for its proposals for reforming the system, provides a clear and readable guide to the present practice. A summary of the Commission's recommendations will be found in Appendix 4.

19.1 PROSECUTING AUTHORITIES

At least three-quarters of the prosecutions in England and Wales are brought by the police, in the sense that a police officer commences the prosecution by laying an information or charging a suspect at the police station. Of the remaining prosecutions, the majority are brought by officials of prosecuting agencies which are each responsible for numerous prosecutions. Local authorities, the Inland Revenue, the Department of Health and Social Security, the Factory Inspectorate, the British Transport Police and many other governmental and quasi-governmental bodies undertake, as part of their wider duties, the responsibility for prosecuting those who offend against the legislation which it is their task to administer. Only a small minority of prosecutions are carried on by persons acting in a purely private capacity. The commonest examples of such prosecutions are prosecutions for assault arising out of neighbour disputes, and prosecutions for shoplifting brought by retail stores. Occasionally, an individual may bring a prosecution because he feels that the police are failing in their duty by not taking action. One recent example is *Whitehouse v Gay News Ltd and Lemon* (1979) 68Cr App R 381 in which Mrs Mary Whitehouse brought a prosecution for blasphemous libel, her prosecution being the first since 1922 for that offence.

The classic view of the police role in enforcing the criminal law is that they only do what any private citizen could do had he the time and inclination. The Royal Commission on Police Powers and Procedure of 1929 (Command 3297) expressed it thus:

> The police of this country have never been recognised, either in law or by tradition, as a force distinct from the general body of citizens... The principle remains that a policeman, in the view of the common law, is only 'a person paid to perform, as a

matter of duty, acts which if he were so minded he might have done voluntarily.'
Indeed, a policeman possesses few powers not enjoyed by the ordinary citizen, and
public opinion…has shown great jealousy of any attempts to give increased
authority to the police.

Those words may still be an accurate description of constitutional theory, but in
practice the police and, to a lesser extent, the other major prosecuting agencies, have
great advantages over the private prosecutor, so that if they are willing to prosecute it
is plainly sensible to leave the matter in their hands. The advantages the police have
include the following:

(a) Although a private citizen can make an arrest, the police powers of arrest are
significantly greater (see Para 19.2.1).

(b) Whereas a private citizen who makes an arrest must bring the person arrested
before a magistrate or hand him over to the police as soon as possible, the police can
delay an appearance before the magistrates' court while they question the person
arrested or conduct other inquiries into the alleged offence.

(c) A private citizen has no right to search another's person or premises. At
common law and by statute the police have wide powers to search for and retain
evidence (see Para. 19.4).

(d) A private citizen who wishes to commence a prosecution must do so by laying
an information before a magistrate or a magistrates' clerk. The police can make use of
what is often a much more convenient procedure, namely charging the suspect at the
police station with the alleged offence (see Para. 19.2.2).

(e) If a private citizen needs legal advice in connection with his prosecution, he
must instruct solicitors privately in the normal way and pay them. At the end of the
trial he will probably be awarded his costs either from the accused or out of central
funds, but in the meantime he has to meet the expenses of the prosecution. Most
police forces, on the other hand, are served by a prosecuting solicitor with a
department who advises, if necessary, on the merits of a prosecution and the evidence
which will be required, and arranges for legal representation at the trial. Those forces
which do not have a prosecuting solicitor instruct solicitors in private practice, but, of
course, the individual police officer who takes the decision to prosecute does not have
to worry about the costs involved.

(f) Lastly, the police resources for investigating crime and gathering evidence are
immeasurably greater than those of the private citizen

The police prosecutor, then, has great advantages over the private prosecutor.
However, there is one important respect in which they are on an equal footing.
Neither, in carrying on the prosecution, acts as an agent of the state. The English
system for prosecutions is unusual in that there is no centralised prosecuting authority.
The Director of Public Prosecutions and his department play an important
supervisory role, but they do not, in general, control police decisions on whether to
prosecute, or the way in which a police prosecution is conducted. Responsibility for
these matters rests ultimately with the chief officers of police

Policing in England and Wales is carried on by 43 separate police forces, each
operating in its own geographical area. At the head of each force is a chief officer,
who is known in the City of London and Metropolitan Forces as the Commissioner
and in other forces has the title of Chief Constable. The chief officer is answerable for

the general efficiency of his force to a police authority, which is made up of local authority members and magistrates from the areas served by the force, save that the police authority for the Metropolitan Police is the Home Secretary. Despite their role in overseeing the work of police forces, the police authorities cannot dictate to a chief officer the policy his force should adopt in investigating and prosecuting offences. Nor can they order a chief officer or his men to prosecute or refrain from prosecuting in an individual case. Similarly, the Home Secretary and members of the government have no power to control chief officers in this aspect of their work. The only possible method of forcing a chief officer to change his prosecuting policy is to obtain an order of mandamus from the Divisional Court. Such an order would only be issued in the unlikely event of the chief officer making a decision which amounted to a dereliction of his duty to uphold the law (e.g. a decision not to prosecute in any case of theft where the value of the goods stolen is under £100). Lord Denning MR in *R v Metropolitan Police Commissioner* ex parte *Blackburn (No. 1)* [1968] 2QB 118, summarised the position as follows:

> I hold it to be the duty of the Commissioner of Police of the Metropolis, as it is of every chief constable, to enforce the law of the land... He must decide whether or not suspected persons are to be prosecuted; and, if need be, bring the prosecution or see that it is brought. But in all these things he is not the servant of anyone, save of the law itself. No Minister of the Crown can tell him... that he must, or must not, prosecute this man or that one. Nor can any police authority tell him so. The responsibility for law enforcement lies on him. He is answerable to the law and to the law alone.

The position as described by Lord Denning is subject to the qualification that in certain classes of cases the Director of Public Prosecutions may assist in or himself conduct the prosecution (see Paras. 2.4.4 and 2.5 for further details on the office and work of the Director). It is the Director's duty to 'institute, undertake or carry on' such criminal proceedings as may be prescribed by the Attorney-General, and to give advice to chief officers of police, justices' clerks and others concerned in the conduct of any criminal proceedings: Prosecution of Offences Act 1979 s. 2(1). The Prosecution of Offences Regulations 1978 provide for the Director's taking action in cases which appear to him to be of importance or difficulty. So that the Director will be aware of cases in which he might want to intervene, the Regulations also provide that he must be informed by the police whenever they have *prima facie* evidence of the commission of certain offences. Offences which must be notified to the Director are those of especial gravity and those in which the decision to prosecute may raise questions of a particularly sensitive nature. They include robbery where firearms are used and injury is caused, robbery where property to a value of £250,000 or more is stolen, arson involving grave damage to public property, rape where one woman is raped by more than one man on the same occasion or where one man rapes several women, offences against the Perjury Act 1911, major drugs and immigration offences, causing death by reckless driving where the deceased is a close relative of the accused, criminal libel, and some offences involving obscene exhibitions or publications. In addition, s. 49 of the Police Act 1964 provides that all complaints against police officers, however trivial, must be reported to the Director, unless the chief officer concerned is satisfied that no offence has been committed. Whenever a case is reported to the Director under the Regulations or under s. 49, or comes to his attention in some other way, he may, if he considers that his intervention is called for, either initiate and carry on a prosecution himself or give advice to whoever has commenced, or is proposing to commence, proceedings. Where a prosecution is already in progress, the Director may take it over, rather than merely giving advice. The power is rarely exercised, but it is a useful way of dealing with apparently malicious prosecutions because, having assumed responsibility for the prosecution, the Director may offer no evidence.

The Director's positive powers to conduct prosecutions are supplemented by negative powers to prevent some prosecutions taking place, in that his consent is required before they may be commenced (see Para. 2.4.4). The statistics set out below, which are for the year 1977, show how the Director, by granting or withholding his consent in cases where his consent to prosecution is necessary, significantly restricts the police's freedom to prosecute whom they will:

APPLICATIONS TO THE DIRECTOR FOR CONSENT TO PROSECUTION

Statute under which the Application was Made	Number of Applications	Number of Successful Applications
Criminal Law Act 1967, s. 4(1) (assisting an offender to avoid apprehension or prosecution)	82	54
Criminal Law Act 1967, s. 5(2) (wasting police time)	375	245
Sexual Offences Act 1956, ss. 10, 11 and 37 (incest)	270	207
Sexual Offences Act 1967, s. 8 (buggery and gross indecency where either man involved was under 21 at the time of the offence)	609	492
Theft Act 1968, s. 30 (theft of spouse's property)	161	93

Other prosecutions require the consent of the Attorney-General. The figures given below are again for 1977.

APPLICATIONS TO THE ATTORNEY-GENERAL FOR CONSENT TO PROSECUTION

Statute under which the Application was Made	Number of Applications	Number of Successful Applications
Official Secrets Acts 1911-1939	33	2
Prevention of Corruption Act 1906: (giving or accepting bribes for acts etc. by an agent in relation to his principal's affairs)	317	102
Public Order Act 1936, ss. 1 and 2 (unlawful wearing of uniforms and organising a private army)	3	0
Public Order Act 1936, s. 5A (incitement to racial hatred)	29	2

In 1978 approaching 18,000 cases were referred to the Director of Public Prosecutions, either with a view to obtaining his consent to prosecution or because notification was necessary under the Prosecution of Offences Regulations or the Police Act 1964, s. 49. Proceedings were conducted by the Director against 2,242 persons. In many other cases he gave advice to those responsible for the prosecution. Nevertheless, viewed as a percentage of the total number of prosecutions taking place, the number of cases in which the Director is involved is small. The conduct of most prosecutions is left entirely in the hands of the police, or other prosecuting agency, and their legal advisers. Accordingly, the remainder of this Chapter will concentrate upon the steps taken by the police in bringing a case before the court.

19.2 BRINGING THE ACCUSED BEFORE THE COURT

In most cases, the accused's first appearance in court is preceded either by his being arrested without warrant and charged at the police station, or by his being warned that he is being reported for consideration for prosecution and subsequently having a summons served on him. Proceeding by arrest and charge is usually reserved for indictable offences. Proceeding by way of a summons is more appropriate for summary cases. In 1978, 76% of the prosecutions for indictable offences commenced with arrest and charge, and 87% of the prosecutions for summary offences commenced with the issue of a summons.

19.2.1 Powers of arrest

When a police officer interviewing a suspect about an offence considers that he has, or will be able to obtain, sufficient evidence to bring proceedings against him, he must decide whether or not to make an arrest. Section 2 of the Criminal Law Act 1967 sets out the general powers of arrest without warrant possessed by constables (i.e. any police officer) and members of the public. These powers are given in respect of arrestable offences, which are defined as offences punishable with five years imprisonment or more, and attempts to commit such offences: s. 2(1). Section 2 provides that:

(a) Any person may arrest anyone whom he reasonably suspects to be in the act of committing an arrestable offence.

(b) A constable may arrest anyone whom he reasonably suspects to be about to commit an arrestable offence.

(c) A constable who reasonably suspects that an arrestable offence has been committed may arrest anyone whom he reasonably suspects to have committed the offence.

(d) Where an arrestable offence has been committed, any person may arrest anyone whom he reasonably suspects to have committed the offence.

The powers of arrest possessed by the private citizen under (d) are thus narrower than the powers possessed by a constable under (c). Whereas an arrest by a constable may be lawful even though no arrestable offence at all has been committed, provided the constable reasonably suspects that one has been, an arrest by a private citizen is only justified if somebody (not necessarily the person arrested) committed the offence of which the person arrested was suspected. Thus, if no offence has in fact occurred (e.g. because the person arrested committed the *actus reus* of the offence but did not have the necessary *mens rea*) an arrest by a private citizen will be wrongful, however reasonable his suspicions may have been.

Most serious offences are punishable with five years imprisonment or more, and therefore fall within the definition of arrestable offences (see Para. 15.1.1 for the maximum panelties for the commoner offences). However, numerous statutes give a power of arrest in respect of offences which, being punishable with less than five years imprisonment, are not arrestable under s. 2 of the 1967 Act. Sometimes the power of arrest is granted to constables and private citizens alike, usually it is granted only to constables, or to constables and officials such as customs or immigration officers. Set out below are a few of the many statutes containing powers of arrest.

STATUTORY PROVISION	OFFENCE	POWER OF ARREST
Theft Act 1968, s. 25(3)	Going equipped to steal	Any person may arrest somebody he reasonably suspects to be committing the offence.
Prevention of Offences Act 1851, s. 11	Any indictable offence committed between the hours of 9pm and 6am	Any person may arrest somebody found committing the offence.
Theft Act 1978, s. 3	Making off without payment	Any person may arrest somebody he reasonably suspects to be committing or attempting to commit the offence.
Theft Act 1968, s. 12	Taking a motor vehicle without authority	Deemed to be an arrestable offence within the meaning of s. 2 of the 1967 Act.
Road Traffic Act 1972, s. 5	Driving while unfit through drink or drugs	A constable may arrest a person committing the offence.
s. 8	Excess alcohol in blood when driving	A constable may arrest a person failing or refusing to take a breath test.
s. 100	Driving while disqualified	A constable in uniform may arrest someone he reasonably suspects of the offence.
s. 164(2)	Reckless or careless driving	A constable who sees the offence may arrest the driver unless he gives his name and address or produces his licence.
Prevention of Crime Act, 1953	Having an offensive weapon in a public place	A constable may arrest a person he reasonably suspects of committing the offence if he is not satisfied as to his name or address.
Misuse of Drugs Act 1971, s. 24	All offences under the Act but without prejudice to s. 2 of the 1967 Act which gives wider powers of arrest in respect of offences under the Act carrying 5 years imprisonment or more	A constable may arrest someone he reasonably suspects to have committed the offence if there is reason to believe the suspect will abscond or the officer is not certain of his name and address.
Public Order Act 1936, s. 7(3)	Using threatening words or behaviour conducive to a breach of the peace and incitement to racial hatred	A constable may arrest somebody he reasonably suspects to be committing the offence.

In addition to the statutory powers of arrest, constables and private citizens have, at common law, the right to arrest a person who has, in their presence, committed a breach of the peace or who threatens to renew a breach of the peace. An arrest may also be made if no breach of the peace has actually occurred but the person arresting honestly and reasonably believes that there is an imminent danger of it happening: *R* v *Howell* 1981 'The Times' 13 April.

As will be seen from the above, the precise circumstances in which there is a power of arrest vary depending upon the wording of the relevant statute. Arguably, the law should be simplified so that a police officer, having to make a decision 'on the spot' as to whether or not to arrest, can know what his powers are without needing to be familiar with the terms of numerous statutes.

An arrest is effected either by physically seizing or touching the arrested person's body, or by using a form of words which sufficiently inform the arrested person that he is no longer free to come and go as he chooses: *Alderson* v *Booth* [1969] 2QB 216. A constable making an arrest must inform the person arrested of the reason for his arrest. The constable is not entitled to keep the reason to himself, or to give a false reason (*Christie* v *Leachinsky* [1947] AC 573 see Viscount Simon at pp. 587-8). The reason need not be given in precise or technical language, provided the suspect is told in substance why he is being detained. If the circumstances of the arrest make the reason for it obvious, or if resistance to arrest prevents the constable stating the reason, the person arrested cannot complain at the lack of reasons. Otherwise, failure to give the correct reason for arrest will make the arrest unlawful and render the constable liable to pay damages for false imprisonment.

A person (constable or private citizen) may use such force as is reasonable to effect a lawful arrest: Criminal Law Act 1967, s. 3. A constable intending to make an arrest under s. 2 of the 1967 Act may enter and search any place where he reasonably suspects the person concerned to be. In making the entry, the constable may use force if necessary. He need not first ask permission to enter: *Swales* v *Cox* (1981) 72Cr App R 171.

19.2.2 Charging at the police station

Having arrested a suspect, the police officer conveys him to the police station. Usually he takes him straight there, but, provided the officer's conduct is reasonable, he may go to other addresses en route (*Dallison* v *Caffery* [1965] 1QB 348 in which case the officer was justified in taking the person arrested to his home, which was searched, and to the address where he claimed to have been working at the time of the alleged offence, before going on to the police station).

At the police station, the arresting officer explains to the station sergeant why he has made the arrest. If the arrest does not appear to be justified (e.g. because the offence suspected does not carry a power of arrest) the station sergeant orders that the arrested person be released. Otherwise, he is normally searched, and the property found on him noted on the charge sheet. The charge sheet is what its name suggests — simply a large sheet of paper on which are entered various details about the arrested person's case, including ultimately the formal charge against him. The arrestee is invited to sign the list of his property to show that it is correct. When he is released from police custody, either on bail or into the custody of the magistrates' court, his property is returned to him, save that the police retain property which is the subject of a charge or which may be required for evidence.

At the time the arrestee is brought into the police station, investigations into the suspected offence will probably not be completed. He may be detained at the station, usually in a cell, while further inquiries are made. The inquiries could involve checking on whether property found on the arrestee or at his home is stolen, arranging for the arrestee to be put on an identification parade, taking his fingerprints, interviewing other people about the offence, questioning the arrestee under caution, and taking a written statement from him. Paragraphs 19.3-5 discuss some of the ways in which the police may gather evidence. Once the police have enough evidence to charge the arrestee, they should do that without delay. The only exception is when they decide to proceed by way of summons rather than by way of charge (e.g. because the offence suspected does not appear particularly serious). In such a case, the arrestee, instead of being charged is told that he may be prosecuted for the offence, and is then released. In due course, assuming the police do decide to prosecute, a summons is served on him (see Para. 19.2.4).

The requirement to charge a suspect is contained in principle (d) of the introductory note, or preamble, to the Judges' Rules (see Para. 19.3.3 for the contents and status of the Judges' Rules). Principle (d) reads:

> When a police officer who is making enquiries of any person about an offence has enough evidence to prefer a charge against that person for the offence, he should without delay cause that person to be charged or informed that he may be prosecuted for the offence.

The reason for not delaying a charge is that once a person has been charged he cannot, generally speaking, be asked further questions about the offence (Rule III (b) of the Judges' Rules). Unfortunately, principle (d) does not specify how much evidence the police must have for the duty to charge to arise. However, Lord Devlin has said in *Hussien* v *Chong Fook Kam* [1970] AC 492 that reasonable suspicion that a person has committed an offence does not necessitate a charge, but as soon as there is enough evidence to establish a *prima facie* case he should be charged. The term '*prima facie* case' is an imprecise one, which tends to have different meanings attached to it depending upon the context in which it is used, but *R* v *Hudson* (1981) 72 Cr App R 163 gives some indication of the stage at which the police have a *prima facie* case. H, a local authority planning officer, was arrested on suspicion of receiving bribes. He spent five days at the police station, during which he was questioned for a total of 25 hours. On the first two days of his detention he orally admitted to receiving £600 in bribes, the offence for which he was eventually prosecuted and convicted. Despite the oral admissions, the police, acting on the instructions of the Director of Public Prosecutions, did not charge H, but continued to question him for another three days, at the end of which he made a written confession. One of several points made by the Court of Appeal in quashing H's conviction was that after the oral admissions the police had a *prima facie* case against H, and so should have charged him. His detention and questioning for a further three days was unlawful.

The procedure for charging an arrestee is that the charge is written down on the charge sheet. It is worded so as to comply with r. 100 of the Magistrates' Courts Rules 1981, which governs the wording of informations (see Para. 11.3). The station officer (usually a station or charge sergeant but occasionally an inspector) then decides whether or not to accept the charge. Usually he will accept it. The charge is then formally read to the arrestee, and he is cautioned in the following terms:

> Do you wish to say anything? You are not obliged to say anything unless you wish

to do so but whatever you say will be taken down in writing and may be given in evidence. (Rule III(a) of the Judges' Rules.)

Having been charged, the arrestee is either bailed to appear at the local magistrates' court on a day fixed by the officer bailing him, or he is kept in custody until he can be brought before the court. The charge sheet, meanwhile, is delivered to the court, where the details on it are used to prepare the court register of cases to be heard by the magistrates. When the accused appears before the magistrates, the charge is read out, which may be regarded as the laying of the information against him.

19.2.3 Bail from the police station

The law is surprisingly vague about the period for which an arrestee may be kept at the police station before being released on bail or brought before the magistrates. Section 43(4) of the Magistrates' Courts Act 1980 establishes the general principle that:

> Where a person is taken into custody for an offence without a warrant and is retained in custody, he shall be brought before a magistrates' court as soon as practicable.

This is supplemented by s. 43(1) which provides that where it will not be practicable to bring the arrestee before the magistrates within 24 hours of his arrest a police officer not below the rank of inspector or the police officer in charge of the station must inquire into the case and, 'unless the offence appears to the officer to be a serious one', grant him bail. Since no attempt is made to define a 'serious' offence, the station sergeant or other officer enquiring into the case has a broad discretion in granting or withholding bail. If he does decide that the matter is serious enough to justify withholding bail, no limit is placed on the time for which an arrested person can be kept at the station other than the imprecise requirement of s. 43(4) that he should be brought before the magistrates 'as soon as practicable'. Taking advantage of the vagueness of s. 43(4), the police have occasionally detained an arrestee for several days, during which they have questioned him and investigated the case (e.g. *R v Hudson* (1981) 72Cr App R 163 — see Para. 19.2.2). However, in *Re Sherman and Apps* 'The Times' 9 December 1980, the Divisional Court (Donaldson LJ) held that 's. 43(4) and the authorities point unmistakably to a period of 48 hours as being the maximum period of detention'. In that case, S and A were arrested and kept at a police station for three days without being charged. Only a few hours after their arrest the police were in a position to charge them with handling stolen goods, but delayed doing so because they were gathering evidence concerning a hundred or so burglaries which they thought S and A could have committed. Had S and A been charged with handling, the relatively minor nature of the charge would have necessitated their being bailed under s. 43(1), which would have made investigation of the burglaries more difficult. The detention of S and A was unlawful for two reasons. First, they should have been charged with handling as soon as the police had sufficient evidence (see Para. 19.2.2). Second, on a true understanding of s. 43, 48 hours is the maximum period of detention at a police station, even in serious cases where s. 43(1) does not require release on bail after 24 hours. The period should be loyally observed by the police. On being told of the Divisional Court's provisional view of the case, the police officer concerned arranged for S and A to be charged and bailed, but, had he not done so, a writ of *habeas corpus* would have been issued to secure their release.

Evidence given to the Royal Commission on Criminal Procedure (see Appendix 4) indicates that about 75% of those charged are charged within six hours of being arrested, and 95% are charged within 24 hours. However, in a three month period in 1979 the Metropolitan Police held 212 persons for questioning for a period in excess of 72 hours. Over 80% of those arrested and charged are bailed from the police station.

> Normally a person is not bailed from a police station until he has been charged, in which case the terms of his bail are that he surrender to custody at the magistrates' court on a day fixed by the officer granting bail. Occasionally, however, the police cannot decide whether to charge an arrestee until they know the result of further enquiries, which cannot be completed during the period for which he may lawfully be detained at the police station. In such cases, the arrestee may be bailed to appear, not at court, but back at the police station. Depending on the outcome of the enquiries, he will, on answering to his bail, either be charged or told that proceedings are not being taken.
>
> A person bailed from the police station may be required to provide sureties. Other conditions (e.g. that he live at a certain address or report periodically to the police station), which may be imposed when a court grants bail, may not be attached to police bail: Bail Act 1976 s. 3(4) and (6).
>
> A summary of the options open to the police in respect of a person they have arrested may be of value. There are five main possibilities. Having investigated the case, they may:
>
> (a) Charge him and keep him in custody at the police station until he can be brought before the magistrates, or
> (b) Charge him and bail him to appear at the magistrates' court, or
> (c) Decide that further enquiries must be made, and bail him to appear back at the police station, or
> (d) Decide that any proceedings to be taken would better be taken by way of summons, and release him with a view to a summons subsequently being served on him, or
> (e) Decide that there is not sufficient evidence to take proceedings, and release him.
>
> Once it has become clear that no charges are to be preferred against an arrested person, he should be released at once (*Wiltshire* v *Barrett* [1966] 1QB 312).

19.2.4   Proceeding by way of summons

Proceedings which are not commenced by way of arrest and charge are commenced by laying an information before a magistrate or a magistrates' clerk and obtaining from him a summons to be served on the accused. A summons is a written command, addressed to the accused, requiring him to attend before a magistrates' court to answer one or more informations. As an alternative to issuing a summons, a magistrate (but not a magistrates' clerk) may issue a warrant for the arrest of the accused. The issuing of a or warrant is known as the issue of process.

Proceeding by way of summons is appropriate in the less serious cases. It is the procedure adopted by the police when:

(a) An officer interviews a suspect about an offence which does not carry a power of arrest, or
(b) An officer has power to arrest the suspect but considers that, in all the circumstances, it is unnecessary to do so, or

(c) The suspect has been arrested and taken to the police station, but the police decide that releasing him and serving a summons is preferable to charging him — this is frequently done in the case of juveniles who have been arrested.

When a police officer thinks that proceeding by way of summons may be appropriate, he tells the suspect that he is being reported for consideration of prosecution. The details of the case are then given to the police prosecutions department who decide, if necessary after consultation with the force's prosecuting solicitor, whether to take further action. If they do decide to proceed, an information alleging the offence is laid before a magistrate or a magistrates' clerk.

An information, as explained in Para. 11.3 is an allegation that the person named in it has committed an offence. Laying an information simply means bringing it to the attention of a magistrate or clerk: *R* v *Leeds Justices* ex parte *Hanson* [1981] 3 WLR 315. That may be done orally by going before him, and telling him the nature of the allegation. A private citizen wishing to commence a prosecution would probably lay an oral information. The police and other prosecuting agencies, however, generally adopt the much more convenient practice of putting the information into writing and delivering it to their local magistrates' court, thus avoiding a time consuming appearance before a magistrate or clerk. The written information must describe the offence alleged with the particularity required by r. 100 of the Magistrates' Courts Rules (1981 SI No 552 — see Para. 11.3 for the contents of an information). It must also give the name and address of both the accused and the person laying it. Sometimes a police information is formally in the name of the chief constable of the force concerned, sometimes it is in the name of the officer heading the prosecutions department. In the Metropolitan Police the name of the reporting or arresting officer is given. Who formally lays the information is of minimal importance, as illustrated by *Hawkins* v *Bepey* [1980] 1 WLR 419, where the death of a chief inspector before the hearing of an appeal against dismissal by the magistrates of an information which he had laid did not cause the appeal to lapse. The Divisional Court held that since the information had notionally been laid on the instructions of the chief constable, the prosecutor was either the chief constable or the force of which he had command.

Written informations having been prepared and delivered to the magistrates' court, they are put before a magistrate, or, more probably, a magistrates' clerk. He must look at each information, and decide whether it justifies the issue of a summons. He should only issue a summons if (a) the offence alleged in the information is known to the law; (b) the information is laid within time; (c) any consent necessary to commence the prosecution has been obtained, and (d) he has jurisdiction (see Para. 9.2.7 for jurisdiction to issue a summons). Even where these conditions are satisfied there is a residual discretion not to issue a summons if the prosecution appears frivolous or vexatious (*R* v *Bros* (1901) 66J P 54 — prosecution of a Jew for Sunday trading) or if the evidence is clearly inadequate: *R* v *Mead* (1916) 80JP 382. However, in the case of an information laid by a police officer, the magistrate or clerk will almost certainly assume that it is neither frivolous nor unsupported by evidence — indeed, assuming the information is in writing it is hard to see how he could check on the quality of the evidence even if he wanted to. The checking of the other matters mentioned above is also likely to be perfunctory as far as police informations are concerned. According to the Royal Commission on Criminal Procedure:

Where a summons is applied for by the police or other recognised prosecution agencies, no consideration is given as to whether or not a summons should be issued.

However, the Divisional Court has on a number of occasions emphasised that the issue of a summons is not merely an administrative or even clerical act, but a judicial function. Each time an information is put before him, the magistrate or clerk should ask himself whether a summons is really justified. He should not be a 'rubber-stamp', approving applications for summonses without question. In *R* v *Gateshead Justices* ex parte *Tesco Stores Ltd* [1981] 2WLR 419 Donaldson LJ expressed it thus:

> Not all prosecutions are brought by experienced and responsible prosecuting authorities. And even in the case of such authorities, the requirement that a justice of the peace or the clerk to the justices...shall take personal responsibility for the propriety of taking so serious a step as to require the attendance of a citizen before a criminal court is a constitutional safeguard of fundamental importance. We have no doubt that his function is judicial...This is not an administrative function and still less is it a purely clerical function.

Despite those fine words, the suspicion remains that if each of the tens of thousands of police informations were checked with the care Donaldson LJ considers necessary the system would grind to a halt.

19.2.5   Contents of a summons

Essentially, a summons is a command to the accused to attend at a magistrates' court to answer one or more informations which have been laid against him. The document, an example of which is shown opposite, contains the following details:

(a)   The name and address of the accused,
(b)   The address of the court before which he is to appear,
(c)   The day on and time at which he is to appear,
(d)   The contents of the information or informations he is to answer, and
(e)   The name and address of the informant (in the case of a police information the address of the police station will be given).

The summons must be signed by the magistrate or clerk who issued it, or, if it was issued by a magistrate, it may state his name and be authenticated by the clerk's signature: Magistrates' Courts Rules 1981, r. 98. To save magistrates and clerks the tedium of signing hundreds of summonses, the practice has grown up of rubber-stamping the relevant signature onto the summons. Provided the magistrate or clerk has personally sanctioned the issue of the summons, the manual task of affixing the signature may be carried out by assistants in the clerk's office: *R* v *Brentford Justices* ex parte *Catlin* [1975] QB 455. Once the summons has been issued and signed it is returned to the police for service on the accused.

19.2.6   Summons taken out by a private citizen

Section 1 of the Magistrates' Courts Act 1980, which gives magistrates jurisdiction to

SUMMONS (M.C. Act 1980 s. 1: M.C. Rules 1981 r. 98)
CASTERBRIDGE Magistrates' Court (Court Code 1234)

To

> Mr. John David DOE
> 1 Port Bredy Road
> CASTERBRIDGE
> Hardyshire

Ref Number MN 0220 (P)

You are hereby summoned to appear
on 27.7.1981   at 10.00am
before the Magistrates' Court
at 50 Egdon Street, CASTERBRIDGE
to answer to the following information laid
today   that you

Alleged
Offence:

on 1st June 1981 at Bridge Lane, Casterbridge did wilfully
obstruct Richard Roe a constable of the Hardyshire Police
Force in the execution of his duty.

Contrary to Section 51(3) of the Police Act 1964

Informant
Address
Date

Police Inspector 30 (B) Brown
Casterbridge Police Station
30 June 1981

John Clerk
~~Stipendiary Magistrates~~/Justices' Clerk/ ~~Justice of the Peace~~

PLEASE READ THE IMPORTANT NOTICE OVERLEAF
Complete and sign the tear off acknowledgement slip below and return it to the
Clerk of the Court forthwith. The correct postage must be paid.

issue a summons or warrant for arrest, draws absolutely no distinction between informations laid by police officers or officials of other prosecuting agencies and, informations laid by private citizens. Like the police, the private citizen may, if he so chooses, put his information into writing and hope to secure the issue of a summons without appearing in person before the magistrate. On receiving an information from a private citizen, the magistrate's powers of issuing a summons or warrant are precisely the same as on receiving an information from a police officer. However, in practice, a private citizen is much more likely than a police officer to lay his information orally, and the magistrate will exercise greater caution in deciding whether to issue a summons. The Royal Commission on Criminal Procedure, after implying that police informations resulted automatically in the issue of a summons (see Para. 9.2.4) stated:

> Where a private person lays an information a magistrate or justices' clerk will seek to ensure the propriety of the prosecution and the technical correctness of the information.

Oral informations are normally laid privately, not in open court. For that reason, the precise procedure is difficult to ascertain, but it appears to involve the informant telling the magistrate the nature of his allegation. If the informant's case appears flimsy, or possibly vexatious, the magistrate may ask questions to ascertain whether a summons is justified. He may even give the person accused in the information leave to oppose the issue of a summons, but the accused has no right to be heard: *R* v *West London Justices* ex parte *Klahn* [1979] 1WLR 933. Having heard what the informant has to say, the magistrate writes down the substance of the information, using a form based upon one set out in the Magistrates' Courts (Forms) Rules (1981 SI No 553). He signs the form to show that the information was taken before him, and, assuming he is satisfied with the information, issues a summons. An example of an information taken in this way will be found at p. 125.

For the sake of convenience, this Paragraph has so far referred to an informant going before a magistrate to lay his information. An oral information, like a written one, may, in fact, be laid before either a magistrate or a magistrates' clerk. The one difference is that only a magistrate may take an information from an informant who is on oath. The significance of the restriction is that it prevents a clerk issuing a warrant for arrest (see Para. 19.2.9). It has no relevance to his power to issue a summons.

19.2.7 Jursidiction to issue a summons

As stated above, both a magistrate and magistrates' clerk have jurisdiction to receive an information and issue a summons: Magistrates' Courts Act 1980, s. 1 and Justices' Clerks Rules 1970, SI No 231. The jurisdiction does not extend to assistant clerks working in the clerk's office, even if they are qualified to sit as clerks in court, although they may assist administratively by (e.g.) putting into one batch informations having similar characteristics or identifying those which may cause difficulties: *R* v *Gateshead Justices* ex parte *Tesco Stores Ltd* [1981] 2WLR 419.

Section 1 of the Magistrates' Courts Act 1980 places territorial limits upon a magistrate's jurisdiction to issue a summons. The restrictions apply equally to magistrates' clerks. The general effect of the section is that:

(a) If the offence alleged in the information is summary, the magistrate may issue a summons only if the offence alleged in the information occurred in the county for which he acts. This is subject to (c) and (d) below.

(b)   If the offence alleged is indictable, he may issue a summons if the offence occurred in the county, or the accused is believed to live in the county, or (c) below applies.

(c)   Whether the offence alleged is indictable or summary and irrespective of where it occurred, a summons may be issued if it is desirable for the accused to be tried jointly with or in the same place as somebody already being proceeded against within the county (e.g. if a thief is to appear before a magistrates' court for the county, a summons can be issued against the handler of the goods stolen, even if he lives outside the county and received the goods outside the county).

(d)   If the information alleges a summary offence, and the accused is already being tried for an offence (indictable or summary) by a magistrates' court within the county, a summons may be issued even if the offence alleged in the information allegedly occured outside the county so that (a) above does not apply.

The summons must require the accused to appear before a magistrates' court for the county for which the magistrate issuing the summons acts.

Although a magistrate always has jurisdiction to issue a summons in respect of an offence occurring within his county, even if it took place outside the petty sessional division to which he is assigned, it is normal to lay an information before a magistrate or clerk of the petty sessional division which was the venue of the offence, and the summons will require the accused to appear before the court for that division.

19.2.8   Service of a summons and non-appearance

Service of a summons may be effected (*inter alia*) by delivering it personally to the accused or posting it to his last known or usual address: Magistrates' Courts Rules 1981, r. 99. However, a magistrates' court may not treat service by post as proved unless either they are satisfied that the summons came to the knowledge of the accused, or the summons was issued in respect of a summary offence and it was sent by registered letter or recorded delivery service.

Where the accused fails to appear in answer to a summons alleging a summary offence, the magistrates may, in any case, simply adjourn the proceedings to another day: Magistrates' Courts Act 1980, s. 10. If it is proved that the summons was served on the accused a reasonable time before the hearing, they may, instead of adjourning, try the case in the accused's absence (s. 11 of the 1980 Act — see Para. 11.4.1). They have the further option of adjourning and issuing a warrant for the arrest of the accused if:

(a)   Service of the summons a reasonable time before the hearing is proved, and

(b)   The information has been substantiated on oath, and

(c)   Either the accused is a juvenile, or the offence alleged is punishable with imprisonment, or they have convicted the accused in his absence and propose to disqualify him from driving (s. 13 of the 1980 Act).

The requirement that the information be substantiated on oath means that, unless the informant orginally laid his information orally on oath, either he or somebody else with knowledge of the case must formally testify that the allegation in the information is correct.

If the accused fails to appear in answer to a summons alleging an indictable offence the magistrates may issue a warrant for his arrest provided only that the information is in writing and substantiated on oath: Magistrates' Courts Act 1980, s. 1(3) and (6). They cannot proceed in his absence except in the limited circumstances mentioned in ss. 4(4) and 23 of the 1980 Act (committal proceedings and proceedings for determining the mode of trial conducted in the accused's absence).

Where the magistrates issue a warrant for arrest it may be 'backed for bail' (see Para. 19.2.9).

19.2.9   Issue of a warrant for arrest

Where a magistrate has jurisdiction to issue a summons in respect of the offence

COURT CODE 1234

CASTERBRIDGE MAGISTRATES' COURT

Date: 30th June 1981

Accused: John David DOE

Address: 1, Port Bredy Road
                   CASTERBRIDGE

Alleged offence: On 1st June 1981 at Bridge Lane, Casterbridge did wilfully
                   obstruct Richard Roe a constable of the Hardyshire Police
                   Force in the execution of his duty contrary to s. 51(3) of the
                   Police Act 1964.

                   Information having been laid before me (on oath) by
                   Richard Roe on 30th June 1981
                   that the accused committed the above offence

Direction: You, the constables of the Hardyshire Police Force are
                   hereby required to arrest the accused and to bring the
                   accused before the Magistrates' Court at 50 Egdon Street,
                   Casterbridge immediately (unless the accused is released on
                   bail as directed below).

Bail: On arrest, after complying with the condition(s) specified in
                   Schedule 1 hereto, the accused shall be released on bail,
                   subject to the condition(s) specified in Schedule II hereto,
                   and with a duty to surrender to the custody of the above
                   magistrates' court on 27th July 1981 at 10.00am.

                                                            John Justice
                                                       Justice of the Peace

Schedule 1
Conditions to be complied with before release on bail

1. To provide 2 suret(y)(ies) in the sum of £50 (each) to
secure the accused's surrender to custody at the time and
place appointed.

2.

Schedule II
Conditions to be complied with after release on bail

1.   To report to Casterbridge Police Station daily between 6
and 7pm.

they have been told about the confession prior to their decision to exclude it. Rules of evidence thus influence the conduct of police questioning in that if something is done to render a suspect's confession involuntary, or if it is obtained following a breach of the Judges' Rules, it must in the former case and may in the latter case be excluded from evidence at the suspect's trial.

19.3.1 Involuntary confessions

If the admissibility of a confession is disputed the prosecution must satisfy the judge beyond reasonable doubt that the confession was made voluntarily: *R* v *Sartori* [1961] Crim L R 397. An involuntary confession is one made as a result of 'fear of prejudice or hope of advantage, excited or held out by a person in authority' (per Lord Sumner in *Ibrahim* v *R* [1914] AC 599 at p.609, and quoted in numerous cases since including *DPP* v *Ping Lin* [1975] 3WLR 419). Principle (e) of the preamble to the Judges' Rules (see Para 19.3.3) adds to Lord Sumner's classic formulation of the rule on involuntary confessions a further condition of voluntariness, namely that a confession must not be obtained by oppression.

A police officer is a person in authority. Therefore, if in questioning a suspect he makes any promise or threat which, as a matter of causation, leads to the suspect confessing, the confession will be involuntary and will be excluded from evidence at the suspect's trial (unless, of course, the officer denies having made the threat or promise and is believed by the judge). The nature of the threat or promise is irrelevant, save that if it was of a very trivial nature the judge may hold that it could not have had any bearing on the accused's decision to confess. Where, however, a threat or promise was made, and the prosecution are unable to satisfy the judge that it had no influence on the accused, the confession must be excluded even if the judge considers that no reasonable man, if innocent, would have confessed as a result of such a minor inducement. Indeed, the majority of their Lordships in the Privy Council case of *Wong Kam-ming* v *R* [1979] 1 All ER 939 held that during the trial on the voire dire the accused may not even be asked whether his confession is true — at that stage the question is whether the confession is voluntary, not whether it is reliable. The case law on what does and what does not amount to a promise or threat is copious. To say to a suspect 'Be sure to tell the truth' is not a threat, but to say 'You had better tell the truth' is (*R* v *Holmes* (1843) 1Cox 9 and *R* v *Fennell* (1881) 7QBD 147 respectively). To use or threaten to use violence on a suspect obviously renders a confession involuntary, but 'even the most gentle . . . threat or slight inducement will taint a confession': *R* v *Smith* [1959] 2 QB 35. A promise to grant bail if the suspect will make a confession is an inducement even if the suggestion originated with the suspect: *R* v *Zaveckas* (1970) 1WLR 516. So is a promise to allow the suspect to have an offence taken into consideration if he confesses instead of being charged with it: *R* v *Northam* [1967] 52Cr App R 97. The promise or threat need not relate to the contemplated charge against the suspect, but could be concerned with some other matter — e.g. a prosecution for a different offence: *Commissioners of Customs and Excise* v *Harz and Power* [1967] 1AC 760. It need not even relate directly to the suspect himself. It could be a promise or threat directed at his girlfriend or a member of his family: *R* v *Middleton* (1975) QB 191. Moreover, where somebody not in authority (e.g. the suspect's father) makes in the presence of a police officer and the suspect a statement amounting to a promise or threat, any resultant confession is involuntary unless the officer dissociates himself from what the third person has said: *R* v *Cleary* (1964) 48CR App R 116.

The cases mentioned above show how, in theory at any rate, a police officer must be very careful about what he says when trying to obtain a confession. In practice, the restrictions upon him may be less stringent, since usually only the suspect and police officers are present at an interrogation. If the suspect confesses, is charged and at his trial claims that he only confessed because he was promised bail if he did so, the judge, assuming the officers deny any such promise, will have a straight choice between believing the officers and believing the accused. The probability is that he will do the former, and if this is the case the confession is allowed into evidence. The evidence about the promise of bail may be repeated before the jury, and they may be more ready to believe the accused on the point than the judge was. However, their concern is with the weight of the evidence, not its admissibility, and they may well conclude that, even if the accused was promised bail, he would not have confessed unless he was guilty of the offence.

19.3.2   Confessions obtained by oppression

Even if no specific promise or threat is employed, a confession is involuntary if it is obtained by oppression. Sachs J. in *R* v *Priestley* (1966) 51Cr App R 1 defined oppression as 'something which tends to sap and has sapped that free will which must exist before a confession is voluntary.' Whether a suspect's will has been so overborne that he cannot genuinely choose whether to confess or not depends on all the circumstances of the case, including the total length of time for which he is questioned, the intervals between periods of questioning, the place where he is questioned, the refreshment and rest he is allowed to have, and, above all, the characteristics of the individual suspect. Thus, 'what may be oppressive as regards a child, an invalid or an old man, or somebody inexperienced in the ways of the world may turn out not to be oppressive when one finds that the accused person is of tough character and an experienced man of the world' (per Sachs J. in *R* v *Priestley* supra). Generally speaking, the courts are reluctant to hold that police questioning has been oppressive: see e.g. *R* v *Prager* [1972] 1WLR 260. However, *R* v *Hudson* (1981) 72CR App R 163 (see Para. 19.2.2) is a good recent example of a confession which ought to have been excluded on that basis. H. was aged 59, and of good character. He was arrested at 6.30 a.m. at his home in Farnham and taken to Chelsea police station, where he spent the next five days, either alone in his cell or accompanied by police officers. He was asked some 700 questions during a total period of 25 hours questioning. At the end of that time he made a written statement confessing to an offence of accepting a bribe. The Court of Appeal held that the statistics of his detention, combined with his age and character and the fact that he should have been charged at a much earlier stage of the enquiry (see Para. 19.2.2) showed that the confession was obtained by oppression. The conviction was quashed.

19.3.3   The Judges' Rules

The common law on involuntary confessions is supplemented by rules of practice which have been drawn up by the judges for the guidance of police officers questioning suspects. These rules of practice are known as the Judges' Rules. They were first formulated in 1912. The present rules were issued to the police in 1964, and are to be found in a Home Office Circular (H.O. Circ. 89/1978). They consist of the Rules proper, together with a note or preamble containing five principles which are unaffected by the Rules, and an appendix consisting of detailed administrative directions to the police, drawn up by the Home Office and approved by the judges. Two of the five introductory principles have already been mentioned — principle (d), dealing with the charging of the accused (see Para. 19.2.2) and principle (e), confirming the common law on involuntary confessions (see Para. 19.3.1).

Whenever a confession is obtained through a breach of the Judges' Rules which is not, of itself, sufficient to render the confession involuntary, the judge has a discretion to exclude the confession from evidence: *R v May* (1952) 36CR App R 91. Most judges seem to approach the exercise of their discretion on the basis that if the breach of the rules, together with any other relevant circumstances, has not rendered the confession unreliable or involuntary they will admit it as evidence. This approach was approved in *R v Prager* [1972] 1WLR 260, where Lord Widgery CJ. (the trial judge) decided that P.'s confession had been voluntary, despite the fact that he had not been cautioned (see below) at the point in his interrogation when he ought to have been. Having so decided, Lord Widgery declined to consider, as a separate question, the possibility of excluding the confession simply because there had been a breach of the Judges' Rules. The Court of Appeal dismissed P.'s appeal — 'ultimately all turns on the judge's decision as to whether, breach or no breach, the confession has been shown to have been made voluntarily.' A similar approach, albeit leading to a different conclusion, is illustrated in *R v Hudson* (supra), where breach of the preamble to the Rules, through failing to charge H., was one of the factors leading the Court of Appeal to conclude that his confession was obtained through oppression. Occasionally, however, a judge will exclude a confession simply because there has been a breach of the Rules. In *R v Allen* (1977) Crim L R 163, for example, McKenna J. ruled a confession inadmissible on the ground that A. had wrongly been refused access to a solicitor, even though no question of oppression or involuntariness arose.

The effect of the Judges' Rules is to divide police questioning into three main stages. The first stage is the gathering of information. Rule I states that a police officer investigating an offence may question any person, whether a suspect or not, from whom he thinks that useful information may be obtained. The questioning may continue even if the person questioned has been arrested and is in custody at the police station. There is no legal duty to answer the questions put (*Rice v Connelly* [1966] 2QB 414), although principle (a) of the preamble refers to a citizen's duty to 'help a police officer to discover and apprehend offenders'. The duty is merely a moral one. A person cannot be detained against his will for questioning unless he has been arrested (principle (b) and *R v Lemsatef* [1977] 1WLR 812). If a person declines a request to accompany a police officer to the station to assist him in his enquiries, or, having complied with the request, decides that he wants to leave, the officer must either allow him to do as he wishes or formally arrest him and give him the reason for the arrest. As Lawton LJ. put it in *R v Lemsatef* (supra at p. 816):

> The law is clear . . . There is no such offence as 'helping police with their inquiries' .
> . . If the idea is getting around amongst . . . police officers that they can arrest or
> detain people, as the case may be, for this particular purpose, the sooner they
> disabuse themselves of that idea, the better

Whether the average suspect, asked to go with a police officer to the station but not under arrest, understands his right not to go or would care to insist upon his right if he did understand it, is open to question.

The second stage in the process of questioning arrives when the police officer questioning a suspect 'has evidence (against him) which would afford reasonable grounds for suspecting that (he) has committed an offence'. At that point the suspect must be cautioned in the following terms: 'You are not obliged to say anything unless you wish to do so but what you say may be put into writing and given in evidence.' (Rule II) The requirement to caution does not arise at the stage of mere surmise or conjecture that the person being interviewed might have committed an offence. It only arises when the officer has evidence against the suspect which could be put before a court as the beginnings of a case: *R v Osbourne and Virtue* [1973] QB 678. In most cases where a suspect is arrested without warrant under the Criminal Law Act 1967, s. 2, the requirement to caution will coincide with the decision to arrest, since the power to arrest arises when the officer reasonably suspects that the arrestee has committed an arrestable offence. The caution could be delayed until after arrest in a case where the suspicion justifying the arrest is based upon information which could not be put before a court. The usual pattern, however, is for the suspect to be cautioned before or at the time of arrest, taken to the police station, and questioned there following a reminder that he is still under caution. A record must be kept of the time and place at which questioning after caution occurs,

The final stage of questioning (or rather non-questioning) is after the suspect has been charged with an offence (see Para. 19.2.2 for the duty to charge and the procedure on charging). He may not be asked further questions about the offence unless that is necessary (a) to prevent or minimise harm or loss to another person or to the public, or (b) to clear up an ambiguity in a previous answer or statement: Rule III (b). A caution must be administered before the further questions are put. Also, Rule V permits a person who has been charged to be shown a statement made by somebody else who has been charged with the same offence. He must not be invited to comment on the statement, and, if he starts to say something, he must be cautioned, but if he chooses to speak what he says is noted, and *prima facie* is admissible in evidence.

Rule IV deals with taking written statements from suspects. If a suspect indicates that he wants to make a statement about the alleged offence, he must be asked whether he wishes to write it himself or would prefer a police officer to write it for him. Most statements are written by a police officer. At the beginning of the statement is the following rubric, signed by the suspect:

I, AB, wish to make a statement. I want someone to write down what I say. I have been told that I need not say anything unless I wish to do so and that whatever I say may be given in evidence.

A suspect writing his own statement puts:

I make this statement of my own free will. I have been told etc.

Then follows the body of the statement. If it has been dictated to a police officer, the suspect is asked to read it, and to make any corrections, alterations or additions he wishes. He is than asked to sign the following certificate:

I have read the above statement and I have been told that I can correct, alter or add anything I wish. This statement is true. I have made it of my own free will.

A police officer taking down a statement should write the exact words spoken by the suspect, and should only ask such questions as may be necessary to make the statement intelligible and relevant. Similarly, a person writing his own statement should not be prompted by the officer attending him, although the officer may indicate what matters are material.

19.3.4 The right to silence

The caution given under Rule II of the Judges' Rules enshrines the suspect's right to silence — i.e. his right not to run the risk of incriminating himself by answering questions from the police or by giving evidence at his trial. In the sense that there is no offence of failing to answer questions or failing to cooperate with the police, every suspect has a right to silence: see *Rice* v *Connelly* [1966] 2QB 414 — Para 19.3.3. The point now for consideration is whether, if a suspect chooses to say nothing and is subsequently charged with an offence, the judge and prosecuting counsel at his trial may comment adversely on his silence. A full answer is not within the compass of this book, but it is suggested that the position is as follows:

(a)   If the accused stayed silent after he had been cautioned, it is presumed that that was because he had been told that he was not obliged to say anything. Therefore, if the judge or prosecuting counsel make any comment at all about his silence, it should be to remind the jury that he was merely exercising his rights, and to warn them not to hold that in any way against him: *R* v *Gilbert* (1978) 66Cr App R 237.

(b)   The effect of silence before caution is less easy to determine. The general principle was stated by Lord Diplock in the Privy Council case of *Hall* v *R* [1971] 1WLR 298:

The caution merely serves to remind the accused of a right which he already possesses at common law. The fact that in a particular case he has not been reminded of it is no ground for inferring that his silence was not in exercise of that right, but was an acknowledgement of the truth of the accusation.

The principle was qualified by the Court of Appeal in *R* v *Chandler* [1976] 1WLR 585. If, prior to caution, a police officer and suspect are speaking on even terms, and the former makes an accusation against the latter that an innocent man would be expected to deny, the suspect's silence can be treated as an acknowledgement that the accusation is true. The jury decide whether to interpret the silence in that way, or to attribute it to some other cause (e.g. the suspect's believing that one should always say as little as possible to the police). It must be emphasised that the reasoning in *R* v *Chandler* only applies when police officer and suspect are on even terms. Except in cases where the suspect's solicitor is present during the questioning, the position of authority enjoyed by a police officer will usually put him at an advantage over the suspect so that, both before and after caution, no adverse inferences can be drawn from the suspect's silence. As an example of a suspect who, even in the absence of his solicitor, would be on an equal footing with a police officer, Lawton LJ in *R* v *Chandler* instanced the case of a well known local politician being interviewed by a junior officer about an allegation of bribery. The politician's status and presumed ability to express his side of the story would place him and the police officer on the same level, so that failure to deny any allegations put could be evidence against him. Such cases are the exception not the rule. Despite *R* v *Chandler,* the average suspect, interviewed without his solicitor, has a right to silence both before and after caution.

(c) It has sometimes been suggested that failure to reveal a defence at the first reasonable opportunity is something a jury may take into account when assessing the credibility of the defence — i.e. the accused's silence prior to trial as to the nature of his defence is not evidence of guilt as such, but it may undermine the case he puts forward at trial. In *R* v *Gilbert* (supra), however, the Court of Appeal held that no adverse inferences whatsoever may be drawn against the accused on account of his silence. The facts of the case were that G, at his trial for murder, put forward the defence that in killing the victim he was acting in reasonable self-defence. When questioned by the police he had begun to make a written statement, but had dealt only with his relationship with the victim prior to the time of the alleged offence. He was asked about the killing itself, but said — 'I am not doing any more. I don't think it is in my interest to make a detailed statement at this stage'. The judge, in summing up the case to the jury, said:

> Bear in mind we have heard of this matter of self-defence for the first time. Ask yourselves the question: if it is the real explanation of what happened, do you or do you not think it remarkable that when making the statement, the accused says nothing whatever about it? That may help you, applying your commonsense, to test the substance of the matter of self-defence.

As the judge implied, commonsense may well suggest that had G really been acting in self-defence he would have said so to the police. Nevertheless, the Court of Appeal held that the comment should not have been made. In *R* v *Gilbert* there was no question of the accused being on equal terms with the police officers who questioned him. Had they been on such terms then, presumably, following *R* v *Chandler* (supra), G's failure to disclose his defence could have been used against him.

(d) Complementing the right to silence before trial is the right of the accused not to give evidence at trial (see Para. 8.5.2 on the position of the accused as a competent but not compellable witness). The judge, but not prosecuting counsel, may comment on the accused not testifying. If the judge does comment it should usually be along the lines suggested by Lord Parker CJ in *R* v *Bathurst* [1968] 2QB 99, pointing out to the jury that the accused is not bound to testify, and that, although they have been deprived of the opportunity of hearing his story tested in cross examination, they must not assume that 'he is guilty because he has not gone into the witness box'.

Despite the right to silence, research carried out for the Royal Commission on Criminal Procedure (see 'Confessions in Crown Court Trials' by Baldwin and McConville — Royal Commission on Criminal Procedure Research Study No. 5) suggests that only a minority of suspects do in fact say nothing to the police. Most give some kind of statement or an explanation for their conduct. Perhaps they are wise, for the law can only control what a judge or prosecuting counsel says to a jury. It cannot control the reasoning employed by the jurors in the privacy of their jury room, and they may well argue that any innocent man would have denied the allegation put by the police officer or, in a case such as *R* v *Gilbert* (supra), have given details of his defence at an earlier stage. The point was taken by Salmon LJ in *R* v

Sullivan (1966) 51Cr App R 102. Having held that it was a misdirection for the judge to say to the jury — 'You may think that if S was innocent he would be anxious to answer questions' — his Lordship went on to remark:

It seems pretty plain that all the members of the jury, if they had any commonsense at all, must have been saying to themselves precisely what the learned judge said to them.

19.3.5 'Right' to see a solicitor

Principle (c) of the preamble to the Judges' Rules states:

Every person at any stage of an investigation should be able to communicate and to consult privately with a solicitor. This is so even if he is in custody provided that in such case no unreasonable delay or hindrance is caused to the processes of investigation or the administration of justice by his doing so.

The 'right' given by the principle is somewhat illusory. First, it is only a right to consult with a solicitor. There is no right to have one's solicitor present at an interrogation, although the police, in their discretion, may allow this, as they did in *R* v *Chandler* (supra). Second, if postponing an interrogation until the suspect has seen his solicitor would cause unreasonable delay or hindrance the police may proceed with their questioning immediately. Thus, access to a solicitor may be refused where the suspect has been arrested in the early hours of the morning, and a solicitor could not come to the police station until office hours. The fact that the suspect has not made any oral or written admission is not a good reason for refusing to allow him to see his solicitor: *R* v *Lemsatef* [1977] 1WLR 812. Third, even where, as in *R* v *Lemsatef*, a solicitor is refused for no good reason and the suspect makes a confession, the evidence of the confession is unlikely to be excluded at his trial. In *R* v *Lemsatef*, L was detained at 12.40am and not allowed to see his solicitor until 6.18pm, by which time he had made oral and written confessions. Except during the early period of L's detention, there was no justification for not giving him an opportunity to speak with the solicitor. The trial judge held that L's confession had been voluntary, that the breach of the Judges' Rules gave him a discretion to exclude it, but that, since it was a voluntary confession, he would admit it into evidence. The Court of Appeal criticised the refusal of a solicitor, but upheld the judge's exercise of his discretion. The judge's decision in *R* v *Lemsatef* may be compared with that of McKenna J in *R* v *Allen* [1977] Crim L R 163, who excluded a confession which was obtained after A had been refused a solicitor on the inadequate basis that he had not yet made any admissions. Most judges, it is thought, will follow the course adopted in *R* v *Lemsatef* in preference to that adopted in *R* v *Allen*.

The administrative directions appended to the Judges' Rules state that persons in custody should be informed orally of the rights and facilities available to them (e.g. the right to consult a solicitor). In addition, notices describing those rights should be displayed at 'convenient and conspicuous places at police stations and the attention of persons in custody should be drawn to these notices'. Research carried out for the Royal Commission on Criminal Procedure (see 'Police Interrogation: An Observational Study in Four Police Stations' by Softley and others — Royal Commission on Criminal Procedure Research Study No. 4) indicated that only about one in ten persons in police custody asked to see a solicitor, about a third of the requests being refused.

19.3.6 'Right' to inform another of an arrest

Section 62 of the Criminal Law Act 1977 provides that:

Where any person has been arrested and is being held in custody in a police station...he shall be entitled to have intimation of his arrest and of the place where he is being held sent to one person reasonably named by him, without delay or, when some delay is necessary in the interest of the investigation or prevention of crime or the apprehension of offenders, with no more delay than is so necessary.

A person 'reasonably named' would include a member of the arrested person's family, or somebody else known personally to him, or a solicitor. Delay in communicating information about the arrest is justified for example where the arrested person's accomplices in crime might make their escapes or destroy the evidence of his or their offences if they were told immediately of the arrest. If the police decide that the arrest can be revealed without prejudice to their investigations, they try to contact the person named by telephone. If that is not possible, an officer is sent round to the person's address. Section 62 does not specify a sanction for failing to comply with its provisions. Perhaps, a confession obtained after breach of the section is excludable from evidence at the judge's discretion.

Under s. 62 a police officer is responsible for informing the person reasonably named of the arrest — the arrestee has no right to make the telephone call himself. However, the administrative directions say that a person in custody should be allowed to 'speak on the telephone to his solicitor or to his friends', and send letters with 'the least possible delay'. This is subject to the proviso that 'no hindrance is reasonably likely to be caused to the processes of investigation or the administration of justice'. Therefore, permission to make a telephone call etc. is in the discretion of the police.

19.4 POLICE POWERS OF SEARCH

A second major way in which the police obtain evidence of crime is through searching the person or home of an arrested person.

19.4.1 Powers of search on arrest

Donaldson LJ in *Lindley* v *Rutter* [1980] 3WLR 660 stated at p. 665 that:

It is the duty of any constable who lawfully has a prisoner in his charge to take all reasonable measures to ensure that the prisoner does not escape or assist others to do so, does not injure himself or others, does not destroy or dispose of evidence and does not commit further crime such as, for example, malicious damage to property.

To carry out this duty, the constable will normally have to search a person he has arrested either on arrest or, more probably, at the police station. The procedure for carrying out a search at the police station, noting on the charge sheet the property found, and returning such property as is not required for evidential purposes to the arrestee when he is released from police custody, has already been described (see Para. 19.2.2). The extent of the search which may lawfully be carried out depends on what is reasonable in the circumstances of the case. While a search of pockets, bags, wallet etc. is standard routine and on the face of it unobjectionable, a body search is far harder to justify. In *Lindley* v *Rutter* (supra) a woman police constable who forcibly removed L's brassiere was, in the circumstances of the case, not acting in the execution of her duty. L had been arrested for being drunk and disorderly, and, because at the police station she continued to shout and scream, she was placed in a cell. In accordance with what were understood to be standing orders for whenever a female prisoner was placed in a cell, attempts were made to remove her brassiere. L resisted, but her conviction for assaulting a police constable in the execution of her duty was quashed by the Divisional Court. Had there been reason to suppose that L was concealing drugs about her person, or had a weapon with which she might injure herself, or might even have used the brassiere to injure herself, the body search would have been justified. Since none of these justifications applied, it was unlawful.

In addition to searching the person of an arrestee, the police may search the premises where he lives, provided there is some connection between the purpose of the search and the offence for which he has been arrested. Thus, in *Jeffrey* v *Black* [1978] 1QB 490 B's lodgings were searched without his consent, following his arrest for stealing a sandwich from a public house. Cannabis was found as a result of the search. Since the police had no reason to suppose that B had in his lodgings a store of stolen sandwiches, the search had no connection with the arrest and was unlawful. Had cannabis been found on B's person, a search of his premises might have been justified as a person found in possession of drugs may well have further supplies at his home.

Where the police arrest a person in his house they are always entitled to search the house, and may seize any articles which they reasonably believe to be material evidence in relation to the crime for which the arrest is made: *Dillon* v *O'Brien and Davies* (1887) 16Cox 245. Provided they act reasonably, they may seize other articles found in the course of their search which implicate the arrestee in other offences.

19.4.2 Powers to search premises

Unless acting within the scope of a power given to them by statute or common law the police may not enter private premises without the consent of the occupier. As already mentioned there is power under the Criminal Law Act 1967, s. 2(6), for a constable to enter premises with a view to effecting an arrest without warrant for an arrestable offence (see Para. 19.2.1). There is also power at common law, subject to the limitations explained in *Jeffrey* v *Black* (supra), to search the home of an arrested person. In addition, numerous statutes empower magistrates to grant warrants authorising the police to enter premises in order to search for and seize evidence of crime. The most important of these provisions is s. 26 of the Theft Act 1968. It states that a magistrate who, as a result of an information laid before him on oath, has reasonable cause to believe that 'any person has in his custody or possession or on his premises any stolen goods' may 'grant a warrant to search for and seize the same'. The warrant may only be issued to a police officer. It names the premises to be searched and the property to be seized, but if, in the course of their search, the police find other property they believe to be stolen they may seize that also: s. 26(3). 'Stolen property' is defined so as to include property obtained by deception or blackmail.

A magistrate should not issue a search warrant without first satisfying himself that, in all the circumstances, it is right to do so. The practical steps which he can take to ascertain that the warrant is justified would seem, however, to be limited. The Lord Chancellor has stated that an officer applying for a warrant may be questioned by the magistrate, but should not be required to identify his informants, although he may be asked whether the informant is known to him, and whether any further enquiries have been made to verify what the informant has said.

As an alternative to obtaining a search warrant a police officer may be given by an officer not below the rank of superintendent written authority to search any premises for stolen goods if:

(a)   the person occupying the premises has been convicted within the preceding five years of any imprisonable offence involving dishonesty, or

(b)   a person who within the preceding five years has been convicted of handling stolen goods and has within the preceding twelve months been in occupation of the premises: Theft Act 1968, s. 26(2).

> The law on powers of search contains some surprising lacunae. For example, there is no power to issue a warrant authorising a police officer to search private premises in order to discover evidence of a murder. As Lord Denning MR. observed in *Ghani* v *Jones* [1970] 1QB 693 at p.705 —
> 'The police have to get the consent of the householder to enter if they can; or, if not, to do it by stealth or by force. Somehow they seem to manage. No decent person refuses them permission. If he does, he is probably implicated in some way or other. So the police risk an action for trespass. It is not much risk.'
> If, otherwise than in the course of executing a search warrant or searching the person or premises of an arrestee, the police discover an article which could be of evidential value, they may take and retain it if:
>
>   (a)   they have reasonable grounds for believing that so serious an offence has been committed that it is of the first importance that the offenders should be brought to justice, and
>   (b)   they have reasonable grounds for believing that the article is either the fruit of the crime, or the instrument by which the crime was committed, or material evidence to prove the commission of the crime, and
>   (c)   they have reasonable grounds for believing that the person in possession of the article has himself committed the crime or is implicated in it, or at any rate that his refusal to hand over the article is quite unreasonable. (*Ghani* v *Jones* supra). Having taken an article the police should not keep it for longer than is reasonably necessary to complete their investigations or preserve it as evidence (e.g. by taking a copy of it if a copy will suffice).

19.4.3   Powers to stop and search

Except when they are acting in execution of a warrant, the police powers of search normally arise after they have arrested a suspect. They do not, generally speaking, have power to search a person in order to obtain the evidence which would justify an arrest. However, various statutes give to the police limited powers to stop and search people without prior arrest. Under the Misuse of Drugs Act 1971, s. 23, for example, a constable who reasonably suspects that a person is in possession of a controlled drug may search him and detain him for that purpose. There is a similar power under the Firearms Act 1968, s. 47, to search anybody reasonably suspected of having a firearm in a public place. In both cases, vehicles may also be stopped and searched. Within the Metropolitan Police Area persons may be searched on reasonable suspicion of 'having or conveying in any manner anything stolen or unlawfully obtained': Metropolitan Police Act 1839, s. 66. Depending on what is found as a result of searches under these and similar provisions, the police officer concerned may be able to arrest and charge the suspect.

19.4.4   Unlawful searches

Until the case of *R* v *Sang* [1979] 3WLR 263, it was thought that where relevant evidence had been obtained by unlawful or unfair means (e.g. an illegal search) it was *prima facie* admissible in a criminal trial but the judge had a discretion to exclude it. According to *Jeffrey* v *Black* [1978] 1QB 490 (see Para. 19.4.1) the discretion could only be exercised where the police in obtaining the evidence had not merely been guilty of technical infringements of the law, but had used trickery, or had misled someone, or had behaved in a manner which was unfair, oppressive or otherwise morally reprehensible. Limited though the application of the discretion was, three successive Lord Chief Justices (Lords Goddard, Parker and Widgery) affirmed that it existed. However, in *R* v *Sang* (supra) the House of Lords held that:

> Save with regard to admissions and confessions and generally with regard to evidence obtained from the accused after commission of the offence the judge has no discretion to refuse to admit relevant evidence on the grounds that it was obtained by improper or unfair means. The court is not concerned with how it was obtained.

While agreeing on that statement of the law, the Law Lords interpreted it in slightly different ways. On the specific point of whether the judge has a discretion to exclude evidence obtained through an unlawful search of the accused's person or premises, they held by a majority of three or two to one that there is no such discretion (Lords Dilhorne, Diplock and probably Scarman were in the majority; Lord Fraser said that in England, as in Scotland, there is a discretion, and Lord Salmon declined to comment). As a result of *R* v *Sang* there is little to discourage the police from taking the risk of making an unlawful search, apart from their own integrity and disciplinary procedures. The legality or illegality of the search by means of which evidence was discovered has no bearing whatsoever on its admissibility, and, as Lord Denning MR remarked in *Ghani* v *Jones* (supra), there is little chance of the victim of an unlawful search bringing a civil action for trespass.

19.5 OBTAINING EVIDENCE OF IDENTITY

It is undesirable to ask a witness to identify the accused for the first time when he (the accused) is standing in the dock. Since the witness knows that the person in the dock is the person suspected of the offence, there is a risk that he will identify him even if he is not really sure of the correctness of his identification. Therefore, if the police have arrested a suspect, and hope that a witness will be able to pick him out as the person he saw committing the offence, they should arrange for the witness to attend at an identification parade.

The rules for the holding of identification parades are set out in a Home Office circular (No. 109 of 1978). The main points about the procedure are:

(a) The parade should normally be held at a police station. If the suspect is in prison, having already been charged and remanded in custody by the magistrates, the parade may take place at the prison if bringing the suspect to the police station for it would create a serious security problem.

(b) The police officer in charge of the parade should not be below the rank of inspector. No officer concerned with the investigation of the case may take part in the arrangements for or conduct of the parade, although he may be present at it provided he does not intervene in any way.

(c) Prior to the arranging of a parade, the suspect must be told that he is not obliged to take part in one, but that if he does he is entitled to have a solicitor or friend present at it unless that would cause unreasonable delay or difficulty.

Immediately before a parade, the officer in charge explains the procedure to the suspect.

(d)   In addition to the suspect there should be on the parade at least eight members of the public who are 'as far as possible of the same age, height, general appearance (including standard of dress and grooming) and position in life as the suspect.' One suspect only should be included in a parade, unless there are two suspects of roughly similar appearance, in which case they may be paraded together with at least twelve other persons. The suspect must be allowed to choose his own position in the line of the parade. He is also asked whether he has any objections to the members of the parade (e.g. on the ground that they do not resemble him in appearance). Any objection is recorded and, if possible, steps are taken to overcome it.

(e)   Before the parade, the witness should be prevented from seeing any member of it. No information should be given to him as to the identity of the suspect, and especial care must be taken to avoid his seeing the suspect 'in circumstances indicating that he is the suspect' (e.g. emerging from a prison van after being brought from prison to stand on the parade). Immediately before the witness inspects the parade he is told that the person he saw may or may not be on the parade. The witness then inspects the parade. If he is able to make an identification, he touches the relevant person or, if he is too nervous to do that, points him out. The witness should be told that if he cannot make a positive identification he should say so.

(f)   If more than one witness has been asked to attend the parade, they are brought in to inspect it one at a time. After each witness has left the room the suspect is asked whether he wishes to change his position in the line.

(g)   After the last witness has left the suspect is given an opportunity to comment on the conduct of the parade, and anything he says is noted.

The Attorney-General stated in his guidelines on identification evidence (27 May 1976 Hansard Vol. 912 No. 115) that, in deciding whether to institute proceedings, the Director of Public Prosecutions would take into account any failure to comply with the Home Office guidance on the holding of identification parades. The Attorney-General and the DPP both hoped that other prosecutors, although not bound by the guidelines, would adopt the approach recommended in them. If a prosecution does take place despite an error in the conduct of a parade at which the accused was identified, the unsatisfactory nature of the parade will affect the quality of the identification evidence. It may be a contributory factor in leading the judge to withdraw the case from the jury. Even if the case is left to the jury to decide, the judge in his summing up should remind them of what went wrong at the parade and its possible effect on the reliability of the identification: see *R* v *Turnbull* [1977] QB 224 for the principles governing cases where identity is in issue.

A suspect is always entitled to refuse to stand on an identification parade. If he does refuse, the police may, if it is possible, arrange for the witness to see him in a group of people so as to test whether the witness can pick him out. A witness should only be allowed to confront the suspect if no alternative method of identification is possible (e.g. because the suspect is of such singular appearance that he would stand out in any group). A 'dock identification' (i.e. an identification of an accused in court by a witness who has not previously identified him either on a parade or otherwise) is undesirable, but may be permitted for instance where the accused has refused to take part in a parade, or where the witness has been too ill to attend a parade as a result of injuries received through the offence alleged against the accused (*R* v *John* [1973] Crim L R 113 and *R* v *Caird and others* (1970) 54 Cr App R 499 respectively).

A witness should not, generally speaking, have seen a photograph of the suspect before attempting to pick him out at an identification parade. If a witness sees a photograph, there is a danger of his identifying the suspect not because he saw him committing the offence but because he saw him in a photograph. Therefore, if the police have a suspect who is available to stand on a parade, they should not show a witness photographs but should arrange a parade as soon as possible. Sometimes, however, the police do not have a definite suspect. In such cases they may ask a witness to look at photographs of people who might have been involved in the offence: *R* v *Palmer* (1914) 10Cr App R 77. Usually, of course, the photographs will be of persons who, as a result of previous convictions, appear in police records. If the witness makes a positive identification from a photograph, no more should be shown either to him or to other witnesses, but both he and the other witnesses should be asked to attend an identification parade. Where a witness picks out the suspect on a parade after first identifying him by photograph, the defence should be informed of the fact. It is rarely referred to in court since the jury are likely to conclude that, as the police had a picture of the accused, he must have previous convictions.

The Home Office circular No. 109 of 1978 gives detailed guidance on how photographs are to be shown to witnesses. The main point is that not less than 12 photographs should be shown at a time.

19.5.1 Fingerprint evidence

By far the safest form of identification evidence is that provided by fingerprints or palmprints. If the police do not have a suspect's prints in their records, they can always, with his consent, take them at the police station. Where they obtain his consent without warning him that the prints could be used in evidence against him or where they use trickery to obtain his consent, the prints are still, as a matter of law, admissible in evidence: *Callis* v *Gunn* [1964] 1QB 495. According to Lord Parker CJ. in *Callis* v *Gunn* there is a discretion, in such cases, to exclude the evidence, but it is not clear whether the discretion has survived the decision of the House of Lords in *R* v *Sang* [1979] 3WLR 263.

If a suspect refuses to have his finger or palmprints taken, a magistrates' court may order that they be taken: Magistrates' Courts Act 1980, s. 49. An order may only be made upon the application of a police officer not below the rank of inspector. The person in respect of whom the order is made must be aged at least 14 and must either:

(a) have been taken into custody and be charged with an offence before a magistrates' court, or

(b) appear before a magistrates' court in answer to a summons for an imprisonable offence.

If an order is made, the prints are taken by a constable who may use reasonable force for that purpose. Should the person concerned be acquitted of the offence alleged, the prints and any copies made of them must be destroyed.

19.6 SPECIAL CASES

The procedures which have been described in the preceding Paragraphs of this Chapter are varied in the cases of certain classes of suspects.

19.6.1   Terrorist offences

A constable may arrest a person whom he reasonably suspects to be guilty of an offence under certain provisions of the Prevention of Terrorism (Temporary Provisions) Act 1976, including the offence of belonging to a proscribed organisation (i.e. the I.R.A. or the Irish National Liberation Army). A person so arrested may be detained in right of the arrest for up to 48 hours, and the Home Secretary may extend that period for up to a further five days. Section 43 of the Magistrates' Courts Act (bail from the police station, bringing the arrestee before a magistrates' court as soon as practicable etc.) does not apply (s. 12 of the 1976 Act).

19.6.2   Juveniles

A juvenile may be arrested with or without warrant in the same circumstances as justify the arrest of an adult. Having been arrested, the officer in charge of the station to which he is brought or other officer not below the rank of inspector must enquire into his case and release him unless either:

(a)   the officer considers that he ought in his own interests to be further detained, or

(b)   the officer has reason to believe that he has committed a grave crime, or that his release would defeat the ends of justice, or that if released he would fail to appear to answer to any charge which might be made: Children and Young Persons Act 1969, s. 29(1).

If the juvenile is not released, arrangements must be made for him to be taken into the care of and detained by the local authority, unless the officer who enquired into his case certifies that it is impracticable to make such arrangements or, having regard to the juvenile's unruly character, such arrangements would be inappropriate: s. 29(3). A juvenile detained under s. 29(3) must be brought before a magistrates' court within 72 hours of his arrest: s. 29(5). The period is longer than that within which, according to *Re Sherman and Apps* (1980) 'The Times' December 9th, an adult should either be brought before the magistrates or released, but, whereas an adult is kept at the police station unless released, a juvenile, subject to a certificate of unruliness, is either released or put into the local authority's care.

Section 34 of the Children and Young Persons Act 1933 provides that a person who arrests a juvenile must take all practicable steps to inform at least one of his parents of what has occurred. The administrative directions appended to the Judges' Rules state that a juvenile (whether suspected of crime or not) should as far as practicable only be interviewed in the presence of a parent or, if that is not possible, in the presence of a non-police officer of the same sex as the juvenile (e.g. a social worker). If it is proposed to put a juvenile on an identification parade, his parents should be invited to be present, and the parade should not be held unless a parent, solicitor or other adult who is not a police officer attends. As to the arrangements which should be made for the detention of juveniles at police stations, the Home Office has advised that secure accommodation, other than cells, should be provided. Juveniles should not be placed in cells unless they are so unruly as to be likely to cause damage if placed in other accommodation (Home Office Consolidated Circular to the Police on Crime and

Kindred Matters, 1977). In some cases it may not even be necessary to put the juvenile in a secure room.

Rather than being charged at the police station, a juvenile is usually released without charge so that the police may take advice on whether to prosecute or not. If they decide to proceed, an information is laid and summons issued. About half the police forces have specialised juvenile bureaux which advise on whether a prosecution is appropriate. It is common practice in all forces to liaise with for instance the local authority social services department or the probation service. The Home Office recommend that juveniles should not be prosecuted if that can be avoided. One way of avoiding a prosecution is formally to caution a juvenile. This involves the juvenile and his parents attending at the police station where a senior police officer administers the caution. The juvenile must admit the offence, and his parents must agree to it being dealt with by means of caution. Although a caution does not amount to a finding of guilt, it is cited in the same way as previous findings of guilt if the juvenile is subsequently found guilty of an offence. The views of the victim of the offence and of the social services department may be taken into account in deciding whether a caution is appropriate. Cautions are not normally considered if the juvenile has previously been cautioned or prosecuted. In 1978, of all juveniles cautioned or found guilty of indictable offences, 49% were cautioned.

19.6.3 'Hard cases'

Trivial road traffic offences committed by adults are often dealt with by way of a caution. The caution is given by a letter sent through the post. The motorist is not required to admit the offence, and the fact that he has been cautioned may not be referred to should he subsequently be prosecuted for another offence. Otherwise, adults suspected of offences are normally prosecuted if the police officer taking the decision on whether to commence proceedings considers that, on the evidence available to him, there is a reasonable chance of securing a conviction. Even where the evidence is strong, however, an element of discretion enters into the officer's decision. He might refrain from prosecuting if the offence alleged was merely a technical or trivial infringement, or if the law contravened is archaic or controversial, or if humanitarian considerations apply (e.g. the suspect is very old or suffering from serious mental or physical disorder). In the last type of case especially a caution might be preferable to a prosecution, but cautions are unusual in the cases of adults suspected of non-motoring offences. If a caution is given, it cannot be referred to in any subsequent proceedings.

> The Director of Public Prosecutions, in a Note provided for the Royal Commission on Criminal Procedure indicated the criteria by which he judged whether or not to commence a prosecution or give his consent to a prosecution. The primary consideration is the quality of the evidence:

> The test normally used in the Department in deciding whether evidence is sufficient to justify proceedings is whether or not there is a reasonable prospect of a conviction; whether, in other words, it seems rather more likely that there will be a conviction than an acquittal.

> But, even if the evidence is good enough, the Director may decide not to prosecute because for example the offence is stale, or the accused is elderly or infirm or suffering from a mental condition which would be worsened by the stress of a trial, or in a case of unlawful sexual

intercourse, the offender and 'victim' are of similar age so that there is no question of an older man corrupting a young girl, or the victim of the offence does not now want a prosecution to be brought.

19.7 ADJOURNMENTS AFTER THE FIRST COURT APPEARANCE

When an accused appears or is brought before magistrates for the first time it is unusual for the case to be dealt with on that occasion. Sometimes the accused wants an adjournment so that he can obtain legal aid and instruct solicitors, sometimes the prosecution are still considering preferring further charges, sometimes either or both parties need more time to prepare statements or interview potential witnesses. Even if the parties are ready to proceed, it may well be that the court will only have time to deal with the case on the basis of a guilty plea or a committal without consideration of the evidence, so if the accused is pleading not guilty or arguing that there is no case to answer there will have to be an adjournment. The magistrates always have a discretion to adjourn a case before or during committal proceedings or summary trial (Magistrates' Courts Act 1980, ss. 5 and 10 — for adjournments after summary conviction, see Para. 11.7). When they adjourn prior to or during trial for a summary offence they may, but need not, remand the accused (s. 10(4) of the 1980 Act). By remanding the accused is meant either committing him to custody to be brought before the court on the day the hearing is to be resumed, or releasing him on bail under a duty to surrender to the custody of the court on that day. If the magistrates adjourn without remanding the accused, he is under no duty to appear for the resumed hearing but obviously runs the risk of being convicted in his absence if he fails to do so. Where the magistrates adjourn prior to or during committal proceedings for an offence triable only on indictment, they must remand the accused: s. 5. Where they adjourn prior to determining the mode of trial for an offence triable either way, they must remand the accused unless he initially appeared in answer to a summons and has not subsequently been remanded: s. 18(4).

Except when the magistrates have summarily convicted an offender and have adjourned for reports under s. 10(3) or s. 30 of the 1980 Act, they may not remand a person in custody for a period exceeding eight clear days: s. 128(6). This means that an accused remanded in custody is brought from prison to the magistrates' court roughly once a week. If there has been any change in the circumstances which might justify the granting of bail, a fresh bail application may be made (see Para. 20.4.1). It should be noted that s. 128(6) only applies to *remands* in custody by magistrates, not to committals for trial or sentence in custody. A person committed in custody will certainly spend more than eight clear days in prison before his case is heard in the Crown Court, but there is no requirement to bring him before either the magistrates or the Crown Court every eight days. A remand on bail may be for more than eight clear days if the prosecution and defence consent. There is absolutely no reason why they should not consent.

20   Bail

Bail is the release of a person subject to a duty to surrender to custody at an appointed time and place. The time when the person bailed is to surrender to custody may be fixed when bail is granted or, in the case of a person committed on bail to the Crown Court for trial or sentence, it may be notified to him subsequently. The place where he is to surrender to custody is either a court or a police station. The granting of bail in criminal proceedings is governed by the Bail Act 1976.

20.1 OCCASIONS ON WHICH A PERSON MAY BE GRANTED BAIL

Most of the occasions on which a court or judge or police officer is faced with the decision to grant or refuse bail have been mentioned in the course of the preceding Chapters. Those occasions are as follows:

(a) A station sergeant or officer not below the rank of inspector must consider releasing on bail any person who, having been arrested without warrant and taken to the police station, cannot be brought before a magistrates' court within 24 hours: Magistrates' Courts Act 1980, s. 43 — see Para. 19.2.3. Where a juvenile is taken to the station under arrest and cannot immediately be brought before a juvenile court, the officer must forthwith consider releasing him, whether on bail or otherwise: Children and Young Persons Act 1969, s. 29 — see Para. 19.6.2.

(b) A magistrate issuing a warrant for the arrest of the person named in an information laid on oath before him should consider whether to endorse the warrant for bail: Magistrates' Courts Act 1980, s. 117 — see Para. 19.2.9. Similarly, a magistrates' court or the Crown Court on issuing a warrant may back it for bail: s. 117 and Courts Act 1971 s. 13(6).

(c) A magistrates' court has jurisdiction to grant bail when:

(i) it remands an accused for the period of an adjournment prior to committal proceedings or summary trial: Magistrates' Courts Act 1980, ss. 5, 10(4) and 18(4) — see Para. 19.7, or

(ii) it remands an offender after conviction for the period of an adjournment for reports under s. 10(3) or s. 30 of the 1980 Act: see Para. 11.7, or

(iii) it commits an accused to the Crown Court for trial on indictment or commits an offender to the Crown Court for sentence (ss. 6(3) and 38 of the 1980 Act which provide respectively that committals for trial and sentence may be in custody or on bail), or

(iv) a person in custody is appealing to the Crown Court or the Divisional Court against one of its (the magistrates' court's) decisions: s. 113 of the 1980 Act — see Para. 18.1.2 and 18.2.2.

Remanding the accused means releasing him on bail or committing him to custody until the day to which the case has been adjourned. Prior to committal proceedings or summary trial the maximum period for a remand in custody is eight clear days: s. 128(6). A remand under s. 10(3) or s. 30 for reports on an offender may be for up to three weeks if it is in custody, or for up to four weeks if it is on bail. The decision to grant or refuse bail when committing for trial or sentence is probably the most important decision taken concerning bail, since a period of several weeks or months will elapse between the committal and the accused's case being heard at the Crown Court. If he is refused bail, he will be in custody for the whole of that period, unless he makes a successful bail application to either the Crown Court or the High Court.

(d) The Crown Court has jurisdiction to grant bail when a person has been committed to it by the magistrates for trial or sentence, or is appealing to it against conviction or sentence by the magistrates, or is appealing from it to the Divisional Court by way of case stated, or is applying for *certiorari* to quash one of its decisions: Courts Act 1971, s. 13(4). The Crown Court also has jurisdiction to grant bail during a trial on indictment. If the accused was on bail prior to the commencement of his trial and surrenders to custody at the appointed time, it is normal practice to renew his bail for the period of any overnight adjournments. Bail may be withdrawn, however, where there is a real danger that the accused might abscond (e.g. because the case is going badly for him), or interfere with witnesses or jurors. The former reason often leads to bail not being renewed after the judge has commenced his summing up (see Practice Note 1974 1WLR 770). After conviction, bail may be granted during an adjournment for reports prior to sentence.

(e) The High Court has jurisdiction to grant bail when:

(i) a magistrates' court withholds bail: Criminal Justice Act 1967, s. 22, or

(ii) a person is applying to it for *certiorari* to quash a magistrates' court's decision: Criminal Justice Act 1948, s. 37, or

(iii) a person is appealing to it by way of case stated from the Crown Court, or is applying to it for *certiorari* to quash a Crown Court decision: s. 37 of the 1948 Act. There is also jurisdiction to vary any conditions of bail imposed by a magistrates' court. The High Court's jurisdiction to grant or vary the terms of bail is exercised by a judge in chambers.

(f) The Criminal Division of the Court of Appeal has jurisdiction to grant bail both to a person appealing to it against conviction or sentence in the Crown Court, and to a person who, after an unsuccessful appeal to it, is further appealing to the House of Lords: Criminal Appeal Act 1968, ss. 19 and 36 — see Paras. 17.6.6 and 17.8. The power of the Court of Appeal to grant bail is one of the powers exercisable by a single judge.

20.2 PRINCIPLES ON WHICH THE DECISION TO GRANT OR REFUSE BAIL IS TAKEN

Section 4 of the Bail Act 1976 gives to an accused person what may usefully, if slightly inaccurately, be described as a right to bail. The section does not apply at all stages of the criminal process, and, even if it does apply, the accused may be refused bail if the circumstances of his case fall within one of a number of sets of circumstances defined in Schedule 1 to the Act. Where the accused is charged with an offence punishable with imprisonment, the circumstances mentioned in Schedule 1 as justifying the refusal of bail are just those circumstances in which, prior to the passing of the Act, judges and magistrates would, as a matter of practice, have tended to remand or commit in custody. Nevertheless, the right to bail is of value to an accused because it emphasises that it is for the prosecution to show a good reason why bail should be withheld, not for the defence to plead for bail as a favour to which the accused is not *prima facie* entitled.

20.2.1 Occasions on which there is a 'right to bail'

Section 4 provides that a person to whom it applies 'shall be granted bail except as provided in Schedule 1'. The section applies whenever a person accused of an offence appears or is brought before a magistrates' court or the Crown Court in the course of or in connection with proceedings for the offence. Thus, at his first court appearance before the magistrates and at all subsequent appearances before the magistrates or the Crown Court up to the occasion on which he is convicted or acquitted, the accused has a right to bail. Even following conviction, he still has a right to bail if his case is adjourned for reports prior to sentencing. He can also rely on the right to bail if, during these stages of the proceedings, he applies to the High Court or the Crown Court for bail following a refusal of bail by the magistrates. There is no right to bail when:

(a) the station sergeant or officer not below the rank of inspector is considering bailing an arrestee from the police station, or

(b) the magistrates, having summarily convicted an offender, commit him to the Crown Court for sentence, or

(c) a person who has been convicted and sentenced, whether by the magistrates or in the Crown Court, is appealing against conviction or sentence.

Of course, in all three cases the police officer or court has power to grant bail, but the matter is entirely one of discretion — there is no initial presumption in favour of bail. Indeed, where the person seeking bail has been committed for sentence, or has been convicted and sentenced but is appealing, there are strong arguments against bail. In the former case, the magistrates have indicated by their decision that they think a custodial sentence of some length is called for, so granting bail is almost an invitation to the offender to abscond. In the latter case, it is undesirable to release on bail a person who, if his appeal fails, will have to be recalled to prison.

20.2.2 Refusing bail for a defendant charged with an imprisonable offence

Schedule 1 to the Bail Act 1976 sets out the circumstances in which a person to whom s. 4 applies (i.e. a person with a right to bail) may be refused bail. The Schedule refers to a person with a right to bail as 'the defendant'.

Part I of the Schedule applies when the defendant stands accused or convicted of at least one offence punishable with imprisonment. He need not be granted bail if:

(a) the court is satisfied that there are substantial grounds for believing that, if released on bail, he would:

(i) fail to surrender to custody, or

(ii)   commit an offence while on bail, or

(iii)   interfere with witnesses or otherwise obstruct the course of justice whether in relation to himself or some other person, or

(b)   the court is satisfied that he should be kept in custody for his own protection or, if he is a juvenile, for his own welfare, or

(c)   he is already serving a custodial sentence, or

(d)   the court is satisfied that lack of time since the commencement of the proceedings has made it impracticable to obtain the information needed to decide properly the questions raised in (a) to (c) above, or

(e)   he has already been bailed during the course of the proceedings, and has been arrested under s. 7 of the Act (arrest of absconders etc. — see Para. 20.6.1).

Some of the above reasons for refusing bail call for little comment. A defendant accused of an offence which has roused much local or national anger may be refused bail for his own protection. In the case of a juvenile, the justification for refusing bail is a little wider, and includes not just his protection but his welfare. Thus, he might be remanded in the care of the local authority if, were he to be released on bail, he would return to a very undesirable environment. Where the defendant is serving a custodial sentence for some other matter, there is little point in going through the motions of a bail application, and where he has already been granted bail in the proceedings but has absconded the court is entitled to say the legal equivalent of 'once bitten twice shy'. Reason (d) for refusing bail is likely to be relevant if the defendant was arrested without warrant and kept in custody at the police station until his first appearance before the magistrates. He will probably not have been able to instruct solicitors, so, unless he is more articulate than the average defendant, the arguments for bail are unlikely to be cogently presented. If there is a duty solicitor present in court, the magistrates may assign him to act for the defendant, but the shortness of time in which to take instructions still militates against an effective bail application. The police may be equally embarrassed in presenting the objections to bail. In the day or so, or possibly only hours, since the defendant was arrested, they may not have been able to check on the information he has given them about himself. He may have claimed to have no convictions, but, even if a check with the criminal records department reveals that nobody of the name given by the defendant is on the files, it is possible that he has given a false name. Again, he may have claimed to have a permanent address and be in steady employment — both factors which increase his chances of bail — but the police will not have had time to confirm or contradict what he asserts. In such cases, the magistrates often play safe by remanding the defendant in custody for a week, at the end of which time, it is hoped, the question of bail can be properly argued on both sides.

The commonest reasons for refusing bail are that, if granted bail, the defendant would fail to surrender to custody, or commit an offence on bail, or interfere with witnesses. Paragraph 9 of Part I of Schedule 1 mentions four considerations which, together with any other relevant factors, the court is to take into account when deciding whether one of these reasons applies. The first consideration is the 'nature and seriousness of the offence and the probable method of dealing with the defendant for it.' There is no rule that a defendant charged with a grave offence (e.g. murder) cannot be granted bail, but the graver the offence charged the more likely it is that the defendant, realising that conviction will result in a substantial prison sentence, would abscond if granted bail. Similarly, the risk of absconding increases where the defendant, if convicted, will be in breach of a suspended sentence. Secondly, the court must consider the 'character, antecedents, associations and community ties of the defendant.' Previous convictions are thus relevant to the granting of bail both for the light they shed on the defendant's character and for the probable effect they will have on sentence should there be a conviction. In considering the community ties of the defendant the court assesses how much he has to lose by absconding. A man who is married with children, who has a steady job and who is buying his own home has much more to lose, if he absconds, than a teenager who is out of work and living in a hostel. Nevertheless, a Home Office circular of 1975 (No. 155) stated that a defendant should not be regarded as more likely to abscond merely because he lives in a bedsitter or a hostel — it is one factor which, combined with others, may show a lack of roots in the community and therefore a likelihood of absconding. Thirdly, in the case of a defendant who has been granted bail in connection with previous criminal proceedings, the court considers whether he answered to his bail and whether he committed any offences while on bail. Lastly, the court considers the strength of the prosecution case against the defendant — the weaker it is the more likely the defendant is to be granted bail for fear of an innocent man spending a substantial time in custody prior to his trial. One problem is that the strength or weakness of the prosecution case may not be disclosed until committal proceedings.

In addition to the considerations mentioned in paragraph 9, the court bears in mind any other relevant factors. For example, the number and quality of the sureties available may reduce the risk of the defendant absconding, the fact that the defendant allegedly committed the offence now charged while on bail for another offence increases the risk that he will commit further offences if again granted bail, and colour may be leant to a suggestion that the defendant would interfere with witnesses by a police officer giving evidence that a potential prosecution witness has complained of threatening telephone calls.

If the defendant's case has been adjourned for reports following conviction and prior to sentencing, there is one further reason for refusing bail. The reason is that the necessary inquiries could not be completed or the report made without the defendant being kept in custody.

20.2.3 Refusing bail for a defendant charged with a non-imprisonable offence

Part II of Schedule 1 applies when none of the offences of which the defendant stands accused or convicted is punishable with imprisonment. He need not be granted bail if reasons (b), (c) or (e) for refusing to grant bail to a defendant accused of an imprisonable offence apply in his case (i.e. he should be kept in custody for his own protection, he is already serving a custodial sentence, or he has been bailed in the course of the proceedings and arrested under s. 7). There is no general power to refuse bail on the grounds that he might abscond, but, if he failed to surrender to custody after being bailed in previous criminal proceedings and the court therefore believes that, if now granted bail, he would again fail to surrender, bail may be refused.

20.3 REQUIREMENTS IMPOSED WHEN GRANTING BAIL

A defendant may be granted bail unconditionally, in which case he is not required to provide sureties before being released and, having been released, the only obligation he is under is that of surrendering to custody at the appointed place and time. Alternatively, s. 3 of the Bail Act allows the police or the courts to attach requirements to a grant of bail.

The most common of the requirements attached to bail is that of providing one or more sureties. Both the police when bailing an arrestee from the station and the courts may require sureties, but they should only do so if it is necessary to ensure that the defendant surrenders to custody. A surety is a person who undertakes to pay the court a specified sum of money in the event of the defendant failing to surrender to custody as he ought. The undertaking into which the surety enters is called a recognisance. If the defendant absconds the surety may be ordered to pay part or all of the sum in which he stood surety. This is known as forfeiting or estreating the recognisance. A surety whose recognisance has been estreated is dealt with as if he had been fined, so if he fails to pay the sum forfeited a means inquiry is held and, ultimately, he could be committed to prison. The possibly serious consequences of being a surety mean that no person proffered as a surety should be accepted as such unless he apparently has the means to satisfy his potential liability under the recognisance. On granting bail, the police officer or court fixes the number and amount of the sureties which will be required, and the defendant must remain in custody until suitable sureties in the stated sums have entered into their recognisances. If the sureties are not forthcoming the defendant, at his next appearance before the court or on an application to a High Court judge in chambers, may argue that the requirement for sureties should be varied or dispensed with all together.

A requirement for sureties does not involve the sureties or the defendant himself paying money to the court as a pre-condition of his release on bail. Where, however, the defendant is unlikely to remain in Great Britain until the time appointed for his surrender to custody he 'may be required before release on bail to give security for his surrender to custody': s. 3(5). Giving security means that the defendant or somebody on his behalf deposits money or other property with the court, which will be forfeited if he absconds. The requirement is rarely imposed but could be useful for instance where a wealthy businessman is planning trips abroad before his next court appearance.

Instead of or in addition to imposing a requirement for sureties or, where appropriate, a requirement for the giving of security, a court but not the police may require the defendant to comply with such other conditions of bail as appear necessary to ensure that he does not abscond, or commit offences while on bail, or interfere with witnesses. Requirements thus imposed may include ordering the defendant to report to a police station once a week or even once a day, ordering him to surrender his passport, ordering him to live at a certain address (e.g. with parents) or to report any change of address, placing him under a curfew so that he has to be indoors by a certain time each night, forbidding his speaking to potential prosecution witnesses, and forbidding his going within a certain distance of the address where a prosecution witness resides. Where the defendant's case has been adjourned after conviction so that reports can be prepared on him, he may be required to make himself available for the purpose of enabling the reports to be made. In particular, if a magistrates' court adjourns under s. 30 of the Magistrates' Courts Act 1980 for medical reports it may be made a condition of bail that the defendant attend at a hospital etc. to undergo the necessary examinations.

In the case of an adult defendant, the sureties have no responsibility for ensuring that the defendant complies with conditions of bail such as those just described — provided the defendant duly surrenders to custody the surety's recognisance is safe even if for example the defendant failed to report to the police station as required by the court. However, where a juvenile defendant's parent stands surety for him, the parent may, with his consent, be required to secure the juvenile's compliance with any conditions of bail imposed, but the sum to be forfeited in the event of non-compliance must not exceed £50.

20.4 PROCEDURE AT AN APPLICATION FOR BAIL IN A MAGISTRATES' COURT

Most bail applications are made in the magistrates' courts. The essentials of the procedure are as follows:

(a)   the officer dealing with the case or, if the police are legally represented, counsel or solicitor for the prosecution is asked by the court whether there are any objections to bail. Although the granting or refusal of bail is always a matter for the magistrates not the police, the former will obviously be much influenced by the latter having no objections to it. Therefore, if there are no police objections the magistrates normally agree without further question that bail should be granted, and the only live issue is what, if any, requirements should be attached to it.

(b)   Assuming there are objections, defence counsel or solicitor is asked whether he is applying for bail. If there is realistically no chance of bail being granted, he may refrain from making an application, but normally one is made, if only to satisfy the defendant that everything possible is being done on his behalf.

(c)   The officer takes the oath and gives his objections to bail. If the defendant has a right to bail under s. 4, the officer will have to show that one of the reasons for refusing bail applies. He could say for instance that the seriousness of the offence and the fact that the defendant has previously 'jumped bail' lead him to believe that, if granted bail, the defendant would fail to appear, or he could mention threats that the defendant has allegedly made against the prosecution witnesses, or he might remind the magistrates that the offence charged was allegedly committed while on bail for another offence. If one of the objections to bail is that the defendant has previous convictions, the better practice is to hand the magistrates a list of those convictions rather than referring to them orally: *R* v *Dyson* (1943) 29Cr App R 104. Defence counsel or solicitor may question the officer. Since much of the officer's evidence is in the realm of speculation and opinion rather than fact, effective cross-examination is difficult, but it could be suggested that the provision of sureties and/or the imposition of other requirements will overcome the officer's objections.

(d)   Defence counsel or solicitor makes a speech dealing with the objections, and stressing the points in favour of bail (e.g. the defendant can provide substantial sureties, has a fixed address, is in work and when granted bail in the past has always surrendered to custody).

(e)   The magistrates announce their decision.

20.4.1   Successive bail applications

The rule that a remand in custody prior to committal proceedings or summary trial must not exceed eight clear days sometimes leads to there being a series of adjournments and remands before the effective hearing of the case. Although the defendant must, subject to limited exceptions, be present for each remand hearing, the magistrates are not always obliged to hear a full bail application on his behalf. At the defendant's first court appearance, the magistrates must, of course, consider whatever he or his representative has to say in favour of bail. Indeed, even if no bail application is made they should satisfy themselves that the circumstances justify refusing bail. At subsequent hearings, however, they should bear in mind that a bench has already enquired into the defendant's case and found that one of the Schedule 1 reasons for refusing bail applies — otherwise the defendant would not have been remanded in custody. The principle of *res judicata,* or something analagous to it, applies to that finding: *R* v *Nottingham Justices* ex parte *Davies* [1980] 3WLR 15. Therefore, the magistrates need not, and indeed should not, consider a full bail application unless there are new considerations relevant to bail which were not before the bench which originally refused bail. The strictness of this rule is relaxed somewhat in that the Divisional Court in ex parte *Davies* (supra) recognised that where a defendant is arrested without warrant and brought from the police station to the court any bail application made on his behalf is likely to be inadequately presented through lack of time to prepare it properly. Their Lordships accordingly approved the practice of always hearing two full bail applications — i.e. one on the occasion of the defendant's first court appearance and a second when, as a result of an eight day remand in custody, the defence have had time to marshal their arguments and find sureties. If the second application fails, a third application can only be made if the defence satisfy the magistrates that new considerations have arisen. At the stage of committal for trial, however, new considerations will nearly always be present in that it will be easier to assess the strength or weakness of the prosecution case, and the seriousness of the alleged offence: per Donaldson LJ in *R* v *Reading Crown Court* ex parte *Malik* [1981] 2WLR 473. To summarise the position, a defendant charged with an indictable offence who is remanded on a series of occasions prior to committal proceedings may make full bail applications on his first two appearances and following his committal for trial. Any other applications to the magistrates are subject to his demonstrating that new considerations have arisen.

20.4.2 Taking sureties

If the magistrates grant bail subject to the provision of sureties, and the necessary sureties are present at court, they may enter into their undertakings before the magistrates. Section 8(2) of the Bail Act provides that, in considering the suitability of a proposed surety, regard may be had to his financial resources, character and previous convictions, and connection with the defendant (e.g. is he a relative, friend, neighbour etc.?). Before he formally agrees to be a surety, it is normal practice to explain to him the nature of his obligations and the possible consequences to him of the defendant absconding. He is also asked whether he is worth the sum involved after all his debts are paid. If the sureties are not at court when bail is granted, they may enter into their recognizances subsequently before a magistrate, magistrates' clerk, station sergeant or officer not below rank of inspector, or governor of the prison etc. where the defendant is in custody. Until they have done so, the defendant must remain in custody. If a surety attempts to enter into a recognizance before one of the persons mentioned above, but he declines to take the recognizance because he considers the surety unsuitable, the surety may apply to the court to take the recognizance.

To avoid the inconvenience to the sureties of their having to enter into recognizances every time the defendant's case is adjourned, the magistrates may make bail continuous. This means that on the occasion when bail is first granted the surety undertakes to pay the specified sum if the defendant fails to appear on any of the occasions to which his case is adjourned. If the offence charged is indictable the recognizance may be further extended to secure the defendant's appearance before the Crown Court should he be committed for trial: Magistrates' Courts Act 1980, s. 128(4).

Similar provisions to those described above apply when the Crown Court, Divisional Court or Court of Appeal grants bail subject to sureties. Continuous bail is particularly useful where, following the defendant's surrender to custody on the first day of his trial on indictment, he is granted bail for the overnight adjournments. If bail is made continuous the sureties only need to be present to enter into their recognizances on the occasion of the first adjournment: Criminal Justice Administration Act 1914, s. 19.

20.4.3 Recording and giving reasons for decisions on bail

Section 5 of the Bail Act sets out some administrative procedures which must be followed when decisions on bail are taken. If the police or a court grant bail, or a court withholds bail from a defendant with a right to bail under s. 4, a record must be made of the decision and, upon request, a copy of the record must be given to the defendant. Where a magistrates' court or the Crown Court withholds bail from a defendant with a right to bail, or imposes conditions on bail granted to such a defendant, it must give reasons for its decision. The reasons should be such as to help the defendant in deciding whether to make a further bail application to another court (see Para. 20.5). A note should be made of the reasons and a copy of the note given to the defendant (unless the decision was taken by the Crown Court and the defendant is represented by counsel or solicitor who does not request a copy). Magistrates who withhold bail from a defendant who is not legally represented must inform him that he may apply for bail to a judge in chambers, or, if he is being committed for trial in custody, that he may apply to a judge in chambers or the Crown Court.

20.4.4 Variations in the conditions of bail etc.

Where a court has granted bail either the prosecution or the defence may apply to it for a variation in the conditions of bail, or, if bail was granted unconditionally, the prosecution may apply for conditions to be imposed: Bail Act 1976, s. 3(8). If the defendant has been committed on bail to the Crown Court for trial or sentence, an application for variation may be made to either the Crown Court or the magistrates' court. Should the court decide to vary or impose conditions a record must be made of its decision. If the defendant has a right to bail, reasons for the decision are required, and the defendant is entitled to a copy of the note of the reasons: s. 5.

A magistrates' court which has remanded a defendant on bail to appear before it on a certain date may, if it is convenient, appoint a later date for the defendant to appear and amend the recognizances of any sureties accordingly: Magistrates' Courts Act 1980, s. 129(3). This power is useful if, for example, the court will not have time to deal with the defendant's case on the day originally fixed. Where a defendant who has been remanded in custody or on bail cannot be brought or appear before the magistrates on the day appointed because of illness or accident, the magistrates may further remand him in his absence, and a remand in custody may exceed eight clear days: Magistrates' Courts Act 1980, s. 129(1).

A defendant who is already serving a custodial sentence may be remanded in custody for up to 28 clear days, unless his sentence is expected to have been completed before the expiration of 28 days: Magistrates' Courts Act 1980, s. 131. For as long as he is still serving his custodial sentence, applications for further remands in custody may be made in his absence provided he is legally represented and consents to not being present.

20.5 APPLICATIONS TO THE CROWN COURT AND HIGH COURT FOR BAIL

Whenever a magistrates' court withholds bail or imposes conditions in granting bail the defendant may make an application to the High Court, which has jurisdiction to grant bail or vary the conditions of bail as the case may be: Criminal Justice Act 1967, s. 22. Whenever a defendant is committed in custody to the Crown Court for trial or sentence, or is in custody as a result of a sentence passed by a magistrates' court and is appealing to the Crown Court against his conviction or sentence, he may apply to the Crown Court for bail: Courts Act 1971, s. 13(4). Thus, a defendant who has been refused bail by the magistrates may always challenge the decision by applying to the High Court for bail, and sometimes has the additional option of applying to the Crown Court.

20.5.1 Applications to the High Court for bail

An application to the High Court for bail is made to a judge in chambers. The procedure is set out in Order 79 r.9 of the Rules of the Supreme Court 1965. It is to be followed both when an application is made under s. 22 of the 1967 Act after magistrates have refused bail, and when the High Court has jurisdiction under s. 37 of the Criminal Justice Act 1948 to grant bail to a person who has applied to the Crown Court to state a case or who is applying for *certiorari* to quash a Crown Court or a magistrates' court decision (see Para. 20.1).

The application is made by summons. The summons must be served on the prosecutor at least 24 hours before the hearing date, and must be supported by an affidavit setting out the grounds of the application. The summons calls upon the respondents to the application (i.e. the prosecution) to show cause why the defendant should not be granted bail or, if the defendant has been granted bail, to show cause why the conditions of bail should not be varied. If the application fails the defendant is not allowed to make a fresh application to another judge or to the Divisional Court (Ord. 79 r.9(12)), nor is there any appeal to the House of Lords (Supreme Court of Judicature (Consolidation) Act 1925, s. 31). If bail is granted subject to sureties being provided, the sureties may enter into their recognizances before any of the persons who may take a surety following a grant of bail by a magistrates' court (see Para. 20.4.2).

A defendant who is not legally represented will have great difficulty in swearing an affidavit and arranging for a summons to be served on the prosecutor. Since legal aid is not available for applications to a judge in chambers for bail, a method has had to be devised to enable defendants without the means to instruct solicitors to have their cases heard. The procedure they must adopt is laid down by paragraphs 4 and 5 of Order 79 r.9. Paragraph 4 states that a defendant who is in custody and desires to apply for bail, but is unable through lack of means to instruct a solicitor, may give written notice to the judge in chambers that he wishes the Official Solicitor to act for him for purposes of a bail application. If the judge, in his discretion, accedes to the defendant's request, the Official Solicitor makes all arrangements necessary for the proper presentation of the application. Having assigned the Official Solicitor to act for the defendant, the judge may, if he thinks fit, dispense with the requirements of serving a summons on the prosecutor and filing an affidavit in support. This will enable what seems to be on the face of it, a meritorious application to be brought before the judge with a minimum of dela

20.5.2 Applications to the Crown Court for bail

A defendant who has been committed in custody to the Crown Court, or who is appealing to the Crown Court and has been refused bail by the magistrates, may choose to apply to the Crown Court for bail in preference to or in addition to applying to a judge in chambers. The advantage of applying to the Crown Court is that if, as is probably the case, the defendant has been granted legal aid for the Crown Court proceedings that aid covers a bail application. The application, which may be heard in chambers, is normally listed for hearing by a circuit judge or recorder. If an unsuccessful application for bail has already been made to a judge in chambers, the Crown Court should be informed of that fact (Rule 18 of the Crown Court Rules 1971 SI No 1292), but it still has jurisdiction to hear the application: *R* v *Reading Crown Court* ex parte *Malik* [1981] 2WLR 473. Conversely, a judge in chambers may grant bail notwithstanding a prior application to the Crown Court — the jurisdictions of the High Court and Crown Court in relation to bail are distinct and independent of each other.

> The procedure for applying to the Crown Court for bail is to serve written notice on the prosecutor of intention to make the application. The notice must be served at least 24 hours before the application. The prosecutor must then do one of three things. He may either notify the appropriate officer of the Crown Court and the defendant that he wishes to be represented at the hearing of the application, or he may give notice that he does not oppose the application, or he may give to the appropriate officer, for the consideration of the Crown Court, a written statement of his reasons for opposing the application. A copy of the written statement must be sent to the defendant. Although he may be given leave to attend the hearing of the application, the defendant has no right to be present. If bail is granted subject to the provision of sureties, they may enter into their recognisances before an appropriate officer of the Crown Court or before any of the persons who may take a surety following a grant of bail by magistrates (see Para. 20.4.2).
>
> The above procedure is not applicable where a bail application is made during the course of the Crown Court proceedings (e.g. for bail during the period of an overnight adjournment). Such applications are made without notice to the judge trying the case. Probably counsel would wait for the jury to leave court before making the application.

20.6 CONSEQUENCES OF A DEFENDANT ABSCONDING

If a defendant who has been granted bail fails to surrender to custody at the appointed time and place, three questions arise for the court's consideration. There is the immediate question of how to secure the defendant's attendance before the court, and there are the further questions of how to deal with him for his breach of bail and how to deal with the sureties for breach of their recognizances.

20.6.1 Powers in respect of an absconder

Section 7(1) of the Bail Act 1976 provides that if a defendant has been bailed to appear before a court and fails to do so, the court before which he should have appeared may issue a warrant for his arrest. This is known as a bench warrant. Although it could be endorsed for bail, it is unlikely that the court would want to take the risk of the defendant again absconding. Where a person was arrested without warrant and bailed by the police to appear back at the police station, s. 7 does not apply, but should the person fail to answer to his bail, the police will have power to arrest him without warrant.

In order to prevent possible breaches of bail, a police officer may arrest without warrant a defendant whom he reasonably believes is unlikely to surrender to custody:

s. 7(3). The power only applies if the defendant was bailed to surrender to the custody of a court. A police officer also has power to arrest a defendant whom he reasonably suspects of having broken, or reasonably believes will break, a condition of his bail. Thus, if it was a condition of bail that the defendant report to a police station, and he fails to report, he may forthwith be arrested without warrant. Similarly, if a surety notifies the police in writing that the defendant is unlikely to surrender to custody and that he (the surety) therefore wishes to be relieved of his obligations, the defendant may be arrested. A defendant who is arrested for suspected or anticipated breach of bail must be brought before a magistrate as soon as practicable and, in any event, within 24 hours of arrest (unless he was to have surrendered to custody within 24 hours in which case he is brought before the appropriate court). If the magistrate is of the opinion that the defendant has broken or is likely to break any condition of his bail, or is not likely to surrender to custody, he may remand him in or commit him to custody, or impose more stringent conditions of bail. Otherwise, he must release him on bail on the same conditions, if any, as were originally imposed.

20.6.2 The offence of absconding

A defendant granted bail in criminal proceedings may not be required to enter into a recognizance to secure his surrender to custody: Bail Act 1976, s. 3(2). However, failure by him to surrender may amount to an offence. Section 6 of the 1976 Act provides that if 'a person who has been released on bail in criminal proceedings fails without reasonable cause to surrender to custody he shall be guilty of an offence.' A person also commits an offence if, having had reasonable cause for not surrendering at the time he should have done, he fails to surrender as soon after as is reasonably practicable. It is for the defendant to prove, on a balance of probabilities, that he had reasonable cause for not surrendering.

The offence of absconding may be dealt with in three ways. First, the defendant may be tried summarily for the offence, even if the offence alleged consists in failing to surrender to the custody of a court other than a magistrates' court. If convicted, the defendant may be sentenced by the magistrates to three months imprisonment and/or a £400 fine. Secondly, a defendant may be summarily convicted and committed, in custody or on bail, to the Crown Court for sentence. The magistrates may commit for sentence if either the circumstances of the offence are such that their powers of punishment are inadequate, or they are committing the defendant for trial in respect of some other offence and they consider that the Crown Court ought to deal with him both for the absconding and, if convicted, the other offence. Thirdly, if the defendant fails to surrender to the custody of the Crown Court, Divisional Court or Court of Appeal the court may deal with him as if he had committed a criminal contempt. This means that a judge of the court concerned may himself decide whether an offence under s. 6 has been proved without the necessity of indicting the defendant for criminal contempt or empanelling a jury: *R* v *Harbax Singh* [1979] 2WLR 100. It is a swift and semi-informal way of dealing with the matter. If the defendant disputes failing to surrender, however, it may be preferable for the judge to direct that a summary prosecution be commenced:

One can imagine circumstances in which there might be a dispute whether or not particular facts amounted to absconding; the trial judge might then think that that was not a suitable matter for determination by him summarily . . . In such a case he might think it right to direct that summary proceedings should be begun before a magistrates' court, or he might think that he could deal with the matter adequately himself. (per Roskill LJ. in *Harbax Singh* supra at p.104).

A defendant who is committed to the Crown Court for sentence for an offence of absconding, or is dealt with for the offence as if he had committed a criminal contempt, is liable to imprisonment for up to 12 months and/or an unlimited fine.

20.6.3 Estreating a surety's recognizance

Where bail was granted subject to sureties being provided, and the defendant absconds, the court before which he should have appeared may order that the recognisances of the sureties be estreated (i.e. they have to pay the sums in which they stood surety): Magistrates' Courts Act 1980, s. 120, r.18A of the Crown Court Rules 1971, SI No 1292 and r.6 of the Criminal Appeal Rules 1968, SI No 1262. Forfeiture of the recognisance is not automatic. The court should consider the means of the surety, and the extent to which he was to blame for the defendant absconding — e.g. did he, on first having reason to suspect that the defendant would abscond, give written notice to the police and ask to be relieved of his obligations as a surety? Failure to consider these matters may lead to the quashing of a decision by magistrates to forfeit a recognisance: *R v Southampton Justices* ex parte *Green* [1976] 1QB 11. However, the presumption is that the defendant's absconding will lead to the surety having to pay the whole sum in which he stood surety. As it was put in *R v Horseferry Road Magistrates' Court* ex parte *Pearson* [1976] 2AllER 264:

The surety has seriously entered into a serious obligation and ought to pay the amount which he or she has promised unless there are circumstances in the case, relating either to means or culpability, which make it fair and just to pay a smaller sum.

20.7 DETENTION OF DEFENDANT WHEN BAIL IS REFUSED

The arrangements for detaining a defendant who is refused bail are as follows:

(a) If he has attained the age of 21, he is committed to prison.

(b) If he is aged 17 to 20 inclusive he is committed to a remand centre, provided that one is available 'for the reception from the court of persons of his class or description': Criminal Justice Act 1948, s. 27. If a remand centre is not available he is committed to prison.

(c) If he is a juvenile he is committed to the care of a local authority: Children and Young Persons Act 1969, s. 23. However, should the court certify, in the case of a young person, that he is of so unruly a character that he cannot safely be committed to the care of a local authority, he is committed instead to a remand centre. If he is male, aged at least 15 and no remand centre is available, he must be committed to prison.

Whenever a magistrates' court has power to remand a person in custody it may, if the remand is for a period not exceeding three clear days, commit him to the custody of a constable: Magistrates' Courts Act 1980, s. 128(7).

20.8 APPLICATION FOR A WRIT OF HABEAS CORPUS

Paragraph 20.5 dealt with the way in which a defendant refused bail by a magistrates' court can challenge the refusal by applying for bail to the High Court or, in some cases, to the Crown Court. However, such applications presuppose that the defendant has been brought before the magistrates. If he has not made a court appearance because he is being detained at the police station, no court has jurisdiction to hear a bail application, but, in order to secure his release, an application may be made on his behalf to the High Court for the issue of the writ of habeas corpus. The writ of habeas corpus is the means by which, for many centuries, the courts have tested the legality of a prisoner's detention. It requires the person to whom it is addressed (e.g. a prison governor or officer in charge of a police station) to produce at court the person named in it, and to give reasons for his detention. The court can then decide whether the detention is lawful and, if it is not, direct the prisoner's release. However, on an application for the issue of habeas corpus the court always has power simply to order that the prisoner be released: Rules of the Supreme Court 1965, Ord.54 r.4. Such an order is sufficient authority for the prison governor, police officer etc. having custody of the prisoner to release him, and it is generally preferable to the rather cumbersome procedure of actually issuing a writ.

The procedure for applying for habeas corpus is contained in Order 54 of the Rules of the Supreme Court. The application must be made ex parte to a judge in court except that:

(a)   it is made to a Divisional Court of the Queen's Bench Division if the court so directs, and

(b)   it may be made to a judge otherwise than in court (e.g. at his private home) should no judge be sitting in court.

The application must be supported by an affidavit showing that the prisoner's detention is unlawful, and that the application is made at his instance. If, for any reason, the prisoner is unable to make the affidavit it may be made by some other person on his behalf. The application, which should normally be made by counsel, is given precedence over the court's other business for the day since a subject's liberty is at stake. Although the writ is sometimes issued on the ex parte application, it is more usual for the application to be adjourned so that notice of it can be served on the person having custody of the prisoner, and on such other persons as the judge directs should be served. The resumed hearing will be before a Divisional Court. Having heard argument on behalf of both the prisoner and the respondent to the application (if he appears), the court may (a) rule that the detention is lawful and refuse to issue the writ, or (b) issue the writ and give directions as to when the prisoner is to be brought before the court, or (c) make an order under r.4 (see above) that the prisoner be released.

Either party may appeal to the House of Lords against the Divisional Court's decision, but leave of either the Divisional Court or the House of Lords is required: Administration of Justice Act 1960, s. 15.

21 Ancillary Financial and Property Orders

The subject of this Chapter is the various financial and property orders which may be made during the course of criminal proceedings. The orders to be discussed are — legal aid orders, orders for the payment of costs, orders to compensate the victims of crime, orders to restore to the rightful owner property which has been stolen, orders to forfeit articles used in the commission of crime, and criminal bankruptcy orders. An order for legal aid is, and an order for costs may be, for the benefit of the accused. Although the remaining orders involve the accused in paying money or surrendering property, they should not, with the exception of forfeiture orders, be regarded as part of the penalty for the offence. They are intended, rather, to give to a victim of crime, who clearly has a good claim against the accused which he could pursue in the civil courts, a swift and efficient remedy enforceable through the criminal courts. Nevertheless, in deciding whether to make an order the court takes into account factors which would be irrelevant in civil proceedings. A compensation order, for example, does not reflect only the loss suffered by the victim, but also the ability of the offender to pay compensation. A civil court would simply assess the damages, give judgement for the plaintiff in the full amount, and worry about the defendant's ability to pay at the stage of enforcing the judgement. Of the orders mentioned above, legal aid, costs and compensation orders are of greatest significance, and it is upon them that the Chapter will concentrate.

21.1 LEGAL AID

Where a legal aid order is made in favour of an accused, the costs incurred in conducting the defence are paid, not by the accused, but out of government money. His costs in the magistrates' court are met out of the legal aid fund, which is a central fund administered by the Law Society, his costs in the Crown Court or Court of Appeal are met by the Home Secretary out of moneys provided by Parliament: Legal Aid Act 1974, s. 37. The provision of legal aid in criminal proceedings is governed principally by Part II of the Legal Aid Act 1974.

21.1.1 The granting of legal aid

Legal aid for criminal proceedings before a magistrates' court (adult or juvenile) may be granted by the magistrates' court concerned. Legal aid for criminal proceedings in the Crown Court may be granted by the Crown Court or, much more conveniently, by the magistrates' court which commits for trial or sentence. Legal aid for an appeal to or from the Court of Appeal may be granted by the Criminal Division: Legal Aid Act 1974, s. 28. Legal aid for an appeal to the Divisional Court by case stated or for an application for one of the prerogative orders is only available under Part I of the 1974 Act. This means that the appellant/applicant must seek a legal aid certificate from the local legal aid committee run by the Law Society. They have a more stringent approach to the granting of legal aid than that adopted by the courts when considering aid under Part II of the Act. In particular, they, unlike the courts, consider the merits of the case which the person applying for legal aid wishes to put before the court, and only accede to the application if they think he is likely to succeed. A person appealing from a magistrates' court to the Crown Court, as opposed to an appellant to the Divisional Court, may be granted legal aid by either the magistrates or the Crown Court: s. 28.

The principles governing the granting of legal aid by the criminal courts are laid down in s. 29 of the 1974 Act. The pre-condition of any grant of aid is that it must appear to the court that the applicant's means are such that he requires assistance to meet the costs of the proceedings in question: s. 29(2). So that the court may know whether this condition is satisfied, the applicant must, before being granted legal aid, be required to provide a written statement of his means: s. 29(4). A statement of means may be dispensed with if either the applicant is physically or mentally incapable of completing one, or he is under 16: see Para. 21.1.3. The financial limitations placed upon the granting of legal aid in criminal matters are far from strict, so an applicant is unlikely to be refused on the grounds of means.

Subject to means, a legal aid order must be made when:

(a)   a person is committed for trial on a charge of murder, or

(b)   a person who is not, but wishes to be, legally represented is brought before a magistrates' court charged with an offence and is at risk of a second remand in custody, he not having been legally represented on the occasion of the first remand, or

(c)   a person who is to be sentenced by a magistrates' court or the Crown Court is remanded in custody so that reports on him can be made, or

(d)   the prosecution are appealing to the House of Lords against the Court of Appeal's decision to allow an appellant's appeal: s. 29(1).

The purpose of making legal aid mandatory in the circumstances of (b) above is to prevent, as far as possible, unnecessary remands in custody. The legal aid may be limited to that necessary to meet the costs of a bail application — i.e. the accused need not be granted aid for purposes of defending himself against the charge which has put him at risk of being remanded in custody.

Where a court may, but is not obliged to, grant legal aid it should make an order if 'it appears . . . desirable to do so in the interests of justice': s. 29(1). This vague phraseology obviously gives the court a broad discretion in the matter, which is reflected in the fact that the availability of legal aid for proceedings in magistrates' courts varies considerably from court to court. At Crown Court level, a person who has been committed for trial or sentence is almost invariably legally aided, unless his means are too great. The Report of the Departmental Committee on Legal Aid in Criminal Proceedings (The Widgery Committee) in 1966 suggested that legal aid is *prima facie* justified when:

(a)   the charge is a grave one, so that the accused is in real jeopardy of losing his liberty or livelihood or suffering serious damage to his reputation, or

(b)   the charge raises a substantial question of law, or

(c)   inadequate knowledge of English or mental or physical disability make it impossible for the accused to follow the proceedings or state his own case, or

(d)   the nature of the defence involves the tracing and interviewing of witnesses or expert cross-examination of prosecution witnesses, or

(e)   legal representation is desirable in the interests of someone other than the accused (e.g. where it is undesirable that the child victim of an alleged sexual offence should be cross-examined directly by the accused).

Some charges are so grave that, even though legal aid is not mandatory, it would in practice always be granted. Thus, no court would refuse aid (except on grounds of means) to a person charged with manslaughter for example, or causing grievous bodily harm with intent, or rape, or robbery. Other charges may or may not justify aid depending on the facts of the particular case. Thus, although the offence of assault occasioning actual bodily harm carries five years imprisonment, magistrates are not obliged to make a legal aid order if the allegations against the accused are in fact of a trivial nature. They should consider how serious the charge is, and, if they have done that and decide that legal aid is unnecessary, the Divisional Court will not interfere with their decision unless it is plainly unreasonable: *R* v *Highgate Justices* ex parte *Lewis* [1977] Crim L R 611. The factors mentioned by the Widgery Committee illustrate how sometimes the granting of legal aid is as much an assistance to the court as it is to the accused. Where the accused would not be able to present his case adequately much time is saved by providing him with a lawyer. Similarly, where cross-examination of a witness by the accused personally would cause distress, the public interest is served by having the cross-examination carried out by a professional man. But, however desirable it is that the accused be legally represented, he cannot be forced to have a lawyer — the court can do no more than offer him legal aid, it cannot make him accept.

21.1.2   Contributions and down payments

After the conclusion of the case for which he was granted aid, the legally aided person may be ordered to contribute towards the costs incurred: Legal Aid Act 1974, s. 32. The contribution order may be for a single lump sum or for payment by instalments, it may be for the full amount, or part only, of the costs incurred. An order may be made even where the legally aided person has been acquitted: ex parte *Meredith* [1973] 2 AllER 234. In every case the order should be 'reasonable having regard to (the legally aided person's) resources and commitments': s. 32(1).

The court with power to make a contribution order is the court finally disposing of the legally aided person's case — i.e. if an accused was legally aided both for committal proceedings in the magistrates' court and for his trial on indictment, it is the Crown Court which decides what contribution he should make not only in respect of his costs in the Crown Court but also in respect of his magistrates' court's costs. Where legal aid is granted for purposes of an appeal to the Crown Court, Court of Appeal or House of Lords, the appellate court orders any contribution towards the costs of the appeal, but has no jurisdiction to interfere with the decision of the court below on the contribution which should be made to the costs of the proceedings which resulted in the appeal. To assist the court in deciding what contribution is reasonable, either the court with power to make the contribution order or the court which originally granted the legal aid may and, on an application from the legally aided person, must request the Supplementary Benefits Commission to enquire into his means: s. 33 of the 1974 Act. If a report from the Commission is available in time, the court must consider it before ordering a contribution. If the report is not received by the court until after it has made an order, it must reconsider its order in the light of this report and, if necessary, vary the order.

Where, having regard to the statement of means supplied by an applicant for legal aid, it seems likely that he will be required to make a contribution to his legal aid costs the court may refuse to grant him legal aid unless he first makes a down-payment on account of any such contribution: s. 29(3). If a down-payment is made but no contribution is subsequently ordered, the amount of the down-payment is refunded to the legally aided person.

21.1.3 Procedure for applying for legal aid

An accused wishing to be legally aided for proceedings in a magistrates' court must first obtain from the clerk's office an application form and a statement of means form. The application form asks for details of the proceedings for which legal aid is sought, and for reasons why legal aid is appropriate (e.g. does the applicant consider that he is in danger of a custodial sentence, or does he regard his case as a particularly complex one?). An application in respect of a juvenile may be made either by the juvenile or his parent: s. 40(2) of the 1974 Act. In the case of a juvenile under 16, his parents may be required to complete a statement of means in addition to or instead of the juvenile completing one: s. 29(5). They may also be ordered, at the conclusion of the case, to make a contribution to the legal aid costs. If an accused is brought before the court unrepresented following arrest without warrant, and the magistrates adjourn the case, they will probably indicate to him the possibility of completing the necessary forms and obtaining legal aid before the next court appearance. If the accused has been summoned or bailed to appear before the magistrates, it is desirable that he should take steps to obtain legal aid before his first appearance. He may go to a solicitor who can then tell him about legal aid and assist him in making his application.

The application is first put before the magistrates' clerk, who may either grant it, or grant it subject to the applicant (or, in the case of an applicant under 16, his parent) making a down-payment, or refer the application to an individual magistrate or to the court: Legal Aid in Criminal Proceedings (General) Regulations 1968, SI No 1231. The clerk has no power to refuse an application. If he grants an application subject to a down-payment being made, the applicant is entitled to have the matter determined by a magistrate. Where counsel or solicitor appears for an accused, and legal aid has not been granted (e.g. because the accused has only just instructed solicitors) an oral application may be made in court, which the magistrates could grant subject to the forms being completed and the accused's means not disqualifying him from aid.

When magistrates commit an accused for trial or sentence, it is normal to ask them for legal aid for the proceedings in the Crown Court. Assuming the accused has been legally aided in the magistrates' court it is almost automatic to extend the aid, provided his means have not changed dramatically for the better. Where magistrates do refuse legal aid for the Crown Court proceedings or, for some reason, the defence omit to ask them for it, an application may be made to the Crown Court. The procedure is similar to that governing applications to a magistrates' court.

The procedure for obtaining legal aid for an appeal to the Court of Appeal is dealt with in Para. 17.6.9.

21.1.4 Scope of legal aid

A legal aid order names the solicitors assigned to represent the accused, he having been asked on the application form which firm he wishes to act for him. Legal aid in the magistrates' court does not normally include the costs of representation by counsel: s. 30(2) of the 1974

Act. This does not mean that counsel do not represent legally aided clients before the magistrates — it merely means that the sum paid to the solicitors out of the legal aid fund does not include a component to cover counsel's fees. In fact, many solicitors find it more profitable or convenient to brief counsel even if the legal aid is for solicitor only. Where the accused is charged with an indictable offence, and the case is unusually grave or difficult, the magistrates may order that the legal aid cover representation by solicitor and counsel.

Legal aid for proceedings in the Crown Court is usually for solicitor and counsel: s. 30(1). In a case of urgency (e.g. where an unrepresented accused decides at the last moment that he wishes to be represented) it may be made for counsel only. Legal aid in the Court of Appeal is either for solicitor and counsel or for counsel only, depending on how much work needs to be done in preparation for the hearing of the appeal: see Para. 17.6.9.

21.1.5 Assistance under s. 2

When a person who has not had a legal aid order made in his favour appears before magistrates unrepresented, they may ask a solicitor who is present within the court precincts to represent him. If the solicitor agrees to the request, the costs of the representation will be met by the legal aid fund up to a maximum of £40, subject to the means of the person concerned not disqualifying him from receiving aid: s. 2 of the 1974 Act, and Legal Advice and Assistance Regulations 1980 SI No 477. The provisions of s. 2 are a useful way of providing an accused with immediate legal assistance for a limited purpose. A solicitor could, for example, be asked to make a bail application or present a plea in mitigation, but if more extensive work needs to be done on behalf of the accused, costing more than £40, he must either apply for a proper legal aid order or pay solicitors privately. In many magistrates' courts a 'duty solicitor' scheme ensures that a solicitor is always available at court to accept work paid for under s. 2.

21.1.6 Challenging a refusal to grant legal aid

Where magistrates refuse to order legal aid for proceedings in the Crown Court, the disappointed applicant can, in effect, challenge the refusal by making an application to the Crown Court itself. If magistrates refuse to make an order for proceedings in the magistrates' court, the only remedy is to apply to the Divisional Court for orders of *certiorari* to quash the refusal and mandamus to compel them to grant aid. However, mandamus will only issue if the magistrates have failed to apply the correct principles in deciding the application (e.g. have not enquired into the gravity of the charge against the applicant), or have clearly been unreasonable in not making an order: *R v Highgate Justices* ex parte *Lewis* [1977] Crim L R 611. There is no appeal against a legal aid contribution order. Since it may be made even when the accused has been acquitted, such an order is not within the definition of 'sentence' (see Paras. 17.3.1 and 18.1.1).

21.2 ORDERS TO PAY COSTS

The award of costs to or against the parties to criminal proceedings is governed by the Costs in Criminal Cases Act 1973. The order may be either for the payment of costs out of central funds (i.e. government money) or for the payment of costs by the unsuccessful party to the successful party. The costs paid out of central funds must be reasonably sufficient to compensate the party in whose favour the award is made for the expenses properly incurred by him in carrying on the proceedings, and to compensate any witnesses called by him for the trouble and expense involved in attending court: s. 1(3) and s. 3(3) of the 1973 Act. The amount to be paid must be ascertained as soon as practicable by the magistrates' clerk or the appropriate officer of the Crown Court depending on whether the award is made by a magistrates' court or the Crown Court. Where magistrates make an award of costs as between the parties they must specify the amount to be paid at the time they make the order: s. 2(3).

Where the Crown Court makes such an order, it may order that the unsuccessful party pay the full amount of the successful party's costs as subsequently ascertained by an appropriate officer of the court. The risk in making an order in that form is that the costs may be greater than expected, and amount to an unfair burden on the party ordered to pay them. Therefore, in most cases the Crown Court, like the magistrates, specifies the amount of costs to be paid. Alternatively, it can order that the party pay the costs as ascertained by the appropriate officer or a specified sum, whichever is the less: *R* v *Hier* (1976) 62CR App R 233 and s. 4(2).

Where an accused is tried summarily for an indictable offence or tried on indictment the court may order that the prosecution's costs be paid out of central funds, whether or not the proceedings end in conviction. The defence may only be awarded their costs out of central funds if the accused is acquitted. If proceedings are in respect of a summary offence there is no power to order costs from central funds, whether in favour of the prosecution or defence. In all cases, whether the offence charged is summary or indictable, the court may order that the unsuccessful party pay costs to the successful party. If the court orders that a party is both to receive his costs out of central funds and to be paid costs by the other party, the full amount is paid to him out of central funds but, when he receives payment from the other party, those payments are passed on to the Home Secretary (i.e. the government). The above is a summary of ss. 1—4 and 16 of the Costs in Criminal Cases Act. Full details are given below.

Practice Directions from the Lord Chief Justice (1973 2AER 592 and 1977 1WLR 537) indicate when the Crown Court should order costs out of central funds. An order should be made in favour of the prosecution unless the proceedings have been brought without reasonable cause, but, to emphasise that the court has a discretion in the matter, there must be a formal application for costs after each case. A successful accused should receive his costs out of central funds unless:

(a)   he has brought suspicion upon himself or misled the prosecution, or

(b)   there is ample evidence to convict him but he is acquitted on a procedural irregularity, or

(c)   he is acquitted on one charge and convicted on another, or

(d)   the prosecution has acted spitefully or unreasonably.

In cases (a) and (b) the accused should be left to pay his own costs. In case (c) the decision will depend largely on the relative importance of the two charges, and in case (d) the costs should come from the prosecution rather than central funds.

The Practice Directions apply only to the Crown Court. In the magistrates' courts there is a greater reluctance to award a successful accused his costs, whether out of central funds or direct from the prosecution. It should also be noted that the Directions assume that there is some point in making an order for costs. If the accused is legally aided and no contribution order is made against him, he pays nothing towards the expenses of his defence, and so has no reason to seek an order for costs. Should an order be made, the money paid under it goes to the legal aid fund or the Home Secretary, depending on whether the legal aid was for proceedings in the magistrates' court or Crown Court. That means, in the great majority of cases, that one arm of government would be paying money to another arm of government. Therefore, a legally aided accused who is acquitted is rarely awarded costs either out of central funds or from the prosecution.

A convicted accused is frequently ordered to pay to the prosecution a specified sum in costs. The actual costs of the prosecution may be well in excess of whatever the accused has to pay since the order will take into account the means of the accused and any other financial orders made in the case (e.g. fine, legal aid contribution order or compensation order).

The circumstances in which the courts may make an order for costs are summarised above, but a fuller account may be of assistance. Orders may be made as follows:

(a) Magistrates dealing summarily with an indictable offence or holding committal proceedings may, whatever the outcome of the proceedings, order payment of prosecution costs out of central funds: s. 1(1) of the 1973 Act.

(b) The Crown Court, following a trial on indictment may, whatever the outcome of the trial, order payment of prosecution costs out of central funds: s. 3(1).

(c) Magistrates who acquit an accused tried summarily for an indictable offence or who discharge an accused following committal proceedings may order payment of defence costs out of central funds: s. 1(2).

(d) The Crown Court, following the accused's acquittal on indictment, may order payment of defence costs out of central funds: s. 3(1).

(e) The Crown Court following a trial on indictment and the magistrates following committal proceedings or summary trial of an indictable offence may, notwithstanding that no order is made for defence costs, order that sums be paid out of central funds to compensate any defence witness for the 'expense, trouble or loss of time' caused through his attendance at court: ss. 1(4) and 3(4).

(f) Following summary trial of an offence (whether summary or indictable) magistrates may, if the accused is convicted, order him to pay costs to the prosecution or, if he is acquitted, order that the prosecution pay costs to him: s. 2(1) and (2).

(g) Following conviction on indictment the Crown Court may order the accused to pay costs to the prosecution; following acquittal on indictment, it may order the prosecution to pay costs to the accused: s. 4(1).

(h) Where magistrates decide not to commit the accused for trial, they may, if of the opinion that the charge was not made in good faith, order the prosecution to pay costs to the defence. If the accused is committed for trial and acquitted, costs awarded to him out of central funds may include the costs of the committal proceedings: s. 3(9).

For the award of costs after an appeal to the Crown Court, Divisional Court or Court of Appeal, see Paras. 18.1.3, 18.2.3, and 17.6.9 respectively.

21.3 COMPENSATION ORDERS

Section 35 of the Powers of Criminal Courts Act 1973 provides that a court dealing with an offender for an offence may, in addition to dealing with him in any other way, order that he pay compensation to the victim of the offence. The main points about compensation orders are:

(a) An order may be made in respect of 'any personal injury, loss or damage resulting from' the offence: s. 35(1). Where an offence under the Theft Act 1968 leads to property being taken out of and later restored to the owner's possession, any damage occurring to the property while it is out of his possession is deemed to have resulted from the offence, however it was caused: s. 35(2). Section 35(3) places two limitations on the scope of compensation. It cannot be ordered in respect of loss suffered by dependants through a person's death, nor can it be ordered for injury, loss or damage caused in a road traffic accident, unless damage caused can be brought within the principle of s. 35(2) above. The effect of this is that if O takes A's car without his consent and has an accident in which both A's car and B's car are damaged, A may, but B may not, claim compensation from O.

(b)   The court may order compensation on its own initiative, even if no formal application is made for it by the victim of the offence: s. 35(1). Normally, the victim is asked when he makes a statement under s. 102 of the Magistrates' Courts Act 1980 whether he wishes to claim compensation or not. If he does, prosecuting counsel may mention the matter to the judge or magistrates. An order should not be made unless either the offender agrees he is liable to pay compensation in the sum proposed or clear evidence is led to show that he is so liable: *R* v *Inwood* (1975) 60Cr App Rep 70 and *R* v *Vivian* [1979] 1 All ER 48. When there is any doubt as to the liability to compensate, the victim should be left to his civil remedies.

(c)   Compensation orders are not intended as the means by which an offender can buy himself out of the penalties of crime. Nor are they intended as punishment for the offender. They are rather 'a convenient and rapid means of avoiding the expense of resorting to civil litigation when the criminal clearly has means which would enable the compensation to be paid' (per Scarman LJ in *R* v *Inwood* supra). Any order should be related to the offender's ability to pay. It must not be oppressive or constitute a temptation to commit further crime. Although the order may be for payment by instalments, it is generally desirable that the period for which payments have to made should be kept relatively short. Thus, in *R* v *Daly* [1974] 1WLR 133 the Court of Appeal reduced a compensation order which would otherwise have required payments over a period of some six years, but held that a second order made in the same case (for payment of £37.40 at 50p per week) was a 'model application' of s. 35.

(d)   The principles explained in *R* v *Inwood and R* v *Daly* (supra) result in compensation orders often being for sums well below the actual loss suffered by the victim. The making of a compensation order does not affect the victim's right to take civil proceedings against the offender, but the damages he can recover are reduced by the amount of the compensation order: s. 38.

(e)   Where an offender is convicted of two or more offences and one or more compensation orders are made, the court should make it clear to which offence each compensation order relates. A single compensation order to cover several offences is bad practice, and may be a nullity: *R* v *Miller* (1979) 68Cr App R 56. An order may be made in respect of an offence which the offender has taken into consideration: s. 35(1). Compensation ordered by magistrates in respect of any one offence must not exceed £1,000. If they take offences into consideration, compensation for those must not exceed the difference between the maximum compensation they could have awarded for the offences of which they have convicted the offender and the compensation they have actually awarded for those offences: s. 35(5).

21.4   RESTITUTION ORDERS

Section 28 of the Theft Act 1968 provides that where goods have been stolen, and an offender is convicted of an offence with reference to the theft (or has such an offence taken into consideration) the court may order anyone having possession or control of the goods to restore them to any person entitled to recover them from him. 'Stolen goods' include goods obtained by deception or through blackmail, and 'an offence with reference to theft' includes handling stolen goods and, possibly, conspiracy to steal or assisting a thief. Persons other than the offender may be ordered to restore goods under s. 28, but the court would only make an order against a third party in the clearest of cases. The obvious application of s. 28 is where a convicted thief or handler was caught in possession of the stolen goods. If there is no doubt as to the true owner, the court can, at the conclusion of the trial, order that the goods be restored to him.

There is also power under s. 28 to order that goods in the offender's possession which directly or indirectly represent the stolen goods be transferred to the person entitled to the stolen goods (e.g. if O steals A's television set and exchanges it for a tape recorder, O could be ordered to transfer the tape recorder to A). Lastly, the court may order that, out of money taken from the offender's possession on his arrest, the person entitled to the stolen goods shall be paid a sum not exceeding their value. In view of the wide powers the courts now have to order compensation under the Powers of Criminal Courts Act 1973, s. 35, orders for payment of money under s. 28 seem to be of limited value.

21.5 FORFEITURE ORDERS

Section 43 of the Powers of Criminal Courts Act 1973 provides that where an offender is convicted on indictment of an offence punishable with at least two years imprisonment, and, at the time of his arrest, he had in his possession or under his control property which the court is satisfied had been, or was intended to be used in committing or facilitating the commission of an offence, the court may make an order depriving him of his rights in the property. If the property is not already in the possession of the police, it is taken into their possession. Facilitating the commission of an offence includes taking steps to dispose of any property to which it related, and taking steps to avoid detection or arrest. If a person other than the offender claims to be entitled to the property, he has six months from the making of the forfeiture order in which to apply to a magistrates' court for an order that the property be returned to him. To succeed, he must satisfy the magistrates that either he did not consent to the offender having the property or he did not know the purpose for which it was to be used.

An order under s. 43 is intended as an additional penalty *R* v *Lidster* [1976] Crim LR 80. Unlike the other orders discussed in this Chapter, it should not be combined with an absolute discharge or, presumably, with a conditional discharge or probation: *R* v *Hunt* [1978] Crim LR 697. *R* v *Lidster* (supra) provides an example of the use of s. 43. L pleaded guilty to handling in that he used his car to transport stolen goods at the request of the thieves. The Court of Appeal upheld an order depriving him of the car.

21.6 CRIMINAL BANKRUPTCY ORDERS

Where an offender is convicted on indictment of one or more offences and, as a result of those offences and any other offences taken into consideration, one or more persons whose identities are known have suffered loss or damage (not due to personal injury) to an aggregate amount of at least £15,000, the Crown Court may make a criminal bankruptcy order: Powers of Criminal Courts Act 1973, s. 39. A criminal bankruptcy order is made in addition to dealing with the offender in any other way, save that it may not be combined with a compensation order. The order names the victims of the offence, and the amount of loss or damage which each has suffered. The offender is then treated as a person who, for purposes of the Bankruptcy Act 1914, has committed an act of bankruptcy on the date of the order, and the victims named in the order are treated as creditors who may prove in the bankruptcy for the amount of loss or damage which, according to the order, they have suffered.

A criminal bankruptcy is, in most respects, identical to an ordinary bankruptcy. The main differences are that the petition must always be presented in the High Court, either a creditor or the Director of Public Prosecutions may present it, the act of bankruptcy and the criminal bankruptcy debts are conclusively proved by production of a copy of the criminal bankruptcy order, and the Official Receiver is always the trustee in bankruptcy. Also, any person who, after the date of the earliest of the offences which resulted in the making of the order, received property from the offender either by way of gift or at an under-value may be ordered to transfer that property to the trustee in bankruptcy. Once the assets of the offender/bankrupt have been realised, they are shared out amongst the creditors named in the criminal bankruptcy order and any other creditors who have proved in the bankruptcy.

alleged in an information laid before him, he may, instead of issuing a summons, issue a warrant for the arrest of the accused provided:

(a)   the information is in writing and substantiated on oath, and

(b)   either the accused is a juvenile, or his address cannot be sufficiently established for a summons to be served on him, or the offence alleged in the information is punishable with imprisonment: Magistrates' Courts Act 1980, s.1(3) and (4).

A warrant for arrest is a document commanding the constables of the police force for the area in which it is issued to arrest the accused and bring him before the magistrates' court named in it. The warrant must contain particulars of the offence alleged in the information which led to its being issued, and must be signed by the magistrate who issued it. Since a magistrates' clerk cannot receive an information laid on oath, he has no jurisdiction to issue a warrant for arrest. An example of a warrant is shown opposite.

Any constable of the police force named in the warrant may execute the warrant (i.e. arrest the accused) anywhere in England and Wales. In addition, a constable of another force may execute the warrant within the area policed by his force: Magistrates' Courts Act 1980, s. 125(2). Reasonable force may be used in making the arrest (Criminal Law Act 1967, s. 3), and force may also be used to enter premises where the accused is known to be: *Launock* v *Brown* (1819) 2B and Ald 592. Although the officer effecting the arrest need not have the warrant in his possession at the time of doing so, he must, on demand, show it to the accused as soon as practicable: Magistrates' Courts Act 1980, s. 125(3). Following the arrest the accused must, unless the warrant was backed for bail, be brought forthwith before the magistrates' court named in the warrant. The magistrates may then release him on bail or remand him in custody.

As a compromise between issuing a summons and issuing an unconditional warrant for arrest, a magistrate may issue a warrant but endorse it with a direction that, having been arrested, the accused shall be released on bail subject to a duty to appear at the magistrates' court at a time specified in the endorsement: Magistrates' Courts Act 1980, s. 117. This is known as 'backing the warrant for bail'. The bail may be made subject to conditions — e.g. providing sureties or reporting to the police station at specified intervals or living at a certain address. If the accused cannot comply with those conditions (e.g. he is unable to find a surety), he is brought before the magistrates who will either vary the terms of bail or remand him in custody. Whenever a magistrate or a magistrates' court has jurisdiction to issue a warrant for arrest, it may be backed for bail. The power is particularly useful when an accused fails to appear in answer to a summons or fails to answer to his bail, but the magistrates feel that this is due to inadvertence rather than design. The shock of being arrested should ensure that he attends for the adjourned hearing, while the endorsement for bail saves him from an unnecessary period of custody.

It is rare for proceedings to commence with the laying of an information and the issue of a warrant for arrest. Apart from the limitations which ss. 1(3) and (4) of the Magistrates' Courts Act 1980 place on the issue of warrants for arrest, there is a general principle that a warrant ought not to be issued when a summons would be equally effectual: *O'Brien* v *Brabner* (1885) 49 JPN 227. Provided the accused's address is sufficiently well established for a summons to be served on him, there is no reason on the face of it why he should not appear at court to answer a charge of a minor nature. If the charge is more serious, it will almost certainly carry a power of arrest without warrant, so obtaining a warrant would be superfluous.

19.3 POLICE QUESTIONING OF A SUSPECT

No book on criminal procedure would be complete without a brief description of some of the ways in which the police gather evidence against a suspect. This and the succeeding two Paragraphs will summarise the rules governing the questioning of suspects, the searching of a suspect's person or home, and the obtaining of identification evidence.

A confession made by an accused prior to his trial is admissible in evidence against him at his trial to prove the facts admitted in it. By a confession is meant an oral or written statement by the accused in which he admits he committed the offence charged, or admits to facts which tend to show that he committed the offence charged. The prosecution can prove an oral confession by calling a witness who heard it being made; they can prove a written confession by producing it as an exhibit, and adducing evidence to show that it was written and/or signed by the accused (e.g. a police officer testifies that he wrote the confession at the accused's dictation, after which the accused signed it of his own free will). A confession is obviously valuable evidence for the prosecution — indeed, it has been held that an accused may be convicted solely on the evidence of his confession, even if that confession was oral: *R* v *Sykes* (1913) 8Cr App R 233 and *R* v *Mallinson* [1977] Crim LR 161. Proof of a confession is not conclusive against the accused, since the jury or magistrates may take the view that he made a false confession because for instance he was in a state of panic or hoped to be granted bail if he made a statement. Nevertheless, if the prosecution can convince the jury or bench that the accused has confessed their chances of a conviction are much improved. Therefore, if the police believe that a suspect they are interviewing has committed an offence they will be anxious to elicit from him a confession to that offence. If he makes an oral confession, they will probably invite him to put it into writing, as a written confession is much easier to prove than an oral one. Where the accused's admissions are verbal, made in the presence only of police officers, he can deny making the admissions alleged, and it is then a question of the word of police officers against the word of the accused. Where, on the other hand, the accused has signed a written confession he cannot realistically deny making the confession, but is thrown back on the argument that the document he put his signature to was untrue.

Because a confession by the accused is so useful to the police the methods by which they can persuade him to make one must be regulated, so as to ensure as far as possible that any confession made is genuine. This is done by excluding from evidence confessions which have been improperly obtained. The general statement made above, that a confession is admissible in evidence against an accused, must now be qualified. It is admissible provided it is voluntary, and provided the judge does not, in his discretion, exclude it because of a breach of the Judges' Rules. If the defence object to the admissibility of a confession, the judge decides the issue in the absence of the jury at a trial on the 'voire dire' (see Para. 8.3.5 for the procedure). If he rules the confession to be inadmissible, the jury hear nothing of it, and the police's object in obtaining the confession is defeated. Similarly, at a summary trial the magistrates may be asked to exclude a confession. If they do so, they ignore as far as they can whatever

(e)   Confessions obtained by violence or the threat of it should be inadmissible as at present, but confessions obtained through some other inducement or through breach of the rules on the conduct of questioning should be admissible although the irregularity would affect their reliability.

5   Prosecuting authorities

The proposal is that a local prosecuting service should be set up for each of the police force areas of England and Wales, which would be responsible for the conduct of prosecutions initiated by the police. Each local service would be headed by a Crown prosecutor, who would be accountable to a police and prosecutions authority. Central government through either the Home Secretary or the Attorney-General would set general standards to which the local services should conform. The functions of the Crown prosecutor and his department would be:

(a)   to conduct criminal cases after the police have decided to commence a prosecution,

(b)   to provide legal advice to the police on prosecution matters,

(c)   to provide advocates in the magistrates' courts (the practice of police officers in the magistrates' courts conducting the case for the prosecution should end), and

(d)   to brief counsel for the Crown Court.

Thus, the decision to take proceedings will remain with the police, but subsequent control of the prosecution, including the dropping and amending of charges, will be in the hands of the Crown prosecutor. This contrasts with the present position where a police prosecuting solicitor merely advises the police in the way that any solicitor advises his client.

The right to bring a private prosecution would be preserved, but the person concerned would have to apply to the Crown prosecutor to take over the case. If the Crown prosecutor refused, leave to commence proceedings would have to be granted by a magistrates' court. The conduct of prosecutions initiated by prosecuting agencies other than the police (e.g. the Department of Health and Social Security or the Inland Revenue) will be unaffected by the introduction of the Crown prosecutor system.

6   Commencing proceedings

The Commission sees little value in the present system of laying informations to obtain the issue of a summons, believing that, at least where the information is that of a police officer, the issue of a summons is a pure formality. It recommends that all police prosecutions should commence with the making of an accusation. The accusation should contain the details about the offence alleged which are now included in an information, and should also give the time and place of the accused's first court appearance. The accusation could either be made at the police station, in which case it would be analogous to a charge, or it could be sent through the post after the fashion of a summons. In neither case would the police need authority from a magistrate or magistrates' clerk to make the accusation. Prosecuting agencies other than the police would also be able to make accusations, but, as explained in (5) above, private prosecutions not taken over by the Crown prosecutor would require leave from a magistrates' court.

7 Committal proceedings

Of the many changes recommended by the Commission perhaps the most important from the viewpoint of the practising lawyer is the abolition of committal proceedings. The Commission wants the Crown prosecutor and other official prosecutors to send direct to the Crown Court cases which are to be tried on indictment. It recognises that arrangements will have to be made to decide questions such as bail, legal aid and the mode of trial, but it does not specify what those arrangements should be. In cases where the period between making the accusation and the start of the trial on indictment is likely to exceed eight weeks the defence should be able to apply for a discharge. If (and only if) they do so, the magistrates will consider the statements of the prosecution witnesses and discharge the accused if there is no case to answer. Although an application for discharge will in some ways resemble a committal with consideration of the evidence, the two will differ in that oral evidence will never be received at an application for discharge.

Despite the abolition of committal proceedings the prosecution would still be under a duty to supply the defence with copies of the statements made by their witnesses before the start of a trial on indictment. To assist the defence at summary trial, the Commission recommends that they be given on request a summary of the prosecution case.

8 Enforcing the rules

In making recommendations about powers to search persons and property, powers to arrest and detain suspects and the conduct of police interrogations, the Commission faced the problem of enforcing the rules it proposed should be made. Like the House of Lords in *R* v *Sang* [1979] 3WLR 263 it is against excluding evidence merely because it was obtained through breach of the rules. The one exception it makes is in the case of a confession obtained through violence or threat of violence which should continue to be inadmissible so as to mark society's disapproval of such methods of obtaining evidence. Otherwise the Commission relies upon police disciplinary procedures and the civil law to secure compliance with the laws and rules governing the investigation of crime. It makes several recommendations, which it has only been possible to touch upon in the preceeding paragraphs, for recording the treatment of suspects, and decisions taken in respect of them. By giving the person concerned access to these records, the Commission hopes to discourage unlawful conduct by the police or others investigating offences, and to facilitate civil or disciplinary proceedings when infringements do occur.

The Schedule lists those offences which are triable either way even though the statute creating them gives no indication to that effect. The most important of them are mentioned in the extract from the Schedule set out below.

SCHEDULE 1

OFFENCES TRIABLE EITHER WAY BY VIRTUE OF SECTION 17

5. Offences under the following provisions of the Offences against the Person Act 1861:
   (a) section 16 (threats to kill);
   (b) section 20 (inflicting bodily injury with or without a weapon);
   (g) section 38 (assault with intent to resist apprehension);
   (h) section 47 (assault occasioning bodily harm — common assault);
   (i) section 57 (bigamy).

14. All offences under the Perjury Act 1911 except offences under:
   (a) section 1 (perjury in judicial proceedings);
   (b) section 3 (false statements etc. with reference to marriage);
   (c) section 4 (false statements etc. as to births or deaths).

15. The following offences under the Forgery Act 1913:
   (a) offences under section 2(2)(a) (forgery of valuable security etc.) in relation to:
      (i) any document being an accountable receipt, release, or discharge, or any receipt or other instrument evidencing the payment of money, or the delivery of any chattel personal; or
      (ii) any document being an authority or request for the payment of money or for the delivery or transfer of goods and chattels, where the amount of money or the value of the goods or chattels does not exceed £1,000;
   (b) offences under section 4 (forgery of documents in general); and
   (c) offences under paragraph (a) of section 7 (demanding property on forged documents), where the amount of the money or the value of the property in respect of which the offence is committed does not exceed £1,000.

21. Offences under the following provisions of the Coinage Offences Act 1936:
   (a) section 4(1) (defacing coins);
   (b) section 5(1) (uttering counterfeit coin);

23. Offences under the following provisions of the Sexual Offences Act 1956:
   (a) section 6 (unlawful sexual intercourse with a girl under 16);
   (b) section 13 (indecency between men);
   (c) section 26 (permitting a girl under 16 to use premises for sexual intercourse).

26.   The following offences are triable either way where the offence to which they relate is triable either way, under the Criminal Law Act 1967:
    (a)   offences under section 4(1) (assisting offenders); and
    (b)   offences under section 5(1) (concealing arrestable offences and giving false information).

27.   Offences under section 4(1) of the Sexual Offences Act 1967 (procuring others to commit homosexual acts).

28.   All indictable offences under the Theft Act 1968 except:
    (a)   robbery, aggravated burglary, blackmail and assault with intent to rob;
    (b)   burglary comprising the commission of, or an intention to commit, an offence which is triable only on indictment;
    (c)   burglary in a dwelling if any person in the dwelling was subjected to violence or the threat of violence.

29.   Offences under the following provisions of the Criminal Damage Act 1971:
    (a)   section 1(1) (destroying or damaging property);
    (b)   section 1(1) and (3) (arson);
    (c)   section 2 (threats to destroy or damage property);
    (d)   section 3 (possessing anything with intent to destroy or damage property).

31.   Uttering any forged document the forgery of which is an offence listed in this Schedule.

32.   Committing an indecent assault upon a person whether male or female.

33.   Aiding, abetting, counselling or procuring the commission of any offence listed in the preceding paragraphs of this Schedule except paragraph 26.

34.   Attempting to commit an offence triable either way except an offence mentioned in paragraph 26 or 33 above.

35.   Any offence consisting in the incitement to commit an offence triable either way except an offence mentioned in paragraph 33 or 34 above.

Appendix 2　The White Paper on Young Offenders (1980 Cmnd 8045)

The White paper, which was presented to Parliament in October 1980, makes proposals for strengthening the law relating to juvenile and young adult offenders. By 'young adult' is meant a person aged 17 to 20 inclusive. The implementation of the proposals 'will depend on the enactment of the necessary legislation which in turn depends on the provision of the necessary resources.' The main recommendations are as follows:

1　Sentences of 'Youth Custody'

A custodial sentence of more than four months passed on a young adult should no longer take the form of Borstal or imprisonment, but should be a sentence of youth custody. Borstal training will cease to be a separate form of sentence, although the existing Borstal institutions will continue to be used to accommodate offenders sentenced to youth custody. Unlike Borstal, youth custody is to be a determinate sentence — i.e. the court fixes the maximum term when it passes the sentence, and release prior to the expiration of that term will depend upon the offender earning remission or being granted parole. The length of sentence will be entirely within the court's discretion save that it must not exceed the maximum term of imprisonment which the court could impose were the offender aged 21 or over, and it must not, subject to the exceptions mentioned below, be for four months or less. Section 3 of the Criminal Justice Act 1961 is to be repealed.

A sentence of youth custody will be served either in a Borstal or in a young prisoner centre or in a young prisoner's wing of an adult prison. The decision as to where the offender will be detained is to be in the hands of the prison authorities, but those offenders sentenced to 18 months or less will be guaranteed a place in a training establishment — i.e. in what is now a Borstal or an instituion run on similar lines. Those receiving longer sentences will be placed in training establishments as far as vacancies permit. Arrangements as to remission and release on licence will be analagous to those now applying to young offenders who are sent to prison. After release, the offender will be subject to supervision for three months or until the date on which his sentence would have expired whichever is the longer, but subject to a maximum of twelve months. A breach of the conditions of the supervision order will be punishable by 30 days in custody or a fine not exceeding £200. A further offence committed while under supervision would be a breach of supervision, and the penalty mentioned above could be imposed in addition to any sentence for the offence itself.

Section 19 of the Powers of Criminal Courts Act 1973 (imprisonment not to be imposed on an offender under 21 unless no other method of dealing with him is appropriate) is to be applied to youth custody sentences. There will not, however, be a power to suspend such a sentence.

Just as the courts can at present pass a sentence of Borstal training on offenders aged 15 and 16, so offenders of that age will be liable to sentences of youth custody, but the maximum term will be one of 12 months.

2 Detention centre

The Government sees value in short custodial sentences for some male offenders in both the 14 to 16 and 17 to 20 age brackets. It will indicate this by repealing s. 7(3) of the Children and Young Persons Act 1969 which, although never brought into effect, had envisaged the phasing out of detention centre sentences for juveniles. The periods of detention which may be imposed will, however, be varied. The minimum sentence will be reduced from three months to three weeks, and the maximum from six months to four months. The theory behind the very short minimum permissible sentence is that the deterrent effect of the sentence diminishes considerably after the first few weeks.

Since the government regards detention in a detention centre as the appropriate way of dealing with males aged 14 to 20 inclusive who should be punished by a short custodial sentence, the minimum sentence of youth custody for males will normally be one exceeding four months. However, where the offender's physical or mental state makes him unsuitable for the detention centre regime, or he has already served two custodial sentences, youth custody for four months or less will be permitted. Since there are no detention centre facilities for girls, youth custody for them may always be for a period of four months or less.

3 Care orders

To help meet the problem of juveniles who offend while in the care of a local authority, the White Paper proposes that a juvenile who has been placed in care following his being found guilty of an offence, and who is then found guilty of an imprisonable offence, shall be liable to a residential care order. The order will be to the effect that for a specified period, not exceeding six months, the juvenile is not to be allowed to remain at home. If a juvenile subject to a residential care order commits an imprisonable offence, a fresh residential order may be made, again for a period not exceeding six months. Once the residential order expires, the local authority will again have complete discretion under the care order to decide whether the juvenile should be returned to his home or not. The government envisages that the power to make a residential care order will be used where, if the juvenile were not already in care, the court would choose to make a care order, and where, in the case of an offender over 14, they would otherwise consider a custodial sentence.

4 Supervision orders and intermediate treatment

The government approves of supervision orders for juveniles with provision for intermediate treatment (i.e. orders under which the juvenile is, for a period not exceeding 90 days, obliged to take part in activities specified by his supervisor). However, it considers that the courts should have more power to control the type of treatment the juvenile receives under such an order. The proposal is that the court should be able to require a juvenile it places under supervision to undertake a programme of activities which has been agreed between the supervisor and the court as being appropriate to the juvenile's needs. The agreed programme could include community work. The White Paper also suggests that the minimum age for community service orders proper should be reduced from 17 to 16.

5   Responsibility of parents

It is thought that the courts are reluctant to order parents to pay fines imposed upon their juvenile children because of uncertainty as to the scope of the relevant provisions. Section 55 of the Children and Young Persons Act 1933 states that a parent shall not be ordered to pay if he has not 'conduced' to the commission of the offence, but exactly what amounts to conducing to an offence may be unclear. The government proposes to clarify the law so that parents will be required to pay fines imposed upon their children under 17 unless it would be unreasonable to make them do so. The riots which, in July 1981, occurred in many cities have given added significance to this proposal as blame for the rioting has, by some, been placed upon parents who failed to control the activities of their children.

Appendix 3   The Transport Act 1981

Section 19 of the Transport Act 1981 contains provisions which will significantly alter the law on disqualifications under the 'totting up' procedure (see Road Traffic Act 1972 s. 93(3) and Para. 15.10 for the present law. Although the Act received the Royal assent in July 1981, s. 19 is not expected to be brought into effect until late 1982. When in force it will provide that if the court orders an offender's licence to be endorsed but does not disqualify him, the endorsement will include, in addition to the particulars now endorsed under s. 101 of the 1972 Act, the date of the offence and the number of penalty points. Each endorsable offence will carry a certain number of points, as illustrated by the table below:

Reckless driving	10 points
Taking a motor vehicle without the owner's consent; going equipped for stealing with reference to the theft or taking of a motor vehicle	8 points
Failing to stop after accident	5-9 points
Failing to give particulars or report accident	4-9 points
Driving while disqualified by order of a court	6 points
Using a vehicle without insurance	4-8 points
Careless or inconsiderate driving	2-5 points
Offences carrying obligatory endorsement (drink/driving offences and causing death by reckless driving)	4 points
Speeding; failing to comply with traffic directions; contravention of Construction and Use Regulations	3 points
Driving while disqualified as being under age	2 points

Where the offence carries a range of penalty points (e.g. careless driving) the court is to fix the number to be endorsed on the licence, having regard, presumably, to the gravity of the particular offence. If particulars of two or more offences committed on the same occasion are to be endorsed, the number of penalty points will be the highest appropriate to any one of the offences.

When a person is convicted of an endorsable offence (the present offence), the court decides how many points will be endorsed on his licence assuming he is not disqualified. If that number added to the points endorsed for any offences committed within the three years preceeding the date of the present offence (the previous offences) comes to 12 or more, the offender must be disqualified for at least six months unless there are special circumstances. The present fairly liberal interpretation of the phrase 'special circumstances' is to be tightened. Only exceptional hardship to the offender will be taken into account, and the triviality of the present offence is to be ignored. The new legislation is, however, more generous to the motorist than the existing law in that:

(a)   If an offender is disqualified (whether under the 'totting up' provisions or otherwise) the 'slate is wiped clean'. Previous offences committed before a disqualification are to be ignored in calculating the number of points an offender has against him, and on the occasion of disqualification no penalty points are endorsed. However, the minimum period of a 'totting up' disqualification is increased to one year in the case of an offender who has been disqualified in the three years preceeding the present offence, and to two years in the cases of offenders disqualified more than once during that period.

(b)   An offender convicted of two or more endorsable offences who becomes liable to a 'totting up' disqualification is only to be liable to one such disqualification, not to a series of them in respect of each offence to run consecutively.

The broad effect of the Act, will be to make liability to disqualification under the 'totting up' provisions reflect more accurately the seriousness of the offences committed. Thus, three offences of speeding within three years will not, as now, attract disqualification, but one offence of reckless driving followed by almost any other endorsable offence will.

Appendix 4 The Report of the Royal Commission on Criminal Procedure (the Philips Commission)

In February 1978 a Royal Commission was set up to examine and make recommendations concerning:

(a) the powers and duties of the police in respect of the investigation of criminal offences, and the rights and duties of suspects and accused persons,

(b) the process of and responsibility for the prosecution of criminal offences, and

(c) other features of criminal procedure and evidence relating to the above.

The Commission, under the Chairmanship of Sir Cyril Philips, reported in January 1981. In addition to the report itself (1980 Command 8092), the Commission produced a 'Law and Procedure Volume' (1980 Command 8092-1), describing the present law and practice on matters such as arrest, powers of search, questioning by the police and commencement of proceedings. It also produced a helpful summary of its findings — 'The Balance of Criminal Justice' obtainable from HMSO. The report contains wide-ranging recommendations which, if adopted, would significantly alter the system for investigating offences prior to the accused's first court appearance (see Chapter 19 for the present law), and would completely abolish committal proceedings (see Chapter 3), replacing them with a procedure known as 'application for discharge'. The Commission's aim was to produce proposals which would be fair, open and workable. Fairness, they suggest, involves *inter alia* the making of rules which will be clear and understood by police and suspect alike. Openness means that decisions affecting him should, as far as possible, be explained to the suspect. Those decisions should be recorded in writing and available for subsequent inspection by the suspect or his advisers. Workable rules must both enable the police to discharge their duty in investigating crime and protect the rights of the suspect. Only a brief summary of the report can be attempted here. The major proposals are as follows:

1 Powers to stop and search

The existing hotch-potch of powers to stop and search people without arresting them should be replaced by a single statutory provision enabling a police officer (uniformed or otherwise) to stop and, if necessary, search any person in a public place whom he reasonably suspects of conveying stolen goods or of being in possession of anything whose possession in a public place is of itself a criminal offence (e.g. controlled drugs, house breaking implements or offensive weapons). There should be an analagous power to search vehicles, but the authority to stop a vehicle would only be given to a constable in uniform. To minimise abuse of these powers, the police officer concerned would have to give the reason for the search, and record it in his notebook. The person searched would be entitled to a copy of the record of the reason.

The power to stop vehicles mentioned above should be supplemented by a limited power to set up road checks at which all vehicles would be stopped. A road check would have to be authorised by an officer not below the rank of assistant chief constable, and would only be permitted where a grave offence has been or may be

committed.

2   Powers to search premises

The Commission's suggestions in this area of the law are that:

(a)   A magistrate should be able to issue a warrant to search premises if prohibited goods are reasonably suspected to be therein. By 'prohibited goods' the Commission means stolen goods and other items which it is an offence knowingly to possess (e.g. drugs, firearms and explosives). This is a simplification, although not a major extension, of the present law. An interesting procedural change proposed is that the police officer applying for a warrant should give his reasons for wanting it in the form of deposition, which would subsequently be open to inspection by the person whose premises were searched. The officer need not, however, name any informants.

(b)   An officer not below the rank of uniformed superintendant should, in cases of particular urgency, be able to authorise a search of premises for prohibited goods. This is similar to, but a considerable extension of, the powers now possessed by superintendants under the Theft Act 1968, s. 26(2).

(c)   A circuit judge should be able to issue a warrant to search premises for evidence. Such a warrant should only be issued as a last resort where the evidence it is hoped to find would be of substantial value, and other methods of investigation have or would prove unsuccessful. Furthermore, before a warrant is granted, the person concerned should be given an opportunity to produce the evidence in obedience to a court order to that effect, unless the making of an order might lead to the evidence being disposed of. This proposal is designed to meet the problem mentioned by Lord Denning MR in *Ghani* v *Jones* [1970] 1QB 693 that, in theory, the police cannot, without the owner's consent, search premises to find, for example, a murder weapon.

(d)   Following arrest, the police should be able to search the arrestee's premises without warrant if they reasonably suspect that items connected with the offence for which he has been arrested will be found. This is similar to the law as stated in *Jeffrey* v *Black* [1978] 1QB 490.

3   Powers of arrest and detention

The Commission wants the power of arrest without warrant simplified and extended. An arrestable offence should be defined as any imprisonable offence. In addition, a police officer who sees a non-imprisonable offence being committed should be able to arrest the offender if he refuses to give his name and address. This extension in the power of arrest should be balanced by the requirement that continued detention must be justified by reference to one of five considerations. The Commission calls this 'the necessity principle'. The five considerations are:

(a)   the arrestee's unwillingness to identify himself so that a summons may be served on him,

(b)   the need to prevent the continuation or repetition of the offence for which the arrest was made,

(c)   the need to protect the arrested person himself or other persons or property,

(d)   the need to secure or preserve evidence relating to the offence or to obtain

evidence from the arrestee by questioning him,

(e) the risk of the arrestee failing to appear at court to answer any charge made against him.

On the arrestee's arrival at the police station, the Commission suggests, the station sergeant should enquire not only into the validity of the arrest, as he would now do, but also into whether there is a necessity for the continued detention of the arrestee. If there is, the reason should be recorded on a document to be known as a 'custody sheet'.

The further safeguards against unjustified detention proposed are that:

(a) After six hours in police detention without charge an arrestee's case should be considered by an officer, if possible of the rank of inspector, who should order his release unless satisfied that there is still a necessity for detaining him.

(b) After 24 hours without charge, the arrestee should be brought before a magistrates' court sitting in private which, in a grave case, may sanction his detention for a further period of up to 24 hours.

(c) At the end of the period, if any, sanctioned by the magistrates, the arrestee must again be brought before them, and they may again permit him to be detained for up to 24 hours. If they do so, it will be possible to appeal against the decision. Over the weekend period, when it might not be possible to bring an arrestee before a magistrates' court, an arrestee detained for more than 24 hours should be visited by a solicitor who can check that he is being properly treated.

The Commission's proposals are intended to reflect the current pattern of questioning at police stations. Roughly 75% of arrestees are released or charged within 24 hours. Detention for more than 48 hours without charge is rare but by no means unknown.

5 Police questioning

The Commission wants the Judges' Rules put on a statutory basis, but the changes it recommends for this aspect of the investigative process are not as fundamental as the changes it recommends in other areas. It suggests that:

(a) The right to silence should be preserved, but the wording of the caution should be improved.

(b) The method of noting oral answers and statements made by suspects should be improved: In particular, the interviewing officer should note the main points emerging from an interview, read them over to the suspect and invite him to comment if he wishes.

(c) In addition to the above, a system for the tape recording of a summary of interviews between a police officer and suspect should be introduced wherever practicable.

(d) Duty solicitor schemes should be set up under which solicitors would be available to attend at police stations to advise suspects who wished to take advantage of their right to have legal advice. But the Commission are against having independent third parties present at all interviews between police and suspect.

Appendix 5 Imaginary Brief

John Michael Smith has been charged with burglary from a sweet shop and, in the alternative, handling part of the proceeds of the burglary. He is to stand trial at Barchester Crown Court. The following pages represent the brief which might be sent to counsel instructed to defend Smith. The brief contains illustrations of some of the comments which have been referred to in the course of this book. In particular, it contains an indictment, statements tendered at commital proceedings under s. 102 of the Magistrates' Courts Act 1980, a notice of particulars of alibi, an antecedents form and a social enquiry report.

IN THE BARCHESTER CROWN COURT

BETWEEN

REGINA
and
John Michael SMITH

BRIEF TO COUNSEL TO APPEAR
ON BEHALF OF THE DEFENDANT

In this matter Instructing Solicitors act on behalf of the Defendant who was committed for trial from the Barchester Magistrates' Court on July 22nd on charges of burglary of a sweet shop situated at 123, High Street, Barchester, and in the alternative, handling 5 boxes of chocolates, part of the proceeds of the burglary. He will plead not guilty to both charges.

Basically the prosecution will allege that the Defendant, together with two persons unknown, went to the aforesaid premises, broke in through a back door, and stole a quantity of sweets and cigarettes. The Defendant's van, according to the prosecution, was used in committing the burglary, and they will call a Mr Charles Watchman to state that he saw the burglars making their 'getaway' in a van number XYZ 999M. That is the number of the Defendant's van. The Defendant will state that he was not involved in any way in the burglary. Either the witness made a mistake about the number of the van he saw, or the burglars, whoever they were, took the van without the Defendant's consent and returned it to where it had been parked, so that the Defendant did not know it had been taken. Unfortunately, the Defendant made a written statement at the police station in which he admitted driving two persons, whom he does not name, to 123 High Street. These two persons broke into the shop, according to the statement, while the Defendant drove around in the van. At a pre-arranged time the Defendant drove back to the rear entrance of the shop, where the van was loaded with the stolen goods and then driven away. The Defendant will say that he only made the statement because the police said he would not get bail unless he made a statement, and he was anxious about his wife, who was expecting a baby at the time.

As to the chocolates, these were found in the Defendant's sideboard. Apparently chocolates of this brand were stolen in the course of the burglary. The Defendant states that he bought the chocolates on the Saturday before the alleged offence. He bought them from a stall-holder in Barchester Market who was selling them cheaply. Counsel is asked to consider whether there is a case to answer as regards handling the chocolates, as there does not seem to be any evidence that they were stolen. The prosecution may try to rely on *R* v Fuschillo [1940] 2 All ER 489, but instructing solicitors suggest that the Defendant's case is clearly distinguishable from that of Fuschillo.

At the time of the alleged burglary, the Defendant was in bed with his wife. A notice of particulars of alibi has been served on the prosecution.

Counsel is asked to advise generally, in conference if so desired, and thereafter appear on behalf of the Defendant.

No. 1234

INDICTMENT

The Crown Court at BARCHESTER

THE QUEEN v JOHN MICHAEL SMITH

JOHN MICHAEL SMITH is CHARGED AS FOLLOWS:—

Count 1   *Statement of Offence*
                     Burglary contrary to section 9(1)(b) of the Theft Act 1968.

                     Particulars of Offence
                     JOHN MICHAEL SMITH, on the 2nd day of July 1981,
                     having entered as a trespasser a building known as 123 High
                     Street, Barchester, stole therein 100 packets of Coffanchoke
                     cigarettes, 100 packets of Coolsmoke cigarettes, 30 boxes of
                     chocolates and 20 boxes of chocolate liqueurs.

Count 2   *Statement of Offence*
                     Handling stolen goods, contrary to section 22(1) of the Theft
                     Act 1968.

                     Particulars of Offence
                     JOHN MICHAEL SMITH, on the 2nd day of July 1981,
                     dishonestly received stolen goods, namely 5 boxes of chocolates
                     belonging to Stewart Sweetman, knowing or believing the same
                     to be stolen goods.

                                          A. N. Other
Date: 29th July 1981   *Officer of the Crown Court*

STATEMENT OF WITNESS

(M.C. Act 1980 s. 102; C.J. Act 1967 s. 9: M.C. Rules 1981 r.70)

Statement of: Stewart SWEETMAN

Age of Witness: (Date of Birth) 33 (born 30.1.'48)

Occupation of Witness: Shop-owner

Address and Telephone Number: 1, Proudie Crescent,

Barchester

Barsetshire

This statement consisting of 1 page, signed by me, is true to the best of my knowledge and belief and I make it knowing that, if it is tendered in evidence, I shall be liable to prosecution if I have wilfully stated in it anything which I know to be false or do not believe to be true.

Dated the 8th day of July 1981

Signed: S. Sweetman

Signature witnessed by: G. Regan

I am the owner of 'Sweet-tooth's', a tobacconists and confectioners of 123 High Street, Barchester. Last week, on the 1st July I think it was, I locked and made secure the premises of my shop before going home at about 6pm. The next morning, at about 8am, I opened up the shop. As I went in I noticed the burglar alarm lying on the floor. There were no other signs of an intruder in the shop itself, but when I went through to my stockroom at the rear of the shop I noticed that the door to the yard was open and the lock had apparently been forced. I checked on my stock, and found that these items had been stolen

1 carton containing 100 packets of 'Coffanchoke' cigarettes, valued at £70 — I produce the invoice No. 2468, Exhibit SS/1

1 carton containing 100 packets of 'Coolsmoke' filter cigarettes, valued at £75 — invoice No. 987, Exhibit SS/2

1 case containing 30 boxes of 'Naughty but Nice' chocolates, valued at £55 — invoice No. 2992, Exhibit SS/3

1 case containing 20 boxes of 'Flavourful' chocolate liqueurs, valued at £40 — invoice No. 5665, Exhibit SS/4

I have been shown 5 boxes of 'Naughty but Nice' chocolates (Exhibit No. GR/1). They are like the chocolates which were stolen from my shop but I cannot positively identify them. I can say that my shop is the only one in Barchester which sells this brand of chocolates. I cannot remember selling 5 boxes to any one customer — if I had done I would remember.

I did not give any one permission to enter my shop or take any property. I am willing to attend court and give evidence. I wish to claim compensation for all the property stolen from me, and also for the cost of repairing the alarm and the back door, which I estimate will come to £100.

Signed: S. Sweetman   Signature witnessed by: G. Regan

STATEMENT OF WITNESS
(M.C. Act 1980 s. 102; C.J. Act 1967 s. 9; M.C. Rules 1981 r. 70)

<u>Statement of:</u>   Charles WATCHMAN

<u>Age of Witness:</u>   (Date of Birth) 51 (born 17.5.'30)

<u>Occupation of Witness:</u>   Fireman

<u>Address and Telephone Number:</u>   10, Cathedral Street,

Barchester

Barsetshire

This statement consisting of 1 page signed by me is true to the best of my knowledge and belief and I make it knowing that, if it is tendered in evidence, I shall be liable to prosecution if I have willfully stated in it anything which I know to be false or do not believe to be true.

<u>Dated the</u> 8th day of July 1981

<u>Signed:</u> C. Watchman

<u>Signature witnessed by:</u> G. Regan

I live at the above address. Opposite my house are the back of entrances of a row of shops which face on to the High Street. One of the shops is a sweet shop called 'Sweet-tooth's'. About a week ago I remember getting up at about 1.30 in the morning. I had to get up at that time as I am a fireman, and that week I was on the early morning shift, so I had to be at the fire-station at 2am. As I was getting dressed I noticed the sound of an alarm coming from across the road. I did not worry about it as the alarms are always going off for no reason, but I thought it went on for rather a long time. Then it stopped, and I forgot about it. I had a cup of tea, and left the house at roughly 1.45. As I opened the front gate I noticed a small, dark coloured van parked about 20 yards down the road on the opposite side. It was parked just by the back entrance to 'Sweet-tooth's'. Two men seemed to be lifting something into the back of the van. Then one of the men climbed into the back of the van and the other got into the front passenger seat, and the van drove quickly off. When I first saw the van, I remembered the burglar alarm which had gone off earlier and that made me suspicious of what the men were doing. Just before the van drove off I was able to see clearly, in the light of a street lamp, what the number was. It was XYZ 999M. I wrote the number down on the back of an envelope which I had in my pocket. I still have the envelope. Then I went back to my house and telephoned the police.

I am willing to attend court and give evidence.

The two men I saw seemed to be fairly young and above average height, but I would not be able to recognise them if I saw them again. It was dark and they had their backs to me.

<u>Signed:</u>   C. Watchman   <u>Signature witnessed by:</u>   G. Regan

STATEMENT OF WITNESS
(M.C. Act 1980 s. 102; C.J. Act 1967 s. 9; M.C. Rules 1981 r. 70)

Statement of: Brian BEATMAN

Age of Witness: (Date of Birth) Over 21

Occupation of Witness: Police Constable 'C'

Address and Telephone Number: Barchester Police Station,

1, Copper Street,
Barchester

This statement, consisting of 1 page signed by me, is true to the best of my knowledge and belief and I make it knowing that, if it is tendered in evidence, I shall be liable to prosecution if I have wilfully stated in it anything which I know to be false or do not believe to be true.

Dated the 2nd day of July 1981.

Signed: B. Beatman

Signature w.tnessed by: J. Carter

On Thursday 2nd July 1981 at 9am I attended at Barchester Fire Station where I saw a Mr Watchman who lives at 10, Cathedral Street. As a result of what he told me I wrote an index mark, XYZ 999M, on a piece of paper. I later transferred this number to crime sheet 1234. I did a vehicle check, and the vehicle owner came back as a Mr John Michael SMITH of 50, Fiddlers Lane, Barchester.

Signed: B. Beatman   Signature witnessed by: J. Carter

STATEMENT OF WITNESS
(M.C. Act 1980 s. 102; C.J. Act 1967 s. 9; M.C. Rules 1981 r. 70)

Statement of: George REGAN

Age of Witness: (Date of Birth) Over 21

Occupation of Witness: Detective Sergeant 'C'

Address and Telephone Number: Barchester Police Station

1, Copper Street,

Barchester

This statement, consisting of 2 pages, each signed by me, is true to the best of my knowledge and belief and I make it knowing that, if it is tendered in evidence, I shall be liable to prosecution if I have wilfully stated in it anything which I know to be false or do not believe to be true.

Dated the 2nd day of July 1981

Signed: G. Regan

Signature witnessed by: J. Carter

On Thursday 2nd July at about 10.30am, in company with D.C. 100 'C' CARTER, I went to 50, Fiddlers Lane, Barchester where I saw John Michael SMITH. I told him we were police officers and showed him my warrant card. He invited us into his flat.

I said to him, 'I'm making enquiries into a burglary at a sweet shop and tobacconists called "Sweet-tooth's" at 123, High Street, Barchester, which occurred last night. I believe you can help me with these enquiries.'

He said, 'I don't know what you're talking about.'

I said, 'Are you the owner of a van number XYZ 999M?'

He said, 'Why are you asking?'

I said, 'That van was used in the commission of the burglary.'

He said, 'Well, I used to own it, but I sold it about a month ago, and I forgot to register the change of ownership.'

I said, 'Who did you sell it to?'

Before he could answer, the street door bell rang, and a woman I now know to be Mrs Janet SMITH walked into the room. In the presence and hearing of SMITH, I said to Mrs Smith, 'Does your husband own a van number XYZ 999M?'

She said, 'Yes, I'm sure that's the number.'

I said, 'So he hasn't sold it recently.'

She said, 'No, of course not.'

Then SMITH said, 'All right, then, I do still own the van but I had nothing to do with the burglary you're asking about.'

I said, 'I'm arresting you on suspicion of burglary,' cautioned him and he said 'It's got nothing to do with me.'

Signed: G. Regan   Signature witnessed by: J. Carter

STATEMENT OF WITNESS
(M.C. Act 1980 s. 102; C.J. Act 1967 s. 9; M.C. Rules 1981 r. 70)

I said, 'Before we go to the police station, I am going to search the flat for any proceeds of the burglary.' In the sideboard in the back room I found 5 one pound boxes of 'Naughty but Nice' chocolates (Exhibit GR/1). I said to SMITH, 'Where did you get these chocolates from? Chocolates like these were stolen in the burglary.'

He said, 'I'm not saying nothing until I've seen a solicitor. I know my rights.'

He was then taken to Barchester Police Station.

Later I saw SMITH at the police station in company with D.C. CARTER. I reminded him of the caution, and said, 'Do you want to tell us about the burglary last night at "Sweet-tooth's"?'

He said, 'I don't know nothing about a burglary. You know me, I've settled down since I got married.'

D.C. CARTER said, 'Your van was seen being used to carry the goods away. First, you tell us you'd sold it, then you admit you've still got it, and we find five boxes of chocolates at your flat just like the chocolates stolen. Now you ask us to believe that you had nothing to do with the burglary.'

SMITH was silent for a short time. Then he said, 'What do you think I'll get?'

I said, 'That's a matter entirely for the judge.'

He said, 'All right, I suppose I had better make a statement. Will you right down what I say?'

I said, 'Yes of course.'

I then wrote at SMITH's dictation a statement which he then signed. The statement was written between 1 and 1.15pm without any break. I now produce the statement Exhibit No. GR/2.

On Thursday 2nd July 1981 at 2pm, SMITH was charged, the charge read over and cautioned and he made no reply.

Signed: G. Regan   Signature witnessed by: J. Carter

STATEMENT UNDER CAUTION

Barchester Police Station
Date: 2 July 1981
Time: 1pm

Statement of: John Michael SMITH
Address: 50, Fiddlers Lane, Barchester
Age: 22
Occupation: Factory worker

I, John Michael SMITH, wish to make a statement. I want someone to write down what I say. I have been told that I need not say anything unless I wish to do so and that whatever I say may be given in evidence.

Signed: J. M. Smith
Signature witnessed by: G. Regan

About a week ago two mates of mine that I used to be friendly with but I haven't seen since I got married came round to see me. They said there was a sweet shop in the High Street that they could break into with no trouble, and they knew a man who would buy off them any sweets or cigarettes they could nick. They said they hadn't got a motor of their own to use on the job, and they didn't think it was worth the risk of nicking one. I said I was married now, and going straight, but they kept on pestering me, and at last I said I would drive my van for them when they did the break-in.

In the early hours of this morning I drove these two mates — I don't want to give their names — to the shop in the High Street. The arrangement was that I would drive around for about ten minutes while they broke into the place, then I would park the van at the back entrance· to the shop, and they would load up the van with whatever they had nicked. Everything went as planned. I drove the van to where one of them lives where we unloaded what they had stolen. They gave me £25 for driving the van and five boxes of chocolates you found at my flat.

I want to say how sorry I am for what happened. I would not have done it if my mates had not kept on at me, even though I said no at first.

J. M. Smith

I have read the above statement and I have been told that I can correct, alter or add anything I wish. This statement is true. I have made it of my own free will.

Signed: J. M. Smith
Signature witnessed by: G. Regan

Statement taken by me George Regan between 1pm and 1.15pm. No breaks for refreshments.

Signed: G. Regan

JOHN MICHAEL SMITH
50, Fiddlers Lane,
Barchester.   d.o.b. 1.5.59

will say
I have been charged with burglary and handling stolen goods and intend to plead
not guilty to both charges.
The facts of the matter are as follows.

On July 1st 1981 I came home from work at about 6pm, and parked my van
outside my flat as I usually do. I then had my dinner, and spent the evening
watching television with my wife — I remember that the tennis was on in the
early part of the evening. We went to bed at about 11pm, and got up at about
8.30am the next morning. I was not at work that day, as we are on short time. At
no time during the night did I leave the house. My wife can confirm this because
if I had done so I would have woken her up. I know nothing about the burglary.
    Turning to the statements of the prosecution witnesses. It is true that when
D.S. Regan asked me if I owned the van, I panicked, and said that I had sold it.
It was a stupid thing to do, but I thought that he would never believe me if I just
said I had nothing to do with the burglary. About the chocolates, I bought them
from a stall in Barchester Market on the Saturday before all this happened. The
man was selling them cheaply, and that is why I bought five boxes. I told the
police that when they found the chocolates. It is not true that I said 'I'm not
saying nothing until I've seen my solicitor'.
    At the police station I was left for about an hour in a cell. I was getting very
worried about my wife, because she was pregnant, and I knew she would be
anxious about me. When the police questioned me in the interview room, I asked
them when I could go home because I had to see my wife. They said I could go as
soon as I told them everything that had happened. I thought that things looked so
bad anyway that making a statement could not make matters worse. D.S. Regan
told me what to write. The statement is not true. I only made it to get bail.
    I work on the production line at 'Wellmade Engineering Works'. My normal
take home pay is about £80 per week, but I am presently on short time, so I only
take home £65. I have several previous convictions, but since marrying in
December last year I have settled down and gone straight. Two weeks ago my
wife gave birth to a baby boy.

Signed: John Smith

Barchester Police
Solicitors Department
Barchester Crown Court

23 July 1981

Dear Sirs,
 re: <u>John Michael SMITH committed from Barchester Magistrates' Court</u>
 <u>on 22nd July</u>

We act on behalf of the above named person who seeks to put forward alibi evidence in support of his defence at his trial. Our Client will state that on the night in question he was at home from 6pm on the evening of 1st July until the time when the police arrived on the morning of the 2nd July. At all times his wife, Mrs Janet SMITH, was at home with Our Client, save that at about 9am she left the house to do some shopping. It is intended to call Mrs Smith at the trial.

Yours faithfully,
I. M. Sharp
Sharp and Practice
Solicitors for the Defendant

BARSETSHIRE POLICE

Division C
                                                Station   Barchester Central
                                                3 July 1981

For the information of the Chief Clerk of the Crown Court/Counsel for the
Prosecution/the Prison Governor/the Court Probation Liaison Officer

Antecedents of: John Michael SMITH
Committed for trial: Barchester Crown Court
For offences of: Burglary and Handling stolen goods
Date and place of birth: 1.5.59 (Puddingdale, Barsetshire) aged 22
Date of first entry in UK: —   Nationality   British
Date of arrest: 2.7.81   ~~In custody~~/On bail
Brief summary of convictions: He has 8 findings of guilt as a juvenile and 7
                                   previous convictions recorded against him
Education: He attended Bishop Grantley's Comprehensive,
                                   leaving at the age of 16

Main employments since leaving school
He was an apprentice at 'Precision Manufacturing' engineering works, but was
dismissed in March 1976 for bad time-keeping. After that he had several jobs of a
casual nature. On his release from Borstal in August 1977 he was employed as a
warehouseman for about a year. Subsequently he worked on building sites between
periods of unemployment.

Present employment
He has worked at 'Wellmade Engineering' since his release from prison in April 1980.
He earns about £80 per week take-home pay.

Address, home conditions and domestic circumstances
He lives at 50, Fiddlers Lane, Barchester, with his wife who is expecting a child. He
pays £20 per week rent, and gives his wife £35 per week housekeeping money. He has
hire-purchase repayments on a television set and washing machine totalling £30 per
month.

Any other antecedent information likely to assist:

List of previous convictions attached	☑	No known previous convictions	☐

G. Regan   Officer in   Supervising
                                case   Officer
Detective   Rank   Rank
Sergeant   55C

Convictions Recorded Against: John Michael SMITH   C.R.O. No. 98765/73
Charged in name of   John Michael SMITH

DATE	COURT	OFFENCES	SENTENCE	DATE OF RELEASE
8.10.73	Barchester Juvenile Court	Theft of a pedal cycle, value £30	Conditional discharge for 12 months	
25.11.73	Barchester Juvenile Court	(1) Burglary, (2) Criminal Damage (two cases t.i.c.)	Supervision Order for 2 years	
7.6.75	Fulchester Juvenile Court	(1) and (2) Taking away m/v without lawful authority (3) and (4) Driving under age	3 months detention centre	2.8.75
1.12.76	Casterbridge Crown Court	(1) Robbery (2) Taking away m/v without lawful authority (3) No insurance (4 cases t.i.c.)	Borstal training. On (2) and (3) l/e disqual. from driving for 12 months	1.8.77
23.12.77	Barchester Crown Court	(1) Assault occasioning ABH (2) Criminal Damage	6 months imprisonment on each concurrent suspended 2 years	
15.4.79	Barchester Crown Court	(1) Burglary (2) Handling stolen goods	(1) 18 months imprisonment (2) 6 months concurrent with (1) Suspended sentence (23.12.77) brought into effect to run concurrently	15.4.80

CONFIDENTIAL
BARCHESTER AREA PROBATION AND AFTER-CARE SERVICE

Probation Officer: MR V. GOOD

Address: Probation Office, Reform Close, Barchester

PROBATION OFFICER'S REPORT to the

Barchester Crown Court   on

Full name: John Michael SMITH

Address: 50, Fiddlers Lane, Barchester

Relevant P.S.D.:   Barchester (City)

Present offence: Burglary and Handling

Previous: As police antecedents
This report is based on one interview with Mr Smith. I have also consulted previous Probation records.

Family and background

John Smith tells me he spent the early years of his life in the small Barsetshire village of Puddingdale. At the age of 10 his family moved to Barchester, where his mother still lives. His father now lives apart from his mother, and Mr Smith has had no contact with him for at least three years. Mr Smith has an older brother and sister who are living away from home, and a younger brother who still lives with his mother.

Recent history

On his release from prison in April 1980 Mr Smith was assisted by the probation service in finding accommodation and his present employment with Wellmade Engineering Works, Barchester. Soon after starting work he met his present wife, who then worked as a typist at Wellmade. They married in December 1980, and moved to their present address in Fiddlers Lane in May of this year. It is a privately-rented two-bedroomed flat with one reception room, for which Mr Smith pays £20 per week rent. I understand that on July 15 Mrs Smith gave birth to a baby boy.

Employment and financial situation

Mr Smith's average take-home pay is £80 per week, but this can rise to £90 with overtime. At present, owing to the recession, he is on short-time and only taking home £65. However, there is not thought to be any risk of Mr Smith being made redundant, and he expects to return to full-time working in September. Mr Smith tells me that there is a chance of his going on a course to qualify as a fitter, which

would result in promotion to a higher grade at Wellmade. He gives his wife £35 per week housekeeping. In addition to the rent of £20, he has repayments on a television set and washing machine totalling £30 per month.

Present offence

I understand that Mr Smith is pleading not guilty to the present charges, and I have therefore not discussed those matters with him.

Conclusion

Mr Smith gives the impression of being a pleasant young man who, after a troubled youth, has settled down happily with his young wife, and feels a proper sense of responsibility for her and his child. He tells me that while in prison he thought seriously about his future, and resolved not to commit any further offences. His behaviour on release bears that out because he has worked steadily, and probation records show that while under supervision on licence he cooperated fully with his supervisor. If he should be convicted of these present charges, I feel that he would benefit from the assistance of the probation service.

Vernon Good
Probation Officer
Petty Sessional Division of Barchester (City)
28 July 1981

NOTE ON CONTENTS OF THE BRIEF

In addition to the documents contained in this imaginary brief, there would, in real life, be a further witness statement under s. 102 of the Magistrates' Court Act 1980 from D.C. Carter, who accompanied D.S. Regan throughout his investigations. For all practical purposes, D.C. Carter' statement will be idential to Regan's. This is because both officers will have prepared their statements from notes written in their note-books soon after the conclusion of the interview with Smith. It is normal police practice for officers to confer together when writing their notes, and arrive at an agreed version of what took place. Since the statements repeat what is in the notes, they, like the notes, will be identical.

Defence solicitors, in addition to taking a statement from the accused, will have taken a statement from Mrs Smith confirming that on the night in question her husband did not leave the house. They may also have made efforts to trace the person who sold the accused the five boxes of chocolates. For purposes of illustration, antecedents and a social enquiry report have been put in the brief, although the defence are unlikely to receive them until the trial.

Subject Index

abuse of process of court
  committal, repeated attempts 21
  discretion to halt prosecution 66
  discretion not to try case 128
accused
  committal proceedings, in 16
  competence and compellability 93, 134
  detention pending charge 275
  dismissal of counsel 95
  mode of trial hearing 144-5
  presence of
    at appeal 239
    to plead 96
    to secure 124
    when essential 133
  proceedings in absence of 129-130
  questioning of 94
  right to
    defend himself 133
    see solicitor 293
    silence 98, 133, 291-3
  sentence, in absence of 132
  unaware of proceedings 129-130
  unrepresented 95
  unsworn statement, by 94
admissibility
  defence objection before trial 88
  written statements, of 134
adjournment
  after first court appearance 302
  before sentence 169
  for reports on accused 137
aiding and abetting
  joint counts 48
alibi
  evidence 94-5, 134
  warning
    committal proceedings, in. 20, 25-6
    dispensing with 26
ancillary orders 181, 317-326
appeal
  against
    conviction 226, 228-231
    sentence 227, 233
  bail pending hearing 239
  case stated, by way of 250, 253-5
  Court of Appeal, Criminal Division,
    to 223

appeal—*continued*
  Crown Court, to 31, 250
    constitution of 35
  effect of, if successful 231-2, 233
  history of criminal appeals 223
  House of Lords, to 244-5, 265
  leave to appeal 225-6, 228
  loss of time 238-9
  jury, appeal against composition of 76-8
  powers of court 252-3
  procedure 234-5
    case stated, for 255-9
    evidence to be received 240
    Crown Court, to 252
    notice of application for leave to
      appeal 235
    Grounds of Appeal, preparation
      of 236
    plea of insanity 243-4
    single judge, application to 237-8
    transcripts 237
  proviso, to avoid miscarriage of
    justice 52, 232
  reference to Court of Appeal
    by Attorney-General 243
    by Home Secretary 242
  right of appeal 224, 250-2
  Rule against Duplicity 41, 44-5
arraignment
  ambiguity of answer 53
  plea on each count 53
  procedure on 53
attachment of earnings order 197
attendance centre orders
  juvenile, subject to 164, 181
  summary conviction, on 136
Attorney-General
  consent required for prosecution 7, 9, 272
  role of 10-11
Autrefois acquit and convict
  application of plea 63-5
  plea of 62-3, 133

Bail
  absconding, consequences of 313-4
  application for, to Crown Court and High
    Court 311-313
  application procedure 309

bail—*continued*
 applications, successive 309-310
 arrest warrant for failure to answer 96
 criteria for granting or withholding 304-5
 custody, when bail refused 315
 estreat of recognizances 315
 from police station 277
 pending appeal 239
 prior to
  committal proceedings 15
  Crown Court hearing 26-7
 procedure for granting 311
 refusal of
  imprisonable offence 305-7
  non-imprisonable offence 307
 requirement of sureties 307-9, 310-311
 'right to bail' 305
 variation of conditions 311
 when bail may be granted 303
bankruptcy
 criminal bankruptcy orders 325-6
bias
 pecuniary interest of magistrate 123
bigamy
 jurisdiction to try 7
bill of indictment, preferring 39, 52
binding over 201-2
Borstal
 committal to Crown Court with Borstal
  recommendation 149-150
 powers of court 203-5
 regime described 203-5
 sentence to 160, 185-7
 sentencing policy 215, 216

care orders, juveniles subject
 to 161-2, 181, 330
case stated, appeal by way of 250, 253
 from Crown Court 258-9
 judicial review, compared with 264-5
 method of hearing 258
 procedure 255-8
 right of appeal 253-5
caution
 accused unrepresented at committal
  proceedings 20
 police officer, by 276-7
certiorari (See also judicial review)
 bias, for 123
character and antecedents
 challenge to accuracy of 172
 committal for sentence, at 147
 sentence, given before 171
charge
 caution 276
 police station, at 275
 without delay 276
child, defined 155

committal proceedings
 bail or custody 145-6
 Borstal recommendation 149-150
 challenge to conduct of 28
 character and antecedents, in 147
 consent to summary trial withheld 142
 in camera 16
 multiple offences, for 151
 'no case to answer' submission of 19
 offences other than those charged, for 20
 'old fashioned' committals 17
 parole 150
 powers of sentence 149-150
 presence of accused, in 22
 prima facie case 15
 procedure 15
  with consideration of evidence 17
  without consideration of
   evidence 21, 22
 'section 1' committals 17, 22-3
 sentence, for, under s. 38 145-7
 sentence, suspended 150
 trial on indictment, prior to 15
 witness orders 24-5
community service orders 181
 juveniles 160
 powers of court 202-3
 report by probation officer 175
 summary conviction, on 136
compensation orders 181, 323-4
confessions
 admissibility of 88
 involuntary 278, 287-8
 Judges' Rules 288-291
conspiracy, joinder of counts 48
convictions, previous
 given before sentence 171
 spent convictions 173-4
corroboration 98
costs, contribution to 181
 order to pay 321-3
counsel
 closing speeches, by 96-7
 defence, approach of 81
 duty to court 82
 judge, seeing in private 82-3
 prosecuting
  approach of 81
  duty to reveal antecedents 81
counts in indictment
 alternate 47
 contents of 40
 duplicity, the rule against 41-5
 essential elements of offence 40
 examples of 42-3
 'founded on the same facts', to be 45
 joinder of counts 45-8
 joinder of defendants 48-50
 more than one accused 29

counts in indictment—*continued*
more than one count 37
more than one linked offence 44-5
'same or similar character' 46
courts, composition of
committal proceedings, in 16
Court of Appeal, Criminal Division 223
Crown Court appeals, in 35
criminal damage charges 151-3
cross-examination
committal proceedings, in 17
limits of 87-8
statements under s. 102, on 18-19
unsworn statements, not allowed 20
Crown Court
appeals from magistrates' court 31
change of venue 34
civil jurisdiction, of 31
classes of offence, in 33
committal for sentence to 31, 142, 145-6, 148-9
distribution of work in 33
judge's view of law prevails in 36
jurisdiction of 31
licensing appeals in 31
location 21, 34-5
organisation of 33-4
revocation of parole, by 188
trial on indictment, in 3
custody, without charge 277

day training centres
probation order, for 198
defence
counsel, approach of 81
evidence, no obligation to adduce 93
opening speech, right of 93
demurrer 67
deportation, powers of court to
recommend 211
depositions (see also Statements under s. 102)
advantages and disadvantages of 19
at trial 89-91
committal proceedings, in 17
juveniles, from 27
persons dangerously ill, from 27
strict conformity with rules 17
detention centre orders
juveniles, sentence to 160, 161, 181
powers of court 205-6
sentencing policy 215, 330
'short, sharp shock' 206
social enquiry report 176
summary conviction, on 136
detention during Her Majesty's pleasure
juveniles 160-1
Director of Public Prosecutions
appointment by Home Secretary 10

DPP—*continued*
consent required for prosecution,
when 7, 9, 272
decision to prosecute, by 6
offences, to be informed of 271
Police, Chief Officer of, relation to 271
role of 10-11
serious prosecutions, report to 10
discharge 181
absolute 136, 199-200
conditional 136, 199-200
breach of conditions 150, 175
offences during 200-1
juveniles 160
discretion, judicial
absence of accused, to proceed in 129
absence of prosecution, to proceed
in 132
alibi evidence, to admit 94-5
amendment to information, to hear 128
change of plea, to allow 59
co-accused, to sentence 55
evidence out of order, to admit 100-1
fitness to plead, postponement of 61-2
jury to separate, to allow 103
juvenile cases, to hear 157
lesser offences 107
mode of trial, to allow change of 145
plea by post, not to accept 131
process, abuse of, not to try for 128
prosecution, to halt 66
trials, to order separate 46, 48, 50
driving offences 208-211
duplicity, the rule against
alternative charges 44
appeal, grounds for 41, 44-5
summary trials, in 126

evidence
additional 89
after jury retires 103
committal proceedings, in 17
Court of Appeal, before 240-2
defence not obliged to adduce 93, 134
fingerprints 299
identification, of 297-9
out of normal order 100-1
strength of, to prosecute 7
examination-in-chief
committal proceedings, in 17
examining justices
certificate of depositions 17
committal proceedings, in 16
extended sentences
persistent offenders, for 187-8
tariff, above 220

fines
attachment of earnings order 197

fines—*continued*
   combined with other sentences   195
   enforcement of   195-7
   imprisonment for non-payment   196
   powers of court   194
   probation officer, to supervise   197
   statement of means   196
   time to pay   194
   warrant of distress   197
   when appropriate   195
fingerprints
   evidence   299
   on arrest   276
forteiture orders   325

habeas corpus, writ of   278, 315-6
hospital order (see also mental abnormality)
   magistrates, by   133
   medical report, following   137
   Mental Health Act orders   206-7
   unfitness to plead   61

identification
   assailant, of   54
   evidence, obtaining   296-9
   guidelines on   86
   parades   276, 297-9
   Section 1 committals, in   23
immunity to prosecution   8
imprisonment (see also Sentence)   181
   courts, general approach of   190
   immediate   182
   juveniles, not allowed   160, 182
   life, for murder   182, 190
   maximum terms of   183
   non-payment of fines, for   196
   remission and release on
     licence   182, 188-190
   restrictions on   185-7
   sentencing regulations   182-190
   summary convictions, on   136
   tariff sentence, as   215
indictable offences   4, 139-141
indictment
   alternative offences, in   44
   application
     to amend   41, 51
     to sever   50
   bill of, preferring   39
   counts
     adding to   51
     joinder of   45-8
     more than one   37
     separate   49
     inclusion of   39, 40
   defects in   51
   defendants, in
     joinder of   48-50
     numerous   50

indictment—*continued*
   drafting of   37, 39, 40
   Duplicity, Rule against   41, 44-5
   examples given of   38
   motion to quash   52
   one offence per count   37
   out of time   39
   particulars of offence   37
   separate trials, discretion to order   46
   statement of offence   37
   statutory offences, to be named in   37
information
   amendment of   128
   charge sheet serves as   126
   counts in   126
   defects in   128
   drafting of   126-7
   duplicity, rule against   126
   laying of   6, 124
   more than one accused   127
   more than one, hearing of   127
   one offence only in count   126
   particulars to be included in   126
   standard form of   125
   summons, procedure for issue   278-280
   time limit for laying   127
   trial on   3
insanity, plea of   243-4
issue estoppel   65-6

judge, Crown Court
   casting vote   35
   mode of address   33
   power to call witnesses   101
   seeing counsel in private   82-3
   verdict of must be accepted   110
Judges' Rules
   charge without delay   276
   confessions   288-291
judicial review
   application for   263-4
   case stated, method compared   264-5
   challenge to magistrates' decision   250
   prerogative orders   259-260
     certiorari   260-2
     mandamus   262-3
     prohibition   262-3
jurisdiction
   committal proceedings, in   16
   Crown Court, of   31
   offences triable wherever committed   7-8
   magistrates' court, of   121-3
   territorial scope, of   7, 121
jury
   autrefois, in question of   62-3
   bias of juror   78
   challenge to juror   71-5
   Crown Court, in   3
   discharge of   78-80, 109-110

jury— *continued*
eligibility for service on 68-9
empanelling of 54, 70-1
appeals against 76-7
excusal 70
irregularities, result of 103
issues triable by one jury 76
jury in waiting 53
leniency, recommendation of 169
misconduct by juror 79
muteness, in question of 60
'no case to answer', absence for 92
non-attendance, penalty for 70
oath 71
overnight accommodation 103
pressure from judge 110
privacy of jury room 104
questions for judge 102, 103-4
retirement of, procedure for 102-3
separation of 103
summoning and remuneration of 69-70
unfitness to plead, in questions of 61
vetting of 75-6
'voire dire', hearing on the 88
jury bailiff 102
juvenile
arrest of 300-1
court 3
special rules in 158-9
costs and compensation against 160
defined 155
detention of, at Home Secretary's
direction 156, 160
fines, policy 160
mode of trial 155-7
procedure of trial 156-7
sentencing of 159-166
trial jointly with adult 155-6

law officers of the crown 10-11
legal aid
appeal against refusal of 321
appeal to Court of Appeal, for 242
committal proceedings, before 15
contribution by accused 319-320
Crown Court proceedings, for 26-7
grant of 317-321
mitigation, for 177
legal representation
magistrates' court in 132-3
mitigation, for 177
Lord Chancellor
lay magistrates, appointment of 116-7
location of stipendiary magistrates 119

magistrates
appointment and qualifications 116-7
arrest warrant, power to issue 115
cannot hear both case and appeal 36

magistrates— *continued*
chairmen, election of 119
Crown Court, as judges in 35
equally divided, when 135
examining justices, as, in committal
proceedings 16, 116
functions of 115-6
history of office 115
juvenile court panel 157
pecuniary interest, disqualification
for 123
powers of sentence 135-7
proceedings against 119
removal and retirement of 118
stipendiary 4, 118
summary trials, in 3
training and attendance of 117
magistrates' clerk
administrative duties of 120
advice from 4, 137
appointment of 119
assistants to 119
function of 4
pecuniary interest in case 124
retiring with magistrates 137
summary trial, in 137
Magistrates' Court
appeal from, to Crown Court 31
committal to Crown Court 31
composition of 123
juvenile cases, in 157
jurisdiction of 121
organisation of 118-9
powers of sentence 135-7
Magistrates' Court committee 119
manslaughter, jurisdiction to try 7
mental abnormality (see also hospital order)
orders under Mental Health Act 181
powers of court 206-8
report on condition of accused 137
restriction order 207
mistaken identity
'no case to answer' 92
mitigation, plea of 'guilty' 55
procedure 176-8
mode of trial
advantages to accused 153-4
change of decision 145
criteria in deciding 141-4
juveniles, of 155-7
procedure for determining 143-4
failure to comply with 144
murder, life imprisonment for 190
jurisdiction to try 7

'no case to answer'
committal proceedings, at 19-20, 23
magistrates' court, in 134
trial, at 91-3

nolle prosequi 10
notice, service of for additional
   witnesses 89

oaths and affirmation
   committal proceedings, in 17
   juror, by 71
   juveniles, by 158
   'voire dire', on the 89
offences
   classification of 4, 139-141
   fresh, after discharge 21
   list of 140-1
   mode of trial, to determine 141-4
   other than those charged in committal
      proceedings 20
   taken into consideration 178-9
   triable either way 4, 121, 139
   triable summarily, with consent 142
Official Secrets Act offences
   jurisdiction to try 7
Order to trial, more than one accused 95

pardon 66
parole 182, 188-190
   local review committee 189
   Parole Board 188, 189
particulars of offence, in indictment 37, 40
perjury
   direction to prosecute for, without
      committal proceedings 30
   jurisdiction to try 7
petty sessional divisions 119
Philips Commission — see Royal
   Commission on criminal procedure,
      Report on
plea bargaining 59-60
pleas
   accused, by, personally 54
   ambiguous 53, 55-6, 133
   autrefois acquit and convict 62-3
   change of plea 59
   defendant, more than one 55
   equivocal 251
   'guilty' 54, 133
      lesser offence, of 57-9
      post, by 130-1
   insanity, of 243-4
   mitigation, in 176-8
   mute of malice 60-1
   mute by visitation of God 60-1
   'not guilty' 54
   pressure on accused 56-7, 96
   special pleas in bar 66-7
   time-span before arraignment 53
   unfitness to plead 61-2, 133
   whole case in issue 54
plea to the jurisdiction 67

police
   Chief Officer of
      Director of Public Prosecutions,
         directions from 271
      mandamus, to control 271
      power and duty of 271
   officer
      application for summons by 6
      character and antecedents given by 171
      decision to prosecute by 6
      powers of
         arrest 270, 335-6
         search 294-6, 335
         stop and search 296, 334
      questioning 336-7
      suspect charged by 6
      unlawful search, by 296
   prosecuting authority, as 269-272
post, pleading guilty by 130-1
powers of arrest 270, 273-5
prerogative orders
   Chief Officer of Police, to control 271
   magistrates' courts, to control 28, 250
   quash for bias, to 123
private prosecutions 7, 269
   information, laying 124
probation 181
   ancillary orders, together with 197
   breach of 150, 175, 198-9
   day training centre 198
   juveniles, of 160
   powers of court 197-8
   sentencing policy 215
   summary conviction, on 136
   with other punishments 197
probation and after care committee 175
prohibition, order of
   attempts at repeated committals 21
proof
   by formal admission 91
   onus of 54
   whole prosecution case, of 54
prosecution
   advance notice of case 134
   commencement of 6-10
   consent of Attorney-General or DPP,
      where required 7, 9
   counsel 81
   duty to reveal to defence
      inconsistent statements 87, 134
      witness, existence of 86, 134
   non-appearance of 132
   opening of case 83
   out of time 9
   private 7, 280-2
   strength of evidence 7
   witnesses to be called 84-6
prosecuting authorities 269-272
   constitutional position 270

prosecuting authorities—*continued*
  police and private prosecutors 269-270
public policy, consideration by Attorney
  General 9

questioning
  of suspects by police 286-7
  of witnesses 85

recidivist offenders
  extended sentences 182, 197-8
  sentencing policy 215
recognizance
  estreat of 315
  parent of juvenile offender, by 163
re-examination in committal
  proceedings 17
rehabilitation period 173-4
remission 182, 188-190
reports on accused
  adjournment for 137
  Home Secretary, on behalf of 176
  imprisonment, before sentence of 185
  medical and mental 137, 176
  sentence, to be read before 175
  social enquiry 137, 175
reports in media
  committal proceedings, of 24
  on discharge of accused 24
  juvenile cases, in 159
  lifting of restrictions 24
restitution orders 324-5
retrial
  accused does not plead personally 54
  Court of Appeal, by order of 29
  magistrates equally divided, where 135
right of audience
  committal proceedings, in 17
  Crown Court, in 36
  magistrates' court, in 132
Royal Commission on Criminal Procedure
  (the Philips Commission), Report
  on 334-8

sentence
  accused, in absence of 132
  co-accused, of 55
  committal to Crown Court, for 142,
    145-6
  consecutive and concurrent 136, 182
  deferment of 211-213
  follows 'guilty' plea 55, 133
  imprisonment
    immediate 182
    life, for murder 190
    maximum terms of 183
  individual 215-7
  juveniles, of 159-166
  mitigating factors 218-220

sentence—*continued*
  policy 214
  powers of courts 146, 179-180, 181
  procedure before 169
  suspended 136, 150, 181, 184-5, 191
    activation of 174-5
    breach, consequences of 191-2
    committal to Crown Court for
      breach 193
    power of court 191, 192-3
    where appropriate 193
  remission 182
  tariff 215-6, 217, 220
service of summons 129
social enquiry reports 175
social workers
  duties under supervision orders 162
solicitor, adjournment to instruct 15
Solicitor General, role of 10-11
special pleas in bar
  demurrer 67
  pardon 66
  plea to the jurisdiction 67
speeches, right of 135
standard of proof
  advice from clerk on 138
  'beyond reasonable doubt' 54
  committal proceedings, in 15, 19
  summing up, in 98
statement of offence, in indictment 37, 40
statements (see also depositions)
  children, from 27
  under s. 102
    admissibility 18
    advantages and disadvantages 18-19
    objections to 18
    trial, at 89-91
  summary trial, in 134
  unsworn
    committal proceedings, in 20
    trial on indictment, at 94
summary offences
  described 4, 139
  penalties for 139
summary trial
  accused, in absence of 129-130
  conduct of 121
  consent to 142
  information, in 124
summing up
  jury, to 3
  matters to be included 97-100
  misdirection to be corrected 100
summons (see also information)
  failure to answer 283
  jurisdiction of court to issue 282-3
  private citizen, by 280-2
  procedure for issue of 124, 278
  service of 283

summons — *continued*
  warrant for arrest, issue of   283-6
supervision orders, juveniles   162-3, 181, 330
suspended sentence supervision orders   199

terrorist offences, power to detain
  suspect   300
transcripts of proceedings   237
trial on indictment   3
  committal proceedings, without   28
  Crown Court, before   31
  period before trial   53
trial on information   3
trials, types of   3

verdict
  alternative counts   105
ambiguous or inconsistent   110-111
  'guilty' of lesser offence   105-8
  return of
    majority   108-9
    unanimous   104-5, 109
voire dire   88-9, 171
voluntary bill of indictment
  committal proceedings, without   28-9
  Court of Appeal, by direction of   29

voluntary bill of indictment — *continued*
  fresh charges   21, 28
  preferment of   28-9

'Walhein direction'   110
warrant of distress, non-payment of
  fines   197
witnesses
  accused as   93
  additional evidence, by   89
  arrest warrant, for   87, 134
  attendance of, securing   87
  committal proceedings, at   19
  contempt of court   87
  Court of Appeal, in   240-2
  prosecution   84-6
  summons   134
witness orders
  full and conditional   24-5, 87
  non-compliance with   25

young offenders, The White Paper
  on   329-31
young person
  defined   155
  social enquiry report on   176
'youth custody'   204, 329